BRIGHTON ROCK

BY THE SAME AUTHOR

Graham Greene

BRIGHTON ROCK

New York
THE VIKING PRESS
1949

PUBLISHED IN JUNE 1938
SECOND PRINTING JULY 1938
THIRD PRINTING SEPTEMBER 1948
FOURTH PRINTING JANUARY 1949

PRINTED IN THE UNITED STATES OF AMERICA

"This were a fine reign:
To do ill and not hear of it again."

THE WITCH OF EDMONTON

NOTE

During the summer season in England certain popular newspapers organize treasure hunts at the seaside. They publish the photograph of a reporter and print his itinerary at the particular town he is visiting. Anyone who, while carrying a copy of the paper, addresses him, usually under some fantastic name, in a set form of words, receives a money prize; he also distributes along his route cards which can be exchanged for smaller prizes. Next day in the paper the reporter describes the chase. Of course, the character of Hale is not drawn from that of any actual newspaperman. —G. G.

Brighton Rock is a form of stick candy as characteristic of English seaside resorts as salt-water taffy is of the American. The word "Brighton" appears on the ends of the stick at no matter what point it is broken off. —Ed.

PART ONE

HALE knew they meant to murder him before
he had been in Brighton three hours. With his
inky fingers and his bitten nails, his manner
cynical and nervous, anybody could tell he didn't belong—belong to the early summer sun, the cool Whitsun wind off the sea, the holiday crowd. They came in
by train from Victoria every five minutes, rocked down

Queen's Road standing on the tops of the little local trams, stepped off in bewildered multitudes into fresh and glittering air. the new silver paint sparkled on the piers, the cream houses ran away into the west like a pale Victorian water-colour; a race in miniature motors, a band playing, flower gardens in bloom below the front, an aeroplane advertising something for the health in pale vanishing clouds across the sky.

It had seemed quite easy to Hale to be lost in Brighton. Fifty thousand people besides himself were down for the day, and for quite a while he gave himself up to the good day, drinking gins and tonics wherever his programme allowed. For he had to stick closely to a programme: from ten till eleven Queen's Road and Castle Square, from eleven till twelve the Aquarium and Palace Pier, twelve till one the front between the Old Ship and West Pier, back for lunch between one and two in any restaurant he chose round the Castle Square, and after that he had to make his way all down the parade to West Pier and then to the station by the Hove streets. These were the limits of his absurd and widely advertised sentry go.

Advertised on every *Messenger* poster: "Kolley Kibber in Brighton today." In his pocket he had a packet of cards to distribute in hidden places along his route: those who found them would receive ten shillings from the *Messenger*, but the big prize was reserved for whoever challenged Hale in the proper form of words and with a copy of the *Messenger* in his hand: "You are Mr. Kolley Kibber. I claim the *Daily Messenger* prize."

This was Hale's job, to do sentry go, until a chal-

lenger released him, in every seaside town in turn:
yesterday Southend, today Brighton, tomorrow——

He drank his gin and tonic hastily as a clock struck
eleven, and moved out of Castle Square. Kolley Kibber
always played fair, always wore the same kind of hat
as in the photograph the *Messenger* printed, was always on time. Yesterday in Southend he had been un-
challenged: the paper liked to save its guineas occasionally; but not too often. It was his duty today to be
spotted—and it was his inclination too. There were
reasons why he didn't feel too safe in Brighton, even
in a Whitsun crowd.

He leant against the rail near the Palace Pier and
showed his face to the crowd as it uncoiled endlessly
past him, like a twisted piece of wire, two by two,
each with an air of sober and determined gaiety.
They had stood all the way from Victoria in crowded
carriages, they would have to wait in queues for lunch,
at midnight half asleep they would rock back in trains
an hour late to the cramped streets and the closed pubs
and the weary walk home. With immense labour and
immense patience they extricated from the long day
the grain of pleasure: this sun, this music, the rattle
of the miniature cars, the ghost train diving between
the grinning skeletons under the Aquarium promenade,
the sticks of Brighton rock, the paper sailors' caps.

Nobody paid any attention to Hale; no one seemed
to be carrying a *Messenger*. He deposited one of his
cards carefully on the top of a little basket and moved
on, with his bitten nails and his inky fingers, alone. He
felt his loneliness only after his third gin: until then

he despised the crowd, but afterwards he felt his kinship. He had come out of the same streets, but he
was condemned by his higher pay to pretend to want
other things; and all the time the piers, the peep shows,
pulled at his heart. He wanted to get back—but all he
could do was to carry his sneer along the front, the
badge of loneliness. Somewhere out of sight a woman
was singing: "When I came up from Brighton by the
train": a rich Guinness voice, a voice from a public
bar. Hale turned into the private saloon and watched
her big blown charms across two bars and through a
glass partition.

She wasn't old—somewhere in the late thirties or
the early forties—and she was only a little drunk in a
friendly accommodating way. You thought of sucking
babies when you looked at her, but if she'd borne them
she hadn't let them pull her down: she took care of
herself. Her lipstick told you that, the confidence of
her big body. She was well covered, but she wasn't
careless; she kept her lines for those who cared for
lines.

Hale did. He was a small man and he watched her
with covetous envy over the empty glasses tipped up in
the lead trough, over the beer handles, between the
shoulders of the two serving in the public bar. "Give
me another, Lily," one of them said and she began:
"One night—in an alley—Lord Rothschild said to
me." She never got beyond a few lines. She wanted to
laugh too much to give her voice a chance, but she had
an inexhaustible memory for ballads. Hale had never
heard one of them before; with his glass to his lips he
watched her with nostalgia, she was off again on a

song which must have dated back to the Australian gold rush.

"Fred," a voice said behind him, "Fred."

The gin slopped out of Hale's glass onto the bar. A boy of about seventeen watched him from the door. A shabby smart suit, the cloth too thin from much wear, a face of starved intensity, a kind of hideous and unnatural pride.

"Who are you Freding?" Hale said. "I'm not Fred."

"It don't make any difference," the boy said. He turned back towards the door, keeping an eye on Hale over his narrow shoulder.

"Where are you going?"

"Got to tell your friends," the boy said.

They were alone in the saloon bar except for an old commissionaire, who slept over a pint glass of old and mild. "Listen," Hale said, "have a drink. Come and sit down over here and have a drink."

"Got to be going," the boy said. "You know I don't drink, Fred. You forget a lot, don't you?"

"It won't make any difference having one drink. A soft drink."

"It'll have to be a quick one," the boy said. He watched Hale all the time, closely and with wonder; you might expect a hunter searching through the jungle for some half-fabulous beast to look like that—at the spotted lion or the pygmy elephant—before the kill. "A grapefruit squash," he said.

"Go on, Lily," the voices implored in the public bar. "Give us another, Lily," and the boy took his eyes for the first time from Hale and looked across the partition at the big breasts and the blown charm.

"A double whisky and a grapefruit squash," Hale said. He carried them to a table, but the boy didn't follow. He was watching the woman with an expression of furious distaste. Hale felt as if hatred had been momentarily loosened like handcuffs to be fastened round another's wrists. He tried to joke: "A cheery soul."

"Soul," the boy said. "You've no cause to talk about souls." He turned his hatred back on Hale, drinking down the grapefruit squash in a single draught.

Hale said: "I'm only here for my job. Just for the day. I'm Kolley Kibber."

"You're Fred," the boy said.

"All right," Hale said, "I'm Fred. But I've got a card in my pocket which'll be worth ten bob to you."

"I know all about the cards," the boy said. He had a fair smooth skin, the faintest down, and his grey eyes had an effect of heartlessness like those of an old man in whom human feeling has died. "We were all reading about you," he said, "in the paper this morning," and suddenly he sniggered as if he'd just seen the point of a dirty story.

"You can have one," Hale said. "Look, take this *Messenger*. Read what it says there. You can have the whole prize. Ten guineas," he said. "You'll only have to send this form to the *Messenger*."

"Then they don't trust you with the cash," the boy said, and in the other bar Lily began to sing: "We met —'twas in a crowd—and I thought he would shun me." "Christ," the boy said, "won't anybody stop that buer's mouth?"

"I'll give you a fiver," Hale said. "It's all I've got on me. That and my ticket."

"You won't want your ticket," the boy said.

"I wore my bridal robe, and I rivall'd its whiteness."

The boy rose furiously and, giving way to a little vicious spurt of hatred—at the song? at the man?—he dropped his empty glass onto the floor. "The gentleman'll pay," he said to the barman and swung through the door of the private lounge. It was then Hale realized that they meant to murder him.

> "A wreath of orange blossoms,
>> When next we met, she wore;
> The expression of her features
>> Was more thoughtful than before."

The commissionaire slept on and Hale watched Lily from the deserted elegant lounge. Her big breasts pointed through the thin vulgar summer dress, and he thought: I must get away from here, I must get away: sadly and desperately watching her, as if he were gazing at life itself in the public bar. But he couldn't get away: he had his job to do, they were particular on the *Messenger*; it was a good paper to be on, and a little flare of pride went up in Hale's heart when he thought of the long pilgrimage behind him: selling newspapers at street corners, the reporter's job at thirty bob a week on the little local paper with a circulation of ten thousand, the five years in Sheffield. He was damned, he told himself with the temporary courage of another whisky, if he'd let that mob frighten him into spoiling his job. What could they do while he had people round him? They hadn't the nerve to kill him in broad day before witnesses; he was safe with the fifty thousand visitors.

"Come on over here, lonely heart." He didn't realize at first she was speaking to him, until he saw all the
faces in the public bar grinning across at him, and
suddenly he thought how easily the mob could get at
him with only the sleeping commissionaire to keep
him company. There was no need to go outside to
reach the other bar, he had only to make a semi-circle
through three doors, by way of the saloon bar, the "ladies only." "What'll you have?" he said, approaching
the big woman with starved gratitude. She could save
my life, he thought, if she'd let me stick to her.

"I'll have a port," she said.

"One port," Hale said.

"Aren't you having one?"

"No," Hale said, "I've drunk enough. I mustn't get
sleepy."

"Why ever not—on a holiday? Have a Bass on me."

"I don't like Bass." He looked at his watch. It was
one o'clock. His programme fretted at his mind. He
had to leave cards in every section · the paper in that
way kept a check on him; they could always tell if he
scamped his job. "Come and have a bite," he implored
her.

"Hark at him," she called to her friends. Her warm
port-winy laugh filled all the bars. "Getting fresh, eh?
I wouldn't trust myself."

"Don't you go, Lily," they told her. "He's not
safe."

"I wouldn't trust myself," she repeated, closing one
soft friendly cow-like eye.

There was a way, Hale knew, to make her come. He
had known the way once. On thirty bob a week he

would have been at home with her; he would have
known the right phrase, the right joke, to cut her out
from among her friends, to be friendly at a snack bar.
But he'd lost touch. He had nothing to say; he could
only repeat: "Come and have a bite."

"Where shall we go, Sir Horace? To the Old Ship?"

"Yes," Hale said. "If you like. The Old Ship."

"Hear that?" she told them in all the bars, the two
old dames in black bonnets in the ladies', the commissionaire who slept on alone in the private, her own
half-dozen cronies. "This gentleman's invited me to
the Old Ship," she said in a mock-refined voice. "Tomorrow I shall be delighted, but today I have a prior
engagement at the Dirty Dog."

Hale turned hopelessly to the door. The boy, he
thought, would not have had time to warn the others
yet. He would be safe at lunch; it was the hour he had
to pass after lunch he dreaded most. The woman said:
"Are you sick or something?"

His eyes turned to the big breasts; she was like darkness to him, shelter, knowledge, common-sense; his
heart ached at the sight; but, in his little bitten inky
cynical framework of bone, pride bobbed up again,
taunting him "back to the womb . . . be a mother to
you . . . no more standing on your own feet."

"No," he said, "I'm not sick. I'm all right."

"You look queer," she said in a friendly concerned
way.

"I'm all right," he said. "Hungry. That's all."

"Why not have a bite here?" the woman said. "You
could do him a ham sandwich, couldn't you, Bill?" and
the barman said, Yes, he could do a ham sandwich.

"No," Hale said, "I've got to be getting on."

—Getting on. Down the front, mixing as quickly as possible with the current of the crowd, glancing to right and left of him and over each shoulder in turn. He could see no familiar face anywhere, but he felt no relief. He thought he could lose himself safely in a crowd, but now the people he was among seemed like a thick forest in which a native could arrange his poisoned ambush. He couldn't see beyond the man in flannels just in front, and when he turned, his vision was blocked by a brilliant scarlet blouse. Three old ladies went driving by in an open horse-drawn carriage : the gentle clatter faded like peace. That was how some people still lived.

Hale crossed the road away from the front. There were fewer people there : he could walk faster and go further. They were drinking cocktails on the terrace of the Grand, a delicate pastiche of a Victorian sunshade twisted its ribbons and flowers in the sun, and a man like a retired statesman, all silver hair and powdered skin and double old-fashioned eyeglass, let life slip naturally, with dignity, away from him, sitting over a sherry. Down the steps of the Cosmopolitan came a couple of expensive women with bright brass hair and ermine coats and heads close together like parrots exchanging metallic confidences. "My dear, I said quite coldly, if you haven't learnt the Del Rey perm, all I can say——" and they flashed their pointed painted nails at each other and cackled. For the first time in five years Kolley Kibber was late in his programme. At the foot of the Cosmopolitan steps, in the shadow the huge bizarre building cast, he remembered that the mob had bought his paper. They hadn't needed to watch the public house for him: they knew where to expect him.

A mounted policeman came up the road: the lovely cared-for chestnut beast stepping delicately on the hot macadam, like an expensive toy a millionaire buys for his children; you admired the finish, the leather as deeply glowing as an old mahogany table top, the bright silver badge; it never occurred to you that the toy was for use. It never occurred to Hale, watching the policeman pass; he couldn't appeal to him. A man stood by the kerb selling objects on a tray; he had lost the whole of one side of the body: leg and arm and shoulder; and the beautiful horse as it paced by turned its head aside delicately like a dowager. "Shoe-laces," the man said hopelessly to Hale, "matches." Hale didn't hear him. "Razor blades." Hale went by, the words lodged securely in his brain: the thought of the thin wound and the sharpness of the agony. That was how Kite was killed.

Twenty yards down the road he saw Cubitt. Cubitt was a big man, with red hair cut *en brosse* and freckles. He saw Hale, but he made no sign of recognition, leaning carelessly against a pillar box watching Hale. A postman came to collect and Cubitt shifted. Hale could see him exchanging a joke with the postman and the postman laughed and filled his bag and all the time Cubitt looked away from him down the street waiting for Hale. Hale knew exactly what he'd do; he knew the whole bunch; Cubitt was slow and had

a friendly way with him. He'd simply link his arm
with Hale's, draw him on where he wanted him to go.

But the old desperate pride persisted, a pride of
intellect. He was scared sick, but he told himself: "I'm
not going to die." He jested hollowly: "I'm not front-
page stuff"; this was real: the two women getting
into a taxi, the band playing on the Palace Pier, "tablets" fading in white smoke on the pale pure sky; not
red-haired Cubitt waiting by the pillar box. Hale
turned again and crossed the road, made back towards
the West Pier walking fast; he wasn't running away,
he had a plan.

He had only, he told himself, to find a girl; there
must be hundreds waiting to be picked up on a Whitsun holiday, to be given a drink and taken to dance at
Sherry's and presently home, drunk and affectionate,
in the corridor carriage. That was the best way: to
carry a witness round with him. It would be no good,
even if his pride had allowed him, to go to the station
now. They would be watching it for certain, and it
was always easy to kill a lonely man at a railway
station: they had only to gather close round a carriage
door or fix you in the crush at the barrier; it was at a
station that Colleoni's mob had killed Kite. All down
the front the girls sat in the twopenny deck chairs,
waiting to be picked, all who had not brought their
boys with them: clerks, shop girls, hairdressers—you
could pick out the hairdressers by their new and daring perms, by their beautifully manicured nails: they
had all waited late at their shops the night before,
preparing each other till midnight. Now they were
sleepy and sleek in the sun.

In front of the chairs the men strolled in twos and threes, wearing their summer suits for the first time, knife-edged silver-grey trousers and elegant shirts; they didn't look as if they cared a damn whether they got a girl or not, and among them Hale went in his seedy suit and his string tie and his striped shirt and his inkstains, ten years older, and desperate for a girl. He offered them cigarettes and they stared at him like duchesses with large cold eyes and said: "I don't smoke, thenk you," and twenty yards behind him he knew, without turning his head, that Cubitt strolled.

It made Hale's manner strange. He couldn't help showing his desperation. He could hear the girls laughing at him after he'd gone, at his clothes and the way he talked. There was a deep humility in Hale; his pride was only in his profession: he disliked himself before the glass, the bony legs and the pigeon breast, and he dressed shabbily and carelessly as a sign—a sign that he didn't expect any woman to be interested. Now he gave up the pretty ones, the smart ones, and looked despairingly down the chairs for someone plain enough to be glad of his attentions.

Surely, he thought, *this* girl, smiling with hungry hope at a fat spotty creature in pink whose feet hardly touched the ground. He sat down in an empty chair beside her and gazed at the remote and neglected sea coiling round the piles of the West Pier.

"Cigarette?" he said presently.

"I don't mind if I do," the girl said. The words were sweet, like a reprieve.

"It's nice here," the fat girl said.

"Down from town?"

"Yes."

"Well," Hale said, "you aren't going to sit here alone all day, are you?"

"Oh, I don't know," the girl said.

"I thought of going to have something to eat, and then we might——"

"*We*," the girl said; "you're a fresh one."

"Well, you aren't going to sit here alone all day, are you?"

"Who said I was?" the fat girl said. "Doesn't mean I'm going with *you*."

"Come and have a drink anyway and talk about it."

"I wouldn't mind," the girl said, opening a compact and covering her spots deeper.

"Come along then," Hale said.

"Got a friend?" the girl said.

"I'm all alone," Hale said.

"Oh, then, I couldn't," the girl said. "Not possibly. I couldn't leave my friend all alone," and for the first time Hale observed in the chair beyond her a pale bloodless creature waiting avidly for his reply.

"But you'd like to come?" Hale implored.

"Oh, yes, but I couldn't possibly."

"Your friend won't mind. She'll find someone."

"Oh, no. I couldn't leave her alone." She stared pastily and impassively at the sea.

"You wouldn't mind, would you?" Hale leant forward and begged the bloodless image, and it screeched with embarrassed laughter back at him.

"She doesn't know anyone," the fat girl said.

"She'll find somebody."

"Would you, Delia?" The pasty girl leant her head

close to her friend's and they consulted together; every now and then Delia squealed.

"That's all right then," Hale said, "you'll come?"

"Couldn't you find a friend?"

"I don't know anyone here," Hale said. "Come along. I'll take you anywhere you like for lunch. All I want"—he grinned miserably—"is for you to stick close."

"No," the fat girl said. "I couldn't possibly—not without my friend."

"Well, both of you come along then," Hale said.

"It wouldn't be much fun for Delia," the fat girl said.

A boy's voice interrupted them. "So there you are, Fred," it said, and Hale looked up at the grey inhuman seventeen-year-old eyes.

"Why," the fat girl squealed, "he said he hadn't got a friend."

"You can't believe what Fred says," the voice said.

"Now we can make a proper party," the fat girl said. "This is my friend Delia. I'm Molly."

"Pleased to meet you," the boy said. "Where are we going, Fred?"

"I'm hungry," the fat girl said. "I bet you're hungry too, Delia?" and Delia wriggled and squealed.

"I know a good place," the boy said.

"Do they have sundaes?"

"The best sundaes," he reassured her in his serious dead voice.

"That's what I want, a sundae. Delia likes splits best."

"We'll be going, Fred," the boy said.

Hale rose. His hands were shaking. This was real now : the boy, the razor cut, life going out with the blood in pain; not the deck chairs and the permanent waves, the miniature cars tearing round the curve on the Palace Pier. The ground moved under his feet, and only the thought of where they might take him while he was unconscious saved him from fainting. But even then common pride, the instinct not to make a scene, remained overpoweringly strong; embarrassment had more force than terror, it prevented his crying his fear aloud, it even urged him to go quietly. If the boy had not spoken again, he might have gone.

"We'd better get moving, Fred," the boy said.

"No," Hale said. "I'm not coming. I don't know him. My name's not Fred. I've never seen him before. He's just getting fresh," and he walked rapidly away, with his head down, hopeless now : there wasn't time; only anxious to keep moving, to keep out in the clear sun; until from far down the front he heard the woman's winy voice singing, singing of brides and bouquets, of lilies and mourning shrouds, a Victorian ballad, and he moved towards it as someone who has been lost a long while in a desert makes for the glow of a fire.

"Why," she said, "if it isn't lonely heart," and to his astonishment she was all by herself in a desert of chairs. "They've gone to the Gents'," she said.

"Can I sit down?" Hale said. His voice broke with relief.

"If you've got twopence," she said. "I haven't." She began to laugh, the great breasts pushing at her dress. "Someone pinched my bag," she said. "Every penny I've got." He watched her with astonishment. "Oh," she said, "that's not the funny part. It's the letters. He'll have had all Tom's letters to read. Were they passionate! Tom'll be crazy when he hears."

"You'll be wanting some money," Hale said.

"Oh," she said, "I'm not worrying. Some nice feller will lend me ten bob—when they come out of the Gents'."

"They your friends?" Hale said.

"I met 'em in the pub," she said.

"You think," Hale said, "they'll come back from the Gents'?"

"My," she said, "you don't think—?" She gazed up the parade, then looked at Hale and began to laugh again. "You win," she said. "They've pulled my leg properly. But there was only ten bob—and Tom's letters."

"Will you have lunch with me now?" Hale said.

"I had a snack in the pub," she said. "They treated me to that, so I got something out of my ten bob."

"Have a little more."

"No, I don't fancy any more," she said, and leaning far back in the deck chair with her skirt pulled up to her knees exposing her fine legs, with an air of ribald luxury she added: "What a day!" sparkling back at the bright sea. "All the same," she said, "they'll wish they'd never been born. I'm a sticker where right's concerned."

"Your name's Lily?" Hale asked. He couldn't see the boy any more: he'd gone; Cubitt had gone. There was nobody he could recognize as far as he could see.

"That's what *they* called me," she said. "My real

name's Ida." The old and vulgarized Grecian name
recovered a little dignity. She said: "You look poorly.
You ought to go off and eat somewhere."

"Not if you won't come," Hale said. "I only want
to stay here with you."

"Why, that's a nice speech," she said. "I wish Tom
could hear you—he writes passionate, but when it
comes to talking——"

"Does he want to marry you?" Hale said; she smelt
of soap and wine; comfort and peace and a slow sleepy
physical enjoyment, a touch of the nursery and the
mother stole from the big tipsy mouth, the magnificent breasts and legs, and reached Hale's withered and
frightened brain.

"He *was* married to me once," Ida said. "But he
didn't know when he was lucky. Now he wants to
come back. You should see his letters. I'd show them
you if they hadn't been stolen. He ought to be
ashamed," she said, laughing with pleasure, "writing
such things. You'd never think. And he was such a
quiet fellow too. Well, I always say it's fun to be
alive."

"Will you take him back?" Hale said, peering out
from the valley of the shadow with sourness and envy.

"I should think not," Ida said. "I know all about
him. There'd be no thrill. If I wanted a man, I could
do better than that now." She wasn't boastful: only a
little drunk and happy. "I could marry money if I
chose."

"And how do you live now?" Hale said.

"From hand to mouth," she said and winked at him

and made the motion of tipping a glass. "What's your name?"

"Fred." He said it automatically: it was the name he always gave to chance acquaintances; from some obscure motive of secrecy he shielded his own name, Charles; from childhood he had loved secrecy, a hiding place, the dark; but it was in the dark he had met Kite, the boy, Cubitt, the whole mob.

"And how do you live?" she asked cheerfully. Men always liked to tell, and she liked to hear. She had an immense store of masculine experiences.

"Betting," he said promptly, putting up his barrier of evasion.

"I like a flutter myself. Could you give me a tip, I wonder, for Brighton on Saturday?"

"Black Boy," Hale said, "in the four o'clock."   .

"He's twenty to one."

Hale looked at her with respect. "Take it or leave it."

"Oh, I'll take it," Ida said. "I always take a tip."

"Whoever gives it you?"

"That's my system. Will you be there?"

"No," Hale said. "I can't make it." He put his hand on her wrist. He wasn't going to run any more risks. He'd tell the news editor he was taken ill; he'd resign; he'd do anything. Life was here beside him, he wasn't going to play around with death. "Come to the station with me," he said. "Come back to town with me."

"On a day like this?" Ida said. "Not me. You've had too much town. You look stuffed up. A blow along the front'll do you good. Besides there's lots of things I want to see. I want to see the Aquarium and Black Rock and I haven't been on the Palace Pier yet today. There's always something new on the Palace Pier. I'm out for a bit of fun."

"We'll do those and then———"

"When I make a day of it," Ida said, "I like to make a real day of it. I told you—I'm a sticker."

"I don't mind," Hale said, "if you'll stay with me."

"Well, *you* can't steal my bag," Ida said. "But I warn you—I like to spend. I'm not satisfied with a ring here and a shot there: I want all the shows."

"It's a long walk," Hale said, "to the Palace Pier in this sun. We better take a taxi." But he made no immediate pass at Ida in the taxi, sitting there bonily crouched with his eyes on the parade: no sign of the boy or Cubitt in the bright broad day sweeping by. He turned reluctantly back, and with the sense of her great open friendly breasts, fastened his mouth on hers and received the taste of port wine on his tongue, and saw in the driver's mirror the old 1925 Morris following behind, with its split and flapping top, its bent fender and cracked and discoloured windscreen. He watched it with his mouth on hers, shaking against her as the taxi ground slowly along beside the parade.

"Give me breath," she said at last, pushing him off and straightening her hat. "You believe in hard work," she said. "It's you little fellows—" She could feel his nerves jumping under her hand, and she shouted quickly through the tube at the driver: "Don't stop. Go on back and round again." He was like a man with fever.

"You're sick," she said. "You oughtn't to be alone. What's the matter with you?"

He couldn't keep it in. "I'm going to die. I'm scared."

"Have you seen a doctor?"

"They are no good. They can't do anything."

"You oughtn't to be out alone," Ida said. "Did they tell you that—the doctors, I mean?"

"Yes," he said and put his mouth on hers again because when he kissed her he could watch in the mirror the old Morris vibrating after them down the parade.

She pushed him off again, but kept her arms round him. "They're crazy. You aren't that sick. You can't tell me I wouldn't know if you were that sick," she said. "I don't like to see a fellow throw up the sponge that way. It's a good world if you don't weaken."

"It's all right," he said, "long as you are here."

"That's better," she said, "be yourself," and letting down the window with a rush for the air to come in, she pushed her arm through his and said in a frightened gentle way: "You were just kidding, weren't you, when you said that about the doctors? It wasn't true, was it?"

"No," Hale said wearily, "it wasn't true."

"That's a boy," Ida said. "You nearly had me scared for a moment. Nice thing it would have been for me if you'd passed out in this taxi. Something for Tom to read about in the paper, I'd say. But men are funny with me that way. Always trying to make out there's something wrong, money or the wife or the heart. You aren't the first who said he was dying.

Never anything infectious though. Want to make the
most of their last hours and all the rest of it. It comes
of me being so big, I suppose. They think I'll mother
them. I'm not saying I didn't fall for it the first time.
'The doctors only give me a month,' he said to me—
that was five years ago. I see him regular now in
Henneky's. 'Hullo, you old ghost,' I always say to
him, and he stands me oysters and a Guinness.''

"No, I'm not sick," Hale said. "You needn't be
scared." He wasn't going to let his pride down as much
as that again, even in return for the peaceful and
natural embrace. The Grand went by, the old statesman dozing out the day, the Metropolitan. "Here we
are," Hale said, "You'll stay with me, won't you, even
if I'm not sick?"

"Of course I will," Ida said, hiccuping gently as
she stepped out. "I like you, Fred. I liked you the
moment I saw you. You're a good sport, Fred. What's
that crowd, there?" she asked with joyful curiosity,
pointing to the gathering of neat and natty trousers,
of bright blouses and bare arms and bleached and per-
fumed hair.

"With every watch I sell," a man was shouting in
the middle of it all, "I give a free gift worth twenty
times the value of the watch. Only a shilling, ladies
and gents, it's only a shilling. With every watch I
sell . . ."

"Get me a watch, Fred," Ida said, pushing him
gently, "and give me threepence before you go. I
want to get a wash." They stood on the pavement at
the entrance to the Palace Pier; the crowd was thick
around them, passing in and out of the turnstiles,

watching the pedlar; there was no sign anywhere of
the Morris car.

"You don't want a wash, Ida," Hale implored her.
"You're fine."

"I've got to get a wash," she said, "I'm sweating
all over. You just wait here. I'll only be two minutes."

"You won't get a good wash here," Hale said.
"Come to a hotel and have a drink——"

"I can't wait, Fred. Really I can't. Be a sport."

Hale said: "That ten shillings. You'd better have
that too while I remember it."

"It's real good of you, Fred. Can you spare it?"

"Be quick, Ida," Hale said. "I'll be here. Just here.
By this turnstile. You won't be long, will you? I'll be
here," he repeated, putting his hand on a rail of the
turnstile.

"Why," Ida said, "anyone'd think you were in
love," and she carried the image of him quite tenderly
in her mind down the steps to the Ladies' Lavatory:
the small rather battered man with the nails bitten
close (she missed nothing) and the inkstains and the
hand clutching the rail. He's a good geezer, she said
to herself, I liked the way he looked in that bar even
if I did laugh at him, and she began to sing again,
softly this time, in her warm winy voice: "One night
—in an alley—Lord Rothschild said to me . . ." It
was a long time since she'd hurried herself so for a
man, and it wasn't more than four minutes before,
cool and powdered and serene, she mounted into the
bright Whitsun afternoon, to find him gone. He
wasn't by the turnstile, he wasn't in the crowd by the
pedlar; she forced herself into that to make sure and

found herself facing the flushed, permanently irritated salesman. "What? Not give a shilling for a watch, and a free gift worth exactly twenty times the watch? I'm not saying the watch is worth much more than a shilling, though it's worth that for the looks alone, but with it a free gift twenty times—" She held out the ten-shilling note and got her small package and the change, thinking: he's probably gone to the Gents'; he'll be back; and taking up her place by the turnstile, she opened the little envelope which wrapped the watch round. "Black Boy," she read, "in the four o'clock at Brighton," and thought tenderly and proudly: "That was his tip. He's a fellow who knows things," and prepared patiently and happily to wait for his return. She was a sticker. A clock away in the town struck half past one.

2

The Boy paid his threepence and went through the turnstile. He moved rigidly past the rows of deck chairs four deep where people were waiting for the orchestra to play. From behind he looked younger than he was, in his dark thin ready-made suit a little too big for him at the hips; but when you met him face to face he looked older; the slaty eyes were touched with the annihilating eternity from which he had come and to which he went. The orchestra began to play; he felt the music as a movement in his belly: the violins wailed in his guts. He looked neither right nor left but went on.

In the Palace of Pleasure he made his way past the

peep shows, the slot machines, and the quoits to a shooting booth. The shelves of dolls stared down with glassy innocence, like Virgins in a church repository. The Boy looked up: chestnut ringlets, blue orbs, and painted cheeks; he thought—Hail Mary . . . in the hour of our death. "I'll have six shots," he said.

"Oh, it's you, is it?" the stall-holder said, eyeing him with uneasy distaste.

"Yes, it's me," the Boy said. "Have you got the time on you, Bill?"

"What do you mean—the time? There's a clock up there in the hall, isn't there?"

"It says nearly a quarter to two. I didn't think it was that late."

"That clock's always right," the man said. He came down to the end of the booth, pistol in hand. "It's always right, see?" he said. "It doesn't stand for any phony alibis. Never again," he said. "A quarter to two, that's the time."

"That's all right, Bill," the Boy said. "A quarter to two. I just wanted to know. Give me that pistol." He raised it; the young bony hand was steady as a rock: he put six shots inside the bull. "That's worth a prize," he said.

"You can take your bloody prize," Bill said, "and hop it. What do you want? Chocolates?"

"I don't eat chocolates," the Boy said.

"Packet of Players?"

"I don't smoke."

"You'll have to have a doll then or a glass vase."

"The doll'll do," the Boy said. "I'll have that one—the one up there with the brown hair."

"You getting a family?" the man said, but the Boy
didn't answer, walking rigidly away past the other
booths, with the smell of gunpowder on his fingers,
holding the Mother of God by the hair. The water
washed round the piles at the end of the pier, dark
poison-bottle green, mottled with seaweed, and the
salt wind smarted on his lips. He climbed the ladder
onto the tea terrace and looked around; nearly every
table was full. He went inside the glass shelter and
round into the long narrow tea room which faced
west, perched fifty feet above the slow withdrawing
tide. A table was free and he sat down where he could
see all the room and across the water to the pale
parade.

"I'll wait," he said to the girl who came for his
order. "I've got friends coming." The window was
open and he could hear the low waves beating at the
pier and the music of the orchestra—faint and sad,
borne away on the wind towards the shore. He said:
"They are late. What time is it?" His fingers pulled
absent-mindedly at the doll's hair, detaching the
brown wool.

"It's nearly ten to two," the girl said.

"All the clocks on this pier are fast," he said.

"Oh, no," the girl said. "It's reel London time."

"Take the doll," the Boy said. "It's no good to me.
I just won it in one of those shooting booths. It's no
good to me."

"Can I reely?" the girl said.

"Go on. Take it. Stick it up in your room and
pray." He tossed it at her, watching the door im-

patiently. His body was stiffly controlled. The only sign of nervousness he showed was a slight tic in his cheek, through the soft chicken down, where you might have expected a dimple. It beat more impatiently when Cubitt appeared, and with him Dallow, a stout muscular man with a broken nose and an expression of brutal simplicity.

"Well?" the Boy said.

"It's all right," Cubitt said.

"Where's Spicer?"

"He's coming," Dallow said. "He's just gone into the Gents' to have a wash."

"He ought to have come straight," the Boy said. "You're late. I said a quarter to two sharp."

"Don't take on so," Cubitt said. "All you'd got to do was come straight across."

"I had to tidy up," the Boy said. He beckoned to the waitress. "Four fish and chips and a pot of tea. There's another coming."

"Spicer won't want fish and chips," Dallow said. "He's not got any appetite."

"He'd better have an appetite," the Boy said and, leaning his face on his hands, he watched Spicer's pale-faced progress up the tea room and felt anger grinding at his guts like the tide at the piles below. "It's five to two," he said. "That's right, isn't it? It's five to two?" he called to the waitress.

"It took longer than we thought," Spicer said, dropping into the chair, dark and pallid and spotty. He looked with nausea at the brown crackling slab of fish the girl set before him. "I'm not hungry," he said. "I can't eat this. What do you think I am?" and they all three left their fish untasted as they stared at the Boy like children before his ageless eyes.

The Boy poured anchovy sauce out over his chips. "Eat," he said. "Go on. Eat." Dallow suddenly grinned. "He ain't got no appetite," he said and stuffed his mouth with fish. They all talked low, their words lost to those around in the hubbub of plates and voices and the steady surge of the sea. Cubitt followed suit, picking at his fish; only Spicer wouldn't eat. He sat stubbornly there, grey-haired and sea-sick.

"Give me a drink, Pinkie," he said. "I can't swallow this stuff."

"You aren't going to have a drink, not today," the Boy said. "Go on. Eat."

Spicer put some fish to his mouth. "I'll be sick," he said, "if I eat."

"Spew then," the Boy said. "Spew if you like. You haven't any guts to spew." He said to Dallow: "Did it go all right?"

"It was perfect," Dallow said. "Me and Cubitt planted him. We gave the cards to Spicer."

"You put 'em out all right?" the Boy said.

"Of course I put 'em out," Spicer said.

"All along the parade?"

"Of course I put 'em out. I don't see why you get so fussed about the cards."

"You don't see much," the Boy said. "They're an alibi, aren't they?" He dropped his voice and whispered it over the fish. "They prove he kept to programme. They show he died after two." He raised his voice again. "Listen. Do you hear that?"

Faintly in the town a clock chimed and struck twice.
. "Suppose they found him already?" Spicer said.

"Then that's just too bad for us," the Boy said.

"What about that polony he was with?"

"She don't matter," the Boy said. "She's just a
buer—he gave her a half. I saw him hand it out."

"You take account of most things," Dallow said
with admiration. He poured himself a cup of black
tea and helped himself to five lumps of sugar.

"I take account of what I do myself," the Boy said.
"Where did you put the cards?" he said to Spicer.

"I put one of 'em in Snow's," Spicer said.

"What do you mean? Snow's?"

"He had to eat, hadn't he?" Spicer said. "The paper
said so. You said I was to follow the paper. It'd look
odd, wouldn't it, if he didn't eat? And he always puts
one where he eats."

"It'd look odder," the Boy said, "if the waitress
spotted your face wasn't right and she found it soon
as you left. Where did you put it in Snow's?"

"Under the tablecloth," Spicer said. "That's what
he always does. There'll have been plenty at that table
since me. She won't know it wasn't him. I don't suppose she'll find it before night, when she takes off the
cloth. Maybe it'll even be another girl."

"You go back," the Boy said, "and bring that card
here. I'm not taking chances."

"I'll not go back," Spicer's voice broke above a
whisper, and once again they all three stared at the
Boy in silence.

"You go, Cubitt," the Boy said. "Maybe it had better not be him again."

"Not me," Cubitt said. "Suppose they'd found the card and saw me looking. Better take a chance and leave it alone," he urged in a whisper.

"Talk natural," the Boy said, "talk natural," as the waitress came back to the table.

"Do you boys want any more?" she said.

"Yes," the Boy said, "we'll have ice-cream."

"Stow it, Pinkie," Dallow protested when the girl had left them, "we don't want ice-cream. We ain't a lot of tarts, Pinkie."

"If you don't want ice-cream, Dallow," the Boy said, "you go to Snow's and get that card. You've got guts, haven't you?"

"I thought we was done with it all," Dallow said. "I've done enough. I've got guts, you know that, but I was scared stiff. . . . Why, if they've found him before time, it'd be crazy to go into Snow's."

"Don't talk so loud," the Boy said. "If nobody else'll go," he said, "I'll go. I'm not scared. Only I get tired sometimes of working with a mob like you. Sometimes I think I'd be better alone." Afternoon moved across the water. He said: "Kite was all right, but Kite's dead. Which was your table?" he asked Spicer.

"Just inside. On the right of the door. A table for one. It's got flowers on it."

"What flowers?"

"I don't know what flowers," Spicer said. "Yellow flowers."

"Don't go, Pinkie," Dallow said, "better leave it alone. You can't tell what'll happen," but the Boy was already on his feet, moving stiffly down the long narrow room above the sea. You couldn't tell if he was scared; his young ancient poker-face told nothing.

In Snow's the rush was over and the table free. The wireless droned a programme of dreary music, broadcast by a cinema organist—a great *vox humana* trembled across the crumby stained desert of used cloths: the world's wet mouth lamenting over life. The waitress whipped the cloths off as soon as the tables were free and laid tea things. Nobody paid any attention to the Boy; they turned their backs when he looked at them. He slipped his hand under the cloth and found nothing there. Suddenly the little spurt of vicious anger rose again in the Boy's brain and he smashed a salt sprinkler down on the table so hard that the base cracked. A waitress detached herself from a gossiping group and came towards him, cold-eyed, acquisitive, ash-blonde. "Well?" she said, taking in the shabby suit, the too young face.

"I want service," the Boy said.

"You're late for the lunch."

"I don't want lunch," the Boy said. "I want a cup of tea and a plate of biscuits."

"Will you go to one of the tables laid for tea, please?"

"No," the Boy said. "This table suits me."

She sailed away again, superior and disapproving, and he called after her. "Will you take that order?"

"The waitress serving your table will be here in a minute," she said, and moved away to the gossips by the service door. The Boy shifted his chair, the nerve in his cheek twitched, again he put his hand under the cloth: it was a tiny action, but it might hang him if he was observed. Still he could feel nothing, and he thought with fury of Spicer: he'll muddle once too often, we'd be better without him.

"Was it tea you wanted, sir?" He looked sharply up with his hand under the cloth· one of those girls who creep about, he thought, as if they were afraid of their own footsteps: a pale thin girl younger than himself.

He said: "I gave the order once."

She apologized abjectly: "There's been such a rush. And it's my first day. This was the only breathing spell. Have you lost something?"

He withdrew his hand, watching her with dangerous and unfeeling eyes; his cheek twitched again; it was the little things which tripped you up; he could think of no reason at all for having his hand under the table. She went on helpfully: "I'll have to change the cloth again for tea, so if you've lost——" In no time she had cleared the table of pepper and salt and mustard, the cutlery and the O.K. sauce, the yellow flowers, had nipped together the corners of the cloth and lifted it in one movement from the table, crumbs and all.

"There's nothing there, sir," she said. He looked at the bare table top and said: "I hadn't lost anything." She began to lay a fresh cloth for tea. She seemed to find something agreeable about him which made her talk, something in common perhaps—youth and shabbiness and a kind of ignorance in the dapper café. Already she had apparently forgotten his exploring hand. But would she remember, he wondered, if later people asked her questions? He despised her quiet, her pallor, her desire to please; did she also observe, remember . . . ? "You wouldn't guess," she said, "what

I found here only ten minutes ago. When I changed the cloth."

"Do you always change the cloth?" the Boy said.

"Oh, no," she said, putting out the tea things, "but a customer upset his drink and when I changed it, there was one of Kolley Kıbber's cards, worth ten shillings. It was quite a shock," she said, lingering gratefully with the tray, "and the others don't like it. You see, it's only my second day here. They say I was a fool not to challenge him and get the prize."

"Why didn't you challenge him?"

"Because I never thought. He wasn't a bit like the photograph."

"Maybe the card had been there all the morning."

"Oh, no," she said, "it couldn't have been. He was the first man at this table."

"Well," the Boy said, "it don't make any odds. You've *got* the card."

"Oh, yes, I've got it. Only it don't seem quite fair— you see what I mean—him being so different. I *might* have got the prize. I can tell you I ran to the door when I saw the card; I didn't wait."

"And did you see him?"

She shook her head.

"I suppose," the Boy said, "you hadn't looked at him close. Else you'd have known."

"I always look at you close," the girl said, "the customer, I mean. You see, I'm new. I get a bit scared. I don't want to do anything to offend. Oh," she said aghast, "like standing here talking when you want a cup of tea."

"That's all right," the Boy said. He smiled at her stiffly; he couldn't use those muscles with any naturalness. "You're the kind of girl I like——" The words were the wrong ones; he saw it at once and altered them. "I mean," he said, "I like a girl who's friendly. Some of these here—they freeze you."

"They freeze me."

"You're sensitive, that's what it is," the Boy said, "like me." He said abruptly: "I suppose you wouldn't recognize that newspaper man again? I mean, he may be still about."

"Oh, yes," she said, "I'd know him. I've got a memory for faces."

The Boy's cheek twitched. He said: "I see you and I've got a bit in common. We ought to get together one evening. What's your name?"

"Rose."

He put a coin on the table and got up. "But your tea?" she said.

"Here we been talking, and I had an appointment at two sharp."

"Oh, I'm so sorry," Rose said. "You should've stopped me."

"That's all right," the Boy said. "I liked it. It's only ten past anyway—by your clock. When do you get off of an evening?"

"We don't close till half past ten except on Sundays."

"I'll be seeing you," the Boy said. "You an' me have things in common."

Ida Arnold broke her way across the Strand; she couldn't be bothered to wait for the signals, and she didn't trust the Belisha beacons. She made her own way under the radiators of the buses; the drivers ground their brakes and glared at her, and she grinned back at them. She was always a little flushed as the clock struck eleven and she reached Henneky's, as if she had emerged from some adventure which had given her a better opinion of herself. But she wasn't the first in Henneky's. "Hullo, you old ghost," she said, and the sombre thin man in black with a bowler hat sitting beside a wine barrel said: "Oh, forget it, Ida. Forget it."

"You in mourning for yourself?" Ida said, cocking her hat at a better angle in a mirror which advertised White Horse; she didn't look a day over thirty-five.

"My wife's dead. Have a Guinness, Ida?"

"Yes. I'll have a Guinness. I didn't even know you had a wife."

"We don't know much about each other, that's what it is, Ida," he said. "Why, I don't even know how you live or how many husbands you've had."

"Oh, there's only been one Tom," Ida said.

"There's been more than Tom in *your* life."

"You ought to know," Ida said.

"Give me a glass of Ruby," the sombre man said. "I was just thinking when you came in, Ida, why shouldn't we two come together again?"

"You and Tom always want to start again," Ida

57

said. "Why don't you keep tight hold when you've got a girl?"

"What with my little bit of money and yours——"

"I like to start something fresh," Ida said. "Not off with the new and on with the old."

"But you've a kind heart, Ida."

"That's what you call it," Ida said, and in the dark depth of her Guinness kindness winked up at her, a bit sly, a bit earthy, having a good time. "Do you ever have a bit on the horses?" she said.

"I don't believe in betting. It's a mug's game."

"That's it," Ida said. "A mug's game. You never know whether you'll be up or down. I like it," she said with passion, looking across the wine barrel at the thin pale man, her face more flushed than ever, more young, more kind. "Black Boy," she said softly.

"Eh, what's that?" the ghost said sharply, snatching a glance at his face in the White Horse mirror.

"It's the name of a horse," she said, "that's all. A fellow gave it me at Brighton. I was wondering if maybe I'd see him at the races. He got lost somehow. I liked him. You didn't know whatever he'd be saying next. I owe him money too."

"You saw about this Kolley Kibber at Brighton the other day?"

"Found him dead, didn't they? I saw a poster."

"They've had the inquest."

"Did he kill himself?"

"Oh, no. Just his heart. The heat knocked him over. But the paper's paid the prize to the man who found him. Ten guineas," the ghost said, "for finding a corpse." He laid the paper bitterly down on the wine barrel. "Give me another Ruby."

"Why!" Ida said. "Is that picture the man who found him? The little rat. That's where he went to. No wonder he didn't need his money back."

"No, no, that's not *him*," the ghost said. "That's Kolley Kibber." He took a little wooden pick out of a paper packet and began to scrape his teeth.

"Oh," Ida said. It was like a blow. "Then he wasn't trying it on," she said. "He *was* sick." She remembered how his hand had shaken in the taxi and how he had implored her not to leave him, just as if he had known he was going to die before she came back. But he hadn't made a scene. "He was a gentleman," she said gently. He must have fallen there by the turnstile as soon as she had turned her back, and she had gone on down without knowing into the Ladies'. A sense of tears came to her now in Henneky's; she measured those polished white steps down to the wash basins as if they were the slow stages of a tragedy.

"Ah, well," the ghost said gloomily, "we've all got to die."

"Yes," Ida said, "but he wouldn't've wanted to die any more than I want to die." She began to read and exclaimed almost at once: "What made him walk all that way in that heat?" For he hadn't dropped at the turnstile: he'd gone back all the way they'd come, sat in a shelter. . . .

"He'd got his job to do."

"He didn't say anything to me about a job. He said: 'I'll be here. Just here. By this turnstile.' He said:

'Be quick, Ida. I'll be here,' " and as she repeated what
she could remember of his words she had a feeling
that later, in an hour or two, when things got straightened out, she would want to cry a bit for the death of
that scared passionate bag of bones who called himself——

"Why," she said, "whatever do they mean? Read
here."

"What about it?" the man said.

"The bitches!" Ida said. "What would they go and
tell a lie like that for?"

"What lie? Have another Guinness. You don't want
to fuss about that."

"I don't mind if I do," Ida said, but when she had
taken a long draught she returned to the paper. She
had instincts; and now her instincts told her there was
something odd, something which didn't smell right.
"These girls," she said, "he tried to pick up, they say
a man came along who called him 'Fred,' and he said
he wasn't Fred and he didn't know the man."

"What about it? Listen, Ida, let's go to the pictures."

"But he *was* Fred. He told me he was Fred."

"He was Charles. You can read it there. Charles
Hale."

"That don't signify," Ida said. "A man always has
a different name for strangers. You aren't telling me
your real name's Clarence. And a man don't have a
different name for every girl. He'd get confused. You
know you always stick to Clarence. You can't tell me
much about men I don't know."

"It don't mean anything. You can read how it was.

They just happened to mention it. Nobody took any notice of that."

She said sadly: "Nobody's taken any notice of anything. You can read it here. He hadn't got any folks to make a fuss. 'The Coroner asked if any relations of the deceased were present, and the police witness stated that they could trace no relations other than a second cousin in Middlesbrough.' It sounds kind of lonely," she said. "Nobody there to ask questions."

"I know what loneliness is, Ida," the sombre man said. "I've been alone a month now."

She took no notice of him · she was back at Brighton on Whit Monday; thinking how while she waited there, he must have been dying, walking along the front to Hove, dying, and the cheap drama and pathos of the thought weakened her heart towards him. She was of the people, she cried in cinemas at *David Copperfield*, when she was drunk all the old ballads her mother had known came easily to her lips, her homely heart was touched by the word "tragedy." "The second cousin in Middlesbrough—he was represented by counsel," she said. "What does that mean?"

"I suppose if this Kolley Kibber hasn't left a will, he gets any money there is He wouldn't want any talk of suicide because of the life assurance."

"He didn't ask any questions."

"There wasn't any need. No one made out he'd killed himself."

"Perhaps he did all the same," Ida said. "There was something queer about him. I'd like to 'ave asked some questions."

"What about? It's plain enough."

A man in plus fours and a striped tie came to the bar. "Hullo, Ida," he called.

"Hullo, Harry," she said sadly, staring at the paper.

"Have a drink."

"I've got a drink, thank you."

"Swallow it down and have another."

"No, I don't want any more, thank you," she said. "If I'd been there——"

"What'd have been the good?" the sombre man said.

"I could've asked questions."

"Questions, questions," he said irritably. "You keep on saying questions. What about, beats me."

"Why he said he wasn't Fred."

"He wasn't Fred. He was Charles."

"It's not natural." The more she thought about it the more she wished she had been there : it was like a pain in the heart, the thought that no one at the inquest was interested, the second cousin stayed in Middlesbrough, his counsel asked no questions, and Fred's own paper gave him only half a column. On the front page was another photograph : the new Kolley Kibber; he was going to be at Bournemouth tomorrow. They might have waited, she thought, a week. It would have shown respect.

"I'd like to have asked them why he left me like that, to go scampering down the front in that sun."

"He had his job to do. He had to leave those cards."

"Why did he tell me he'd wait?"

"Ah," the sombre man said, "you'd have to ask *him* that," and at the words it was almost as if he *was* trying to answer her, answer her in his own kind of hieroglyphics, in the obscure pain, speaking in her nerves as a ghost would have to speak. Ida believed in ghosts.

"There's a lot he'd say if he could," she said. She took up the paper again and read slowly. "He did his job to the end," she said tenderly; she liked men who did their jobs: there was a kind of vitality about it. He'd dropped his cards all the way down the front; they'd come back to the office: from under a boat, from a litter basket, a child's pail. He had only a few left when "Mr. Alfred Jefferson, described as a chief clerk, of Clapham," found him. "If he did kill himself," she said (she was the only counsel to represent the dead), "he did his job first."

"But he didn't kill himself," Clarence said. "You've only got to read. They cut him up and they say he died natural."

"That's queer," Ida said. "He went and left one in a restaurant. I knew he was hungry. He kept on wanting to eat, but whatever made him slip away like that all by himself and leave me waiting? It sounds crazy."

"I suppose he changed his mind about you, Ida."

"I don't like it," Ida said. "It sounds strange to me. I wish I'd been there. I'd have asked 'em a few questions."

"What about you and me going across to the flickers, Ida?"

"I'm not in the mood," Ida said. "It's not every day you lose a friend. And you oughtn't to be in the mood, either, with your wife just dead."

"She's been gone a month now," Clarence said; "you can't expect anyone to go on mourning for ever."

"A month's not so long," Ida said sadly, brooding over the paper. A day, she thought, that's all he's been gone, and I dare say there's not another soul but me thinking about him: just someone he picked up for a drink and a cuddle, and again the easy pathos touched her friendly and popular heart. She wouldn't have given it all another thought if there had been other relations besides the second cousin in Middlesbrough, if he hadn't been so alone as well as dead. But there *was* something fishy to her nose, though there was nothing she could put her finger on except that "Fred" —and everyone would say the same: "He wasn't Fred. You've only to read. Charles Hale."

"You oughtn't to fuss about that, Ida. It's none of your business."

"I know," she said, "it's none of mine." But it's none of anybody's, her heart repeated to her; that was the trouble: no one but her to ask questions. She knew a woman once who'd seen her husband, after he was dead, standing by the wireless set trying to twiddle the knob: she twiddled the way he wanted and he disappeared and immediately she heard an announcer say on Midland Regional: "Gale warning in the Channel." She had been thinking of taking one of the Sunday day trips to Calais, that was the point. It just showed: you couldn't laugh at the idea of ghosts. And if Fred, she thought, wanted to tell someone something, it wouldn't be to his second cousin in Middlesbrough that he'd go; why shouldn't he come to me? He had left her waiting there; she had waited nearly half an hour: perhaps he wanted to tell her why. "He was a gentleman," she said aloud, and with bolder resolution she cocked her hat and smoothed her hair and rose from the wine barrel. "I've got to be going," she said. "So long, Clarence."

"Where to? I've never known you in such a hurry, Ida," he complained bitterly.

Ida put her finger on the paper. "Someone ought to be *there*," she said, "even if second cousins aren't."

"He won't care who's putting him in the ground."

"You never know," Ida said, remembering the ghost by the radio set. "It shows respect. Besides—I *like* a funeral."

But he wasn't exactly being put in the ground in the bright new flowery suburb where he had lodged. There were no unhygienic buryings in that place. Two stately brick towers, like those of a Scandinavian town hall, cloisters with little plaques along the walls like war memorials, a bare cold secular chapel which could be adapted quietly and conveniently to any creed: no cemetery, wax flowers, impoverished jam-pots of wilting wild flowers. Ida was late. Hesitating a moment outside the door for fear the place might be full of Fred's friends, she thought someone had turned on the National Programme. She knew that cultured inexpressive heartless voice, but when she opened the door, a man, not a machine, stood up in a black cassock, saying: "Heaven." There was nobody there but some-one like a landlady, a servant who had parked her pram outside, two men impatiently whispering.

"Our belief in heaven," the clergyman went on, "is not qualified by our disbelief in the old medieval hell. We believe," he said, glancing swiftly along the smooth polished slipway towards the New Art doors through which the coffin would be launched into the flames, "we believe that this our brother is already at one with the One." He stamped his words, like little pats of butter, with his personal mark. "He has attained unity. We do not know what that One is with whom (or with which) he is now at one. We do not retain the old medieval beliefs in glassy seas and golden crowns. Truth is beauty and there is more beauty for us, a truth-loving generation, in the certainty that our brother is at this moment reabsorbed in the universal spirit." He touched a little buzzer, the New Art doors opened, the flames flapped, and the coffin slid smoothly down into the fiery sea. The doors closed, the nurse rose and made for the door, the clergyman smiled gently from behind the slipway, like a conjurer who has produced his nine hundred and fortieth rabbit without a hitch.

It was all over. Ida squeezed out with difficulty a last tear into a handkerchief scented with Californian Poppy. She liked a funeral—but it was with horror— as other people like a ghost story. Death shocked her, life was so important. She wasn't religious. She didn't believe in heaven or hell, only in ghosts, ouija boards, tables that rapped and little inept voices speaking plaintively of flowers. Let Papists treat death with flippancy : life wasn't so important perhaps to them as what came after; but to her death was the end of everything. At one with the One, it didn't mean a thing beside a glass of Guinness on a sunny day. She believed in ghosts, but you couldn't call that thin transparent existence life eternal : the squeak of a board, a piece of ectoplasm in a glass cupboard at the psychical research headquarters, a voice she'd heard once at a séance saying: "Everything is very beautiful on the upper plane. There are flowers everywhere."

Flowers, Ida thought scornfully; that wasn't life. Life was sunlight on brass bedposts, ruby port, the leap of the heart when the outsider you have backed passes the post and the colours go bobbing up. Life was poor Fred's mouth pressed down on her in the taxi, vibrating with the engine along the parade. What was the sense of dying if it made you babble of flowers? Fred didn't want flowers, he wanted—and the enjoyable distress she had felt in Henneky's returned. She took life with a deadly seriousness: she was prepared to cause any amount of unhappiness to anyone in order to defend the only thing she believed in. To lose your lover—"broken hearts," she would say, "always mend"—to be maimed or blinded—"lucky," she'd tell you, "to be alive at all." There was something dangerous and remorseless in her optimism, whether she was laughing in Henneky's or weeping at a funeral or a marriage.

She came out of the crematorium, and there from the twin towers above her head fumed the very last of Fred, a thin stream of grey smoke from the ovens. People passing up the flowery suburban road looked up and noted the smoke; it had been a busy day at the furnaces. Fred dropped in indistinguishable grey ash on the pink blossoms: he became part of the smoke nuisance over London, and Ida wept.

But while she wept a determination grew. it grew all the way to the tram lines which would lead her back to her familiar territory, to the bars and the elec-

tric signs and the variety theatres. Man is made by
the places in which he lives, and Ida's mind worked
with the simplicity and the regularity of a sky sign:
the ever-tipping glass, the ever-revolving wheel, the
plain question flashing on and off: "Do You Use
Forhan's for the Gums?" I'd do as much for Tom, she
thought, for Clarence, that old deceitful ghost in
Henneky's, for Harry. It's the least you can do for
anyone—ask questions, questions at inquests, questions at séances. Somebody had made Fred unhappy,
and somebody was going to be made unhappy in turn.
An eye for an eye. If you believed in God, you might
leave vengeance to Him, but you couldn't trust the
One, the universal spirit. Vengeance was Ida's, just as
much as reward was Ida's, the soft gluey mouth affixed
in taxis, the warm handclasp in cinemas, the only reward there was. And vengeance and reward—they
both were fun.

The tram tingled and sparked down the Embankment. If it was a woman who had made Fred unhappy,
she'd tell her what she thought. If Fred had killed
himself, she'd find it out, the papers would print the
news, someone would suffer. Ida was going to begin
at the beginning and work right on. She was a sticker.

The first stage (she had held the paper in her hand
all through the service) was Molly Pink, "described as
a private secretary," employed by Messrs. Carter &
Galloway.

Ida came up from Charing Cross Station into the
hot and windy light in the Strand flickering on the
carburetors; in an upper room of Stanley Gibbons's a
man with a long grey Edwardian moustache sat in a

window examining a postage stamp through a magnifying glass; a great dray laden with barrels stamped by, and the fountains played in Trafalgar Square, a cool translucent flower blooming and dropping into the drab sooty basins. It'll cost money, Ida repeated to herself, it always costs money if you want to know the truth, and she walked slowly up St. Martin's Lane, calculating, while all the time beneath the melancholy and the resolution, her heart beat faster to the refrain: it's exciting, it's fun, it's living. In Seven Dials the Negroes were hanging round the Royal Oak doors in tight natty suitings and old school ties, and Ida recognized one of them and passed the time of day. "How's business, Joe?" The great white teeth went on like a row of lights in the darkness above the bright striped shirt. "Fine, Ida, fine."

"And the hay fever?"

"Tur'ble, Ida, tur'ble."

"So long, Joe."

"So long, Ida."

It was a quarter of an hour's walk to Messrs. Carter & Galloway's, who were at the very top of a tall building on the outskirts of Gray's Inn. She had to economize now: she wouldn't even take a bus; and when she got to the dusty antiquated building, there wasn't a lift. The long flights of stone stairs wearied Ida. She'd had a long day and nothing to eat but a bun at the station. She sat down on a window sill and took off her shoes. Her feet were hot, she wiggled her toes. An old gentleman came down. He had a long moustache and a sidelong raffish look. He wore a check coat, a yellow waistcoat, and a grey bowler. He took off his bowler.

"In distress, madam?" he said, peering down at Ida with little bleary eyes. "Be of assistance?"

"I don't allow anyone else to scratch my toes," Ida said.

"Ha, ha," the old gentleman said, "a card. After my own heart. Up or down?"

"Up. All the way to the top."

"Carter & Galloway. Good firm. Tell 'em I sent you."

"What's your name?"

"Moyne. Charlie Moyne. Seen you here before."

"Never."

"Some place else. Never forget fine figure of a woman. Tell 'em Moyne sent you. Give you special terms."

"Why don't they have a lift in this place?"

"Old-fashioned people. Old-fashioned myself. Seen you at Epsom."

"You might have."

"Always tell a sporting woman. Ask you round the corner to split a bottle of fizz if those beggars hadn't taken the last fiver I came out with. Wanted to go and lay a couple. Have to go home first. Odds'll go down while I'm doing it. You'll see. You couldn't oblige me, I suppose? Two quid, Charlie Moyne." The bloodshot eyes watched her without hope, a little aloof and careless; the buttons on the yellow waistcoat stirred as the old heart hammered.

"Here," Ida said, "you can have a quid; now run along."

"Awfully kind of you. Give me your card. Post you a cheque tonight."

"I haven't got a card," Ida said.

"Came out without mine too. Never mind. Charlie Moyne. Care of Carter & Galloway. All know me here."

"That's all right," Ida said. "I'll see you again. I've got to be going on up."

"Take my arm." He helped her up. "Tell 'em Moyne sent you. Special terms." She looked back at the turn of the stairs. He was tucking the pound note away in his waistcoat, smoothing the moustache which was still golden at the tips, like a cigarette smoker's fingers, setting his bowler at an angle. Poor old geezer, Ida thought, he never expected to get that, watching him go off down the stairs in his jaunty and ancient despair.

There were only two doors on the top landing. She opened one marked "Inquiries," and there without a doubt was Molly Pink. In a little room hardly larger than a broom cupboard she sat beside a gas ring sucking a sweet. A kettle hissed at Ida as she entered. A swollen spotty face glared back at her without a word.

"Excuse me," Ida said.

"The partners is out."

"I came to see you."

The mouth fell a little open, a lump of toffee stirred on the tongue, the kettle whistled.

"Me?"

"Yes," Ida said. "You'd better look out. The kettle'll boil over. You *are* Molly Pink?"

"You want a cup?" The room was lined from floor to ceiling with files. A little window disclosed through the undisturbed dust of many years another block of buildings with the same arrangement of windows staring dustily back like a reflection. A dead fly hung in a broken web.

"I don't like tea," Ida said.

"That's lucky. There's only one cup," Molly said, filling a thick brown teapot with a chipped spout.

"A friend of mine called Moyne . . ." Ida began.

"Oh, him!" Molly said. "We just turned him out of house and home." A copy of *Woman and Beauty* was propped open on her typewriter, and her eyes slid continually back to it.

"Out of house and home?"

"House and home. He came to see the partners. He tried to blarney."

"Did he see them?"

"The partners is out. Have a toffee?"

"It's bad for the figure," Ida said.

"I make up for it. I don't eat breakfast."

Over Molly's head Ida could see the labels on the files: "Rents of 1-6 Mud Lane." "Rents of Wainage Estate, Balham." "Rents of . . ." They were surrounded by the pride of ownership, property. . . .

"I came here," Ida said, "because you met a friend of mine."

"Sit down," Molly said. "That's the clients' chair. I has to entertain 'em. Mr. Moyne's not a friend."

"Not Moyne. Someone called Hale."

"I don't want any more to do with that business. You ought to 'ave seen the partners. They was furious. I had to have a day off for the inquest. They kept me hours late next day."

"I just want to hear what happened."

"What happened? The partners is awful when roused."

"I mean about Fred—Hale."

"I didn't exactly know him."

"That man you said at the inquest came up——"

"He wasn't a man. He was just a kid. He knew Mr. Hale."

"But in the paper it said——"

"Oh, Mr. Hale *said* he didn't know him. I didn't tell them different. They didn't ask me. Except was there anything odd in his manner. Well, there wasn't anything you'd call odd. He was just scared, that's all. We get lots like that in here."

"But you didn't tell them that?"

"That's nothing uncommon. I knew what it was at once. He owed the kid money. We get lots like that. Like Charlie Moyne."

"He was scared, was he? Poor old Fred."

" 'I'm not Fred,' " he said, "sharp as you please. But I could tell all right. So could my girl friend."

"What was the kid like?"

"Oh, just a kid."

"Tall?"

"Not particularly."

"Fair?"

"I couldn't say that."

"How old was he?"

" 'Bout my age, I dessay."

"What's that?"

"Eighteen," Molly said, staring defiantly across the typewriter and the steaming kettle, sucking a toffee.

"Did he ask for money?"

"He didn't have time to ask for money."

"You didn't notice anything else?"

"He was awful anxious for me to go along with him. But I couldn't, not with my girl friend there."

"Thanks," Ida said, "it's something learnt."

"You a woman detective?" Molly asked.

"Oh, no, I'm just a friend of his."

There *was* something fishy: she was convinced of it now. She remembered again how scared he'd been in the taxi, and going down Holborn towards her digs behind Russell Square, in the late afternoon sun, she thought again of the way in which he had handed her the ten shillings before she went down into the Ladies'. He was a real gentleman; perhaps it was the last few shillings he had; and those people—that boy—dunning him for money. Perhaps he was another one ruined like Charlie Moyne, and now that her memory of his face was getting a bit dim, she couldn't help lending him a few of Charlie Moyne's features, the bloodshot eyes if nothing else. Sporting gentlemen, freehanded gentlemen, real gentlemen. The commercials drooped their dewlaps in the hall of the Imperial, the sun lay flat across the plane trees, and a bell rang and rang for tea in a boarding house in Coram Street.

I'll try the Board, Ida thought, and then I'll know.

When she got in, there was a card on the hall table, a card of Brighton Pier; if I was superstitious, she thought, if I was superstitious. She turned it over. It was only from Phil Corkery, asking her to come down. She had the same every year from Eastbourne, Hastings, and once from Aberystwyth. But she never went.

He wasn't someone she liked to encourage. Too quiet. Not what she called a man.

She went to the basement stairs and called Old Crowe. She needed two sets of fingers for the board and she knew it would give the old man pleasure. "Old Crowe," she called, peering down the stone stairs. "Old Crowe."

"What is it, Ida?"

"I'm going to have a turn at the Board."

She didn't wait for him, but went on up to her bed-sitting-room to make ready. The room faced east and the sun had gone. It was cold and dusk. Ida turned on the gas fire and drew the old scarlet velvet curtains to shut out the grey skies and the chimney pots. Then she patted the divan bed into shape and drew two chairs to the table. In a glass-fronted cupboard her life stared back at her, a good life: pieces of china bought at the seaside, a photograph of Tom, an Edgar Wallace, a Netta Syrett from a second-hand stall, some sheets of music, *The Good Companions*, her mother's picture, more china, a few jointed animals made of wood and elastic, trinkets given her by this, that, and the other, *Sorrell and Son*, the board.

She took the board gently down and locked the cupboard. A flat oval piece of polished wood on tiny wheels, it looked like something that had crept out of a drawer in a basement kitchen. But in fact it was Old Crowe who had done that, knocking gently on the door, sidling in, white hair, grey face, short-sighted pit-pony eyes, blinking at the bare globe in Ida's reading lamp. Ida tossed a pink netty scarf over the light and dimmed it for him.

"You got something to ask it, Ida?" Old Crowe said.
He shivered a little, frightened and fascinated. Ida
sharpened a pencil and inserted it in the prow of the
little board.

"Sit down, Old Crowe. What you been doing all
day?"

"They had a funeral at twenty-seven. One of those
Indian students."

"I been to a funeral too. Was yours a good one?"

"There aren't any good funerals these days. Not
with plumes."

Ida gave the little board a push. It slid sideways
across the polished table more than ever like a beetle.
"The pencil's too long," Old Crowe said. He sat, hugging his hands between his knees, bent forward watching the board. Ida screwed the pencil a little higher.
"Past or future?" Old Crowe said, panting a little.

"I want to get into touch today," Ida said.

"Dead or alive?" Old Crowe said.

"Dead. I seen him burnt this afternoon. Cremated.
Come on, Old Crowe, put your fingers on."

"Better take off your rings," Old Crowe said. "Gold
confuses it."

Ida unclothed her fingers, laid the tips on the board,
which squeaked away from her across the sheet of
foolscap. "Come on, Old Crowe," she said.

Old Crowe giggled. He said: "It's naughty," and
placed his bony digits on the very rim, where they
throbbed a tiny nervous tattoo. "What you going to
ask it, Ida?"

"Are you there, Fred?"

The board squeaked away under their fingers, drawing long lines across the paper this way and that. "It's got a will of its own," Ida said.

"Hush," said Old Crowe.

The board bucked a little with its hind wheel and came to a stop. "We might look now," Ida said. She pushed the board to one side, and they stared together at the network of pencilling.

"You might make out a Y there," Ida said.

"Or it might be an N."

"Anyway something's there. We'll try again." She put her fingers firmly on the board. "What happened to you, Fred?" and immediately the board was off and away. All her indomitable will worked through her fingers: she wasn't going to have any nonsense this time, and across the board the grey face of Old Crowe frowned with concentration.

"It's writing—real letters," Ida said with triumph, and as her own fingers momentarily loosened their grip she could feel the board slide firmly away as if on another's errand.

"Hush," said Old Crowe, but it bucked and stopped. They pushed the board away, and there, unmistakably, in large thin letters was a word, but not a word they knew: "SUKILL."

"It looks like a name," Old Crowe said.

"It must mean something," Ida said. "The Board always means something. We'll try again," and again the little wooden beetle scampered off, drawing its tortuous trail. The globe burnt red under the scarf, and Old Crowe whistled between his teeth. "Now," Ida said and lifted the board. A long ragged word ran diagonally across the paper: "FRESUICILLEYE."

"Well," Old Crowe said, "that's a mouthful. You can't make anything out of that, Ida."

"Can't I though?" Ida said. "Why, it's clear as clear. *Fre* is short for Fred and *Suici* for Suicide and Eye; that's what I always say—an eye for an eye and a tooth for a tooth."

"What about those two L's?"

"I don't know yet, but I'll bear them in mind." She leant back in her chair with a sense of power and triumph. "I'm not superstitious," she said, "but you can't get over that. The Board knows."

"She knows," Old Crowe said, sucking his teeth.

"One more try?" The board slid and squeaked and abruptly stopped. Clear as clear the name stared up at her: "PHIL."

"Well," Ida said, "well." She blushed a little. "Like a sugar biscuit?"

"Thank you, Ida, thank you."

Ida took a tin out of the cupboard drawer and pushed it over to Old Crowe. "They drove him to death," Ida said happily. "I knew there was something fishy. See that *Eye*. That as good as tells me what to do." Her eye lingered on *Phil*. "I'm going to make those people sorry they was ever born." She drew in her breath luxuriously and stretched her monumental legs. "Right and wrong," she said, "I believe in right and wrong," and delving a little deeper, with a sigh of happy satiety, she said: "It's going to be exciting, it's going to be fun, it's going to be a bit of life, Old Crowe," giving the highest praise she could give to anything, while the old man sucked his tooth and the pink light wavered on the Warwick Deeping.

PART TWO

1

THE Boy stood with his back to Spicer staring out
across the dark wash of sea. They had the end
of the pier to themselves; everyone else at that
hour and in that weather was in the concert hall. The
lightning went on and off above the horizon and the
rain dripped. "Where've you been?" the Boy said.

"Walking around," Spicer said.

"You been There?"

"I wanted to see it was all safe, that there wasn't anything you'd forgotten."

The Boy said slowly, leaning out across the rail into the doubtful rain: "When people do one murder, I've read they sometimes have to do another—to tidy up." The word "murder" conveyed no more to him than the words "box," "collar," "giraffe." He said: "Spicer, you keep away from there."

The imagination hadn't awakened. That was his strength. He couldn't see through other people's eyes, or feel with their nerves. Only the music made him uneasy, the cat-gut vibrating in the heart; it was like nerves losing their freshness, it was like age coming on, other people's experience battering on the brain. "Where are the rest of the mob?" he said.

"In Sam's, drinking."

"Why aren't you drinking too?"

"I'm not thirsty, Pinkie. I wanted some fresh air. This thunder makes you feel queer."

"Why don't they stop that bloody noise in there?" the Boy said.

"You not going to Sam's?"

"I've got a job of work to do," the Boy said.

"It's all right, Pinkie, ain't it? After that verdict it's all right? Nobody asked questions."

"I just want to be sure," the Boy said.

"The mob won't stand for any more killing."

"Who said there was going to be any killing?" The lightning flared up and showed his tight shabby jacket, the bunch of soft hair at the nape. "I've got a date, that's all. You be careful what you say, Spicer. You aren't milky, are you?"

"I'm not milky. You got me wrong, Pinkie. I just don't want another killing. That verdict sort of shook us all. What did they mean by it? We *did* kill him, Pinkie?"

"We got to go on being careful, that's all."

"What did they mean by it though? I don't trust the doctors. A break like that's *too* good."

"We got to be careful."

"What's that in your pocket, Pinkie?"

"I don't carry a gun," the Boy said. "You're fancying things." In the town a clock struck eleven; three strokes were lost in the thunder coming down across the Channel. "You better be off," the Boy said. "She's late already."

"You've got a razor there, Pinkie."

"I don't need a razor with a polony. If you want to know what it is, it's a bottle."

"You don't drink, Pinkie."

"Nobody would want to drink this."

"What is it, Pinkie?"

"Vitriol," the Boy said. "It scares a polony more than a knife." He turned impatiently away from the sea and complained again: "That music"; it moaned in his head in the hot electric light, it was the nearest he knew to sorrow, just as a faint secret sensual pleasure he felt, touching the bottle of vitriol with his fingers as Rose came hurrying by the concert hall, was his nearest approach to passion. "Get out," he said to Spicer. "She's here."

"Oh," Rose said, "I'm late. I've run all the way," she said. "I thought you might have thought——"

"I'd have waited," the Boy said.

"It was an awful night in the café," the girl said. "Everything went wrong. I broke two plates. And the cream was sour." It all came out in a breath. "Who was your friend?" she asked, peering into the darkness.

"He don't matter," the Boy said.

"I thought somehow—I couldn't see properly———"

"He don't matter," the Boy repeated.

"What are we going to do?"

"Why, I thought we'd talk a little here first," the Boy said, "and then go on somewhere—Sherry's? I don't care."

"I'd love Sherry's," Rose said.

"You got your money yet for that card?"

"Yes. I got it this morning."

"Nobody came and asked you questions?"

"Oh, no. But wasn't it dreadful, his being dead like that?"

"You saw his photograph?"

Rose came close to the rail and peered palely up at the Boy. "But it wasn't him. That's what I don't understand."

"People look different in photographs."

"I've got a memory for faces. It wasn't him. They must have cheated. You can't trust the newspapers."

"Come here," the Boy said. He drew her round the corner until they were a little further from the music, more alone with the lightning on the horizon and the thunder coming closer. "I like you," the Boy said, an unconvincing smile forking his mouth, "and I want to warn you. This fellow Hale, I've heard a lot about him. He got himself mixed up with things."

"What sort of things?" Rose whispered.

"Never mind what things," the Boy said. "Only I'd warn you for your own good—you've got the money —if I was you I'd forget it, forget all about that fellow who left the card. He's dead, see? You've got the money. That's all that matters."

"Anything you say," Rose said.

"You can call me Pinkie if you like. That's what my friends call me."

"Pinkie," Rose repeated, trying it out shyly as the thunder cracked overhead.

"You read about Peggy Baron, didn't you?"

"No, Pinkie."

"It was in all the papers."

"I didn't see any papers till I got this job. We couldn't afford papers at home."

"She got mixed up with a mob," the Boy said, "and people came asking her questions. It's not safe."

"I wouldn't get mixed up with a mob like that," Rose said.

"You can't always help it. It kind of comes that way."

"What happened to her?" Rose said.

"They spoilt her looks. She lost one eye. They splashed vitriol on her face."

Rose whispered. "Vitriol? What's vitriol?" and the lightning showed a strut of tarred wood, a wave breaking, and her pale bony terrified face.

"You never seen vitriol?" the Boy said, grinning through the dark. He showed her the little bottle. "That's vitriol." He took the cork out and spilled a lit-

tle on the wooden plank of the pier; it hissed like
steam. "It burns," the Boy said. "Smell it," and he
thrust the bottle under her nose.

She gasped at him. "Pinkie, *you* wouldn't—" and
"I was pulling your leg," he smoothly lied to her.
"That's not vitriol, that's just spirit. I wanted to warn
you, that's all. You and me's going to be friends. I
don't want a friend with her skin burned off. You tell
me if anyone asks questions. Anyone, mind. Get me on
the blower at Billy's straight off. Three sixes. You can
remember that." He took her arm and propelled her
away from the lonely pier end, back by the lit concert
hall, the music drifting landwards, grief in the guts.
"Pinkie," she said, "I wouldn't want to interfere. I
don't interfere in anyone's business. I've never been
nosy. Cross my heart."

"You're a good kid," he said.

"You know an awful lot about things, Pinkie," she
said with horror and admiration, and suddenly at the
stale romantic tune the orchestra was playing—"lovely
to look at, beautiful to hold, and heaven itself"—a little venom of anger and hatred came out on the Boy's
lips. "You've got to know a lot," he said, "if you get
around. Come on, we'll go to Sherry's."

Once off the pier they had to run for it; taxis
splashed them with water; the strings of coloured bulbs
down the Hove parade gleamed like pools of petrol
through the rain. They shook themselves like dogs on
the floor of Sherry's and Rose saw the queue waiting
all the way upstairs for the gallery. "It's full," she
said with disappointment.

"We'll go on the floor," the Boy said, paying his

three shillings as carelessly as if he always went there, and walked out among the little tables where the dancing partners sat with bright metallic hair and little black bags, while the coloured lights flashed green and pink and blue. Rose said: "It's lovely here. It reminds me," and all the way to their table she counted over aloud all the things of which it reminded her, the lights, the tune the band was playing, the crowd on the floor trying to rumba. She had an immense store of trivial memories and when she wasn't living in the future she was living in the past. As for the present— she got through that as quickly as she could, running away from things, running towards things, so that her voice was always a little breathless, her heart pounding at an escape or an expectation. "I whipped the plate under the apron and she said: 'Rose, what are you hiding there?' " and a moment later she was turning wide unfledged eyes back to the Boy with a look of the deepest admiration, the most respectful hope.

"What'll you drink?" the Boy said.

She didn't even know the name of a drink. In Nelson Place, from which she had emerged like a mole into the daylight of Snow's restaurant and the Palace Pier, she had never known a boy with enough money to offer her a drink. She would have said "beer" but she had had no opportunity of discovering whether she liked beer. A twopenny ice from an Everest tricycle was the whole extent of her knowledge of luxury. She goggled hopelessly at the Boy. He asked her sharply: "What d'you like? *I* don't know what you like."

"An ice," she said with disappointment, but she couldn't keep him waiting.

"What kind of an ice?"

"Just an ordinary ice," she said. Everest hadn't in all the slum years offered her much choice.

"Vanilla?" the waiter said. She nodded; she supposed that that was what she had always had, and so it proved, only a size larger; otherwise she might just as well have been sucking it between wafers by a tricycle.

"You're a soft sort of kid," the Boy said. "How old are you?"

"I'm seventeen," she said defiantly; there was a law which said a man couldn't go with you before you were seventeen.

"I'm seventeen too," the Boy said, and the eyes which had never been young stared with grey contempt into the eyes which had only just begun to learn a thing or two. He said: "Do you dance?" and she replied humbly: "I haven't danced much."

"It don't matter," the Boy said. "I'm not one for dancing." He eyed the slow movement of the two-backed beasts: pleasure, he thought, they call it pleasure: he was shaken by a sense of loneliness, an awful lack of understanding. The floor was cleared for the last cabaret of the evening. A spotlight picked out a patch of floor, a crooner in a dinner jacket, a microphone on a long black movable stand. He held it tenderly as if it were a woman, swinging it gently this way and that, wooing it with his lips while from the loudspeaker under the gallery his whisper reverberated hoarsely over the hall, like a dictator announcing victory, like the official news following a long censorship. "It gets you," the Boy said, "it gets you," surrendering himself to the huge brazen suggestion:

"Music talks, talks of our love.
  The starling on our walks talks, talks of our love,
  The taxis tooting,
  The last owl hooting,
  The tube train rumbling,
  Busy bee bumbling,
    Talk of our love.

"Music talks, talks of our love,
  The west wind on our walks talks, talks of our love,
  The nightingale singing,
  The postman ringing,
  Electric drill groaning,
  Office telephoning,
    Talk of our love."

The Boy stared at the spotlight; music, love, night-ingale, postman: the words stirred in his brain like po-etry; one hand caressed the vitriol bottle in his pocket, the other touched Rose's wrist. The inhuman voice whistled round the gallery and the Boy sat silent. It was he this time who was being warned; life held the vitriol bottle and warned him: I'll spoil your looks. It spoke to him in the music, and when he protested that he for one would never get mixed up, the music had his own retort at hand: "You can't always help it. It kind of comes that way."

"The watchdog on our walks talks, talks of our love."

The crowd stood at attention six deep behind the tables (there wasn't enough room on the floor for so many). They were dead quiet. It was like the anthem on Armistice Day when the King has deposited his

wreath, the hats off, and the troops turned to stone. It
was love of a kind, music of a kind, truth of a kind
they listened to.

"Gracie Fields funning,
The gangsters gunning,
Talk of our love."

The music pealed on under the Chinese lanterns and
the pink spotlight featured the crooner with the microphone close to his starched shirt. "You been in love?"
the Boy asked sharply and uneasily.

"Oh, yes," Rose said.

The Boy retorted with sudden venom: "You would
have been. You're green. You don't know what people
do." The music came to an end and in the silence he
laughed aloud. "You're innocent." People turned in
their chairs and looked at them; a girl giggled. His fingers pinched her wrist. "You're green," he said again.
He was working himself into a little sensual rage, as
he had done with the soft kids at the council school.
"You don't know anything," he said, with contempt
in his nails.

"Oh, no," she protested. "I know a lot."

The Boy grinned at her. "Not a thing"—pinching
the skin of her wrist until his nails nearly met. "You'd
like me for your boy, eh? We'll keep company?"

"Oh," she said, "I'd love it." Tears of pride and
pain pricked behind her lids. "If you like doing that,"
she said, "go on."

The Boy let go. "Don't be soft," he said. "Why
should I like it? You think you know too much," he

complained. He sat there, anger like a live coal in his belly, as the music came on again; all the good times he'd had in the old days with nails and splinters, the tricks he'd learnt later with a razor blade: what would be the fun if people didn't squeal? He said furiously: "We'll be going. I can't stand this place," and obediently Rose began to pack her handbag, putting back her Woolworth compact and her handkerchief. "What's that?" the Boy said when something clinked in her bag; she showed him the end of a string of beads.

"You a Catholic?" the Boy said.

"Yes," Rose said.

"I'm one too," the Boy said. He gripped her arm and pushed her out into the dark dripping street. He turned up the collar of his jacket and ran as the lightning flapped and the thunder filled the air. They ran from doorway to doorway until they were back on the parade in one of the empty glass shelters. They had it to themselves in the noisy stifling night. "Why, I was in a choir once," the Boy confided, and suddenly he began to sing softly in his spoilt boy's voice: "Agnus dei qui tollis peccata mundi, dona nobis pacem." In his voice a whole lost world moved; the lighted corner below the organ, the smell of incense and laundered surplices, and the music. Music, it didn't matter what music— "Agnus dei," "lovely to look at, beautiful to hold," "the starling on our walks," "credo in unum Dominum"—any music moved him, speaking of things he didn't understand.

"Do you go to Mass?" he said.

"Sometimes," Rose said. "It depends on work. Most weeks I wouldn't get much sleep if I went to Mass."

"I don't care what you do," the Boy said sharply. "I don't go to Mass."

"But you believe, don't you," Rose implored him, "you think it's true?"

"Of course it's true," the Boy said. "What else could there be?" he went scornfully on. "Why," he said, "it's the only thing that fits. These atheists, they don't know nothing. Of course there's Hell. Flames and damnation," he said with his eyes on the dark shifting water and the lightning and the lamps going out above the black struts of the Palace Pier, "torments."

"And Heaven too," Rose said with anxiety, while the rain fell interminably on.

"Oh, maybe," the Boy said, "maybe."

Wet to the skin, the trousers sticking to his thin legs, the Boy went up the long unmatted flight to his bedroom at Billy's. The banister shook under his hand, and when he opened the door and found the mob there, sitting on his brass bedstead smoking, he said furiously: "When's that banister going to be mended? It's not safe. Someone'll take a fall one day." The curtain wasn't drawn, the window was open, and the last lightning flapped across the grey roofs stretching to the sea. The Boy went to his bed and swept off the crumbs of Cubitt's sausage roll. "What's this," he said, "a meeting?"

"There's trouble about the subscriptions, Pinkie," Cubitt said. "There's two not come in. Brewer and Tate. They say now Kite's dead——"

"Do we carve 'em up, Pinkie?" Dallow said. Spicer

stood at the window watching the storm. He said nothing, staring out at the flames and chasms of the sky.

"Ask Spicer," the Boy said. "He's been doing a lot of thinking lately." They all turned and watched Spicer. Spicer said: "Maybe we ought to lay off awhile. You know a lot of the boys cleared out when Kite got killed."

"Go on," the Boy said. "Listen to him. He's what they call a philosopher."

"Well," Spicer said angrily, "there's free speech in this mob, ain't there? Those that cleared out, they didn't see how a kid could run this show."

The Boy sat on the bed watching him with his hands in his damp pockets. He shivered once.

"I was always against murder," Spicer said. "I don't care who knows it. What good's revenge? It's sentiment."

"Sour and milky," the Boy said.

Spicer came into the middle of the room. "Listen, Pinkie," he said. "Be reasonable." He appealed to them all: "Be reasonable."

"There's things in what he says," Cubitt suddenly put in. "We had a lucky break. We don't want to draw attention to ourselves. We'd better let Brewer and Tate be for a while."

The Boy got up. A few crumbs stuck to his wet suit. "You ready, Dallow?" he said.

"What you say, Pinkie," Dallow said, grinning like a large friendly dog.

"Where you going, Pinkie?" Spicer said.

"I'm going to see Brewer."

Cubitt said: "You act as if it was last year we killed Hale, not last week. We got to be cautious."

"That's over and done," the Boy said. "You heard the verdict. Natural causes," he said, looking out at the dying storm.

"You forget that girl in Snow's. She could hang us."

"I'm looking after the girl. She won't talk."

"You're marrying her, aren't you?" Cubitt said. Dallow laughed.

The Boy's hands came out of his pockets, the knuckles clenched white. He said: "Who told you I was marrying her?"

"Spicer," Cubitt said.

Spicer backed away from the Boy. He said: "Listen, Pinkie. I only said as it would make her safe. A wife can't give evidence. . . ."

"I don't need to marry a squirt to make her safe. How do we make you safe, Spicer?" His tongue came out between his teeth, licking the edges of his dry cracked lips. "If carving'd do it . . ."

"It was just a joke," Cubitt said. "You don't need to take it so solemn. You want a sense of humour, Pinkie."

"You think that was funny, eh?" the Boy said. "Me—marrying—that cheap polony." He croaked: "Ha, ha," at them. "I'll learn. Come on, Dallow."

"Wait till morning," Cubitt said. "Wait till some of the other boys come in."

"You milky too?"

"You don't believe that, Pinkie. But we got to go slow."

"You with me, Dallow?" the Boy said.

"I'm with you, Pinkie."

"Then we'll be going," the Boy said. He went across

to the washstand and opened the little door where the
jerry stood. He felt at the back behind the jerry and
pulled out a tiny blade, like the blades women shave
with but blunt along one edge and mounted with sticking plaster. He stuck it under his long thumb nail, the
only nail not bitten close, and drew on his glove. He
said: "We'll be back with the sub in half an hour,"
and led the way bang straight down Billy's stairs. The
cold of his drenching had got under his skin: he came
out onto the front a pace ahead of Dallow, his face
contorted with ague, a shiver twisting the narrow
shoulders. He said over his shoulder to Dallow: "We'll
go to Brewer's. One lesson'll be enough."

"What you say, Pinkie," Dallow said, plodding
after. The rain had stopped; it was low tide and the
shallow edge of the sea scraped far out at the rim of
the sand. A clock struck midnight. Dallow suddenly
began to laugh.

"What's got you, Dallow?"

"I was just thinking," Dallow said. "You're a grand
little geezer, Pinkie. Kite was right to take you on.
You go straight for things, Pinkie."

"You're all right," the Boy said, staring ahead, the
ague wringing his face. They passed the Cosmopolitan, the lights on here and there up the huge front to
the turrets against the clouded moving sky. In Snow's
when they passed a single light went out. They turned
up the Old Steyne. Brewer had a house near the tram
lines on the Lewes road almost under the railway viaduct.

"He's gone to bed," Dallow said. Pinkie rang the
bell, holding his finger on the switch. Low shuttered

shops ran off on either hand; a tram went by with nobody in it, labelled Depot only, ringing and swinging
down the empty road, the conductor drowsing on a seat
inside, the roof gleaming from the storm. Pinkie kept
his finger on the bell.

"What made Spicer say that—about me marrying?" the Boy said.

"He just thought it'd close her clapper," Dallow
said.

"She's not what keeps me awake," the Boy said,
pressing on the bell. A light went on upstairs, a window creaked up, and a voice called: "Who's that?"

"It's me," the Boy said. "Pinkie."

"What do you want? Why don't you come around
in the morning?"

"I want to talk to you, Brewer."

"I've got nothing to talk about, Pinkie, that can't
wait."

"You'd better open up, Brewer. You don't want the
mob along here."

"The old woman's awful sick, Pinkie. I don't want
any trouble. She's asleep. She hasn't slept for three
nights."

"This'll wake her," the Boy said with his finger on
the bell. A slow goods train went by across the viaduct,
shaking smoke down into the Lewes Road.

"Leave off, Pinkie, and I'll open up."

Pinkie shivered as he waited, his gloved hand deep
in his damp pocket. Brewer opened the door, a stout
elderly man in soiled white pyjamas. The bottom button was missing and the coat swung from the bulging
belly and the deep navel. "Come in, Pinkie," he said,

"and walk quiet. The old woman's bad. I've been worrying my head off."

"That why you haven't paid your subscription, Brewer?" the Boy said. He looked with contempt down the narrow hall—the shell case converted into an umbrella stand, the moth-eaten stag's head bearing on one horn a bowler hat, a steel helmet used for ferns. Kite ought to have got them into better money than this. Brewer had only just graduated from the street-corner, saloon-bar betting. A welsher. It was no good trying to draw more than ten per cent of his bets.

Brewer said: "Come in here and be snug. It's warm in here. What a cold night!" He had a hollow cheery manner even in pyjamas. He was like a legend on a racing card: The Old Firm—You Can Trust Bill Brewer. He lit the gas fire, turned on a stand lamp in a red silk shade with a bobble fringe. The light glowed on a silver-plated biscuit box, a framed wedding group. "Have a spot of Scotch?" Brewer invited them.

"You know I don't drink," the Boy said.

"Ted will," Brewer said.

"I don't mind a spot," Dallow said. He grinned and said: "Here's how."

"We've called for that subscription, Brewer," the Boy said.

The man in white pyjamas hissed soda into his glass. His back turned, he watched Pinkie in the glass above the sideboard until he caught the other's eye. He said: "I been worried, Pinkie. Ever since Kite was croaked."

"Well?" the Boy said.

"It's like this. I said to myself if Kite's mob can't even protect—" He stopped suddenly and listened.

"Was that the old woman?" Very faintly from the room above came the sound of coughing. Brewer said: "She's woke up. I got to go and see her."

"You stay here," the Boy said, "and talk."

"She'll want turning."

"When we've finished you can go."

Cough, cough, cough: it was like a machine trying to start and failing. Brewer said desperately: "Be human. She won't know where I've got to. I'll only be a minute."

"You don't need to be longer than a minute here," the Boy said. "All we want's what's due to us. Twenty pounds."

"I haven't got it in the house. Honest I haven't."

"That's too bad for you." The Boy drew off his right glove.

"It's like this, Pinkie. I paid it all out yesterday. To Colleoni."

"What in Jesus' name," the Boy said, "has Colleoni to do with it?"

Brewer went rapidly and desperately on, listening to the cough, cough, cough upstairs. "Be reasonable, Pinkie. I can't pay both of you. I'd have been carved if I hadn't paid Colleoni."

"Is he in Brighton?"

"He's stopping at the Cosmopolitan."

"And Tate—Tate's paid Colleoni too?"

"That's right, Pinkie. He's running the business in a big way." A big way—it was like an accusation, a reminder of the brass bedstead at Billy's, the crumbs on the mattress.

"You think I'm finished?" the Boy said.

"Take my advice, Pinkie, and go in with Colleoni."

The Boy suddenly drew his hand back and slashed with his razored nail at Brewer's cheek. He struck blood out along the cheekbone. "Don't," Brewer said, "don't," backing against the sideboard, upsetting the biscuit box. He said: "I've got protection. You be careful. I've got protection."

Dallow refilled his glass with Brewer's whisky. The Boy said: "Look at him. He's got protection." Dallow took a splash of soda.

"You want any more?" the Boy said. "That was just to show you who's protecting you."

"I can't pay both, Pinkie. God's sake, keep back."

"Twenty pounds is what we've come for, Brewer."

"Colleoni'll have my blood, Pinkie."

"You needn't worry. We'll protect you."

Cough, cough, cough, went the woman upstairs, and then a faint cry like a sleeping child's. "She's calling me," Brewer said.

"Twenty pounds."

"I don't keep my money in here. Let me fetch it."

"You go with him, Dallow," the Boy said. "I'll wait here," and he sat down on a straight carved dining-room chair and stared out—at the mean street, the dustbins along the pavement, the vast shadow of the viaduct. He sat perfectly still with his grey ancient eyes giving nothing away.

A big way—Colleoni come into it in a big way—he knew there wasn't a soul in the mob he could trust —except perhaps Dallow. That didn't matter. You couldn't make mistakes when you trusted nobody. A cat coasted cautiously round a bin on the pavement stopped suddenly, crouched back, and in the semi-dark its agate eyes stared up at the Boy. Boy and cat, they didn't stir, watching each other, until Dallow returned.

"I've got the money, Pinkie," Dallow said. The Boy turned his head and grinned at Dallow; suddenly his face was convulsed: he sneezed twice, violently. Overhead the coughing died away. "He won't forget this visit," Dallow said. He added anxiously: "You ought to have a spot of whisky, Pinkie. You've caught cold."

"I'm all right," the Boy said. He got up. "We won't stop and say good-bye."

The Boy led the way down the middle of the empty road, between the tram lines. He said suddenly: "Do you think I'm finished, Dallow?"

"You?" Dallow said. "Why, you haven't even begun." They walked for a while in silence, the water from the gutters dripped on the pavement. Then Dallow spoke:

"You worrying about Colleoni?"

"I'm not worrying."

Dallow said suddenly: "You're worth a dozen Colleonis. The Cosmopolitan!" he exclaimed and spat.

"Kite thought he'd go in for the automatic machines. He learned different. Now Colleoni thinks the coast's clear. *He's* branching out."

"He ought to have learned from Hale."

"Hale died natural."

Dallow laughed. "Tell that to Spicer." They turned the corner by the Royal Albion and the sea was with them again—the tide had turned—a movement, a splashing, a darkness. The Boy looked suddenly sideways and up at Dallow—he could trust Dallow—receiving from the ugly and broken face a sense of triumph and companionship and superiority. He felt as a physically weak but cunning schoolboy feels who has attached to himself in an undiscriminating fidelity the strongest boy in the school. "You mug," he said and pinched Dallow's arm. It was almost like affection.

A light still burned in Billy's, and Spicer was waiting in the hall. "Anything happened?" he asked anxiously. His pale face had come out in spots round the mouth and nose.

"What do you think?" the Boy said, going upstairs. "We brought the subscription."

Spicer followed him into his bedroom. "There was a call for you just after you'd gone."

"Who from?"

"A girl called Rose."

The Boy sat on the bed undoing his shoe. "What did she want?" he said.

"She said while she was out with you, somebody had been in asking for her."

The Boy sat still with the shoe in his hand. "Pinkie," Spicer said, "was it *the* girl? The girl from Snow's?"

"Of course it was."

"I answered the phone, Pinkie."

"Did she know your voice?"

"How do I know, Pinkie?"

"Who was asking for her?"

"She didn't know. She said tell you because you wanted to hear. Pinkie, suppose the bogies have got that far?"

"The bogies aren't as smart as that," Pinkie said.

"Maybe it's one of Colleoni's men, poking around after their pal Fred." He took off his other shoe. "You don't need to turn milky, Spicer."

"It was a woman, Pinkie."

"I'm not troubling. Fred died natural. That's the verdict. You can forget it. There's other things to think of now." He put his shoes side by side under the bed, took off his coat, hung it on a bed ball, took off his trousers, lay back in his underpants and shirt on top of the bed. "I'm thinking, Spicer, you oughter take a holiday. You look all in. I wouldn't want anyone seeing you like that." He closed his eyes. "You be off, Spicer, and take things easy."

"If that girl ever knew *who* put the card . . ."

"She'll never know. Turn out the light and get."

The light went out and the moon went on like a lamp outside, slanting across the roofs, laying the shadow of clouds across the downs, illuminating the white empty stands of the racecourse above White-hawk Bottom like the monoliths of Stonehenge, shining across the tide which drove up from Boulogne and washed against the piles of the Palace Pier. It lit the washstand, the open door where the jerry stood, the brass balls at the bed end.

2

The Boy lay on the bed. A cup of coffee went cold on the washstand, and the bed was sprinkled with flakes of pastry. The Boy licked an indelible pencil, his mouth was stained purple at the corners, he wrote: "Refer you to my previous letter" and concluded it at

last: "P. Brown, Secretary, the Bookmakers' Protection . . ." The envelope addressed "Mr. J. Tate" lay
on the washstand, the corner soiled with coffee. When
he had finished writing, he put his head back on the
pillow and closed his eyes. He fell asleep at once: it
was like the falling of a shutter, the pressure of the
bulb which ends a time exposure. He had no dreams.
His sleep was functional. When Dallow opened the
door he woke at once. "Well?" he said, lying there
without moving, fully dressed among the pastry
crumbs.

"There's a letter for you, Pinkie. Judy brought
it up."

The Boy took the letter. Dallow said: "It's an elegant letter, Pinkie. Smell it."

The Boy held the mauve envelope to his nose. It
smelt like a cachou for bad breath. He said: "Can't
you keep off that bitch? If Billy knew . . ."

"Who'd be writing an elegant letter like that,
Pinkie?"

"Colleoni. He wants me to call in for a talk at the
Cosmopolitan."

"The Cosmopolitan," Dallow repeated with disgust. "You won't go, will you?"

"Of course I'll go."

"It's not the sort of place where you'd feel at home."

"Elegant," the Boy said, "like his notepaper. Costs a
lot of money. He thinks he can scare me."

"Perhaps we'd better lay off Tate."

"Take that jacket down to Billy. Tell him to sponge
it quick and put an iron over it. Give these shoes a
brush." He kicked them out from under the bed and

sat up. "He thinks he'll have the laugh on us." In the tipped mirror on the washstand he could see himself, but his eyes shifted quickly from the image of smooth, never shaven cheek, soft hair, old eyes · he wasn't interested. He had too much pride to worry about appearances.

So that later he was quite at ease waiting in the great lounge under the domed lights for Colleoni; young men kept on arriving in huge motoring coats accompanied by small tinted creatures, who rang like expensive glass when they were touched but who conveyed an impression of being as sharp and as tough as tin. They looked at nobody, sweeping through the lounge as they had swept in racing models down the Brighton Road, ending on high stools in the American Bar. A stout woman in a white fox fur came out of a lift and stared at the Boy, then she got back into the lift again and moved weightily upwards. A little Jewess sniffed at him bitchily and then talked him over with another little Jewess on a settee. Mr. Colleoni came across an acre of deep carpet from the Louis Seize Writing Room, walking on tiptoe in glacé shoes.

He was a small Jew with a neat round belly; he wore a grey double-breasted waistcoat, and his eyes gleamed like raisins. His hair was thin and grey. The little bitches on the settee stopped talking as he passed and concentrated. He clinked very gently as he moved; it was the only sound.

"You were asking for me?" he said.

"You asked for me," the Boy said. "I got your letter."

"Surely," Mr. Colleoni said, making a little bewildered motion with his hands, "you are not Mr. P. Brown?" He explained: "I expected someone a good deal older."

"You asked for me," the Boy said.

The little raisin eyes took him in: the sponged suit and the narrow shoulders, the cheap black shoes. "I thought Mr. Kite . . ."

"Kite's dead," the Boy said. "You know that."

"I missed it," Mr. Colleoni said. "Of course that makes a difference."

"You can talk to me," the Boy said, "instead of Kite."

Mr. Colleoni smiled. "I don't think it's necessary," he said.

"You'd better," the Boy said. Little chimes of laughter came from the American Bar and the chink, chink, chink of ice. A page came out of the Louis Seize Writing Room, called: "Sir Joseph Montagu, Sir Joseph Montagu," and passed into the Pompadour Boudoir. The spot of damp, where Billy's iron had failed to pass, above the Boy's breast pocket was slowly fading out in the hot Cosmopolitan air.

Mr. Colleoni put out a hand and gave him a quick pat, pat, pat on the arm. "Come with me," he said. He led the way, walking on glacé tiptoe past the settee, where the Jewesses whispered, past a little table where a man was saying· "I told him ten thousand's my limit" to an old man who sat with closed eyes above his chilling tea. Mr. Colleoni looked over his shoulder and said gently: "The service here is not what it used to be."

He looked into the Louis Seize Writing Room. A

woman in mauve with an untimely tiara was writing a letter in a vast jumble of chinoiserie. Mr. Colleoni withdrew. "We'll go where we can talk in peace," he said and tiptoed back across the lounge. The old man had opened his eyes and was testing his tea with his finger. Mr. Colleoni led the way to the gilt grille of the lift. "Number fifteen," he said. They rose angelically towards peace. "Cigar?" Mr. Colleoni asked.

"I don't smoke," the Boy said. A last squeal of gaiety came from below, from the American Bar, the last syllable of the page boy returning from the Pompadour Boudoir: "Gu," before the gates slid back and they were in the padded sound-proof passage. Mr. Colleoni paused and lit his cigar.

"Let's have a look at that lighter," the Boy said.

Mr. Colleoni's small shrewd eyes shone blankly under the concealed pervasive electric glow. He held it out. The Boy turned it over and looked at the hall mark. "Real gold," he said.

"I like things good," Mr. Colleoni said, unlocking a door. "Take a chair." The armchairs, stately red velvet couches stamped with crowns in gold and silver thread, faced the wide seaward windows, and the wrought-iron balconies. "Have a drink."

"I don't drink," the Boy said.

"Now," Mr. Colleoni said, "who sent you?"

"No one sent me."

"I mean who's running your mob if Kite's dead."

"I'm running it," the Boy said.

Mr. Colleoni politely checked a smile, tapping his thumb nail with the gold lighter.

"What happened to Kite?"

"You know that story," the Boy said. He gazed across at the Napoleonic crowns, the silver thread. "*You* won't want to hear the details. It wouldn't have happened if we hadn't been crossed. A journalist thought he could put over one on us."

"What journalist's that?"

"You ought to read the inquests," the Boy said, staring out through the window at the pale arch of sky against which a few light clouds blew up.

Mr. Colleoni looked at the ash on his cigar; it was half an inch long; he sat deep down in his armchair, and crossed his little plump thighs contentedly.

"I'm not saying anything about Kite," the Boy said. "He trespassed."

"You mean," Mr. Colleoni said, "you aren't interested in automatic machines?"

"I mean," the Boy said, "that trespassing's not healthy."

A little wave of musk came over the room from the handkerchief in Mr. Colleoni's breast pocket.

"It'd be you who'd need protection," the Boy said.

"I've got all the protection I need," Mr. Colleoni said. He shut his eyes; he was snug; the huge moneyed hotel lapped him round; he was at home. The Boy sat on the edge of his chair because he didn't believe in relaxing during business hours; it was he who looked like an alien in this room, not Mr. Colleoni.

"You are wasting your time, my child," Mr. Colleoni said. "You can't do me any harm." He laughed gently. "If you want a job though, come to me. I like push. I dare say I could find room for you. The world needs young people with energy." The hand with the cigar moved expansively, mapping out the world as Mr. Colleoni visualized it: lots of little electric clocks controlled by Greenwich, buttons on a desk, a good suite on the first floor, accounts audited, reports from agents, silver, cutlery, glass.

"I'll be seeing you on the course," the Boy said.

"You'll hardly do that," Mr. Colleoni said. "I haven't been to a racecourse, let me see, it must be twenty years." There wasn't a point, he seemed to be indicating, fingering his gold lighter, at which their worlds touched: the week-end at the Cosmopolitan, the portable dictaphone beside the desk, had not the smallest connexion with Kite slashed quickly with razors on a railway platform, the grubby hand against the skyline signalling to the bookie from the stand, the heat, the dust fuming up over the half-crown enclosure, the smell of bottled beer.

"I'm just a business man," Mr. Colleoni softly explained. "I don't need to see a race. And nothing you might try to do to my men could affect me. I've got two in hospital now. It doesn't matter. They have the best attention. Flowers, grapes . . . I can afford it. I don't have to worry. I'm a business man," Mr. Colleoni went expansively and good-humouredly on. "I like you. You're a promising youngster. That's why I'm talking to you like a father. You can't damage a business like mine."

"I could damage you," the Boy said.

"It wouldn't pay. There wouldn't be any faked alibis for you. It would be *your* witnesses who'd be scared. I'm a business man." The raisin eyes blinked as the sun slanted in across a bowl of flowers and fell on the deep carpet. "Napoleon the Third used to have this room," Mr. Colleoni said, "and Eugénie."

"Who was she?"

"Oh," Mr. Colleoni said vaguely, "one of those foreign polonies." He plucked a flower and stuck it in his buttonhole, and something a little doggish peeped out of the black buttony eyes, a hint of the seraglio.

"I'll be going," the Boy said. He rose and moved to the door.

"You do understand me, don't you?" Mr. Colleoni said without moving; holding his hand very still he kept the cigar ash, quite a long ash now, suspended. "Brewer's been complaining. You don't do that again. And Tate . . . you mustn't try tricks with Tate." His old Semitic face showed few emotions but a mild amusement, a mild friendliness; but suddenly sitting there in the rich Victorian room, with the gold lighter in his pocket and the cigar case on his lap, he looked as a man might look who owned the whole world, the whole visible world, that is: the cash registers and policemen and prostitutes, Parliament and the laws which say "this is Right and this is Wrong."

"I understand all right," the Boy said. "You think our mob's too small for you."

"I employ a great many people," Mr. Colleoni said.

The Boy closed the door; a loose shoelace tapped all the way down the passage; the huge lounge was almost empty: a man in plus fours waited for a girl. The visible world was all Mr. Colleoni's. The spot where the iron hadn't passed was still a little damp over the Boy's breast.

A hand touched the Boy's arm. He looked round

and recognized the man in a bowler hat. He nodded guardedly. "Morning."

"They told me at Billy's," the man said, "you'd come here."

The Boy's heart missed a beat: for almost the first time it occurred to him that the law could hang him, take him out in a yard, drop him in a pit, bury him in lime, put an end to the great future. . . .

"You want me?"

"That's right."

He thought: Rose, the girl, someone asking questions. His memory flashed back: he remembered how she caught him with his hand under the table, feeling for something. He grinned dully and said: "Well, they haven't sent the Big Four anyway."

"Mind coming round to the station?"

"Got a warrant?"

"It's only Brewer been complaining you hit him. You left your scar all right."

The Boy began to laugh. "Brewer? Me? I wouldn't touch him."

"Come round and see the inspector?"

"Of course I will."

They came out onto the parade. A pavement photographer saw them coming and lifted the cap from his camera. The Boy put his hands in front of his face and went by. "You ought to put a stop to those things," he said. "Fine thing it'd be to have a picture postcard stuck up on the pier, you and me walking to the station."

"They caught a murderer once in town with one of those snaps."

"I read about it," the Boy said and fell silent. This is Colleoni's doing, he thought, he's showing off: he put Brewer up to this.

"Brewer's wife's pretty bad, they say," the detective remarked softly.

"Is she?" the Boy said. "I wouldn't know."

"Got your alibi ready, I suppose?"

"How do I know? I don't know when he said I hit him. A geezer can't have an alibi for every minute of the day."

"You're a wide kid," the detective said, "but you needn't get fussed about this. The inspector wants to have a friendly chat, that's all."

He led the way through the charge room. A man with a tired ageing face sat behind a desk. "Sit down, Brown," he said. He opened a cigarette box and pushed it across.

"I don't smoke," the Boy said. He sat down and watched the inspector alertly. "Aren't you going to charge me?"

"There's no charge," the inspector said. "Brewer thought better of it." He paused. He looked more tired than ever. He said: "I want to talk straight for once. We know more about each other than we admit. I don't interfere with you and Brewer: I've got more important things to do than prevent you and Brewer—arguing. But you know just as well as I do that Brewer wouldn't come here to complain if he hadn't been put up to it."

"You've certainly got ideas," the Boy said.

"Put up to it by someone who's not afraid of your mob."

"There's not much escapes the bogies," the Boy said, grimacing derisively.

"The races start next week, and I don't want to have any big-scale mob fighting in Brighton. I don't mind you carving each other up in a quiet way, I don't give a penny for your worthless skins, but when two mobs start scrapping, people who matter may get hurt."

"Meaning who?" the Boy said.

"Meaning decent innocent people. Poor people out to put a shilling on the tote. Clerks, charwomen, navvies. People who wouldn't be seen dead talking to you —or to Colleoni."

"What are you getting at?" the Boy said.

"I'm getting at this. You aren't big enough for your job, Brown. You can't stand against Colleoni. If there's any fighting I shall come down like a ton of bricks on both of you—but it will be Colleoni who'll have the alibis. No one's going to fake you an alibi against Colleoni. You take my advice. Clear out of Brighton."

"Fine," the Boy said. "A bogy doing Colleoni's job for him."

"This is private and unofficial," the inspector said. "I'm being human for once. I don't care if you get carved or Colleoni gets carved, but I'm not going to have innocent people hurt if I can help it."

"You think I'm finished?" the Boy said. He grinned uneasily, looking away, looking at the walls plastered with notices. Dog Licences. Gun Licences. Found Drowned. A dead face met his eye staring from the wall, unnaturally pasty. Unbrushed hair. A scar by the mouth. "You think Colleoni'll keep the peace better?" He could read the writing: "One nickel watch, waistcoat and trousers of grey cloth, blue striped shirt, aertex drawers.''

"Well?"

"It's valuable advice," the Boy said, grinning down at the polished desk, the box of Players, a crystal paperweight. "I'll have to think it over. I'm young to retire."

"You're too young to run a racket if you ask me."

"So Brewer's not bringing a charge?"

"He's not afraid to. I talked him out of it. I wanted to have a chance to speak to you straight."

"Well," the Boy said, standing up, "maybe I'll be seeing you, maybe not." He grinned again, passing through the charge room, but a bright spot of colour stood out on each cheekbone. There was poison in his veins, though he grinned and bore it. He had been insulted. He was going to show the world. They thought because he was only seventeen . . . he jerked his narrow shoulders back at the memory that he'd killed his man, and these bogies who thought they were clever weren't clever enough to discover that. He trailed the clouds of his own glory after him : hell lay about him in his infancy. He was ready for more deaths.

PART THREE

2

IDA ARNOLD sat up in the boarding-house bed.
For a moment she didn't know where she was.
Her head ached with the thick night at Sherry's.
It came slowly back to her as she stared at the heavy
ewer on the floor, the basin of grey water in which
she had perfunctorily washed, the bright pink roses
on the wallpaper, a wedding group—Phil Corkery

dithering outside the front door, pecking at her lips, swaying off down the parade as if that was all he could expect, while the tide receded. She looked round the room: it didn't look so good in the morning light as when she had booked it, but "it's homely," she thought with satisfaction, "it's what I like."

The sun was shining; Brighton was at its best. The passage outside her room was gritty with sand; she felt it under her shoes all the way downstairs; and in the hall there were a pail, two spades, and a long piece of seaweed hanging by the door as a barometer. There were a lot of sandshoes lying about, and from the dining room came a child's querulous voice repeating over and over: "I don't want to dig. I want to go to the pictures. I don't want to dig."

At one she was meeting Phil Corkery at Snow's. Before that there were things to do; she had to go easy on the money, not put away too much in the way of Guinness. It wasn't cheap living down at Brighton, and she wasn't going to take cash from Corkery—she had a conscience, she had a code, and if she took cash she gave something in return. Black Boy was the answer: she had to see about it first thing before the odds shortened: sinews of war; and she made her way towards Kemp Town to the only bookie she knew: old Jim Tate, "Honest Jim" of the half-crown enclosure.

He bellowed at her as soon as she got inside his office: "Here's Ida. Sit down, Mrs. Turner," getting her name wrong. He pushed a box of Gold Flake across to her. "Inhale a cheroot." He was a little more than life size. His voice, after the race meetings of twenty years, could hit no tone which wasn't loud and hoarse. He was a man you needed to look at through the wrong end of a telescope if you were to believe him the fine healthy fellow he made himself out to be. When you were close to him, you saw the thick blue veins on the left forehead, the red money-spider's web across the eyeballs. "Well, Mrs. Turner—Ida, what is it you fancy?"

"Black Boy," Ida said.

"Black Boy," Jim Tate repeated. "That's ten to one."

"Twelve to one."

"The odds have shortened. There's been a packet laid on Black Boy this week. You wouldn't get ten to one from anyone but your old friend."

"All right," Ida said. "Put me on twenty-five pounds. And my name's not Turner. It's Arnold."

"Twenty-five nicker. That's a fat bet for you, Mrs. Whatever you are." He licked his thumb and began to comb the notes. Half-way through he paused, sat still like a large toad over his desk, listening. A lot of noise came in through the open window, feet on stone, voices, distant music, bells ringing, the continuous whisper of the Channel. He sat quite still with half the notes in his hand. He looked uneasy. The telephone rang. He let it ring for two seconds, his veined eyes on Ida; then he lifted the receiver. "Hullo. Hullo. This is Jim Tate." It was an old-fashioned telephone. He screwed the receiver close in to his ear and sat still while a low voice buzzed like a bee.

One hand holding the receiver to his ear Jim Tate shuffled the notes together, wrote out a slip. He said hoarsely: "That's all right, Mr. Colleoni. I'll do that, Mr. Colleoni," and planked the receiver down.

"You've written Black Dog," Ida said.

He looked across at her. It took him a moment to understand. "Black Dog," he said, and then laughed, hoarse and hollow. "What was I thinking of? Black Dog indeed."

"That means Care," Ida said. "The Popes used to find them under the bed."

"Well," he barked with unconvincing geniality, "we've always something to worry about." The telephone rang again. Jim Tate looked as if it might sting him.

"You're busy," Ida said. "I'll be going."

When she went out into the street she looked this way and that to see if she could find any cause for Jim Tate's uneasiness; but there was nothing visible: just Brighton about its own business on a beautiful day.

Ida went into a pub and had a glass of Douro port. It went down sweet and warm and heavy. She had another. "Who's Mr. Colleoni?" she said to the barman.

"You don't know who Colleoni is?"

"I never heard of him till just now."

The barman said: "He's taking over from Kite."

"Who's Kite?"

"Who *was* Kite? You saw how he got croaked at St. Pancras?"

"No."

"I don't suppose they meant to do it," the barman said. "They just meant to carve him up, but a razor slipped."

"Have a drink."

"Thanks. I'll have a gin."

"Cheerio."

"Cheerio."

"I hadn't heard all this," Ida said. She looked over his shoulder at the clock: nothing to do till one: she might as well have another and gossip awhile. "Give me another port. When did all this happen?"

"Oh, before Whitsun." The word Whitsun always caught her ear now: it eant a lot of things, a grubby ten-shilling note, the white steps down to the Ladies', Tragedy in capital letters. "And what about Kite's friends?" she said.

"They don't stand a chance now Kite's dead. The mob's got no leader. Why, they tag round after a kid of seventeen. What's a kid like that going to do against Colleoni?" He bent across the bar and whispered: "He cut up Brewer last night."

"Who? Colleoni?"

"No, the kid."

"I dunno who Brewer is," Ida said, "but things seem lively."

"You wait till the races start," the man said. "They'll be lively all right then. Colleoni's out for a monopoly. Quick, look through the window there and you'll see him."

Ida went to the window and looked out, and again she saw only the Brighton she knew; she hadn't seen anything different even the day Fred died: two girls in beach pyjamas arm in arm, the buses going by to Rottingdean, a man selling papers, a woman with a shopping basket, a boy in a shabby suit, an excursion

steamer edging off from the pier, which lay long,
luminous, and transparent, like a shrimp in the sunlight. She said: "I don't see anyone."

"He's gone now."

"Who? Colleoni?"

"No, the kid."

"Oh," Ida said, "that boy," coming back to the bar,
drinking up her port.

"I bet he's worried plenty."

"A kid like that oughtn't to be mixed up with
things," Ida said. "If he was mine I'd just larrup it
out of him." With those words she was about to dismiss him, to turn her attention away from him, moving her mind on its axis like a great steel dredger,
when she remembered: a face in a bar seen over Fred's
shoulder, the sound of a glass breaking, "The gentleman will pay"—she had a royal memory. "You ever
come across this Kolley Kibber?" she asked.

"No such luck," the barman said.

"It seemed odd his dying like that. Must have made
a bit of gossip."

"None I heard of," the barman said. "He wasn't a
Brighton man. No one knew him round these parts.
He was a stranger."

A stranger; the word meant nothing to her: there
was no place in the world where she felt a stranger.
She circulated the dregs of the cheap port in her glass
and remarked to no one in particular: "It's a good
life." There was nothing with which she didn't claim
kinship: the advertising mirror behind the barman's
back flashed her own image at her; the beach girls
went giggling across the parade; the gong beat on the

steamer for Boulogne—it was a good life. Only the
darkness in which the Boy walked, going from Billy's,
going back to Billy's, was alien to her: she had no pity
for something she didn't understand. She said: "I'll
be getting on."

It wasn't one yet, but there were questions she
wanted to ask before Mr. Corkery arrived. She said to
the first waitress she saw: "Are you the lucky one?"

"Not that I know of," the waitress said coldly.

"I mean the one who found the card—the Kolley
Kibber card."

"Oh, that was *her*," the waitress said contemptuously, nodding a pointed powdered chin.

Ida changed her table. She said: "I've got a friend
coming. I'll have to wait for him, but I'll try to pick.
Is the shepherd's pie good?"

"It looks lovely."

"Nice and brown on top?"

"It's a picture."

"What's your name, dear?"

"Rose."

"Why, I do believe," Ida said, "you were the lucky
one who found a card?"

"Did *they* tell you that?" Rose said. "They haven't
forgiven me. They think I didn't ought to be lucky
like that my second day."

"Your second day? That *was* a bit of luck. You won't
forget that day in a hurry."

"No," Rose said, "I'll remember that always."

"I mustn't keep you here talking."

"If you only would. If you'd sort of look as if you
was ordering things. There's no one else wants to be

attended to and I'm ready to drop with these trays."

"You don't like the job?"

"Oh," Rose said quickly. "I didn't say that. It's a good job. I wouldn't have anything different for the world. I wouldn't be in a hotel, or in Chessman's, not if they paid me twice as much. It's elegant here," Rose said, gazing over the waste of green-painted tables, the daffodils, the paper napkins, the sauce bottles.

"Are you a local?"

"I've always lived here—all my life," Rose said, "in Nelson Place. This is a fine situation for me because they have us sleep in. There's only three of us in my room, and we have two looking glasses."

"How old are you?"

Rose leant gratefully across the table. "Sixteen," she said. "I don't tell them that. I say seventeen. They'd say I wasn't old enough if they knew. They'd send me"—she hesitated a long while at the grim word—"home."

"You must have been glad," Ida said, "when you found that card."

"Oh, I was."

"Do you think I could have a glass of stout, dear?"

"We have to send out," Rose said. "If you give me the money——"

Ida opened her purse. "I don't suppose you'll ever forget the little fellow."

"Oh, he wasn't so . . ." Rose began and suddenly stopped, staring out through Snow's window across the parade to the pier.

"He wasn't what?" Ida said. "What was it you were going to say?"

"I don't remember," Rose said.

"I just asked if you'd ever forget the little fellow."

"It's gone out of my head," Rose said. "I'll get your drink. Does it cost all that—a glass of stout?" she asked, picking up the two shilling pieces.

"One of them's for you, dear," Ida said. "I'm inquisitive. I can't help it. I'm made that way. Tell me how he looked?"

"I don't know. I can't remember. I haven't got any memory for faces."

"You can't have, can you, dear, or you'd have challenged him. You must have seen his picture in the papers."

"I know. I'm silly that way." She stood there, pale and determined and out of breath and guilty.

"And then it would have been ten pounds not ten shillings."

"I'll get your drink."

"Perhaps I'll wait after all. The gentleman who's giving me lunch, he can pay." Ida picked up the shillings again, and Rose's eyes followed her hand back to her bag. "Waste not, want not," Ida said gently, taking in the details of the bony face, the large mouth, the eyes too far apart, the pallor, the immature body, and then suddenly she was loud and cheerful again, calling out: "Phil Corkery, Phil Corkery," waving her hand.

Mr. Corkery wore a blazer with a badge and a stiff collar underneath. He looked as if he needed feeding up, as if he was wasted with passions he had never had the courage to pursue far enough.

"Cheer up, Phil. What are you having?"

"Steak and kidney," Mr. Corkery said gloomily. "Waitress, we want a drink."

"We have to send out."

"Well, in that case make it two large bottles of Guinness," Mr. Corkery said.

When Rose came back Ida introduced her to Mr. Corkery: "This is the lucky girl who found a card."

Rose backed away, but Ida detained her, grasping firmly her black cotton sleeve. "Did he eat much?" she said.

"I don't remember a thing," Rose said, "really I don't." Their faces, flushed a little with the warm summer sun, were like posters announcing danger.

"Did he look," Ida said, "as if he was going to die?"

"How can I tell?" Rose said.

"I suppose you talked to him?"

"I didn't talk to him. I was rushed. I just fetched him a Bass and a sausage roll, and I never saw him again." She snatched her sleeve from Ida's hand and was gone.

"You can't get much from her," Mr. Corkery said.

"Oh, yes, I can," Ida said, "more than I bargained for."

"Why, whatever's wrong?"

"It's what that girl said."

"She didn't say much."

"She said enough. I always had a feeling it was fishy. You see, he told me in the taxi he was dying and I believed him for a moment: it gave me quite a turn till he told me he was just spinning a tale."

"Well, he *was* dying."

"He didn't mean it that way. I have my instincts."

"Anyway," Mr. Corkery said, "there's the evidence, he died natural. I don't see as there's anything to worry about. It's a fine day, Ida. Let's go on the *Brighton Belle* and talk it over there. No closing hours at sea. After all if he did kill himself, it's his business."

"If he killed himself," Ida said, "he was driven to it. I heard what the girl said, and I know this—it wasn't him that left the ticket here."

"Good God!" Mr. Corkery said. "What do you mean? You oughtn't to talk like that. It's dangerous." He swallowed nervously and the Adam's apple bobbed up and down under the skin of his scrawny neck.

"It's dangerous all right," Ida said, watching the thin sixteen-year-old body shrink by in its black cotton dress, hearing the clink, clink, clink of a glass on a tray carried by an unsteady hand, "but who to's another matter."

"Let's go out in the sun," Mr. Corkery said. "It's not so warm here." He hadn't got an undershirt on, or a tie; he shivered a little in his cricket shirt and blazer.

"I've got to think," Ida repeated.

"I shouldn't get mixed up in anything, Ida. He wasn't anything to you."

"He wasn't anything to anyone, that's the trouble," Ida said. She dug down into her deepest mind, the plane of memories, instincts, hopes, and brought up from them the only philosophy she lived by. "I like fair play," she said. She felt better when she'd said that and added with terrible lightheartedness: "An eye for an eye, Phil. Will you stick by me?"

The Adam's apple bobbed. A draught from which

all the sun had been sifted swung through the revolving door and Mr. Corkery felt it on his bony breast. He said: "I don't know what's given you the idea, Ida, but I'm for law and order. I'll stick by you." His daring went to his head. He put a hand on her knee. "I'd do anything for you, Ida."

"There's only one thing to do after what *she* told me," Ida said.

"What's that?"

"The police."

Ida blew in to the police station with a laugh to this man and a wave of the hand to that. She didn't know them from Adam. She was cheerful and determined, and she carried Phil along in her wake.

"I want to see the inspector," she told the sergeant at the desk.

"He's busy, ma'am; what was it you wanted to see him about?"

"I can wait," Ida said, sitting down between the police capes. "Sit down, Phil." She grinned at them all with brassy assurance. "Pubs don't open till six," she said. "Phil and I haven't anything to do till then."

"What was it you wanted to see him about, ma'am?"

"Suicide," Ida said, "right under your noses and you call it natural death."

The sergeant stared at her, and Ida stared back. Her large clear eyes (a spot of drink now and then didn't affect them) told nothing, gave away no secrets. Camaraderie, good nature, cheeriness, fell like shutters before a plate-glass window. You could only guess at the goods behind : sound old-fashioned hall-marked goods, justice, an eye for an eye, law and order, capital punishment, a bit of fun now and then, nothing nasty, nothing shady, nothing you'd be ashamed to own, nothing mysterious.

"You aren't pulling my leg, are you?" the sergeant said.

"Not this time, Sarge."

He passed through a door and shut it behind him, and Ida settled herself more firmly on the bench, made herself at home. "Bit stuffy in here, boys," she said. "What about opening another window?" and obediently they opened one.

The sergeant called to her from the door. "You can go in," he said.

"Come on, Phil," Ida said, and bore him with her into the tiny cramped official room, which smelt of French polish and fish glue.

"And so," the inspector said, "you wanted to tell me about a suicide, Mrs. . . . ?" He had tried to hide a tin of fruit drops behind a telephone and a manuscript book.

"Arnold, Ida Arnold. I thought it might be your line, Inspector," she said with heavy sarcasm.

"This your husband?"

"Oh, no, a friend. I wanted a witness, that's all."

"And who is it you're concerned about, Mrs. Arnold?"

"Hale's the name, Fred Hale. I beg your pardon. Charles Hale."

"We know all about Hale, Mrs. Arnold. He died quite naturally."

"Oh, no," Ida said, "you don't know all. You don't know he was with me, two hours before he was found."

"You weren't at the inquest?"

"I didn't know it was him till I saw his picture."

"And why do you think there's anything wrong?"

"Listen," Ida said. "He was with me and he was scared about something. We were at the Palace Pier. I had to have a wash and brush up, but he didn't want me to leave him. I was only away five minutes and he'd gone. Where'd he gone to? You say he went and had lunch at Snow's and then went on down the pier to the shelter in Hove. You think he just gave me the slip, but it wasn't Fred—I mean Hale—who had lunch at Snow's and left that card. I've just seen the waitress. Hale didn't like Bass—he wouldn't drink Bass—but the man at Snow's sent out for a bottle."

"That's nothing," the inspector said. "It was a hot day. He was feeling bad too. He got tired of doing all the things he'd got to do. I wouldn't be surprised if he cheated and got someone else to go into Snow's."

"The girl won't say a thing about him. She knows but she won't say."

"I can think of an explanation easily enough, Mrs. Arnold. The man may have left a card on condition she didn't say anything."

"It's not that. She's scared. Someone's scared her. Maybe the same person who drove Fred . . . And there are other things."

"I'm sorry, Mrs. Arnold. It's just a waste of time getting fussed like this. You see, there was a post-mortem. The medical evidence shows without any doubt that he died naturally. He had a bad heart. The medical name for it is myocarditis. I'd call it just heat and crowds and exertion—and a weak heart."

"Could I see the report?"

"It wouldn't be usual."

"I was a friend of his, you see," Ida said softly. "I'd like to be satisfied."

"Well, to put your mind at rest, I'll stretch a point. It's here now on my desk."

Ida read it carefully. "This doctor," she said, "he knows his stuff?"

"He's a first-class doctor."

"It seems clear, doesn't it?" Ida said. She began to read it all over again. "They do go into details, don't they? Why, I wouldn't know more about him if I'd married him. Appendix scar, supernumerary nipples, whatever they are, suffered from wind—I do that myself on a bank holiday. It's almost disrespectful, isn't it? He wouldn't have liked this." She brooded over the report with easy kindliness. "Varicose veins. Poor old Fred. What's this mean about the liver?"

"Drank too much, that's all."

"I wouldn't be surprised. Poor Fred. So he had ingrowing toe nails. It doesn't seem right to know that."

"You were a great friend of his?"

"Well, we only knew each other that day. But I liked him. He was a real gentleman. If I hadn't been a bit lit this wouldn't have happened." She blew out her bust. "He wouldn't have come to any harm with me."

"Have you quite finished with the report, Mrs. Arnold?"

"He does mention everything, this doctor of yours, doesn't he? Bruises, superficial, whatever that means, on the arms. What do you think of that, Inspector?"

"Nothing at all. Bank holiday crowds, that's all. Pushed here and there."

"Oh, come off it," Ida said, "come off it." Her tongue flared up. "Be human. Were *you* out on bank holiday? Where do you find a crowd like that? Brighton's big enough, isn't it? It's not a tube lift. I was here. I know."

The inspector said stubbornly: "You've got fancies, Mrs. Arnold."

"So the police won't do a thing? You won't question that girl in Snow's?"

"The case is closed, Mrs. Arnold. And even if it had been suicide, why open old wounds?"

"Someone drove him . . . maybe it wasn't suicide at all . . . maybe . . ."

"I've told you, Mrs. Arnold, the case is closed."

"That's what you think," Ida said. She rose to her feet; she summoned Phil with a jerk of the chin. "Not half, it isn't," she said. "I'll be seeing you." She looked back from the door at the elderly man behind the desk and threatened him with her ruthless vitality. "Or maybe not," she said. "I can manage this my own way. I don't need your police." (The constables in the outer room stirred uneasily; somebody laughed; somebody dropped a tin of boot polish.) "I've got my friends."

Her friends—they were everywhere under the

bright glittering Brighton air. They followed their wives obediently into fishmongers', they carried the children's buckets to the beach, they lingered round the bars waiting for opening time, they took a penny peep on the pier at "A Night of Love." She had only to appeal to any of them, for Ida Arnold was on the right side. She was cheery, she was healthy, she could get a bit lit with the best of them. She liked a good time, her big breasts bore their carnality frankly down the Old Steyne, but you had only to look at her to know that you could rely on her. She wouldn't tell tales to your wife, she wouldn't remind you next morning of what you wanted to forget, she was honest, she was kindly, she belonged to the great middle law-abiding class, her amusements were their amusements, her superstitions their superstitions (the planchette scratching the French polish on the occasional table, and the salt over the shoulder), she had no more love for anyone than they had.

"Expenses mounting up," Ida said. "Never mind. Everything will be all right after the races."

"You got a tip?" Mr. Corkery asked.

"Straight from the horse's mouth. I shouldn't say that. Poor Fred."

"Tell a pal," Mr. Corkery implored.

"All in good time," Ida said. "Be a good boy and you don't know what mayn't happen."

"You don't still think, do you?" Mr. Corkery sounded her. "Not after what the doctor wrote?"

"I've never paid any attention to doctors."

"But why?"

"We've got to find out."

"And how?"

"Give me time. I haven't started yet."

The sea stretched like a piece of gay common washing in a tenement square across the end of the street. "The colour of your eyes," Mr. Corkery interjected thoughtfully and with a touch of nostalgia. He said: "Couldn't we now—just go for a while on the pier, Ida?"

"Yes," Ida said. "The pier. We'll go to the Palace Pier, Phil," but when they got there she wouldn't go through the turnstile, but took up her stand like a huckster facing the Aquarium, the Ladies' Lavatory. "This is where I start from," she said. "He waited for me here, Phil," and she stared out over the red and green lights, the heavy traffic of her battlefield, laying her plans, marshalling her cannon fodder, while five yards away Spicer stood, too, waiting for an enemy to appear. Only a slight doubt troubled her optimism. "That horse has got to win, Phil," she said. "I can't hold out else."

2

Spicer was restless these days. There was nothing for him to do. When the races began again he wouldn't feel so bad, he wouldn't think so much about Hale. It was the medical evidence that upset him: "Death from natural causes," when with his own eyes he'd seen the Boy . . . It was fishy, it wasn't straight. He told himself that he could face a police inquiry, but he couldn't stand this not knowing, the false security of the verdict. There was a catch in it somewhere, and all through the long summer sunlight Spicer wandered uneasily, watching out for trouble: the police station, the Place where It had been done, even Snow's came into his promenade. He wanted to be satisfied that the cops were doing nothing (he knew every plainclothes man in the Brighton force), that no one was asking questions or loitering where they had no reason to loiter. He knew it was just nerves. "I'll be all right when the races start," he told himself, like a man with a poisoned body who believes that all will be well when a single tooth is drawn.

He came up the parade cautiously, from the Hove end, from the glass shelter where Hale's body had been set, pale, with bloodshot eyes and nicotined finger ends. Spicer had a corn on his left foot and limped a little, dragging after him a bright orange-brown shoe. He had come out in spots too round his mouth, and that also was caused by Hale's death. Fear upset his bowels, and the spots came: it was always that way.

He limped cautiously across the road when he was close to Snow's: that was another vulnerable place. The sun caught the great panes of plate glass and flashed back at him like headlamps. He sweated a little passing by. A voice said: "Well, if it isn't Spicey!" He had had his eyes on Snow's across the road, he hadn't noticed who was beside him on the parade, leaning on the green railing above the shingle. He turned his damp face sharply. "What are you doing here, Crab?"

"It's good to be back," said Crab, a young man in a mauve suit, with shoulders like coat hangers and a small waist.

"We ran you out once, Crab. I thought you'd stay

out. You've altered." His hair was carroty, except at the roots, and his nose was straightened and scarred. He had been a Jew once, but a hairdresser and a surgeon had altered that. "Afraid we'd lamp you if you didn't change your mug?"

"Why, Spicey, me afraid of your lot? You'll be saying 'sir' to me one of these days. I'm Colleoni's right-hand man."

"I always heard as how he was left-handed," Spicer said. "Wait till Pinkie knows you're back."

Crab laughed. "Pinkie's at the police station," he said.

The police station: Spicer's chin went down, he was off, his orange shoe sliding on the paving, his corn shooting. He heard Crab laugh behind him, the smell of dead fish was in his nostrils, he was a sick man. The police station; the police station: it was like an abscess jetting its poison through the nerves. When he got to Billy's there was no one there. He creaked his tortured way up the stairs, past the rotten banister, to Pinkie's room: the door stood open, vacancy stared in the swing mirror; no message, crumbs on the floor; it looked as a room would look if someone had been called suddenly away.

Spicer stood at the chest of drawers (the walnut stain splashed unevenly): no scrap of written reassurance in a drawer, no warning. He looked up and down, the corn shooting through his whole body to the brain, and suddenly there was his own face in the glass: the coarse black hair greying at the roots, the small eruptions on the face, the bloodshot eyeballs, and it occurred to him, as if he were looking at a close-up on a screen, that that was the kind of face a nark might have, a man who grassed to the bogies.

He moved away · flakes of pastry ground under his foot; he told himself he wasn't a man to grass : Pinkie, Cubitt, and Dallow, they were his pals. He wouldn't let them down—even though it wasn't he who'd done the killing. He'd been against it from the first; he'd only laid the cards; he only *knew*. He stood at the head of the stairs looking down past the shaky banister. He would rather kill himself than squeal, he told the empty landing in a whisper, but he knew really that he hadn't got that courage. Better run for it; and he thought with nostalgia of Nottingham and a pub he knew, a pub he had once hoped to buy when he had made his pile. It was a good spot, Nottingham, the air was good, none of this salt smart on the dry mouth, and the girls were kind. If he could get away—but the others would never let him go : he knew too much about too many things. He was in the mob for life now; he looked down the drop of the staircase to the tiny hall, the strip of linoleum, the old-fashioned telephone on a bracket by the door.

As he watched, it began to ring. He stared down at it with fear and suspicion. He couldn't stand any more bad news. Where had everybody gone to? Had they run and left him without a warning? Even Billy wasn't in the basement. There was a smell of scorching as if he'd left his iron burning. The bell rang on and on. Let them ring, he thought. They'll tire of it in time; why should I do all the work of this bloody gaff? On and on and on. Whoever it was didn't tire easily. He came to the head of the stairs and scowled down

at the vulcanite spitting noise through the quiet house.
"The trouble is," he said aloud, as if he were rehears-
ing a speech to Pinkie and the others, "I'm getting too
old for this game. I got to retire. Look at my hair. I'm
grey, ain't I? I got to retire." But the only answer was
the regular ring, ring, ring.

"Why can't someone answer the bloody blower?"
he shouted down the well of the stairs. "I got to do all
the work, have I?" and he saw himself dropping a
ticket into the child's bucket, slipping a ticket under
an upturned boat, tickets which could have hanged
him. He suddenly ran down the stairs in a kind of
simulated fury and lifted the receiver. "Well," he
bellowed, "well, who the hell's there?"

"Is that Billy's?" a voice said. He knew the voice
now. It was the girl in Snow's. He lowered the receiver
in a panic and waited, and a thin doll's voice came out
at him from the orifice: "Please, I've got to speak to
Pinkie." It was almost as if listening betrayed him.
He listened again and the voice repeated with desperate anxiety: "Is that Billy's?"

Keeping his mouth away from the phone, curling
his tongue in an odd way, mouthing hoarsely and
crookedly, Spicer in disguise replied: "Pinkie's out.
What do you want?"

"I've got to speak to him."

"He's out, I tell you."

"Who's that?" the girl suddenly said in a scared
voice.

"That's what I want to know. Who are you?"

"I'm a friend of Pinkie's. I got to find him. It's
urgent."

"I can't help you."

"Please. You've got to find Pinkie. He told me I
was to tell him—if ever—" The voice died away.

Spicer shouted down the phone. "Hullo. Where
you gone? If ever what?" There was no reply. He
listened, with the receiver pressed against his ear, to
silence buzzing up the wires. He began to jerk at the
hook, "Exchange. Hullo. Hullo. Exchange," and then
suddenly the voice came on again as if somebody had
dropped a needle into place on a record. "Are you
there? Please, are you there?"

"Of course I'm here. What did Pinkie tell you?"

"You got to find Pinkie. He said he wanted to know.
It's a woman. She was in here with a man."

"What do you mean—a woman?"

"Asking questions," the voice said. Spicer put down
the receiver; whatever else the girl had to say was
strangled on the wire. Find Pinkie? What was the
good of finding Pinkie? It was the others who had
done the finding. And Cubitt and Dallow: they'd
slipped away without even warning him. If he did
squeal it would be only returning them their own
coin. But he wasn't going to squeal. He wasn't a nark.
They thought he was yellow. *They'd think* he'd
squeal. He wouldn't even get the credit . . . a few tears
of self-pity came pricking out of the dry ageing ducts.

I got to think, he repeated to himself, I got to think.
He opened the street door and went out. He didn't even
wait to fetch his hat. His hair was thin on top, dry and
brittle over the dandruff. He walked rapidly, going
nowhere in particular, but every road in Brighton
ended on the front. I'm too old for the game, I got to

get out, Nottingham; he wanted to be alone, he went
down the stone steps to the level of the beach; it was
early closing and the small shops facing the sea under
the promenade were shut. He walked on the edge of
the asphalt, scuffling in the shingle. I wouldn't grass,
he remarked dumbly to the tide as it lifted and withdrew, but it wasn't my doing, I never wanted to kill
Fred. He passed into shadow under the pier, and a
cheap photographer with a box camera snapped him
as the shadow fell and pressed a paper into his hand.
Spicer didn't notice. The iron pillars stretched down
across the wet dimmed shingle holding up above his
head the motor-track, the shooting booths and peep
machines, mechanical models, "the Robot Man will
tell your fortune." A seagull flew straight towards
him between the pillars like a scared bird caught in a
cathedral, then swerved out into the sunlight from the
dark iron nave. I wouldn't grass, Spicer said, unless I
had to. . . . He stumbled on an old boot and put his
hand on the stones to save himself: they had all the
cold of the sea and had never been warmed by sun
under these pillars.

He thought: that woman—how does she know anything—what's she doing asking questions? I didn't
want to have Hale killed; it wouldn't be fair if I took
the drop with the others; I told 'em not to do it. He
came out into the sunlight and climbed back onto the
parade. It'll be this way the bogies will come, he
thought, if they know anything; they always recon-
struct the crime. He took up his stand between the
turnstile of the pier and the Ladies' Lavatory. There
weren't many people about: he could spot the bogies

easily enough—if they came. Over there was the
Royal Albion; he could see all the way up the Grand
Parade to Old Steyne; the pale green domes of the
Pavilion floated above the dusty trees; he could see
anyone in the hot empty midweek afternoon who went
down below the Aquarium, the white deck ready for
dancing, to the little covered arcade where the cheap
shops stood between the sea and the stone wall, selling
Brighton rock.

3

The poison twisted in the Boy's veins. He had been
insulted. He had to show someone he was—a man.
He went scowling into Snow's, young, shabby, and
untrustworthy, and the waitresses with one accord
turned their backs. He stood there looking for a table
(the place was full), and no one attended to him. It
was as if they doubted whether he had the money to
pay for his meal. He thought of Colleoni padding
through the enormous rooms, the embroidered crowns
on the chair-backs. He suddenly shouted aloud: "I
want service!" and the pulse beat in his cheek. All the
faces round him shivered into motion, and then were
still again like water. Everyone looked away. He was
ignored. Suddenly a sense of weariness overtook him.
He felt as if he had travelled a great many miles to
be ignored like this.

A voice said: "There isn't a table." They were still
such strangers that he didn't recognize the voice, until
it added: "Pinkie." He looked round and there was
Rose, dressed to go out in a shabby black straw which

made her face look as it would look in twenty years' time, after the work and the child-bearing.

"They got to serve me," the Boy said. "Who do they think they are?"

"There isn't a table."

Everyone was watching them now—with disapproval.

"Come outside, Pinkie."

"What are you all dressed up for?"

"It's my afternoon off. Come outside."

He followed her out and suddenly taking her wrist he brought the poison onto his lips: "I could break your arm."

"What have I done, Pinkie?"

"No table. They don't like serving me in there, I'm not class. They'll see—one day——"

"What?"

But his mind staggered before the extent of his ambitions. He said: "Never mind—they'll learn——"

"Did you get the message, Pinkie?"

"What message?"

"I phoned you at Billy's. I told him to tell you."

"Told who?"

"I don't know." She added casually: "I think it was the man who left the ticket."

He gripped her wrist again. He said: "The man who left the ticket's dead. You read it all." But she showed no sign of fear this time. He'd been too friendly. She ignored his reminder.

"Did he find you?" she asked, and he thought to himself: she's got to be scared again.

"No one found me," he said. He pushed her roughly

forward. "Come on. We'll walk. I'll take you out."

"I was going home."

"You won't go home. You'll come with me. I want exercise," he said, looking down at his pointed shoes, which had never walked further than the length of the parade.

"Where'll we go, Pinkie?"

"Somewhere," Pinkie said, "out in the country. That's where people go on a day like this." He tried to think for a moment of where the country was: the racecourse, that was country; and then a bus came by marked Peacehaven, and he waved his hand to it. "There you are," he said, "that's country. We can talk there. There's things we got to get straight."

"I thought we were going to walk."

"This is walking," he said roughly, pushing her up the steps. "You're green. You don't know a thing. You don't think that people really *walk?* Why—it's miles."

"When people say: Come for a walk, they mean a bus?"

"Or a car. I'd have taken you in the car, but the mob are out in it."

"You got a car?"

"I couldn't get on without a car," the Boy said, as the bus climbed up behind Rottingdean: red brick buildings behind a wall, a great stretch of parkland, one girl with a hockey stick staring at something in the sky, with cropped expensive turf all round her. The poison drained back into its proper glands: he was admired, no one insulted him, but when he looked at the girl who admired him, the poison oozed out

again. He said: "Take off that hat. You look awful."
She obeyed him: her mousy hair lay flat on the small
scalp; he watched her with distaste. That was what
they'd joked about him marrying: that. He watched
her with his soured virginity, as one might watch a
draught of medicine offered that one would never,
never take; one would die first—or let others die. The
chalky dust blew up round the windows.

"You told me to ring up," Rose said, "so
when——"

"Not here," the Boy said. "Wait till we're alone."
The driver's head rose slowly against a waste of sky:
a few white feathers blown backward into the blue;
they were on top of the downs and turned eastwards.
The Boy sat with his pointed shoes side by side, his
hands in his pockets, feeling the throb of the engine
come up through the thin soles.

"It's lovely," Rose said, "being out here—in the
country with you." Little tarred bungalows with tin
roofs paraded backwards, gardens scratched in the
chalk, dry flower beds like Saxon emblems carved on
the downs. Notices said: "Pull in Here," "Mazawattee
Tea," "Genuine Antiques"; and, hundreds of feet
below, the pale green sea washed into the scarred and
shabby side of England. Peacehaven itself dwindled
out against the downs: half-made streets turned into
grass tracks. They walked down between the bungalows to the cliff edge; there was nobody about; one of
the bungalows had broken windows, in another the
blinds were down for a death. "It makes me giddy,"
Rose said, "looking down." It was early closing, and
the store was shut; closing time and no drinks obtain-

able at the hotel; a vista of To Let boards running back along the chalky ruts of unfinished roads. The Boy could see over her shoulder the rough drop to the shingle. "It makes me feel I'll fall," Rose said, turning from the sea. He let her turn; no need to act prematurely; the draught might never be offered.

"Tell me," he said, "now—who rang up who and why?"

"I rang up *you*, but you weren't in. *He* answered."

"He?" the Boy repeated.

"The one who left the ticket that day you came in. You remember—you were looking for something." He remembered all right—the hand under the cloth, the stupid innocent face he had expected would so easily forget. "You remember a lot," he said, frowning at the thought.

"I wouldn't forget that day," she said abruptly and stopped.

"You forget a lot too. I just told you that wasn't the man you heard speak. That man's dead."

"It doesn't matter anyway," she said. "What matters is—someone was in asking questions."

"About the ticket?"

"Yes."

"A man?"

"A woman. A big one with a laugh. You should have heard the laugh. Just as if she'd never had a care. I didn't trust her. She wasn't our kind."

"Our kind"; he frowned again towards the shallow wrinkled tide at the suggestion that they had something in common and spoke sharply: "What did she want?"

"She wanted to know everything. What the man who left the card looked like."

"What did you tell her?"

"I didn't tell her a thing, Pinkie."

The Boy dug with his pointed shoe into the thin dry turf and sent an empty corn-beef tin rattling down the ruts. "It's only you I'm thinking of," he said. "It don't matter to me. I'm not concerned. But I wouldn't want you getting mixed up in things that might be dangerous." He looked quickly up at her, sideways. "You don't seem scared. It's serious what I'm telling you."

"I wouldn't be scared, Pinkie—not with you about."

He dug his nails into his hands with vexation. She remembered everything she ought to forget, and forgot all that she should remember—the vitriol bottle. He'd scared her all right then; he'd been too friendly since: she really believed that he was fond of her. Why, this, he supposed, was "walking out," and he thought again of Spicer's joke. He looked at the mousy skull, the bony body, and the shabby dress, and shuddered—involuntarily, a goose flying across the final bed. "Saturday," he thought, "today's Saturday," remembering the room at home, the frightening weekly exercise of his parents which he watched from his single bed. That was what they expected of you, every polony you met had her eye on the bed; his virginity straightened in him like sex. That was how they judged you; not by whether you had the guts to kill a man, to run a mob, to conquer Colleoni. He said:

"We don't want to stay round here. We'll be getting back."

"We've only just come," the girl said. "Let's stay a bit, Pinkie. I like the country," she said.

"You've had a look," he said. "You can't *do* anything with the country. The pub's closed."

"We could just sit. We've got to wait for the bus anyway. You're funny. You aren't scared of anything, are you?"

He laughed queerly, sitting awkwardly down in front of the bungalow with the shattered glass. "Me scared? That's funny." He lay back against the bank, his waistcoat undone, his thin frayed tie bright and striped against the chalk.

"This is better than going home," Rose said.

'Where's home?"

"Nelson Place. Do you know it?"

"Oh, I've passed through," he said airily, but he could have drawn its plan on the turf as accurately as a surveyor: the barred and battlemented Salvation Army gaff at the corner, his own home beyond in Paradise Piece, the houses which looked as if they had passed through an intensive bombardment, flapping gutters and glassless windows, an iron bedstead rusting in a front garden, the smashed and wasted ground in front where houses had been pulled down for model flats which had never gone up.

They lay on the chalk bank side by side with a common geography, and a little hate mixed with his contempt. He thought he had made his escape, and here his home was: back beside him, making claims.

Rose said suddenly: "*She's* never lived there."

"Who?"

"That woman asking questions. Never a care."

"Well," he said, "we can't all 'ave been born in Nelson Place."

"You weren't born there—or somewhere round?"

"Me. Of course not. What do you think?"

"I thought—maybe you were. You're a Roman too. We were all Romans in Nelson Place. You believe in things. Like Hell. But you can see she doesn't believe a thing." She said bitterly: "You can tell the world's all dandy with her."

He defended himself from any connexion with Nelson Place: "I don't take any stock in religion. Hell—it's just there. You don't need to think of it—not before you die."

"You might die sudden."

He closed his eyes under the bright empty arch, and a memory floated up imperfectly into speech. "You know what they say—'Between the stirrup and the ground, he something sought and something found.'"

"Mercy."

"That's right: Mercy."

"It would be awful though," she said slowly, "if they didn't give you time." She turned her cheek onto the chalk towards him and added, as if he could help her: "That's what I always pray. That I don't die sudden. What do you pray?"

"I don't," he said, but he was praying even while he spoke to someone or something: that he wouldn't need to carry on any further with her, get mixed up again with that drab dynamited plot of ground they both called home.

"You angry about anything?" Rose asked.

"A man wants to be quiet sometimes," he said, lying rigidly against the chalk bank, giving nothing away. In the silence a shutter flapped and the tide lisped; two people walking out: that's what they were, and the memory of Colleoni's luxury, the crowned chairs at the Cosmopolitan, came back to taunt him. He said: "Talk, can't you? Say something."

"You wanted to be quiet," she retorted with a sudden anger which took him by surprise. He hadn't thought her capable of that. "If I don't suit you," she said, "you can leave me alone. I didn't ask to come out." She sat up with her hands round her knees and her cheeks burned on the tip of the bone: anger was as good as rouge on her thin face. "If I'm not grand enough—your car and all——"

"Who said——?"

"Oh," she said, "I'm not that dumb. I've seen you looking at me. My hat . . ."

It occurred to him suddenly that she might even get up and leave him, go back to Snow's with her secret for the first comer who questioned her kindly; he had to conciliate her, they were walking out, he'd got to do the things expected of him. He put out his hand with repulsion; it lay like a cold paddock on her knee. "You took me up wrong," he said, "you're a sweet girl. I've been worried, that's all. Business worries. You and me"—he swallowed painfully—"we suit each other down to the ground." He saw the colour go, the face turn to him with a blind willingness to be deceived, saw the lips waiting. He drew her hand up quickly and put his mouth against her fingers; anything was better than the lips; the fingers were rough on his skin and tasted a little of soap. She said: "Pinkie, I'm sorry. You're sweet to me."

. He laughed nervously: "You and me," and heard the hoot of a bus with the joy of a besieged man listening to the bugles of the relieving force. "There," he said, "the bus. Let's be going. I'm not much of a one for the country. A city bird. You too." She got up and he saw the skin of her thigh for a moment above the artificial silk, and a prick of sexual desire disturbed him like a sickness. That was what happened to a man in the end: the stuffy room, the wakeful children, the Saturday night movements from the other bed. Was there no escape—anywhere—for anyone? It was worth murdering a world.

"It's beautiful here all the same," she said, staring up the chalky ruts between the To Let boards, and the Boy laughed again at the fine words people gave to a dirty act: love, beauty . . . all his pride coiled like a watch spring round the thought that *he* wasn't deceived, that *he* wasn't going to give himself up to marriage and the birth of children, he was going to be where Colleoni now was and higher . . . he knew everything, he had watched every detail of the act of sex, you couldn't deceive him with lovely words, there was nothing to be excited about, no gain to recompense you for what you lost, but when Rose turned to him again, with the expectation of a kiss, he was aware all the same of a horrifying ignorance. His mouth missed hers and recoiled. He'd never yet kissed a girl.

She said: "I'm sorry. I'm stupid. I've never had——"
and suddenly broke off to watch a gull rise from one
of the little parched gardens and drop over the cliff
towards the sea.

He didn't speak to her in the bus, sullen and ill at
ease, sitting with his hands in his pockets, his feet
close together, not knowing why he'd come this far
out with her, only to go back again with nothing settled; the secret, the memory, still lodged securely in
her skull. The country unwound the other way: Mazawattee tea, antique dealers, pull-ins, the thin grass
petering out on the first asphalt.

From the pier the Brighton anglers flung their
floats. A little music ground mournfully out into the
windy sunlight. They walked on the sunny side past
"A Night of Love," "For Men Only," "The Fan
Dancer." Rose said: "Is business bad?"

"There's always worries," the Boy said.

"I wish I could help, be of use."

He said nothing, walking on. She put out a hand
towards the thin rigid figure, seeing the smooth cheek,
the fluff of fair hair at the nape. "You're so young,
Pinkie, to get worries." She put her hand through his
arm. "We're both young, Pinkie," and felt his body
stonily withdrawn.

A photographer said: "Snap you together against
the sea," raising the cap from his camera, and the Boy
flung up his hands before his face and went on.

"Don't you like being snapped, Pinkie? We might
have had our pictures stuck up for people to see. It
wouldn't have *cost* anything."

"I don't mind what things cost," the Boy said, rattling his pockets, showing how much cash he had.

"We might 'ave been stuck up there," Rose said, halting at the photographer's kiosk, at the pictures of the bathing belles and the famous comedians and the anonymous couples, "next—" and exclaimed with surprise: "Why—there *he* is!"

The Boy was staring over the side where the green tide sucked and slid like a wet mouth round the piles. He turned unwillingly to look and there was Spicer fixed in the photographer's window for the world to gaze at, striding out of the sunlight into the shadow under the pier, worried and hunted and in haste, a comic figure at which strangers could laugh and say: "He's worried right enough. They caught *him* unawares."

"The one who left the card," Rose said. "The one you said was dead. *He's* not dead. Though it almost looks"—she laughed with amusement at the blurred black and white haste—"that he's afraid he will be if he doesn't hurry."

"An old picture," the Boy said.

"Oh, no, it's not. This is where today's pictures go. For you to buy."

"You know a lot."

"You can't miss it, can you?" Rose said. "It's comic. Striding along. All fussed up. Not even seeing the camera."

"Stay here," the Boy said. Inside the kiosk it was dark after the sun. A man with a thin moustache and steel-rimmed spectacles sorted piles of prints.

"I want a picture that's up outside," the Boy said.

"Slip please," the man said and put out yellow
fingers which smelt faintly of hypo.

"I haven't got a slip."

"You can't have the picture without the slip," the
man said and held a negative up to the electric globe.

"What right have you," the Boy said, "to stick up
pictures without a by-your-leave? You let me have
that picture," but the steel rims glittered back at him,
without interest—a fractious boy. "You bring that
slip," the man said, "and you can have the picture.
Now run along. I'm busy." Behind his head were
framed snapshots of King Edward VII—Prince of
Wales—in a yachting cap and a background of peep
machines, going yellow from inferior chemicals and
age; Vesta Tilley signing autographs; Henry Irving
muffled against the Channel winds—a nation's history. Lily Langtry wore ostrich feathers, Mrs. Pank-
hurst hobble skirts, the English Beauty Queen of 1923
a bathing dress. It was little comfort to know that
Spicer was among the immortals.

4

"Spicer," the Boy called, "Spicer!" He climbed up
from Billy's small dark hall towards the landing, leaving a smear of country, of the downs, white on the
linoleum. "Spicer!" He felt the broken banister tremble under his hand. He opened the door of Spicer's
room and there he was upon the bed, asleep face down.
The window was closed, an insect buzzed through the

stale air, and there was a smell of whisky from the
bed. Pinkie stood looking down on the greying hair;
he felt no pity at all; he wasn't old enough for pity.
He pulled Spicer round; the skin round his mouth was
in eruption. "Spicer."

Spicer opened his eyes. He saw nothing for a while
in the dim room.

"I want a word with you, Spicer."

Spicer sat up. "My God, Pinkie, I'm glad to see
you."

"Always glad to see a pal, eh, Spicer?"

"I saw Crab. He said you were at the police station."

"Crab?"

"You weren't at the station then?"

"I was having a friendly talk—about Brewer."

"Not about—?"

"About Brewer." The Boy suddenly put his hand
on Spicer's wrist. "Your nerves are all wrong, Spicer.
You want a holiday." He sniffed with contempt the
tainted air. "You drink too much." He went to the
window and threw it open on the vista of grey wall.
A leather-jacket buzzed up the pane and the Boy
caught it in his hand. It vibrated like a tiny watch
spring in his palm. He began to pull off the legs and
wings one by one. "She loves me," he said, "she loves
me not. I've been out with my girl, Spicer."

"The one from Snow's?"

The Boy turned the denuded body over on his palm
and puffed it away over Spicer's bed. "You know who
I mean," he said. "You had a message for me, Spicer.
Why didn't you bring it?"

"I couldn't find you, Pinkie. Honest I couldn't.

And anyway it wasn't that important. Some old busy-body asking questions."

"It scared you all the same," the Boy said. He sat down on the hard deal chair before the mirror, his hands on his knees watching Spicer. The pulse beat in his cheek.

"Oh, it didn't scare me," Spicer said.

"You went walking blind straight to There."

"What do you mean—there?"

"There's only one There to you, Spicer. You think about it and you dream about it. You're too old for this life."

"This life?" Spicer said, glaring back at him from the bed.

"This racket, of course, I mean. You get nervous and then you get rash. First there was that card in Snow's and now you let your picture be stuck up on the pier for anyone to see. For Rose to see."

"Honest to God, Pinkie, I never knew that."

"You forget to walk on your toes."

"She's safe. She's stuck on you, Pinkie."

"I don't know anything about women. I leave that to you and Cubitt and the rest. I only know what you tell me. You've told me time and again there never was a safe polony yet."

"That's just talk."

"You mean I'm a kid and you tell me good-night stories. But I've got so I believe them, Spicer. It don't seem safe to me that you and Rose are in the same town. Apart from this other buer asking questions. You'll have to disappear, Spicer."

"What do you mean," Spicer said, "disappear?"

He fumbled inside his jacket and the Boy watched him, his hands flat on his knees. "You wouldn't do anything," he said, fumbling in his pocket.

"Why," the Boy said, "what do you think I mean? I mean take a holiday, go away somewhere for a while."

Spicer's hand came out of his pocket. He held out a silver watch towards the Boy. "You can trust me, Pinkie. Look there, what the boys gave me. Read the inscription: 'Ten Years a Pal. From the Boys at the Stadium.' I don't let people down. That was fifteen years ago, Pinkie. Twenty-five years on the tracks. You weren't born when I started."

"You need a holiday," the Boy said. "That's all I said."

"I'd be glad to take a holiday," Spicer said, "but I wouldn't want you to think I'm milky. I'll go at once. I'll pack a bag and clear out tonight. Why, I'd be glad to be gone."

"No," the Boy said, staring down at his shoes. "There's not all that hurry." He lifted a foot. The sole was worn through in a piece the size of a shilling. He thought again of the crowns on Colleoni's chairs at the Cosmopolitan. "I'll need you at the races." He smiled across the room at Spicer. "A pal I can trust."

"You can trust me, Pinkie." Spicer's fingers smoothed the silver watch. "What are you smiling at? Have I got a smut or something?"

"I was just thinking of the races," the Boy said. "They mean a lot to me." He got up and stood with his back to the greying light, the tenement wall, the smut-smeared pane, looking down at Spicer with a kind of curiosity. "And where will you go, Spicer?" he said. His mind was quite made up, and for the second time in a few weeks he looked at a dying man. He couldn't help feeling inquisitive. Why, it was even possible that old Spicer was not set for the flames, he'd been a loyal old geezer, he hadn't done as much harm as the next man, he might slip through the gates into—but the Boy couldn't picture any eternity except in terms of pain. He frowned a little in the effort: a glassy sea, a golden crown, old Spicer.

"Nottingham," Spicer said. "A pal of mine keeps the Blue Anchor in Union Street. A free house. High class. Lunches served. He's often said to me: 'Spicer, why don't you come into partnership? We'd make the old place into a hotel with a few more nickers in the till.' If it wasn't for you and the boys," Spicer said, "I wouldn't want to come back. I wouldn't mind staying away for keeps."

"Well," the Boy said, "I'll be off. We know where we are now anyway." Spicer lay back on the pillow and put up the foot with the shooting corn. There was a hole in his woollen sock, and a big toe showed through, hard skin calcined with middle age. "Sleep well," the Boy said.

He went downstairs; the front door faced east, and the hall was dark. He switched on a light by the telephone and then switched it out again, he didn't know why. Then he rang up the Cosmopolitan. When the hotel exchange answered he could hear the dance music in the distance, all the way from the Palm House (thés dansants, three shillings) behind the Louis Seize Writing Room. "I want Mr. Colleoni." The nightingale singing, the postman ringing—the tune was abruptly cut off, and a low Semitic voice purred up the line.

"That Mr. Colleoni?"

He could hear a glass chink and ice move in a shaker. He said: "This is Mr. P. Brown. I've been thinking things over, Mr. Colleoni." Outside the little dark linoleumed hall a bus slid by, the lights faint in the grey end of the day. The Boy put his mouth close to the mouth of the telephone and said: "He won't listen to reason, Mr. Colleoni." The voice purred happily back at him. The Boy explained slowly and carefully: "I'll wish him good luck and pat him on the back." He stopped and said sharply: "What's that you say, Mr. Colleoni? No. I just thought you laughed. Hullo. Hullo." He banged the receiver down and turned with a sense of uneasiness towards the stairs. The gold cigar lighter, the grey double-breasted waistcoat, the feeling of a racket luxuriously successful for a moment dominated him: the brass bedstead upstairs, the little pot of violet ink on the washstand, the flakes of sausage roll. His board school cunning wilted for a while; then he turned on the light, he was at home. He climbed the stairs, humming softly: "The nightingale singing, the postman ringing," but as his thoughts circled closer to the dark, dangerous, and deathly centre the tune changed: "Agnus dei qui tollis peccata mundi . . ."; he walked stiffly, the jacket sagging across his immature shoulders, but when he opened the door of his room—— "Dona nobis pacem"—his pallid face peered dimly back at him full of pride from the mirror over the ewer, the soap dish, the basin of stale water.

PART FOUR

1

IT WAS a fine day for the races. People poured into Brighton by the first train; it was like bank holiday all over again, except that these people didn't spend their money; they harboured it. They stood packed deep on the tops of the trams rocking down to the Aquarium, they surged like some natural and irrational migration of insects up and down the front. By eleven o'clock it was impossible to get a seat on the buses going out to the course. A Negro wearing a bright striped tie sat on a bench in the Pavilion garden and smoked a cigar. Some children played touch wood from seat to seat, and he called out to them hilariously, holding his cigar at arm's length with an air of pride and caution, his great teeth gleaming like an advertisement. They stopped playing and stared at him, backing slowly. He called out to them again in their own tongue, the words hollow and unformed and childish like theirs, and they eyed him uneasily and backed further away. He put his cigar patiently back between the cushiony lips and went on smoking. A band came up the pavement through Old Steyne, a blind band playing drums and trumpets, walking in the gutter, feeling the kerb with the edge of their shoes, in Indian file. You heard the music a long way off, persisting through the rumble of the crowd, the shots of exhaust pipes, and the grinding of the buses starting uphill for the racecourse. It rang out with spirit, marched like a regiment, and you raised your eyes in expectation of the tiger skin and the twirling drumsticks and saw the pale blind eyes, like those of pit ponies, going by along the gutter.

In the great public-school grounds above the sea the girls trooped solemnly out to hockey: stout goalkeepers padded like armadillos; captains discussing tactics with their lieutenants; junior girls running amuck in the bright day. Beyond the aristocratic turf, through the wrought-iron main gates they could see the plebeian procession, those whom the buses wouldn't hold, plodding up the down, kicking up the dust, eating buns out of paper bags. The buses took the long way round through Kemp Town, but up the steep hill came the crammed taxicabs—a seat for anyone at ninepence a time—a Packard for the members' enclosure, old Morrises, strange high cars with family parties, keeping the road after twenty years. It was as if the whole road moved upwards like an Underground staircase in the dusty sunlight, a creaking, shouting, jostling crowd of cars moving with it. The junior girls took to their heels like ponies racing on the turf, feeling the excitement going on outside, as if this were a day on which life for many people reached a kind of climax. The odds on Black Boy had shortened, nothing could ever make life quite the same after that rash bet of a fiver on Merry Monarch. A scarlet racing model, a tiny rakish car which carried about it the atmosphere of innumerable roadhouses, of totsies gathered round swimming pools, of furtive encounters in by-lanes off the Great North Road, wormed through the traffic with incredible dexterity. The sun caught it: it winked as far as the dining-hall windows of the girls' school. It was crammed tight: a woman sat on a man's knee, and another man clung on the running board as it swayed and hooted and cut in and out uphill towards the downs. The woman was singing, her voice faint and disjointed through the horns, something traditional about brides and bouquets, something which went with stout and oysters, and the old Leicester Lounge, something out of place in the little bright racing car. Upon the top of the down the words blew back along the dusty road to meet an ancient Morris rocking and receding in their wake at forty miles an hour, with flapping top, bent fender, and discoloured windscreen.

The words came through the flap, flap, flap of the old top to the Boy's ears. He sat beside Spicer, who drove the car. Brides and bouquets: and he thought of Rose with sullen disgust. He couldn't get the suggestion of Spicer out of his mind: it was like an invisible power working against him: Spicer's stupidity, the photograph on the pier, that woman—who the hell was she?—asking questions . . . If he married her, of course, it wouldn't be for long: only as a last resort to close her mouth and give him time. He didn't want *that* relationship with anyone: the double bed, the intimacy, it sickened him like the idea of age. He crouched in the corner away from where the ticking pierced the seat, vibrating up and down in bitter virginity. To marry—it was like ordure on the hands.

"Where's Dallow and Cubitt?" Spicer asked.

"I didn't want them here today," the Boy said. "We've got something to do today the mob are better out of." Like a cruel child who hides the dividers behind him, he put his hand with spurious affection on Spicer's arm. "I don't mind telling you. I'm going to make it up with Colleoni. I wouldn't trust *them.* They are violent. You and I, we'll handle it properly between us."

"I'm all for peace," Spicer said. "I always have been."

The Boy grinned through the cracked windscreen at the long disorder of cars. "That's what I'm going to arrange," he said.

"A peace that lasts," Spicer said.

"No one's going to break this peace," the Boy said. The faint singing died in the dust and the bright sun:

a final bride, a final bouquet, a word which sounded like "wreath." "How do you set about getting married?" the Boy unwillingly asked. "If you've got to in a hurry?"

"Not so easy for you," Spicer said. "There's your age." He ground the old gears as they climbed a final spur towards the white enclosure on the chalky soil, the gipsy vans. "I'd have to think about it."

"Think quick," the Boy said. "You don't forget you're clearing out tonight."

"That's right," Spicer said. Departure made him a little sentimental. "The eight-ten. You ought to see that pub. You'd be welcome. Nottingham's a fine town. It'll be good to rest up there awhile. The air's fine, and you couldn't ask for a better bitter than you get at the Blue Anchor." He grinned. "I forgot you didn't drink."

"Have a good time," the Boy said.

"You'll be always welcome, Pinkie."

They rolled the old car up into the park and got out. The Boy passed his arm through Spicer's. Life was good walking outside the white sun-drenched wall— past the loudspeaker vans, the man who believed in a second coming, towards the finest of all sensations, the infliction of pain. "You're a fine fellow, Spicer," the Boy said, squeezing his arm, and Spicer began to tell him in a low friendly confiding way all about the Blue Anchor. "It's not a tied house," he said; "they've a reputation. I've always thought when I'd made enough money I'd go in with my friend. He still wants me to. I nearly went when they killed Kite."

"You get scared easy, don't you?" the Boy said. The

loudspeakers on the vans advised them whom to put
their money with, and gipsy children chased a rabbit
with cries across the trampled chalk. They went down
into the tunnel under the course and came up into the
light and the short grey grass sloping down by the
bungalow houses to the sea. Old race cards rotted into
the chalk: "Barker Will Bet You," a smug smiling
nonconformist face printed in yellow; "Don't Worry,
I Pay," and old tote tickets among the stunted plan-
tains. They went through the wire fence into the half-
crown enclosure. "Have a glass of beer, Spicer," the
Boy said, pressing him on.

"Why, that's good of you, Pinkie. I wouldn't mind a
glass," and while he drank it by the wooden trestles,
the Boy looked down the line of bookies. There were
Barker and Macpherson and George Beale ("The Old
Firm") and Bob Tavell of Clapton, all the familiar
faces, full of blarney and fake good-humour. The first
two races had been run; there were long queues at the
tote windows. The sun lit the white Tattersall stand
across the course, and a few horses galloped by to the
start. "There goes General Burgoyne," a man said,
"he's restless," starting off to Bob Tavell's stand to
cover his bet. The bookies rubbed out and altered the
odds as the horses went by, their hoofs padding like
boxing gloves on the turf.

"You going to take a plunge?" Spicer asked, finish-
ing his Bass, blowing a little gaseous malted breath towards the bookies.

"I don't bet," the Boy said.

"It's the last chance for me," Spicer said, "in good
old Brighton. I wouldn't mind risking a couple of

nicker. Not more. I'm saving my cash for Nottingham."

"Go on," the Boy said, "have a good time while you can."

They walked down the row of bookies towards Brewer's stand; there were a lot of men about. "He's doing good business," Spicer said. "Did you see the Merry Monarch? He's going up," and while he spoke, all down the line the bookies rubbed out the old sixteen-to-one odds. "Ten to one," Spicer said.

"Have a good time while you're here," the Boy said.

"Might as well patronize the old firm," Spicer said, detaching his arm and walking across to Tate's stand. The Boy smiled. It was as easy as shelling peas. " Memento Mori," Spicer said, coming away card in hand. "That's a funny name to give a horse. Five to one, for a place. What does Memento Mori mean?"

"It's foreign," the Boy said. "Black Boy's shortening."

"I wish I'd covered myself with Black Boy," Spicer said. "There was a woman down there saying she'd put a pony on Black Boy. It sounds crazy to me. But think if he wins," Spicer said. "My God, what wouldn't I do with two hundred and fifty pounds? I'd take a share in the Blue Anchor straight away. You wouldn't see me back here," he said, staring round at the brilliant sky, the dust over the course, the torn betting cards and the short grass towards the slow dark sea beneath the down.

"Black Boy won't win," the Boy said. "Who was it put the pony on?"

"Some polony or other. She was over there at the

bar. Why don't you have a fiver on Black Boy? Have a bet for once to celebrate?"

"Celebrate what?" the Boy said quickly.

"I forgot," Spicer said. "This holiday's perked me up, so's I think everyone's got something to celebrate."

"If I did want to celebrate," the Boy said, "it wouldn't be with Black Boy. Why, that used to be Fred's favourite. Said he'd be a Derby winner yet. I wouldn't call that a lucky horse," but he couldn't help watching him canter up by the rails: a little too young, a little too restless. A man on top of the half-crown stand signalled with his hand to Bob Tavell of Clapton and a tiny man who was studying the ten-shilling enclosure through binoculars suddenly began to saw the air, to attract the attention of the Old Firm. "There," the Boy said, "what did I tell you? Black Boy's going down again."

"Twelve to one Black Boy, twelve to one," George Beale's representative called, and "They're off," somebody said. People pressed out from the refreshment booth towards the rails carrying glasses of Bass and currant buns. Barker, Macpherson, Bob Tavell, all wiped the odds from their boards, but the Old Firm remained game to the last: "Fifteen to one on Black Boy"; while the little man made masonic passes from the top of the stand. The horses came by in a bunch, with a sharp sound like splintering wood, and were gone. "General Burgoyne," somebody said, and somebody said: "Merry Monarch." The beer drinkers went back to the trestle boards and had another glass, and the bookies put up the runners in the four o'clock and began to chalk a few odds.

"There," the Boy said, "what did I tell you? Fred never knew a good horse from a bad one. That crazy polony's dropped a pony. It's not *her* lucky day. Why—" but the silence, the inaction after a race is run and before the results go up, had a daunting quality. The queues waited outside the totes: everything on the course was suddenly still, waiting for a signal to begin again; in the silence you could hear a horse whinny all the way across from the weighing-in. A sense of uneasiness gripped the Boy in the quiet and the brightness. The soured false age, the concentrated and limited experience of the Brighton slum, drained out of him. He wished he had Cubitt there and Dallow. There was too much to tackle by himself at seventeen. It wasn't only Spicer. He had started something on Whit Monday which had no end. Death wasn't an end; the censer swung and the priest raised the Host, and the loudspeaker intoned the winners: "Black Boy. Memento Mori. General Burgoyne."

"By God," Spicer said, "I've won! Memento Mori for a place," and remembering what the Boy had said, he added: "And she's won too. A pony. What a break! Now what about Black Boy?" Pinkie was silent. He told himself: Fred's horse. If I was one of those crazy geezers who touch wood, throw salt, won't go under ladders, I might be scared to——

Spicer plucked at him. "I've won, Pinkie. A tenner. What do you know about that?"

——To go on with what he'd planned with care. Somewhere from further down the enclosure he heard a laugh, a female laugh, mellow and confident, perhaps the polony who'd put a pony on Fred's horse. He turned on Spicer with secret venom, cruelty straightening his body like lust.

"Yes," he said, putting his arm round Spicer's shoulder, "you'd better collect now."

They moved together towards Tate's stand. A young man with oiled hair stood on a wooden step paying out money. Tate himself was away in the ten-shilling enclosure, but they both knew Samuel. Spicer called out to him quite jovially as he advanced: "Well, Sammy, now the pay-off."

Samuel watched them, Spicer and the Boy, come across the shallow threadbare turf, arm in arm like very old friends. Half a dozen men collected and stood round, waiting; the last creditor slipped away; they waited in silence; a little man holding an account book put out a tip of tongue and licked a sore lip.

"You're in luck, Spicer," the Boy said, squeezing his arm. "Have a good time with your tenner." .

"You aren't saying good-bye yet, are you?" Spicer said.

"I'm not waiting for the four-thirty. I won't be seeing you again."

"What about Colleoni?" Spicer said. "Aren't you and I . . . ?" The horses cantered by for another start; the odds were going up; the crowd moved in towards the tote and left them a clear lane. At the end of the lane the little group waited.

"I've changed my mind," the Boy said. "I'll see Colleoni at his hotel. You get your money." A hatless tout delayed them: "A tip for the next race. Only a shilling. I've tipped two winners today." His toes showed through his shoes. "Tip yourself off," the Boy said. Spicer didn't like good-byes: he was a sentimental soul; he shifted on his corn-sore feet. "Why," he said, looking down the lane to the fence, "Tate's lot haven't written up the odds yet."

"Tate always was slow. Slow in paying out too. Better get your money." He urged him nearer, his hand on Spicer's elbow.

"There's not anything wrong, is there?" Spicer said. He looked at the waiting men; they stared through him.

"Well, this is good-bye," the Boy said.

"You remember the address," Spicer said. "The Blue Anchor, you remember, Union Street. Send me any news. I don't suppose there'll be any for *me* to send."

The Boy put his hand up as if to pat Spicer on the back and let it fall again: the group of men stood in a bunch waiting. "Maybe——" the Boy said; he looked round: there wasn't any end to what he had begun. A passion of cruelty stirred in his belly. He put up his hand again and patted Spicer on the back. "Good luck to you," he said in a high broken adolescent voice, and patted him again.

The men with one accord came round them. He heard Spicer scream: "Pinkie!" and saw him fall; a boot with heavy nails was lifted, and then he felt pain run like blood down his own neck.

The surprise at first was far worse than the pain (a nettle could sting as badly). "You fools," he said, "it's not me, it's him you want," and turned and saw Semitic faces ringing him all round. They grinned back at him: every man had his razor out; and he remem-

bered for the first time Colleoni laughing up the telephone wire. The crowd had scattered at the first sign
of trouble; he heard Spicer call out: "Pinkie. For
Christ's sake"; an obscure struggle reached its climax
out of his sight. He had other things to watch: the
long cut-throat razors which the sun caught slanting
low down over the downs from Shoreham. He put his
hand to his pocket to get his blade, and the man immediately facing him leant across and slashed his
knuckles. Pain happened to him; and he was filled with
horror and astonishment as if one of the bullied brats
at school had stabbed first with the dividers.

They made no attempt to come in and finish him.
He sobbed at them: "I'll get Colleoni for this." He
shouted "Spicer" twice before he remembered that
Spicer couldn't answer. The mob were enjoying themselves, just as he had always enjoyed himself. One of
them leant forward to cut his cheek and when he put
up his hand to shield himself they slashed his knuckles
again. He began to weep, as the four-thirty went by in
a drumbeat of hoofs beyond the rail.

Then somebody from the stand shouted: "Bogies,"
and they all moved together, coming quickly at him
in a bunch. Somebody kicked him on the thigh, he
clutched a razor in his hand and was cut to the bone.
Then they scattered as the police ran up the edge of
the course, slow in their heavy boots, and he broke
through them. A few followed him, out of the wire
gate and straight down the side of the down towards
the houses and the sea. He wept as he ran, lame in one
leg, from the kick; he even tried to pray. You could be
saved between the stirrup and the ground, but you

couldn't be saved if you didn't repent, and he hadn't time, scrambling down the chalk down, to feel the least remorse. He ran awkwardly, tripping, bleeding down his face and from both hands.

Only two men followed him now, and they followed him for the fun of it, shooing him as they might shoo a cat. He reached the first houses in the bottom, but there was no one about. The races had emptied every house: nothing but crazy paving and little lawns, stained-glass doors and a lawn mower abandoned on a gravel path. He didn't dare to take refuge in a house—while he rang and waited they would reach him. He had his razor blade out now, but he had never yet used it on an armed enemy. He had to hide, but he left a track of blood along the road.

The two men were out of breath: they had wasted it on laughter, and he had young lungs. He gained on them; he wrapped his hand in a handkerchief and held his head back so that the blood ran down his clothes; he turned a corner and was into an empty garage before they had reached it. There he stood, in the dusky interior, with his razor out, trying to repent. He thought: "Spicer," "Fred," but his thoughts would carry him no further than the corner where his pursuers might reappear; he discovered that he hadn't the energy to repent.

And when a long while later the danger seemed to be over, and there was a long dusk on his hands, it wasn't eternity he thought about but his own humiliation. He had wept, begged, run: Dallow and Cubitt would hear of it. What would happen to Kite's mob now? He tried to think of Spicer, but the world held

him. He couldn't order his thoughts. He stood with
weak knees against the concrete wall with the blade
advanced and watched the corner. A few people passed,
the faintest sound of music from the Palace Pier bit,
like an abscess, into his brain, the lights came out in
the neat barren bourgeois road.

The garage had never been used for a garage; it had
become a kind of potting shed; little green shoots
crept, like caterpillars, out of shallow boxes of earth; a
spade, a rusty lawn mower, and all the junk the owner
had no room for in the tiny house: an old rocking
horse, a pram which had been converted into a wheel-
barrow, a pile of ancient records: "Alexander's Rag
Time Band," "Pack Up Your Troubles," "If You
Were the Only Girl"; they lay with the trowels, what
was left of the crazy paving, a doll with one glass eye
and a dress soiled with mould. He took it all in with
quick glances, his razor blade ready, the blood clotting
on his neck, dripping from his hand, where the handkerchief had slipped. Whatever jackdaw owned this
house would have that much added to his possessions:
the little drying stain on the concrete floor.

Whoever the owner was, he had come a long way to
land up here. The pram-wheelbarrow was covered
with labels—the marks of innumerable train jour-
neys: Doncaster, Lichfield, Clacton (that must have
been a summer holiday), Ipswich, Northampton—
roughly torn off for the next journey they left, in the
litter which remained, an unmistakable trail. And this,
the small villa under the racecourse, was the best finish
he could manage. You couldn't have any doubt that
this was the end, the mortgaged home in the bottom;

like the untidy tidemark on a beach, the junk was piled
up here and would never go further.

And the Boy hated him. He was nameless, faceless,
but the Boy hated him. The doll, the pram, the broken
rocking horse. The small pricked-out plants irritated
him like ignorance. He felt hungry and faint and
shaken. He had known pain and fear.

Now, of course, was the time, while darkness drained
into the bottom, for him to make his peace. Between
the stirrup and the ground there wasn't time: you
couldn't break in a moment the habit of thought: habit
held you closely while you died, and he remembered
Kite, after they'd got him at St. Pancras, passing out
in the waiting room, while a porter poured coal dust
on the dead grate, talking all the time about someone's
tits.

But "Spicer," the Boy's thoughts came inevitably
back with a sense of relief. "They've got Spicer." It
was impossible to repent of something which made
him safe. The nosy woman hadn't got a witness now,
except for Rose, and he could deal with Rose; and then
when he was thoroughly secure, he could begin to
think of making peace, of going home, and his heart
weakened with a faint nostalgia for the tiny dark confessional box, the priest's voice, and the people waiting
under the statue, before the bright lights burning
down in the pink glasses, to be made safe from eternal
pain. Eternal pain had not meant much to him; now it
meant the clash of razor blades infinitely prolonged.

He sidled out of the garage. The new raw street cut
in the chalk was empty except for a couple pressed
against each other out of the lamplight by a wooden

fence. The sight pricked him with nausea and cruelty. He limped by them, his cut hand close on the blade, with his cruel virginity, which demanded some satisfaction different from theirs, habitual, brutish, and short.

He knew where he was going. He wasn't going to return to Billy's like this with the cobwebs from the garage on his clothes, defeat cut in his face and hand. They were dancing in the open air on the white stone deck above the Aquarium, and he got down onto the beach where he was more alone, the dry seaweed left by last winter's gales cracking under his shoes. He could hear the music, "The One I Love." "Wrap it up in cellophane," he thought, "put it in silver paper." A moth wounded against one of the lamps crawled across a piece of driftwood and he crushed it out of existence under his chalky shoe. One day, one day—he limped along the sand with his bleeding hand hidden, a young dictator. He was head of Kite's gang; this was a temporary defeat. One confession when he was safe to wipe out everything. The yellow moon slanted up over Hove, the exact mathematical Regency Square, and he day-dreamed, limping in the dry unwashed sand, by the closed bathing huts : I'll give a statue.

He climbed up from the sand just past the Palace Pier and made his painful way across the parade. Snow's Restaurant was all lit up. A radio was playing. He stood on the pavement outside until he saw Rose serve a table close to the window, then went and pressed his face to it. She saw him at once; his attention rang in her brain as quickly as if he had dialled her on an automatic phone. He took his hand from his pocket, but his wounded face was anxiety enough to her. She tried to tell him something through the glass; he couldn't understand her: it was as if he were listening to a foreign language. She had to repeat it three times: "Go to the back," before he could read her lips. The pain in his leg was worse; he trailed round the building, and as he turned, a car went by, a Lancia, a uniformed chauffeur, and Mr. Colleoni, Mr. Colleoni in a dinner jacket with a white waistcoat, who leant back and smiled and smiled in the face of an old lady in purple silk. Or perhaps it was not Mr. Colleoni at all, they went so smoothly and swiftly past, but any rich middle-aged Jew returning to the Cosmopolitan after a concert in the Pavilion.

He bent and looked through the letterbox of the back door; Rose came down the passage towards him with her hands clenched and a look of anger on her face. He lost some of his confidence: she's noticed, he thought, how done in . . . he'd always known a girl looked at your shoes and coat. If she sends me away, he thought, I'll crack this vitriol bottle . . . but when she opened the door she was as dumb and devoted as ever she'd been. "Who's done it?" she whispered. "If I could get at them."

"Never mind," the Boy said and boasted experimentally: "You can leave them to me."

"Your poor face." He remembered with disgust that they were always said to like a scar, that they took it as a mark of manhood, of potency.

"Is there somewhere," he said, "where I can wash up?"

She whispered: "Come quietly. Through here's the

cellar," and she led the way into a little closet, through which the hot pipes ran, where a few bottles lay on a small bin.

"Won't they be coming here?" he asked.

"No one here orders wine," she said. "We haven't got a licence. It's what was left when we took over. The manageress drinks it for her health." Every time she mentioned Snow's she said "we" with faint self-consciousness. "Sit down," she said. "I'll fetch some water. I'll have to put the light out or someone might see." But the moon lit the room enough for him to look around; he could even read the labels on the bottles: Empire wines, Australian hocks, and harvest burgundies.

She was gone only a little while but immediately she returned she began humbly to apologize: "Someone wanted a bill and Cook was watching." She had a white pudding basin of hot water and three handkerchiefs. "They're all I've got," she said, tearing them up, "the laundry's not back," and added firmly, as she dabbed the long shallow cut, like a line drawn with a pin down his neck: "If I could get at them . . ."

"Don't talk so much," he said and held out his slashed hand. The blood was beginning to clot; she tied it unskilfully.

"Has anyone been around again talking, asking questions?"

"That man the woman was with."

"A bogy?"

"I don't think so. He said his name was Phil."

"*You* seem to have done the asking."

"They all tell you things."

"I don't understand it," the Boy said. "What do
they want if they aren't bogies?" He put out his un-
wounded hand and pinched her arm. "You don't tell
them a thing?"

"Not a thing," she said and watched him with devotion through the dark. "Were you afraid?"

"They can't put anything on me."

"I mean," she said, "when they did this," touching
his hand.

"Afraid?" he lied. "Of course I wasn't afraid."

"Why did they do it?"

"I told you not to ask questions." He got up, unsteady on his bruised leg. "Brush my coat. I can't go
out like this. I've got to be respectable." He leant
against the harvest burgundy while she brushed him
down with the flat of her hand. The moonlight shad-
owed the room, the small bin, the bottles, the narrow
shoulders, the smooth scared adolescent face.

He was aware of an unwillingness to go out again
into the street, back to Billy's and the unending calcu-
lations with Cubitt and Dallow of the next move. Life
was a series of complicated tactical exercises, as complicated as the alinements at Waterloo, thought out on
a brass bedstead among the crumbs of sausage roll.
Your clothes continually needed ironing, Cubitt and
Dallow quarrelled, or else Dallow went after Billy's
wife, the old box telephone under the stairs rang and
rang, and the extras were always being brought in and
thrown on the bed by Judy, who smoked too much and
wanted a tip—a tip—a tip. How could you think out a
larger strategy under those conditions? He had a sudden nostalgia for the small dark cupboard room, the si-

lence, the pale light on the harvest burgundy. To be alone awhile . . .

But he wasn't alone. Rose put her hand on his and asked him with fear: "They aren't waiting for you, are they, out there?"

He shrank away and boasted. "They aren't waiting anywhere. They got more than they gave. They didn't reckon on me, only on poor Spicer."

"Poor Spicer?"

"Poor Spicer's dead," and just as he spoke a loud laugh came down the passage from the restaurant, a woman's laugh, full of beer and good fellowship and no regrets. "*She's* back," the Boy said.

"It's her all right." One had heard that laugh in a hundred places: dry-eyed, uncaring, looking on the bright side, when boats drew out and other people wept; saluting the bawdy joke in music halls; beside sick beds and in crowded Southern Railway compartments; when the wrong horse won, a good sportswoman's laugh. "She scares me," Rose whispered. "I don't know what she wants."

The Boy pulled her up to him; tactics, tactics: there was never any time for strategy; and in the grey night light he could see her face lifted for a kiss. He hesitated, with repulsion; but tactics. He wanted to strike her, to make her scream, but he kissed her inexpertly, missing her lips. He took his crinkling mouth away, and said: "Listen."

She said: "You haven't had many girls, have you?"

"Of course I have," he said, "but listen . . ."

"You're my first," she said. "I'm glad." When she said that, he began again to hate her. She wouldn't

even be something to boast of : her first; he'd robbed
nobody, he had no rival, no one else would look at her,
Cubitt and Dallow wouldn't give her a glance—her in-
determinate natural hair, her simpleness, the cheap
clothes he could feel under his hand. He hated her as
he had hated Spicer and it made him circumspect; he
pressed her breasts awkwardly under his palms, with
a grim opportunist pretence of another's man's passion, and thought : it wouldn't be so bad if she was
more dolled up, a bit of paint and henna, but this—
the cheapest, youngest, least experienced skirt in all
Brighton—to have *me* in her power.

"Oh, God," she said, "you're sweet to me, Pinkie. I
love you."

"You wouldn't give me away—to *her?*"

Somebody in the passage shouted : "Rose"; a door
slammed.

"I'll have to go," she said. "What do you mean—
give you away?"

"What I said. Talk. Tell her who left that ticket.
That it wasn't you know who."

"I won't tell her." A bus went by in West Street;
the lights came through a little barred window straight
onto her white determined face : she was like a child
who crosses her fingers and swears her private oath.
She said gently : "I don't care what you've done," as
she might have denied interest in a broken window
pane or a smutty word chalked on someone else's door.
He was speechless; and some knowledge of the astuteness of her simplicity, the long experience of her sixteen years, the possible depths of her fidelity, touched
him like cheap music as the light shifted from cheek-

bone to cheekbone and across the wall as the gears
ground outside.

He said: "What do you mean? I've done nothing."

"I don't know," she said. "I don't care."

"Rose," a voice cried, "Rose."

"It's Her," she said, "I'm sure it's Her. Asking
questions. Soft as butter. What does she know about
us?" She came closer. She said: "I did something once
too. A mortal sin. When I was twelve. But she—she
doesn't know what a mortal sin is."

"Rose. Where are you? Rose."

The shadow of her sixteen-year-old face shifted in
the moonlight on the wall. "Right and wrong. That's
what she talks about. I've heard her at the table. Right
and wrong. As if she knew." She whispered with contempt: "Oh, she won't burn. She couldn't burn if she
tried." She might have been discussing a damp Cath-
erine wheel. "Molly Carthew burnt. She was lovely.
She killed herself. Despair. That's mortal sin. It's un-
forgivable. Unless—what is it you said about the stirrup?"

He told her unwillingly: "The stirrup and the
ground. That doesn't work."

"What you did," she persisted, "did you confess it?"

He said evasively, a dark stubborn figure resting his
bandaged hand on the Australian hock: "I haven't
been to Mass for years."

"I don't care," she repeated. "I'd rather burn with
you than be like Her." Her immature voice stumbled
on the word: "She's ignorant."

"Rose." The door opened on their hiding place. A
manageress in a sage-green uniform, glasses hanging

from a button on her breast, brought in with her the
light, the voices, the radio, the laugh, dispelled the
dark theology between them. "Child," she said, "what
are you doing here? And who's the other child?" she
added peering at the thin figure in the shadows, but
when he moved into the light she corrected herself:
"This boy." Her eye ran along the bottles, counting
them. "You can't have followers here."

"I'm going," the Boy said.

She watched him with suspicion and distaste: the
cobwebs had not all gone. "If you weren't so young,"
she said, "I'd call the police."

He said with the only flash of humour he ever
showed: "I'd have an alibi."

"And as for you"—the manageress turned on Rose
—"we'll talk about you later." She watched the Boy
out of the room and said with disgust: "You're both
too young for this sort of thing."

Too young—that was the difficulty. Spicer hadn't
solved that difficulty before he died. Too young to close
her mouth with marriage, too young to stop the police
putting her in the witness box, if it ever came to that.
To give evidence that—why, to say that Hale had
never left the card, that Spicer had left it, that he himself had come and felt for it under the cloth. She remembered even that detail. Spicer's death would add
suspicion. He'd got to close her mouth one way or another · he had to have peace.

He slowly climbed the stairs to the bed sitting room
at Billy's. He had the sense that he was losing grip, the
telephone rang and rang, and as he lost grip he began
to realize all the things he hadn't years enough to

know. Cubitt came out of a downstairs room, his cheek was stuffed with apple, he had a broken penknife in his hand. "No," he said, "Spicer's not here. He's not back yet."

The Boy called down from the first landing. "Who wants Spicer?"

"She's rung off."

"Who was she?"

"I don't know. Some skirt of his. He's soft on a girl he sees at the Queen of Hearts. Where *is* Spicer, Pinkie?"

"He's dead. Colleoni's men killed him."

"God," Cubitt said. He shut the knife and spat the apple out. "I said we ought to lay off Brewer. What are we going to do?"

"Come up here," the Boy said. "Where's Dallow?"

"He's out."

The Boy led the way into the bed sitting room and turned on the single globe. He thought of Colleoni's room in the Cosmopolitan. But you had to begin somewhere. He said: "You've been eating on my bed again."

"It wasn't me, Pinkie. It was Dallow. Why, Pinkie, they've cut *you* up."

Again the Boy lied. "I gave them as good." But lying was a weakness. He wasn't used to lying. He said: "We needn't get worked up about Spicer. He was milky. It's a good thing he's dead. The girl at Snow's saw him leave the ticket. Well, when he's buried, no one's going to identify him. We might even have him cremated."

"You don't think the bogies—?"

"I'm not afraid of the bogies. It's others who are nosing round."

"They can't get over what the doctors said."

"You know we killed him and the doctors knew he died natural. Work it out for yourself, I can't." He sat down on the bed and swept off Dallow's crumbs. "We're safer without Spicer."

"Maybe you know best, Pinkie. But what made Colleoni—?"

"He was scared, I suppose, that we'd let Tate have it on the course. I want Mr. Drewitt fetched. I want him to fix me something. He's the only lawyer we can trust round here—if we can trust him."

"What's the trouble, Pinkie? Anything serious?"

The Boy leant his head back against the brass bedpost. "Maybe I'll have to get married after all."

Cubitt suddenly bellowed with laughter, his large mouth wide, his teeth carious. Behind his head the blind was half drawn down, shutting out the night sky, leaving the chimney pots, black and phallic, palely smoking up into the moonlit air. The Boy was silent, watching Cubitt, listening to his laughter as if it were the world's contempt.

When Cubitt stopped he said: "Go on. Ring Mr. Drewitt up. He's got to come round here," staring past Cubitt at the acorn gently tapping on the pane at the end of the blind cord, at the chimneys and the early summer night.

"He won't come here."

"He's got to come. I can't go out like *this*." He touched the marks on his neck where the razors had cut him. "I've got to get things fixed."

"You dog you," Cubitt said. "You're a young one at
the game." The game: and the Boy's mind turned
with curiosity and loathing to the small cheap ready-
for-anyone face, the bottles catching the moonlight on
the bin, and the word "burn," "burn," repeated. What
did people mean by "the game"? He knew everything
in theory, nothing in practice; he was only old with
the knowledge of other people's lusts, those of strangers who wrote their desires on the walls in public lavatories. He knew the moves, he'd never played the
game. "Maybe," he said, "it won't come to that. But
fetch Mr. Drewitt. He knows."

Mr. Drewitt knew. You were certain of that at the
first sight of him. He was a stranger to no wangle,
twist, contradictory clause, ambiguous word. His yellow shaven middle-aged face was deeply lined with legal decisions. He carried a little brown leather portfolio and wore striped trousers which seemed a little
too new for the rest of him. He came into the room
with hollow joviality, a dockside manner; he had long
pointed polished shoes which caught the light. Everything about him, from his breeziness to his morning
coat, was brand-new, except himself and that had aged
in many law courts, with many victories more damag-
ing than defeats. He had acquired the habit of not listening: innumerable rebukes from the bench had
taught him that. He was deprecating, discreet, sympathetic, and as tough as leather.

The Boy nodded to him without getting up, sitting
on the bed. "Evening, Mr. Drewitt," and Mr. Drewitt

smiled sympathetically, put his portfolio on the floor, and sat down on the hard chair by the dressing table. "It's a lovely night," he said. "Oh, dear, oh, dear, you've been in the wars." The sympathy didn't belong; it could be peeled off his eyes like an auction ticket from an ancient flint instrument.

"It's not *that* I want to see you about," the Boy said. "You needn't be scared. I just want information."

"No trouble, I hope?" Mr. Drewitt said.

"I want to avoid trouble. If I wanted to get married what'd I do?"

"Wait a few years," Mr. Drewitt said promptly, as if he were calling a hand in cards.

"Next week maybe," the Boy said.

"The trouble is," Mr. Drewitt thoughtfully remarked, "you're under age."

"That's why I've called *you* in."

"There are cases," Mr. Drewitt said, "of people who give their ages wrong. I'm not suggesting it, mind you. What age is the girl?"

"Sixteen."

"You're sure of that? Because if she was under sixteen you could be married in Canterbury Cathedral by the Archbishop himself, and it wouldn't be legal."

"That's all right," the Boy said. "But if we give our ages wrong, are we married all right—legally?"

"Hard and fast."

"The police wouldn't be able to call the girl—?"

"In evidence against you? Not without her consent. Of course you'd have committed a misdemeanour. You could be sent to prison. And then—there are other difficulties." Mr. Drewitt leant back against the wash-stand, his grey neat legal hair brushing the ewer and eyed the Boy.

"You know I pay," the Boy said.

"First," Mr. Drewitt said, "you've got to remember it takes time."

"It mustn't take long."

"Do you want to be married in a church?"

"Of course I don't," the Boy said. "This won't be a real marriage."

"Real enough."

"Not real like when the priest says it."

"Your religious feelings do you credit," Mr. Drewitt said. "This, I take it then, will be a civil marriage. You could get a licence—fifteen days' residence—you qualify for that—and one day's notice. As far as that's concerned you could be married the day after tomorrow—in your own district. Then comes the next difficulty. A marriage of a minor's not easy."

"Go on. I'll pay."

"It's no good you just saying you're twenty-one. No one would believe you. But if you said you were eighteen you could be married provided you had your parents' or your guardian's consent. Are your parents alive?"

"No."

"Who's your guardian?"

"I don't know what you mean."

Mr. Drewitt said thoughtfully: "We might arrange a guardian. It's risky though. It might be better if you'd lost touch. He'd gone to South Africa and left you. We might make quite a good thing out of that,"

Mr. Drewitt added softly. "Flung on the world at an early age you've bravely made your own way." His eyes shifted from bedball to bedball. "We'd ask for the discretion of the registrar."

"I never knew it was all that difficult," the Boy said. "Maybe I can manage some way else."

"Given time," Mr. Drewitt said, "anything can be managed." He showed his tartar-coated teeth in a fatherly smile. "Give the word, my boy, and I'll see you married. Trust me." He stood up, his striped trousers were like a wedding guest's, hired for the day at Moss's; when he crossed the room, yellowly smiling, he might have been about to kiss the bride. "If you'll let me have a guinea now for the consultation, there are one or two little purchases—for the spouse . . ."

"Are *you* married?" the Boy said with sudden eagerness. It had never occurred to him that Drewitt . . . He gazed at the smile, the yellow teeth, the lined and wasted and unreliable face as if *there* possibly he might learn . . .

"It's my silver wedding next year," Mr. Drewitt said. "Twenty-five years at the game." Cubitt put his head in at the door and said: "I'm going out for a turn." He grinned. "How's the marriage?"

"Progressing," Mr. Drewitt said, "progressing," patting the portfolio as if it had been the plump cheek of a promising infant. "We shall see our young friend spliced yet."

Just till it all blows over, the Boy thought, leaning back on the grey pillow, resting one shoe on the mauve eiderdown: not a real marriage, just something to keep her mouth shut for a time. "So long," Cubitt said,

giggling at the bed end. Rose, the small devoted Cock-
ney face, the sweet taste of human skin, emotion in the
dark room by the bin of harvest burgundy; lying on
the bed he wanted to protest "not yet" and "not with
her." If it had to come some time, if he had to follow
everyone else into the brutish game, let it be when he
was old, with nothing else to gain, and with someone
other men could envy him. Not someone immature,
simple, as ignorant as himself.

"You've only to give the word," Mr. Drewitt said.
"We'll fix it together." Cubitt had gone. The Boy
said: "You'll find a nicker on the washstand."

"I don't see one," Mr. Drewitt said anxiously, shifting a toothbrush.

"In the soap dish—under the cover."

Dallow put his head into the room. "Evening," he
said to Mr. Drewitt. He said to the Boy: "What's up
with Spicer?"

"It was Colleoni. They got him on the course," the
Boy said. "They nearly got me too," and he raised his
bandaged hand to his scarred neck.

"But Spicer's in his room now. I heard him."

"*Heard?*" the Boy said. "You're imagining things."
He was afraid for the second time that day: a dim
globe lit the passage and the stairs; the walls were unevenly splashed with walnut paint. He felt the skin of
his face contract as if something repulsive had touched
him. He wanted to ask whether you could do more
than hear this Spicer, if he was sensible to the sight
and the touch. He stood up: it had to be faced whatever it was, passed Dallow without another word. The
door of Spicer's room swung in a draught to and fro.

He couldn't see inside. It was a tiny room; they had all
had tiny rooms but Kite, and he had inherited that.
That was why his room was the common room for
them all. In Spicer's there would be space for no one
but himself—and Spicer. He could hear little creaking
leathery movements as the door swung. The words,
"Dona nobis pacem," came again to mind; for the second time he felt a faint nostalgia, as if for something
he had lost or forgotten or rejected.

He walked down the passage and into Spicer's room.
His first feeling when he saw Spicer bent and tighten-
ing the straps of his suitcase was relief—that it was
undoubtedly the living Spicer, whom you could touch
and scare and command. A long strip of sticking plaster lined Spicer's cheek; the Boy watched it from the
doorway with a rising cruelty; he wanted to tear it
away and see the skin break. Spicer looked up, put
down the suitcase, shifted uneasily towards the wall.
He said: "I thought—I was afraid—Colleoni had got
you." His fear gave away his knowledge. The Boy said
nothing, watching him from the door. As if he were
apologizing for being alive at all he explained · "I got
away . . ." His words wilted out like a line of seaweed,
along the edge of the Boy's silence, indifference, and
purpose.

Down the passage came the voice of Mr. Drewitt:
"In the soap dish. He said it was in the soap dish," and
the clatter of china noisily moved about.

"I'm going to work on that kid every hour of the day until I get something." She rose formidably and moved across the restaurant, like a warship going into action, a warship on the right side in a war to end wars, the signal flags proclaiming that every man would do his duty. Her big breasts, which had never suckled a child of her own, felt a merciless compassion. Rose fled at the sight of her, but Ida moved relentlessly towards the service door. Everything now was in train, she had begun to ask the questions she had wanted to ask when she had read about the inquest in Henneky's, and she was getting the answers. And Fred too had done his part, had tipped the right horse, so that now she had funds as well as friends: an infinite capacity for corruption: two hundred pounds.

"Good evening, Rose," she said, standing in the kitchen doorway, blocking it. Rose put down a tray and turned with all the fear, obstinacy, incomprehension, of a small wild animal who will not recognize kindness.

"You again?" she said. "I'm busy. I can't talk to you."

"But the manageress, dear, has given me leave."

"We can't talk here."

"Where can we talk?"

"In my room if you'll let me out."

Rose went ahead up the stairs behind the restaurant to the little linoleumed landing. "They do you well here, don't they?" Ida said. "I once lived in at a pub-

lic, that was before I met Tom—Tom's my husband,"
she patiently, sweetly, implacably explained to Rose's
back. "They didn't do you so well there. Flowers on
the landing!" she exclaimed, with pleasure, at the
withered bunch on a deal table, pulling at the petals,
when a door slammed. Rose had shut her out, and as
she gently knocked she heard an obstinate whisper:
"Go away. I don't want to talk to you."

"It's serious. Very serious." The stout that Ida had
been drinking returned a little; she put her hand up to
her mouth and said mechanically: "Pardon," belching
towards the closed door.

"I can't help you. I don't know anything."

"Let me in, dear, and I'll explain. I can't shout
things on the landing."

"Why should you care about *me?*"

"I don't want the innocent to suffer."

"As if you knew," the soft voice accused her, "who
was innocent."

"Open the door, dear." She began, but only a little,
to lose her patience; her patience was almost as deep as
her goodwill. She felt the handle and pushed; she
knew that waitresses were not allowed keys; but a
chair had been wedged under the handle. She said with
irritation· "You won't escape me this way." She put
her weight against the door and the chair cracked and
shifted, the door opened a slit.

"I'm going to make you listen," Ida said. When you
were life saving you must never hesitate, so they
taught you, to stun the one you rescued. She put her
hand in and detached the chair, then went in through
the open door. Three iron bedsteads, a chest of draw-

ers, two chairs, and a couple of cheap mirrors : she took it all in and Rose against the wall as far as she could get, watching the door with terror through her innocent and experienced eyes, as if there was nothing which mightn't come through.

"Don't be silly now," Ida said. "I'm your friend. I only want to save you from that boy. You're crazy about him, aren't you? But don't you understand—he's wicked?" She sat down on the bed and went gently and mercilessly on.

Rose whispered · "You don't know a thing."

"I've got my evidence."

"I don't mean *that*," the child said.

"He doesn't care for you," Ida said. "Listen, I'm human. You can take my word I've loved a boy or two in my time. Why, it's natural. It's like breathing. Only you don't want to get all worked up about it. There's not one who's worth it—leave alone *him*. He's wicked. I'm not a Puritan, mind. I've done a thing or two in my time—that's *natural*. Why," she said, extending towards the child her plump and patronizing paw, "it's in my hand · the girdle of Venus. But I've always been on the side of Right. You're young. You'll have plenty of boys before you've finished. You'll have plenty of fun—if you don't let them get a grip on you. It's natural. Like breathing. Don't take away the notion I'm against Love. I should say not. Me. Ida Arnold. They'd laugh." The stout came back up her throat again and she put a hand before her mouth. "Pardon, dear. You see we can get along all right when we are together. I've never had a child of my own and somehow I've taken to you. You're a sweet little thing." She suddenly barked: "Come away from that wall and act sensible. He doesn't love you."

"I don't care," the childish voice stubbornly murmured.

"What do you mean, you don't care?"

"I love him."

"You're acting morbid," Ida said. "If I was your mother I'd give you a good hiding. What'd your father and mother say if they knew?"

"*They* wouldn't care."

"And how do you think it will all end?"

"I don't know."

"You're young. That's what it is," Ida said, "romantic. I was like you once. You'll grow out of it. All you need is a bit of experience." The Nelson Place eyes stared back at her without understanding; driven to her hole the small animal peered out at the bright and breezy world: in the hole were murder, copulation, extreme poverty, fidelity, and the love and fear of God; but the small animal had not the knowledge to deny that only in the glare and open world outside was something which people called experience.

3

The Boy looked down at the body, spreadeagled like Prometheus, at the bottom of Billy's stairs. "Good God," Mr. Drewitt said, "how did it happen?"

The Boy said: "These stairs have needed mending a long while. I've told Billy about it, but you can't make the bastard spend money." He put his bound hand on the rail and pushed until it gave. The rotten wood lay across Spicer's body, a walnut-stained eagle couched over the kidneys.

"But that happened *after* he fell," Mr. Drewitt protested; his insinuating legal voice was tremulous.

"You've got it wrong," the Boy said. "You were here in the passage and you saw him lean his suitcase against the rail. He shouldn't have done that. The case was too heavy."

"My God, you can't mix me up in this," Mr. Drewitt said. "I saw nothing. I was looking in the soap dish, I was with Dallow."

"You both saw it," the Boy said. "That's fine. It's a good thing we have a fine respectable lawyer like you on the spot. Your word will do the trick."

"I'll deny it," Mr. Drewitt said. "I'm getting out of here. I'll swear I was never in the house."

"Stay where you are," the Boy said. "We don't want another accident. Dallow, go and telephone for the police—and a doctor, it looks well."

"You can keep me here," Mr. Drewitt said, "but you can't make me say——"

"I only want you to say what you want to say. But it wouldn't look good, would it, if I was taken up for killing Spicer, and you were here—looking in the soap dish. It would be enough to ruin some lawyers."

Mr. Drewitt stared over the broken gap at the turn of the stairs where the body lay. He said slowly: "You'd better lift that body and put the wood under it. The police would have a lot to ask if they found it that way." He went back into the bedroom and sat down on the bed and put his head in his hands. "I've got a headache," he said, "I ought to be at home." Nobody paid him any attention. Spicer's door rattled in the draught. "I've got a splitting headache," Mr. Drewitt said.

Dallow came lugging the suitcase down the passage; the cord of Spicer's pyjamas squeezed out of it like toothpaste. "Where was he going?" Dallow said.

"The Blue Anchor, Union Street, Nottingham," the Boy said. "We'd better wire them. They might want to send flowers."

"Be careful about finger prints," Mr. Drewitt implored them from the washstand without raising his aching head, but the Boy's steps on the stairs made him look up. "Where are you going?" he asked sharply. The Boy stared up at him from the turn in the stairs. "Out," he said.

"You can't go now," Mr. Drewitt said.

"I wasn't here," the Boy said. "It was just you and Dallow. You were waiting for me to come in."

"You'll be seen."

"That's your risk," the Boy said. "I've got things to do."

"Don't tell me," Mr. Drewitt cried hastily and checked himself, "don't tell me," he repeated in a low voice, "what things . . ."

"We'll have to fix that marriage," the Boy said, sombrely. He gazed at Mr. Drewitt for a moment—the spouse, twenty-five years at the game—with the air of someone who wanted to ask a question, almost as if he were prepared to accept advice from a man so much older, as if he expected a little human wisdom from the old shady legal mind.

"It had better be soon," the Boy went softly and sadly on. He still watched Mr. Drewitt's face for some reflection of the wisdom twenty-five years at the game must have given him, but saw only a frightened face, boarded up like a store when a riot is on. He went on down the stairs, dropping into the dark well where Spicer's body had fallen. He had made his decision; he had only to move towards his aim; he could feel his blood pumped from the heart and moving indifferently back along the arteries like trains on the inner circle. Every station was one nearer safety, and then one farther away, until the bend was turned and safety again approached, like Notting Hill, and afterwards receded. The middle-aged whore on Hove front never troubled to look round as he came up behind her like electric trains moving on the same track there was no collision. They both had the same end in view, if you could talk of an end in connexion with that circle. Outside the Norfolk bar two smart scarlet racing models lay along the kerb like twin beds. The Boy was not conscious of them, but their image passed automatically into his brain, released his secretion of envy.

Snow's was nearly empty. He sat down at the table where once Spicer had sat, but he was not served by Rose. A strange girl came to take his order. He said awkwardly: "Isn't Rose here?"

"She's busy."

"Could I see her?"

"She's talking to someone up in her room. You can't go there. You'll have to wait."

The Boy put half a crown on the table. "Where is it?"

The girl hesitated. "The manageress would bawl hell."

"Where's the manageress?"

"She's out."

The Boy put another half-crown on the table.

"Through the service door," the girl said, "and straight up the stairs. There's a woman with her though——"

He heard the woman's voice before he reached the top of the stairs. She was saying: "I only want to speak to you for your own good," but he had to strain to catch Rose's reply.

"Let me be, why won't you let me be?"

"It's the business of anyone who thinks right."

The Boy could see into the room now from the head of the stairs, though the broad back, the large loose dress, the square hips of the woman nearly blocked his view of Rose, who stood back against the wall in an attitude of sullen defiance. Small and bony in the black cotton dress and the white apron, her eyes stained but tearless, startled and determined, she carried her courage with a kind of comic inadequacy, like the little man in the bowler put up by the management to challenge the strong man at a fair. She said: "You'd better let me be."

It was Nelson Place and Manor Street which stood there in the servant's bedroom, and for a moment he felt no antagonism but a faint nostalgia. He was aware that she belonged to his life, like a room or a chair: she was something which completed him; he thought: "She's got more guts than Spicer." What was most evil in him needed her: it couldn't get along without goodness. He said softly. "What are you worrying my girl about?" and the claim he made was curiously sweet to his ears, like a refinement of cruelty. After all, though he had aimed higher than Rose, he had this comfort: she couldn't have gone lower than himself. He stood there, with a smirk on his face, when the woman turned; "between the stirrup and the ground," he had learned the fallacy of that comfort; if he had attached to himself some bright brassy skirt, like the ones he'd seen at the Cosmopolitan, his triumph after all wouldn't have been so great. He smirked at the pair of them, nostalgia driven out by a surge of sad sensuality. She was good, he'd discovered that, and he was damned: they were made for each other.

"You leave her alone," the woman said. "I know all about you." It was as if she were in a strange country: the typical Englishwoman abroad. She hadn't even got a phrase book. She was as far from either of them as she was from Hell—or Heaven. Good and evil lived in the same country, spoke the same language, came together like old friends, feeling the same completion, touching hands beside the iron bedstead. "You want to do what's Right, Rose?" she implored.

Rose whispered again: "You let us be."

"You're a Good Girl, Rose. You don't want anything to do with Him."

"You don't know a thing."

There was nothing she could do at the moment but threaten from the door: "I haven't finished with you yet. I've got friends."

The Boy watched her go with amazement. He said: "Who the hell is she?"

"I don't know," Rose said.

"I've never seen her before." The vaguest memory pricked him and passed.

"What did she want?"

"I don't know."

"You're a good girl, Rose," the Boy said, pressing his fingers round the small sharp wrist.

She shook her head. "I'm bad." She implored him: "I want to be bad if she's good and you———"

"You'll never be anything but good," the Boy said. "There's some wouldn't like you for that, but I don't care."

"I'll do anything for you. Tell me what to do. I don't want to be like her."

"It's not what you do," the Boy said, "it's what you think." He boasted. "It's in the blood. Perhaps when they christened me, the holy water didn't take. I never howled the devil out."

"Is *she* good?" She came weakly to him for instruction.

"She?" The Boy laughed. "She's just nothing."

"We can't stay here," Rose said. "I wish we could." She looked round her, at a badly foxed steel engraving of Van Tromp's victory, the three black bedsteads, the two mirrors, the single chest of drawers, the pale mauve knots of flowers on the wallpaper, as if she was safer here than she could ever be in the squally summer night outside. "It's a nice room." She wanted to share it with him till it became a home for both of them.

"How'd you like to leave this place?"

"Snow's? Oh, no, it's a good place. I wouldn't want to be anywhere else than Snow's."

"I mean marry me."

"We aren't old enough."

"It could be managed. There are ways." He dropped her wrist and put on a careless air. "If you wanted. I don't mind."

"Oh," she said. "I want it. But they'll never let us."

He explained airily. "It couldn't be in church, not at first. There'd be difficulties. Are you afraid?"

"I'm not afraid," she said. "But will they let us?"

"My lawyer'll manage somehow."

"Have you got a lawyer?"

"Of course I have."

"It sounds somehow—grand—and old."

"A man can't get along without a lawyer."

She said: "It's not where I always thought it would be."

"Where what would be?"

"Someone asking me to marry him. I thought—in the pictures or maybe at night on the front. But this is best," she said, looking from Van Tromp's victory to the two looking glasses. She came away from the wall and lifted her face to him; he knew what was expected of him; he regarded her unmade-up mouth with faint nausea. Saturday night, eleven o'clock, the primeval exercise. He pressed his hard puritanical mouth on hers; and tasted again the sweetish smell of the human skin. He would have preferred the taste of Coty powder or Kissproof lipstick, of any chemical compound. He shut his eyes and when he opened them again, it was to see her waiting, like a blind girl, for further alms. It shocked him that she had been unable to detect his repulsion. She said : "You know what that means?"

"What means?"

"It means I'll never let you down, never, never, never."

She belonged to him like a room or a chair : the Boy fetched up a smile for the blind lost face, uneasily, with obscure shame.

PART FIVE

EVERYTHING went well: the inquest never even got onto the newspaper posters; no questions asked. The Boy walked back with Dallow, he should have felt triumphant. He said: "I wouldn't trust Cubitt if Cubitt knew."

"Cubitt won't know. Drewitt is scared to say a thing —and you know I don't talk, Pinkie."

"I've got a feeling we're being followed, Dallow."

Dallow looked behind. "No one. I know every bogy in Brighton."

"No woman?"

"No. Who are you thinking of?"

"I don't know."

The blind band came up the kerb, scraping the sides of their shoes along the edge, feeling their way in the brilliant light, sweating a little. The boy walked up the side of the road to meet them; the music they played was plaintive, pitying, something out of a hymn book about burdens; it was like a voice prophesying sorrow at the moment of victory. The boy met the leader and pushed him out of the way, swearing at him softly, and the whole band, hearing their leader move, shifted uneasily a foot into the roadway and stood there stranded till the boy was safely by, like barques becalmed on a huge and landless Atlantic. Then they edged back, feeling for the landfall of the pavement.

"What's up with you, Pinkie?" Dallow said. "They're blind."

"Why should I get out of my way for a beggar?" But he hadn't realized they were blind; he was shocked by his own action. It was as if he was being driven too far down a road he wanted to travel only a certain distance. He stood and leant on the rail of the front while the midweek crowd passed and the hard sun flattened.

"What's on your mind, Pinkie?"

"To think of all this trouble over Hale. He deserved what he got, but if I'd known how it would go maybe

I'd have let him live. Maybe he wasn't worth killing. A dirty little journalist who played in with Colleoni and got Kite killed. Why should anyone bother about him?" He looked suddenly over his shoulder. "Have I seen that geezer before?"

"He's only a visitor."

"I thought I'd seen his tie."

"Hundreds in the shops. If you were a drinking man I'd say what you needed was a pick-up. Why, Pinkie, everything's going fine. No questions asked."

"There were only two people could hang us, Spicer and the girl. I've killed Spicer and I'm marrying the girl. Seems to me I'm doing everything."

"Well, we'll be safe now."

"Oh, yes, *you*'ll be safe. It's me who runs all the risk. *You* know I killed Spicer. Drewitt knows. It only wants Cubitt and I'll need a massacre to put me right this time."

"You oughtn't to talk that way to me, Pinkie. You've been all bottled up since Kite died. What you want's a bit of fun."

"I liked Kite," the Boy said. He stared straight out towards France, an unknown land. At his back beyond the Cosmopolitan, Old Steyne, the Lewes Road, stood the downs, villages and cattle round the dewponds, another unknown land. This was his territory: the populous foreshore, a few thousand acres of houses, a narrow peninsula of electrified track running to London, two or three railway stations with their buffets and buns. It had been Kite's territory, it had been good enough for Kite, and when Kite had died in the waiting room at St. Pancras, it had been as if a father had died, leaving him an inheritance it was his duty never to leave for strange acres. He had inherited even the mannerisms, the bitten thumb nail, the soft drinks. The sun slid off the sea and like a cuttlefish shot into the sky the stain of agonies and endurances.

"Break out, Pinkie. Relax. Give yourself a chance. Come out with me and Cubitt to the Queen of Hearts and celebrate."

"You know I never touch a drink."

"You'll have to on your wedding day. Whoever heard of a dry wedding?"

An old man went stooping down the shore, very slowly, turning the stones, picking among the dry seaweed for cigarette ends, scraps of food. The gulls which had stood like candles down the beach rose and cried under the promenade. The old man found a boot and stowed it in his sack, and a gull dropped from the parade and swept through the iron nave of the Palace Pier, white and purposeful in the obscurity: half vulture and half dove. In the end one always had to learn.

"All right, I'll come," the Boy said.

"It's the best roadhouse this side of London," Dallow encouraged him.

They drove out in the old Morris into the country. "I like a blow in the country," Dallow said. It was between lighting-up time and the real dark when the lamps of cars burned in the grey visibility as faintly and unnecessarily as the night lights in nurseries. The advertisements trailed along the arterial road; bungalows and a broken farm, short chalky grass where a

hoarding had been pulled down, a windmill offering
tea and lemonade, the great sails gaping.

"Poor old Spicer would have liked this ride," Cubitt
said. The Boy sat beside Dallow, who drove, and Cubitt
sat in the rumble. The Boy could see him in the driving mirror bouncing gently up and down on the de-
fective springs.

The Queen of Hearts was floodlit behind the petrol
pumps: a Tudor barn converted, a vestige of a farmyard left in the arrangement of the restaurant and bars,
a swimming pool where the paddock had been. "We
ought to 'ave brought some girls with us," Dallow
said. "You can't pick 'em up in this gaff. It's real
class."

"Come in the bar," Cubitt said and led the way.
He stopped on the threshold and nodded towards the
girl who sat and drank alone at the long steel bar
under the old rafters. "We better say something,
Pinkie. You know the kind of thing—he was a real
good old pal, we sympathize with what you feel."

"What are you clapping about?"

"That's Spicer's girl," Cubitt said.

The Boy stood in the doorway and took her reluctantly in: hair fair as silver, wide vacuous brow,
trim little buttocks shaped by the high seat, alone with
her glass and her grief.

"How's things, Sylvie?" Cubitt said.

"Awful."

"Terrible, wasn't it? He was a good pal. One of the
best."

"You were there, weren't you?" she said to Dallow.

"Billy ought to 'ave mended that stair," Dallow said. "Meet Pinkie, Sylvie, the best one in our mob."

"Were you there too?"

"He wasn't there," Dallow said.

"Have another drink?" the Boy said.

Sylvie drained her glass. "I don't mind if I do. A sidecar."

"Two Scotch, a sidecar, a grapefruit squash."

"Why," Sylvie said, "don't you drink?"

"No."

"I bet you don't go with girls either."

"You got him, Sylvie," Cubitt said, "first shot."

"I admire a man like that," Sylvie said. "I think it's wonderful to be fit. Spicie always said you'd break out one day—and then—oh, gosh, how wonderful!" She put down her glass, miscalculated, upset the cocktail. She said: "I'm not drunk. I'm upset about poor Spicie."

"Go on, Pinkie," Dallow said, "have a drink. It'll jerk you up." He explained to Sylvie: "He's upset too." In the dance hall the band was playing: "Love me tonight, And forget in daylight, All our delight . . ."

"Have a drink," Sylvie said. "I've been awful upset. You can see I've been crying. Aren't my eyes awful? . . . Why, I hardly dared show myself. I can see why people go into monasteries." The music beat on the boy's resistance; he watched with a kind of horror and curiosity Spicer's girl friend: she knew the game. He shook his head, speechless in his scared pride. He knew what he was good at: he was the top: there was no limit to his ambition: nothing must lay him open

to the mockery of people more experienced than he.
To be compared with Spicer and found wanting . . .
his eyes shifted miserably and the music wailed its
tidings—"forget in daylight"—about the game of
which they all knew so much more than he did.

"Spicie said he didn't think you'd ever had a girl,"
Sylvie said.

"There was plenty Spicer didn't know."

"You're awful young to be so famous."

"You and me had better go away," Cubitt said to
Dallow. "Seems we're not wanted. Come an' lamp the
bathing belles." They moved heavily out of sight.
"Dallie just knows when I like a boy," Sylvie said.

"Who's Dallie?"

"Your friend, Mr. Dallow, silly. Do you dance—
why, I don't even know your proper name?" He
watched her with scared lust: she had belonged to
Spicer; her voice had wailed up the telephone wires
making assignations; he had had signed letters in
mauve envelopes, addressed to him; even Spicer had
had something to be proud of, to show to friends—
"my girl." He remembered some flowers which had
come to Billy's labelled "Brokenhearted." He was fascinated by her infidelity. She belonged to nobody—
unlike a table or a chair. He said slowly, putting his
arm round her to take her glass and pressing her breast
clumsily: "I'm going to be married in a day or two."
It was as if he were staking a claim to his share of
infidelity: he wasn't to be beaten by experience. He
lifted her glass and drank it; the sweetness dripped
down his throat, his first alcohol touched the palate
like a bad smell: this was what people called pleasure

—this and the game. He put his hand on her thigh
with a kind of horror; Rose and he; forty-eight hours
after Drewitt had arranged things; alone in God
knows what apartment—what then, what then? He
knew the traditional actions as a man may know the
principles of gunnery in chalk on a blackboard, but to
translate the knowledge to action, to the smashed village and the ravaged woman, one needed help from
the nerves. His own were frozen with repulsion: to be
touched, to give oneself away, to lay oneself open—
he had held intimacy back as long as he could at the
end of a razor blade.

He said: "Come on. Let's dance."

They circulated slowly in the dance hall. To be
beaten by experience was bad enough, but to be beaten
by greenness and innocence, by a girl who carried
plates at Snow's, by a little bitch of sixteen years . . .

"Spicie thought a lot of you," Sylvie said.

"Come out to the cars," the boy said.

"I couldn't, not with Spicie dead only yesterday."

They stood and clapped and then the dance began
again. The shaker clacked in the bar, and the leaves
of one small tree were pressed against the window beyond the big drum and the saxophone.

"I like the country. It makes me feel romantic. Do
you like the country?"

"No."

"This is *real* country. I saw a hen just now. They
use their own eggs in the gin slings."

"Come out to the cars."

"I feel that way too. Oh, gosh, wouldn't it be fine?
But I can't, not with poor Spicie . . ."

"You sent flowers, didn't you, you been crying . . ."

"My eyes are awful."

"What more can you do?"

"It broke my heart. Poor Spicie going off like that."

"I know. I saw your wreath."

"It does seem awful, doesn't it? Dancing with you like this and him . . ."

"Come to the cars."

"Poor Spicie," but she led the way, and he noticed with uneasiness how she ran—literally ran across the lit corner of what had once been a farmyard—towards the dark car park and the game. He thought with sickness: "In three minutes I shall know."

"Which is your car?" Sylvie said.

"That Morris."

"No good to us," Sylvie said. She darted down the line of cars. "This Ford." She pulled the door open, said: "Oh, pardon me," and shut it, scrambled into the back of the next car in the line, and waited for him. "Oh," her voice softly and passionately pronounced from the dim interior, "I love a Lancia." He stood in the doorway and the darkness peeled away between him and the fair and vacuous face. Her skirt drawn up above her knees she waited for him with luxurious docility.

He was conscious for a moment of his enormous ambitions under the shadow of the hideous and commonplace act: the suite at the Cosmopolitan, the gold cigar lighter, chairs stamped with crowns for a foreigner called Eugénie. Hale dropped out of sight, like a stone thrown over a cliff; he was at the beginning of a long

polished parquet walk, there were busts of great men
and the sound of cheering, Mr. Colleoni bowed like a
shopwalker, stepping backwards, an army of razors
was at his back: a conqueror. Hoofs drummed along
the straight and a loudspeaker announced the winner;
music was playing. His breast ached with the effort
to enclose the whole world.

"You've got the doings, haven't you?" Sylvie said.

With fear and horror he thought: next move, what
is it?

"Quick," Sylvie said, "before they find us here."

The parquet floor rolled up like a carpet. The moonlight touched a Woolworth ring and a plump knee.
He said in a bitter and painful rage: "Wait there. I'll
get Cubitt for you," and turned his back on the Lancia
and walked back towards the bar. Laughter from the
bathing pool deflected him. He stood in the doorway
with the taste of the alcohol on his tongue watching a
thin girl in a red rubber cap giggle under the flood-
lighting. His mind tracked inevitably back and forth
to Sylvie like a model engine electrically driven. Fear
and curiosity ate at the proud future, he was aware of
nausea and retched. Marry, he thought, hell, no; I'd
rather hang.

A man in a bathing slip came running down the
highboard, jumped and somersaulted in the pearly
brilliant light, struck the dark water; the two bathers
swam together, stroke by stroke, towards the shallows,
turned and came back, side by side, smooth and un-
hurried, playing a private game, happy and at ease.

The Boy stood and watched them, and as they came
down the pool a second time he saw in the floodlit

water his own image shiver at their stroke, the narrow
shoulders and the hollow breast, and he felt the brown
pointed shoes slip on the splashed and shining tiles.

2

Cubitt and Dallow chattered all the way back, a
little lit; the Boy stared ahead into the bright core of
the darkness. He said suddenly with fury: "You can
laugh."

"Well, you didn't do so bad," Cubitt said.

"You can laugh. You think you're safe. But I'm
tired of the lot of you. I've got a good mind to clear
out."

"Take a long honeymoon," Cubitt said and grinned,
and an owl cried with painful hunger swooping low
over a filling station, into the headlights and out
again, on furry and predatory wings.

"I'm not going to marry," the Boy said.

"I knew a geezer once," Cubitt said, "was so scared
he killed himself. They had to send back the wedding
presents."

"I'm not going to marry."

"People often feel that way."

"Nothing's going to make me marry."

"You've got to marry," Dallow said. A woman
stared from a window of Charlie's Pull-in Café waiting for someone: she didn't look at the car going by,
waiting.

"Have a drink," Cubitt said: he was more drunk
than Dallow. "I brought a flask away. You can't say
you don't drink now: we saw you, Dallow and me."

The Boy said to Dallow: "I won't marry. Why should I marry?"

"It was your doing," Dallow said.

"What was his doing?" Cubitt said. Dallow didn't reply, laying his friendly and oppressive hand on the Boy's knee. The boy took a squint at the stupid devoted face and felt anger at the way another's loyalty could hamper and drive. Dallow was the only man he trusted, and he hated him as if he was his mentor. He said weakly: "Nothing will make me marry," watching the long parade of posters going by in the submarine light—Guinness Is Good for You, Try a Worthington, Keep that Schoolgirl Complexion—a *long* series of adjurations, people telling you things: Own Your Own Home, Bennett's for Wedding Rings.

And at Billy's they told him: "Your girl's here." He went up the stairs to his room in hopeless rebellion: he would go in and say—I've changed my mind, I can't marry you. Or perhaps: The lawyers say it can't be managed after all. The banisters were still broken and he looked down the long drop to where Spicer's body had lain. Cubitt and Dallow were standing on the exact spot laughing at something; the sharp edge of a broken banister scratched his hand. He put it to his mouth and went in. He thought: I've got to be calm, I've got to keep my wits about me, but he felt his integrity stained by the taste of the spirit at the bar. You could lose vice as easily as you lost virtue, going out of you from a touch.

He took a look at her. She was scared when he said softly: "What are you doing here?" She had on the hat he disliked and she made a snatch at it as soon

as he looked. "At this time of night," he said in a
shocked way, thinking there was a quarrel to be picked
there if he went about it in the right way.

"You've seen this?" Rose implored him. She had
the local paper; he hadn't bothered to read it, but there
on the front page was the picture of Spicer striding
in terror under the iron arches. They'd been more
successful at the kiosk than he'd been. Rose said: "It
says here—it happened———"

"On the landing," the boy said. "I was always telling Billy to mend those banisters."

"But you said they got him on the course. And he
was the one who———"

He faced her with spurious firmness: "Gave you the
ticket? So you said. Maybe he knew Hale. He knew
a lot of geezers I didn't. What of it?" With confidence
he repeated his question before her dumb stare:
"What of it?" His mind, he knew, could contemplate
any treachery, but she was a good kid, she was bound-
aried by her goodness; there were things she couldn't
imagine, and he thought he saw her imagination wilting now in the vast desert of dread.

"I thought," she said, "I thought . . ." looking beyond him to the shattered banister on the landing.

"What did you think?"

His fingers curled with passionate hatred round the
small bottle in his pocket.

"I don't know. I didn't sleep last night. I had such
dreams."

"What dreams?"

She looked at him with horror. "I dreamed you
were dead."

He laughed. "I'm young and spry," thinking with nausea of the car park and the invitation in the Lancia.

"You aren't going to stay here, are you?"

"Why not?"

"I'd have thought——" she said, her eyes back again in their gaze at the banisters. She said: "I'm scared."

"You've no cause to be," he said, tickling the vitriol bottle.

"I'm scared for you. Oh," she said, "I know I'm no account. I know you've got a lawyer and a car and friends, but this place——" she stumbled hopelessly in an attempt to convey the sense she had of the territory in which he moved: a place of accidents and unexplained events, the stranger with a card, the fight on the course, the headlong fall. A kind of boldness and brazenness came into her face, so that he felt again the faintest stirring of sensuality. "You've got to come away from here. You've got to marry me like you said."

"It can't be done after all. I've seen my lawyer. We're too young."

"I don't mind about that. It's not a *real* marriage anyway. A register's doesn't make any difference."

"You go back where you came from," he said harshly, "you little buer."

"I can't," she said. "I'm sacked."

"What for?" It was as if the handcuffs were meeting. He suspected her.

"I was rude to a customer."

"Why? What customer?"

"Can't you guess?" she said, and went passionately

on: "Who is she anyway? Interfering . . . pestering
. . . *you* must know."

"I don't know her from Adam," the boy said.

She put all her full experience—drawn from the
twopenny library—into the question: "Is she jealous?
Is she someone . . . you know what I mean?" and
ready then, masked behind the ingenuous question
like the guns in a Q ship, was possessiveness: she was
his like a table or a chair, but a table owned you too—
by your finger prints.

He laughed uneasily. "What, she? She's old enough
to be my mother."

"Then what does she want?"

"I wish I knew."

"Do you think," she said, "I ought to take this"—
she held out the paper to him—"to the police?"

The ingenuousness—or the shrewdness—of the
question shocked him. Could one ever be safe with
someone who realized so little how she had got mixed
up in things? He said: "You got to mind your step,"
and thought with dull and tired distaste (it had been
the hell of a day) : I shall have to marry her after
all. He managed a smile—those muscles were beginning to work—and said: "Listen. You don't need to
think about those things. I'm going to marry you.
There are ways of getting round the law."

"Why bother about the law?"

"I don't want any loose talk. Only marriage," he
said with feigned anger, "will do for me. We got to
be married properly."

"We won't be that, whatever we do. The father up
at St. John's—he says——"

"You don't want to listen too much to priests," he said. "They don't know the world like I do. Ideas change, the world moves on. . . ." His words stumbled before her carved devotion. That face said as clearly as words that ideas never changed, the world never moved: it lay there always the ravaged and disputed territory between the two eternities. They faced each other as it were from opposing territories, but like troops at Christmas time they fraternized. He said: "It's the same to you anyway—and I want to be married—legally."

"If you want to . . ." she said and made a small gesture of complete assent.

"Maybe," he said, "we could work it this way. If your father wrote a letter . . ."

"He can't write."

"Well, he could make his mark, couldn't he, if I got a letter written? . . . I don't know how these things work. Maybe he could come to the magistrate's. Mr. Drewitt could see about that."

"Mr. Drewitt?" she asked quickly. "Wasn't he the one—the one at the inquest who was here? . . ."

"What of it?"

"Nothing," she said. "I just thought . . ." but he could see the thoughts going on and on, out of the room to the banisters and the drop, out of that day altogether. . . . Somebody turned on the radio down below: some jest of Cubitt's perhaps to represent the right romantic atmosphere. It wailed up the stairs past the telephone and into the room, somebody's band from somebody's hotel, the end of a day's programme. It switched her thoughts away and he wondered for

how long it would be necessary for him to sidetrack
her mind with the romantic gesture or the loving act,
how many weeks and months—his mind wouldn't
admit the possibility of years. Some day he would be
free again; he put out his hands towards hers as if she
were the detective with the cuffs and said · "Tomorrow
we'll see about things, see your father. Why"— the
muscles of his mouth faltered at the thought— "it
only takes a couple of days to get married in."

3

He was scared, walking alone back towards the territory he had left—oh, years ago. The pale green sea
curdled on the shingle and the green tower of the
Metropole looked like a dug-up coin verdigrised with
age-old mould. The gulls swooped up to the top promenade, screaming and twisting in the sunlight, and a
well-known popular author displayed his plump, too-
famous face in the window of the Royal Albion, staring out to sea. It was so clear a day you looked for
France.

The Boy crossed over towards Old Steyne walking
slowly. The streets narrowed uphill above the Steyne:
the shabby secret behind the bright corsage, the de-
formed breast. Every step was a retreat. He thought
he had escaped for ever by the whole length of the
parade, and now extreme poverty took him back:
Salome's shop where a shingle could be had for two
shillings in the same building as a coffin-maker who
worked in oak, elm, or lead; no window dressing but
one child's coffin dusty with disuse and the list of

Salome's prices. The Salvation Army Citadel marked
with its battlements the very border of his home. He
began to fear recognition and feel an obscure shame
as if it were his native streets which had the right to
forgive and not he to reproach them with the dreary
and dingy past. Past the Albert Hostel ("Good Accom-
modation for Travellers") and there he was, on the
top of the hill, in the thick of the bombardment. A
flapping gutter, glassless windows, an iron bedstead in a
front garden the size of a table top. Half Paradise Piece
had been torn up as if by bomb bursts: the children
played about the steep slope of rubble; a piece of fireplace showed houses had once been there, and a municipal notice announced new flats on a post stuck in the
torn gravel and asphalt facing the little dingy damaged
row, all that was left of Paradise Piece. His home was
gone: a flat place among the rubble may have marked
its hearth; the room at the bend of the stairs where the
Saturday night exercise had taken place was now just
air. He wondered with horror whether it all had to be
built again for him; it looked better as air.

He had sent Rose back the night before and now
draggingly he rejoined her. It was no good rebelling
any more; he had to marry her; he had to be safe.
The children were scouting among the rubble with
pistols from Woolworth's; a group of girls surlily
watched. A child with its leg in an iron brace limped
blindly into him; he pushed it off; someone said in a
high treble: "Stick 'em up." They took his mind back
and he hated them for it; it was like the dreadful
appeal of innocence, but *there* was not innocence: you

had to go back a long way further before you got innocence; innocence was a slobbering mouth, a toothless
gum pulling at the teats, perhaps not even that; innocence was the ugly cry of birth.

He found the house in Nelson Place, but before he
had time to knock the door opened. Rose had spied
him through the broken glass. She said: "Oh, how
glad I am! . . . I thought perhaps . . ." In the awful
little passage which stank like a lavatory she ran
quickly and passionately on. "It was awful last night
. . . you see, I've been sending them money . . . they
don't understand everyone loses a job some time or
another."

"I'll settle them," the Boy said. "Where are they?"

"You got to be careful," Rose said. "They get
moods."

"Where are they?"

But there wasn't really much choice of direction:
there was only one door and a staircase matted with
old newspapers. On the bottom steps between the
mud marks stared up the tawny child face of Violet
Crow violated and buried under the West Pier in
1936. He opened the door and there beside the black
kitchen stove with cold dead charcoal on the floor sat
the parents. They had a mood on: they watched him
with silent and haughty indifference—a small thin
elderly man, his face marked deeply with the hieroglyphics of pain and patience and suspicion; the
woman middle-aged, stupid, vindictive. The dishes
hadn't been washed and the stove hadn't been lit.

"They got a mood," Rose said aloud to him. "They

wouldn't let me do a thing. Not even light the fire. I like a clean house, honest I do. Ours wouldn't be like this."

"Look here, Mr.——" the Boy said.

"Wilson," Rose said.

"Wilson. I want to marry Rose. It seems as she's so young I got to get your permission."

They wouldn't answer him. They treasured their mood as if it was a bright piece of china they alone possessed, something they could show to neighbours as "mine."

"It's no use," Rose said, "when they get a mood."

A cat watched them from a wooden box.

"Yes or no?" the Boy said.

"It's no good," Rose said, "not when they've got a mood."

"Answer a plain question," the Boy said. "Do I marry Rose or don't I?"

"Come back tomorrow," Rose said. "They won't have a mood then."

"I'm not going to wait on them," he said. "They oughter be proud——"

The man suddenly got up and kicked the dead coke furiously across the floor. "You get out of here," he said. "We don't want any truck with you," he went on, "never, never, never," and for a moment in the sunk lost eyes there was a kind of fidelity which reminded the Boy dreadfully of Rose.

"Quiet, Father," the woman said, "don't talk to them," treasuring her mood.

"I've come to do business," the Boy said. "If you don't want to do business . . ." He looked round the battered and hopeless room. "I thought maybe ten pounds would be of use to you," and he saw swimming up through the blind vindictive silence incredulity, avarice, suspicion. "We don't want—" the man began again and then gave out like a gramophone. He began to think; you could see the thoughts bob up one after another.

"We don't want your money," the woman said. They each had their own kind of fidelity.

Rose said; "Never mind what they say. I won't stay here."

"Stop a moment. Stop a moment," the man said. "You be quiet, Mother." He said to the Boy: "We couldn't let Rose go—not for ten nickers—not to a stranger. How do we know you'd treat her right?"

"I'll give you twelve," the Boy said.

"It's not a question of money," the man said. "I like the look of you. We wouldn't want to stand in the way of Rose bettering herself—but you're too young."

"Fifteen's my limit," the Boy said, "take it or leave it."

"You can't do anything without we say yes," the man said.

The Boy moved a little away from Rose. "I'm not all that keen."

"Make it guineas."

"You've had my offer." He looked with horror round the room: nobody could say he hadn't done right to get away from this, to commit any crime . . . when the man opened his mouth he heard his father speaking; that figure in the corner was his mother; he bargained for his sister and felt no desire. . . . He turned to Rose, "I'm off," and felt the faintest twinge of pity for goodness which couldn't murder to escape. They said that saints had got—what was the phrase? —"heroic virtues," heroic patience, heroic endurance, but there was nothing he could see that was heroic in the bony face, protuberant eyes, pallid anxiety, while they bluffed each other and her life was confused in the financial game. "Well," he said, "I'll be seeing you," and made for the door. At the door he looked back; they were like a family party. Impatiently and contemptuously he gave in to them. "All right. Guineas. I'll be sending my lawyer," and as he passed into the evil passage Rose was behind him panting her gratitude.

He played the game to the last card, fetching up a grin and a compliment: "I'd do more for you."

"You were wonderful," she said, loving him among the lavatory smells, but her praise was poison: it marked her possession of him; it led straight to what she expected from him, the horrifying act of a desire he didn't feel. She followed him out into the fresh air of Nelson Place. The children played among the ruins of Paradise Piece, and a wind blew from the sea across the site of his home. A dim desire for annihilation stretched in him, the vast superiority of vacancy.

She said, as she had said once before: "I always wondered how it'd be." Her mind moved obscurely among the events of the afternoon, brought out the unexpected discovery. "I've never known a mood go so quick. They must have liked you."

4

Ida Arnold bit an éclair and the cream spurted between the large front teeth. She laughed a little thickly in the Pompadour Boudoir and said: "I haven't had as much money to spend since I left Tom." She took another bite and a wedge of cream settled on the plump tongue. "I owe it to Fred too. If he hadn't tipped me Black Boy . . ."

"Why not give everything up," Mr. Corkery said, "and just have a bit of fun? It's dangerous."

"Oh, yes, it's dangerous," she admitted, but no real sense of danger could lodge behind those large vivacious eyes. Nothing could ever make her believe that one day she too, like Fred, would be where the worms . . . her mind couldn't take that track: she could go only a short way before the switch automatically shifted and set her vibrating down the accustomed line, the season ticket line marked by desirable residences and advertisements for cruises and small fenced boskages for rural love. She said, eyeing her éclair: "I never give in. They didn't know what a packet of trouble they were stirring up."

"Leave it to the police."

"Oh, no. I know what's right. You can't tell me. Who's that, do you think?"

An elderly Jew in glacé shoes, with a white slip to his waistcoat and a jewelled pin, came padding across the Boudoir. "Distinguay," Ida Arnold said.

A secretary trotted a little way behind him, reading out from a list. "Bananas, oranges, grapes, peaches . . ."

"Hothouse?"

"Hothouse."

"Who's that?" Ida Arnold said.

"That was all, Mr. Colleoni?" the secretary asked.

"What flowers?" Mr. Colleoni demanded. "And could you get any nectarines?"

"No, Mr. Colleoni."

"My dear wife," Mr. Colleoni said, his voice dwindling out of their hearing. They could catch only the word "passion." Ida Arnold swivelled her eyes round the elegant furnishing of the Pompadour Boudoir. They picked out like a searchlight a cushion, a couch, the thin clerkly mouth of the man opposite her. She said: "We could have a fine time here," watching his mouth.

"Expensive," Mr. Corkery said nervously; a too sensitive hand stroked his thin shanks.

"Black Boy will stand it. And we can't have—you know—fun at the Belvedere. Strait-laced."

"You wouldn't mind a bit of fun here?" Mr. Corkery said. He blinked. You couldn't tell from his expression whether he desired or dreaded her assent.

"Why should I? It doesn't do anyone any harm that I know of. It's human nature." She bit at her éclair and repeated the familiar password. "It's only fun after all." Fun to be on the right side, fun to be human . . .

"You go and get my bag," she said, "while I book a room."

Mr. Corkery flushed a little. "Half and half," he said.

She grinned at him. "It's on Black Boy."

"A man likes—" Mr. Corkery said weakly.

"Trust me, I know what a man likes." The éclair and the deep couch and the gaudy furnishings were like an aphrodisiac in her tea. She was shaken by a Bacchic and a bawdy mood. In every word either of them uttered she detected the one meaning. Mr. Corkery blushed, plunged deeper in his embarrassment. "A man can't help feeling," and was shaken by her immense glee.

"You're telling me," she said, "you're telling me?"

While Mr. Corkery was gone she made her preparations for carnival, the taste of the sweet cake between her teeth. The idea of Fred Hale dodged backwards like a figure on a platform when the train goes out; he belonged to somewhere left behind; the waving hand only contributes to the excitement of the new experience. The new—and yet the immeasurably old. She gazed round the big padded pleasure dome of a bedroom with bloodshot and experienced eyes: the long mirror and the wardrobe and the enormous bed. She settled frankly down on it while the clerk waited. "It springs," she said, "it springs," and sat there for quite a long while after he'd gone, planning the evening's campaign. If somebody had said to her then: "Fred Hale," she would hardly have recognized the name; there was another interest: for the next hour let the police have him.

Then she got up slowly and began to undress. She

never believed in wearing much: it wasn't any time
at all before she was exposed in the long mirror—a
body firm and bulky, a proper handful. She stood on a
deep soft rug, surrounded by gilt frames and red velvet hangings, and a dozen common and popular
phrases bloomed in her mind—"A Night of Love,"
"You Only Live Once," and the rest. She bore the same
relation to passion as a peep show. She sucked the chocolate between her teeth and smiled, her plump toes
working in the rug, waiting for Mr. Corkery—just a
great big blossoming surprise.

Outside the window the sea ebbed, scraping the
shingle, exposing a boot, a piece of rusty iron, and the
old man stooped, searching between the stones. The
sun dropped behind the Hove houses and dusk came,
the shadow of Mr. Corkery lengthened, coming slowly
up from Belvedere carrying the suitcases, saving on
taxis. A gull swooped screaming down to a dead crab
beaten and broken against the iron foundation of the
pier. It was the time of near-darkness and of the evening mist from the Channel and of love.

5

The Boy closed the door behind him and turned to
face the expectant and amused faces.

"Well," Cubitt said, "is it all fixed up?"

"Of course it is," the Boy said; "when I want a
thing . . ." His voice wavered out unconvincingly.
There were half a dozen bottles on his washstand: his
room smelt of stale beer.

"Want a thing," Cubitt said. "That's good." He

opened another bottle, and in the warm stuffy room the froth rose quickly and splashed on the marble top.

"What do you think you're doing?" the Boy said.

"Celebrating," Cubitt said. "You're a Roman, aren't you? A betrothal, that's what Romans call it."

The Boy watched them: Cubitt a little drunk, Dallow preoccupied, one or two lean hungry faces he hardly knew—hangers-on at the fringes of the great game who smiled when you smiled and frowned when you frowned. But now they smiled when Cubitt smiled, and suddenly he saw the long way he had slipped since that afternoon on the pier when he arranged the alibi, gave the orders, did what they hadn't got the nerve to do themselves.

Billy's wife Judy put her head in at the door. She was wearing a dressing gown. Her Titian hair was brown at the roots. "Good luck, Pinkie," she said, blinking mascara'd lashes. She had been washing her brassière: the little piece of pink silk dripped on the linoleum. Nobody offered her a drink. "Work, work, work," she moued at them, going on down the passage to the hot-water pipes.

A long way . . . and yet he hadn't made a single false step: if he hadn't gone to Snow's and spoken to the girl, they'd all be in the dock by now. If he hadn't killed Spicer . . . Not a single false step, but every step conditioned by a pressure he couldn't even place: a woman asking questions, messages on the telephone scaring Spicer. He thought: when I've married the girl, will it stop then? Where else can it drive me; and with a twitch of the mouth, he wondered—what worse . . . ?

"When's the happy day?" Cubitt said, and they all smiled obediently except Dallow.

The Boy's brain began to work again. He moved slowly towards the washstand. He said: "Haven't you got a glass for me? Don't I do any celebrating?"

He saw Dallow astonished, Cubitt thrown off his mark, the hangers-on doubtful whom to follow, and he grinned at them, the one with brains.

"Why, Pinkie . . ." Cubitt said.

"I'm not a drinking man and I'm not a marrying man," the Boy said. "So *you* think. But I'm liking one, so why shouldn't I like the other? Give me a glass."

"Liking," Cubitt said and grinned uneasily, "you *liking* . . ."

"Haven't you seen her?" the Boy said.

"Why, me and Dallow just lamped her. On the stairs. But it was too dark . . ."

"She's a lovely," the Boy said, "she's wasted in a kip. And intelligent. Don't make any mistake. Of course I didn't see any cause to *marry* her, but as it is—" Somebody handed him a glass; he took a long draught; the bitter and bubbly fluid revolted him—so this was what they liked—he tightened the muscles of his mouth to hide his revulsion. "As it is," he said, "I'm glad," and eyed with hidden disgust the pale inch of liquid in the glass before he drained it down.

Dallow watched in silence and the Boy felt more anger against his friend than against his enemy: like Spicer he knew too much; but what he knew was far more deadly than what Spicer had known. Spicer had known only the kind of thing which brought you to the dock, but Dallow knew what your mirror and your bedsheets knew: the secret fear and the humiliation. He said with hidden fury: "What's getting you, Dallow?"

The stupid and broken face was hopelessly at a loss.

"Jealous?" the Boy began to boast. "You've cause when you've seen her. She's not one of your dyed totsies. She's got class. I'm marrying her for your sake, but I'm laying her for my own." He turned fiendishly on Dallow. "What's on *your* mind?"

"Well," Dallow said, "it's the one you met on the pier, isn't it? I didn't think she was all that good."

"You," the Boy said, "you don't know anything. You're ignorant. You don't know class when you see it."

"A duchess," Cubitt said and laughed.

An extraordinary indignation jerked in the Boy's brain and fingers. It was almost as if someone he loved had been insulted. "Be careful, Cubitt," he said.

"Don't mind him," Dallow said. "We didn't know you'd fallen. . . ."

"We got some presents for you, Pinkie," Cubitt said. "Furniture for the home," and indicated two little obscene objects beside the beer on the washstand; the Brighton stationers were full of them: a tiny doll's commode in the shape of a radio set labelled: "The smallest A.1 two-valve receiving set in the world," and a mustard pot shaped like a lavatory seat with the legend, "For me and my girl." It was like a return of all the horror he had ever felt, the hideous loneliness of his innocence. He struck at Cubitt's face and Cubitt dodged, laughing. The two hangers-on slipped out of the room. They hadn't any taste for rough houses. The

Boy heard them laugh on the stairs. Cubitt said:
"You'll need 'em in the home. A bed's not the only
furniture." He mocked and backed at the same time.

The Boy said: "By God, I'll treat you like I treated
Spicer."

No meaning reached Cubitt at once. There was a
long time lag. He began to laugh and then saw Dallow's startled face and *heard*. "What's that?" he said.

"He's crazy," Dallow intervened.

"You think yourself smart," the Boy said. "So did
Spicer."

"It was the banister," Cubitt said. "You weren't
here. What are you getting at?"

"Of course he wasn't here," Dallow said.

"You think you know things." All the Boy's hatred
was in the word "know" and his repulsion: he knew—
as Drewitt knew after twenty-five years at the game.
"You don't know everything." He tried to inject himself with pride, but all the time his eyes went back to
the humiliation. "The smallest A.1 . . ." You could
know everything there was in the world and yet if you
were ignorant of that one dirty scramble you knew
nothing.

"What's he getting at?" Cubitt said.

"You don't need to listen to him," Dallow said.

"I mean this," the Boy said; "Spicer was milky
and I'm the only one in this mob knows how to act."

"You act too much," Cubitt said. "Do you mean—
it wasn't the banisters?" The question scared himself:
he didn't want an answer. He made uneasily for the
door, keeping his eye on the Boy.

Dallow said: "Of course it was the banisters. I was there, wasn't I?"

"I don't know," Cubitt said, "I don't know," making for the door. "Brighton's not big enough for him. I'm through."

"Go on," the Boy said. "Clear out. Clear out and starve."

"I won't starve," Cubitt said. "There's others in this town . . ."

When the door closed the Boy turned on Dallow. "Go on," he said, "you go too. You think you can get on without me, but I've only got to whistle . . ."

"You don't need to talk to me like that," Dallow said. "I'm not leaving you. I don't fancy making friends with Crab again so soon."

But the Boy paid him no attention. He said again · "I've only got to whistle . . ." He boasted: "They'll come tumbling back." He went over to the brass bed and lay down; he had had a long day; he said · "Get me Drewitt on the blower. Tell him there's no difficulty at *her* end. Let him fix things quick."

"The day after tomorrow if he can?" Dallow asked.

"Yes," the Boy said. He heard the door close and lay with twitching cheek staring at the ceiling; he thought: it's not my fault they get me angry so I want to do things; if people would leave me in peace . . . His imagination wilted at the word. He tried in a half-hearted way to picture "peace"—his eyes closed and behind the lids he saw a grey darkness going on and on without end, a country of which he hadn't seen as much as a picture postcard, a place far stranger

than the Grand Canyon and the Taj Mahal. He opened
them again and immediately poison moved in the vein;
for there on the washstand were Cubitt's purchases.
He was like a child with hæmophilia: every contact
drew blood.

6

A bell rang muffled in the Cosmopolitan corridor;
through the wall against which the bed end stood, Ida
Arnold could hear a voice talking on and on: somebody
reading a report perhaps in a conference room or dic-
tating to a dictaphone. Phil lay asleep on the bed in
his pants, his mouth a little open showing one yellow
tooth and a gob' of metal filling. Fun . . . human
nature . . . does no one any harm . . . regular as clockwork the old excuses came back into the alert sad and
dissatisfied brain—nothing ever matched the deep excitement of the regular desire. Men always failed you
when it came to the act. She might just as well have
been to the pictures.

But it did no one any harm, it was just human
nature, no one could call her really bad—a bit free and
easy perhaps, a bit Bohemian; it wasn't as if she got
anything out of it, as if like some people she sucked a
man dry and cast him aside like a cast-off—threw him
aside like a cast-off glove. She knew what was Right
and what was Wrong. God didn't mind a bit of human
nature—what He minded—and her brain switched
away from Phil in pants to her Mission, to doing good,
to seeing that the evil suffered . . .

She sat up in bed and put her arms round her large
naked knees and felt excitement stirring again in the

disappointed body. Poor old Fred—the name no longer
conveyed any sense of grief or pathos. She couldn't remember anything much about him now but a monocle
and a yellow waistcoat and that belonged to poor old
Charlie Moyne. The hunt was what mattered. It was
like life coming back after a sickness.

Phil opened an eye—yellow with the sexual effort
—and watched her apprehensively. She said: "Awake,
Phil?"

"It must be nearly time for dinner," Phil said. He
gave a nervous smile. "A penny for your thoughts,
Ida."

"I was just thinking," Ida said, "that what we
really need now is one of Pinkie's men. Somebody
scared or angry. They must get scared some time.
We've only got to wait."

She got out of the bed, opened her suitcase, and
began to lay out the clothes she thought were suitable
for dinner in the Cosmopolitan. In the pink read-
ing-lamp, love-lamp light spangles glittered. She
stretched her arms; she no longer felt desire or disappointment; her brain was clear. It was almost dark
along the beach; the edge of sea was like a line of
writing in whitewash: big sprawling letters. They
meant nothing at this distance. A shadow stooped with
infinite patience and disinterred some relic from the
shingle.

PART SIx

1

WHEN Cubitt got outside the front door the hangers-on had already vanished. The street was empty. He felt in a dumb, bitter, and uncomprehending way like a man who had destroyed his home without having prepared another. The mist was coming up from the sea, and he hadn't got his coat. He was as angry as a child: he wouldn't

go back for it; it would be like admitting he was
wrong. The only thing to be done now was to drink
a strong whisky at the Crown.

At the saloon bar they made way for him with
respect. In the mirror marked Booth's Gin he could
see his own reflection : the short flaming hair, the blunt
and open face, broad shoulders; he stared like Nar-
cissus into his pool and felt better; he wasn't the sort
of man to take things lying down; he was valuable.
"Have a whisky?" somebody said. It was the green-
grocer's assistant from the corner shop. Cubitt laid a
heavy paw across his shoulder, accepting, patronizing ·
the man who had done a thing or two in his time
chummy with the pale ignorant fellow who dreamed
from his commercial distance of a man's life. The relationship pleased Cubitt. He had two more whiskies
at the grocer's expense.

"Got a tip, Mr. Cubitt?"

"I've got other things to think of beside tips," Cubitt
said darkly, adding a splash.

"We were having an argument in here about Gay
Parrot for the two-thirty. Seemed to me . . ."

Gay Parrot . . . the name didn't mean a thing to
Cubitt; the drink warmed him; the mist was in his
brain; he leant forward towards the mirror and saw
"Booth's Gin . . . Booth's Gin," haloed above his head.
He was involved in high politics : men had been killed;
poor old Spicer; allegiances shifted like heavy balances
in his brain; he felt as important as a prime minister
making treaties.

"There'll be more killings before we're through," he
mysteriously pronounced. He had his wits about him :

he wasn't giving anything away; but there was no harm in letting these poor sodden creatures a little way into the secrets of living. He pushed his glass forward and said: "A drink all round," but when he looked to either side they'd gone; a face took a backward look through the pane of the saloon door, vanished; they couldn't stand the company of a Man.

"Never mind," he said, "never mind," and drank down his whisky and left. The next thing, of course, was to see Colleoni. He'd say to him: "Here I am, Mr. Colleoni. I'm through with Kite's mob. I won't work under a boy like that. Give me a Man's job and I'll do it." The mist got at his bones: he shivered involuntarily; a grey goose . . . He thought: if only Dallow too . . . and suddenly loneliness took away his confidence: all the heat of the drink seeped out of him, and the mist like seven devils went in. Suppose Colleoni simply wasn't interested? He came down onto the front and saw through the thin fog the high lights of the Cosmopolitan; it was cocktail time.

Cubitt sat down chilled in a glass shelter and stared out towards the sea. The tide was low and the mist hid it: it was just a sliding and a sibilation. He lit a cigarette; the match warmed for a moment the cupped hands. He offered the packet to an elderly gentleman wrapped in a heavy overcoat who shared the shelter. "I don't smoke," the old gentleman said sharply and began to cough: a steady hack, hack, hack towards the invisible sea.

"A cold night," Cubitt said. The old gentleman swivelled his eyes on him like opera glasses and went on coughing: hack, hack, hack, the vocal cords dry

as straw. Somewhere out at sea a violin began to play:
it was like a sea beast mourning and stretching towards
the shore. Cubitt thought of Spicer, who'd liked a good
tune. Poor old Spicer. The mist blew in, heavy compact drifts of it like ectoplasm. Cubitt had been to a
séance once in Brighton; he had wanted to get in touch
with his mother, dead twenty years ago. It had come
over him quite suddenly—the old girl might have a
word for him. She had · she was on the seventh plane
where all was very beautiful; her voice had sounded
a little boozed, but that wasn't really unnatural. The
boys had laughed at him about it, particularly old
Spicer. Well, Spicer wouldn't laugh now. He could be
summoned himself any time to ring a bell and shake a
tambourine. It was a lucky thing he liked music.

Cubitt got up and strolled to the turnpike of the
West Pier, which straddled into the mist and vanished
towards the violin. He walked up towards the Concert
Hall, passing nobody. It wasn't a night for courting
couples to sit out. Whatever people there were upon
the pier were gathered every one inside the Concert
Hall; Cubitt turned round it on the outside looking in:
a man in evening dress fiddling to a few rows of people
in overcoats, islanded fifty yards out to sea in the
middle of the mist. Somewhere in the Channel a boat
blew its siren and another answered, and another, like
dogs at night waking each other.

Go to Colleoni and say . . . it was all quite easy; the
old geezer ought to be grateful. . . . Cubitt looked back
towards the shore and saw above the mist the high
lights of the Cosmopolitan, and they daunted him. He
wasn't used to that sort of company. He went down the

iron companionway to the Gents' and drained the
whisky out of him into the movement under the piles
and came up onto the deck lonelier than ever. He took
a penny out of his pocket and slipped it into an automatic machine: a robot face, behind which an electric
bulb revolved, iron hands for Cubitt to grip. A little
blue card shot out at him: "Your Character Delin-
eated." Cubitt read: "You are mainly influenced by
your surroundings and inclined to be capricious and
changeful. Your affections are more intense than en-
during. You have a free, easy, and genial nature. You
make the best of whatever you undertake. A share of
the good things of life can always be yours. Your lack
of initiative is counterbalanced by your good common-
sense, and you will succeed where others fail."

He dragged slowly on past the automatic machines,
delaying the moment when there would be nothing
for him to do but go to the Cosmopolitan. "Your lack
of initiative . . ." Two leaden football teams waited
behind glass for a penny to release them; an old witch
with the stuffing coming out of her claw offered to tell
his fortune. "A Love Letter" made him pause. The
boards were damp with mist, the long deck was empty,
the violin ground on. He felt the need of a deep sentimental affection, orange blossoms and a cuddle in a
corner. His great paw yearned for a sticky hand. Somebody who wouldn't mind his jokes, who would laugh
with him at the two-valve receiving set. He hadn't
meant any harm; the cold reached his stomach, and a
little stale whisky returned into his throat. He almost
felt inclined to go back to Billy's. But then he remembered Spicer. The boy was mad, killing mad, it wasn't

safe. Loneliness dragged him down the solitary boards. He took out his last copper and thrust it in. A little pink card came out with a printed stamp: a girl's head, long hair, the legend, "True Love." It was addressed to "My Dear Pet, Spooner's Nook, With Cupid's Love," and there was a picture of a young man in evening dress kneeling on the floor, kissing the hand of a girl carrying a big fur. Up in a corner two hearts were transfixed by an arrow just above Reg. No. 745812. Cubitt thought: It's clever. It's cheap for a penny. He looked quickly over his shoulder—not a soul—and turned it quickly and began to read. The letter was addressed from Cupid's Wings, Amor Lane. "My dear little girl. So you have discarded me for the Squire's son. You little know how you have ruined my life in breaking faith with me, you have crushed the very soul out of me, as the butterfly on the wheel; but with it all I do not wish anything but your happiness."

Cubitt grinned uneasily. He was deeply moved. That was what always happened if you took up with anything but a buer; they gave you the air. Grand Renunciations, Tragedies, Beauty moved in Cubitt's brain. If it was a buer, of course you took a razor to her, carved her face, but this love printed here was class. He read on: it was literature; it was the way he'd like to write himself. "After all, when I think of your wondrous, winsome beauty and culture, I feel what a fool I must have been to dream that you ever really loved me." Unworthy. Emotion pricked behind his eyelids and he shivered in the mist with cold and beauty. "But remember, dearest, always, that I love you, and if ever you want a friend just return the little token of love I gave you and I will be your servant and slave. Yours brokenheartedly, John." It was his own name: an omen.

He moved again past the lighted Concert Hall and down the deserted deck. Loved and Lost. Tragic griefs flamed under his carrot hair. What can a man do but drink? He got another whisky just opposite the pier head and moved on, planting his feet rather too firmly, towards the Cosmopolitan—plank, plank, plank along the pavement as if he were wearing iron weights under his shoes, as a statue might move, half flesh, half stone.

"I want to speak to Mr. Colleoni." He said it defiantly. The plush and gilding smoothed away his confidence. He waited uneasily beside the desk while a page boy searched through the lounges and boudoirs for Mr. Colleoni. The clerk turned over the leaves of a big book and then consulted a *Who's Who*. Across the deep carpet the page returned and Crab followed him, sidling and triumphant with his black hair smelling of pomade.

"I said Mr. Colleoni," Cubitt said to the clerk, but the clerk took no notice, wetting his finger, skimming through *Who's Who*.

"You wanted to see Mr. Colleoni?" Crab said.

"That's right."

"You can't. He's occupied."

"Occupied," Cubitt said. "That's a fine word to use. Occupied."

"Why, if it isn't Cubitt," Crab said. "I suppose you

want a job." He looked round in a busy preoccupied way and said to the clerk: "Isn't that Lord Heversham over there?"

"Yes, sir," the clerk said.

"I've often seen him at Doncaster," Crab said, squinting at a nail on his left hand. He swept round on Cubitt. "Follow me, my man. We can't talk here," and before Cubitt could reply he was sidling off at a great rate between the gilt chairs.

"It's like this," Cubitt said, "Pinkie———"

Half-way across the lounge Crab paused and bowed and, moving on, became suddenly confidential. "A fine woman." He flickered like an early movie. He had picked up between Doncaster and London a hundred different manners; travelling first class after a successful meeting he had learnt how Lord Heversham spoke to a porter; he had seen old Digby scrutinize a woman.

"Who is she?" Cubitt said.

But Crab took no notice of the question. "We can talk here." It was the Pompadour Boudoir. Through the gilt and glass door beyond the boule table you could see little signboards pointing down a network of passages—tasteful little chinoiserie signboards with a Tuileries air: "Ladies," "Gentlemen," "Ladies' Hairdressing," "Gentlemen's Hairdressing."

"It's Mr. Colleoni I want to talk to," Cubitt said. He breathed whisky over the marquetry, but he was daunted and despairing. He resisted with difficulty the temptation to say "sir." Crab had moved on since Kite's day, almost out of sight. He was part of the great racket now—with Lord Heversham and the fine woman; he had grown up.

"Mr. Colleoni hasn't time to see anyone," Crab said. "He's a busy man." He took one of Mr. Colleoni's cigars out of his pocket and put it in his mouth; he didn't offer one to Cubitt. Cubitt with uncertain hand offered him a match. "Never mind, never mind," Crab said, fumbling in his double-breasted waistcoat. He fetched out a gold lighter and flourished it at his cigar. "What do you want, Cubitt?" he asked.

"I thought maybe," Cubitt said, but his words wilted among the gilt chairs. "You know how it is," he said, staring desperately round. "What about a drink?"

Crab took him quickly up. "I wouldn't mind one—just for old times' sake." He rang for a waiter.

"Old times," Cubitt said.

"Take a seat," Crab said, waving a possessive hand at the gilt chairs. Cubitt sat gingerly down. The chairs were small and hard. He saw a waiter watching them and flushed. "What's yours?" he said.

"A sherry," Crab said. "Dry."

"Scotch and splash for me," Cubitt said. He sat waiting for his drink, his hands between his knees, silent, his head lowered. He took furtive glances. This was where Pinkie had come to see Colleoni—he had nerve all right.

"They do you pretty well here," Crab said. "Of course Mr. Colleoni likes nothing but the best." He took his drink and watched Cubitt pay. "He likes things smart. Why, he's worth fifty thousand nicker if he's worth a penny. If you ask me what I think," Crab said, leaning back, puffing at the cigar, watching Cubitt through black, remote, and supercilious eyes, "he'll go in for politics one day. The Conservatives think a lot of him—he's got contacts."

"Pinkie—" Cubitt began and Crab laughed. "Take my advice," Crab said. "Get out of that mob while there's time. There's no future . . ." He looked obliquely over Cubitt's head and said: "See that man going to the Gents'? That's Mais. The brewer. He's worth a hundred thousand nicker."

"I was wondering," Cubitt said, "if Mr. Colleoni . . ."

"Not a chance," Crab said. "Why, ask yourself— what good would you be to Mr. Colleoni?"

Cubitt's humility gave way to a dull anger. "I was good enough for Kite."

Crab laughed. "Excuse me," he said, "but Kite . . ." He shook his ash out onto the carpet and said: "Take my advice. Get out. Mr. Colleoni's going to clean up this track. He likes things done properly. No violence. The police have great confidence in Mr. Colleoni." He looked at his watch. "Well, well, I must be going. I've got a date at the Hippodrome." He put his hand with patronage on Cubitt's arm. "There," he said, "I'll put in a word for you—for old times' sake. It won't be any good, but I'll do that much. Give my regards to Pinkie and the boys." He passed—a whiff of pomade and Havana, bowing slightly to a woman at the door, an old man with a monocle on a black ribbon. "Who the hell—?" the old man said.

Cubitt drained his drink and followed. An enormous depression bowed his carrot head, a sense of illtreatment moved through the whisky fumes—some-

body sometime had got to pay for something. All that
he saw fed the flame: he came out into the entrance
hall; a page boy with a salver infuriated him. Everybody was watching him, waiting for him to go, but he
had as much right there as Crab. He glanced round
him, and there alone at a table with a glass of port
was the woman Crab knew.

She smiled at him—"I think of your wondrous,
winsome beauty and culture." A sense of the immeasurable sadness of injustice took the place of
anger. He wanted to confide, to lay down burdens
. . . he belched once . . . "I will be your servant and
slave." The great body turned like a door, the heavy
feet altered direction and padded towards the table
where Ida Arnold sat.

"I couldn't help hearing," she said, "when you
went across just now that you knew Pinkie."

He realized with immense pleasure when she spoke
that she wasn't class. It was to him like the meeting
of two fellow-countrymen a long way from home. He
said: "You a friend of Pinkie's?" and felt the whisky
in his legs. He said: "Mind if I sit down?"

"Tired?"

"That's it," he said, "tired." He sat down with his
eyes on her large friendly bosom. He remembered the
lines on his character. "You have a free, easy, and
genial nature." By God, he had. He only needed to be
treated right.

"Have a drink?"

"No, no," he said with woolly gallantry, "it's on
me," but when the drinks came he realized he was out

of cash. He had meant to borrow from one of the boys
—but then the quarrel . . . He watched Ida Arnold
pay with a five-pound note.

"Know Mr. Colleoni?" he asked.

"I wouldn't call it *know*," she said.

"Crab said you were a fine woman. He's right."

"Oh—Crab," she said vaguely, as if she didn't
recognize the name.

"You oughta steer clear though," Cubitt said.
"You've got no call to get mixed up in things." He
stared into his glass as into a deep darkness: outside
innocence, winsome beauty, and culture—unworthy,
a tear gathered behind the bloodshot eyeball.

"You a friend of Pinkie's?" Ida Arnold asked.

"Christ, no," Cubitt said and took some more
whisky.

A vague memory of the Bible, where it lay in the
cupboard next the Board, the Warwick Deeping, *The
Good Companions*, stirred in Ida Arnold's memory.
"I've seen you with him," she lied; a courtyard, a
sewing wench beside the fire, the cock crowing.

"I'm no friend of Pinkie's."

"It's not safe being friends with Pinkie," Ida
Arnold said. Cubitt stared into his glass like a diviner
into his soul, reading the dooms of strangers. "Fred
was a friend of Pinkie's," she said.

"What you know about Fred?"

"People talk," Ida Arnold said. "People talk all the
time."

"You're right," Cubitt said. The stained eyeballs
lifted; they gazed at comfort, understanding; he
wasn't good enough for Colleoni; he had broken with

Pinkie; behind her head through the window of the
lounge—darkness and the retreating sea; through a
ruined Tintern picture postcard arch lay desolation.
"Christ," he said, "you're right." He had an enormous urge to confession, but the facts were confused.
He knew only that these were the times when a man
needed a woman's understanding. "I've never held
with it," he told her. "Carving's different."

"Of course, carving's different," Ida Arnold
smoothly and deftly agreed.

"And Kite—that was an accident. They only meant
to carve him. Colleoni's no fool. Somebody slipped.
There wasn't any cause for bad feeling."

"Have another drink?"

"It oughta be on me," Cubitt said. "But I'm cleaned
out. Till I see the boys."

"It was fine of you—breaking with Pinkie like that.
It needed courage after what happened to Fred."

"Oh, he can't scare me. No broken banisters . . ."

"What do you mean—broken banisters?"

"I wanted to be friendly," Cubitt said. "A joke's a
joke. When a man's getting married, he oughta take
a joke."

"Married? Who married?"

"Pinkie, of course."

"Not to the little girl at Snow's?"

"Of course."

"The little fool," Ida Arnold said with sharp anger.
"Oh, the little fool."

"He's not a fool," Cubitt said. "He knows what's
good for him. If she chose to say a thing or two——"

"You mean, say it wasn't Fred left the ticket?"

"Poor old Spicer," Cubitt said, watching the bubbles rise in the whisky. A question floated up: "How did you . . . ?" but broke in the doped brain. "I want air," he said, "stuffy in here. What say you and I . . . ?"

"Just wait awhile," Ida Arnold said. "I'm expecting a friend. I'd like you and him to be acquainted."

"This central heating," Cubitt said. "It's not healthy. You go out and catch a chill and the next you know——"

"When's the wedding?"

"Whose wedding?"

"Pinkie's."

"I'm no friend of Pinkie's."

"You didn't hold with Fred's death, did you?" Ida Arnold softly persisted.

"You understand a man."

"Carving would have been different."

Cubitt suddenly, furiously, broke out: "I can't see a piece of Brighton rock without . . ." He belched and said with tears in his voice: "Carving's different."

"The doctors said it was natural causes. He had a weak heart."

"Come outside," Cubitt said. "I got to get some air."

"Just wait a bit. What do you mean—Brighton rock?"

He stared inertly back at her. He said: "I got to get some air. Even if it kills me. This central heating . . ." he complained. "I'm liable to colds."

"Just wait two minutes." She put her hand on his arm, feeling an intense excitement, the edge of discovery above the horizon, and was aware herself for the first time of the warm close air welling up round them from hidden gratings, driving them into the open. She said: "I'll come out with you. We'll take a walk . . ." He watched her with nodding head, an immense indifference as if he had lost grip on his thought as you loose a dog's lead and it has disappeared, too far to be followed, in what wood . . . He was astonished when she said: "I'll give you—twenty pounds." What had he said that was worth that money? She smiled enticingly at him. "Just let me put on a bit of powder and have a wash." He didn't respond, he was scared, but she couldn't wait for a reply; she dived for the stairs—no time for the lift. A wash: they were the words she had used to Fred. She ran upstairs, people were coming down, changed, to dinner. She hammered on her door and Phil Corkery let her in. "Quick," she said, "I want a witness." He was dressed, thank goodness, and she raced him down, but immediately she got into the hall she saw that Cubitt had gone. She ran out onto the steps of the Cosmopolitan, but he wasn't in sight.

"Well?" Mr. Corkery said.

"Gone. Never mind," Ida Arnold said. "I know now all right. It wasn't suicide. They murdered him." She said slowly over to herself: ". . . Brighton rock . . ." The clue would have seemed hopeless to many women, but Ida Arnold had been trained by the Board. Queerer things than that had spidered out under her fingers and Old Crowe's; with complete confidence her mind began to work.

The night air stirred Mr. Corkery's thin yellow hair. It may have occurred to him that on an evening like this—after the actions of love—romance was required by any woman. He touched her elbow timidly. "What a night," he said. "I never dreamed—what a night," but words drained out of him as she switched her large thoughtful eyes towards him, uncomprehending, full of other ideas. She said slowly: "The little fool . . . to marry him . . . why, there's no knowing what he'll do." A kind of righteous mirth moved her to add with excitement: "We got to save her, Phil."

2

At the bottom of the steps the Boy waited. The big municipal building lay over him like a shadow—departments for births and deaths, for motor licences, for rates and taxes, somewhere in some long corridor the room for marriages. He looked at his watch and said to Mr. Drewitt: "God damn her. She's late."

Mr. Drewitt said: "It's the privilege of a bride."

Bride and groom: the mare and the stallion which served her; like a file on metal or the touch of velvet to a sore hand. The Boy said: "Me and Dallow—we'll walk and meet her."

Mr. Drewitt called after him: "Suppose she comes another way. Suppose you miss her . . . I'll wait here."

They turned to the left out of the official street. "This ain't the way," Dallow said.

"There's no call on us to wait on her," the Boy said.

"You can't get out of it now."

"Who wants to? I can take a bit of exercise, can't I?" He stopped and stared into a small newsagent's window—two-valve receiving sets, the grossness everywhere.

"Seen Cubitt?" he asked, staring in.

"No," Dallow said. "None of the boys either."

The daily and the local papers, a poster packed with news: Scene at Council Meeting, Woman Found Drowned at Black Rock, Collision in Clarence Street; a Wild West magazine, a copy of *Film Fun*, behind the inkpots and the fountain pens and the paper plates for picnics and the little gross toys; the works of Marie Stopes: *Married Love*. The Boy stared in.

"I know how you feel," Dallow said. "I was married once myself. It kind of gets you in the stomach. Nerves. Why," Dallow said, "I even went and got one of those books, but it didn't tell me anything I didn't know. Except about flowers. The pistils of flowers. You wouldn't believe the funny things that go on among flowers."

The Boy turned and opened his mouth to speak, but the teeth snapped to again. He watched Dallow with pleading and horror. If Kite had been there, he thought, he could have spoken—but if Kite had been there, he would have had no need to speak . . . he would never have got mixed up.

"These bees . . ." Dallow began to explain and stopped. "What is it, Pinkie? You don't look too good."

"I know the rules all right," the Boy said.

"What rules?"

"You can't teach me the rules," the Boy went on with gusty anger. "I watched 'em every Saturday night, didn't I? Bouncing and ploughing." His eyes flinched as if he were watching some horror. He said in a low voice: "When I was a kid, I swore I'd be a priest."

"A priest? You a priest? That's good," Dallow said. He laughed without conviction, shifted his foot uneasily, so that it trod in a dog's ordure.

"What's wrong with being a priest?" the Boy said. "They know what's what. They keep away"—his whole mouth and jaw loosened; he might have been going to weep; he beat out wildly with his hands towards the window: Woman Found Drowned, two-valve, *Married Love*, the horror—"from this."

"What's wrong with a bit of fun?" Dallow took him up, scraping his shoe against the pavement edge. The word "fun" shook the boy like malaria. He said: "You wouldn't have known Annie Collins, would you?"

"Never heard of her."

"She went to the same school I did," the Boy said. He took a look down the grey street and then the glass before *Married Love* reflected his young and hopeless face. "She put her head on the line," he said, "up towards Hassocks. She had to wait ten minutes for the seven-five. Fog made it late from Victoria. Cut off her head. She was fifteen. She was going to have a baby and she knew what it was like. She'd had one two years before, and they could 'ave pinned it on twelve boys."

"It does happen," Dallow said. "It's the luck of the game."

"I've read love stories," the Boy said. He had never been so vocal before, staring in at the paper plates with frilly edges and the two-valve receiving set: the daintiness and the grossness. "Billy's wife read them. You know the sort. Lady Angeline turned her starry eyes towards Sir Mark. They make me sick. Sicker than the other kind"—Dallow watched with astonishment this sudden horrified gift of tongues—"the kind you buy under the counter. Spicer used to get them. About girls being beaten. Full of shame to expose herself thus before the boys she stooped . . . It's all the same thing," he said, turning his poisoned eyes away from the window, from point to point of the long shabby street · a smell of fish, the sawdusted pavement below the carcasses. "It's love," he said, grinning mirthlessly up at Dallow. "It's fun. It's the game."

"The world's got to go on," Dallow said uneasily.

"Why?" the Boy said.

"You don't need to ask me," Dallow said. "You know best. You're a Roman, aren't you? You believe . . ."

"Credo in unum Satanum," the Boy said.

"I don't know Latin. I only know . . ."

"Come on," the Boy said. "Let's have it. Dallow's creed."

"The world's all right if you don't go too far."

"Is that all?"

"It's time for you to be at the registrar's. Hear the clock? It's striking two now." A peal of bells stopped their cracked chime and struck—one, two——

The Boy's whole face loosened again; he put his hand on Dallow's arm. "You're a good sort, Dallow. You know a lot. Tell me—" his hand fell away. He looked beyond Dallow down the street. He said hopelessly: "Here she is. What's she doing in *this* street?"

"She's not hurrying either," Dallow commented, watching the thin figure slowly approach. At that distance she didn't even look her age. He said: "It was clever of Drewitt to get the license at all, considering."

"Parents' consent," the Boy said dully. "Best for morality." He watched the girl as if she were a stranger he had got to meet. "And then, you see, there was a stroke of luck. I wasn't registered. Not anywhere they could find. They added on a year or two. No parents. No guardian. It was a touching story old Drewitt spun."

She had tricked herself up for the wedding, discarded the hat he hadn't liked, a new mackintosh, a touch of powder and cheap lipstick. She looked like one of the small gaudy statues in an ugly church: a paper crown wouldn't have looked odd on her or a painted heart; you could pray to her but you couldn't expect an answer.

"Where've you been?" the Boy said. "Don't you know you're late?"

They didn't even touch hands. An awful formality fell between them.

"I'm sorry, Pinkie. You see"—she brought the fact out with shame, as if she were admitting conversation with his enemy—"I went into the church."

"What for?" he said.

"I don't know, Pinkie. I got confused. I thought I'd go to confession."

He grinned at her. "Confession? That's rich."

"You see, I wanted—I thought——"

"For Christ's sake, what?"

"I wanted to be in a state of grace when I married you." She took no notice at all of Dallow. The theological term lay oddly and pedantically on her tongue. They were two Romans together in the grey street. They understood each other. She used terms common to Heaven and Hell.

"And did you?" the Boy said.

"No. I went and rang the bell and asked for Father James. But then I remembered. It wasn't any good confessing. I went away." She said with a mixture of fear and pride: "We're going to do a mortal sin."

The Boy said, with bitter and unhappy relish: "It'll be no good going to confession ever again—as long as we're both alive." He had graduated in pain: first the school dividers had been left behind, next the razor. He had a sense now that the murders of Hale and Spicer were trivial acts, a boy's game, and he had put away childish things. Murder had only led to this—this corruption. He was filled with awe at his own powers. "We'd better be moving," he said and touched her arm with next to tenderness. As once before he had a sense of needing her.

Mr. Drewitt greeted them with official mirth. All his jokes seemed to be spoken in court, with an ulterior motive, to catch a magistrate's ear. In the great institutional hall from which the corridors led off to deaths and births there was a smell of disinfectant. The walls were tiled like a public lavatory. Somebody had dropped a rose. Mr. Drewitt quoted promptly, inaccurately: "Roses, roses all the way, and never a sprig of yew." A soft hollow hand guided the Boy by the elbow. "No, no, not that way. That's taxes. That comes later." He led them up great stone stairs. A clerk passed them carrying printed forms. "And what is the little lady thinking?" Mr. Drewitt said. She didn't answer him. . . .

The bride and groom only were allowed to mount the sanctuary steps, to kneel down within the sanctuary rails with the priest and the Host.

"Parents coming?" Mr. Drewitt said. She shook her head. "The great thing is," Mr. Drewitt said, "it's over quickly. Just sign the names along the dotted line. Sit down here. We've got to wait our turn, you know."

They sat down. A mop leant in a corner against the tiled wall. The footsteps of a clerk squealed on the icy paving down another passage. Presently a big brown door opened; they saw a row of clerks inside who didn't look up; a man and wife came out into the corridor. A woman followed them and took the mop. The man—he was middle-aged—said: "Thank you," gave her sixpence. He said: "We'll catch the three-fifteen after all." On the woman's face there was a look of faint astonishment, bewilderment, nothing so definite as disappointment. She wore a brown straw and carried an attaché case. She was middle-aged too. She might have been thinking: "Is that all there is to it—after all these years?" They went down the big stairs walking a little apart, like strangers in a store.

"Our turn," Mr. Drewitt said, rising briskly. He led the way through the room where the clerks worked. Nobody bothered to look up. Nibs wrote shrill numerals and ran on. In a small inner room with green washed walls like a clinic's the registrar waited: a table, three or four chairs against the wall. It wasn't what she thought a marriage would be like—for a moment she was daunted by the cold poverty of a state-made ceremony.

"Good morning," the registrar said. "If the witnesses will just sit down—would you two—?" he beckoned them to the table. He was like a provincial actor who believes too much in his part. he stared at them with gold-rimmed and glassy importance; it was as if he considered himself on the fringe of the priestly office. The Boy's heart beat; he was sickened by the reality of the moment. He wore a look of sullenness and of stupidity.

"You're both very young," the registrar said.

"It's fixed," the Boy said. "You don't have to talk about it. It's fixed."

The registrar gave him a glance of intense dislike; he said venomously · "Repeat after me," and then ran too quickly on : "I do solemnly declare that I know not of any lawful impediments," so that the Boy couldn't follow him. The registrar said sharply: "It's quite simple. You've only to repeat after me . . ."

"Go slower," the Boy said. He wanted to lay his hand on speed and break it down, but it ran on : it was no time at all, a matter of seconds, before he was repeating the second formula: "My lawful wedded wife." He tried to make it careless, he kept his eyes off Rose, but the words were weighted with shame.

"No ring?" the registrar asked sharply.

"We don't need any ring," the Boy said. "This isn't a church," feeling he could never now rid his memory of the cold green room and the glassy face. He heard Rose repeating by his side : "I call upon these persons

here present to witness . . ." and then the word "husband," and he looked sharply up at her. If there had
been any complacency in her face then he would have
struck it. But there was only surprise as if she were
reading a book and had come to the last page too soon.

The registrar said: "You sign here. The charge is
seven and sixpence." He wore an air of official uncon-
cern while Mr. Drewitt fumbled.

"These persons," the Boy said and laughed bro-
kenly. "That's you, Drewitt and Dallow." He took
the pen and the government nib scratched into the
page, gathering fur; in the old days, it occurred to
him, you signed covenants like this in your blood. He
stood back and watched Rose awkwardly sign—his
temporal safety in return for two immortalities of
pain. He had no doubt whatever that this was mortal
sin, and he was filled with a kind of gloomy hilarity
and pride. He saw himself now as a full-grown man
for whom the angels wept.

"These persons," he repeated, ignoring the registrar altogether. "Come and have a drink."

"Well," Mr. Drewitt said, "that's a surprise from
you."

"Oh, Dallow will tell you," the Boy said, "I'm a
drinking man these days." He looked across at Rose.
"There's nothing I'm not now," he said. He took her
by the elbow and led the way out to the tiled passage
and the big stairs; the mop was gone and somebody
had picked up the flower. A couple rose as they came
out: the market was firm. He said: "That was a wedding. Can you beat it? We're—" He meant to say

"husband and wife" but his mind flinched from the defining phrase. "We got to celebrate," he said, and like an old relation you can always trust for the tactless word his brain beat on : "celebrate what?" and he thought of the girl sprawling in the Lancia and the long night coming down.

They went to the pub round the corner. It was nearly closing time, and he stood them pints of bitter and Rose took a port. She hadn't spoken since the registrar had given her the words to say and Mr. Drewitt took a quick look round and parked his portfolio. With his dark striped trousers he might really have been at a wedding. "Here's to the bride," he said with a jocularity which petered unobtrusively out; it was as if he had tried to crack a joke with a magistrate and scented a rebuff; the old face recomposed itself quickly on serious lines. He said reverently : "To your happiness, my dear."

She didn't answer; she was looking at her own face in a glass marked Extra Stout : in the new setting with a foreground of beer handles, it was a strange face. It seemed to carry an enormous weight of responsibility.

"A penny for your thoughts," Dallow said to her. The Boy put the glass of bitter to his mouth and tasted for the second time—the nausea of other people's pleasures stuck in his throat. He watched her sourly as she gazed wordlessly back at his companions; and again he was sensible of how she completed him. *He* knew her thoughts : they beat unregarded in his own nerves. He said with triumphant venom : "I can tell you what she's thinking of. Not much of a wedding, she's thinking. She's thinking—it's not what I pictured. That's right, isn't it?"

She nodded, holding the glass of port as if she hadn't learned the way to drink.

"With my body I thee worship," he began to quote at her, "with all my worldly goods . . . and then," he said, turning to Mr. Drewitt, "I give her a gold piece."

"Time, gentlemen," the barman said, swilling not quite empty glasses into the lead trough, mopping with a yeasty cloth.

"We're up in the sanctuary, do you see, with the priest . . ."

"Drink up, gentlemen."

Mr. Drewitt said uneasily: "One wedding's as good as another in the eyes of the law." He nodded encouragingly at the girl, who watched them with famished immature eyes. "You're married all right. Trust me."

"Married?" the Boy said. "Do you call that married?" He screwed up the beery spittle on his tongue.

"Easy on," Dallow said. "Give the girl a chance. You don't need to go too far."

"Come along, gentlemen, empty your glasses."

"Married!" the Boy repeated. "Ask her." The two men drank up in a shocked furtive way and Mr. Drewitt said: "Well, I'll be getting on." The Boy regarded them with contempt; they didn't understand a thing, and again he was touched by the faintest sense of communion between himself and Rose— she too knew that this evening meant nothing at all, that there hadn't been a wedding. He said with rough kindness: "Come on. We'll be going," and raised a hand to put it on her arm—then saw the double image in the mirror (Extra Stout) and let it fall; a married couple, the image winked at him.

"Where?" Rose said.

Where? He hadn't thought of that—you had to take them somewhere—the honeymoon, the week-end at the sea, the present from Margate on the mantelpiece his mother'd had; from one sea to another, a change of pier.

"I'll be seeing you," Dallow said; he paused a moment at the door, met the Boy's eye, the question, the appeal, understood nothing, and sloped away, cheerily waving, after Mr. Drewitt, leaving them alone.

It was as if they'd never been alone before in spite of the barman drying the glasses not really alone in the room at Snow's, nor above the sea at Peacehaven—not alone as they were now.

"We'd better be off," Rose said.

They stood on the pavement and heard the door of the Crown closed and locked behind them—a bolt grind into place; they felt as if they were shut out from an Eden of ignorance. On this side there was nothing to look forward to but experience.

"Are we going to Billy's?" the girl said. It was one of those moments of sudden silence that fall on the busiest afternoon: not a tram bell, not a cry of steam from the terminus; a flock of birds shot up together into the air above Old Steyne and hovered there as if a crime had been committed on the ground. He thought with nostalgia of the room at Billy's—he knew exactly where to put his hand for money in the soap dish; everything was familiar; nothing strange there; it shared his bitter virginity.

"No," he said, and again, as noise came back, the clang and crash and cry of afternoon: "No."

"Where?"

He smiled with hopeless malice—where did you bring a swell blonde to if not to the Cosmopolitan, coming down by Pullman at the week-end, driving over the down in a scarlet roadster? Expensive scent and furs, sailing like a new-painted pinnace into the restaurant, something to swank about in return for the nocturnal act. He absorbed Rose's shabbiness like a penance in a long look. "We'll take a suite," he said, "at the Cosmopolitan."

"No, but where—really?"

"You heard me—the Cosmopolitan." He flared up. "Don't you think I'm good enough?"

"You are," she said, "but I'm not."

"We're going there," he said. "I can afford it. It's the right place. There was a woman called—Eugeen —used to go there. That's why they have crowns on the chairs."

"Who was she?"

"A foreign polony."

"Have you been there then?"

"Of course I've been there."

Suddenly she put her hands together in an excited gesture. "I dreamed," she said and then looked sharply up to see if he was only mocking after all.

He said airily: "The car's being repaired. We'll walk and send them round for my bag. Where's yours?"

"My what?"

"Your bag."

"It was so broken, dirty . . ."

"Never mind," he said with desperate swagger, "we'll buy you another. Where's your things?"

"Things . . . ?"

"Christ, how dumb you are!" he said. "I mean . . ." but the thought of the night ahead froze his tongue. He drove on down the pavement, the afternoon waning on his face.

She said: "There was nothing . . . nothing I could marry you in, only this. I asked them for a little money. They wouldn't give it me. They'd a right. It was theirs."

They walked a foot apart along the pavement. Her words scratched tentatively at the barrier like a bird's claws on the window pane: he could feel her all the time trying to get at him; even her humility seemed to him a trap. The crude quick ceremony was a claim on him. *She* didn't know the reason; she thought—God save the mark—he wanted her. He said roughly: "You needn't think there's going to be a honeymoon. That nonsense. I'm busy. I've got things to do. I've got . . ." He stopped and turned to her with a kind of scared appeal—let this make no difference. "I got to be away a lot."

"I'll wait," she said. He could already see the patience of the poor and the long-married working up under her skin like a second personality, a modest and shameless figure behind a transparency.

They came out onto the front, and evening stood back a pace; the sea dazzled the eyes; she watched it with pleasure as if it was a different sea. He said: "What did your Dad say today?"

"He didn't say a thing. He'd got a mood."

"And the old woman?"

"She had a mood too."

"They took the money all right."

They came to a halt on the front opposite the Cosmopolitan and under its enormous bulk moved a few inches closer. He remembered the page boy calling a name and Colleoni's gold cigarette case. . . . He said slowly and carefully, shutting uneasiness out: "Well, we oughta be comfortable there." He put a hand up to his withered tie, straightened his jacket, and set unconvincingly his narrow shoulders. "Come on." She followed a pace behind, across the road, up the wide steps. Two old ladies sat on the terrace in wicker chairs in the sun, wrapped round and round with veils; they had an absolute air of security; when they spoke they didn't look at each other, just quietly dropped their remarks into the understanding air. "Now Willie . . ." "I always liked Willie." The Boy made an unnecessary noise coming up the steps.

He walked across the deep pile to the reception desk, Rose just behind him. There was nobody there. He waited furiously—it was a personal insult. A page called: "Mr. Pinecoffin, Mr. Pinecoffin," across the lounge. The Boy waited. A telephone rang. When the entrance door swung again they could hear one of the old ladies say: "It was a great blow to Basil." Then a man in a black coat appeared and said: "Can I do anything for you?"

The Boy said furiously: "I've been waiting here——"

"You could have touched the bell," the clerk said coldly and opened a large register.

"I want a room," the Boy said. "A double room."

The clerk stared past him at Rose, then turned a page. "We haven't a room free," he said.

"I don't mind what I pay," the Boy said. "I'll take a suite."

"There's nothing vacant," the clerk said without looking up.

The page boy returning with a salver paused and watched. The Boy said in a low furious voice: "You can't keep me out of here. My money's as good as anybody else's. . . ."

"No doubt," the clerk said, "but there happens to be no room free." He turned his back and picked up a jar of Stickphast.

"Come on," the Boy said to Rose, "this gaff stinks." He strode back down the steps, past the old ladies, tears of humiliation pricked behind his eyes. He had an insane impulse to shout out to them all that they couldn't treat him like that, that he was a killer, he could kill men and not be caught. He wanted to boast. He could afford that place as well as anyone: he had a car, a lawyer, two hundred pounds in the bank. . . .

Rose said: "If I'd had a ring . . ."

He said furiously: "A ring . . . what sort of a ring? We aren't married. Don't forget that. We aren't married." But outside on the pavement he restrained himself with immense difficulty and remembered bitterly that he still had a part to play—they couldn't *make* a wife give evidence, but nothing could prevent a wife except—love, lust, he thought with sour horror, and turning back to her he unconvincingly apologized. "They get me angry," he said. "You see I'd promised you——"

"I don't care," she said. Suddenly with wide astonished eyes she made the foolhardy claim: "Nothing can spoil today."

"We got to find somewhere," he said.

"I don't mind where—Billy's?"

"Not tonight," he said. "I don't want any of the boys around tonight."

"We'll think of a place," she said. "It's not dark yet."

These were the hours—when the races were not on, when there was no one to see on business—that he spent stretched on the bed at Billy's. He'd eat a packet of chocolate or a sausage roll, watch the sun shift from the chimney pots, fall asleep and wake and eat again and sleep with the dark coming in through the window. Then the boys would return with the evening papers and life would start again. Now he was at a loss: he didn't know how to spend so much time when he wasn't alone.

"One day," she said, "let's go into the country like we did that time. . . ." Staring out to sea she planned ahead . . . he could see the years advancing before her eyes like the line of the tide.

"Anything you say," he said.

"Let's go on the pier," she said. "I haven't been since we went that day—you remember?"

"Nor've I," he lied quickly and smoothly, thinking of the first time, Spicer, and the lightning on the sea—

the beginning of something of which he couldn't see
the end. They went through the turnstile; there were
a lot of people about; a row of anglers watched their
floats in the thick green swell; the water moved under
their feet.

"Do you know that girl?" Rose said. The Boy
turned his head apathetically. "Where?" he said. "I
don't know any girls in this place."

"There," Rose said. "I bet she's talking about
you."

The fat stupid spotty face swam back into his memory, nuzzled the glass like some monstrous fish in
the Aquarium—dangerous—a stingray from another
ocean. Fred had spoken to her and he had come up to
them upon the front; she'd given evidence—he
couldn't remember what she had said—nothing important. Now she watched him, nudged her pasty girl
friend, spoke of him, told he didn't know what lies.
Christ! he thought. Had he got to massacre a world?

"*She* knows you," Rose said.

"I've never seen her," he lied, walking on.

Rose said: "It's wonderful being with you. Everyone knows you. I never thought I'd marry someone
famous."

Who next, he thought, who next? An angler drew
back across their path to make his cast, whirling his
line, dropped it far out; the float was caught in the
cream of a wave and drove a line's length towards the
shore. It was cold on the sunless side of the pier; on
one side of the glass division it was day, on the other
evening advanced. "Let's cross over," he said. He
began to think again of Spicer's girl: why had he left

her in the car? God damn it, after all, she knew the
game.

Rose stopped him. "Look," she said, "won't you
give me one of those? As a souvenir. They don't cost
much," she said, "only sixpence." It was a small glass
box like a telephone cabinet. "Make a record of your
own voice," the legend ran.

"Come on," he said. "Don't be soft. What's the
good of that?"

For the second time he came up against her sudden
irresponsible resentment. She was soft, she was dumb,
she was sentimental—and then suddenly she was dangerous. About a hat, about a gramophone record. "All
right," she said, "go away. You've never given me a
thing. Not even today you haven't. If you don't want
me why don't you go away? Why don't you leave me
alone?" People turned and looked at them—at his acid
and angry face, at her hopeless resentment. "What do
you want me for?" she cried at him.

"For Christ's sake . . ." he said.

"I'd rather drown," she began, but he interrupted
her: "You can have your record." He smiled nervously. "I just thought you were crazy," he said.
"What do you want to hear me on a record for?
Aren't you going to hear me every day?" He squeezed
her arm. "You're a good kid. I don't grudge you
things. You can have anything you say." He thought·
She's got me where she wants . . . how long? "You
didn't mean those things now, did you?" he wheedled
her. His face crinkled in the effort of amiability like
an old man's.

"Something came over me," she said, avoiding his

eyes with an expression he couldn't read, obscure and despairing.

He felt relieved—but reluctant. He didn't like the idea of putting anything on a record: it reminded him of finger prints. "Do you really," he said, "want me to get one of those things? We haven't got a gramophone anyway. You won't be able to hear it. What's the good?"

"I don't want a gramophone," she said. "I just want to have it there. Perhaps one day you might be away somewhere and I could borrow a gramophone. And you'd speak," she said with a sudden intensity that scared him.

"What do you want me to say?"

"Just anything," she said. "Say something to me. Say Rose and—something."

He went into the box and closed the door. There was a slot for his sixpence, a mouthpiece, an instruction: "Speak clearly and close to the instrument." The scientific paraphernalia made him nervous; he looked over his shoulder and there outside she was watching him—without a smile; he saw her as a stranger, a shabby child from Nelson Place, and he was shaken by an appalling resentment. He put in a sixpence and speaking in a low voice for fear it might carry beyond the box he gave his message up to be graven on vulcanite: "God damn you, you little bitch, why can't you go back home for ever and let me be?"; he heard the needle scratch and the record whir, then a click and silence.

Carrying the black disk he came out to her. "Here," he said, "take it. I put something on it—loving."

She took it from him carefully, carried it like something to be defended from the crowd. Even on the sunny side of the pier it was getting cold; and the cold fell between them like an unanswerable statement— you'd better be getting home now. He had the sense of playing truant from his proper work—he should be at school, but he hadn't learned his lesson. They passed through the turnstile, and he watched her out of the corner of an eye to see what she expected now; if she had shown any excitement he would have slapped her face. But she hugged the record as chilled as he.

"Well," he said, "we got to go somewhere."

She pointed down the steps to the covered walk under the pier. "Let's go there," she said, "it's sheltered there."

The Boy looked sharply round at her; it was as if deliberately she had offered him an ordeal. For a moment he hesitated; then he grinned at her. "All right," he said, "we'll go there." He was moved by a kind of sensuality: the coupling of good and evil.

In the trees of the Old Steyne the fairy lights were switched on; it was too early, their pale colours didn't show in the last of the day. The long tunnel under the parade was the noisiest, lowest, cheapest section of Brighton's amusements: children rushed past them in paper sailor caps marked "I'm No Angel"; a ghost train rattled by carrying courting couples into a squealing and shrieking darkness. All the way along the landward side of the tunnel were the amusements; on the other little shops: Magpie Ices, Photoweigh, Shellfish, Rock. The shelves rose to the ceiling; little doors let you into the obscurity behind, and on the sea side there were no doors at all, no windows, nothing but shelf after shelf from the pebbles to the roof, a breakwater of Brighton rock facing the sea. The lights were always on in the tunnel; the air was warm and thick and poisoned with human breath.

"Well," the Boy said, "what's it to be—winkles or Brighton rock?" He watched her as if something important really depended on her answer.

"I'd like a stick of Brighton rock," she said.

Again he grinned; only the devil, he thought, could have made her answer that. She was good, but he'd got her like you got God in the Eucharist—in the guts. God couldn't escape the evil mouth which chose to eat its own damnation. He padded across to a doorway and looked in. "Miss," he said. "Miss. Two sticks of rock." He looked around the little pink barred cell as if he owned it; his memory owned it, it was stamped with footmarks, a particular patch of floor had eternal importance; if the cash register had been moved he'd have noticed it. "What's that?" he said and nodded at a box, the only unfamiliar object there.

"It's broken rock," she said, "going cheap."

"From the maker's?"

"No. It got broken. Some clumsy fools—" she complained.

He took the sticks and turned; he knew what he would see—nothing; the promenade was shut out behind the rows of Brighton rock. He had a momentary sense of his own immense cleverness. "Good night," he said, stooped in the little doorway, and went out. If only one could boast of one's cleverness, relieve the enormous pressure of pride . . .

They stood side by side sucking their sticks of rock; a woman bustled them to one side. "Out of the way, you children." Their glances met: a married couple.

"Where now?" he said uneasily.

"Perhaps we ought to find—somewhere," she said.

"There's not all that hurry." His voice caught a little with anxiety. "It's early yet. Like a movie?" He wheedled her again. "I've never took you to a movie."

But the sense of power left him. Again her passionate assent—"You're good to me"—repelled him.

Slumped grimly in the three-and-sixpenny seat, in the half-dark, he asked himself crudely and bitterly what she was hoping for; beside the screen an illuminated clock marked the hour. It was a romantic film: magnificent features, thighs shot with studied care, esoteric beds shaped like winged coracles. A man was killed, but that didn't matter. What mattered was the game. The two main characters made their stately progress towards the bed sheets: "I loved you that first time in Santa Monica . . ." A song under a window, a girl in a nightdress, and the clock beside the screen moving on. He whispered suddenly, furiously, to Rose: "Like cats." It was the commonest game under the sun—why be scared at what the dogs did in the streets? The music moaned: "I know in my heart you're divine." He whispered: "Maybe we'd better go to Billy's after all," thinking: we won't be alone there; something may happen; maybe the boys will have drinks; maybe they'll celebrate—there won't be any bed for anyone tonight. The actor with a lick of black hair across a white waste of face said: "You're mine. All mine." He sang again under the restless stars in a

wash of incredible moonshine, and suddenly, inexplicably, the Boy began to weep. He shut his eyes to
hold in his tears, but the music went on—it was like a
vision of release to an imprisoned man. He felt con-
striction and saw—hopelessly out of reach—a limitless
freedom : no fear, no hatred, no envy. It was as if he
were dead and were remembering the effect of a good
confession, the words of absolution; but being dead
it was a memory only—he couldn't experience contrition—the ribs of his body were like steel bands
which held him down to eternal unrepentance. He
said at last · "Let's go. We'd better go."

It was quite dark now; the coloured lights were on
all down the Hove front. They walked slowly past
Snow's, past the Cosmopolitan. An aeroplane flying
low burred out to sea, a red light vanishing. In one of
the glass shelters an old man struck a match to light
his pipe and showed a man and girl cramped in the
corner. A wail of music came off the sea. They turned
up through Norfolk Square towards Montpellier Road;
a blonde with Garbo cheeks paused to powder on
the steps up to the Norfolk bar. A bell tolled somewhere for someone dead and a gramophone in a basement played a hymn. "Maybe," the Boy said, "after
tonight we'll find some place to go."

He had his latchkey but he rang the bell. He wanted
people, talk . . . but no one answered. He rang again.
It was one of those old bells you have to pull; it jangled
on the end of its wire, the kind of bell that knows from
long experience of dust and spiders and untenanted
rooms how to convey that a house is empty. "They
can't 'ave all gone out," he said, slipped in his latchkey.

A globe had been left burning in the hall; he saw at once the note stuck under the telephone: "Two's company"; he recognized the drab and sprawling hand of Billy's wife. "We gone out to celebrate the wedding. Lock your door. Have a good time." He crumpled the paper up and dropped it on the linoleum. "Come on," he said, "upstairs." At the top he put his hand on the new banister rail and said: "You see. We've got it mended." A smell of cabbages and cooking and burnt cloth hung about the dark passage. He nodded. "That was old Spicer's room. Do you believe in ghosts?"

"I don't know."

He pushed open his own door and switched on the naked dusty light. "There," he said, "take it or leave it," and drew aside to expose the big brass bed, the washstand and chipped ewer, the varnished wardrobe with its cheap glass front.

"It's better than a hotel," she said, "it's more like home."

They stood in the middle of the room as if they didn't know what their next move should be. She said · "Tomorrow I'll tidy up a bit."

He banged the door to. "You won't touch a thing," he said. "It's my home, do you hear? I won't have you coming in, changing things. . . ." He watched her with fear—to come into your own room, your cave, and find a strange thing there . . . "Why don't you take off your hat?" he said. "You're staying, aren't you?" She took off her hat, her mackintosh—this was the ritual of mortal sin: this, he thought, was what people damned each other for . . . the bell in the hall clanged. He paid it no attention. "It's Saturday night," he said with a bitter taste on his tongue, "it's time for bed."

"Who is it?" she said, and the bell jangled again—its unmistakable message to whoever was outside that the house was no longer empty. She came across the room to him; her face was white. "Is it the police?" she said.

"Why should it be the police? Some friend of Billy's." But the suggestion startled him. He stood and waited for the clang. It didn't come again. "Well," he said, "we can't stand here all night. We better get to bed." He felt an appalling emptiness as if he hadn't fed for days. He tried to pretend, taking off his jacket and hanging it over a chair-back, that everything was as usual. When he turned she hadn't moved; a thin and half-grown child, she trembled between the washstand and the bed. "Why," he mocked her with a dry mouth, "you're scared." It was as if he had gone back four years and was taunting a schoolfellow into some offence.

"Aren't you scared?" Rose said.

"Me?" He laughed at her unconvincingly and advanced, an embryo of sensuality—he was mocked by the memory of a gown, a back, "I loved you that first time in Santa Monica . . ." Shaken by a kind of rage, he took her by the shoulders. He had escaped from Paradise Piece to this; he pushed her against the bed. "It's mortal sin," he said, getting what savour there was out of innocence, trying to taste God in the mouth: a brass bedball, her dumb frightened and acquiescent eyes—he blotted everything out in a sad

brutal now-or-never embrace: a cry of pain and then
the jangling of the bell beginning all over again.
"Christ," he said, "can't they let a man alone?" He
opened his eyes on the grey room to see what he had
done: it seemed to him more like death than when
Hale and Spicer had died.

Rose said: "Don't go. Pinkie, don't go."

He had an odd sense of triumph: he had graduated
in the last human shame—it wasn't so difficult after
all. He had exposed himself and nobody had laughed.
He didn't need Mr. Drewitt or Spicer, only—a faint
feeling of tenderness woke for his partner in the act.
He put out a hand and pinched the lobe of her ear.
The bell clanged in the empty hall. An enormous
weight seemed to have lifted. He could face anyone
now. He said: "I'd better see what the bugger wants."

"Don't go. I'm scared, Pinkie."

But he had a sense that he would never be scared
again: running down from the track he had been
afraid, afraid of pain and more afraid of damnation—
of the sudden and unshriven death. Now it was as if
he was damned already and there was nothing more
to fear ever again. The ugly bell clattered, the long
wire humming in the hall, and the bare globe burnt
above the bed—the girl, the washstand, the sooty window, the blank shape of a chimney, a voice whispered.
"I love you, Pinkie." This was hell then, it wasn't
anything to worry about: it was just his own familiar
room. He said:

"I'll be back. Don't worry. I'll be back."

At the head of the stairs he put his hand on the new
unpainted wood of the mended banister. He pushed it

gently and saw how firm it was. He wanted to crow
at his own cleverness. The bell shook below him. He
looked down: it was a long drop, but you couldn't
really be certain that a man from that height would
be killed. The thought had never occurred to him before, but men sometimes lived for hours with broken
backs, and he knew an old man who went about to this
day with a cracked skull which clicked in cold weather
when he sneezed. He had a sense of being befriended.
The bell jangled: it knew he was at home. He went
on down the stairs, his toes catching in the worn linoleum—he was too good for this place. He felt an in-
vincible energy—he hadn't lost vitality upstairs, he'd
gained it. What he had lost was a fear. He hadn't any
idea who stood outside the door, but he was seized by
a sense of wicked amusement. He put up his hand to
the old bell and held it silent: he could feel the pull at
the wire. An odd tug of war went on with the stranger
down the length of the hall, and the Boy won. The
pull ceased and a hand beat at the door. The Boy released the bell and moved softly towards the door, but
immediately behind his back the bell began to clap
again, cracked and hollow and urgent. A ball of paper
—"Lock your door. Have a good time"—scuffled at
his toes.

He swung the door boldly open, and there was
Cubitt, Cubitt hopelessly and drearily drunk; somebody had blacked his eye and his breath was sour:
drink always spoiled his digestion.

The Boy's sense of triumph increased: he felt an
immeasurable victory. "Well," he said, "what do *you*
want?"

"I got my things here," Cubitt said. "I want to get my things."

"Come in and get 'em then," the Boy said.

Cubitt sidled in. He said: "I didn't think I'd see you . . ."

"Go on," the Boy said. "Get your things and clear out."

"Where's Dallow?"

The Boy didn't answer.

"Billy?"

Cubitt cleared his throat; his sour breath reached the Boy. "Look here, Pinkie," he said, "you and me —why shouldn't we be friends? Like we always was."

"*We* were never friends," the Boy said.

Cubitt took no notice. He got his back to the telephone and watched the Boy with his drunken and cautious eyes. "You and me," he said, the sour phlegm rising in his throat and thickening every word, "you and me can't get on separate. Why," he said, "we're kind of brothers. We're tied together."

The Boy watched him, standing against the opposite wall.

"You an' me—it's what I said. We can't get on separate," Cubitt repeated.

"I suppose," the Boy said, "Colleoni wouldn't touch you—not with a stick, but I'm not taking his leavings, Cubitt."

Cubitt began to weep a little—it was a stage he always reached; the Boy could measure his glasses by his tears: they squeezed reluctantly out, two tears like drops of spirits squeezed out of the yellow eyeballs.

"You've no cause to take on like that," he said, "Pinkie."

"You better get your things."

"Where's Dallow?"

"He's out," the Boy said. "They're all out." The spirit of cruel mischief moved again. "We're quite alone, Cubitt," he said. He glanced down the hall at the new patch of linoleum over the place where Spicer had fallen. But it didn't work: the stage of tears was transitory—what came after was sullenness, anger. . . .

Cubitt said: "You can't treat me like dirt."

"That how Colleoni treated you?"

"I came here to be friendly," Cubitt said. "You can't afford not to be friendly."

"I can afford more than you'd think," the Boy said.

Cubitt took him quickly up. "Lend me five nicker."

The Boy shook his head. He was shaken by a sudden impatience and pride · he was worth more than this— this squabble on worn linoleum under the bare and dusty globe with—Cubitt. "For Christ's sake," he said, "get your things and clear out."

"I've got things I could tell about you. . . ."

"Nothing."

"Fred . . ."

"You'd hang," the Boy said. He grinned. "But not me. I'm too young to hang."

"There's Spicer too."

"Spicer fell down there."

"I heard you . . ."

"You heard me? Who's going to believe that?"

"Dallow heard."

"Dallow's all right," the Boy said. "I can trust

Dallow. Why, Cubitt," he went quietly on, "if you
were dangerous, I'd do something about you. But
thank your lucky stars you aren't dangerous." He
turned his back on Cubitt and mounted the stairs. He
could hear Cubitt behind him—panting; he had no
wind.

"I didn't come here to give hard words. Lend me a
couple of nicker, Pinkie. I'm broke."

The Boy didn't answer—"For the sake of old
times"—turned off at the bend of the stairs to his
own room.

Cubitt said: "Wait a moment and I'll tell you a
thing or two, you bloody little geezer. There's someone'll give me money—twenty nicker. You—why,
you—I'll tell you what you are."

The Boy stopped in front of his door. "Go on," he
said, "tell me."

Cubitt struggled to speak: he hadn't got the right
words. He flung his rage and resentment away in
phrases light as paper. "You're mean," he said,
"you're yellow. You're so yellow you'd kill your best
friend to save your own skin. Why"—he laughed
thickly—"you're scared of a girl. Sylvie told me—"
but that accusation had come too late. He had graduated now in knowledge of the last human weakness.
He listened with amusement, with a kind of infernal
pride; the picture Cubitt drew had got nothing to do
with him: it was like the pictures men drew of Christ
in the image of their own sentimentality. Cubitt
couldn't know. He was like a professor describing to a
stranger some place he had only read about in books—
statistics of imports and exports, tonnage and mineral

resources and if the budget balanced—when all the time it was a country the stranger *knew* from thirsting in the desert and being shot at in the foothills. Mean . . . yellow . . . scared; he laughed gently with derision: it was as if he had outsoared the shadow of any night Cubitt could be aware of. He opened his door, went in, closed it, and locked it.

Rose sat on the bed with dangling feet like a child in a classroom waiting for a teacher in order to say her lesson. Outside the door Cubitt swore and hacked with his foot, rattled the handle, and moved off. She said with immense relief—she was used to drunken men: "Oh, then it's not the police."

"Why should it be the police?"

"I don't know," she said, "I thought maybe——"

"Maybe what?"

He could only just catch her answer. "Kolley Kibber."

For a moment he was amazed. Then he laughed softly with infinite contempt and superiority at a world which used words like innocence. "Why," he said, "that's rich. You knew all along. You guessed. And I thought you were so green you hadn't lost the eggshell. And there you were"—he built her up in the mind's eye that day at Peacehaven, among the Empire wines at Snow's—"there you were, knowing."

She didn't deny it; sitting there with her hands locked between her knees she accepted everything. "It's rich," he said. "Why, when you come to think of it—you're as bad as me." He came across the room and added with a kind of respect: "There's not a pin to choose between us."

She looked up with childish and devoted eyes and swore solemnly: "Not a pin."

He felt desire move again, like nausea in the belly. "What a wedding night!" he said. "Did you think a wedding night would be like this?" . . . the piece of gold in the palm, the kneeling in the sanctuary, the blessing . . . footsteps in the passage, Cubitt pounded on the door, pounded and lurched away, the stairs creaked, a door slammed. She made her vow again, holding him in her arms, in the attitude of mortal sin: "Nothing to choose."

The Boy lay on his back—in his shirt sleeves—and dreamed. He was in an asphalt playground: one plane tree withered; a cracked bell clanged and the children came out to him. He was new; he knew no one; he was sick with fear—they came towards him with a purpose. Then he felt a cautious hand on his sleeve and in a mirror hanging on the tree he saw the reflection of himself and Kite behind—middle-aged, cheery, bleeding from the mouth. "Such tits," Kite said and put a razor in his hand. He knew then what to do: they only needed to be taught once that he would stop at nothing, that there were no rules.

He flung out his arm in a motion of attack, made some indistinguishable comment, and turned upon his side. A piece of blanket fell across his mouth; he breathed with difficulty. He was upon the pier and he could see the piles breaking—a black cloud came racing up across the Channel and the sea rose; the whole pier lurched and settled lower. He tried to scream; no death was so bad as drowning. The deck of the pier

lay at a steep angle like that of a liner on the point of
its deadly dive; he scrambled up the polished slope
away from the sea and slipped again, down and down
into his bed in Paradise Piece. He lay still thinking.
"What a dream!" and then heard the stealthy movement of his parents in the other bed. It was Saturday
night. His father panted like a man at the end of a race
and his mother made a horrifying sound of pleasurable
pain. He was filled with hatred, disgust, loneliness; he
was completely abandoned: he had no share in their
thoughts—for the space of a few minutes he was dead,
he was like a soul in purgatory watching the shameless act of a beloved person.

Then quite suddenly he opened his eyes; it was as if
nightmare couldn't go further; it was black night, he
could see nothing and for a few seconds he believed he
was back in Paradise Piece. Then a clock struck three,
clashing close by like the lid of a dustbin in the backyard, and he remembered with immense relief that he
was alone. He got out of bed in his half-drowse (his
mouth was clotted and evil-tasting) and felt his way
to the washstand. He took up his tooth mug, poured
out a glass of water, and heard a voice say: "Pinkie?
What is it, Pinkie?" He dropped the glass and as the
water spilt across his feet he bitterly remembered.

He said cautiously into the dark: "It's all right. Go
to sleep." He no longer had a sense of triumph or
superiority. He looked back on a few hours ago as if
he had been drunk then or dreaming—he had been
momentarily exhilarated by the strangeness of his
experience. Now there would be nothing strange ever
again—he was awake. You had to treat these things

with common-sense—she knew. The darkness thinned before his wide-awake and calculating gaze—he could see the outline of the bedknobs and a chair. He had won a move and lost a move: they couldn't *make* her give evidence, but she knew. . . . She loved him, whatever that meant, but love was not an eternal thing like hatred and disgust. They saw a better face, a smarter suit . . . The truth came home to him with horror that he had got to keep her love for a lifetime; he would never be able to discard her; if he climbed he had to take Nelson Place with him like a visible scar; the registry office marriage was as irrevocable as a sacrament. Only death could ever set him free.

He was taken by a craving for air, walked softly to the door. In the passage he could see nothing; it was full of the low sound of breathing—from the room he had left, from Dallow's room. He felt like a blind man watched by people he couldn't see. He felt his way to the stairhead and on down to the hall, step by step, creakingly. He put out his hand and touched the telephone, then with his arm outstretched made for the door. In the street the lamps were out, but the darkness no longer enclosed between four walls seemed to thin out across the vast expanse of a city. He could see basement railings, a cat moving, and reflected on the dark sky the phosphorescent glow of the sea. It was a strange world; he had never been alone in it before. He had a deceptive sense of freedom as he walked softly down towards the Channel.

The lights were on in Montpellier Road; nobody about, and an empty milk bottle outside a gramophone shop; far down the illuminated clock tower and the

public lavatories; the air was fresh, like country air. He
could imagine he had escaped. He put his hands for
warmth into his trouser pockets and felt a scrap of paper which should not have been there. He drew it out
—a scrap torn from a notebook—big, unformed,
stranger's writing. He held it up into the grey light
and read—with difficulty: "I love you, Pinkie. I don't
care what you do. I love you for ever. You've been
good to me. Wherever you go, I'll go too." She must
have written it while he talked to Cubitt and slipped it
into his pocket while he slept. He crumpled it in his
fist; a dustbin stood outside a fishmonger's—then he
held his hand. An obscure sense told him you never
knew—it might prove useful one day.

He heard a whisper, looked sharply round, and
thrust the paper back. In an alley between two shops,
an old woman sat upon the ground; he could just see
the rotting and discoloured face: it was like the sight
of damnation. Then he heard the whisper: "Blessed
art thou among women," saw the grey fingers fumbling at the beads. This was not one of the damned; he
watched with horrified fascination: this was one of the
saved.

PART SEVEN

1

IT SEEMED not in the least strange to Rose that
she should wake alone——she was a stranger in the
country of mortal sin, and she assumed that everything was customary. He was, she supposed, about his
business. No alarm clock dinned her to get up, but the
morning light woke her, pouring through the uncur-
tained glass. Once she heard footsteps in the passage,
277

and once a voice called "Judy" imperatively. She lay there wondering what a wife had to do—or rather a mistress.

But she didn't lie long—that was frightening, the unusual passivity. It wasn't like life at all—to have nothing to do. Suppose they assumed she knew—about the stove to be lit, the table to be laid, the debris to be cleared away. A clock struck seven: it was an unfamiliar clock (all her life she had lived in hearing of the same one till now), and the strokes seemed to fall more slowly and more sweetly through the early summer air than any she had ever heard before. She felt happy and scared: seven o'clock was a terribly late hour. She scrambled out and was about to mutter her quick "Our Fathers" and "Hail Marys" while she dressed, when she remembered again. . . . What was the good of praying now? She'd finished with all that: she had chosen her side; if they damned him they'd got to damn her too.

In the ewer there was only an inch of water with a grey heavy surface, and when she lifted the lid of the soap box she found three pound notes wrapped round two half-crowns. She put the lid back: that was just another custom you had to get used to. She took a look round the room, opened a wardrobe and found a tin of biscuits and a pair of boots; some crumbs crunched under her tread. The gramophone record caught her attention on the chair where she'd laid it; she stowed it in the cupboard for greater safety. Then she opened the door—not a sound or sign of life—looked over the banisters; the new wood squeaked under her pressure. Somewhere down below must be the kitchen, the liv-

ing room, the places where she had to work. She went
cautiously down—seven o'clock—what furious faces!
—in the hall a ball of paper scuffled under her feet.
She smoothed it out and read a pencilled message:
"Lock your door. Have a good time." She didn't understand it: it might as well have been in code—she
assumed it must have something to do with this foreign world where you sinned on a bed and people lost
their lives suddenly and strange men hacked at your
door and cursed you in the night.

She found the basement stairs; they were dark where
they dropped under the hall, but she didn't know
where to find a switch. Once she nearly tripped and
held the wall close with beating heart, remembering
the evidence at the inquest, how Spicer had fallen. His
death gave the house a feeling of importance: she had
never been on the scene of a recent death. At the bottom of the stairs she opened the first door she came to,
cautiously, expecting a curse; it was the kitchen all
right, but it was empty. It wasn't like either of the
kitchens she knew: the one at Snow's clean, polished,
busy; the one at home which was just the room where
you sat, where people cooked and ate and had moods
and warmed themselves on bitter nights and dozed in
chairs. This was like the kitchen in a house for sale:
the stove was full of cold coke; on the window sill there
were two empty sardine tins; a dirty saucer stood under the table for a cat which wasn't there; a cupboard
stood open full of empties.

She went and raked at the dead coke; the stove was
cold to the touch; there hadn't been a fire alight there
for hours or days. The thought struck her that she'd

been deserted; perhaps this was what happened in *this* world: the sudden flight, leaving everything behind, your empty bottles and your girl and the message in code on a scrap of paper. When the door opened she expected a policeman.

It was a man in pyjama trousers. He looked in, said: "Where's Judy?" then seemed to notice her. He said: "You're up early."

"Early?" She couldn't understand what he meant.

"I thought it was Judy rooting around. You remember me. I'm Dallow."

She said: "I thought maybe I'd better light the stove."

"What for?" ·

"Breakfast."

He said: "If that polony's gone and forgotten—" He went to a dresser and pulled open a drawer. "Why," he said, "what's got you? You don't want a stove. There's plenty here." Inside the drawer were stacks of tins: sardines, herrings. . . . She said: "But tea."

He looked at her oddly. "Anyone'd think you wanted work. No one here wants any tea. Why take the trouble? There's beer in the cupboard, and Pinkie drinks the milk out of the bottle." He padded back to the door. "Help yourself, kid, if you're hungry. Pinkie want anything?"

"He's gone out."

"Christ's sake, what's come over this house?" He stopped in the doorway and took another look at her as she stood with helpless hands near the dead stove. He said: "You don't *want* to work, do you?"

"No," she said doubtfully.

He was puzzled. "I wouldn't want to stop you," he said. "You're Pinkie's girl. You go ahead and light that stove if you want. I'll shut up Judy if she barks, but Christ knows where you'll find the coke. Why, that stove's not been lit since March."

"I don't want to put anyone out," Rose said. "I came down . . . I thought . . . I'd *got* to light it."

"You don't need to do a stroke," Dallow said. "You take it from me, this is Liberty Hall." He said: "You've not seen a bitch with red hair rooting around, have you?"

"I haven't seen a soul."

"Well," Dallow said, "I'll be seeing you." She was alone again in the cold kitchen. Needn't do a stroke . . . Liberty Hall . . . she leant against the whitewashed wall and saw an old flypaper dangling above the dresser; somebody a long time ago had set a mousetrap by a hole, but the bait had been stolen and the trap had snapped on nothing at all. It was a lie when people said that sleeping with a man made no difference: you emerged from pain to this—freedom, liberty, strangeness. A stifled exhilaration moved in her breast, a kind of pride. She opened the kitchen door boldly and there at the head of the basement stairs was Dallow and the red-haired bitch, the woman he'd called Judy. They stood with lips glued together in an attitude of angry passion: they might have been inflicting on each other the greatest injury of which either was capable. The woman wore a mauve dressing gown with a dusty bunch of paper poppies, the relic of an old November. As they fought mouth to mouth the sweet-toned clock sounded the half-hour. Rose watched them from the foot of the stairs. She had lived years in a night. She knew all about this now.

The woman saw her and took her mouth from Dallow's. "Well," she said, "who's here?"

"It's Pinkie's girl," Dallow said.

"You're up early. Hungry?"

"No. I just thought—maybe I ought to light the fire."

"We don't use that fire often," the woman said. "Life's too short." She had little pimples round her mouth and an air of ardent sociability. She stroked her carrot hair and coming down the stairs to Rose fastened a mouth wet and prehensile, like a sea anemone, upon her cheek. She smelt faintly, stalely of Californian Poppy. "Well, dear," she said, "you're one of us now," and she seemed to present to Rose in a generous gesture the half-naked man, the bare dark stairs, the barren kitchen. She whispered softly so that Dallow couldn't hear: "You won't tell anyone you saw us, dear, will you? Billy gets worked up, an' it don't mean anything, not anything at all."

Rose dumbly shook her head; this foreign land absorbed her too quickly—no sooner were you past the customs than the naturalization papers were signed, you were conscripted. . . .

"There's a duck," the woman said. "Any friend of Pinkie's is a friend of all of us. You'll be meeting the boys before long."

"I doubt it," said Dallow from the top of the stairs.

"You mean . . . ?"

"We got to talk to Pinkie serious."

"Did you have Cubitt here last night?" the woman asked.

"I don't know," Rose said. "I don't know who anyone is. Someone rang the bell and swore a lot and kicked the door."

"That was Cubitt," the woman gently explained.

"We got to talk to Pinkie serious. It's not safe," Dallow said.

"Well, dear, I'd better be getting back to Billy." She paused on a step just above Rose. "If you ever want a dress cleaned, dear, you couldn't do better than give it to Billy. Though I say it who shouldn't. There's no one like Billy for getting out grease marks. An' he hardly charges a thing to lodgers." She bent down and laid a freckled finger on Rose's shoulder. "It could do with a sponge now."

"But I haven't got anything to wear, only this."

"Oh, well, dear, in that case"——she bent and whispered confidentially——"make your hubby buy you one"; then gathered the faded dressing gown around her and loped up the stairs. Rose could see a dead white leg, like something which has lived underground, covered with russet hairs, a dingy slipper flapped a loose heel. It seemed to her that everyone was very kind: there seemed to be a companionship in mortal sin.

Pride swelled in her breast as she came up from the basement. She was accepted. She had experienced as much as any woman. Back in the bedroom she sat on the bed and waited and heard the clock strike eight; she wasn't hungry; she was sensible of an immense freedom—no time table to keep, no work which had

to be done. You suffered a little pain and then came
out on the other side to this amazing liberty. There
was only one thing she wanted now—to let others see
her happiness. She could walk into Snow's now like
any other customer, rap the table with a spoon, and demand service. She could boast . . . it was a fantasy, but
sitting on the bed while time drifted by it became an
idea, something she was really able to do. In less than
half an hour they would be opening for breakfast. If
she had the money . . . she brooded with her eyes on
the soap dish. She thought: after all we are married—
in a way; he's given me nothing but that record; he
wouldn't grudge me—half a crown. She stood up and
listened, then walked softly over to the washstand.
With her fingers on the lid of the soap dish she waited
—somebody was coming down the passage: it wasn't
Judy and it wasn't Dallow—perhaps it was the man
they called Billy. The footsteps passed; she lifted the
lid and unwrapped half a crown. She had stolen biscuits, she had never stolen money before. She expected
to feel shame, but it didn't come—only again the odd
swell of pride. She was like a child in a new school who
finds she can pick up the esoteric games and passwords
in the cement playground, at once, by instinct.

In the world outside it was Sunday—she'd forgotten that: the church bells reminded her, shaking over
Brighton. Freedom again in the early sun, freedom
from the silent prayers at the altar, from the awful demands made on you at the sanctuary rail. She had
joined the other side now for ever. The half-crown was
like a medal for services rendered. People coming back
from seven-thirty Mass, people on the way to eight-

thirty Matins—she watched them in their dark clothes like a spy. She didn't envy them and she didn't despise them; they had their salvation and she had Pinkie and damnation.

At Snow's the blinds had just gone up: a girl she knew, called Maisie, was laying a few tables—the only girl she cared about, a new girl like herself and not much older. She watched her from the pavement—and Doris, the senior waitress with her habitual sneer, doing nothing at all except flick a duster where Maisie had already been. Rose clutched the half-crown closer; well, she had only got to go in, sit down, tell Doris to fetch her a cup of coffee and a roll, tip her a couple of coppers—she could patronize the whole lot of them. She was married. She was a woman. She was happy. What would they feel like when they saw her coming through the door?

And she didn't go in. That was the trouble. Suppose Doris should weep? How would she feel then, flaunting her freedom? Then through the pane she caught Maisie's eye; she stood there with a duster staring back, bony, immature, like her own image in a mirror. And *she* stood now where Pinkie had stood—outside, looking in. This was what the priests meant by one flesh. And just as she, days ago, had motioned, Maisie motioned—a slant of the eyes, an imperceptible nod towards the side door. There was no reason at all why she shouldn't go in at the front, but she obeyed Maisie. It was like doing something you'd done before.

The door opened and Maisie was there. "Rose, what's wrong?" She ought to have had wounds to show; she felt guilty at having only happiness. "I thought I'd come," she said, "and see you. I'm married."

"Married?"

"Kind of."

"Oh, Rose, what's it like?"

"Lovely."

"You got rooms?"

"Yes."

"What do you do all day?"

"Nothing at all. Just lie about."

The childish face in front of her took on the wrinkled expression of grief. "God, Rosie, you're lucky. Where did you meet him?"

"Here."

A hand bonier than her own seized her by the wrist. "Oh, Rosie, ain't he got a friend?"

She said lightly: "He's not got friends."

"Maisie," a voice called shrilly from the café. "Maisie." Tears lay ready in the eyes—in Maisie's eyes, not Doris's—she hadn't meant to hurt her friend. An impulse of pity made her say: "It's not all that good, Maisie." She tried to destroy the appearance of her own happiness. "Sometimes he's bad to me. Oh, I can tell you," she urged, "it's not all roses."

But "not roses," she thought as she turned back to the parade, "if it's not all roses, what is it?" And mechanically, walking back towards Billy's without her breakfast, she began to think: What have I done to deserve to be so happy? She'd committed a sin; that was the answer; she was having her cake in this world, not in the next, and she didn't care. She was stamped with him, as his voice was stamped on the vulcanite.

A few doors from Billy's, from a shop where they sold the Sunday papers, Dallow called to her: "Hi, kid." She stopped. "You got a visitor."

"Who?"

"Your mother."

She was stirred by a feeling of gratitude and pity; her mother hadn't been happy like this. She said: "Give me a *News of the World*. Mum likes a Sunday paper." In the back room somebody was playing a gramophone. She said to the man who kept the shop: "Sometime would you let me come here—and play a record I got?"

"O' course he will," Dallow said.

She crossed the road and rang at Billy's door. Judy opened it; she was still in her dressing gown, but underneath she now had on her corsets. "You got a visitor," she said.

"I know." Rose ran upstairs; it was the biggest triumph you could ever expect: to greet your mother for the first time in your own house, ask her to sit down on your own chair, to look at each other with an equal experience. There was nothing now, Rose felt, her mother knew about men she didn't know: that was the reward for the painful ritual upon the bed. She flung the door gladly open and there was the woman.

"What are you—?" she began, then said: "They told me it was my mother."

"I had to tell them something," the woman gently explained. She said: "Come in, dear, and shut the door behind you," as if it were *her* room.

"I'll call Pinkie."

"I'd like a word with your Pinkie." You couldn't

get round her: she stood there like the wall at the end of an alley scrawled with the obscene chalk messages of an enemy. She was the explanation—it seemed to Rose—of sudden harshnesses, of the nails pressing her wrist. She said: "You'll not see Pinkie. I won't have anyone worry Pinkie."

"He's going to have plenty to worry him soon."

"Who are you?" Rose implored her. "Why do you interfere with us? You're not the police."

"I'm like everyone else. I want Justice," the woman cheerfully remarked, as if she were ordering a pound of tea. Her big prosperous carnal face hung itself with smiles. She said: "I want to see *you're* safe."

"I don't want any help," Rose said.

"You ought to go home."

Rose clenched her hands in defence of the brass bed, the ewer of dusty water. "This is home."

"It's no good your getting angry, dear," the woman continued. "I'm not going to lose my temper with you again. It's not your fault. You don't understand how things are. Why, you poor little thing, I pity you," and she advanced across the linoleum as if she intended to take Rose in her arms.

Rose backed against the bed. "You keep your distance."

"Now don't get agitated, dear. It won't help. You see—I'm determined."

"I don't know what you mean. Why can't you talk straight?"

"There's things I've got to break—gently."

"Keep away from me. Or I'll scream."

The woman stopped. "Now let's talk sensible, dear.

I'm here for your own good. You got to be saved. Why—" she seemed for a moment at a loss for words; she said in a hushed voice: "Your life's in danger."

"You go away if that's all———"

"All!" The woman was shocked. "What do you mean, all?" Then she laughed resolutely. "Why, dear, for a moment you had me rattled. All, indeed! It's enough, isn't it? I'm not joking now. If you don't know it, you got to know it. There's nothing he wouldn't stop at."

"Well?" Rose said, giving nothing away.

The woman whispered softly across the few feet between them: "He's a murderer."

"Do you think I don't know *that?*" Rose said.

"God's sake," the woman said, "do you mean—?"

"There's nothing *you* can tell me."

"You crazy little fool—to marry him knowing that. I got a good mind to let you be."

"I won't complain," Rose said.

The woman hooked on another smile, as you hook on a wreath. "I'm not going to lose my temper, dear. Why, if I let you be, I wouldn't sleep at nights. It wouldn't be Right. Listen to me; maybe you don't know what happened. I got it all figured out now. They took Fred down under the parade, into one of those little shops and strangled him—least they would have strangled him, but his heart gave out first." She said in an awe-struck voice: "They strangled a dead man," then added sharply: "You aren't listening."

"I know it all," Rose lied. She was thinking hard— she was remembering Pinkie's warning—"Don't get mixed up." She thought wildly and vaguely: he did

his best for me; I got to help him now. She watched the
woman closely: she would never forget that plump,
good-natured, ageing face; it stared out at her like an
idiot's from the ruins of a bombed home. She said:
"Well, if you think that's how it was, why don't you
go to the police?"

"Now you're talking sense," the woman said. "I
only want to make things clear. This is the way it is,
dear. There's a certain person I've paid money to who's
told me things. And there's things I've figured out for
myself. But that person—he won't give evidence. For
reasons. And you need a lot of evidence—seeing how
the doctors made it natural death. Now if you——"

"Why don't you give it up?" Rose said. "It's over
and done, isn't it? Why not let us all be?"

"It wouldn't be right. Besides—he's dangerous.
Look what happened here the other day. You don't tell
me that was an accident."

"You haven't thought, have you," Rose said, "why
he did it? You don't kill a man for no reason."

"Well, why did he?"

"I don't know."

"Ask him."

"I don't need to know."

"You think he's in love with you," the woman said;
"he's not."

"He married me."

"And why? Because they can't make a wife give
evidence. You're just a witness like that other man
was. My dear"—she again tried to close the gap between them—"I only want to save you. He'd kill *you*
soon as look at you if he thought he wasn't safe."

With her back to the bed Rose watched her approach. She let her put her large cool pastry-making hands upon her shoulders. "People change," she said.

"Oh, no, they don't. Look at me. I've never changed. It's like those sticks of rock: bite it all the way down, you'll still read Brighton. That's human nature." She breathed mournfully over Rose's face—a sweet and winy breath.

"Confession . . . repentance," Rose whispered.

"That's just religion," the woman said. "Believe me. It's the world we got to deal with." She went pat pat on Rose's shoulder, her breath whistling in her throat. "You just pack a bag and come away with me. I'll look after you. You won't have any cause to fear."

"Pinkie . . ."

"I'll look after Pinkie."

Rose said: "I'll do anything—anything you want . . ."

"That's the way to talk, dear."

"If you'll let us alone."

The woman backed away. A momentary look of fury was hung up among the wreaths—discordantly. "Obstinate," she said. "If I was your mother . . . a good hiding." The bony and determined face stared back at her; all the fight there was in the world lay there—warships cleared for action and bombing fleets took flight—between the set eyes and the stubborn mouth. It was like the map of a campaign marked with flags.

"Another thing," the woman bluffed. "They can send you to jail. Because you know. You told me so. An accomplice, that's what you are. After the fact."

"If they took Pinkie, do you think," she asked with astonishment, "I'd mind?"

"Gracious," the woman said, "I only came here for your sake. I wouldn't have troubled to see you first, only I don't want to let the Innocent suffer"—the aphorism came clicking out like a ticket from a slot machine. "Why, won't you lift a finger to stop him killing you?"

"He wouldn't do me any harm."

"You're young. You don't know things like I do."

"There's things *you* don't know." She brooded darkly by the bed, while the woman argued on: a God wept in a garden and cried out upon a cross; Molly Carthew went to everlasting fire.

"I know one thing you don't. I know the difference between Right and Wrong. They didn't teach you *that* at school."

Rose didn't answer; the woman was quite right; the two words meant nothing to her. Their taste was extinguished by stronger foods—Good and Evil. The woman could tell her nothing she didn't know about these—she knew by tests as clear as mathematics that Pinkie was evil—what did it matter in that case whether he was right or wrong?

"You're crazy," the woman said. "I don't believe you'd lift a finger if he was killing you."

Rose came slowly back to the outer world—"greater love hath no man than this." She said: "Perhaps I wouldn't. I don't know. But perhaps . . ."

"If I wasn't a kind woman I'd give you up. But I've got a sense of responsibility." Her smiles hung very insecurely when she paused at the door. "You can warn that young husband of yours," she said, "I'm getting warm to him. I got my plans." She went out and closed the door; then flung it open again for a last attack. "You be careful, dear," she said. "You don't want a murderer's baby," and grinned mercilessly across the bare bedroom floor. "You better take precautions."

Precautions . . . Rose stood at the bed and pressed a hand against her body, as if under that pressure she could discover . . . *That* had never entered her mind; and the thought of what she might have let herself in for came like a sense of glory. A child . . . and that child would have a child . . . it was like raising an army of friends for Pinkie. If They damned him and her, They'd have to damn them too. She'd see to that. There was no end to what the two of them had done last night upon the bed : it was an eternal act.

2

The Boy stood back in the doorway of the newspaper shop and saw Ida Arnold come out. She looked a little flushed, a little haughty sailing down the street; she paused and gave a small boy a penny. He was so surprised he dropped it, staring after her heavy and immaculate retreat.

The Boy gave a sudden laugh, rusty and half-hearted. He thought: She's drunk . . . Dallow said: "That was a narrow squeak."

"What was?"

"Your mother-in-law."

"Her . . . how did *you* know?"

"She asked for Rose."

The Boy put down the *News of the World* upon the
counter; a headline stood up—"Assault on Schoolgirl
in Epping Forest." He walked across to Billy's, thinking hard, and up the stairs. Half-way he stopped; she'd
dropped an artificial violet from a spray; he picked it
off the stair. it smelt of Californian Poppy. Then he
went in, holding the flower concealed in his palm, and
Rose came across to him, welcoming. He avoided her
mouth. "Well," he said and tried to express in his face
a kind of rough and friendly jocularity, "I hear your
Mum's been visiting you," and waited anxiously and
avidly for her reply.

"Oh, yes," Rose said doubtfully, "she did look in."

"Not one of her moody days?"

"No."

He kneaded the violet furiously in his palm. "Well,
did she think it suited you—being married?"

"Oh, yes, I think she did. . . . She didn't say much."

The Boy went across to the bed and slipped on his
coat. He said: "You been out too, I hear."

"I thought I'd go and see friends."

"What friends?"

"Oh—at Snow's."

"You call *them* friends?" he asked with contempt.
"Well, did you see them?"

"Not really. Only one—Maisie. For a minute."

"And then you got back here in time to catch your
Mum. Don't you want to know what I've been up to?"

She stared stupidly at him; his manner scared her.
"If you like."

"What do you mean, if I like? You aren't as dumb as that." The wire anatomy of the flower pricked his palm. He said: "I got to have a word with Dallow. Wait here," and left her.

He called to Dallow across the street, and when Dallow joined him, he said: "Where's Judy?"

"Upstairs."

"Billy working?"

"Yes."

"Come down to the kitchen then." He led the way down the stairs; in the basement dusk his feet crunched on dead coke. He sat down on the edge of the kitchen table and said: "Have a drink."

"Too early," Dallow said.

"Listen," the Boy said. An expression of pain crossed his face as if he was about to wring out an appalling confession. "I trust you," he said.

"Well," Dallow said, "what's getting you?"

"Things aren't too good," the Boy said. "People are getting wise to a lot of things. Christ," he said, "I killed Spicer and I married the girl. Have I got to have a massacre?"

"Was Cubitt here last night?"

"He was and I sent him away. He begged—he wanted a fiver."

"Did you give it him?"

"Of course I didn't. D'you think I'd let myself be blackmailed by a thing like him?"

"You oughta have given him something."

"It's not him I'm worried about."

"You ought to be."

"Be quiet, can't you?" the Boy suddenly and shrilly squealed at him. He jerked his thumb towards the ceiling. "It's *her* I'm worried about." He opened his hand and said: "God damn it, I dropped that flower."

"Flower . . . ?"

"Be quiet, can't you, and listen," he said low and furiously. "That wasn't her Mum."

"Who was it?" Dallow said.

"The buer who's been asking questions . . . the one who was with Fred in the taxi the day . . ." He put his head for a moment between his hands in an attitude of grief or desperation—but it wasn't either. He said: "I got a headache. I got to think clear. Rose told me it was her Mum. What's she after?"

"You don't think," Dallow said, "she's talked?"

"I got to find out," the Boy said.

"I'd have trusted her," Dallow said, "all the way."

"I wouldn't trust anyone that far. Not you, Dallow."

"But if she's talking, why does she talk to *her*—why not to the police?"

"Why don't any of them talk to the police?" He stared with troubled eyes at the cold stove. He was haunted by his ignorance. "I don't know what they're getting at." Other people's feelings bored at his brain; he had never before felt this desire to understand. He said passionately: "I'd like to carve the whole bloody boiling."

"After all," Dallow said, "she don't know much. She only knows it wasn't Fred left the card. If you ask me she's a dumb little piece. Affectionate, I dare say, but dumb."

"You're the dumb one, Dallow. She knows a lot. She knows I killed Fred."

"You sure?"

"She told me so."

"An' she married you?" Dallow said. "I'm damned if I understand what they *want*."

"If we don't do something quick it looks to me as if all Brighton'll know we killed Fred. All England. The whole God-damned world."

"What can *we* do?"

The Boy went over to the basement window crunching on the coke: a tiny asphalt yard with an old dustbin which hadn't been used for weeks, a blocked grating, and a sour smell. He said: "It's no good stopping now. We got to go on." People passed overhead, invisible from the waist upwards; a shabby shoe scuffled the pavement wearing out the toecap; a bearded face stooped suddenly into sight looking for a cigarette end. He said slowly: "It ought to be easy to quiet her. We quieted Fred an' Spicer, an' she's only a kid . . ."

"Don't be crazy," Dallow said. "You can't go on like that."

"Maybe I got to. No choice. Maybe it's always that way—you start and then you go on going on."

"We're making a mistake," Dallow said. "I'd stake you a fiver she's straight. Why—you told me yourself —she's stuck on you."

"Why did she say it was her Mum then?" He watched a woman go by: young as far as the thighs; you couldn't see further up than that. A spasm of disgust shook him; he'd given way; he had even been proud of *that*—what Spicer did with Sylvie in a Lan-

cia. Oh, it was all right, he supposed, to take every
drink once—if you could stop at that, say "never
again," not go on—going on.

"I can tell it myself," Dallow said. "Clear as clear.
She's stuck on you all right."

Stuck; high heels trodden over, bare legs moving
out of sight. "If she's stuck," he said, "it makes it
easier—she'll do what I say." A piece of newspaper
blew along the street: the wind was from the sea.

Dallow said: "Pinkie, I won't stand for any more
killing."

The Boy turned his back to the window and his
mouth made a bad replica of mirth. He said: "But suppose she killed herself?" An insane pride bobbed in his
breast; he felt inspired; it was like a love of life returning to the blank heart: the empty tenement and then
the seven devils worse than the first. . . .

Dallow said: "For Christ's sake, Pinkie. You're
imagining things."

"We'll soon see," the Boy said.

He came up the stairs from the basement, looking
this way and that for the scented flower of cloth and
wire. He could see it nowhere. Rose's voice said:
"Pinkie" over the new banister; she was waiting there
for him anxiously on the landing. She said: "Pinkie, I
got to tell you. I wanted to keep you from worrying—
but there's got to be someone I don't have to lie to.
That wasn't Mum, Pinkie."

He came slowly up, watching her closely, judging.
"Who was it?"

"It was that woman. The one who used to come to
Snow's asking questions."

"What did she want?"

"She wanted me to go away from here."

"Why?"

"Pinkie, she *knows*."

"Why did you say it was your Mum?"

"I told you—I didn't want you to worry."

He was beside her, watching her; she faced him back with a worried candour, and he found that he believed her as much as he believed anyone; his restless cocky pride subsided; he felt an odd sense of peace, as if—for a while—he hadn't got to plan.

"But then," Rose went anxiously on, "I thought—perhaps you ought to worry."

"That's all right," he said and put his hand on her shoulder in an awkward embrace.

"She said something about paying money to some-one. She said she was getting warm to you."

"I don't worry," he said and pressed her back. Then he stopped, looking over her shoulder. In the doorway of the room the flower lay. He had dropped it when he closed the door, and then—he began at once to calculate—she followed me, of course she saw the flower, she knew I *knew*. That explains everything, the confession. . . . All the while he was down there below with Dallow she had been wondering what she had to do to cover her mistake. A clean breast—the phrase made him laugh—a clean tart's breast, the kind of breast Sylvie sported—cleaned up for use. He laughed again; the horror of the world lay like infection in his throat.

"What is it, Pinkie?"

"That flower," he said.

"What flower?"

"The one *she* brought."

"What . . . where . . . ?"

Perhaps she hadn't seen it then . . . maybe she was straight after all . . . who knows? Who, he thought, will ever know? And with a kind of sad excitement— what did it matter anyway? He had been a fool to think it made any difference; he couldn't afford to take risks. If she were straight and loved him it would be just so much easier, that was all. He repeated : "I don't worry. I don't need to worry. I know what to do. Even if she got to know everything I know what to do." He watched her shrewdly. He brought his hand round and pressed her breast. "It won't hurt," he said.

"What won't hurt, Pinkie?"

"The way I'll manage things. . . ." He started agilely away from his dark suggestion. "You don't want to leave me, do you?"

"Never," Rose said.

"That's what I meant," he said. "You wrote it, didn't you. Trust me, I'll manage things if the worst comes to the worst—so it won't hurt either of us. You can trust me," he went smoothly and rapidly on, while she watched him with the dazed tricked expression of someone who has promised too much, too quickly. "I knew," he said, "you'd feel like that. About us never parting. What you wrote."

She whispered with dread. "It's a mortal . . ."

"Just one more," he said. "What difference does it make? You can't be damned twice over, and we're damned already—so they say. And anyway it's only if the worst . . . if she finds out about Spicer."

"Spicer," Rose moaned, "you don't mean Spicer too . . . ?"

"I only mean," he said, "if she finds out that I was here—in the house—but we don't need to worry till she does."

"But Spicer," Rose said.

"I was here," he said, "when it happened, that's all. I didn't even see him fall, but my solicitor . . ."

"He was here too?" Rose said.

"Oh, yes."

"I remember now," Rose said. "Of course I read the paper. They couldn't believe, could they, that he'd cover up anything really wrong? A solicitor."

"Old Drewitt," the Boy said, "why"—again the unused laugh came into rusty play—"he's the Soul of Honour." He pressed her breast again and uttered his qualified encouragement. "Oh, no, there's no cause to worry till *she* finds out. Even then, you see, there's *that* escape. But perhaps she never will. And if she doesn't, why"—his fingers touched her with secret revulsion —"we'll just go on, won't we"—and he tried to make the horror sound like love—"the way we are."

3

But it was the Soul of Honour none the less who really worried him. If Cubitt had given that woman the idea that there was something wrong about Spicer's death as well, whom could she go to but Mr. Drewitt? She wouldn't attempt anything with Dallow; but a man of law—when he was as clever as Drewitt was— was always frightened of the law. Drewitt was like a man who kept a tame lion cub in his house: he could never be quite certain that the lion to whom he had taught so many tricks, to beg and eat out of his hand, might not one day unexpectedly mature and turn on him; perhaps he might cut his cheek shaving—and the law would smell the blood.

In the early afternoon he couldn't wait any longer; he set out for Drewitt's house. First he told Dallow to keep an eye on the girl in case . . . More than ever yet he had the sense that he was being driven further and deeper than he'd ever meant to go. A curious and cruel pleasure touched him—he didn't really care so very much—it was being decided for him, and all he had to do was to let himself easily go. He knew what the end might be—it didn't horrify him: it was easier than life.

Mr. Drewitt's house was in a street parallel to the railway, beyond the terminus; it was shaken by shunting engines; the soot settled continuously on the glass and the brass plate. From the basement window a woman with tousled hair stared suspiciously up at him —she was always there watching visitors from a hard and bitter face; she was never explained: he had always thought she was the cook, but it appeared now she was the "spouse"—twenty-five years at the game. The door was opened by a girl with grey underground skin—an unfamiliar face. "Where's Tilly?" the Boy said.

"She's left."

"Tell Drewitt, Pinkie's here."

"He's not seeing anyone," the girl said. "This is a Sunday, ain't it?"

"He'll see me." The Boy walked into the hall, opened a door, sat down in a room lined with filing boxes; he knew the way. "Go on," he said, "tell him. I know he's asleep. You wake him up."

"You seem to be at home here," the girl said.

"I am." He knew what those filing boxes contained marked Rex *v.* Innes, Rex *v.* T. Collins—they contained just air. A train shunted and the empty boxes quivered on the shelves; the window was open only a crack, but the radio from next door came in—Radio Luxembourg.

"Shut the window," he said. She shut it sullenly. It made no difference; the walls were so thin, you could hear the neighbour move behind the shelves like a rat. He said: "Does that music always play?"

"Unless it's a talk," she said.

"What are you waiting for? Go and wake him."

"He told me not to. He's got indigestion."

Again the room vibrated and the music wailed through the wall.

"He's always got it after lunch. Go on and wake him."

"It's a Sunday."

"You'd better go quick," he obscurely threatened her, and she slammed the door on him—a little plaster fell.

Under his feet in the basement someone was moving the furniture about—the spouse, he thought. A train hooted and a smother of smoke fell into the street. Over his head Mr. Drewitt began to speak—there was nothing anywhere to keep out sound. Then footsteps

Mr. Drewitt's smile went on as the door opened. "What brings our young cavalier?"

"I just wanted to see you," the Boy said. "See how you were getting along." A spasm of pain drove the smile from Mr. Drewitt's face. "You ought to eat more careful," the Boy said.

"Nothing does it any good," Mr. Drewitt said.

"You drink too much."

"Eat, drink, for tomorrow . . ." Mr. Drewitt writhed with his hand on his stomach.

"You got an ulcer?" the Boy said.

"No, no, nothing like that."

"You ought to have your inside photographed."

"I don't believe in the knife," Mr. Drewitt said quickly and nervously, as if it was a suggestion constantly made for which he had to have the answer on the tongue.

"Don't that music ever stop?"

"When I get tired of it," Mr. Drewitt said, "I beat on the wall." He took a paperweight off his desk and struck the wall twice; the music broke into a high oscillating wail and ceased. They could hear the neighbour move furiously behind the shelves. "How now! a rat?" Mr. Drewitt quoted. The house shook as a heavy engine pulled out. "Polonius," Mr. Drewitt explained.

"Polony? What polony?"

"No, no," Mr. Drewitt said. "The rank intruding fool, I mean. In Hamlet."

"Listen," the Boy said impatiently, "has a woman been round here asking questions?"

"What sort of questions?"

"About Spicer."

Mr. Drewitt said with sickly despair: "Are people asking questions?" He sat down quickly and bent with indigestion. "I've just been waiting for this."

"There's no need to get scared," the Boy said. "They can't prove anything. You just stick to your story." He sat down opposite Mr. Drewitt and regarded him with grim contempt. "You don't want to ruin yourself," he said.

Mr. Drewitt looked sharply up. "Ruin?" he said. "I'm ruined now." He vibrated with the engines on his chair, and somebody in the basement slammed the floor beneath their feet. "What ho, old mole!" Mr. Drewitt said. "The spouse—you've never met the spouse."

"I've seen her," the Boy said.

"Twenty-five years. Then this." The smoke came down outside the window like a blind. "Has it ever occurred to you," Mr. Drewitt said, "that you're lucky? The worst that can happen to you is you'll hang. But I can rot."

"What's upsetting you?" the Boy said. He was confused—as if a weak man had struck him back. He wasn't used to this—the infringement of other people's lives. Confession was an act one did—or didn't do —oneself.

"When I took on your work," Mr. Drewitt said, "I lost the only other job I had. The Bakely Trust. And now I've lost you."

"You got everything there is of mine."

"There won't be any more soon. Colleoni's going to take over this place from you, and he's got his lawyer. A man in London. A swell."

"I haven't thrown my sponge in yet." He sniffed the air tainted with gasometers and said: "I know what's wrong with you. You're drunk."

"On Empire burgundy," Mr. Drewitt said. "I want to tell you things. Pinkie, I want"—the literary phrase came glibly out—"to unburden myself."

"I don't want to hear them. I'm not interested in *your* troubles."

"I married beneath me," Mr. Drewitt said. "It was my tragic mistake. I was young. An affair of uncontrollable passion. I was a passionate man," he said, wriggling with indigestion. "You've seen her," he said, "now. My God." He leant forward and said in a whisper: "I watch the little typists go by carrying their little cases. I'm quite harmless. A man may watch. My God, how neat and trim!" He broke off, his hand vibrating on the chair arm. "Listen to the old mole down there. She's ruined me." His old lined face had taken a holiday—from bonhomie, from cunning, from the legal jest. It was a Sunday and it was itself. Mr. Drewitt said: "You know what Mephistopheles said to Faustus when he asked where Hell was? He said: 'Why, this is Hell, nor are we out of it.'" The Boy watched him—with fascination and fear.

"She's cleaning in the kitchen," Mr. Drewitt said, "but she'll be coming up later. You ought to meet her —it'd be a treat. The old hag. What a joke it would be, wouldn't it, to tell her—everything. That I'm concerned in a murder. That people are asking questions. To pull down the whole damned house like Samson." He stretched his arms wide and contracted them in the pain of indigestion. "You're right," he said, "I've got an ulcer. But I won't have the knife. I'd rather die. I'm drunk too. On Empire burgundy. Do you see that photo there—by the door? A school group. Lancaster College. Not one of the great schools perhaps, but you'll find it in the Public Schools Year Book. You'll see me there—cross-legged in the bottom row. In a straw hat." He said softly: "We had field days with Harrow. A rotten set they were. No *esprit de corps.*"

The Boy didn't so much as turn his head to look; he had never known Drewitt like this before: it was a frightening and an entrancing exhibition. A man was coming alive before his eyes: he could see the nerves set to work in the agonized flesh, thought bloom in the transparent brain.

"To think," Mr. Drewitt said, "an old Lancaster boy—to be married to that mole in the cellarage down there and to have as only client"—he gave his mouth an expression of fastidious disgust—"you. What would old Manders say? A great head."

He had the bit between his teeth; he was like a man determined to live before he died; all the insults he had swallowed from police witnesses, the criticisms of magistrates, regurgitated from his tormented stomach. There was nothing he wouldn't tell to anybody. An enormous self-importance was blossoming out of his humiliation; his wife, the Empire burgundy, the empty files, and the vibration of locomotives on the line, they were the important landscape of his great drama.

"You talk too easily," the Boy said.

"Talk?" Mr. Drewitt said. "I could shake the world. Let them put me in the dock if they like. I'll give them —revelation. I've sunk so deep I carry"—he was shaken by an enormous windy self-esteem, he hiccuped twice—"the secrets of the sewer."

"If I'd known you drank," the Boy said, "I wouldn't have touched you."

"I drink—on Sundays. It's the day of rest." He suddenly beat his foot upon the floor and screamed furiously. "Be quiet down there."

"You need a holiday," the Boy said.

"I sit here and sit here—the bell rings, but it's only the groceries—tinned salmon, she has a passion for tinned salmon. Then I ring the bell—and in comes that pasty stupid—I watch the typists going by. I could embrace their little portable machines."

"You'd be all right," the Boy said—nervous and shaken with the conception of another life growing in the brain—"if you took a holiday."

"Sometimes," Mr. Drewitt said, "I have an urge to expose myself—shamefully—in a park."

"I'll give you money."

"No money can heal a mind diseased. This is Hell, nor are we out of it. How much could you spare?"

"Twenty nicker."

"It would go only a little way."

"Boulogne—why not slip across the Channel?" the Boy said with horrified disgust. "Enjoy yourself"— watching the grubby and bitten nails, the shaky hands which were the instruments of pleasure.

"Could you spare some small sum like that, my boy? Don't let me rob you; though, of course, 'I have done the state some service.' "

"You can have it tomorrow—on conditions. You got to leave by the midday boat—stay away as long as you can. Maybe I'll send you more." It was like fastening a leech onto the flesh—he felt weakness and disgust. "Let me know when it's finished and I'll see."

"I'll go, Pinkie—when you say. And—you won't tell my spouse?"

"I keep *my* mouth shut."

"Of course. I trust you, Pinkie, and you can trust me. Recuperated by this holiday I shall return——"

"Take a long one."

"Bullying police sergeants shall recognize my renewed astuteness. Defending the outcast."

"I'll send the money first thing. Till then you don't see anyone. You go back to bed. Your indigestion's cruel. If anyone comes round you're not in."

"As you say, Pinkie, as you say."

It was the best he could do. He let himself out of the house and, looking down, met in the basement the hard suspicious gaze of Mr. Drewitt's spouse; she had a duster in her hand and she watched him like a bitter enemy from her cave, under the foundations. He crossed the road and took one more look at the villa, and there in an upper window half concealed by the curtains stood Mr. Drewitt. He wasn't watching the Boy—he was just looking out—hopelessly, for what might turn up. But it was a Sunday and there weren't any typists.

4

He said to Dallow: "You got to watch the place. I don't trust him a yard. I can just see him looking out there, waiting for something, and seeing *her* . . ."

"He wouldn't be such a fool."

"He's drunk. He says he's in Hell."

Dallow laughed: "Hell. That's good."

"You're a fool, Dallow."

"I don't believe in what my eyes don't see."

"They don't see much then," the Boy said. He left Dallow and went upstairs. But, oh, if this was Hell, he thought, it wasn't so bad: the old-fashioned telephone, the narrow stairs, the snug and dusty darkness—it wasn't like Drewitt's house, comfortless, shaken, with the old bitch in the basement. He opened the door of his room and there, he thought, was *his* enemy—he looked round with angry disappointment at his changed room—the position of everything a little altered and the whole place swept and clean and tidied. He condemned her: "I told you not to."

"I've only cleared up, Pinkie."

It was her room now, not his: the wardrobe and the washstand shifted, and the bed—of course she hadn't forgotten the bed. It was her Hell now if it was anybody's—he disowned it. He felt driven out, but any change must be for the worse. He watched her like an enemy, disguising his hatred, trying to read age into her face, how she would look one day staring up from his basement. He had come back wrapped in another person's fate—a doubled darkness.

"Don't you like it, Pinkie?"

He wasn't Drewitt: he'd got guts; he hadn't lost his fight. He said: "Oh, this—it's fine. It was just I wasn't expecting it."

She misread his constraint. "Bad news?"

"Not yet. We got to be prepared, of course. I *am*

prepared." He went to the window and stared out through a forest of wireless masts towards a cloudy peaceful Sunday sky, then back at the changed room. This was how it might look if he had gone away and other tenants . . . He watched her closely while he did his sleight of hand passing off his idea as hers. "I got the car all ready. We could go out into the country where no one would hear . . ." He measured her terror carefully and before she could pass the card back to him, he changed his tone. "That's only if the worst comes to the worst." The phrase intrigued him; he repeated it: the worst—that was the stout woman with her glassy righteous eye coming up the smoky road— to the worst—and that was drunken ruined Mr. Drewitt watching from behind the curtains for just one typist.

"It won't happen," he encouraged her.

"No," she passionately agreed. "It won't, it can't." Her enormous certainty had a curious effect on him— it was as if that plan of his too were being tidied, shifted, swept until he couldn't recognize his own. He wanted to argue that it *might* happen; he discovered in himself an odd nostalgia for the darkest act of all.

She said: "I'm so happy. It can't be so bad after all."

"What do you mean?" he said. "Not bad? It's mortal sin." He glanced with furious disgust at the made bed as if he contemplated a repetition of the act there and then—to thrust the lesson home.

"I know," she said. "I know, but still——"

"There's only one thing worse," he said. It was as if she were escaping him; already she was domesticating their black alliance.

"I'm happy," she argued bewilderedly. "You're good to me."

"That doesn't mean a thing."

"Listen," she said, "what's that?" A thin wailing came through the window.

"The kid next door."

"Why doesn't somebody quiet it?"

"It's a Sunday. Maybe they're out." He said. "You want to do anything? The flickers?"

She wasn't listening to him; the unhappy continuous cry absorbed her; she wore a look of responsibility and maturity. "Somebody ought to see what it wants," she said.

"It's just hungry·or something."

"Maybe it's ill." She listened with a kind of vicarious agony. "Things happen to babies suddenly. You don't know what it mightn't be."

"It isn't yours."

She turned bemused eyes towards him. "No," she said, "but I was thinking—it might be." She said with passion : "I wouldn't leave it all an afternoon."

He said uneasily : "They haven't either. It's stopped. What did I tell you?" But her words lodged in his brain—"It might be." He had never thought of that; he watched her with terror and disgust as if he were watching the ugly birth itself, the rivet of another life already pinning him down, and she stood there listening—with relief and patience, as if already she had passed through years of this anxiety and knew that the relief never lasted long and that the anxiety always began again.

5

Nine o'clock in the morning; he came furiously out into the passage; the morning sun trickled in over the top of the door below, staining the telephone. He called: "Dallow, Dallow!"

Dallow came slowly up from the basement in his shirt sleeves. He said: "Hallo, Pinkie. You look as if you hadn't slept."

The Boy said: "You keeping away from me?"

"Of course I'm not, Pinkie. Only—you being married—I thought you'd want to be alone."

"You call it," the Boy said, "being alone?" He came down the stairs; he carried in his hand the mauve scented envelope Judy had thrust under the door. He hadn't opened it. His eyes were bloodshot. He carried down with him the marks of a fever—the beating pulse and the hot forehead and the restless brain.

"Johnnie phoned me early," Dallow said. "He's been watching since yesterday. No one's been to see Drewitt. We got scared for nothing."

The Boy paid him no attention. He said: "I want to be alone, Dallow. Really alone."

"You been taking on too much at your age," Dallow said and began to laugh. "Two nights . . ."

The Boy said: "She's got to go before she—" he couldn't express the magnitude of his fear—or its nature to anyone: it was like an ugly secret.

"It's not safe to quarrel," Dallow said quickly and cautiously.

"No," the Boy said, "it won't ever be safe again. I
315

know that. No divorce. Nothing at all except dying.
All the same," he put his hand on the vulcanite for
coolness. "I told you—I had a plan."

"It was crazy. Why should that poor kid want to
die?"

He said with bitterness: "She loves me. She says she
wants to be with me always. And if I don't want to
live . . ."

"Dally," a voice called, "Dally." The Boy looked
sharply and guiltily round; he hadn't heard Judy moving silently above in her naked feet and her corsets.
He was absorbed, trying to get the plan straight in the
confused hot brain, tied up in its complexity, uncertain who it was who had to die . . . himself or her or
both. . . .

"What you want, Judy?" Dallow said.

"Billy's finished your coat."

"Let it be," Dallow said. "I'll fetch it in a shake."

She blew him an avaricious, unsatisfied kiss and
padded back to her room.

"I started something there all right," Dallow said.
"Sometimes I wish I hadn't. I don't want trouble with
poor old Billy, an' she's so careless."

The Boy looked at Dallow broodingly, as if perhaps
he knew from his long service what one did.

"Suppose," he said, "you had a child?"

"Oh," Dallow said, "I leave that to her. It's *her*
funeral." He said: "You got a letter there from Colleoni?"

"But what does she do?"

"The usual, I suppose."

"And if she doesn't," the Boy persisted, "an' she began a child?"

"There's pills."

"They don't always work, do they?" the Boy said. He had thought he'd learned everything now, but he was back in his state of appalled ignorance.

"They never work, if you ask me," Dallow said. "Colleoni written?"

"If Drewitt grassed, there wouldn't be a hope, would there?" the Boy brooded.

"He won't grass. And anyway he'll be in Boulogne tonight."

"But *if* he did . . . or say I thought he had . . . there'd be nothing to do then, would there, but kill myself? And she—she wouldn't want to live without me. If she thought . . . And all the time perhaps it wouldn't be true. They call it—don't they?—a suicide pact."

"What's got you, Pinkie? You're not giving in?"

"I mightn't die."

"That's murder too."

"They don't hang you for it."

"You're crazy, Pinkie. Why, I wouldn't stand for a thing like that." He gave the Boy a shocked and friendly blow. "You're joking, Pinkie—there's nothing wrong with the poor kid—except for liking you." The Boy said not a thing; he had an air of removing his thoughts, like heavy bales, and stacking them inside, turning the key on all the world. "You want to lie down a bit and rest," Dallow said uneasily.

"I want to lie down alone," the Boy said. He went

slowly upstairs; when he opened the door he knew
what he would see; he looked away as if to shut out
temptation from the ascetic and the poisoned brain.
He heard her say:

"I was just going out for a while, Pinkie. Is there
anything I can do for you?"

Anything . . . His brain staggered with the immen-
sity of its demands. He said gently: "Nothing," and
schooled his voice to softness. "Come back soon. We
got things to talk about."

"Worried?"

"Not worried. I got things straight," he gestured
with deadly humour at his head, "in the box here."

He was aware of her fear and tension—the sharp
breath and the silence and then the voice steeled for
despair. "Not bad news, Pinkie?"

He flew out at her: "For Christ's sake, go!"

He heard her coming back across the room to him,
but he wouldn't look up; this was his room, his life; he
felt that if he could concentrate enough, it would be
possible to eliminate every sign of her . . . everything
would be just the same as before . . . before he entered
Snow's and felt under that cloth for a ticket which
wasn't there and began the deception and shame. The
whole origin of the thing was lost: he could hardly remember Hale as a person or his murder as a crime—it
was all now him and her.

"If anything's happened . . . you can tell me . . .
I'm not scared. There must be some way, Pinkie, not
to . . ." She implored him: "Let's talk about it first."

He said: "You're fussed about nothing. I want you
to go all right, you can go," he went savagely on, "to

. . ." But he stopped in time, raked up a smile, ". . . go and enjoy yourself."

"I won't be gone long, Pinkie." He heard the door close, but he knew she was lingering in the passage— the whole house was hers now. He put his hand in his pocket and pulled out the paper—"I don't care what you do. . . . Wherever you go, I'll go too." It sounded like a letter read in court and printed in the newspapers. He heard her feet upon the stairs going down.

Dallow looked in and said: "Drewitt should be starting now. I'll feel better when he's on that boat. You don't think, do you, she'd get the police to hunt him out?"

"She hasn't got the evidence," the Boy said. "You're safe enough when he's out of the way." He spoke dully as if he'd lost all interest in whether Drewitt went or stayed—it was something which concerned other people. He'd gone beyond that.

"You too," Dallow said. "You'll be safe."

The Boy didn't answer.

"I told Johnnie to see he got on the boat safe and then phone us. He'll be ringing up now almost any time. We oughta have a party to celebrate, Pinkie. My God, how sunk she'll feel when she turns up there and finds him gone!" He went to the window and looked out. "Maybe we'll have some peace then. We'll have got out of it easy. When you come to think. Hale and poor old Spicer. I wonder where he is now." He stared sentimentally out through the thin chimney smoke and the wireless masts. "What about you and me—an' the girl, of course—shifting off to some new place? It's not going to be so good here now with Colleoni butting in." He turned back into the room. "That letter"—and the telephone began to ring. He said: "That'll be Johnnie," and hurried out.

It occurred to the Boy that it wasn't the sound of feet on the stairs he recognized, it was the sound of the stairs themselves—he could tell those particular stairs even under a stranger's weight; there was always a creak at the third and seventh step down. This was the place he had come to after Kite had picked him up—he had been coughing on the Palace Pier in the bitter cold, listening to the violin wailing behind the glass; Kite had given him a cup of hot coffee and brought him here—God knows why—perhaps because he was out and wasn't down, perhaps because a man like Kite needed a little sentiment, like a tart who keeps a pekinese. Kite had opened the door of No. 63 and the first thing he'd seen was Dallow embracing Judy on the stairs and the first thing he had smelt was Billy's iron in the basement. Everything had been of a piece: nothing had really changed; Kite had died, but he had prolonged Kite's existence—not touching liquor, biting his nails in the Kite way, until *she* came and altered everything.

Dallow's voice drifted up the stairs: "Oh, I dunno. Send some pork sausages. Or a tin of beans."

He came back into the room. "It wasn't Johnnie," he said. "Just the International. We oughta be hearing from Johnnie." He sat anxiously down on the bed and said: "That letter from Colleoni, what does it say?"

The Boy tossed it across to him. "Why," Dallow said, "you haven't opened it." He began to read: "Well," he said, "it's bad, of course. It's what I thought. And yet it's not so bad either. Not when you come to look at it." He glanced cautiously up over the mauve notepaper at the Boy, sitting there by the wash-stand, thinking. "We're played out here, that's what it comes to. He's got most of our boys and all the bookies. But he doesn't want trouble. He's a business man—he says a fight like you had the other day brings a track into—disrepute. Disrepute," Dallow repeated thoughtfully.

"He means," the Boy said, "the suckers stay away."

"Well, that's sense. He says he'll pay you three hundred nicker for the goodwill. Goodwill?"

"He means not carving his geezers."

"It's a good offer," Dallow said. "It's what I was saying just now—we could clear out right away from this damned town and this phony buer asking ques-tions, start again on a good line—or maybe retire altogether, buy a pub, you an' me—an' the girl, of course." He said: "When the hell's Johnnie going to phone? It makes me nervous."

The Boy said nothing for a while, looking at his bitten nails. Then he said: "Of course—you know the world, Dallow. You've travelled."

"There's not many places I don't know," Dallow agreed, "between here and Leicester."

"I was born here," the Boy said. "I know Good-wood and Hurst Park. I've been to Newmarket. But I'd feel a stranger away from here." He claimed with dreary pride: "I suppose I'm real Brighton"—as if his single heart contained all the cheap amusements, the Pullman cars, the unloving week-ends in gaudy hotels, and the sadness after coition.

A bell rang. "Listen," Dallow said. "Is that Johnnie?"

But it was only the front door. Dallow looked at his watch. "I can't think what's keeping him," he said. "Drewitt oughta be on board by now."

"Well," the Boy said—with gloom, "we change, don't we? It's as you say. We got to see the world. . . . After all I took to drink, didn't I? I can take to other things."

"An' you got a girl," Dallow said with hollow cheeriness. "You're growing up, Pinkie—like your father."

Like my father . . . The Boy was shaken again with his nocturnal Saturday disgust. He couldn't blame his father now . . . it was what you came to . . . you got mixed up, and then, he supposed, the habit grew . . . you gave yourself away weekly. You couldn't even blame the girl. It was life getting at you . . . there even were the blind seconds when you thought it fine. "We'd be safer," he said, "without her," touching the loving message in the trouser pocket.

"She's safe enough now. She's crazy about you."

"The trouble with you is," the Boy said, "you don't look ahead. There's years . . . And any day she might fall for a new face or get vexed or something . . . if I don't keep her smooth . . . there's no security," he said. The door opened and there she was back again; he bit his words short and smirked a welcome. But it wasn't hard—she took deception with such hopeless ease that he could feel a sort of tenderness for her stupidity and a companionship in her goodness—they were both doomed in their own way. Again he got the sense that she completed him.

She said: "I hadn't got a key. I had to ring. I felt afraid soon as I'd gone out that something might be wrong. I wanted to be here, Pinkie."

"There's nothing wrong," he said. The telephone began to ring. "There, you see, there's Johnnie now," he said to Dallow joylessly. "You got your wish."

They heard his voice at the phone shrill with suspense: "That you, Johnnie? Yes? What was that? You don't mean . . . ? Oh, yes, we'll see you later. Of course you'll get your money." He came back up and at the right place the stairs creaked—his broad brutal and innocent face bore good news like a boar's head at a feast. "That's fine," he said, "fine. I was getting anxious, I don't mind telling you. But he's on the boat now an' she left the pier ten minutes ago. We got to celebrate this. By God, you're clever, Pinkie. You think of everything."

6

Ida Arnold had had more than a couple. She sang softly to herself over the stout—"One night in an alley Lord Rothschild said to me . . ." The heavy motion of the waves under the pier was like the sound of bath water; it set her going. She sat there massively alone—no harm in her for anybody in the world—minus one; the world was a good place if you didn't weaken; she was like the chariot in a triumph—be-

hind her were all the big battalions—right's right, an
eye for an eye, when you want to do a thing well, do
it yourself. Phil Corkery made his way towards her—
behind him through the long glass windows of the tea
room you could see the lights of Hove; green copper
Metropole domes lay in the layer of last light under
the heavy nocturnal clouds slumping down. The spray
tossed up like fine rain against the windows. Ida
Arnold stopped singing and said: "Do you see what
I see?"

Phil Corkery sat down; it wasn't like summer at all
in this glass breakwater; he looked cold in his grey
flannel trousers and his blazer with the old something-
or-other arms on the pocket; a little pinched, all passion spent. "It's them," he said wearily. "How did
you know they'd be here?"

"I didn't," Ida said. "It's fate."

"I'm tired of the sight of them."

"But think *how* tired," she said with cheery relish,
"*they* are." They looked across a waste of empty tables
towards France, towards the Boy and Rose—and a
man and woman they didn't recognize. If the party
had come there to celebrate or something, she had
spoiled their fun. The Guinness welled warmly up
into her throat; she had an enormous sense of well-
being; she belched and said: "Pardon me," lifting a
black gloved hand. She said: "I suppose he's gone
too?"

"He's gone."

"We aren't lucky with our witnesses," she said.
"First Spicer, then the girl, then Drewitt, and now
Cubitt."

"He took the first morning train—with your money."

"Never mind," she said. "They're alive. They'll come back. An' I can wait—thanks to Black Boy."

Phil Corkery looked at her askance: it was astonishing that he had ever had the nerve to send her—to send that power and purpose—postcards from seaside resorts; from Hastings a crab from whose stomach you could wind out a series of views; from Eastbourne a baby sitting upon a rock which lifted to disclose the High Street and Boots Library and a fernery; from Bournemouth (was it?) a bottle containing photographs of the promenade, the rock garden, the new swimming pool. . . . It was like offering a bun to an elephant in Africa. He was shaken by a sense of terrific force . . . when she wanted a good time nothing would stop her, and when she wanted justice . . . He said nervously: "Don't you think, Ida, we've done enough? . . ."

She said: "I haven't finished yet," with her eyes on the little doomed party. "You never know. They think they're safe; they'll do something crazy now." The Boy sat there silent beside Rose; he had a glass of drink but he hadn't tasted it; only the man and the woman chattered about this and that.

"We've done our best. It's a matter for the police or no one," Phil said.

"You heard them that first time." She began to sing again: "One night in an alley . . . "

"It's not our business now."

"Lord Rothschild said to me . . ." She broke off to set him gently right. You couldn't let a friend have

wrong ideas. "It's the business of anyone who knows
the difference between Right and Wrong."

"But you're so terribly certain about things, Ida.
You go busting in . . . Oh, you mean well, but how do
we know the reasons he may have had? . . . And besides," he accused her, "you're only doing it because
it's fun. Fred wasn't anyone you cared about."

She switched towards him her large and lit-up eyes.
"Why," she said, "I don't say it hasn't been—exciting." She felt quite sorry it was all over now.
"What's the harm in that? I like doing what's right,
that's all."

Rebellion bobbed weakly up—"And what's wrong
too."

She smiled at him with enormous and remote tenderness. "Oh, that. That's not wrong. That does no
one any harm. That's not like murder."

"Priests say it is."

"Priests!" she exclaimed with scorn. "Why, even
Romans don't believe in *that*. Or that girl wouldn't be
living with him now." She said: "You can trust me.
I've seen the world. I know people," and she turned
her attention heavily back on Rose. "You wouldn't let
me leave a little girl like that—to him? She's vexing,
of course, she's stupid, but she don't deserve that."

"How do you know she doesn't *want* to be left?"

"You aren't telling me, are you, that she wants to
die? Nobody wants that. Oh, no. I don't give up until
she's safe. Get me another Guinness." A long way out
beyond the West Pier you could see the lights of
Worthing, a sign of bad weather; and the tide rolled
regularly in, a gigantic white splash in the dark

against the breakwaters nearer shore. You could hear
it pounding at the piles, like a boxer's fist against a
punchball in training for the human jaw, and softly
and just a little tipsily Ida Arnold began to recall the
people she had saved: a man she had once pulled out
of the sea when she was a young woman, the money
to a blind beggar, and the kind word in season to the
despairing schoolgirl in the Strand.

<h2 style="text-align:center">7</h2>

"Poor old Spicer too," Dallow said, "he got the
same idea—he thought he'd have a pub somewhere
some day." He slapped Judy's thigh and said: "What
about me an' you settling in with the young people?"
He said: "I can see it now. Right out in the country.
On one of those arterials with the charabancs stopping:
the Great North Road. Pull in here. I wouldn't be
surprised if there wasn't more money in the long
run . . ." He stopped and said to the Boy: "What's up?
Take a drink. There's nothing to worry about now."

The Boy looked across the tea room and the empty
tables to where the woman sat. How she hung on!
Like a ferret he'd seen on the down, among the chalky
holes, fastened to the hare's throat. All the same *this*
hare escaped. He had no cause to fear her now. He
said in a dull voice: "The country. I don't know much
about the country."

"It's healthy," Dallow said. "Why, you'll live to
eighty with your missus."

"Sixty-odd years," the Boy said, "it's a long time."
Behind the woman's head the Brighton lamps beaded

out towards Worthing. The last sunset light slid lower
in the sky and the heavy indigo clouds came down over
the Grand, the Metropole, the Cosmopolitan, over the
towers and domes. Sixty years: it was like a prophecy
—a certain future, a horror without end.

"You two," Dallow said, "what's got you both?"

This was the tea room to which they had all come
after Fred's death—Spicer and Dallow and Cubitt.
Dallow was right, of course: they were safe—Spicer
dead and Drewitt out of the way, and Cubitt God
knows where (they'd never get *him* into a witness
box: he knew too well he'd hang—he'd played too big
a part—the prison record of 1923 lay behind him).
And Rose was his wife. As safe as they could ever
be. They'd won out—finally. He had—Dallow right
again—sixty years ahead. His thoughts came to pieces
in his hand: Saturday nights; and then the birth, the
child, habit, and hate. He looked across the tables: the
woman's laughter was like defeat.

He said: "This place is stuffy. I got to have some
air." He turned slowly to Rose. "Come for a stroll,"
he said. Between the table and the door he picked the
right thought out of all the pieces, and when they
came out on the windy side of the pier he shouted to
her: "I got to go away from here." He put his hand
on her arm and guided her with terrible tenderness
into shelter. The waves came breaking up from
France, pounding under their feet. A spirit of reck-
lessness took him; it was like the moment when he had
seen Spicer bending by his suitcase, Cubitt begging
for money in the passage. Through the glass panes
Dallow sat with Judy by the drinks; it was like the

first week of the sixty years—the contact and the sensual tremble and the stained sleep and waking not alone; in the wild and noisy darkness the Boy had the whole future in his brain. It was like a slot machine: you put in a penny and the light goes on, and the doors open and the figures move. He said with agile tenderness: "This was where we met that night. Remember?"

"Yes," she said and watched him with fear.

"We don't want *them* with us," he said. "Let's get into the car an' drive"—he watched her closely—"into the country."

"It's cold."

"It won't be in the car." He dropped her arm and said: "Of course—if you don't want to come—I'll go alone."

"But where?"

He said with studied lightness: "I told you. In the country." He took a penny out of his pocket and slammed it home in the nearest slot machine. He pulled a handle, didn't look at what he did, and with a rattle the packets of fruit gums came dropping out—a bonus—lemon and grapefruit and liquorice all-sorts. He said: "I've got a lucky hand."

"Is something wrong?" Rose said.

He said: "You saw her, didn't you? Believe me—she's never going to leave go. I saw a ferret once—out by the track." As he turned one of the pier lights caught his eyes: a gleam, an exhilaration. He said: "I'm going for a ride. You stay here if you want to."

"I'll come," she said.

"You needn't."

"I'll come."

At the shooting range he paused. He was taken with
a kind of wild humour. "Got the time?" he asked the
man.

"You know what the time is. I've told you before
how I won't stand . . ."

"You needn't get your rag out," the Boy said.
"Give me a gun." He lifted it, got the sight firmly on
the bull, then deliberately shifted it and fired—he
thought: "Something had agitated him, the witness
said."

"What's up with you today?" the man exclaimed.
"You only got an outer."

He laid the rifle down. "We need a freshener.
We're going for a ride in the country. Good night."
He planted his information pedantically, as carefully
as he had had them lay Fred's cards along the route—
for later use. He even turned back and said: "We're
going Hastings way."

"I don't want to know," the man said, "where
you're going."

The old Morris was parked near the pier. The self-
starter wouldn't work; he had to turn the handle. He
stood a moment looking at the old car with an expression of disgust; as if this was all you got out of a
racket . . . He said: "We'll go the way we went that
day. Remember? In the bus." Again he planted his
information for the attendant to hear. "Peacehaven.
We'll get a drink."

They swung out round by the Aquarium and
ground uphill in second gear. He had one hand in his
pocket feeling for the scrap of paper on which she had

written her message. The hood flapped and the split
discoloured glass of the windscreen confined his view.
He said: "It's going to rain like hell soon."

"Will this hood keep it out?"

"It doesn't matter," he said, staring ahead. "*We*
won't get wet."

She didn't dare ask him what he meant—she wasn't
sure, and as long as she wasn't sure she could believe
that they were happy, that they were lovers taking a
drive in the dark with all the trouble over. She put a
hand on him and felt his instinctive withdrawal; for
a moment she was shaken by an awful doubt—if this
was the darkest nightmare of all, if he didn't love her,
as the woman said . . . the wet windy air flapped her
face through the rent. It didn't matter; she loved him;
she had her responsibility. The buses passed them
going downhill to the town: little bright domestic
cages in which people sat with baskets and books; a
child pressed her face to the glass and for a moment
at a traffic light they were so close the face might have
been held against her breast. "A penny for your
thoughts," he said and caught her unawares—"Life's
not so bad."

"Don't you believe it," he said. "I'll tell you what
it is. It's jail, it's not knowing where to get some
money. Worms and cataract, cancer. You hear 'em
shrieking from the upper windows—children being
born. It's dying slowly."

It was coming now—she knew it; the dashboard
light lit the bony mind-made-up fingers; the face was
in darkness, but she could imagine the exhilaration,
the bitter excitement, the anarchy in the eyes. A rich

man's private car—Daimler or Bentley, she didn't know the makes—rolled smoothly past them. He said: "What's the hurry?" He took his hand out of his pocket and laid on his knee a paper she recognized. He said: "You mean that—don't you?" He had to repeat it: "Don't you?" She felt as if she were signing away more than her life—Heaven, whatever that was, and the child in the bus, and the baby crying in the neighbour's house. "Yes," she said.

"We'll go and have a drink," he said, "and then—you'll see. I got everything settled." He said with hideous ease: "It won't take a minute." He put his arm round her waist and his face was close to hers; she could see him now, considering and considering; his skin smelt of petrol; everything smelt of petrol in the little leaking out-dated car. She said: "Are you sure . . . can't we wait . . . one day?"

"What's the good? You saw her there tonight. She's hanging on. One day she'll get her evidence. What's the use?"

"Why not *then?*"

"It might be too late *then*." He said disjointedly through the flapping hood: "A knock and the next thing you know . . . the cuffs . . . too late . . ." He said with cunning: "We wouldn't be together then." He put down his foot and the needle quivered up to thirty-five—the old car wouldn't do more than forty, but it gave an immense impression of reckless speed; the wind battered on the glass and tore through the rent.

He began softly to intone: "Dona nobis pacem."

"He won't."

"What do you mean?"

"Give us peace."

He thought: there'll be time enough in the years ahead—sixty years—to repent of this. Go to a priest. Say: "Father, I've committed murder twice. And there was a girl—she killed herself." Even if death came suddenly, driving home tonight, the smash on the lamp post—there was still: "between the stirrup and the ground." The houses on one side ceased altogether, and the sea came back to them, beating at the undercliff drive, a darkness and deep sound. He wasn't really deceiving himself—he'd learned the other day that when the time was short there were other things than contrition to think about. It didn't matter anyway . . . he wasn't made for peace, he couldn't believe in it. Heaven was a word; Hell was something he could trust. A brain was capable only of what it could conceive, and it couldn't conceive what it had never experienced; his cells were formed of the cement school playground, the dead fire and the dying man in the St. Pancras waiting room, his bed at Billy's and his parents' bed. An awful resentment stirred in him —why shouldn't he have had his chance like all the rest, seen his glimpse of Heaven if it was only a crack between the Brighton walls? . . . He turned as they went down to Rottingdean and took a long look at her as if she might be it—but the brain couldn't conceive —he saw a mouth which wanted the sexual contact, the shape of breasts demanding a child. Oh, she was good all right, he supposed, but she wasn't good enough; he'd got her down.

Above Rottingdean the new villas began: pipe-

dream architecture; up on the down the obscure skele-
ton of a nursing home, winged like an aeroplane. He
said: "They won't hear us in the country." The lights
petered out along the road to Peacehaven; the chalk
of a new cutting flapped like white sheets in the head-
light; cars came down on them, blinding them. He
said: "The battery's low."

   She had the sense that he was a thousand miles
away—his thoughts had gone on beyond the act she
couldn't tell where; he was wise; he was foreseeing,
she thought, things she couldn't conceive—eternal
punishment, the flames . . . She felt terror, the idea of
pain shook her, their purpose drove up in a flurry of
rain against the old stained windscreen. This road led
nowhere else. It was said to be the worst act of all, the
act of despair, the sin without forgiveness; sitting
there in the smell of petrol she tried to realize despair,
the mortal sin, but she couldn't; it didn't feel like
despair. He was going to damn himself, but she was
going to show them that they couldn't damn him without damning her too; there was nothing he could do
she wouldn't do; she felt capable of sharing any murder. A light lit his face and left it; a frown, a thought,
a child's face; she felt responsibility move in her
breasts; she wouldn't let him go into that darkness
alone.

   The Peacehaven streets began, running out towards
the cliffs and the downs; thorn bushes grew up round
the To Let boards; streets ended in obscurity, in a
pool of water and in salty grass. It was like the last
effort of despairing pioneers to break new country.
The country had broken them. He said: "We'll go to

the hotel and have a drink and then—I know the right place."

The rain was coming tentatively down; it beat on the faded scarlet doors of Lureland, the poster of next week's Whist Drive and last week's Dance. They ran for it to the hotel door; in the lounge there was nobody at all—white marble statuettes and on the green dado above the panelled walls Tudor roses and lilies picked out in gold. Siphons stood about on blue-topped tables, and on the stained-glass windows medieval ships tossed on cold curling waves. Somebody had broken the hands off one of the statuettes—or perhaps it was made like that, something classical in white drapery, a symbol of victory or despair. The Boy rang a bell and a boy of his own age came out of the public bar to take his order; they were oddly alike and allusively different—narrow shoulders, thin face, they bristled like dogs at the sight of each other.

"Piker," the Boy said.

"What of it?"

"Give us service," the Boy said. He took a step forward and the other backed and Pinkie grinned at him. "Bring us two double brandies," he said, "and quick." He said softly: "Who would have thought I'd find Piker here?" She watched him with amazement that he could find any distraction from their purpose; she could hear the wind on upstairs windows; where the steps curved another tombstone statuette raised its ruined limbs. He said: "We were at the school together. I used to give him hell in the breaks." The other returned with the brandies and brought, sidelong and scared and cautious, a whole smoky childhood with him. She felt a pang of jealousy against him because tonight she should have had all there was of Pinkie.

"You a servant?" the Boy said.

"I'm not a servant, I'm a waiter."

"You want me to tip you?"

"I don't want your tips."

The Boy took his brandy and drank it down; he coughed when it took him by the throat, it was like the stain of the world in his stomach. He said: "Here's courage." He said to Piker: "What's the time?"

"You can read it on the clock," Piker said, "if you can read."

"Haven't you any music?" the Boy said. "God damn it, we want to celebrate."

"There's the piano. An' the wireless."

"Turn it on."

The wireless was hidden behind a potted plant; a violin came wailing out, the notes shaken by static. The Boy said: "He hates me. He hates my guts," and turned to mock at Piker, but he'd gone. He said to Rose: "You'd better drink that brandy."

"I don't need it," she said.

"Have it your own way."

He stood by the wireless and she by the empty fireplace; three tables and three siphons and a Moorish-Tudor-God-knows-what-of-a-lamp were between them; they were gripped by an awful unreality, the need to make conversation, to say: "What a night" or: "It's cold for the time of year." She said: "So he was at your school?"

"That's right." They both looked at the clock; it

was almost nine, and behind the violin the rain tapped against the seaward windows. He said awkwardly: "We'd better be moving soon."

She began to pray to herself: "Holy Mary, Mother of God," but then she stopped—she was in mortal sin; it was no good praying. Her prayers stayed here below with the siphons and the statuettes; they had no wings. She waited by the fireplace in terrified patience. He said uneasily: "We ought to write—something, so people will know."

"It doesn't matter, does it?" she said.

"Oh, yes," he said quickly, "it does. We got to do things right. This is a pact. You read about them in the newspapers."

"Do lots of people—do it?"

"It's always happening," he said; an awful and airy confidence momentarily possessed him; the violin faded out and the time signal pinged through the rain. A voice behind the plant gave them the weather report —storms coming up from the Continent, a depression in the Atlantic, tomorrow's forecast. She began to listen and then remembered that tomorrow's weather didn't matter at all.

He said: "Like another drink—or something?" He looked round for a Gents' sign—"I just got to go— an' wash." She noticed the weight in his pocket—it was going to be that way. He said: "Just add a piece on that note while I'm gone. Here's a pencil. Say you couldn't live without me, something like that. We got to do this right, as it's always done." He went out into the passage and called to Piker and got his direction, then went up the stairs. At the statuette he turned and

looked down into the panelled lounge. This was the
kind of moment one kept for memory—the wind at
the pier end, Sherry's and the man singing, lamplight
on the harvest burgundy, the crisis as Cubitt battered
at the door. He found that he remembered it all without repulsion; he had a sense that somewhere, like a
beggar outside a shuttered house, tenderness stirred,
but he was bound in a habit of hate. He turned his
back and went on up the stairs. He told himself that
soon he would be free again—they'd see the note: he
hadn't known she was all that unhappy because he'd
said they'd got to part; she must have found the gun
in Dallow's room and brought it with her. They'd test
it for finger prints, of course, and then—he stared out
through the lavatory window: invisible rollers beat
under the cliff. Life would go on. No more human
contacts, other people's emotions washing at the brain
—he would be free again: nothing to think about but
himself. Myself: the word echoed hygienically on
among the porcelain basins, the taps and plugs and
wastes. He took the revolver out of his pocket and
loaded it—two chambers. In the mirror above the
wash basin he could see his hand move round the metal
death, adjusting the safety catch. Down below, the
news was over and the music had begun again—it
wailed upwards like a dog over a grave, and the huge
darkness pressed a wet mouth against the panes. He
put the revolver back and went out into the passage.
That was the next move. Another statuette pointed an
obscure moral with cemetery hands and a chaplet of
marble flowers, and again he felt the prowling presence of pity.

"They've been gone a long while," Dallow said. "What are they up to?"

"Who cares?" Judy said. "They want to be"—she fixed her plump prehensile lips against Dallow's cheek—"alone"—her red hair caught in his mouth —a sour taste. "You know what love is," she said.

"He doesn't." He was uneasy—conversations came back to him. He said: "He hates her guts." He put his arm half-heartedly round Judy—it was no good spoiling a party, but he wished he knew what Pinkie had in mind. He took a long drink out of Judy's glass, and somewhere Worthing way a siren wailed. Through the window he could see a couple mooning at the pier end, and an old man got his fortune card from the witch behind glass.

"Why don't he get clear of her then?" Judy said. Her mouth looked for his mouth down the line of his jaw. She drew herself indignantly up and said: "Who's that polony over there? What does she want lamping us all the time? This is a free country."

Dallow turned and looked. His brain worked very slowly, first the statement, "I never seen her," and then the memory. "Why," he said, "it's that damned buer who's been getting Pinkie rattled." He got cumbrously to his feet and stumbled a little between the tables. "Who are you?" he said. "Who are you?"

"Ida Arnold," she said, "for what it's worth. My friends call me Ida."

"I'm not your friend."

"You better be," she said gently. "Have a drink.
Where's Pinkie gone—and Rose? You ought to 'ave
brought them along. This is Phil. Introduce the lady
friend." She ran softly on: "It's time we all got together. What's your name?"

"Don't you know what people get who poke their
noses—?"

"Oh, I know," she said. "I know all right. I was
with Fred the day you finished him."

"Talk sense," Dallow said. "Who the hell are you?"

"You ought to know. You followed us all the way
up the front in that old Morris of yours." She smiled
quite amiably at him. He wasn't her game. "It seems
an age ago now, doesn't it?"

It was true all right—it seemed an age.

"Have a drink," Ida said, "you may as well. An'
where's Pinkie? He didn't seem to like the look of me
tonight. What were you celebrating? Not what's happened to Mr. Drewitt? You won't have heard that."

"What do you mean?" Dallow said. The wind got
up against the glass and the waitresses yawned.

"You'll see it in the morning papers. I don't want
to spoil your fun. And of course you'll know it sooner
than that if he talks."

"He's gone abroad."

"He's at the police station now," she said with
complete confidence. "They brought him right back,"
she went elaborately on. "You ought to choose your
solicitors better, men who can afford to take a holiday.
They've got him for fraud. Arrested him on the
quay."

He watched her uneasily. He didn't believe her—

but all the same . . . "You know an awful lot," he said. "Do you sleep at night?"

"Do you?"

The big broken face had a kind of innocence about it. "Me?" he said. "I don't know a thing."

"It was a waste giving him all that money. He'd have run anyway—and it didn't look good. When I got hold of Johnnie at the pier——"

He stared at her with hopeless amazement. "You got hold of Johnnie? How the hell . . . ?"

She said simply: "People like me." She took a drink and said: "His mother treated him shameful when he was a kid."

"Whose mother?"

"Johnnie's."

Dallow was impatient, puzzled, scared. "What the hell," he said, "do you know about Johnnie's mother?"

"What he told me," she said. She sat there completely at her ease, her big breasts ready for any secrets. She carried her air of compassion and comprehension about her like a rank cheap perfume. She said gently: "I got nothing against you. I like to be friendly. Bring over your lady friend."

He glanced quickly over his shoulder and back again. "I better not," he said. His voice fell. He too began automatically to confide: "Truth is, she's a jealous bitch."

"You don't say? And her old man . . . ?"

"Oh, her old man," he said, "he's all right. What Billy doesn't see, he doesn't mind." He dropped his voice still lower. "And he can't see much—he's blind."

"I didn't know that," she said.

"You wouldn't," he said. "Not from his pressing and ironing. He's got a wonderful hand with an iron," then broke suddenly off. "What the hell," he said, "did you mean—you didn't know *that?* What did you know?"

"There isn't much," she said, "I've not picked up— here and there. The neighbours always talk." She was barnacled with pieces of popular wisdom.

"Who's talking?" It was Judy now. She'd come across to them. "An' what 'ave they got to talk about? Why, if I chose to put my tongue round some of their doings . . . But I wouldn't like to," Judy said. "I wouldn't like to." She looked vaguely round. "What *has* happened to those two?"

"Perhaps I scared them," Ida Arnold said.

"*You* scared them?" Dallow said. "That's rich. Pinkie's not scared that easy."

"What I want to know is," Judy said, "what neighbours said what?"

Somebody was shooting at the range; when the door opened and a couple came in they could hear the shots—one, two, three. "That'll be Pinkie," Dallow said. "He was always good with a gun."

"You better go an' see," Ida gently remarked, "that he doesn't do something desperate—with his gun— when he gets to know."

Dallow said: "You jump to things. We got no cause to be afraid of Mr. Drewitt."

"You gave him money, I suppose, for Something."

"Aw," he said, "Johnnie's been joking."

"Your friend Cubitt seemed to think . . ."

"Cubitt doesn't know a thing."

"Of course," she admitted, "he wasn't there, was
he? That time, I mean. But you . . ." she said.
"Wouldn't twenty pounds be of use to you? After all
you don't want to get into trouble. . . . Let Pinkie
carry his own crimes."

"You make me sick," he said. "You think you
know a lot and you don't know a thing." He said to
Judy: "I'm goin' to have a drain. You want to keep
your mouth shut or this polony . . ." He stretched a
gesture, hopelessly—he couldn't express what she
mightn't put over on you. He went uneasily out, and
the wind caught him, so that he had to grab at his old
greasy hat and hold it on. Going down the steps to the
Gents' was like going down into a ship's engine room
in a storm. The whole place shook a little under his
feet as the swell came up against the piles and drove
on to break against the beach. He thought: I oughta
warn Pinkie about Drewitt if it's true. . . . He *had*
things on his mind, other things besides old Spicer.
He came up the ladder and looked down the deck—
Pinkie wasn't to be seen. He went on past the peep
machines—not in sight. It was someone else shooting
at the booth.

He asked the man: "Seen Pinkie?"

"What's the game?" the man said. "You know I
seen him. *An'* he's gone for a ride in the country—
with his girl—for a freshener—Hastings way. *An'* I
suppose you want to know the time too. Well," the
man said, "I'm swearing nothing. You can pitch on
someone else for your phony alibis."

"You're crackers," Dallow said. He moved away;
across the noisy sea the hour began to strike in

Brighton churches; he counted one, two, three, four, and stopped. He was scared—suppose it *was* true, suppose Pinkie knew, and it was that mad scheme . . . what the hell was taking anyone for a ride in the country at this hour, except to a roadhouse, and Pinkie didn't go to roadhouses. He said softly: "I won't stand for it," aloud; he was confused, he wished he hadn't drunk all that beer; she was a good kid. He remembered her in the kitchen, going to light the stove. And why not? he thought, staring gloomily out to sea; he was shaken by a sudden sentimental desire which Judy couldn't satisfy; for a paper with your breakfast and warm fires. He began to walk rapidly down the pier towards the turnstiles. There were things he wouldn't stand for.

He knew the Morris wouldn't be on the rank, but all the same he had to go and see for himself. Its absence was like a voice speaking quite plainly in his ear. "Suppose she kills herself . . . A pact may be murder, but they don't hang you for it." He stood there hopelessly, not knowing what to do. Beer clouded his brain; he passed a harassed hand across his face. He said to the attendant: "You see that Morris go out?"

"Your friend and his girl took it," the man said, hobbling between a Talbot and an Austin. One leg was gammy; he moved it with a mechanism worked from his pocket, lurching with an air of enormous strain to pocket sixpence, to say: "It's a fine night"; he looked worn with the awful labour of the trivial act. He said: "They're goin' up to Peacehaven for a drink.

Don't ask me why." Hand in pocket he pulled the
hidden wire and made his unsteady and diagonal way
towards a Ford. "The rain won't hold off long," his
voice came back, and: "Thank you, sir," and then
again the labour of movement as a Morris Oxford
backed in, the pulling at the wire.

Dallow stood there hopelessly at a loss. There were
buses . . . but everything would be over long before a
bus got in. Better to wash his hands of the whole thing
. . . after all he didn't *know*; in half an hour he might
see the old car coming back past the Aquarium, Pinkie
driving and the girl beside him, but he knew very well
in his heart that it would never come, not with both of
them, that way. The Boy had left too many signs
behind him—the message at the shooting range, at
the car park; he wanted to be followed in good time,
in his own time, to fit in with his story. The man came
lurching back. He said: "I thought your friend seemed
queer tonight. Sort of lit up." It was as if he were
talking in the witness box, giving the evidence he was
meant to give.

Dallow turned hopelessly away . . . fetch Judy, go
home, wait . . . and there was the woman standing a
few feet away. She'd followed him and listened. He
said: "God's sakes, this is your doing. You made him
marry her, you made him . . ."

"Get a car," she said, "quick."

"I've not got the money for a car."

"I have. You better hurry."

"There's no cause to hurry," he said weakly.
"They've just gone for a drink."

"You know what they've gone for," she said. "I don't. But if *you* want to keep out of this, you'd better get that car."

The first rain began to blow up the parade as he weakly argued. "I don't know a thing."

"That's right," she said. "You're just taking me for a drive, that's all." She burst suddenly out at him: "Don't be a fool. You better have me for a friend. . . ." She said: "You see what's come to Pinkie."

All the same he didn't hurry. What was the good? Pinkie had laid *this* trail. Pinkie thought of everything, they were meant to follow in due course, and find . . . he hadn't got the imagination to see what they'd find.

9

The Boy stopped at the head of the stairs and looked down. Two men had come into the lounge; hearty and damp in camel hair coats they shook out their moisture like dogs and were noisy over their drinks. "Two pints," they ordered, "in tankards," and fell suddenly silent scenting a girl in the lounge. They were upper-class, they'd learned that tankard trick in class hotels; he watched their gambits with hatred from the stairs. Anything female was better than nothing, even Rose; but he could sense their half-heartedness. She wasn't worth more than a little sidelong swagger. "I think **we** touched eighty."

"I made it eighty-two."

"She's a good bus."

"How much did they sting you?"

"A couple of hundred. She's cheap at the price."

Then they both stopped and took an arrogant look
at the girl by the statuette. She wasn't worth bothering about, but if she absolutely fell, without trouble
. . . one of them said something in a low voice and the
other laughed. They took long swills of bitter from
the tankards.

Tenderness came up to the very window and looked
in. What the hell right had they got to swagger and
laugh . . . if she was good enough for him? He came
down the stairs into the hall; they looked up and
moued to each other, as much as to say: "Oh, well,
she wasn't really worth the trouble."

One of them said: "Drink up. We better get on
with the good work. You don't think Zoe'll be out?"

"Oh, no. I said I might drop in."

"Her friend all right?"

"She's hot."

"Let's get on then."

They drained their beer and moved arrogantly to
the door, taking a passing look at Rose as they went.
He could hear them laugh outside the door. They were
laughing at him. He came a few steps into the lounge;
again they were bound in an icy constraint. He had a
sudden inclination to throw up the whole thing, to get
into the car and drive home, and let her live. It was
less a motion of pity than of weariness—there was such
a hell of a lot to do and think of: there were going to
be so many questions to be answered. He could hardly
believe in the freedom at the end of it, and even that
freedom was to be in a strange place. He said: "The
rain's worse." She stood there waiting; she couldn't
answer; she was breathing hard as if she'd run a long

way—and she looked old. She was sixteen but this was how she might have looked after years of marriage, of the childbirth and the daily quarrel; they had reached death and it affected them like age.

She said: "I wrote what you wanted." She waited for him to take the scrap of paper and write his own message to the coroner, to *Daily Express* readers, to what one called the world. The other boy came cautiously into the lounge and said: "You haven't paid." While Pinkie found the money, she was visited by an almost overwhelming rebellion—she had only to go out, leave him, refuse to play. He couldn't make her kill herself; life wasn't as bad as that. It came like a revelation, as if someone had whispered to her that she was someone, a separate creature—not just one flesh with him. She could always escape—if he didn't change his mind. Nothing was decided. They could go in the car wherever he wanted them to go; she could take the gun from his hand, and even then—at the last moment of all—she needn't shoot. Nothing was decided—there was always hope.

"That's your tip," the Boy said. "I always tip a waiter." Hate came back. He said: "You a good Catholic, Piker? Do you go to Mass on Sundays like they tell you?"

Piker said with weak defiance: "Why not, Pinkie?"

"You're afraid," the Boy said. "You're afraid of burning."

"Who wouldn't be?"

"I'm not." He looked with loathing into the past—a cracked bell ringing, a child weeping under the cane—and repeated: "I'm not afraid." He said to Rose:

"We'll be going." He came tentatively across and put a nail against her cheek—half caress, half threat—and said: "You'd love me always, wouldn't you?"

"Yes."

He gave her one more chance: "You'd always have stuck to me," and when she nodded her agreement, he began wearily the long course of action which one day would let him be free again.

Outside in the rain the self-starter wouldn't work; he stood with his coat collar turned up and pulled the handle. She wanted to tell him that he mustn't stand there, getting wet, because she'd changed her mind—they were going to live, by hook or by crook—but she daren't. She pushed hope back—to the last possible moment. When they drove off she said: "Last night . . . the night before . . . you didn't hate me, did you, for what we did?"

He said: "No, I didn't hate you."

"Even though it was a mortal sin?"

It was quite true—he hadn't hated her; he hadn't even hated the act. There had been a kind of pleasure, a kind of pride, a kind of—something else. The car lurched back onto the main road; he turned the nose to Brighton. An enormous emotion beat on him; it was like something trying to get in, the pressure of gigantic wings against the glass. *Dona nobis pacem.* He withstood it, with all the bitter force of the school bench, the cement playground, the St. Pancras waiting room, Dallow's and Judy's secret lust, and the cold unhappy moment on the pier. If the glass broke, if the beast—whatever it was—got in, God knows what it would do. He had a sense of huge havoc—the confes-

sion, the penance, and the sacrament—an awful distraction, and he drove blind into the rain. He could
see nothing through the cracked stained windscreen.
A bus came up on them and pulled out just in time—
he was on the wrong side. He said, suddenly, at random: "We pull in here."

An ill-made street petered out towards the cliff—
bungalows of every shape and kind, a vacant plot full
of salt grass and wet thorn bushes like bedraggled
fowls, no lights except in three windows. A radio
played, and in a garage a man was doing something
to his motor-bike, which roared and spluttered in the
darkness. He drove a few yards in, turned out his
headlights, switched off his engine. The rain came
noisily in through the rent in the top and they could
hear the sea battering the cliff. He said: "Well, take
a look. It's the world." Another light went on behind
a stained glass door, the Laughing Cavalier between
Tudor roses; and looking out as if it was he who'd got
to take some sort of farewell of the bike and the bungalows and the rainy street, he thought of the words in
the Mass: "He was in the world and the world was
made by Him and the world knew Him not."

It was about as far as hope could be stretched; she
had to say now or never—"I won't do it. I never
meant to do it." It was like some romantic adventure
—you plan to fight in Spain, and then before you
know it the tickets are taken for you, the introductions
are pressed into your hand, somebody has come to see
you off, everything is real. He put his hand in his
pocket and pulled out the gun. He said: "I got it out
of Dallow's room." She wanted to say she didn't know

how to use it, to make any excuse, but he seemed to have thought of everything. He explained: "I've put up the safety catch. All you need do is pull on this. It isn't hard. Put it in your ear—that'll hold it steady." His youth came out in the crudity of his instruction; he was like a boy playing on an ash heap. "Go on," he said, "take it."

It was amazing how far hope could extend. She thought: I needn't say anything yet. I can take the gun and then—throw it out of the car, run away, do something to stop everything. But all the time she felt the steady pressure of his will. *His* mind was made up. She took the gun; it was like a treachery. What will he do, she thought, if I don't . . . shoot? Would he shoot himself alone, without her? Then he would be damned, and she wouldn't have her chance of being damned too, of showing Them they couldn't pick and choose. To go on living for years . . . you couldn't tell what life would do to you in making you meek, good, repentant. Belief in her mind had the bright clarity of images, of the crib at Christmas; here goodness ended, past the cow and the sheep, and there evil began —Herod seeking the child's birthplace from his turreted keep. She wanted to be with Herod—if *he* were there; you could win to the evil side suddenly, in a moment of despair or passion, but through a long life the guardian good drove you remorselessly towards the crib, the "happy death."

He said: "We don't want to wait any longer. Do you want me to do it first?"

"No," she said, "no."

"All right then. You take a walk—or better still

I'll take a walk an' you stay here. When it's over, I'll come back an' do it too." Again he gave the sense that he was a boy playing a game, a game in which you could talk in the coldest detail of the scalping knife or the bayonet wound and then go home to tea. He said: "It'll be too dark for me to see much."

He opened the door of the car. She sat motionless with the gun on her lap. Behind them on the main road a car went slowly past towards Peacehaven. He said awkwardly: "You know what to do?" He seemed to think that some motion of tenderness was expected of him. He put out his mouth and kissed her on the cheek; he was afraid of the mouth—thoughts travel too easily from lip to lip. He said: "It won't hurt," and began to walk back a little way towards the main road. Hope was stretched now as far as it would go. The radio had stopped; the motor-bicycle exploded twice in the garage, feet moved on gravel, and on the main road she could hear a car reversing.

If it was a guardian angel speaking to her now, he spoke like a devil—he tempted her to virtue like a sin. To throw away the gun was a betrayal; it would be an act of cowardice; it would mean that she chose never to see him again for ever. Moral maxims dressed in pedantic priestly tones remembered from old sermons, instructions, confessions—"you can plead for him at the throne of Grace"—came to her like unconvincing insinuations. The evil act was the honest act, the bold and the faithful—it was only lack of courage, it seemed to her, that spoke so virtuously. She put the gun up to her ear and put it down again with a feeling of sickness—it was a poor love that was afraid to die.

She hadn't been afraid to commit mortal sin—it was death not damnation which was scaring her. Pinkie said it wouldn't hurt. She felt his will moving her hand—she could trust him. She put up the gun once more.

A voice called sharply: "Pinkie," and she heard somebody splashing in the puddles. Footsteps ran . . . she couldn't tell where. It seemed to her that this must be news, that this must make a difference. She couldn't kill herself when this might mean good news. It was as if somewhere in the darkness the will which had governed her hand relaxed, and all the hideous forms of self-preservation came flooding back. It didn't seem real—that she had really intended to sit here and press the trigger. "Pinkie," the voice called again, and the splashing steps came nearer. She pulled the car door open and flung the revolver far away from her towards the damp scrub.

In the light from the stained glass she saw Dallow and the woman—and a policeman who looked confused as if he didn't quite know what was happening. Somebody came softly round the car behind her and said: "Where's that gun? Why don't you shoot? Give it me."

She said: "I threw it away."

The others approached cautiously like a deputation. Pinkie called out suddenly in a breaking childish voice: "You bloody squealer, Dallow."

"Pinkie," Dallow said, "it's no use. They got Drewitt." The policeman looked ill at ease like a stranger at a party.

"Where's that gun?" Pinkie said again. He

screamed with hate and fear: "My God, have I got to
have a massacre?"

She said: "I threw it away."

She could see his face indistinctly as it leant in over
the little dashboard light. It was like a child's, badg-
ered, confused, betrayed; fake years slipped away—
he was whisked back towards the unhappy playground.
He said: "You little . . ." he didn't finish—the deputation approached, he left her, diving into his pocket for
something. "Come on, Dallow," he said, "you bloody
squealer," and put his hand up. Then she couldn't
tell what happened: glass—somewhere—broke, he
screamed and she saw his face—steam. He screamed
and screamed, with his hands up to his eyes; he turned
and ran; she saw a police baton at his feet and broken
glass. He looked half his size, doubled up in appalling
agony; it was as if the flames had literally got him and
he shrank—shrank into a schoolboy flying in panic
and pain, scrambling over a fence, running on.

"Stop him," Dallow cried; it wasn't any good; he
was at the edge, he was over; they couldn't even hear
a splash. It was as if he'd been withdrawn suddenly by
a hand out of any existence—past or present, whipped
away into zero—nothing.

10

"It shows," Ida Arnold said, "you only have to hold
on." She emptied her glass of stout and laid it down
on Henneky's upturned barrel.

"And Drewitt?" Clarence said.

"How slow you are, you old ghost! I just made that

up. I couldn't chase over France for him, and the police—you know what police are—they always want evidence."

"They had Cubitt?"

"Cubitt wouldn't talk when he was sober. And you'd never get him drunk enough to talk to them. Why, this is slander what I've been telling you. Or it would be slander—if *he* were alive."

"I wonder you don't feel bad about that, Ida."

"Somebody else would have been dead if we hadn't turned up."

"It was her own choice."

But Ida Arnold had an answer to everything. "She didn't understand. She was only a kid. She thought he was in love with her."

"An' what does she think now?"

"Don't ask me. I've done my best. I took her home. What a girl needs at a time like that is her mother and dad. Anyway she's got me to thank she isn't dead."

"How did you get the policeman to go with you?"

"We told him they'd stolen the car. The poor man didn't know what it was all about, but he acted quick when Pinkie pulled out the vitriol."

"And Phil Corkery?"

"He's talking of Hastings," she said, "next year, but I have a sort of feeling there won't be any post-cards for me after this."

"You're a terrible woman, Ida," Clarence said. He sighed deeply and stared into his glass. "Have another?"

"No, thank you, Clarence. I got to be getting home."

"You're a terrible woman," Clarence repeated; he

was a little drunk, "but I got to give you credit. You act for the best."

"He's not on my conscience anyway."

"As you say, it was him or her."

"There wasn't any choice," Ida Arnold said. She got up; she was like a figurehead of Victory. She nodded to Harry at the bar.

"You've been away, Ida?"

"Just a week or two."

"It doesn't seem so long," Harry said.

"Well, good night, all."

"Good night. Good night."

She took the tube to Russell Square and walked, carrying her suitcase; let herself in and looked in the hall for letters. There was only one—from Tom. She knew what that would be about, and her great warm heart softened as she thought: "After all, when all's said, Tom an' I know what Love is." She opened the door onto the basement stairs and called: "Crowe. Old Crowe."

"You, Ida?"

"Come up for a chat an' we'll have a turn with the Board."

The curtains were drawn as she had left them— nobody had touched the china on the mantelpiece, but Warwick Deeping wasn't in the bookshelf and *The Good Companions* was on its side. The char had been in—she could see that—borrowing. She got out a box of chocolate biscuits for Old Crowe; the lid had not been left properly on and they were a little soft and stale. Then carefully she lifted out the Board, cleared the table, and laid it in the centre. SUICILLEYE, she thought. I know what that means now. The Board had foreseen it all—Sui, its own word for the scream, the agony, the leap. She brooded gently with her fingers on the Board. When you came to think of it, the Board had saved Rose, and a multitude of popular sayings began to pass together into her mind. It was like when the switch shifts and the signal goes down and the red lamp changes to green and the great engine takes the accustomed rails. It's a strange world, there's more things in heaven and earth . . .

Old Crowe came peering in. "What's it to be, Ida?"

"I want to ask advice," Ida said. "I want to ask whether maybe I ought to go back to Tom."

11

Rose could just see the old head bent towards the grille. The priest had a whistle in his breath. He listened—patiently—whistling, while she painfully brought out her whole agony. She could hear the exasperated women creak their chairs outside waiting for confession. She said: "It's *that* I repent. Not going with him." She was defiant and tearless in the stuffy box; the old priest had a cold and smelt of eucalyptus. He said gently and nasally : "Go on, my child."

She said: "I wish I'd killed myself. I oughta 'ave killed myself." The old man began to say something, but she interrupted him. "I'm not asking for absolution. I don't want absolution. I want to be like him— damned."

The old man whistled as he drew in his breath; she felt certain he understood nothing. She repeated

monotonously: "I wish I'd killed myself." She pressed
her hands against her breasts in the passion of misery;
she hadn't come to confess, she had come to think, she
couldn't think at home when the stove hadn't been lit
and her father had got a mood and her mother—she
could tell it in her sidelong questions—was wondering
how much money Pinkie . . . She would have had the
courage now to kill herself if she hadn't been afraid
that somewhere in that obscure countryside of death
they might miss each other—mercy operating somehow for one and not for the other. She said with breaking voice: "That woman. *She* ought to be damned.
Saying he wanted to get rid of me. She doesn't know
about love."

"Perhaps she was right," the old priest murmured.

"And you don't either!" she said furiously, pressing
her childish face against the grille.

The old man suddenly began to talk—whistling
every now and then and blowing eucalyptus through
the grille. He said: "There was a man, a Frenchman,
you wouldn't know about him, my child, who had the
same idea as you. He was a good man, a holy man, and
he lived in sin all through his life, because he couldn't
bear the idea that any soul could suffer damnation."
She listened with astonishment. He said: "This man
decided that if any soul was going to be damned, he
would be damned too. He never took the sacraments,
he never married his wife in church. I don't know,
my child, but some people think he was—well, a saint.
I think he died in what we are told is mortal sin—I'm
not sure; it was in the war; perhaps . . ." He sighed—
and whistled, bending his old head. He said: "You

can't conceive, my child, nor can I or anyone—the . . .
appalling . . . strangeness of the mercy of God."

Outside the chairs creaked again and again—people
impatient to get their own repentance, absolution,
penance finished for the week. He said: "It was a case
of greater love hath no man than this, that he lay down
his soul for his friend."

He shivered and sneezed. "We must hope and
pray," he said, "hope and pray. The Church does not
demand that we believe any soul is cut off from
mercy."

She said with sad conviction: "He's damned. He
knew what he was about. He was a Catholic too."

He said gently: "Corruptio optimi est pessima."

"Yes, Father?"

"I mean—a Catholic is more capable of evil than
anyone. I think perhaps—because we believe in him
—we are more in touch with the devil than other
people. But we must hope," he said mechanically,
"hope and pray."

"I want to hope," she said, "but I don't know how."

"If he loved you, surely," the old man said, "that
shows . . . there was some good . . ."

"Even love like that?"

"Yes."

She brooded on the idea in the little dark box. He
said: "And come back soon—I can't give you absolution now—but come back—tomorrow."

She said weakly: "Yes, Father. . . . And if there's
a baby . . . ?"

He said: "With your simplicity and his force . . .
Make him a saint—to pray for his father."

A sudden feeling of immense gratitude broke through the pain—it was as if she had been given the sight a long way off of life going on again. He said:

"Pray for me, my child."

She said: "Yes, oh, yes."

Outside she looked up at the name on the confessional box—it wasn't any name she remembered. Priests come and go.

She went out into the street—the pain was still there; you couldn't shake it off with a word; but the worst horror, she thought, was over—the horror of the complete circle; to be back at home, back at Snow's—they'd take her back—just as if the Boy had never existed at all. He had existed and would always exist. She had a sudden conviction that she carried life—and she thought proudly: Let them get over that if they can; let them get over that. She turned out onto the front opposite the Palace Pier and began to walk firmly away from the direction of her home towards Billy's. There was something to be salvaged from that house and room, something else they wouldn't be able to get over—his voice speaking a message to her: if there was a child, speaking to the child. "If he loved you," the priest had said, "that shows . . ." She walked rapidly in the thin June sunlight towards the worst horror of all.

PRAISE FOR
Where I'm Bound

"*. . . important story of black soldiers in the Union army . . . [a] good read for anyone interested in the Civil War and the history of African-Americans.*"

— James M. McPherson, Professor of History, Princeton University, Author of *Battle Cry of Freedom: The Civil War Era*

"*. . . a terrific story!*"

— Nell Irvin Painter, Edwards Professor of American History, Princeton University, Author of *Sojourner Truth: A Life, A Symbol*

"*Built around the campaigns of the 3rd U.S. Colored Calvary Regiment; . . . another marvelous and moving epoch of the Black experience. . .*"

— John A. Williams, Author of *The Man Who Cried I Am*

"*Rising from the dead, the voices of black soldiers in the Civil War whisper, shout and wail how that societal conflict really felt, smelled and tasted; . . . Those who want to deepen their knowledge of that horrendous period in American history shouldn't miss the satisfying tale.*"

— Shirlee Taylor Haizlip, Author of *The Sweeter Juice*

"*In* Where I'm Bound, *Allen B. Ballard has given us the smell of combat, the horror and comedy of slavery, the richness and complexities of love, [and] the nuances of history all wrapped in a riveting story about black soldiers making their way through the whirlwind of the Civil War. This is a stunning novel!*"

— Roger Wilkins, Clarence J. Robinson Professor of American History and Culture, George Mason University

WHERE
I'M BOUND

A Civil War Novel

BY ALLEN B. BALLARD

The Education of Black Folk
The Afro-American struggle for knowledge in white America

One More Day's Journey
A Novel of Urban Bravery in America

Breaching Jericho's Walls
A Twentieth-Century African American Life

Where I'm Bound
A Civil War Novel

Carried by Six
A Novel of Urban Bravery in America

Keep on Moving!
*An Old Fellow's Journey Into The World of Rollators,
Mobile Scooters, Recumbent Trikes,
Adult Trikes and Electric Bikes*

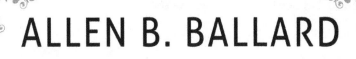

ALLEN B. BALLARD

WHERE I'M BOUND

A Civil War Novel

FIRST STEPS PUBLISHING
OREGON

WHERE I'M BOUND, *A Civil War Novel*
by Allen Ballard
Copyright © 2000, 2006, 2020 by Allen Ballard

Published by

  First Steps Publishing
publish@firststepspublishing.com

ISBN-13:   978-1-944072-49-0 (hc)
            978-1-944072-48-3 (pbk)
            978-1-944072-54-4 (hc Large Print)
            978-1-944072-50-6 (ebk)

Cover / Interior layout & design by Suzanne Fyhrie Parrott
Cover art: "Fort Davis" by Robert Summers. Used with permission.

Ballard, Allen B.
Where I'm bound / Allen B. Ballard.

1. United States—History—Civil War Era, 1861–1865— Participation,
African-American & Black—Fiction. 2. Mississippi—History—Civil War
Era, 1861–1865—African-Americans & Black—Fiction. [1. Slavery—Fiction.
2. African-American & Black soldiers—Fiction.] I. Title.

Previously published by
            Simon & Schuster (October 5, 2000): 978-0684870311 (hc)
            iUniverse (July 21, 2006): 978-0595398560 (pbk)

10 9 8 7 6 5 4 3 2

Printed and bound in the
United States of America.

ACKNOWLEDGMENTS

I would like to thank all of the following people for their help in bringing Where I'm Bound to print: Carson Carr, Richard Farrell, Craig Hancock, Mars Hill, Suzanne Lance, Leonard Slade, Harriet Temps, Stuart Tolnay, Gartrell Turman, and Lillian Williams all read part of all of the manuscript and made helpful suggestions. Two of my then-senior students here at the university, Nyree Busby and Andre Duncan, also read it and made very useful comments. The following scholars in the field of Civil War and Reconstruction history were kind enough to read the manuscript and thus helped me, a newcomer to the study of the Civil War, to avoid major pitfalls: Noah A. Trudeau, Reid Mitchell, and Robert R. Dykstra. And Mr. Trudeau was kind enough to supply me with an area map of the territory in which the Third Cavalry operated. They are hereby absolved of any responsibility for factual error—that still rests on me. My office mate, H. Peter Krosby, also read the manuscript and has been unstinting in his support of the work, as has been Richard Hamm. David H. Wallace of the National Archives responded with alacrity to my request for material on the Third United States Colored Cavalry.

I would also like to thank my colleagues in the Africana Studies Department, particularly Chair Joseph A. Sarfoh, and the History Department, particularly Chair Dan White, here at SUNY-Albany, for their backing over the years. I also received great support at my church, Mount Calvary Baptist, where native-born Mississippians Vera Gray, Ernest Williams, and "Big John" Fountain were kind enough to school me on matters as diverse as the proper techniques for picking cotton to the catching and cooking of catfish in their home state. My pastor, Reverend Robert W. Dixon, himself a former horse soldier who served in the cavalry detachment at West Point during WWII, was generous with his time in explaining technical matters about horses and cavalrymen. I have also benefited from my membership in the Capital District Civil War Roundtable, a group of enthusiasts with a wealth of knowledge about the war and an eagerness to share it with others. Edward Kaprielian, Colonel U.S.A. (Ret.) was of great help with his technical knowledge at critical moments in the writing. Kenneth Botsford, Mary T. Linnane, Susan McCormack, Aimee Tschoop, John Smith, and Bonita Weddle, all graduate students with the distinct misfortune to have offices adjacent to the one where a novelist was writing his book, were frequently corralled by me to read a page or two of freshly typed words and never once refused to give me a minute or two of their precious time and offer valuable opinions as to the flow of the narrative and other vital matters. Departmental secretaries Elaine Sevits, Debby Neuls, and Ronnie Saunders were of great service whenever I called upon them for help.

James M. McPherson, Nell I. Painter, Joseph E. Persico, and John A. Williams all read the manuscript and were kind enough to take the time to comment on it for the book jacket.

Finally, Ross Browne, Mary Costello, and Renni Browne of the Editorial Department put me through a rigorous and intellectually exhilarating "postgraduate" education in the writing of fiction in the course of the past seven years. Owen Laster of the William Morris Agency has been as fine an agent as one could find, and my editor at Simon & Schuster, Dominick Anfuso, has made sagacious and creative suggestions that have substantively reshaped the manuscript for the better.

As life and the passage of time would have it, I've lost some good friends over the past few years. Dean Harrison of the City University Graduate School, Dean Haywood Burns of the City University Law School, Professor Harry Lazer of CCNY, Professors Leslie Berger and Henry Morton of Queens College, and my cousin Charles Blackwell have all passed on. In good times and bad, they were always there to cheer me on, and I sorely miss their comradeship. And even as I pen these words, I've just learned of the death of Professor Adam B. Ulam of Harvard University, a dissertation adviser, mentor, and friend. He too will be missed.

Through all these years, my son, John, and my brother Walter and his wife, Gerry, and my brother Forrest have been supportive of my work.

Thanks for your love, you all!

Post-Script: January, 2021

I've taken the liberty of making a very few editorial changes in the text of this volume, hopefully broadening its reach and making it more suitable and accessible for younger audiences.

For

Nellie R. Bright, *Principal*

Joseph E. Hill Elementary School

Philadelphia, Pennsylvania

~ and ~

The Right Reverend E. Sydnor Thomas, *Rector*

St. Barnabas Protestant Episcopal Church

Philadelphia, Pennsylvania

WHERE I'M BOUND

Who can faint, when such a river
Ever will their thirst assuage—
Grace which, like the Lord, the giver
Never fails from age to age?

John Newton
Franz Joseph Haydn

A FEW CIVIL WAR DATES

April 13, 1861

    Fall of Fort Sumter, South Carolina, to the Southerners

April 15, 1861

    President Abraham Lincoln issues call for 75,000 volunteers to suppress the rebellion.

February 16, 1862

    Fort Donelson, Tennessee, surrenders to General Ulysses S. Grant putting the Confederates in the west on the defensive.

April 6-7, 1862

    The great battle at Shiloh, Tennessee, with 23,746 combined Union and Confederate casualties. General Grant will continue to move south.

January 1, 1863

    The Emancipation Proclamation takes effect.

July 1 –3, 1863

    Battle of Gettysburg. General Robert E. Lee's invasion of Pennsylvania is repulsed and he and his army retreat back into Virginia.

July 4, 1863

> Vicksburg, Mississippi, falls to General Grant, thus split-
> ting the Confederacy in two and opening the Mississippi
> River to Union navigation.

April 12, 1864

> Confederate General Nathan Bedford Forrest captures
> Fort Pillow, Tennessee.

September 2, 1864

> Atlanta falls to Union general William T. Sherman.

December 15–16, 1864

> General George H. Thomas defeats the Confederates at
> the Battle of Nashville, effectively ending the Southern
> threat in the western theater.

December 21, 1864

> General Sherman occupies Savannah.

January 14, 1865

> Fort Fisher, North Carolina, falls to Union forces.

April 9, 1865

> General Lee surrenders to General Grant at Appomattox
> Courthouse, Virginia.

**Operational Area
3rd USCC
1864-1865**

TENNESSEE

• Jackson

• Ft. Pillow
• Memphis

ARKANSAS

Mississippi River

Mississippi Central Railroad

Brice's Cross Roads

• Tupelo

• Okolona
• Egypt

Gaines
Landing •

Big Black
River
Bridge

Yazoo River

• Franklin

Big Black River

Benton •

← Yazoo City
← Satartia

Vicksburg •

• Jackson

• Merdian

LOUISIANA

MISSISSIPPI

Mississippi River

Yazoo River

Haynes
Bluff

Milliken's
Bend

Vicksburg

Railroad ....
River
State Border ────

© 2021 Suzanne Fyhrie Parrott

CHAPTER ONE

THE first thing Joe did when he caught sight of those colored soldiers wearing blue Yankee uniforms was to stand staring at them with his mouth wide open till the captain rode up behind him and whacked him across the shoulder with his riding crop.

"Don't go getting ideas, Joe. We're going to run them niggers right off into the river and drown 'em like rats."

But they hadn't.

And now, on this late June day of 1863, he was in a Confederate camp not far from Milliken's Bend, Louisiana, where a Texas regiment was licking its wounds after fighting against colored Union troops.

It was unusually quiet as the men prepared to bed down for the night. The song of the Negro mule skinners attached to the unit seemed to fit the mood of the camp.

Soon, one morning, death come stealing in your room . . .

"Wish they'd stop that," Zack said. "Make me feel funny, what with all we going to do and all."

"Best for us they keep at it," said Joe, shifting in an effort to get all of his six-foot frame underneath a tattered blanket. "You know these white men must expect it—their niggers supposed to be singing like that, all sorry so many of their masters got killed today. And by colored, too."

"With them long-assed bayonets on they guns," Zack said.

"Oh, my Lord, oh, my Lord, what shall I do . . . ?"

The Yankees were good and close now, him and Zack wouldn't have a chance like this again. Joe felt beneath his rough-cotton trousers for the knife tied around his leg. He'd be out of this damn camp tonight. Or dead trying. After what he'd seen today he didn't much care which.

Zack moved over closer to him. "You sure this the best time to go? These Texas men's just like mad wolves now—got a killing fever on them. They was cutting up colored soldiers every whichaway—even ones already dead. If they catches us . . ."

"And you think if we stay here, they going to sweeten?" Joe said. "I say they'll get meaner. I ain't staying one more night with them. If there's going to be killing, I'm the one's going to do it, not them."

Zack thought about it for a minute. "You right," he said finally. "I'd a heap more rather die fighting with my folk than from some Yankee bullet."

Hush, hush, somebody calling my name . . .

The singers' voices were getting low now. Everybody was tired, and no wonder. Yankee gunboats shelling all day, horses going crazy, pack mules running wild, bumping into trees and spilling food and bullets all over the ground. Then a two-hour march to get away from the river and cannon balls . . .

"How soon you want to light out of here, Joe?"

"Give it another few hours. And don't you be falling asleep like you always do. We leaving soon as the camp's quiet."

* * *

The singing had stopped, and in the quiet Joe could hear crickets chirping. He eyed the sentry closest to him: Massa Clem. Sitting on a log stump, shotgun on his lap, old black hat slouched down over his face like he was asleep. Joe knew better.

Massa Clem liked to brag about how no nigger had ever run away from his mule detail, but he'd not be saying it again. Wouldn't be using that bullwhip of his neither, whipping on them all the way from Texas clear on over to the Mississippi. Well, Massa Clem, you done brought me to just where I want to be—the Yankees. Now I am through with you.

Joe sniffed the air. Rain coming soon. Would make it a little harder for the bloodhounds, if they used them.

"Clem, we took a licking today." That was the sergeant, making his rounds, damn fool talking so loud he might wake some folk up.

"I wouldn't say that. Hadn't been for them gunboats, we'd of whupped the niggers good."

"Except it's us retreating, not them. Stay awake. Don't know what to expect tonight."

The sergeant moved on. The first raindrops fell. Massa Clem's chin fell forward on his chest, his hand still resting on the shotgun in his lap.

Joe nudged Zack. He got up and walked over to Massa Clem, pointed first to his pants, then to the woods. The guard nodded, and Zack went into the trees.

Joe looked around at the other sentries. They were quiet, probably asleep. He pulled the knife out from beneath his britches.

Why was Zack taking so long to pee?

Massa Clem must have been wondering the same thing, for he got up with his back to Joe and took a few steps toward the woods. Joe held his breath. As soon as Zack reappeared, Joe was across the space between him and the sentry, quiet as a panther and just as quick. He threw his arm around the sentry's throat, pulled it tight, and drove the knife into his back—felt the blood spurt out all over his hands. Massa Clem's body stiffened, his right hand releasing the shotgun, then flailing the night air. He tried to straighten up and his hat fell off. He did manage to hit Joe in the belly with his left elbow and was trying to aim another blow when all of a sudden his body relaxed and collapsed into a heap.

Joe pulled the knife out and wiped the blade clean on the dead man's shirt. His hand was trembling. Killing a man wasn't like killing no hog. It was the first time he'd done it.

He grabbed the short-barreled shotgun and Massa Clem's old hat—be better than nothing on the hot days—and followed Zack off into the woods. He hardly noticed that the crickets had stopped chirping.

* * *

They were no more than a couple of hours from the Mississippi and the Yankee lines, Zack behind, Joe in front, and trying to keep the road in sight for a guide.

It was raining steady now, and the water from the swampy ground squished in what was left of Joe's shoes. Of late it seemed like the slightest bit of wet might bring on a coughing fit, and it wouldn't do to have one now. Everybody knew the general kept a lot of his soldiers out on picket duty.

Joe felt Zack's touch on his shoulder and they both hunkered down. Twenty feet ahead of them was a soldier, his horse tied to the branches of a tree. He was facing the river. Thank you, Jesus.

Zack pointed toward the road. Two more troopers, also facing the river. Joe looked to the left, Zack shook his head and pointed again. Joe squinted hard—another trooper was just barely visible through the trees.

Damn. Looked like they'd have to stay put for a while. The soldiers would be moving on in the morning, but once the sun came up he and Zack would be in clear sight. Freedom was on the other side of those soldiers, and that's where he was bound. Only needed a little opening. Joe wasn't part Choctaw for nothing. If they—

A horse came galloping down the road. Its rider pulled up, leaned down, and said something to the trooper at the road. The soldier walked into the woods but was back a minute later. The two still in the woods unhitched their horses, pulled out their guns—six-shot Navy Colts—and started beating the bushes, moving slowly in Joe's and Zack's direction. And far off in the distance, Joe heard the cry of the hounds.

He looked up at the sky. Any minute, dawn would be breaking. He nodded at Zack and held up his hand.

Just another minute or two. Don't jump yet, Zack. Let 'em get real close.

One of the horses neighed. The trooper closest to them straightened up and cocked his revolver.

Too late. Zack ran straight into him with his knife held hard out in front. It went clean into the soldier's chest. The horse bolted and Zack leapt for the reins just in time to dodge a bullet from the other soldier's gun. Joe let out the breath he'd been holding. That shot would be the soldier's last.

Joe leveled the shotgun, blasted the soldier in the stomach, and immediately looked toward the road. The two other men must have heard the commotion and were coming into the woods to help. He didn't see their horses, but they had to be on foot, too—even he couldn't ride a horse through those trees.

The sounds of the dogs were closer now.

He turned to Zack. "You lead the horse, I'll stay about ten yards back. I got one more load in this gun, and we got theirs now."

They made their way toward the road, Joe darting from tree to tree, searching the woods in front of him. Just like hunting wolves, only this quarry was a mite more dangerous. But not more smart, and ain't no wolf ever outsmarted me yet.

His finger tightened on the trigger of the six-shooter. He motioned to Zack to stop, and they crept into a patch of bushes not far from the road. Joe kept looking up and down but couldn't see hide nor hair of the other two soldiers.

"You reckon they scairt off?" Zack whispered.

"Scared to go into the woods after a couple of crazy runaway niggers with guns?" Joe grinned. "Shows they got good sense. Now it's our turn. Let's get out of here."

No sooner were they on the horse and headed down the road than two bloodhounds come busting out the woods, baying and growling like all hell was on the march.

Zack, who had the reins, dug his heels in.

"C'mon, boy!"

"Not so fast," Joe said. "We going to let these sons of bitches get right up close to us."

"How close? Shit, I can feel their breath on my feet."

"Don't worry."

The dogs were blade-thin and black as night. And they were close, all right—close enough for one quick leap to bring the horse down. Then they'd have their day, oh yes they would.

Joe looked back into the red throat of the closest dog, took aim and fired. Then he shot the other one. The hellish baying stopped and the only sound left was that of the horse's hooves clattering on the packed-down surface of the dirt road.

* * *

About three miles farther on, Zack and Joe walked into the Yankee lines, leading the horse and carrying one engraved shotgun, one carbine, and three good-looking sets of revolvers.

"Howdy there, young fellow." Joe grinned at the black soldier who had a gun leveled at them. "Don't be pointing that thing so careless-like. Don't want to spoil the day, do you? Just look at that sun rising high in the sky." He tipped Massa Clem's old black hat to the soldier, walked over to him, and fingered the brass buttons on his uniform. "Now tell me, how do a man go about getting him an outfit like that?"

* * *

Captain William Stiles, Third United States Colored Cavalry, looked up from his desk at the long line of colored men waiting to enlist. Most had the look of the road—dust-covered clothes patched time and time again, battered and torn hats, sweat-stained bandannas knotted around a couple of heads. They'd been following Union troops, working as cooks, teamsters, and laborers, building roads and digging ditches for Grant's army on its way down the Mississippi to capture Vicksburg.

Some of them could ride—they'd been around horses and mules all their lives. Most of them looked hard and lean—strong the way the cavalry needed them to be. Good thing, too, because they'd be going into the fighting right away. With Grant's main units having to move eastward, somebody had to stay back and protect the hard-won Mississippi River passage from the Confederate troops and irregulars out in the woods and the bayous of Mississippi and Louisiana. The Third Cavalry—along with veteran Union outfits—had gotten the job, and by God he'd see they did it well. They had but two weeks before they took to the field.

Time to get moving.

"Name?"

"Joe."

"Joe what?"

"No last name, Massa."

"Don't call me Massa, from now on it's sir. That goes for all soldiers, colored or white."

"Yes, sir."

"Got a last name you like? Everybody has to have one."

"Duckett, sir. That's a good name, I heard tell it was my grandfather's."

"All right, Joe Duckett. Now tell me how you got here."

The captain wrote it all down. A runaway, captured and impressed by them, escaped . . .

There was something familiar about him.

"You the one busted through the Reb lines up at Milliken's Bend? Rode with General Grant's cavalry escort as a scout up there in the Yazoo?"

A broad smile. "The very same, sir."

Now, this was a piece of luck. The man was practically a legend—a cook for Colonel Osband, one day he begs to tag along with some regulars, they mount him on a mule and give him a musket from the War of 1812, and next thing you know he's come back into camp with five Reb prisoners marching in front of him. The story was that he even had them singing "John Brown's Body," but Stiles wasn't so sure about that part.

"Me too, Cap'n," said the tall man just behind Duckett. "I rode with Colonel Osband too."

"Well, I'm glad to hear it, soldier. I'll get to you in a minute. Now, Duckett, a few questions, and then I want you to go over to the headquarters unit and wait for me. Are you married?"

"Yes, and got three children."

"Names?"

"My wife is Zenobia. She still up at the Kenworthy plantation in the Yazoo with my baby daughter Cally, I think. My boy and other girl—Luke and Milly—they was sold away three years ago. I'll find them someday."

Captain Stiles heard the pain in the man's voice and laid down his pen.

"After this war is over, Duckett. You understand that, don't you?"

His new recruit pulled himself erect, and did it right. The days around Grant's cavalry told.

"I will do my duty, sir."

* * *

An hour later Joe stood at attention in the tent that served as Captain Stiles's company headquarters.

"At ease, Duckett."

"Yes, sir."

"I've got plenty of sergeants, good ones, who rode with me at Fort Donelson and Shiloh. They went through days such as I never want to see again, and they are true as tempered steel. What

I don't have is a sergeant who knows the colored people and the country around here. I want you to be the first colored sergeant in this cavalry regiment."

Now how about that! Joe blessed his lucky stars for landing in the hands of a fellow with sense enough to come to such a conclusion.

"I know the colonel will back me up. General Grant, too. It was you and them colored boys up at Milliken's who brought him around on this whole idea of colored soldiers."

Stiles studied the dark smiling face. The man was clearly of African descent, but his black hair was almost curly, hinting at some Indian blood. He wore it parted in the middle and it fell clear down to his shoulders. He looked to be a few years over thirty, and by all accounts he could ride like a whirlwind.

"I'll be mighty proud to do it, Captain. One thing, can I have Zack Bascom assigned to my troop as a corporal?"

"If you think he can do the job, take him."

The captain wrote their names down on the roll.

"We'll get down to training tomorrow—mainly weapons and firing. The men I've picked can ride, probably better than all of us New Yorkers. But they must learn their weapons and the discipline of drill. That's all for now."

Joe snapped to attention and was about to salute.

"Oh, and one more thing. I heard that while you were up with that cavalry outfit, they did a lot of hard drinking around and with the general. I've found that whiskey and horse soldiering don't go well together. Understood?"

Joe winced, then squared his shoulders and grinned. "Yes, sir."

"Dismissed."

CHAPTER TWO

"ZENOBIA! Oh, Zenobia!"

That was Lisa Mae, so it must be lunchtime. Zenobia straightened up and stretched her back, then looked down the long row of cotton plants she'd been picking. She dropped the bag where it was. About half full. Would it be the second or third she'd filled this morning?

"Come on, honey, time for you and Momma to get something to eat."

She scooped her daughter up with one arm, took the piece of sugarcane out of her mouth, and started walking. It seemed such a long way back to the grove. Long as you were picking, the sun wasn't so bad, but once you stopped, you could feel it beating down on you like Satan was trying to burn you off the face of the earth.

All around her, the women in white shifts—the only folks left on the plantation—had stopped their singing and were calling out to each other as they moved back toward the grove where they would eat.

"Lula Mae, what for you laughing like that? You know something I don't?"

"Doralee, child, you been picking all morning and look at that little bit of cotton you got."

"You always be walking so proud, Rena. Nobody tell you there ain't no men left around here to look at you?"

"Nary a one of them ever looked at you, that's for sure."

Zenobia joined in the teasing as they came together at the end of the rows.

"If'n Sammy boy with all them big fine muscles and such was to suddenly show up around here, bet you-all would hush that fussing and make some fast tracks to see who'd be the first one to catch ahold of him."

The girls tittered and Lula Mae said, "Way I be, they could run to him as fast as they want." She threw her head back to one side, put her hand on her hip, and swayed her body back and forth. "I'd wait right here where I be, and that there sweet-loving man would come flying down the field to me."

The little children who'd been with their mothers in the field trailed behind them, buck naked. Looking ahead to the blessed shade of the trees, Zenobia could see that Drayton had the food ready—one thing that trifling nigger was good for. Ever since the white overseer went to the army and Miss Kenworthy put him in charge, Drayton had made sure they had enough to eat. It wasn't like the old days, but Zenobia had heard from folks who passed through, moving from plantation to plantation, how bad things were all over. She was grateful for the corn bread and fatback and corn or string beans they got every noontime. At night there were only the greens she grew in her garden.

Drayton was waiting for them, cooling himself with his fancy fan and sitting on the little log bench where the old overseer used to sit. He even had on a white vest and a brown stovepipe hat with its top cut off. She wondered if he was fool enough to think his fancy clothes made him any less a slave than the rest of them.

"See how I feeds you?" he said, as the youngsters who were serving put the corn bread and string beans with fatback into the bowls. "Ain't I good to you, children?"

Good for nothing was more like it, trying to climb in bed with every woman on the place since all the men were gone. She watched a few of the women go over to him, hugging and kissing him. You couldn't really blame them. He could make it easier for them on the job, get them something extra to eat.

She fed Cally, then dipped the hem of her shift in the water bucket and wiped the little girl's face and neck.

"You mighty warm, honey, think you might could stay up here with the bigger chilluns this afternoon? It be too hot out in that sun for you."

"I don't want to be away from you. Somebody take me."

"Nobody going to take you, sugar. You can just stay up here and play with Ned—I'll come to take you both home when." She pointed toward the long expanse of cotton waiting to be picked.

Cally started to cry, and Zenobia picked her up. "Your mama's life is hard enough without I worry about the sun burning you up. Remember, honey, I ain't going to let nobody take you. Now you stay up here with them other chilluns. Lisa Mae won't let nobody hurt you neither."

"All right, you all!" Drayton hollered. "Time to get back to the fields."

Zenobia called over to Lisa Mae. "Take Cally and keep her with you this afternoon. And make sure she keeps drinking water." She joined the line of women headed back out into the fields, looked at the children following their mothers, and shook her head. "They should be staying with you too. Sun will burn them hard."

"Wait up there just a minute, girl."

She turned and saw Drayton strutting up behind her.

"Look mighty pretty this noontime. Your walk is something powerful sweet to see. Makes me feel like the earth is shaking."

"Hush your mouth, I gets tired just listening to you."

"Want to take the afternoon off, come on and take a little walk over to my new place? We could look around, drink some lemonade from the big house."

The sweat was already running down her face again, and she'd only just gotten up from the table. She looked out toward the cotton fields where the other women were already picking. They'd started singing too.

> All night, all day,
> Oh God's angels keep watching over me . . .

Drayton had caught up to her now. "Zenobia—"

"Told you once, told you twice, ain't going with you."

"You still think your Joe be coming back for you. Well, I'm here. He ain't. I can feed you. He cain't."

The words cut right to the very bone. Drayton was right. Joe had left her all alone. It was a cruel world and getting crueler every day.

"I got some cotton to pick," she said.

Drayton grabbed hold of her shoulder. "I can make you go with me, you know. I'm the top dog now."

"Dog be the right word, I'd say." She jerked away, quickly putting some distance between them with her long easy stride. He let her go, but she could feel his eyes following every step out to the field.

"Someday you'll need me," he called after her.

All night, all day
Oh, God's angels keep watching over me . . .

* * *

Late in the midnight hour. Cally and Ned were asleep on their wooden pallets, the dog between them. Zenobia wished Brother Caleb hadn't shown up. Every single one of her bones had its own ache, and she wanted nothing more than to climb in bed. But here she and Lisa Mae were, sitting at the old log table listening to the preacher man from the Newton plantation down the road.

It was hard enough just trying to keep herself and the young ones fed and washed up and decent. Now here he come, talking about freedom, about how everybody's leaving. Just make that three days' journey through the swamps and woods to the Mississippi River and they'd be slaves no more. Oh, the way would be hard, but General Grant would soon put an end to all of the colored people's pain.

"No more whips," Caleb was saying. "No more auction blocks, no more children sold down the river. A Mighty Deliverer has come to smite Pharaoh's armies. Just one more river to cross, Zenobia child."

"And when would we be leaving?"

"Tomorrow night."

"That soon?"

"Ought to be leaving tonight. All around us these white folks so scared of losing their niggers, they be running colored folks—putting them in big gangs and taking them far away from the Mississippi River so's the Yankee soldiers cain't free them."

"How many of us would be going?"

"About ten, with those from our place."

"Cally and Ned too little to go," Zenobia said. "There's snakes and wildcats and things out there in the swamps, and—"

"Best to leave them here, anyway. We go, we'll have to move fast, and they would slow us down. The white folks ain't taking children, just folks old enough to work."

Lisa Mae leaned forward. "You sure enough don't know Zenobia or me if you think we leaving Cally and Ned nowhere," she said.

"Aw, Ned ain't even your child, Zenobia," Caleb said. "And I tell you, nothing would happen to them here."

Luke and Milly are out there somewhere. Is there a chance I could find them? And Joe . . .

She looked at Cally, the only one of her children she could still protect, the only one she could still see and touch and hold. And Ned, just eight years old and already done had his folks sold away from him. She got up from the table to get a dipper of water, took her time drinking it, looking off into the night.

"I guess you better go on without us."

"Well, now, Zenobia, the thing is, we was counting on you to lead us." Brother Caleb got up and came over to stand beside her. "See, Joe done taught you all about them woods, how to find old Injun paths through the swamps, how to read signs on them trees."

"I ain't going without Cally and Ned."

"But we needs you—"

"If you needs me, you needs them."

Brother Caleb sighed. "All right, they can go too. Be ready tomorrow night when you hears the hoot owl calling."

But come morning, Cally was sweating and whimpering. Zenobia wiped her hot forehead and knew they'd not be going anywhere any time soon.

That night the hoot owl called and called, seemed like all the night long.

* * *

Zenobia had to admit Drayton was mighty good to them when Cally took sick. Miss Sue acted half crazy most of the time now, but somehow he got her to listen to him and give them a room up in the big house, quiet and peaceful, with clean white sheets on their bed. He even fixed it so Zenobia could stay in the house with Cally and take care of Miss Sue's children instead of working in the fields.

A week after they moved into the big house, Cally was well enough to play outside, running all over the big green lawn with Miss Sue's children. Zenobia was watching them from a rocking chair on the front porch when a horseman pulled up wearing a white shirt with a blue bandanna around his neck. He was off the horse and past Zenobia in a minute, like he hadn't even seen her. And before she had time to wonder why he was in such a powerful hurry, he was back out of the house and galloping away.

"Zenobia, fetch Drayton from down the field," said Miss Sue, who had come out on the porch. "And hurry up, it's mighty important."

"It's almost supper time, Miss Sue. You reckon I could take Cally and stay down at our cabin after I give him your message?"

"Oh, for goodness' sakes! I don't care where you stay, just make sure Drayton gets up here in a hurry."

By sundown there wasn't a woman in the long line of cabins who would be able to sleep that night.

"Something bad about to happen," Zenobia had told them. "Feel it in my bones. You pack up everything you care about tonight, or you be sorry tomorrow."

"How you know?" one young woman asked.

"She always do," another woman said. "You heard tell about that shooting star that fell just before the war started? Back before you came here? Well, Zenobia told everybody it was coming and that was a whole week before."

Long after all the children were asleep, a knock came at her door.

"Who that?"

"It's me, Drayton. Come on out here. I got some mighty important news and I don't want the children to hear it."

Was he making it up just to get her outside alone? He had been good the whole week. Zenobia looked over at the children and Lisa Mae, saw they were still asleep, then slipped out of the cabin and closed the door softly behind her.

"They coming in the morning, so you got to make up your mind."

"Who's coming?"

"Major Kenworthy, he done sent a messenger to tell Miss to move everybody over to Alabama, away from the Yankees, 'cause they robbing and stealing and killing folks something awful. They burning niggers."

"That ain't what I heard. I heard they coming to make us free."

"Don't matter what you hear, the slave-running gang be here in the morning to take everybody. Miss and me and her chilluns, we're going up to a little town other side of Jackson, stay with some of her kin."

"Why you telling me all this?"

"You can come with me and Miss Sue, don't have to go to Alabama. Miss took a liking to you, said you can take care of her chilluns and bring yours and Lisa Mae with you."

"I don't know . . ."

"They coming at sunup, whole plantation be gone by the time the sun's high."

"And if I don't want to go with Miss Sue?"

"Don't make her no difference, plenty other women here will want to go." He looked at her and shrugged. "I'll be by in the morning, hope you got sense enough to leave with us."

Zenobia went back into the hut and shook Lisa Mae.

"Get up, honey, come on outside, we got some talking to do."

Lisa Mae's deep brown face stayed calm as Zenobia told her about Drayton's visit, but she kept tugging on one of the long plaited braids that fell down almost to her shoulders.

"I can't see the chillun making it all the way to Alabama, Zee. Way I see it, we got to go with Drayton and Miss and trust in God. Besides, further away we go from the Yankees, the less chance we got to get free."

"That sorry-assed Drayton think the Yankee soldiers going to tar and feather him," Zenobia said.

"He ain't so bad, Zee. Stop talking so mean about him."

"Then when he ask, you can be the one to lay down with him, 'cause I ain't."

"I'd say you may have to if times get hard. It's you he's sweet on, anyway."

Zenobia sighed. "You right about one thing—it don't make sense to start for Alabama with Ned and Cally, especially with her just over being sick."

"So we'll go with Miss and Drayton?"

"And when the time comes," Zenobia said, "we'll get through to the Yankees."

* * *

The roosters crowed so loud that morning Zenobia thought they must know what was happening. She wanted to turn away from the sight in front of her, but she couldn't. This was something she would have to remember. Brother Caleb had been so wrong when he said they weren't running children over to Alabama. They were taking everybody except them and Miss Sue's old house slaves Linus and Mary.

Out of the cabins came the women, some so light-skinned they almost might have been white, some black as night. They carried bundles of clothes over their shoulders, and some of them balanced another bundle on their heads. They walked oh, so slowly down the path to where Drayton waited with some white men. Some of them held guns and others played with the whips in their hands. Merciful Lord! What had they to fear from a bunch of women weighted down with bundles?

Two old wooden wagons hitched to a couple of mules were being loaded up with water, flour, bacon. Two white men sat with the reins in their hands. The boss of the train stood talking to Drayton, counting out the people and checking their names off on a sheet of paper as they fell in line on the road.

"Rena Mae and two young 'uns, Lawrence and Lionel?" The man lifted his head and glanced at the coffee-colored woman kneeling down in the road to fasten her sons' sandals. He checked them off the list and moved on.

"Annie and Ruth . . ." The two sisters were holding hands. One was about twelve, with big doe-like brown eyes set in a pool of white, the other fourteen but with a body so like a full-grown woman's that the man looked every inch of it over before he put a check beside their names.

Zenobia lifted Cally up and turned to Lisa Mae. "Take Ned's hand, we got to go down and say goodbye. We ain't never going to see a one of them again."

When she got to the road there were many, many more than she had expected. There were colored folks, mostly women, from plantations down the road and up by the river—a long line of them, stretched back almost as far as you could see. More white men with guns and whips moved along beside the women and children to make sure no one strayed. She walked down to the line, Cally right beside her.

"Matty Lou, you don't lose your faith in God, you hear? Zelma, you look after your auntie Lena real good, you promise? Sarah, don't let your mamma carry that bundle, it too heavy for her."

Up and down the line she went, scolding and hugging and crying, till finally she reached Aunt Garry. The gray-haired old woman had been here when Zenobia came, brought in chains over those same hills where the line would soon disappear. She'd been there when Zenobia and Joe jumped the broom, too, and when Luke and Milly got sold away. She'd sung Zenobia to sleep when she cried like a little baby the night a half-crazed Joe ran off into the woods after the children. Like he could bring them back—the big brave fool. Instead she lost them all at once . . .

She put her arms around Aunt Garry and hugged her tight.

"Now don't you go worrying about me, Zenobia. The Good Lord done look after me over all my long journey this far, I don't reckon He going to stop now. And don't you feel bad 'cause we got to go and you ain't, either. You hear me, child?"

"I hears you." She reached down into a pocket and pulled out some Yankee coins she'd dug up out of a secret hiding place the night before. "Here, take this little bit of money, I got some more. Just in case you need to buy some food on the way."

"Keep it, girl. Where I'm going I won't need no money, and you got to have enough for all of you. Now you better be off, 'fore Miss change her mind and send you along with us."

Zenobia stepped back. Somewhere down the line somebody was singing:

"Jesus have gone to Galilee."

In front of Zenobia, a smiling Aunt Garry picked up the song:

"And how do you know that Jesus is gone?"

A low moaning sound, then the women sang:

"I tracked Him by His drops of blood."

Aunt Garry sang:

"And every drop He dropped in love."

Zenobia picked up Cally and headed back to the hilltop. Right in front of the big house, she put Cally down and shaded her eyes so she could follow her friends' white shifts as they walked down the road, little puffs of red dust rising in their wake.

Soon—so soon—the last of them had rounded the bend, and she could no longer hear their voices.

Zenobia lifted her head and sang out, loud as she could:

"And every drop He dropped in love."

CHAPTER THREE

MAJOR Richard Kenworthy was bone-weary of this riding. He had served the Confederacy since the eighth day of May, 1861—how long ago was that? It was now December 14, 1863—that made it more than two and a half years. He should be doing a real soldier's job, should be galloping across open fields charging Union cavalry. Not stuck on patrol over in Louisiana raiding abandoned plantations along the Mississippi where Grant had escaped slaves raising cotton and food for his armies.

It was only when he thought about Clifton, the Kenworthy plantation, and what he'd lost that the raids seemed to make any kind of sense. Grant had taken Vicksburg, but even a fallen city had to be supplied—and too many Yankees still thought they could do it with food from nearby plantations. Just as too many coloreds thought they could collaborate with the Yankees now that their masters had all gone away. An idea like that could cause God knows how much trouble on plantations whose slaves weren't free yet.

Behind the major rode Clinton Adams, Kenworthy's oldest friend and for the past two years captain in charge of the second troop of Caper's battalion of Confederate cavalry. Kenworthy slowed down so their horses were side by side.

"How much farther to the Ransome place?" Kenworthy asked.

"I'd say three miles," Adams said.

"All right, we'll stop here for the night. Make sure the men see to the horses. And no fires."

Kenworthy had wondered what kind of officer his old schoolmate and drinking buddy would make, but he needn't have worried. Adams was a trustworthy officer, who had, of late, begun to show the marks of real leadership. The men liked him even though he was hard on them. Seemed to have the knack of getting them to be comfortable with him without being too familiar.

After Adams passed the word down the line and set out the pickets, Kenworthy waited for him to return to the little knoll before going over plans with two other officers.

"After tomorrow," he said, "we'll have to head northwest up along the Boeuf River. The Yankees must be real tired of these raids—just got word they're sending out some light cavalry to wipe us out. We have to do a good job with the Ransome place, then light out of there. Fast."

When he'd finished going over the disposition of their forces, the two lieutenants went off to sleep, but not Captain Adams.

"Something on your mind, Clint?"

"Need to talk with you a few minutes before I turn in."

"Long as it's not hours instead of minutes," the major said. "I remember some long nights at Mississippi College."

"I don't like it," Adams said. "I don't like what we're doing."

"Meaning what?"

"What we got to do to those niggers tomorrow."

Kenworthy began to unroll his blanket. "We didn't tell these Yankees to come down here. We didn't destroy the Constitution, tromp all over the rights of property holders. We didn't—"

"But there have to be limits, Richard. Even in war. And these darkies aren't combatants."

"Don't matter. Vicksburg's gone, and what we do this next few months will tell if we get the Yankees to go home or not. Can't you see? Any sign of weakness and it's all over for us."

Adams got up from his seat on a rock. "I seem to remember a friend of mine who used to say maybe slavery was bad, maybe we should gradually abolish it. You didn't say abolish the slaves."

"The Yankees took that option away from us, Captain Adams." Damn, Clint was his friend and he hadn't meant to speak to him from such a height, but war didn't allow for all this second-guessing, thinking, and philosophizing. It was just a job, something to be done. "Catch you some sleep, Clint, we've got to be up early in the morning."

* * *

It was about as challenging as a springtime stroll in the woods. When the sun came up the major's forty men surrounded the plantation, shot the only armed black guard, then rounded up every escaped slave who hadn't managed to run off.

One big yellow-skinned nigger seemed to be in charge of the gang of men who'd been working the farm. He was sitting on the ground in the middle of them, surrounded by five guards with double-barreled shotguns.

Kenworthy looked up at the sky. The sun was climbing fast, they'd have to get out of there in a hurry. His orders were explicit. Confiscate all the cattle and kill the colored who couldn't be taken along and used as laborers. He sure didn't have time to take them with the Yankee cavalry all about.

"Captain Adams, burn the buildings and cotton. Get the cattle moving, we'll get them up the road a bit and run 'em off in the woods, maybe three or four miles away."

"And the niggers?"

"Tie their hands behind. Line 'em up single file, backs to the river. Form a firing squad. Oh, and send that yellow one over to me."

A cavalryman marched the man over to Kenworthy at saber-point. He had a bruise on his cheek. Something about him rubbed the major the wrong way, maybe it was because he had the same arrogant look that Joe used to have sometimes back on the plantation.

"Where you from, boy?"

"Squires plantation, 'cross the river."

"How long you darkies been here, squatting on white folks' land?"

"'Bout three months."

"Heard anything about Yankee cavalry coming this way?"

"No, suh, Massa.'"

"I doubt it. If I had time, I'd whip your lying black ass."

"Yeessuh, Massa."

Kenworthy turned to the guard. "Take him back with the rest of them."

As soon as the men gathered the cattle, Adams assembled a firing squad. The major trotted his horse over to where the colored stood, some singing, some praying. A wretched-looking lot, pants threadbare, shoes broken down, shirts ripped or no shirts at all.

He rode slowly down the line and looked directly into the eyes of each man. He stopped when he saw a boy about eleven.

"Take him out, and set him free."

He brought his horse to a halt in front of the big yellow man, looked hard into his blazing eyes.

"You poor miserable darkies have been tricked into believing you are free. And you've been helping the Yankees against your lawful masters. It's a sin and a shame you've been so misled, boys. Because now we're going to have to put an end to you."

He backed the horse a few steps and looked over at Adams.

"Too bad they didn't stay on their masters' plantations. Prepare your firing squad."

"Order arms!" Adams shouted. "Right shoulder arms!"

A minute passed.

What the hell was wrong with Clint? Why wasn't he giving the aim-and-fire command?

What the—

Adams was turning his horse, riding up so close only Richard could hear him.

"You can't do this, Richard. It's wrong and you know it."

The condemned men were as still as the men on the firing squad.

Kenworthy grabbed the reins of his friend's horse. "Clint, do your duty!" he hissed. He released the reins. "Now!"

Instead, Adams made as if to dismount.

"Captain Adams! Attention!" Major Richard Kenworthy sat bolt upright on his horse, his knuckles white from gripping the pommel so tight and hard.

Adams was a soldier, and the order stopped him. He sat at attention on his mount, his eyes straight ahead.

"Captain Adams, I am giving you a direct order. You will obey it."

Adams's horse was pawing the earth, as if he sensed the tension.

"Major Kenworthy, sir, I will not. If their blood is shed, it won't be on my hands."

In all that damn quiet every man must have heard every word. Now they were waiting, all of them, black, white, condemned, free, for his next move.

Dear God—would it be to execute his best friend?

He unbuckled his burnished black leather holster. Felt his fingers tremble as they touched the butt of his ten-shot French-made revolver.

The sound of a scout galloping into the yard broke the silence. "They're coming. Yankee cavalry's three miles down the road. And they're colored cavalry."

"Mount up the men. Leave the niggers where they are." Kenworthy rode up to the yellow man. "Looks like your God spared you today."

"We serves the same one, sir."

"I don't have time to argue theology with you, but somebody's God must have been looking out for you." He nodded toward Captain Adams. "And him."

And me.

* * *

That night—miles, he hoped, from the Union cavalry—he called Captain Adams over. His friend stood at attention before him, and Kenworthy felt the anger rise up in him again over this rotten assignment.

"I expect you see what happened today as God's hand and there I'd agree with you. I'm glad I didn't have to kill them, but by His holy name, I will surely shoot you on the spot should you ever again refuse to obey an order."

* * *

Sergeant Joe Duckett stood up in his stirrups and looked behind him at the long line of black troopers. They'd come a good long way since that first little fight back in October. This would be their first real raid up into Confederate country in Louisiana, about twenty miles below the Arkansas State Line. Joe was mighty proud that Colonel Osband said he'd be counting on him to be the scout. He spurred his horse and rode up beside Captain Stiles, who was leading the column.

"Horses and men all ready, Sergeant? I'm thinking we're in for some heavy fighting, and soon."

"Couldn't be more ready, Captain."

Stiles looked over at Joe's horse. "You know that roan of yours may be the damnedest sorriest-looking animal I ever saw. A sergeant ought to be riding something better."

"Begging your pardon, Captain, but the day you find a horse anywhere that can beat Hawk running, then I'll get rid of her and give her to one of the bugle boys."

The captain laughed. "If we weren't getting ready to go into some fighting, I'd like to have a run at you myself. In fact, I think I will once we get back in camp."

"Captain, can I ask you something?"

"You can. What is it?"

"We riding together with that white outfit, right?"

"And?"

"Them men been saying niggers ain't going to fight."

The captain pulled down the brim of his hat. The sun was getting hot. "So?"

"You think they going to back us up like they should if the fighting gets hard?"

The captain frowned. "They will, Duckett. Because out there if one falters, everybody falters, and everybody dies. They're

Union soldiers, I've ridden with them and seen them in action. They'll fight with you."

"We heard tell that a whole Yankee regiment tried to run off rather than fight with us."

"General Grant took care of that. Anyway, you know you can't do a blessed thing about what other folk think. Just do your best to make sure our boys are ready, and everything will turn out fine. Now I think you'd better go back and prepare to turn the company over to Zack. It's time for you to go up to the colonel for your briefing."

An hour later, at the noontime break, Joe—dressed like a field hand and wearing his big black country hat—rode up to report to Captain Stiles. In front of them was the Mississippi, muddy and swirling.

"The colonel wants me to find where that Rebel cavalry at, sir."

"Where's your weapon?"

Joe smiled, reached down inside his pants leg, and took out a six-shot Colt polished so brightly it might have just come out of the factory up in Springfield.

"Son of a bitch. Good luck. See you tomorrow. And don't forget about our race."

"Captain, next thing you know you be walking around buck naked," said Zack, who'd come to tell Joe good-bye. "Joe done already won himself a heap of money with that broken-down horse of his."

Joe stroked Hawk's mane. "Baby, they talking about you mighty bad, but I wouldn't trade you for nothing." He saluted the captain and rode away.

* * *

Traveling in this country, not more than a few days' ride from Clifton, made Joe sad. Zenobia and Cally were over there somewhere. Oh, what wouldn't he give for just a glimpse of his daughter, see those sparkly black eyes . . . give Zenobia a pat on her sweet ass. It was hard being a free man with family near, close as your breath and you couldn't go to them. But he was a soldier man now, he knew where he had to be.

About an hour up the road he came to a path that led down to the river. He guided Hawk down the hill to where an old black man sat on a little ferryboat. A rope ran from one side of the river to the other.

"Morning, Uncle," Joe said. "You got a nice little boat there."

"Makes me a living. Who you be?"

Joe pulled out a dollar coin. "You take me across and wait for me, I give you two more."

The man took the money and waved Joe on board.

"Careful, now. Two horses as much as this little thing can take." He began to draw the ferry across the river. "You with them Yankees, ain't you?"

"I is a free man. And we fighting to make you free too."

"Better watch yourself when we get to the other side. Them gray-boys all around, they catching and killing any colored man they don't know. Say any lone nigger by hisself got to be with the Yankees. They sure going to wonder where somebody tall and strong as you come from. You look like you been eating too good."

The ferry came to the other bank and slid to a halt in the mud. Joe rode Hawk onto solid ground and turned back.

"Don't forget to wait for me."

"I'll say you a prayer, too, expect you'll be needing it." He grinned. "But by the look of you some of them folks might be needing a little prayer soon too."

Joe rode off into the woods with the old man
heavy on his mind. If they caught him, they'd hang him ... one
of those tall dark oak trees in the forest he was riding through. He
caressed his neck softly with his right hand, then reached down
into his pants for the flask of bourbon. He took a good long swig
and wiped his mouth with the cuff of his blue cotton blouse.
There, that felt better. Good thing Captain Stiles hadn't asked
what else he was carrying. But the captain wasn't out here alone in
these dark woods, the trees so thickly branched they must block
out the sky when they were in leaf. As it was, not much of the
weak sunshine could make it through.

He took another long sip of whiskey, got off of Hawk, and
cut him a good stout club. Might need it if he couldn't get to his
gun.

Squirrels was everywhere, jumping from tree to tree, sometimes stopping to look at him. Wasn't used to having no company
in their forest. If Zenobia was here she'd be teasing him about
squirrel stew. Always had fun with him about how much he liked
to eat, and he'd rather eat squirrel than anything. Zenobia—

Come on, man, you a soldier in the army, ain't got no time
to be thinking about no family—you getting back to them the
best way you know how. You—

"Nigger, what you doing out here in the woods on that rag-
gedy-looking horse?"

Shit! Put a little whiskey in your belly, take your mind off a
job, and you ride right out into a road and a Rebel trooper. With
a gun pointed right at your daydreaming head.

"Oh, Massa, you liked to scared this poor nigger to death. I
done told Massa George, if he put me on a horse to catch that runaway Amos, then some Yankee soldiers be surely going to catch

me and he'll have done lost hisself two niggers 'stead of one. That's just what I told him."

"We ain't no Yankees, boy. Whose nigger are you, anyway?"

"Like I done told you—I belongs to Massa George. He done sent me after Amos. If'n I don't come back soon, he—"

"Well, you ain't going back right now. I'm taking you to the colonel."

"What for, Massa?"

"Just come on up the road with me, boy."

When they got to a fork a little ways down the road, Joe saw more Rebel cavalry than he'd ever thought about, much less laid eyes on. Had to be at least four companies of them. And there, riding beside what must be the colonel, was Massa Richard Kenworthy, standing up in his stirrups, one hand cupped over his eyes so he didn't have to squint to see the black man riding alongside his scout.

Joe's legs gripped Hawk like he feared he might fall off. "That the colonel way over yonder?" His right hand closed around the big wooden stick, and he pointed with the other.

When the scout turned to look, Joe swung the stick. The blow landed just where neck met shoulder and knocked the Reb right off his horse.

Joe spurred Hawk into a gallop, and they tore down the road with three Rebel troopers hot behind them.

Damn, got me a race today!

Joe put his head down alongside Hawk's neck and whispered in her ear. "Don't forget, I knows there ain't no horse lives can catch you."

The Rebels were whooping that god-awful yell of theirs, sounding like a pack of hounds.

"Gonna hang you when we catch you, nigger," one of them shouted. Joe shouted, too, but not at the Rebs. "Go, Hawk!"

When he took a second to look back, he felt like giving a whooping yell himself. They was falling back. Couldn't keep up with him—except, damn, one of them's still there and gaining. Hawk was all wet and lathered. Wasn't no way to get more speed out of her.

"Come on, baby, it's into the woods."

He could hear the lone trooper crashing through the trees behind him. Good. Come on into my woods. Choctaw woods. Spirits of my ancestors all around me. Big Bear and Little Wolf . . .

He got down off Hawk and threaded his way through clumps of trees along a path that made all kinds of bends. Just past a real sharp one he tied up the horse, pulled out his Colt, and waited for the Reb to round the bend.

That Reb was only a youngster, but his eyes were mean. Joe shot him in the chest.

The Reb's horse bolted away down another path, probably led to the ferry. Joe jumped on Hawk and followed. I ain't about to let a horse fast as you go back to them.

They reached the ferry at a full gallop. "Whoa, girl!" He jumped down and grabbed the reins of both horses.

"Let's get going, Uncle. They right behind me."

"God have mercy."

"You can pray while you pull on that rope."

The old man suddenly didn't seem so old. He pulled like he was twenty, and with Joe helping him, the little ferryboat made its way not so slowly across the Mississippi.

Halfway across, he heard shots and saw the water pinging up, way to the right of them. He looked back. Three Rebs stood at the river's edge, blasting away with their shotguns.

The old man's hands shook something terrible.

"Aren't even coming close," Joe said. "You keep prayin' and pullin'."

Soon as they reached the other bank, he pulled both horses up the hill, tied them to a tree, and looked around.

"Watch them for me," he told the old man. "Got something I need to do."

He spotted an ax propped against the old man's wood supply, picked it up, and returned to the boat.

It took but four blows to split the hull. He cut the rope, shoved what was left of the boat off into the current, watched it list and then sink. With his hands around his mouth he shouted to the Rebs on the other side.

"Any of you cross this river today, it ain't goin' to be here!"

For a moment, the Rebels stopped shooting and the breeze sent their words clear across the water.

"You see how that nigger broke up that boat?"

"Like it were sheet-board!"

"Just like I'd of broke your heads!" Joe shouted back. "If them worn-out nags of yours could of caught me."

Now the Rebs commenced calling him everything except a child of God. And Massa Richard Kenworthy stood right there in the front of them, just waving his fist and shouting God knew what, Joe couldn't tell with all of them yelling. Probably that this was the very last time in life that Joe would ever cross him.

The old man was looking his age again, as if he'd shriveled up even more. Joe offered him the last of the whiskey and it was gone in one long gulp. Joe sighed. It would be a long dry ride back to the regiment.

"Uncle, I sure am sorry I had to sink your boat. But I'll tell my captain how you brought that little bitty boat across the Mississippi with them Rebs firing away, and I reckon he'll make it right with you."

"You tell him that? And they might pay me for my boat?"

"I'll do my damnedest to see they does. Now get up on that horse there—she's a good 'un. We better get out of here fast, it'll go hard with you if they catches you."

"You right about that," the old man said with a broad grin. "I be a surenuff Union man now."

* * *

"We'll grab us any boat comes down the river today and use it to ferry the boys across to the other side," Colonel Osband said when Joe made his report. "Good a time as any to whip them."

The Union detachment crossed over the river into Louisiana and pursued the Reb cavalry up toward the Arkansas line. Then the Rebs turned on them and counterattacked, the weight of their assault falling on the white Illinois troopers, who fought like wildcats. Joe would never doubt them again. Seeing the fight almost lost, Captain Stiles grabbed a squad of men, told Joe to come along, and led them across the field with drawn sabers. And oh, those Rebel cavalry had no taste for that. By day's end, seventy-five white troopers and a hundred twenty-five colored troopers sent close to five hundred Rebs running off into the woods. Not without a price: a good quarter of the Yankees ended up killed, wounded, or taken prisoner.

But now the Rebs knew the colored enemy would fight. And the white enemy would fight right alongside them. Gave you something to think about.

CHAPTER FOUR

IT WAS surprisingly mild and warm for a February day, even in upper Louisiana. Pauline watched rays of bright sunshine playing over the still muddy ground where, just days ago, a sudden ice storm had covered everything with its rigid beauty. The road that led to the great white house was strewn with broken branches.

The morning after the storm, she had walked around the plantation and marveled at the still loveliness of the trees, every branch, every twig encased in glittering ice. When she heard what sounded like shots, she spun around, frightened, looking for the source of the sound—and again was awed by her surroundings. What she'd heard were pine boughs, snapping under the weight of the ice and sending down a shower of shining tubes as the sheaths of ice, one after the other, broke loose. Nature had clothed the branches in that glittering raiment and given them a moment of splendor—then swiftly and cruelly brought it to an end.

Now on this day when she'd have preferred to be outside, Pauline was in the living room of the plantation, watching the woman she called Miss read a letter delivered not five minutes ago by a Rebel soldier.

"I'm afraid you're in for some trouble," Miss said. "Richard's been fighting upcountry. He'll be stopping in here any day now." She saw Pauline shiver. "You can hide out in that hut down by the river, Pauline. You'd better take Milly and Luke with you, he's still angry that we bought them."

"I wish . . ."

"What, dear?"

Pauline sighed. "It's sad, isn't it, that Joe ran off and never got a chance to know his children were safe with us."

"Sad like so much about this terrible war. I wish to God it were over." She took Pauline's hand. "You worry about him a lot, don't you?"

"Joe?"

"Of course."

"I do. He's my only brother and I see his face every day when I look at Luke."

"What a strange world we live in. Richard still loves you, you know. Always has and always will."

Pauline walked over to the window and looked down on Luke, who was washing a horse down near the stables. Milly, his tall and willowy sixteen-year-old sister, stood watching him. The three years Joe's children had spent with the Cannons had brightened Pauline's life in ways she'd never expected. She'd taught them to read and write, loved them, and been loved back.

And now, with the colonel away, there was no telling what Massa Richard would do when he got to the plantation. He must not find them. . . .

She turned back to Miss. "I think I'd better get down to that hut this afternoon and clean it up. Nobody's been there for a good while. I'll come back and start dinner later."

"Stay down there, don't worry about dinner. Times being what they are, we don't know when he might get here or who's with him."

* * *

Pauline spent the night in the slave shack with the children. Milly responded to their situation calmly enough, but Pauline knew better than to expect anything resembling calm from Luke. It wasn't just his looks that reminded her of his father. He had always had a mind of his own, never thought like children his age. Now he was nearly fourteen. His years on the plantation and recent status as blacksmith had made him bold—dangerously bold.

"Aunt Pauline," he said, "this Massa Richard, what can he do to me? We belong to Colonel Cannon, not him. I want to sleep up next to the stables."

"You'll sleep right here. First thing you know, he'll have grabbed you and have you working on some levee."

"Why you always have to argue?" Milly said. "Just do what she says, just once—please? Remember what happened to you when you fought that white boy?"

Two years ago Luke had bloodied the nose of a boy from a neighboring plantation, and the overseer had come over with a gun. Miss Dorothy had had to do some powerful fast talking to stop him from getting killed. He definitely had Joe's temper. Pauline just hoped he never started drinking.

She put her hand on Luke's knee. "You'll do what I say. And you, young lady, just let me say one more time, keep your blouses pulled up on you and don't be wearing those red skirts."

Milly frowned. "But you're the one taught me to care about how I look. And when I do, you get mad and worry how the men will see me. It's not fair—Miss Dorothy's children dress any way they like."

"You ain't her daughter. That's the problem with you being around those white folks all day. You forget you're colored."

"You were raised the same way, Auntie—and look how you talk around them. And treat them. It's almost like Miss Dorothy was your sister. You run the whole house, and you the beautifulest woman on the plantation, ever. Even Miss Dorothy say that, and—"

"That's different. She's different. We played together as children, we been through so many things together.. ." She looked from Luke's face to Milly's. She saw the confusion on their young faces and realized they were right, it didn't make sense. She liked how they made her think about things in a different way. But not right now.

"Both of you, listen to me. These will be some of the most dangerous days in your lives. White folks know the end is near— they're mad enough about it to chew up nails and spit out rust. Don't you see what their faces are like when these soldiers come riding through here?"

"Like they looking in our eyes trying to see what we thinking. See if we want to be free, right?"

"That's it, Luke. We've been their property, and they're losing. It's like somebody losing gold. They're going to fight for it."

Luke came over and sat down on the dirt floor between her knees. "You think all this freedom coming mean we ever going to see Mama and Daddy again?"

Milly's face lit up.

"Things are changing so fast," Pauline said. "Runaways coming through here every day, white soldiers leaving their army . . . But I don't know."

"Maybe?"

"It's time for bed. You all keep praying, the Lord might just send them here to you. No way of knowing. One thing I do know—last I heard, your mother was still over at Clifton."

* * *

She spent the next day in the cabin, reading parts of the Old Testament that she loved so well—stories about Ruth and David, the Psalms, and especially the Songs of Songs. She checked every so often to see that Luke and Milly were staying close to the cabin.

"Don't go up by the big house," she'd told them. "But you can visit your friends down here if you want."

At nightfall, she went with them down to the fire where the other slaves were cooking their evening meal. A little food, a few songs, and it was time for Luke and Milly to go to bed. Pauline stayed by the fire and talked for a while. Living up in the big house, she sometimes didn't get to know much about what was happening on the farm, how things were for the rest of them.

"Ain't seen you down here in ages," said a jet-black man with a scar down the right side of his face.

Pauline smiled. She had felt his eyes on her all evening. "I've been real busy. It's a huge house and most of the help is gone. How come you're still around, Woodson? I'd of thought those press gangs would get a man like you the first time around."

"Ain't because they didn't try, that's for sure." His laugh was rich and powerful, seemed to match up with his strong-muscled arms and broad shoulders. "I reckon I be a little too swift for them. Me and my sidekicks, we can smell the grayboys a mile off."

"For a big man, you sure are fast. But one day they might catch you, and Miss won't be able to protect you. Every week she get another order telling her to send men to the army. But she won't do it."

"I reckon we'll have to take our chances. One day I just might run away up into the swamps and stay. They's plenty of colored folks hiding out up there. They got guns, too."

"What are they saying? What have you heard?"

"White folks leaving. Going every which way. Them Yankees, they done taken most of the land along the river, burned down the big houses and stole everything out of them. Won't be long afore they be coming this way, burn down Miss Dorothy's house."

"She's been mighty good to all of us."

"Don't matter. Yankees burn down everybody—the good with the bad. Like the Book say, the just and the unjust." He poked a stick into the embers of the fire. "I'm thinking you and those two children might want to be going off to the woods with me if trouble comes. Them Yankees, they frees the niggers but they makes free with colored women. And you mighty fine-looking, you know. You and the girl."

Woodson was a good man, strong and smart and fearless. He'd been after her for years to be his wife. She always said she had enough on her hands raising the children and running the big house, but now things were really changing fast.

Pauline took hold of Woodson's hand. "That's mighty kind of you, to be always thinking about us. I'll keep what you say in mind."

He kissed her gently on the lips. "Even if I didn't love you, I'd want to keep you safe. You're a woman ought to be kept safe. It's time you were."

* * *

Major Richard Kenworthy spurred his horse and galloped ahead of the five men riding with him. He hadn't realized until he was on the path to his sister's plantation how eager he was to see her, how much he'd missed her. And Pauline. He dismounted, tossed his reins to the trooper behind him, and sent them all down to the stables to water and feed the horses.

"Come on back up for dinner," he said. "You can eat out on the back porch."

He wasn't halfway up the stairs before Dorothy ran down with her arms outstretched.

"Oh, it's been such a long time." She looked up into his face. "You seem . . . goodness, I don't know what. I might not have recognized my big brother if I hadn't known you were coming."

He linked her arm in his. "Am I so different?"

"Just older—I think."

"Years and years, the way it feels. A lot's happened since . . . can you have somebody get some food together for my men?"

She looked over his shoulder at the men leading their horses down to the stable.

"Lottie will take care of them," she said.

Lottie? Not Pauline?

"I've put out some clean clothes of the colonel's for you. Come on in and let's get you settled."

When he had washed and changed, he said hello to his nieces, made them blush and giggle and delighted them with some Yankee chocolate. Dorothy was waiting for him on the front porch with refreshments, lemonade for her, a tumbler of bourbon for him.

God, but it was good to sit here in the quiet. He stretched his long legs out, felt himself beginning to loosen up. His sister knew to give him time, and it wasn't long before he was telling her about how Sue and the children had left Clifton and were now more or less safe up at Meridian, where Drayton, Zenobia, and a few others were staying with them.

"But what will happen to Clifton without someone to look after it?" said Dorothy.

The major looked deep down into his glass. "Nothing left to happen to Clifton, sis. The Yankees already passed through."

"And?"

He stood up and sat down on the porch railing facing his sister. "I haven't seen it yet, but I've been told that it's pretty bad . . ."

"Oh, Richard. How bad?"

He put the glass down on the railing. "Everything's gone. The bastards destroyed everything. All that clearing away of the brush, all those days at the cotton gin, all that trying to buy the best nigras we could . . . When I think how we took care of them, fed them, stayed up all night and nursed them when they were sick—all that's wasted effort. It don't mean a damn thing."

"Oh, I do hope that nothing happened to that little picture of the brook with the deer drinking from it. That was Mama's favorite."

"I honestly don't know, Dorothy. I'm just thankful she didn't live to see this." He picked up his glass and took a deep swallow. "How's Winston? What do you hear from him?"

"Not a thing for six months now. What with the Yankees on the Mississippi, very little mail comes through. As far as I know, he's still fighting with Jubal Early over in Virginia. Why, I don't know. Seems to me he should be here, what with the Yankees so close to overrunning us. Oh, Richard, what can I possibly do if . . ."

He got off the railing, bent over and took her hand. "Well, we do need to talk about what you should do. But right now let's go get some of whatever it is that smells so good."

* * *

Close to ten o'clock, with his men bedded down except for a sentry posted in front of the house against the possibility of some Yankee raiding party, Dorothy offered her brother a glass of cognac.

"I don't know if I should . . ." His head was buzzing from all the wine and whiskey he'd drunk, but he took a sip.

"Better you should drink it than the Yankees," she said. "I've heard they drink as much as they can, then give it to the field niggers so they'll go crazy and rape some white women."

"A lot of what you hear isn't true. Them Yankees don't like the nigras much more than we do—I'd say they would shoot a darky if they caught him trying to rape one of our women. Now, the colored women, that's another story." He shook his head. "Enough of all this gruesome talk. How do you propose to survive if the Yankees come by here, which they surely will soon? I wish you'd take the children and leave. Head on over to Texas till we drive the Yankees out."

No point in telling her the war was finished, it was just a matter of time before the Confederacy fell.

"I'm not letting any Yankees drive me from this land," Dorothy said. "Winston will be coming home, and when he gets here I'll be waiting for him. Me and the children. They miss him something terrible."

Lottie came in to clear away the remaining dishes. Where was Dorothy hiding Pauline? She had to know that was why he'd come.

"What about you?" Dorothy said. "Where are you and those men off to now?"

"We're heading up north in the morning. I've been assigned to General Forrest's cavalry, up in Tennessee."

"That Memphis slave trader, that common little man."

"There's not a Yankee general living can outsmart him or outfight him, believe me."

She walked over to him, sat down, and took his right hand in hers. "Richard, what's this war doing to you?"

For a moment he saw her perched shakily in the swing, when they were children—when he was the one doing the comforting. Hold on tight to the ropes and I'll push you just a little bit. If you get scared, just yell and I'll stop. You'll see, you can swing so high up some day your feet might even touch the sky . . .

It was getting late. He took his hand back.

"I haven't seen Pauline," Richard said. "Or Joe's boy and girl—they must be pretty big by now. Did you know that ungrateful boy is fighting for the Yankees now? I'm going to fix him good when I catch him."

He read the look his sister gave him. She was remembering how Joe had beaten him at lots of things when they were children together at Clifton—from wrestling to skipping rocks on the river to telling which birds were making what sounds. But this time it would be different—he was a crack marksman now and an acknowledged master of the cavalry saber, renowned among his fellow Confederate horse soldiers for his ferocity and bravery in battle.

She picked up a teacup Lottie had overlooked. "Help's getting awful sloppy these days."

"Pauline isn't sloppy," he said as he followed her into the kitchen. "Where is she? Where are Luke and Milly?"

She didn't answer right away, and when he saw her face he knew she was about to tell him a lie.

"I hired them out," she said. "They're at another plantation, about two days from here, close to the Texas border."

He went back into the salon and replenished his snifter.

"I want to see Pauline," he said. "You going to get her, or do I have to find her myself?"

"What about Sue? What about your own children? Do you ever stop to think—"

"I didn't ask for a sermon, I just want to know where Pauline is."

She stood looking at him. Not a word, not a gesture. He picked up his hat with the crossed swords, buckled on his revolver, and walked out to his lookout sentry.

"Think I'll have me a look around down by the niggers' quarters, "he said, loud enough for his sister to hear.

* * *

He pounded on the door of the first cabin he got to.

"Yassuh?" An old man's voice.

"Where's Pauline?"

"She gone this morning."

"Where was she staying?"

He pointed to the hut next door and Richard walked right in. A boy and girl lay sleeping on the pallets. He'd impress Joe's kid Luke, put him to work in the regiment. And the girl, Milly— she'd been a pretty little thing when he last saw her. Not so little now.

"Get up and get outside where I can see you."

The two obeyed.

"Shit, you ain't Joe's kids. Where are they?"

"We don't know, Massa. All we know is, they gone."

He went back up to the big house to Dorothy. "If they're really gone, do you know that makes them fair game for anybody?"

"They've got passes."

He laid his hands gently on her shoulders.

"Sis, I love you too much to dispute with you tonight." He kissed her on her forehead. "I reckon it'll be better if I sleep down in the stables with my men—we have to be out of here at first light."

"You'll take care of yourself? I think it's near the end, Richard. That makes it more dangerous than ever."

"I'll be as careful as I can." He hugged her, started off, then turned back. "When you see Pauline, tell her I love her. And that the world isn't wide enough for her to get away from me."

* * *

He was halfway down to the stables when he saw Sergeant Barclay with his Colt out, pushing a young darky ahead of him.

"Look what we found sleeping in a stall, sir. A good strong boy—we could use him."

"Bring him closer." The major's face broke into a grin. "Well, I'll be damned if it ain't young Luke. Why, you're the spitting image of that father of yours."

The boy stared him straight in the eyes.

"Looks like you got his sass and spunk, too." He turned to Barclay. "Take him back to the stables, bind and gag him—we're taking him out of here with us in the morning. Don't want no fuss from my sister about it."

"Miss Dorothy! Help! They—"

The sergeant slugged him with the revolver, tossed him over his shoulder, and hurried off.

Hell, they'd have to keep Luke bound and gagged. Get nothing out of him about Pauline.

The door of the big house opened.

"Richard?" Dorothy was silhouetted in the doorway. "What's going on out there?"

"Nothing, sis, just some varmint noises. Go on to bed, get yourself a full night's sleep. Wish I could."

* * *

Two days later, after Woodson had scouted the plantation, Pauline and Milly came back.

"Where's Luke?" Pauline said the minute she saw Miss. "When we went to get him and Milly to run off in the swamps, he was gone. Woodson wanted to sneak up toward the big house to see if he could find him, but I wouldn't let him."

Miss walked up to Pauline and hugged her. "You must be strong, Pauline. He's gone. With the Confederates."

Pauline took a step back. "Gone?"

"One of the troopers found him sleeping in the stables. Richard impressed him."

Pauline wanted to scream. And if she'd had Luke in front of her, she didn't know what she'd have done to him. Milly began to cry. Pauline put her arms around her.

"He was like a son to me, too—you know that," Miss said. "The war's done things to Richard. Made him meaner. I never would have thought that he'd abduct a child behind my back. I didn't even know about it till after they were gone. Just wait till the colonel hears. Stealing a slave off his own brother-in-law's property."

"If only he'd listened to me," Pauline said softly.

* * *

After she finally got Milly settled for the night, Pauline went into the living room where Miss sat drinking a cup of tea.

"Oh, Pauline, I don't know when all this evil will cease. God seems to have taken a dislike to folks in these parts, black and white. I just feel so helpless before it all." She brushed her hair back with her hand. "There's one good thing—and only one— that's come out of all this."

How could she say such a thing? What was good about losing Luke?

"Joe's alive, Pauline. Alive and fighting with the Yankees. Richard told me so."

For an instant, Pauline's spirits soared. Then, like a dark cloud covering the sun, she thought of Luke, a boy condemned to face all the hardships and brutalities a war could bring. Who knew what would happen to him now that he was riding with people famous for their cruelty to colored folks? And with Richard, who had more reasons than the color of his skin to hate him?

CHAPTER FIVE

THE Yazoo River meanders its way from a point up above Greenwood, Mississippi, through Yazoo City, down past Haynes Bluff, and into the Mississippi at Vicksburg. In February of 1864, Joe Duckett and a detachment of the Third Cavalry were aboard the paddle-wheel transport *Mirabelle P* in the midst of a flotilla steaming up the Yazoo from Vicksburg to raid the upriver plantations, carry off their slaves, and enlist the men into the army.

Joe stood concealed behind one of the cotton bales that lined the deck to protect the troops. There were Reb sharpshooters hiding up there in the pine trees and rocks on the eastern bank of the Yazoo, firing at anything they could get a bead on. Joe's eyes continually scanned the bluffs, his carbine at the ready. He hoped to get him one of those boys before the day was out.

The Rebs' treatment of the flotilla on this the third day of the expedition had been pure torment. In addition to the sharpshooters, they had a couple of light fieldpieces high up on a cliff. They'd let the escorting gunboats, their stacks belching black smoke, sail by unmolested, then as soon as the gunboats were too far up the river to put down a suppressing fire, the artillery opened up on the troop transports. Sneaky bastards. Withdrew soon as the Yankees put a small landing party ashore to destroy the batteries, then led them on until they ran smack up against a Confederate force that drove them clear back to the river.

Now Joe's transport lay anchored on the west bank of the Yazoo, just out of range of the punishing artillery fire from the Reb batteries again mounted on the hilltop. One thing was for sure; they'd need a lot more troops to push those guns inland, out of range of the river, if they were going to reach Yazoo City and move out into the countryside.

So when Captain Stiles walked over to him, he had a pretty good idea why.

"You're going back, Joe—we need help sent up from Vicksburg. If you and Zack can get through to General McArthur there and tell him what we're up against, he'll send the rest of the regiment here."

Joe nodded. The captain didn't need to tell him how dangerous their position was. Give the Rebs a few more hours and they'd either figure out how they could position those batteries so as to blow the transports to bits or bring up bigger guns with enough range to reach the ships. As it was, the troopships couldn't advance up or down the river without being destroyed.

"Same uniform as last time," Stiles said, "and two separate sets of dispatches sewn into your pockets. And lay off the booze should any come your way. The whole outfit's counting on you. That's General Ross's cavalry over there—might near as good as Forrest's."

Joe saluted, then went in search of Zack. The two of them changed from their blue uniforms into ragged plantation clothes.

"Sarge, we taking bets on what kind of hoodoo you going to put on them Rebs tonight, "one of the men said. "You turning invisible or you fixing to fly over them?"

"He's put his money on you going to make it in under nine hours," another man said. "Me, I reckon more. Maybe twelve, thirteen hours. Any longer than that, and it's our asses anyhow."

Zack laughed. "Joe going to throw a haunt on them bastards, freeze 'em good. They going to see us, good as you all seeing us now, but when they go and try to shoot us, they going to be frozen. He be throwing the haunt on them, you watch and see."

"Ten hours," Joe said. "No more. Ain't but sixty miles to Vicksburg." He looked at Donald, the troop gamble boss. "Put ten dollars on me—I pay you when I get back."

"But, Sarge—"

"When I get back."

They started off to the colonel to get the dispatches secured into their clothing. Behind them Joe heard the men's voices.

"Three dollars on eleven hours."

"Dollar on thirteen hours."

"But suppose—"

"Suppose, nothing. He the Wizard."

* * *

An hour later, when dark had fallen over the Yazoo, Joe and Zack dropped down into a skiff commanded by a midshipman and rowed by four sailors. The oars were muffled with rags; the only sound to be heard was water dripping off an oar when it came out of the water. The men stroked softly, letting the boat drift down the river a bit before trying to make it over to the other side. They knew Reb cavalry on the east side of the Yazoo was thicker than flies on a cow carcass and just dying to get some colored troops to kill. The Texans didn't take black prisoners.

The skiff floated down the river for a mile or so. Then the midshipman poked one of the sailors, and they slowly headed for shore, toward a spot with overhanging pines. Didn't seem there'd be any horse cavalry down there, but if there was . . .

A few minutes later, Joe and Zack slipped ashore and dropped to the ground. It was just a little space, about three feet between the trunk of a big old tree and the water's edge. At least their Colts were dry. They stayed still, listening to see whether the Rebs had heard the landing.

After five minutes with nothing but the sound of the river running, Joe tapped Zack on the shoulder and they started up the bank toward the road that ran alongside the river. Joe motioned Zack to stay still and crawled up behind a big bush near the road to take a good look.

Damn. Up and down the road, every twenty-five yards or so, there was a Reb on a horse. He could get through by himself— God made him invisible. But Zack?

Have to find another way.

He crawled back to Zack and pointed downriver. Hugging the bank, sometimes moving through the water by pulling on low-slung branches, they crept down the side of the riverbank.

Now if he just didn't get himself bitten by a cottonmouth—

Wait a minute. Was that a culvert? Sure enough, going right under the road—right under that Reb picket. Sure to be slimy, and there wouldn't be nothing to hold on to. But the boys on the transport needed help, so there wasn't nothing for it but to crawl in.

It stank something awful. And just like he thought, it was slick with slime. Worst of all, it had barnacles all over it that cut their hands and knees. They kept crawling all the same, didn't slow down, and in a minute Joe was through and out on the other side of the road, Zack right beside him.

"Whoa, Star," came a deep voice. "Something got you spooked?"

Joe and Zack froze.

They were in a pile of rushes on the other side of the culvert, nothing in front of them but swampland and levees. Joe heard the man get off his horse, probably to take it down to a tree and tie it up.

Just enough time.

He felt around till he found a rock, stood up quick, and threw it on the other side of the culvert, into the Yazoo. As the Reb hustled across the road and down the riverbank, Joe and Zack cut off into the swamps. Over fifty miles to go—they needed to get them some horses. The colonel had promised them twenty-four-hours' leave if they made it, even put it in the orders. And that would give Joe a chance to do something important he had to do in Vicksburg.

After walking an hour through the swamps, they came to level ground and spied a good-sized log cabin sitting way out there in the woods. There were lights on inside, and they could hear what sounded like singing.

Joe cupped his hand over his ear to hear better.

> "She's the sweetest rose of color
> This soldier ever knew.
> Her eyes are bright as diamonds . . ."

They were men's voices, raised in that pretty song them Texans sang all the time. The words got more distinct as Joe and

Zack crept up closer to the house.

> *"Where the Rio Grande is flowing*
> *And the starry skies are bright,*
> *She walks along the river*
> *In the quiet summer night.*
> *She thinks, if I remember,*
> *When we parted long ago,*
> *I promised to come back again*
> *And not to leave her so."*

One man's beautiful voice rang through the chill night air clear and pure as a church bell on a bright Sunday morning. For a few seconds there, Joe nearly forgot what he was there for.

When they were about fifty paces from the house, Joe took out his revolver. "I'm going down there and take a look, be back in a minute."

"Let me go," Zack said. "You always taking all the chances."

He was right. About time he started letting Zack take some responsibility.

"Go ahead, but be careful. I give you ten minutes to get back."

Zack disappeared into the darkness.

With nothing to do but wait, Joe realized he was shivering from the cold, and his hands hurt from the barnacles on the culvert. A shot of bourbon would be good along about now. He wished to hell he hadn't minded the captain and had brought his flask. Them fellows down at the house sure were having themselves a good time. There were sure to be some horses down there. And some bourbon, what with all that racket coming from the house.

What was taking Zack so long? Should gone himself.

The singing made him think of Zenobia, the songs she loved, like "It's a Good Time in Heaven, Don't You Want to Go?" That was one singing woman. And she couldn't be more than thirty miles away. Maybe she'd had some word of Luke and Milly by now. Maybe . . . his heart got heavy.

The music from the house stopped. The loud talk died down, then there was silence.

Joe waited another five minutes. No Zack.

Should he go on? Leave Zack and take the chance of finding horses somewhere else? That would be the wise course of action. The Third Cavalry needed help.

But there'd been no shots fired, so Zack was still alive. He could think all he wanted, but there was no way he was going to leave his buddy there. And there wasn't no Reb in this world could capture Joe Duckett. Not while his ancestors watched over him.

He took out his Colt, twirled the cylinder to make sure all six loads were in place, and crept off toward the house, darting from bush to bush until finally he vaulted over a low fence. Tied up at the railing were four of the prettiest horses he had ever laid eyes on, sawed-off shotguns all tucked in their scabbards.

There was a lot of shouting coming from inside the house.

Joe crept up to a window and saw seven or eight women, none of them what you'd call all the way dressed. And he saw Zack.

He was sitting on a table surrounded by four Rebs. The biggest, with gray whiskers and a Union forage cap cocked sideways on his head, had a pistol under Zack's jaw. His left hand held Zack's chin in a claw grip. The three other men, their pistols holstered, were laughing. One of them had a half-empty bottle of whiskey in one hand and an old banjo in the other.

Most of the women had their skirts hiked up and plenty of white flesh spilling out of their bodices. Some stood near the table Zack was sitting on, others sprawled on a couch, and one was in a chair, her legs spread wide open. All of their faces were flushed with excitement and whatever they'd been drinking.

Well, you didn't have to be as smart as Joe to figure out what had happened. All that confounded fool sidekick of his had had to do was get close to the house to see the men and count their horses. Instead he'd looked in, seen all the fun, stared at those pretty women with their hair flowing all down their backs. And got caught. Probably them Rebs didn't know they had a Yankee soldier, thought they had a peeping-Tom nigger.

Hell, he ought to leave him right there. Serve him right if he waited another half-hour just to let him sweat, which he surely would do when they stopped laughing and drinking in there and pulled out their Bowie knives to cut off his dick and balls.

But there wasn't time for no more fooling around. Those boys back up on the Yazoo . . .

Joe went over to one of the horses and drew a shotgun from its sheath. He quieted the nervous horse, reached into the ammunition pouch, and loaded the gun's double barrel. It was, he had reason to know, a weapon deadlier than it looked. A wild-riding secesh had once cut down half a squad of Joe's men with one.

Pistol in one hand, shotgun in the other, he crept around to the front of the house.

Now.

He took a deep breath and kicked the door open.

For a few seconds after he burst in scarcely anything moved in the logwalled room with its flickering wick lamps and roaring fire. The sound of the banjo hitting the floor with clanging strings and a loud thump seemed to bring everybody to life. The women tried to cover themselves, and one man's hand moved halfheartedly toward his holster. Another stood staring, with his mouth wide open and his hands high in the air.

"It's another one! Where'd all these damn niggers come from?"

Somewhere in all the racket Zack called his name. But Joe, his thumb on the hammer of the Colt, his finger tight on its trigger, was watching the man with the Union forage cap. He hadn't fully lowered his revolver yet. Any second now, he would chance turning that pretty double-action Adams revolver of his, of which there were very few in existence, on Joe.

He never got that chance. Joe blew his head apart with a snap shot from his Colt and aimed the shotgun at the other men. The one whose hand had been edging toward his holster raised both hands in the air quick.

"Don't shoot!"

"Sergeant Joe Duckett, Third United States Colored Cavalry at your service, ladies. Please join them gentlemens over in that corner!" A wave of the revolver accompanied the invitation.

"Corporal Zack Bascom!"

"Joe—"

"Relieve them secesh of their sidearms!"

Zack took the three men's Colts from their holsters and wrapped them in a blue shawl that belonged to one of the women. In seconds the men were lined up with their hands against the wall. One of them twisted his head around to look at Joe.

"Keep your eyes on that wall," Joe said. "You done surrendered your weapons without a fight and give Uncle Sam's army them pretty horses and those sweet shooting shotguns. Whoeeee!

They going to put all your asses in the pioneers corps when you get back to camp—that is, if you lives to see camp."

"Why, you low-down stinking polecat of a field nigger, ain't no way you going to get through our patrols. What you going to do with us?"

"Find me a way of teaching you not to call colored folks niggers for one thing."

Using the revolver, he fired a shot that whizzed past the man's right ear and shattered a windowpane next to him.

"Don't! I got kids, I—"

"Nobody else got 'em, right?"

Zack had taken his own Colt from its holster in his trousers. "Joe, I'm sorry—"

"Get them men down on the ground and tie their wrists behind."

When they were secured to Joe's satisfaction, he turned to the women. Five of them were now hunched together on the couch, the other two sitting on the floor in front of it. They had buttoned themselves back up properly, though a bosom or two was having a time of it trying to stay in.

"What you going to do with us?" one of them asked. She had long curly dark hair and a steady gaze. Couldn't be much over twenty.

"Not what you thinking, little miss. I swear you not much older than my Milly. Ain't you ashamed of yourselves, carrying on here like you ain't been raised right?"

"Joe!" Zack said. "We got to move."

One of the soldiers glared at Joe. "Nigger, you lay a finger on them and you'll burn in hell's own fires, so help me God!"

Shit, they'd never learn. Joe drew out his Choctaw knife, walked over to the soldier, and traced the knife's razor-sharp blade across the side of the man's throat, just barely drawing blood.

"No more talk, hear?" He turned to face the young woman. "You, miss, what's your name?"

"Lydia."

"I intends no harm to you, but you all got to be secured so's we can be on our way."

The woman gave him a long look.

"I'll see to it," she said finally. "Jessica, give me a hand tying the others. When we're done, this nigra." She looked at Joe's tattered shirt. "This sergeant can tie our hands up, too."

Ten minutes later, Joe and Zack were ready to leave.

Joe walked over to the man who'd said he had children, bent down, and cut the thongs binding his wrists.

"You a big family fellow," he said, pushing the man ahead of him and toward the door. "What's the names of your chilluns?"

The man hesitated, then said, "Two girls, Mary Ann and Portia. And, three boys—Tom, Lionel, and Crew."

Joe nudged him out the door with the barrel of his newly acquired Adams revolver and yelled over to Zack, who stood holding the horses' reins.

"Keep a gun on this Reb, I got me one more thing to do."

"Aw, Joe, you ain't going back in there, is you?"

"Just be a minute."

He walked back into the cabin, and over to the two prone Rebs. "Ain't it a mite hot in here for you boys? With all them things you got on, you might be tempted to take a walk outside or something stupid like that."

He rolled them both over and proceeded to pull their trousers off. The women tittered, and Joe had to admit the Rebs were a sight in their dirty long white underwear with plenty of holes to show off their skinny knobby legs.

It was too much for the man who'd already told Joe that he would burn in hell.

"If I ever see your black ass again, I'll burn you to gray."

Joe gave him a sweet smile. "That's all right, one good turn deserve another. Right now, I'm going to burn these trousers and boots of yours in this here fireplace. When they put you out working on those roads in them swamps with them pioneers, you going to be in bad shape." He tossed the clothes into the fire, then picked up the banjo. "You knows how us darkies just love to strum and strut. And you'd look like hell strumming in them nasty old britches of yours, so I don't reckon you'll be needing this no more tonight." His eye fell on the bottle of bourbon. "This, neither."

He took a good deep satisfying swig, corked the bottle, and doffed his hat to all.

"I bids you all a good night."

* * *

He stowed the banjo and whiskey in a saddlebag and turned to the Reb Zack was holding a Colt on.

"What your name, man?"

"Andy."

"Do what I say and you lives to see Mary Ann and Portia. Otherwise . . ." Joe laid the six-inch barrel of the Adams in the palm of his hand and kissed it. "Got it?"

The Reb nodded.

"Thought you would. You looks like a right smart man to me, the kind of man what values his life. We sees anybody, you going to give them a good story about what we doing with you.

We make five miles to them good roads over past Satartia, then I let you go, so you can see . . . what the name of your wife? Don't recall you told me."

"Felicia."

"So you can see sweet Miss Felicia and lie in a warm bed with her one more time. Don't that sound good now?" He turned to Zack. "Take the reins of the extra horse and I'll keep my gun on our secesh friend here. Looky here, Andy—see? It's right under this saddle blanket. Let's go now. At a fast trot."

They moved out into the dark night.

About two miles down the road Joe signaled for them to halt.

> *"Gave her my promise true*
> *Which ne'er forgot will be . . ."*

The voices of the men were ragged, and they were messing up the song. Must have been about a half-mile away. Joe looked back. Andy, sitting straight up like a natural-born horse soldier in the saddle, seemed to be thinking up a storm. Zack, on the horse behind him, had a worried frown on his face. Served him right. Hell, if he'd done the right thing in the first place, they'd be past Satartia and on the way to Vicksburg and winning that ten-dollar bet now. Last time, the pool had been a hundred and fifty dollars!

> *"And for Bonnie Annie Laurie . . ."*

Closer now . . .

> *"I'd lay me doon and dee."*

Joe dropped back beside his prisoner. "Remember Felicia, now."

"Don't you worry none, this pilgrim wants shet of you."

Joe could just make out four riders approaching. Not on patrol, for they loudly hailed Joe's prisoner when they got closer.

"Andy, you going the wrong way—we was just coming down to the shindig . . . Hey, what you doing with these two niggers?"

Joe hoped Zack had followed orders this time and had the men covered.

Slowly he edged his horse sideways to the road, never taking his gun off Andy. If he gave them away, Joe would kill him and escape down the road soon as Zack got the others. None of which were paying the least attention to him or Zack.

"Well, boys," Andy said, "these two niggers.. ." He turned and glanced at Joe, then back at his friend. "These two niggers are the best damn buck and wing dancers you ever did see. And that one there"—he pointed at Joe—"he can play that banjo in his saddlebag up a storm. They tell me there's a few more of 'em on a little plantation down the road can come play for us if we ask their missus' permission. That's where we're on our way to now—some of them pretty gals we got down there are just crazy for music."

Joe was glad the Reb couldn't see his grin. Why, that man deserved a place in liar's heaven, bless his seceding soul!

"How many gals?"

"One for each of us. And guess who's waiting for you?"

"Lydia! It's Lydia, ain't it?"

"And she done put on a white dress for you. What there is of it."

"Times a'wasting. Andy, we'll try to keep the girls busy till you get back." The Reb spurred his horse and they were off.

"Save some whiskey for me!" Andy yelled after them.

Joe rode up with his grin still in place. "Andy, you a mighty fine liar, must of had you a whole lot of practice."

Andy sat up even straighter on his horse. "See how good you'd lie if you had some crazy fool nig—crazy fool soldier ready to kill you dead."

Two miles down the road, Joe set him afoot. "We going to leave you here."

"I'm free now?"

"Like I said."

Joe reached down into the saddlebag, pulled out the whiskey bottle, and uncorked it.

"Here, take you a good swig or two, it may be a while afore your boys come back for you, and it getting cold out here."

Andy took a couple of swallows, then handed the bottle back to Joe, who offered it to Zack and then took a couple of good belts himself.

Andy was no more than a few steps down the road before he looked back.

"Thanks, Sarge, you one heap of man for a nigger!"

Joe returned his wave, which was close to a salute.

* * *

Using the back roads and cutting across plantations slowed them down, but they galloped into McArthur's camp exactly ten hours and ten minutes after they'd left. Joe's pocket was already getting warm from the money he knew he'd won. He wondered how many other boys had put their money on ten hours, too.

Soon they were in front of McArthur's tent, and Joe was explaining the situation up there on the Yazoo.

"Go get cleaned up and take your twenty-four-hour liberty," the general said when Joe finished. "You've earned it. And the four horses are a godsend."

* * *

Late afternoon found Joe sitting on a park bench close to the courthouse building, high up in Vicksburg, looking out over the Mississippi River toward the Louisiana shore a half-mile away. What must General Grant have felt when he stood on one of these hills overlooking the great river and thought about the ten thousand men it had cost them to take this fortress city?

Earlier that day, walking through the town in his blue uniform with its bright brass buttons, Joe had been struck by the destruction the war had wrought. No matter where you looked, you saw houses with windows and doors blown away or living rooms exposed to the open air because their roofs had collapsed on them.

He couldn't stop thinking about what a beautiful place Vicksburg had been when he used to come down here with Massa Kenworthy before the war. City of a Hundred Hills, they called it. Well, the Union gunboats with their huge pulverizing mortars and the massed ranks of artillery batteries up there in the hills above the city hadn't left a yard of ground untouched. The general had called thunder and lightning down upon the Rebs' citadel.

Joe took one last look at the sky, red tinged by the setting sun. Seemed like every time there was no action, every time there were no Rebels to kill or outsmart, he got sad and started thinking about Zenobia, Luke, Milly, and Cally. Had to be some way he could find them, save them—put his family back together again, be a proper daddy and all.

He smiled to himself and remembered the time when he'd taken Luke down to the blacksmith hearth and let him pump the bellows for a while, seen the delight in the little seven-year-old's eyes as the flames leapt up and flickered in brilliant colored tongues of red, yellow, and white. He'd let Luke stick a little iron rod in the hearth and leave it there until it had turned almost white from the heat, then put it on the anvil and let the boy pound away at it with a small hammer until he'd formed a hook in the end of it. Then he had shouted with joy along with Luke when the boy plunged the fiery rod into the water bucket and the steam hissed up into their happy faces. Later that day, he'd trailed along behind Luke as he ran to show Zenobia the new fireplace poker that he'd made as a present for her on her birthday. "See, Momma,what Daddy helped me make for you?" Zenobia had swept both of them into her arms. "My mens!"

He got up from the bench and headed down the steep, winding streets toward the little riverfront place where he was supposed to meet Zack. Not much of his leave left, considering that he had to be back at nine in the morning. So far it had been a real bust. They'd slept half their leave away, then took off in separate directions, Zack to see some friends and Joe to a refugee camp to seek out information about his family.

At the camp, old Brother Caleb told him how Zenobia hadn't shown up on the night of the planned escape. "But, you know, it's a funny thing how God do work. The patrollers caught all of us three days after our escape, shot three of the mens and took off the women in chains. I's the only one made it through. And you sees what it's like here." A sweep of his arm took in broken-down shacks, mud puddles, and children running around in ragged shirts and torn britches.

"Every day we losing a dozen or more folks to dysentery," the old preacher man said. "Seem like with all these folk together, disease just jump from one to the other, old devil light on one, get strong, look around and say, 'I sees me another one over there,' then go put the death clamp on them."

"But what you doing to try and keep yourself strong?" Joe said. "You looking mighty poorly, Brother Caleb."

"I got work to do here," he said, with a nod toward the bucket of sand he'd been carrying to the sanitary pits on the edge of the camp. "I'll look after my flock long as my strength hold out.

"You see, son, no matter how bad things get, the good Lord don't ever put more on us than we can bear. He grant his chillun a daily portion of health and strength sufficient to their need." He stopped and put his arm around Joe's shoulder. "The Bible say we shall mount up on wings like eagles, run and not get weary. Don't you ever forget that."

Joe took the bucket from him. "Let me give you a hand, I ain't got nothing else to do for now."

"Ain't changed one bit, have you, boy? The Lord's going to bless you real good, but I don't want you spending your little bit of time off here. No, you young still. Go on out and have you a good time."

"I'll finish helping you with that pile of sand, then I'll be on my way."

"Brother Caleb! Didn't I tell you about carrying them heavy pails? Thank goodness that nice sergeant took it from you."

The low musical voice belonged to a good-looking brown-skinned woman somewhere in her twenties, in the blue uniform with the special green markings of the Medical Department. Even the heavy jacket couldn't hide the shape of a fine body. Her eyes were big and slanted, her features sharp and distinct. Those high cheekbones and that tinge of bronze in her skin meant Indian blood, Joe would have bet on it. She walked proudly, her head thrown back, and beneath her fatigue cap he could see that she wore her hair twisted in braids.

She came abreast of the men and completed her conquest with a smile aimed at Joe. "I'm Nurse Betty Ransome, on loan from the field hospital."

"And I is Sergeant Duckett, now of the Third Cavalry but once from the Kenworthy Clifton plantation, up near where Brother Caleb here come from."

Brother Caleb smiled. "He one hell of a man, but do mind his temper."

"And what brings you over here, Sergeant?"

Joe explained, but it was hard keeping his mind on looking for his family when she reached over and took his hand.

"I'm sorry," she said. "I didn't know—"

Her hand was warm, and, Lordy, but she was one fine-looking woman.

"Ain't no way you supposed to know, ma'am. We all got our troubles."

The three of them walked together to the latrine pits to empty the bucket, then went back to the sand pile. While the nurse and Brother Caleb talked, Joe carried bucket after bucket until he'd transferred the rest of the sand to the latrine area.

As he trod back and forth, a distance of about a quarter of a mile, he thought of various ways he could get Miss Betty Ransome to go out with him that night. He knew she liked him, could tell that from the way she'd looked him up and down when she first saw him. Best to just tell her he'd enjoy her company for the evening.

But when he got back from his last trip with the sand, Brother Caleb was standing there alone.

"A messenger done called her back to the hospital," he said before Joe could ask the question. "Would you like to pray with me for a minute before you leave?"

"I don't reckon it would hurt, considering what I got to go back to tomorrow."

They prayed together right there, in front of Brother Caleb's log hut, then Joe said good-bye and set off toward the river. If the place where he was meeting Zack turned out like the rest of his leave, he'd almost be glad to be back in camp come morning.

But Zack had been right. It was a nice place, a little one-room café that couldn't hold no more than maybe about thirty people. And up at the front of the room was a small band.

A colored man with a bandanna around his neck was playing away at his banjo, just plucking those strings, while a little boy, black as could be, beat with two sticks on a wooden tub turned upside down. Over him stood a yellow man, plucking away at one string stretched out on a long piece of wood. And there was a fiddler, too. They were making some nice music, especially when the string-plucker sang. He had a mighty good voice:

> "Old master's gone away
> And the darkies stayed at home
> Must be now that the kingdom's come
> And the year for Jubilees.

"Look up the road and see the cloud arising
Look like we're gonna' have a storm
Oh, no, you're mistaken,
It's only the darkies' bayonets and buttons on their uniforms

"Darkies, did you see old master
With the mustache on his face?
Left here soon one morning
Says he's going for to leave this place."

Most everybody was laughing or trying to sing along with him, and by the time he'd put down two tumblers of whiskey, Joe was feeling mighty good himself.

"See, ain't us having a good time?" Zack was eating away at a plate of hot biscuits, chicken, greens, and baked beans. Joe had already finished one plate and was about to start in on another.

Next thing he knew, some women were dancing to the music. Just like that, they came into the room, and started moving their bodies. And one of them was sure enough Nurse Betty Ransome.

Well! Brother Caleb had said the Good Lord was going to bless him, and now look what He had done for him.

Body moving like it was a willow tree, with a soft breeze blowing it. No beginning, no end, just one part of her flowing into the next, smooth as a shimmering ripple in a quiet pond. Hands balled up into little fists, moving up and down to the sound of that music.

The man with the banjo saw her dancing and had to get up from his seat. Up and playing like the devil done took over his hands, up and down, trying to keep rhythm with that gal's body.

He got behind her, Betty peeking over one shoulder, making sure he was there, and then the two of them were stepping perfect-like all around that room like they was one person.

Her brown skin was shiny, her braids a-flying, and her white blouse looked like it couldn't hold them titties.

Joe jumped up, moved the banjo player out of the way, and got behind her himself.

She peeked over her shoulder. "Sergeant Duckett?"

"And mighty happy to see you." Matching every step she made.

Every time she twisted that behind, he moved right with her. Next thing you know, she turned around and they were facing each other, banjo ringing and drums beating, and their bodies just swaying back and forth.

Folks made a circle around them and started dancing too, a roomful of men and women shuffling and moving and shaking their bodies round and round in a circle. Finally, Joe's legs gave out. He grabbed Betty's hand, led her over to his table, and sat her down beside him.

"When I got back to Brother Caleb and saw you was gone," he said, "it like to broke my heart."

She smiled. "Mine, too."

Still holding his hand, she rested her elbows on the table. So soft and tender was her touch that Joe felt dizzy. And no wonder. Her leg was right up against his thigh.

"Who you be, Joe?"

Joe briefly told her how he'd come to be in the Third Cavalry.

"And you the first black army nurse I ever seen. How come you to be here?"

She sighed. "We ain't got but so much time, I hate to use it up telling about me. And I'm hungry. Can I have some of your chicken and biscuits?"

Joe had lost all interest in the plate in front of him. She took one of his biscuits, buttered it, then looked at Joe and put it down.

"You might as well know . . ."

Turned out she had been born of a slave-owning Indian father and a black mother. But her father had raised her as if she were free-born and seen to it that she learned to read and write. When he died, his heirs, her blood half-brothers, sold her and her mother away, separating them. From then on her story was like hundreds of others—house slave, two children sold away, the war, escape, and now the army.

By the time she finished, the chicken was cold and Zack and his friend had long since departed. And Joe's hand was on her knee.

"I'm sure glad I met you," he said, "because I think you could stand a lot of care. I don't wants to brag none, but I thinks I be the man for you right now."

"I don't doubt that for a minute. And when you next get back to Vicksburg, we got a lot of talking to do." She kissed him on his cheek and started to get up. Joe glanced over at the table where her friends had been seated. They were gone.

"It's dangerous out there, you can't go home by yourself."

"Corporal Lewis over there, he's assigned to the hospital and he'll see me home. He'll take good care of me."

Joe's heart was doing flip flops. All this time she'd been talking to him, she hadn't said one word about no boyfriend. Not a peep out of her. And what kind of a soldier let his woman sit there all night with another man?

Betty sat back down. "Oh, Joe, you should see yourself, you look like you just lost your last friend on this earth. There ain't nothing between the corporal and me. That's his girlfriend over there, sitting across from him. He takes us both home when we come here."

Joe let out a long breath and laughed. "Tell you what. I'll pay the bill and you just go over there and tell him you got somebody else to do the honors tonight."

* * *

As they walked through the rubble of Vicksburg, Joe began to hum a little tune about "Sally, that old sweet gal," and Betty hummed along with him and squeezed his hand tight. When they got to her place—just a little wooden shack behind one of the big old abandoned houses—she turned to him.

"It's way late—time for you to get back to camp and get you some sleep before you go back up the Yazoo. Besides, my place ain't fit to be seen by no first sergeant of the United States colored cavalry."

"I ain't the man to find fault with your place. I sure would like to lay my head down on your pillow tonight." Surely Zenobia would understand . . .

Betty hesitated so long he thought she was gathering up the words to say no. But then she took him by the hand and drew him into the little house. "You got such a pitiful look on your face, ain't no way I'm going to send you back to no Yazoo City looking like that!"

* * *

Joe woke up the next morning to find Betty propped up on an elbow, looking down on him.

"You must of had some bad dreams last night," she said softly. "You was tossing and turning all night long, and once you yelled out something about blood on your hand."

"What time is it?"

"You got about fifteen–twenty minutes before you got to go back."

"That's just about enough time—"

She laughed. "No, you 'bout wore me out last night. When you come back from Yazoo City."

Joe kissed her nipple. "You one sweet thing. And you made this poor soldier mighty happy."

"Least I can do for a man like you. You made me happy too. Hope you don't think—"

"Come closer to me I'll show you what I think." Joe pulled her tight against him.

"Didn't you say you had to be back by nine o'clock?"

"Hush." He kissed her and held her close. She was like the sweetest honey he'd ever tasted in his life. Zenobia was far away, and Betty was right here. And he had to go back to a war. But not right this minute.

* * *

As a Reb bullet tore off the branch of a tree over his head, Captain Will Stiles was wishing Joe was up here with the unit instead of on temporary assignment briefing the gunboat captain in Yazoo City on currents and depths in the river. Hell, he'd been there ever since he got back up from Vicksburg and collected that two-hun-dred-dollar pot. And Stiles needed him badly, because in front of him and his fifty-man reconnaissance squad, still partially concealed from the enemy by trees and rocks, was a whole damn army of Rebs—cavalry, artillery, and infantry. They weren't supposed to be out there, but there they were, regimental standards flying, not more than three quarters of a mile away.

Through his glasses, he could see the small fieldpieces being wheeled into position, and beyond them, clouds of red dust rising as troops of cavalry massed for an assault. Close to the cavalry was a group of dismounted officers gathered in a circle, some standing, some kneeling on the ground, all listening to a tall bare-headed man giving them orders. The Rebs must have been just as surprised to run into his outfit as he'd been to run into them.

Where had they come from, anyway? In the three months since the Third Cavalry had first come up the Yazoo, the Rebs had pretty much disappeared from this area. But here they were, back again, obviously determined to take Yazoo City and drive them into the river.

The only thing stopping them from getting into the town was a little fort about four hundred yards directly behind the captain and his men—really just a heavily built-up mound of dirt, with trenches deep enough for the men to stand in, and wood planking on top. It dominated the approaches to the city. But right now it was undefended, and until the reinforcements he'd sent for arrived, until he was able to somehow or another maneuver his fifty men back into it, the way to Yazoo City was wide open.

The two sides were going at each other strong, but thank God the Rebs didn't know how few in number they were—if they'd known, they'd have swept right on by them into the fort. His men would have to fall back slowly, buy enough time for the reinforcements to get up.

At least he had Zack. "Corporal! Tell the men to make sure every shot counts. And watch the flanks."

Sure enough, bullets started flying from the woods to his left. But his men were fighting smart, not panicking, keeping their mounts, giving as good as they were getting.

Another half hour of this, and they'd be able to get back to the fort.

Two troopers galloping to reach shelter in the woods went down, almost as though they were twins—the Rebs had shot their horses. Tumbling to the ground, rolling every which way, bodies one direction, guns the other.

Jenkins, a short mulatto from New Orleans, got to his feet. Jones, the other trooper, was still on his knees when the Reb cavalry pulled up. A major, dressed in that gray uniform with its fancy yellow curls, pulled out his revolver as the Rebel color guard rode up beside him, the flag fluttering in the stiff March breeze.

The major cupped his hands and yelled over to the Yankee lines. "Now, hear me, niggers! The Good Book says 'Servants obey your masters. The wages of sin is death.'"

Jenkins and Jones raised their hands in surrender. The major drew his revolver, took careful aim, and shot both of them in the head.

For a moment, silence fell on that section of the battlefield. Stiles closed his eyes, but only for a few seconds. One Rebel yell was followed by another and another till they were all shouting and screaming and blasting away. Seemed to have but one thing in mind—kill the niggers.

Stiles was everywhere on the field, slashing with his saber in one hand and blasting away with his revolver in the other. And right behind him, always, was Zack, handling his saber as if it were a toothpick.

"Captain, the two lieutenants are dead. Don't you join them." He fired and killed a Reb coming in fast on Stiles's right.

They fell back some more, then he dismounted the men, called some horse holders, and yelled, "Back to the rifle pits!" After half an hour, they fell back again. Stiles was the last man into the fort.

Thank God they'd piled those heavy planks of wood on the parapets with little spaces in between so the men could shoot through them. At least their heads would be protected from enemy sharpshooters in the hills all around.

"Come on over, you bastards!" a man yelled.

And now they were all cursing and waving their sabers.

"You wants your niggers, come on and get them!"

He was just wishing his men wouldn't swear so much when a loud hurrah went up from the Reb lines. About a hundred of them got up and started charging over the fifty yards of ground that separated them from the Third Cavalry's lines. They ran fast and low, carrying their sawed-off shotguns and carbines at the ready and shouting that crazy Rebel yell. No matter how many times he heard it, a chill still went up his spine. If only he could have him a war where the only thing that happened was that the colored troops would curse at the Rebs and the Rebs would yell at the Negroes. Put them face to face, ten paces apart—first one to ask the other to quit would have to stack their arms and go home. War over! Shake hands, boys, and go back to the farms! And don't ever bring any of that racket around this poor Adirondack mountain fellow's way again!

That Reb lieutenant with a plume in the band of his hat and a brace of Colts in his hands didn't seem the kind who'd quit till he was laid in his grave by a fast bullet or cold steel. His face contorted and twisted, he was shouting loud in a high-pitched voice as he ran. And he was such a fast runner that he'd gotten five yards out in front of his troops.

"Steady, men, fire at my command!" Stiles looked up and down the line of his troops. They were ready.

For a moment his eyes locked with those of the Lieutenant, now about twenty paces away from the Union lines. The Reb raised his pistols slowly to a firing position and kept on coming. Well, if the young fool was bent on a hero's death, Stiles'd give it to him.

Stiles lifted his Colt and took aim at the gray blouse of the lieutenant.

"Fire!"

All over the field, Rebs fell to the ground. You couldn't see them well in all that acrid-smelling smoke, but you could hear their cries for help. Directly in front of him he saw that the Reb youngster was down, but not what condition he was in—the rest of them kept on coming. Too many to count, and every one of them spoiling for a fight.

Then they were at the ramparts of the fort, and all along the line; man to man, they went at it fast and furious, Rebs and Yanks, blasting away with shotguns and carbines, colored and white swinging sabers, screaming and grunting until he lost all sense of time. He heard the screaming loud as ever, but somehow it seemed far off. He dodged bullets and shotgun blasts and slashing sabers—determined to stay alive in the madness and confusion, and just as determined to kill as many of the enemy as possible. Had to, because it looked for sure like the fort would be lost in a few more minutes. Well, they'd make the enemy pay dearly for their prize.

Just as he was about to give up hope, he heard the sound of a bugle blowing the charge. The Rebs in front of him suddenly turned and bolted. Thank God! Four companies of the 11th Illinois—white infantry—trotting at the quick step into the fort. It would hold for the time being.

He walked a little ways outside the fort to where the boy lieutenant lay in the dirt, groaning and holding his intestines in with his hands. His hat, the plume intact, lay on the ground beside him, brown dirt soiling its crown.

"Water," said the lieutenant, his blue eyes once again fixed on Stiles. The life was fast draining from them, so the water would do him no harm. He took the boy's head onto his right arm and cradled it.

"Here, just take a little sip, Lieutenant." He barely wet the boy's lips with the spout of the canteen, then lowered his head to the ground.

"Thanks."

Stiles took off his own jacket, made a pillow of it and placed it under the lieutenant's head. "Rest easy now, son, we'll get help for you soon. That was a mighty brave charge you led out here."

The boy's eyes brightened with pride, then dimmed. He was about to say something when his head dropped down. Stiles gently retrieved his jacket from under the boy's head and rolled it up under his left arm.

From the fort, his men watched him stand at attention for a minute and salute before walking back to join them.

* * *

The week that followed was a quiet one, so uneventful that Stiles had time to write Eunice. Every two weeks or so he was rewarded with a bundle of letters from her, letters full of her softness and love. He could never write such letters, nor would he have had the time to compose them even if his words were as strong as his feelings. Since the beginning of the campaign up the Yazoo, he'd scarcely had a moment even to think of her, what with the bringing in of cattle and freed slaves, the daily skirmishes with the regular Confederate cavalry, or with bands of guerrillas and deserters . . .

Writing had not come easy to him before, but as he began to tell her about the men, he found the words coming faster than he could write them down:

> Their countenances may be dark, but a great light glows within them. When I first marched off to Albany to come down here to fight this wet and devilish war in a land that could only have been created as a cruel afterthought by God Almighty, I thought solely of saving our sacred Union. I know now that there is something more. We have a duty, I have come to believe, a great mission to help these poor oppressed people out of the Darkness and Ignorance to which both the unfortunate accident of their geographic origins and the state of slavery has condemned them.
>
> I have come to admire their courage and valor and determination. Did I tell you how they yearn more than anything to read and write? Even when we are all weary after a long day of chasing the pesky Rebs, they still come up to my tent and ask that I teach them to read yet another verse of the Bible. Some of them—like our Wizard, Joe Duckett, are quick to

learn and seem to soak up whatever you teach them. Yet there are some for whom it is a painful struggle. It almost broke my heart when a chap of about forty-five came up to me after the eighth lesson with tears in his eyes and said, "Too late, sir, too late."

Eunice, my dearest, of late I have been thinking that when this conflict is over and the Union restored, I would like to stay here, purchase a plantation, settle our men upon it, and teach them animal husbandry, the science of farming, the uses of machinery. This is such a backward land, and such a backward people, even the poor whites. With a little hard work and rolling up of our shirtsleeves, my men and I can make our farm bloom, set an example for colored and white alike of progressive life. Give white and black a place where their children can grow up healthy and wise, daily glorifying God. It would be a blessed work, my darling, yet I hesitate to commit myself to it, lest you, for reasons of health or otherwise, find yourself unable to join me here. This is one more thing of which we must talk sometime. I boldly and with no apology admit that my love of you and my need of you come first.

Have you heard any news of—

He looked up as a shell from a twelve-pounder slammed into the dirt about thirty paces from where he sat writing.

The Rebs were really just getting their strength together. Only a week since the attack on the fort, and there were four to five thousand Rebs surrounding the city. They had the Yankees—just twelve hundred of them— in a noose and were hell-bent on driving them from the fort and the city and sweeping them right down into the Yazoo. And what use were the Yankee gunboats sitting there in the river with their cannon when the Union forces and the city lay between the boats and the Rebels? If they fired, the shells might fall on their own forces.

Now here the Rebs came again. He walked over to where Zack was standing in one of the fort's trenches.

"Wish Joe was back up here. We're going to get it today."

Another shell landed, closer this time, and tore a hole in the ramparts. Zack stood beside the captain, his carbine at the ready.

"Sir, I've a request of you from the men."

Will looked out along the long line of his troopers, who stood waiting for the Rebs. What the hell could they want?

"What is it, Bascom?"

"No surrender. Don't care if all hell descends on this here fort this afternoon. We ask you not to surrender, sir. We done talked it all over, and we is sworn to die to the last man."

That major's assassination of Jenkins and Jones had to be behind this resolution. Will sighed and buckled on his sword belt.

"Then that's the way it will be." He shook Zack's hand. "Just like you said, no surrender."

* * *

That was the last word they exchanged for a good half hour, because the skies opened to pour tons of metal into the Third Cavalry's trenches. The Rebs wanted Yazoo City badly.

When the barrage ceased, Stiles looked out with his binoculars. A Confederate major—he'd swear it was the very one who had a week ago shot down Jenkins and Jones and three more later that same day—was advancing under a flag of truce, a Texas Ranger at his side. Stiles ordered his men to cease fire and went out to meet him.

"General Ross sends his compliments and says your men have fought bravely," the major said. "You've seen the forces we have against you. Surrender the fort and you'll have all the privileges of prisoners of war."

"Privileges? You speak to me of privileges. Why did you kill my troopers out there last week after they'd surrendered?"

"Sir, may I remind you of the rules of war? We may only converse about truce terms."

"And what do the rules say about executing unarmed prisoners? I'd like to wring your cowardly neck."

"Me too." The black trooper who'd escorted him whispered under his breath, so that only Stiles heard him. Even so, he'd pay for that indiscretion if he survived this day.

"Sir," said the major, "will you conduct my superior's terms to your commanding officer or not?"

"Do those terms include sparing the lives of the colored troops should we surrender?"

"Yes. You have ten minutes to give an answer. We'll hold fire during that time."

Stiles turned to go.

"Captain, one more thing, before you go."

"Get on with it."

"If you refuse to surrender, General Ross says he cannot be responsible for what happens to your men. Feelings are running mighty high among our men about that armed nigger rabble. And remember, it's four to one."

Zack was waiting at the ramparts. "Well, Captain?"

"I'll be back in a few minutes."

He went up to Major Wickham, the commander of the fort, and reported both the terms and the colored troopers' oath to fight to the death.

"Hells bells, man! What kind of fool!—what did you tell them, for God's sakes?"

"I gave them my word. No surrender."

"Damn it to hell, Stiles, what's the matter with you ? That's not for you to decide, it's my decision."

"But, sir—"

"But, sir, nothing! There are some white troops and noncoms here and they deserve some damn consideration, don't they?"

Stiles slapped his gauntlets across his open palm. "After what the bastards did to our men last week, you can't—"

"There are thousands of Rebs over there. How long do you think we'll last once they come at us full force? Ten minutes? Fifteen, twenty? Come on, man, they wouldn't kill all your troopers if we surrendered. Probably just a few for show. And maybe not even that. They don't have time, they want to take Yazoo City."

Stiles looked over at his men, who were watching intently. "Major, if you decide to surrender, I ask you to issue me an order detaching me and my men from your command so we can continue to fight. I cannot break my word."

Wickham walked over to Stiles, put his arm around his shoulder, drew him to a spot where the men could no longer observe them.

"I'm an old man, Will, and I've lived through too many battles to want to die now because of some damn niggers. And that's what you're asking me to do."

Stiles nodded his head. At this point he knew the major well enough to know he was no coward. He'd simply assessed the odds and made a realistic judgment based on that assessment.

"Then I'll give you ten of my best, sir, and you can try to make it through to Yazoo City. Just leave me here to defend the fort with the rest of my men."

"And leave me coming into the lines while my command is being destroyed by the enemy?" The old soldier stood for a long moment, glaring. "Damn your eyes, you young pup, we'll fight, we'll fight to the death— which is probably what the damn Rebels are going to be dealing. Now go back and tell that Reb."

Stiles walked back out. "No surrender."

The Confederate major's eyebrows went up. "Well, Captain, we'll be sure to bury you with your niggers when it's over."

"We'll see who does the burying honors." With that, he turned on his heel and nodded to his men. All along the Yankee lines, they began clapping their hands and shouting. "No surrender. No surrender!"

* * *

The exhilaration of the moment was forgotten in the onslaught that followed. From the dugout he dropped into, Stiles could see Zack swinging his carbine like a stick, crushing heads all around him. He also saw the extent of the drubbing the squadron was taking.

Everywhere lay dead and bloodied men. Over the din of screaming horses, colored soldiers and Rebel soldiers tried to out-shout and outcurse each other.

"That's for Jason!" a colored soldier yelled as he ran his saber through a Reb's chest.

"This for Mattie-Lou!" yelled another.

But they fell back. Fighting, yes. Swearing, yes. But still falling back slowly and surely before the enraged Confederate legions.

Stiles felt a bullet whistle through his hat. Then another grazed him hard on the arm, knocking him to the ground. Immediately Zack was by his side, himself bleeding from a cut on his forehead, but ready to help as Stiles struggled to get back on his feet.

"Hold strong, men." His head was spinning—surely he would fall. "Stand fast!" he cried.

A hurrah went up along the Yankee lines.

"The Wizard, he's coming!"

And two seconds later, Joe was in the trenches. "They near broke through in the city, sir, but we held them. Captain Cook, he put a bunch of us together, and we turned them back. In a minute these Rebs in front of you are going to break. When they do the major says give 'em almighty hell."

Sure enough, off on their left flank the Texans began to break and run, and soon all along the line Rebels were turning and running back across the field, some of them throwing their weapons down in their haste to escape.

"Steady, men," Stiles said. "Give 'em a volley to keep them company."

The colored troops poured a withering fire into the Rebs, then with sabers drawn pursued them across the field.

"Kick their asses."

"If they breathe, stick 'em."

It was all he and Joe could do to stop the enraged men from taking the lives of the Reb wounded who littered the field.

They turned back toward their own lines and saw Zack Bascom running toward them.

"Captain, Captain!"

He glanced around the battlefield. Could the enemy possibly have sent a force behind them and attacked from the rear?

As Zack came closer, they saw that he was crying. "Captain! It's the major, sir!"

"Get yourself together, man, what happened?"

"A shell hit near Major Wickham. He dead."

Stiles put his arm around Zack's shoulder. "Take me to him."

Down in the middle of the fort, where the command post had been, almost a dozen men were gathered in a circle swaying gently back and forth and chanting a slow dirge about crossing Chilly Jordan. As he approached, they stopped singing and parted to let him through. Someone had covered the major's remains with a horse blanket and placed his officer's cap on top of it.

Stiles wanted to cry himself. Hell, hadn't he seen the major lead many a charge, like the one outside Jackson that had sent the Rebs packing? Hadn't he seen how day after day he'd forced his tired old body to stay in the saddle when he ought to have been back home in Kingston sitting by a blazing fire with his young wife and three children? Hadn't he traded his life for those of the colored troops when he agreed not to surrender? Well, so be it. It had been his choice, and there were worse ways to die.

The weight of that choice was heavy on Stiles's shoulders, but he looked at the grieving faces of his men, knew that wasn't what they needed. "Cheer, up boys! He'd be proud of you! You sent him off like a soldier!"

CHAPTER SIX

SUE Kenworthy felt like crumpling Dorothy's letter into a little ball and throwing it at somebody. So Richard had stopped in to see Dorothy, which at least placed him in Louisiana—but *when would he be home?* What about *her?* What about *their* children? It was bad enough having to live here in a house that had once been her cousin's. But now the cousin was gone, leaving just her and the five adult Negroes to manage the little holding and take care of her four children. The Yankees were destroying *everything.*

She called out to the kitchen, where she hoped Zenobia was fixing lunch. "You didn't get the laundry done yesterday. Martha and Debbie have just about run out of clean clothes."

"Only got two hands, Miss Sue. Me and Drayton were down all day trying to do some planting for the summer garden. It's already May."

"But that doesn't mean you and Lisa Mae can't do the other work around here. The children come first, after all."

"Children got to eat, too. Miss Sue, we trying our best, but what with the cooking and everything and keeping this big old house clean—"

"Have you forgotten that I saved you and Cally from going on that transport to Alabama? You could at least be grateful, I'd think. Instead it seems to me you don't work as hard as you used to."

"I'm working hard as I can, Miss Sue. It ain't your fault there's so much work—or mine, neither."

"You know, the pressing gangs, they're still in operation if you think you're not up to all this household work."

Zenobia came into the room, that blue calico bandanna tied around her head. She was a handsome woman for a Negro, her narrow black face almost chiseled, her deep-set eyes smart and knowing. Probably came from royalty over there in Africa.

"Miss Sue, I don't mean no disrespect, but it seems to me you can't hardly find no more faithful folk than me, Lisa Mae, Drayton and the old servants been. You know what's happened on all them other places, colored folks running away to the Yankees. Not us, we've stayed right here. Don't seem to me you should be thinking of sending us to no Alabama."

Sue let out a deep sigh. Zenobia was looking righteous.

"I'm sorry I was scratchy. But, Zenobia, everything's changing so fast. Sometimes I just don't know what to make of it."

"You been through a mighty lot, Miss. Reckon it hurt powerful bad to have to leave Clifton. I remembers the day you and Massa Richard was married there. I was working in the kitchen special that day and oh, didn't we cook some spread for you?"

Now, that was something to remember. Before the wedding, Cousin Fred had sung, "Thou Wilt Come No More, Gentle Annie." Sue looked around the room, smiled at the memory of turkey, chicken, potato salad, candied yams, and fresh green beans spread on glistening white tablecloths embroidered in gold, which covered the table from end to end. Bottles of the finest French wines, brought all the way from Paris, France, and a seven-course meal—a different wine for each course. And the smiling nigras, so happy for them, served strawberries with the special whipped cream flavored with a framboise liqueur.

Oh, how they'd danced that night. And as they all sat on the porch, candles lighting up the night, the nigras sang for the wedding party like God had touched their voices in a special way just to bless her nuptials.

"What was that song . . . " She turned to ask Zenobia, but she must have already gone back to the kitchen.

Oh well. Hadn't folks talked about the wedding for years afterward? And then the guests had spilled out onto the lawn and . . . She glanced out the window at the scruffy old brown grass, the path from the house to the road covered with weeds.

She stamped her foot at the unfairness of it all and called to Zenobia. "Just see to it that the children are taken care of when they finish tutoring. And you'll just have to find the time to straighten out the salon before the afternoon. The ladies will be coming over for tea."

* * *

Later, that afternoon, Sue and her friends Mary Reynolds and Doris sat on the porch and spoke for a few minutes about the latest news, how Lee was still outwitting the Northerners over in Virginia and how gallantly their troops were fighting to free Mississippi of the Yankees. But soon they were talking about childhood escapades, visits in better days to one another's homes, when life flowed so easily compared to now.

"You know what I was thinking about the other day?" said Mary Reynolds. "Remember the night that we left to go down to Vicksburg to the winter ball on the Janet Rouse?"

"How could I forget?" said Sue. "Why you'd forgotten two of your bags, and there the boat was, belching smoke and all, bells ringing, and the darkies clapping because we were dressed so pretty and they were so proud of us."

Doris laughed. "Oh, I can see the captain up there on the side of the pilothouse yelling for us to come on board, and dear old Mammy Eunice running down the levee to catch you, hollering, 'Mary Reynolds, don't you dare leave without this!'"

"She like to have jumped out of her skin and fallen into the river when the captain blew the steam whistle three times," said Mary Reynolds.

Sue laughed. "And the next morning, waking up, going on deck, and seeing the flowers all in bloom along the banks of the river—violets, pansies and daisies, bluebells, morning glories, and wild roses everywhere, like the Good Lord had made a special show for us because He knew we were sixteen and on our way to our first ball. As if He'd strewn petals before our feet."

"You have such a way of saying things, Sue. Honestly, sometimes I think you should write stories, or poetry, or something."

"Maybe someday, Mary Reynolds, maybe when . . ."

The women fell silent for a moment.

"You remember that very tall, very black man who worked with your grandfather?" Mary Reynolds said.

"Course I do," Sue said. "Why, that was Luther. I could never, ever forget him."

"What a wonderful old darky he was. I don't think I've ever seen so good a worker."

"We called him Uncle Luther, of course," Sue said. "Why, he could rub the silver, polish the glass, clean the boots, saddle the horse, row the skiff across the Yazoo, and drive us around in the pony cart all in one day. And always smiling, too." She thought of Zenobia and frowned.

"What ever became of him?"

"I'd say he died of sadness, Mary Reynolds. When the war came, and all our nigras started running away, getting ornery, he couldn't stand it."

"How's that?" Doris asked.

"You see, we were truly his family. He didn't have anybody but us. And when all these bad things started happening, it just went to his heart and broke it in two. He tried to make up by himself for all the runaways, just killing himself with work."

Doris set her cup back into the saucer and shook her head.

"One day he just keeled over, dead of some heart ailment out there in that cruel sun."

"They are a faithful and good people," Doris said.

"They were," Sue got up and walked to the end of the porch and looked down the side of the house, then returned.

"They haven't changed, Sue. Well, I mean, I guess they have, but it's not their doing. It's just that the Yankees have influenced some of them and corrupted them to think they're just as good as white folks."

"You're right," Sue said. "And I think the Yankees did it out of spite. We lived so well and in such harmony with the nigras! They couldn't understand it and they couldn't stand it, either! I'd say they'll find out what harm they've done when they've lived with the freed ones for a while."

Mary Reynolds tucked a stray curl back into her swept-up brown hair and took a sip of lemonade. "I am afraid for the future, Sue. Aren't you?"

"Well, sometimes. But I hear that England will soon join in on our side."

"Maybe it will. But in the meantime, every day the nigras become more insolent. I had to call mine together and read them a letter from John where he promised to give them a thrashing once he came home if they didn't mend their ways."

Sue drew her chair closer to the other two and whispered, "I've had to threaten Drayton in the same way. And he was always so obedient. As to Zenobia and the other one, they've become impossible—I'm selling them off."

"When?"

"Mr. Salter will be here in a few days to take them away."

Sue went over to close the window that opened out on to the porch and was startled when five-year-old Debbie poked her head out. "Mommy, surprise!"

"Debbie! How many times have I told you not to listen to grown-up talk? Now, go back outside with the others."

How much had Debbie heard? Should she say something to her about it or just hope that either she hadn't heard it, or if she had heard it, wouldn't tell Zenobia?

She turned back to her friends. "Sometimes I don't know about that child. We were talking about the nigras."

"I'm afraid they're forever spoiled," Doris said. "The spirit of that Haitian rebellion is among them—you remember Toussaint-L'Ouverture and what he did to the white people in Santo Domingo."

Sue shivered at the mention of the bloody black dictator's name. "I think maybe you're right. Under our wings, they're a kind and peaceable people. But once the civilizing example of a higher race is gone from before their eyes, they revert to barbarity."

"It's so sad," Mary Reynolds said. "Soon it will be as if we had never brought them from Africa, never tried to teach them our Christian ways."

Doris said, "What do you hear from the front? Has Richard written lately?"

Sue passed for the third time a plate of the blueberry tarts Zenobia had made that morning. "He used to write so frequently, and now . and it's just hot and heavy all the time for them. He's still with Forrest's cavalry. But every now and then he'll send a gift for me and the children with a little note."

Doris said, "Then he was with our troops who routed the Yankees at Fort Pillow last month."

Sue tapped her teaspoon lightly on the side of her cup. "I've heard that ladies from the neighborhood were so relieved those nigra soldiers and whites were defeated, they held a special service of thanksgiving for the victory and set out the most delicious spread for General Forrest and his men."

"I would hope so," Mary Reynolds said. "Those nigras and Yankees were going all around the countryside, terrorizing and burning and stealing something awful. I heard that half of the nigras were drunk when General Forrest's troops broke into the fort."

Sue shuddered. "And they were standing up on the parapets of the fort, taunting our troops and . . . exposing themselves!"

"Did you hear?" Doris helped herself to another tart. "I swear, Sue, these tarts are just scrumptious. Did you hear how those foolish darkies kept on shooting even after the truce was declared, so that General Forrest had to attack them again?"

"Well, for some of them that will be their last vile act," Mary Reynolds said. "It should show the rest of them that the Yankees are leading them down a terrible path. They'll think twice before they take up arms against us. Leastwise, before fighting General Forrest."

"But the Yankees are calling it a massacre," Doris said. "Why I read in a paper yesterday that the Herald Tribune said in an editorial that General Forrest murdered—in cold blood—the defenders of Fort Pillow. They said—"

"Stop, I will not hear it, even from your lips," Sue said. "Richard would never murder anyone." She stood up. "Where has the afternoon gone? It's time for the children's dinner. I like to sit with them every evening. It calms them. Which is something we could all use nowadays."

An hour later, Sue sat down to dinner with her children and was pleased to see that for once Zenobia had set a good table. There were heaping bowls of turnip greens, mashed potatoes with gravy, and fried ham. And piping hot corn bread, with just-churned butter, and peach cobbler for dessert.

Sue looked at Gregory, her eight-year-old. He and the three girls had been running and playing in the yard all afternoon once the tutor went home.

"Open your hands." It didn't look as if he'd been anywhere near soap and water, but she gave him the benefit of the doubt. "Get up this minute and go wash those hands again. The idea. And you're the oldest, supposed to be the man of the house."

While they waited for him, she turned to Debbie. Was there a funny look in her eyes or was she imagining it? She might not have heard anything, and Sue couldn't think of a way to question her about what she'd heard without giving away that something was wrong. Oh, it was just too much, having to make all these decisions.

When Gregory came back, Sue bowed her head.

"Bless the table, please."

* * *

When dinner was over and all was quiet in the house, Sue went to her room and read once more the lines Richard had written after the battle at Fort Pillow:

> . . . please read these things, then let me know how you feel. My heart is heavy for I saw much blood two days ago. Indeed the river ran red with the blood of the Negroes. We had told them to surrender. And it is the strangest thing with these new, liberated Negroes—as they used to do at corn shucking time, when the whiskey got to them and they started to fight—so it was with those colored soldiers. It was not enough that they would refuse a truce, they found it necessary to engage in the most vituperative abuse against our men, threatening us with everlasting death should we continue our attack on the fort.
>
> They fought hard, indeed some few never even gave up until the end. When we finally got the better of them, our men gave them no mercy, so exasperated were they by the conduct of the darkies. It was a horrid sight, and I hope never to see such again. They begged mercy, still we fired and kept on firing. I attempted to stop the slaughter, but to no avail. General Forrest came over and ordered the men to keep on shooting, even though the victory was won and the Negroes and their white allies defeated . . . Worse, after the battle was over, there was a sort of blood lust in our men. Some found stocks of whiskey and committed depraved acts of which I heard, but did not witness. They nailed the bodies of some wounded

black sergeants to logs by their hands and feet, then fired the logs, making of them one great pyre. And in their drunkenness, someone got the idea that some of the colored wounded should be killed by fire. So they were thrown into buildings, and the buildings were fired. I am told their cries for help were piteous as the flames consumed the buildings. Pray for me, and ask God's forgiveness on my soul.

Your loving husband,
Richard

Sue sat holding the letter for a time, then put a candle to it and burned it up. She sat down at the night table and began her letter to him:

Dearest Richard,

I have your letter. The less said of the painful events at Fort Pillow, the better. God knows your heart, and your morality, and so do I. If there were any sinful acts committed there, I am sure that by your action to try and stop them, God has absolved you of any lasting moral stain. We serve a forgiving God. May He grant our arms victory.

Your loving wife,
Sue

She sealed the envelope and went to bed.

* * *

Zenobia quietly opened the door to the slave hut she shared with Lisa Mae, Cally, and Ned. Everybody was sleeping, the children as tired out from playing as she and Lisa Mae were from working. She was grateful Lisa Mae had fed them and washed their clothes so they'd have something clean for the next day.

She went over to her pallet and shook her awake.

Lisa Mae turned over slowly. It had to be hard for her, too, working as a field hand, watching the two children, and trying to deal with the demands of Drayton. Damn man tried to make them do all the work, including his. All the time saying do this, do that, "else I tell Miss."

Zenobia nodded her head toward the door, the only opening in the shack, and Lisa Mae got up and followed her out.

"I'm so tired, every bone in my body ache. Why you wake me up?"

"We have to leave here."

"Why?"

"In two or three days, that woman going to put us on a transport to Alabama."

"You crazy. Why she want to do something like that?"

"She tired of feeding us and keeping us, and she ain't too happy with me nor you neither."

"Miss Sue wouldn't do that."

"Listen to me." Zenobia put her right hand on Lisa Mae's face, one finger just under her cheekbone and the thumb under her chin. "This afternoon, Debbie come crying to me about not wanting Mommy to send me away. I shushed the child and told her Miss Sue was joking, so stop crying 'cause her auntie Zenobia wasn't going nowhere. That calmed her down a mite."

Lisa Mae grasped her hand. "You know what it is you thinking about doing? It's near three or four days to the river and the Yankees. How you reckon to get there, just us and them two little children?"

Zenobia nodded over at the bushes . "Let's go over there and talk. Cally need her sleep, elsewise that cough will never leave her."

"That's just what I mean," Lisa Mae said. "We should stay here, take our chances—"

"I know white folks and I know when they intend to do something. She been complaining about running out of money all the time. That woman mean to put us on the road, and that may be the end of all of us."

Lisa Mae said, "It such a long way, and swamps and snakes and bears out in them woods."

"They's worse things," Zenobia said. "You only eighteen and born at Clifton, but you know I was marched here, me and my two sisters that you never knowed, all the way from Abbeville Courthouse, South Carolina, down near the Savannah River. It pain me now to think on it, but maybe you'll understand why we got to run if I tell you about what happened when we was just one day outside of Chattanooga. The sun was beating down on us like we was standing right over a forge. We'd been on the road so long that I lost track of the days and nights. And this woman, her name was Mabel and she had a baby—I were only fifteen, but I used to carry it for her some Anyway, they marched us something awful. I just wanted to lay down there and die, but I was young and somehow or other I always managed to get up when the man cracked his whip.

"But Mabel, she say to the man, I can't walk no more, give me some of that water, please, before I die. The man said, 'You'll die, then.' He took the baby from her and give it to me. I won't never forget. For when she lay down, he commenced to beat her with a whip. 'Get up, you nigger, get up, you lazy bitch'—and he beat her and beat her till she quit breathing. And they left her dead, right there in the road. I carried the baby for many a day, till it took sick and died."

Lisa Mae shuddered. Zenobia reached for Lisa Mae's hand and drew her close. "Truth is, I not only think Miss want to send us away, I also think she want to sell me and you away from these children. I do believe that. And the road to the Yankees can't be no worse than that, no matter the danger out there. Even if—"

"What you girls talking about out here in the middle of the night?" It was Drayton. He lived by himself in a shack close by.

"What you hear?"

"Enough, you ain't going nowhere."

"Hush, you'll have somebody down here," Zenobia said. "Let's go in your cabin."

Once they were inside, Drayton said, "Now give me one reason why I shouldn't go up there and tell Miss."

"Well, for one, 'cause if the Yankees win, and Joe alive, he cut your throat, that's why."

Lisa Mae smiled at the prospect.

"I ain't studying no Joe . . . "

"And for another," Zenobia said, "I hear that the colored Yankee soldiers ain't been too nice to no white folks' niggers like you. Been tarring and feathering them."

"My white folks going to protect me, no matter what."

"Their time is over," Lisa Mae said. "You got to know that."

Drayton had walked outside without his shirt and now busied himself putting it on. "All this kind of talk make me nervous, you understand. Miss get wind of this and she sell me, too."

"Oh, so you done heard, Miss done told you." Zenobia waved her finger in front of his face and turned to Lisa Mae. "See?"

"Miss hold me responsible for you," Drayton said. "You run away, she'll whip me something awful. Remember how I saved you all from going to Alabama, neither one of you has repaid me. And it would just have been a little old thing."

Zenobia had had enough of this nigger. "You do what you want, but I'm going to tell you something. Miss Sue ain't got no money left—Mr. Richard ain't got any to send her. And these Confederate soldiers, they be coming every day to take mens away to work for them. They likely to take you away too—you a big strong nigger. Lessen the Yankees gets you first."

"You got any sense, you be begging to go with us," Lisa Mae said. "Yankees ain't that far away. And Abraham Lincoln done freed the slaves—ain't you heard about it?"

Zenobia nodded. "Might be a more better trip if you went with us. You know how to read and write—can make us out some passes."

"This your chance, Mr. Drayton." Lisa Mae unbuttoned the top of her blouse. "Might even think about how I been so mean to you."

Drayton's eyes lit up. "Well, I won't be telling Miss Sue nothing nohow."

He looked back at Zenobia. "How you planning to do this thing? And what you going to do with them children?"

"You'll see if you decide to come with us," Zenobia said. "But with you or without you, we going. We on our way."

CHAPTER SEVEN

JOE sat at the table smoking his corncob pipe. Betty was on the bed, sewing a brass button back on his blue uniform blouse. She'd cooked a dinner of steak, greens in fatback grease, and corn bread with a good brown crust.

"What you thinking?"

"That you mighty pretty, darlin', not to mention a mighty fine cook." Joe didn't know where she'd gotten that steak, but it was some kind of good.

"You always thinking that. But what about the fighting you got to do tomorrow?"

"Ain't going to be no different. We beating the Rebs. Soon won't be no more of them left in Mississippi."

"Couldn't tell that from all the soldiers that keep coming into our ward every day."

"I didn't say that the Rebs couldn't fight, 'cause they can. I'm just saying we ain't found the ones yet that can stop us."

Betty sighed. "I do worry every time you go up the river. I've just seen so much—men with legs gone, arms gone. And worse."

He looked at her head bent over his uniform and felt a wave of tenderness that startled him. "Honey, I think you beginning to get too close to me."

She shook her head, and when she looked up at him she was smiling. But her eyes were serious.

"Too late to worry about that," she said. "Done already happened."

"What I mean is, if I get hurt I don't want you getting all upset about me. Ain't good for you and surely ain't good for me." He put his pipe down, went over and lay down on his side with his head propped up next to her.

Betty put down her sewing and snuggled up to him. "Baby, you got to talk about this thing."

"Ain't that what we doing?"

"Joe. About going up to Clifton."

"And Zenobia?"

She nodded. He ran his hand through her hair and kissed her softly on the cheek.

"It ain't even about her no more. If she still there—and I don't know one way or another—or if anybody's there, then she probably still mad at me, because I let my temper get ahold of me and ran away to try and find my children. She probably think I'm dead."

"And supposing she is there? What then?"

"I don't rightly know." He was quiet for a moment. "I think I'd ask her forgiveness that I left her to carry the burden all alone, leaving her with our three-month-old baby. It was the corn liquor made me run."

"There's a lot more, ain't there?" She got up and poured him a cup of whiskey.

He took a long swallow and coughed when it stuck in his windpipe on the way down. As soon as he recovered, he sat up straight and stared down at the dirt floor, holding the cup in both hands, twisting it round and round.

"I can't never forget the day they come and took my children away."

"What happened?"

"See, Massa Richard, he knew how much I hated what he done to my sister, Pauline, knew I was biding my time . . .

"Oh yes, I remember about Pauline."

"Well, he run into debt and had to start selling off land, then he finally had to sell off slaves. And things being like they was between us, he started with my kids." Joe walked over to the small fireplace, knocked the pipe against the stone, and emptied the tobacco ashes into the fire. "Massa Richard he liked to be the best at everything. And he was a very strong man—heavy-built and all, but every now and then I used to beat him running and even shooting, 'cause his daddy used to let us go hunting together. He always held that against me."

"The way you talk, you must have been one troublesome slave."

"I was surely that."

He walked over to her, bent down and kissed her on the neck. She smiled.

"No, baby, I wasn't ever thinking like some of these niggers that love old Massa. No, I argued with that man all the time. Told him he weren't no better than me, had no right to hold me in bondage, nor to take my people's land—I told you Mama was part colored, part Choctaw. And what right did they have to sell my poor African papa down into Texas a month after I was born?"

Betty poured herself some bourbon. Most likely she'd never met no colored man that thought like he did, much less one who would put it into words. "And he didn't have you whipped?"

"No, because his daddy, old Massa Kenworthy, you see, he liked me a lot, thought somebody like me was good for his own boy to have as a playmate. So I got away with a lot of things other boys couldn't."

"It almost sounds like you was free."

"Not hardly. But there's plenty of men like me—even some in the regiment—wasn't made to be nobody's slave. Nothing the white man could do with us, except shoot us, sell us, or live with us. Because you see a man so mean he ain't afraid to die, he a hard man to control. Ain't but one way to do it."

"By doing harm to those he hold most dear to his bosom."

Joe set down his empty glass and got ready to go. He had to be back at camp by taps.

"Sold Luke and Milly down the river. I don't know where they be, but when we lands up there near Clifton, I may find out."

He kissed the top of her head and left her sitting at the table. She was still there, thinking, long after he was back in camp.

* * *

"Come on over behind the tent," Zack said. "Got us a little jug, and the guys got them a little poker game going. Tucker's dealing."

"You know I don't like that low-down nigger," Joe said. "Always whipping on folk littler than him."

"That don't matter tonight," Zack said. "You play, do you good, what with us going into Clifton tomorrow. Cards will take your mind off all that."

"You go on. Leave me be a little while. I might come back there directly."

Six miles outside of Clifton. Damn. Had sure taken him a long time to get back. Three years of mud, mosquitoes, beatings. Now, in a few more hours, he'd be leading the regiment back into the place where his dear mother had borne him—a slave—close to thirty-five years ago. Never once saw the sun rise on that place in freedom, but tomorrow, Lord willing, he would. He'd sorta be freedom's own personal messenger to Clifton.

For some reason the memory came back of the little brook under a willow tree where he and Zenobia made love sometimes when the heat was so bad you couldn't even turn over in the bed without sweating. Maybe there was still a high singing mocking-bird up in its branches. The clean lines of Zenobia's beautiful face seemed to be in front of him. What did she look like now? And Luke? Was he tall? Did Milly still have that dimple in her smile or had she outgrowed it? And Cally, she'd already know how to talk now. Had to make sure she learned to read and write like proper folks.

Hell, why'd he have that little shot of corn whiskey a while ago? Went right to his head, was splashing through his brains, like some kind of moonshine waterfall. Zenobia, you my soul. Wherever the wind and the water have taken you, if God let me live through these cannon and bullets and shotguns, I'll find you and the young 'uns.

* * *

"Joe?" Zack was back. "Man, that ain't no good, just sitting there staring at the fire. Come on back, have you a little drink, then go to bed. This your homecoming."

"Go to hell."

Zack flinched.

"Sorry." Joe got up. "I'm coming."

He had to smile when he got close enough to the fire to see the serious-faced men sitting in their white underwear tops with their suspenders holding up their blue cavalry trousers.

"Hey, Sarge, sit down. We having us a good time." Patton smiled and moved aside to give Joe a place to sit.

"Don't feel like playing. I'll just sit here and watch awhile."

Slater, a young recruit, was softly trilling on the harmonica. The rest played cards without a word or smile, except maybe when one of them got himself a big pot. When Patton finally won a hand he stood up and pranced around the circle, leaning down and jabbing his finger at each of the other players in turn.

"Told you all don't be sitting down with me! One terrible man! Mountain jack hide when he hear me coming! Lose all your money! All your money, I say!"

Joe laughed and stretched his hand out. "Stop running off at the mouth and hand me back that dollar I lent you to get through the month."

The men broke out laughing.

"Talking about some old mountain jack? Better get out of here while you still got a pot to piss in!"

"Strutting like some damn peacock and ain't won nothing else the whole night long!"

"Why don't you sit in, Joe?"

"Give us a chance to win back some of that two hundred dollars," Tucker said. "Ain't right for no one man to be holding all the money in the outfit. Like you some damn bank."

"All right, I'll give you fools a chance to lose some more of your money. Deal."

He looked over at the razor-cut scars on Tucker's brown face. He was big for a horse soldier, and so strong he'd been known to knock out a mule with his bare fist. Mules wasn't all he hit, though. He had already been busted from corporal twice, once for beating up on the little drummer.

Joe took the tin cup Patton handed him and drained it in two quick gulps. "What's the stake?"

"Dollar a hand."

Tucker was looking at Joe as if he knew he had a turkey. Joe put down a silver coin and started playing. At first things went good, then he started to lose.

"Zack, get me another cup of that rotgut."

"You done had you enough, Joe."

Joe put his cards down. "Ain't you been after me all night to join in? Now . . . hell, man, you won't get it, I'll get it myself."

"Sit, Joe. I'll get it, but this the last one."

Joe drank the whiskey down and wiped his mouth with his hand. Man, that stuff burned your stomach. Did something to your eyes, too—looked like there was two of every man around the slowly dying fire. He looked down at the pile of coins at his side. He'd started with ten dollars, now he had three. He was just thinking he'd go to bed after a couple more hands when he noticed something. Nobody was winning now but Tucker and Easely. The later it got, the more they won. And that damn nine card kept coming up in their hands.

He tried hard to focus on the cards in Tucker's hand. Shit. There was so much whiskey in his brains he could barely see them, much less what Tucker was doing with them. But sure enough, when the deal was done, Easely had won again.

Joe stood up quick and almost fell down again, he was that dizzy. But he reached down and grabbed Tucker by the arm.

"Enough of this shit, give everybody back their money."

Tucker looked at Joe like he was crazy.

"Yeah, you heard him," Zack said. "Give everybody back their money. I seen it too. You cheating."

"Man, that firewater done gone to your head." Tucker looked over at Zack. "You better take this loco Indian nigger and put him to bed before he get hisself hurt."

He shook loose and began to rake in the pile of coins in front of him, but Joe grabbed his hand again.

"Said give the money back, and don't be calling me no names—I'm your superior officer."

Tucker jerked his arm away and leapt to his feet.

"You ain't shit, nothing but a drunken-assed piece of shit. Get out of here before I kick your ass!"

Joe punched him hard and quick in the stomach.

Tucker gasped for breath and bent over like he'd been kicked in the balls. Joe put his two fists together and chopped him hard on the top of his head. Tucker fell to the ground, his big body rolling back and forth in the dirt. He was groaning something awful.

Joe reached down for the money pile. "Zack, count this out and make sure everybody gets what's coming to them. I'm going to bed." He straightened up and started to head toward his tent.

"Look out, Joe!" Zack yelled.

Joe turned and saw that Tucker was back on his feet, a Colt in his hand.

Whoa, Suzy! Turned his back on a hurt animal and look at him now. That gun was gleaming in the glow of the fire, and there was no mistaking the sound of the trigger cocking.

First mistake, Tucker, I still got my Adams double-action on me!

Joe fell to the ground, and rolled fast and hard away from the fire, toward the woods.

A bullet whizzed into the darkness over his head, and he heard Tucker cock the Colt for another shot. The big fool was standing right there against the light of the fire.

Second mistake, Tucker!

Joe sighted the Adams and fired. Tucker dropped the gun and reached for his shoulder, where the blood was gushing out like he was a stuck hog.

"Aw, hell!" cried Tucker. "That red-black nigger done kilt me." He staggered toward Joe like he was going to punch him, then fell to the ground.

In a second, Zack was by his side. Bent over him for a minute, then turned to Joe.

"You knows the penalty for shooting, Joe."

Why they could hang him.

With the whiskey in his brain and his blood up from the fight, Joe didn't stop to think, just lit out for the woods fast as he could.

"Halt!" A bullet whistled through the trees over his head, and he plunged deeper into the woods. He'd have to keep on running, of course. Hell, there wasn't a man in the command could catch him, drunk or sober. I done gone and lost me everything now! But nobody's coming into those woods after me, and I still have got my Adams and my Choctaw dagger.

He knew only one place to go, trotting fast and taking all the old paths where he used to come out into the forest to trap birds or track the bears for old Massa. Wasn't a path around here he didn't know.

* * *

Joe stopped for water at the Newton plantation, about three miles from Clifton, scouted around for a minute, then went down to the slave quarters. All of the little cabins were empty. He pushed open the door of one: nothing in there but the old straw bag the folks used to sleep on, now ripped open and lying all over the floor.

Walking a little farther down, he saw the pickaninnies' trough—he'd eaten out of one like it when he was little, pushing and shoving with the other kids to see if they could get some of the bread and milk Aunt Garry used to pour into the trough. He'd always managed to get himself enough.

He walked over to the well, then remembered how his own troop, under orders, had been going around cutting the ropes in the wells. Sure enough, whoever had come this way—Yankee or Reb—had cut the rope.

Sometimes trotting, sometimes fast walking, and crouching down in the ditches when he had to, he finally reached Clifton. A couple of times, he had to get into the woods quickly because he heard the sound of horses' hooves on the road. Had to be Reb patrols. Wouldn't be any Yankees up here until tomorrow.

Skirting around the outside of Clifton, satisfied that there were no troops about, he then went down to the slave quarters. Same thing as over at Newton's. Seemed like the loudest thing around was the pounding in his head. He remembered how at night, particularly when they were picking cotton in the moonlight to keep up with Massa's schedule, the whole quarters would be lit up, a big fire going in front of the row of cabins, people talking and children singing and shouting . . . Now there was nothing. Quiet like the grave.

The cabin where he and Zenobia had lived together for nearly fifteen years was a wreck. Gourds all over the floor, the wooden table he'd made for her split up—most likely used for firewood. And the trundle beds where Luke and Millie used to sleep—somebody had taken them, too.

Joe closed the cabin door behind him, got down on his hands and knees, and lit a match. Cupping its dim light with his hand, he searched every inch of the floor, looking for something, anything, of Zenobia's or Cally's, maybe even something that would give him a clue as to where they had gone. Surely she knew that someday he'd come back and look for her and that pretty little brown-skinned baby of his.

Shit, Zenobia! You should have left something.

But try as he might and search where he would, Joe couldn't find a thing to remember them by, much less a clue to their whereabouts. Then, just when he was about to blow out the third match, he saw something, almost covered up by the dust. It was the wooden comb he'd made for Zenobia, just about the time Millie was born. He ran his fingers over the smooth wood, felt the pretty carvings he'd put on it. Lord, Zee had been proud the first time she put it in her hair.

Cradling the comb against his heart, Joe closed his eyes, and could see his beloved, a little older but still pretty and haughty, full powerful hips, and skin that shone like fine polished furniture. Oh, it was Zenobia all right, but he couldn't quite make out what she was saying, like something was getting in the way. Then she seemed to fade and rise, go floating up high into some trees, finally drifting away up into some pretty white clouds with little black edges around them.

Gone.

Why hadn't she told him where Luke was? And Millie? Should have waited around, tarried awhile. Damn it, Zee— couldn't hear one word you said. Nary a one!

The door opened. Joe drew his Adams.

"Don't shoot, Joe. It just me."

"Uncle Dan? Ain't you got enough sense not to be poking all around at night? I could have killed you." Joe put the pistol away and hugged his friend.

"I knowed it was you, said you'd be coming back someday. Come on over to my shack. I'm the only one left on the plantation."

The old man was bent over, seemed smaller than before, but he still had that same blue-black skin. Leaning on his oak cane, he led Joe to a shack at the very end of a long row of cabins that stood about two hundred yards from the big house. Inside, he waved his arm for Joe to sit down on one of the two oak-stump stools. He went to light a lamp that hung near the door, but Joe stopped him.

"No need of attracting attention tonight."

As Joe's eyes became accustomed to the dark, he saw there wasn't much inside the shack save for the stools, a straw mattress that lay atop a wooden pallet on the floor, and another pallet where Uncle Dan had piled his clothes, boots, and some jars and dishes he must have scavenged from the abandoned shacks around him.

He reached across, putting his withered right hand on Joe's knee. "I'm mighty glad to see you, son. It gets awful lonesome around here all by myself. Just waiting for the angels to come."

"Don't talk that way, you got some good years left in you."

The old man grinned. "Mighty kind of you to say so, but you knows the only reason I's here is 'cause don't nobody think nothing about me. Ain't worth nothing to nobody, that's why everybody leave me alone—the Yankees, the grayboys, and all them thieves and robbers out there. They comes through here most every day and don't bother me none, one way or another."

"But how do you live?"

"Got me a few chickens out there in a special place in the woods, got me some cornmeal and smoked pork meat. Even got me a little garden. We going to have us some good eating in the morning."

"For now, could I have some water?"

"Sure, and I got something a little stronger than that. Way you look I reckon you could use a good belt or two."

"You guessed right, but I'll just take the water. I'm running away from trouble and headed straight for it. Need to clear my head so's I can think straight. Now, how about you tell me what happened to Zenobia and Cally."

Uncle Dan poured himself a drink. "They gone with Miss Sue up somewhere the other side of Jackson, but you got to know that Cally were sick a lot, and Zenobia, she weren't much better. Her gout done got worse, sometime she couldn't even get out of bed."

He took a sip of whiskey from the cup. "I prayed a lot for them. And I still prays for them every night. Cally, she done took a real liking to me before they left."

"What she look like?"

"Joe, that little thing, she got the shiniest black eyes, and she always smiling. And you know, they could be lots of folks around, and she'd always run right up to me and stick her little hand out for me to shake. She beautiful, Joe."

He was silent for a moment, then pointed with his thumb up toward the big house. "You wouldn't believe what it look like up there."

"What happened?"

"Well, them Yankees—you one of 'em now, but these was white boys— they come through here mighty fast one day— looking to catch Massa Richard, they say he a powerful secesh. They got themselves some liquor, and when they didn't find him, they just naturally commenced to tear up everything."

Joe took Uncle Dan's hand. "Have you seen or heard anything of Luke or—?"

"It were something awful. They ripped up the mattresses looking for money, then commenced to burning the beds, and the tables and the curtains. Burnt everything, then pissed on the floor. Lord, it were bad. Finally, a captain come in and made them stop, made them put out the fires."

Joe said, "We trying to punish these slave masters, break them out of their nasty ways."

"Still weren't right to destroy all them beautiful things. Massa Richard, when he seed it, he were more madder than I ever seen him. And—oh Lord, Joe . "

"What?"

"He had Luke with him, serving as his orderly man."

"You sure?"

Uncle Dan finished the last of his cup of whiskey and put it down on the dirt floor. "Sure as I'm sitting here. I'd know that boy anywhere—he grown big and tall now, look just like you. He Massa Richard's body man and a blacksmith with General Forrest."

"Did Massa Richard say anything about Milly?"

"I didn't have no time to find out, barely had time to talk with him. They was in and out of here mighty fast."

Joe was completely sober now. And tired.

"Uncle Dan, I'm going up in the pine grove over there and get me some sleep. Be too dangerous sleeping down here. In the morning, I need you to give me some clothes to wear 'stead of this uniform, and some food. Then I'll be on my way."

"Where to?"

"Meridian. That's where Zenobia and Cally is and that's where I'm headed."

He went over to the grove, broke some pine branches off the trees, made a litter, and lay down to sleep.

Several times during the night he awoke to the sounds of night critters astir in the woods around him. And when he looked up from his bed of pine he saw bright stars splashed all over God's heaven way above him. He pulled Uncle Dan's blanket up over his head and fell back to sleep.

"Damn!" A sharp pain in his butt brought him awake. In front of him was a pair of brown boots and gray pants.

His eyes followed the pants upward to the open flap of the black holster on the brown leather belt of the Reb above him. He grabbed for his Adams.

"Wouldn't do that if I was you. Get up."

Standing there with four Rebs, and pointing right at him, was Uncle Dan.

"See, I told you there were a Yankee here."

Joe said, "Praise the Lord! I's so glad Uncle Dan went for you. I knowed he would 'cause he a good nigger, sure love his grayboys, just like I do. I thanks you, Uncle."

"It were the least I could do for you, Joe."

"What you talking about, boy?" the corporal said. "You take me for a fool or something? And you with them sergeant stripes on you?"

"I's a deserter, I done run the guards."

"A likely story. We'll see what the colonel says."

They tied Joe up, threw him over the mule's back, and took him over to the woods about a mile away, to a clearing full of Reb cavalry. Their colonel sure didn't look like no easy kind of man, not with that brace of pearl-handled pistols sitting right on the desk while he talked to Joe.

"Like I was telling this lieutenant, sir . . ." Joe pointed to the corporal.

"Damn," the colonel said. "They sure make anybody a sergeant in the nigger cavalry. You don't even know he's a corporal?"

"I's ignorant, Colonel, sir. Like I was saying, I was with Colonel Witherspoon's Texas Brigade, sir, a mule skinner and a cook, sir. I's a good cook."

"And?" He glared at Joe, his hand toying with one of the pistols.

"Dem Yankees captured us'n, and next thing I knowed, Generals Grant and . . . let's see, who was that other one? Was it Sherman, yeah, de very same, and these two generals is arguing about whether to shoot us or not for they didn't want to have to feed no captured niggers."

"Boy, you ain't never seen them men."

"Ain't lying, Massa."

The colonel leaned forward.

"What'd they look like?"

"General Grant, he de one wanted to shoot me, but General Sherman, de redheaded one, he say, this nigger fought against us, now let him fight against them."

The corporal looked hard at Joe. "And?"

"General Grant, he say then I would have to fire against them, and he march me over to a big cannon, make me put three loads of ammunition in it, put in dat big old heavy ball, swab it, and pull the lanyard. It like to knock me off'n my feet. Then he say, now you go fight for us, boy, and they make this poor darky go into a nigger horse regiment."

The colonel roared with laughter. "Sounds just like Ulysses. We were together in Mexico. How came you to be at that plantation over the way?"

"Well, Massa, I was just abiding my time. Just waiting my chance to get away from those Yankees. So now when we gets up here, close to Massa's house, I knowed I could get away 'cause I knows de country 'round here real good."

"So what did you do?"

"Sneaked out the Yankee camp last night, and when the sentry come after me, I shot him square between the eyes and took off in the woods trying to find my white folks. Dat's how I come to be here." Joe fell to his knees in front of the table, rolled his eyes upward in their sockets, and folded his hands together like he was praying. "Oh, Massa, I's so glad to be back with my white folks, you got to save me from dem Yankees."

"How many times did you shoot him?" the colonel asked, tapping his finger on the table. "How many times did you shoot that sentry?"

"Once."

The colonel motioned to the corporal. "Let me see his Adams."

He broke it, and counted the five remaining bullets in the cylinder.

"No nigger could have made up that story about Ulysses S. Grant. Wait till the general hears it. You say you a cook?"

"Best you ever et, Colonel, sir. Why sometimes old Colonel Osband he let me feed all de officers. They loved my cooking something awful. For a while there, sir, I was his orderly too."

The colonel leaned forward over the pistols on his desk. "We could use a real cook. You know how to polish boots and take care of horses?"

Joe, still on his knees, showed a wide row of white teeth and grinned up at the colonel. "I is the best. Used to race for Massa at Natchez."

"You better be, because I got one of the finest horses in the country out there—and that's why I got rid of that other boy.

Couldn't take care of my Princess properly." He turned to the corporal. "Take charge of this man. Show him his duties, and let him prepare the officers' mess for tonight. We'll see how good a cook he is."

"Massa, you ain't never going to regret this. I'm one thankful nigger. You mighty good to me."

"Well now, don't you worry, Joe, you're back with your people, and we appreciate good niggers like you. As a matter of fact, if you're real good, we might let you fight with us, we got one colored boy that rides and fights with us just like white folks. You'll see him when you go get your new clothes."

He motioned to the corporal to escort Joe out of the tent.

"Oh, and, if we get anywhere close to Sherman and his boys, we'll let you load you up a cannon and take a shot at him."

Joe bent over laughing and slapped his hands on his thighs. "That's a good 'un, Colonel, sir. A mighty good 'un."

* * *

That night the colonel and his officers sat down at a table laid with a spotless white tablecloth. Dishes of baked sweet potatoes and slow-cooked string beans were at either end of the table, in the center chickens that had been barbecued on a spit. There were good hot pan biscuits to go along with them. And at the side of the table stood Joe, beaming, a white napkin wrapped over his arm.

"Hope it meets your 'spectations, sir."

Behind him were two waiters, bowing and scraping the way Joe had taught them a few hours earlier.

"Gentlemen, we've found us a chef. This calls for some good wine." The colonel tossed Joe a key. "Go into my tent, you'll find a special liquor chest. Bring us out three bottles of that red wine."

By the time dinner was over, Joe had made two more trips to the wine cabinet, and the colonel and his staff officers were singing "When This Cruel War Is Over." The way they were bellowing, you'd have thought it was already over. And the singing got even louder when the colonel called for some of his men—his choristers, he called them—to come over and sing with them.

Joe was back in the mess area cleaning up when he heard the new voices:

> *When the summer breeze is sighing mournfully along*
> *Or when autumn leaves are falling*
> *Sadly breathes the song . . .*

A beautiful soaring tenor was all too distinct from the rest of the voices. Damn. Wasn't another voice in the whole world like that one. And the last time he'd heard it was the night he and Zack stole those horses. Must be one of them Rebs that had been in that house. Just hoped it wasn't Andy, 'cause he'd be sure to recognize him.

Didn't his troubles ever end?

The field kitchen area wasn't far from the colonel's dinner table, and it was getting dark. Joe decided to walk over so as to get a better look.

> *Oft in dreams I see thee lying on the battle plain*
> *Lonely, wounded, even dying . . .*

Oh, that man sure could sing. His voice was sweeter than the clear juice from a ripe melon at the close of a hot summer day.

Joe got as close as he dared—close enough to see it was Andy, all right. Standing there along with five other Rebs in front of the officers' table, just singing his heart out.

The colonel looked back over his shoulder, and saw Joe.

"Come here, boy. Some of my officers want to personally thank you for that great meal!"

Oh, Lord. He walked over to the officers' table—not ten feet from Andy, who looked him dead in the face.

"Calling but in vain . . ."

He stopped singing, and raised his hand. Joe stood tensed on the balls of his feet. He'd run if he had to, and maybe they'd had enough to drink that they wouldn't be shooting so straight.

Andy kept singing, God bless him.

"Weeping sad and lonely . . ."

* * *

"Best meal I've had since the war started, Joe," the colonel said. "The regiment will be going into the field tomorrow to give that old nigger outfit of yours a whipping. They won't know what hit them. We should polish them off by noon. That should give you time to get my tent in order and give Princess a good grooming."

"I reckon they won't know what hit them, Colonel, sir."

* * *

In the morning, Joe was up early. He helped the colonel into his boots and buckled his saber and saber belt on. When all the troops were assembled and on their horses, he helped the colonel mount up.

"This a fine-looking animal, too, Colonel, sir."

"Never mind about Tornado, just see you take care of Princess. Rub her down good, you hear?"

"Yes, sir. Give those niggers a good licking for me. Stealing me away from General Witherspoon like they did."

The colonel led his regiment out of the camp about an hour before day-break, and Joe went into the colonel's tent to start the cleanup. He was humming "Dixie," but at the same time wondering how the hell he had gotten himself into such a fix.

He folded the colonel's blanket, then pulled down a brace of pearl handled revolvers from a peg, and began to polish the holsters. He eased one of the revolvers out of its holster, broke it, and spun the cylinder. All loaded. It would take the Rebs about an hour and a half to reach the place where they planned to ambush the regiment. Knowing the woods the way he did, he could probably make it in forty-five . . .

But what good would it do him even if he did get there first? He was a wanted man. They'd probably shoot him on sight.

Joe began to polish Colonel Montgomery's camp table. For the moment, he was better off with the Rebs. At least he wouldn't get shot. And he could get away from them any time he wanted.

Outside, there wasn't one sentry left in the camp. Nothing but the wounded and they were still asleep.

It would be stupid to go back.

He walked over to the tree where Princess was tied. She was one fine-looking sorrel. Fast enough to beat Hawk?

A rooster crowed. Soon those wounded Rebs would be up and about. On the ground right close to Princess was a saddle and bridle.

Zack, Captain Stiles, Patton . . . those Rebs would cut them all down. Wouldn't take no nigger prisoners, nor their white captain.

Joe returned to the colonel's tent. He loosened his trousers enough to tie the holsters with the guns around his waist, rebuckled the pants back up over them, and went outside. There wasn't a sound from the camp when he walked Princess a ways off into the woods, saddled her up, and took off to where he figured the Third would be.

The sky in the east was dawn-pink. Couldn't be sure he'd get to Brown's Crossroads before the colonel, but—oh hell he had to. His outfit was in trouble.

He reached the crossroads in just over a half hour. He tied Princess to a tree and squatted down to examine the dirt. Nope, no cavalry horses had passed this way yet. He spurred Princess and cut off the road to make better time. That Reb colonel was right about one thing. Princess could fly.

"Halt, or we'll fire!"

Six black troopers, carbines all leveled at him! More behind them. And at the front, Lieutenant Geary.

"Joe?" One grabbed his reins. "What the hell you doing out here, Joe?"

"Don't worry about that. Lieutenant, a whole regiment of Reb cavalry is right behind me, no more'n a half hour away. Maybe less."

"Be that as it may, you're under arrest. Sergeant, get him back to the colonel and let him report to him. The rest of you men dismount and prepare a skirmish line here." He glared at the sergeant. "Get a move on, man!"

Ten minutes later, the main body of the detachment was in motion.

"We'll see who does the ambushing," Colonel Osband said, then turned to Joe. "Report to your outfit and get that Reb jacket off. We're going to meet Colonel Montgomery."

"You mean I ain't under arrest, sir?"

"I'll deal with that after the fight. Now get the hell out of here."

"Yes, sir."

Twenty minutes later Joe sat on Princess, carbine in hand, Colonel Montgomery's Colts still buckled on, watching from the woods, Zack at his side. A small artillery fieldpiece loaded with grapeshot and its crew stood at the ready. A gunner was poised to set it off with a match. Lieutenant Geary's small detachment, firing carbines from their horses, was riding back across the very field where his men had found Joe.

When they got to the far side of the clearing, they dismounted and fired a volley. Now Colonel Montgomery's men were flooding into the open space. Lieutenant Geary and his men grabbed their horses and ran off into the woods.

From his place of concealment, Joe could hear Colonel Montgomery loud and clear.

"After them, men, we'll teach this nigger cavalry a lesson they'll never forget." The whole Rebel force came into the big field, firing their shotguns into the woods. The only thing Colonel Montgomery didn't know was that on both sides of the field, in the woods there, were the rest of the Third Cavalry, carbines cocked and aimed, just waiting till all the Rebs were in the jaws of the trap.

When Joe saw that saber he'd polished the night before, he felt kind of sorry for Colonel Montgomery. Him and all them officers Joe had fed such a good meal, the way you feed the pigs before the slaughter, they wasn't bad people. Hell, he wouldn't have minded riding with the colonel, if he hadn't wanted him to be a slave.

Here they came, lickity-split across the field, to the awful sound of their Rebel yell. Sounded like a cross between a hound dog baying and a mountain lion's holler.

The woods on three sides exploded with fire and smoke.

Rebs were falling everywhere. And the horses hit with bullets or grapeshot were screaming with pain.

"Fire at will!"

A steady stream of small arms fire poured into the Rebel ranks.

Colonel Montgomery dropped his saber. Was he hurt? If he was, it couldn't be too bad, because he was shouting, "Dismount, form as skirmishers."

These Rebs were some kind of soldiers. In the midst of all that fire, they kept coming on, shooting into the woods, because they would not take low in front of no colored boys.

The little fieldpiece spoke again, and Joe watched first one, then two, then eight Rebs begin to retreat back across the field. Colonel Montgomery stayed forward, near their colors.

"Don't fall back!" he cried.

But even he finally saw that they couldn't stand against the fury pouring out of those woods. They fell back across the field and set up another skirmish line.

Joe knew how good the gunners attached to the Third were. They'd shell them right out of there. And sure enough, it wasn't long—maybe after fifteen more shells from that little artillery piece—before the Rebs broke, got on their horses, and took off back down the road they'd come up just a while ago.

The Third Cavalry followed them, drove them all the way to a bridge. Joe was right in front, leading his company. He wished he'd been a little quicker about it, though. By the time they got to the bridge, the Rebs were already burning it and taking up firing positions to protect their retreat. Colonel Montgomery was busy directing his troops.

And he almost had a fit when he saw Joe riding Princess— jumped up and down, waved his saber, and swore. You could hear him yelling over all the fire.

"Ten dollars and three bottles of my best corn liquor to the man that kills that nigger son of a bitch! But I'll hang the one who hits Princess."

Bullets whistled all around Joe's head.

"Joe, take that damn horse to the rear," Captain Stiles yelled. "The Rebs don't need one more thing to get their dander up."

When the fieldpiece caught up with Joe's company and began to shell the Rebs on the other side of the bridge, they retreated again. The Third Cavalry quickly threw together a make-shift bridge and continued the pursuit, swept right on through the camp where Joe had been a prisoner that morning. The Rebs scattered into the woods and the bayous.

* * *

That evening, when the camp was all policed and the Reb and Yankee casualties taken care of, the colonel had Joe brought to his tent, the very same tent where Colonel Montgomery had slept the night before.

"Joe, you're a most fortunate man," the colonel said. "You just winged Tucker. Probably served the bastard right. It'll teach him not to cheat at cards."

"Yes, sir."

"But you were supposed to set an example. You and firewater don't mix, you know it and I know it. I want your word that you'll not drink whiskey again—not while you're in this regiment."

"Colonel, sir? That's a mighty stiff—"

"Stiff? You say anything but 'Yes, sir' and you'll find out what stiff is.

Your word, Private!"

"Yes, sir. Private, sir?

"I'm demoting you for at least thirty days. And docking you thirty days' pay."

"Yes, sir."

"I'm also putting you in for a citation. That was a hell of an action you engaged in today."

"Thank you, sir . . . Colonel, sir, may I ask something now?"

He nodded, but his look warned Joe to take care what he was about. It told him, better than a demotion, how much he'd disappointed the colonel.

"I was wondering, sir, if you might not like for me to cook you and the other officers a fine victory meal tonight. I know where all the fixings are."

CHAPTER EIGHT

ZENOBIA knew escape would be hard. The dampness in the swamp was bound to make her gout act up. And what would happen when the cold swamp air hit Cally's lungs? Her cough could give them away in the woods.

There were so many patrollers out there, and she'd heard the tales of what had happened to black folk caught by soldiers. On both sides.

That night she prayed on her knees. "Jesus, they about to separate me from my very last child, and I cannot bear it no more. And poor little Ned—all he got is me and Lisa Mae. You a mighty good captain, and I'm calling on you to lead us on this journey."

The next morning, soon as he'd finished cleaning up the yard, Drayton came into the kitchen with a big smile on his face.

"Good morning, good morning . . ."

It wasn't like him to be full of smiles and greetings.

"I've decided to go with you."

"I think you a brave man." Lisa Mae snuggled close up into his arms. "You'll never be sorry for this."

Drayton smiled. "Just don't want to see you two women sold away, that's all."

No, that wasn't all. Zenobia looked at Lisa Mae, then back at Drayton. Had she slipped out during the night and slept with him?

Didn't matter. Probably Drayton had decided that Miss Sue might sell him too.

She slapped at a mosquito buzzing around her ear. There were dozens of them around. "You going to be able to steal some horses and a wagon?" she asked.

"Yes, but that won't get us but a little ways. We going to have to go by the swamps." He frowned. "I still think you wrong to run away. Maybe Miss change her mind."

This man was getting on her last nerve. Wasn't it bad enough that she had decided to go into the marshland with her baby child? She was leaving a place where they had decent food and a sturdy roof over their heads at night. God only knew what dangers lay ahead of them. She didn't need Drayton trying to make her change her mind, weaken her will.

"You going with us or not?"

He grabbed at a fly, caught it, held it in his hand for a second, then released it.

"I'm going. Now, first thing, we got to fix Cally's cough. I'll make up a special medicine—mullein leaves, sugar, and vinegar. Sure to help her some, but she got to take it twice a day."

"I'll see to it. What else?"

"We're in luck, 'cause Miss she going away to Miss Margie's for a few days and she taking the children. And Linus and Mary, they so old, they hardly going to know we gone."

Zenobia smiled. As if the two old house slaves would have said anything anyhow.

"What about the hounds? What we do if they come after us with them hounds?"

"You sure enough full of questions. Tire a man out. Let's sit down over there." He pointed to the pine bench near his cabin. "I done taken my precautions. Took me two pistols out the big house, and some knives. The dogs may be the least of our troubles." He shook his head. "See, Zenobia, you so headstrong. You don't know like I do about all of them dangers. It ain't only all them varmints in the swamps. There's deserters, Yankees and grayboys, and there's bands of irregulars—they's armed and they don't obey nobody, they the law all to themselves. You don't hear the way these white folks talk like I do. Some of them are scared of their own people."

Lisa Mae put her hand on Drayton's. "You shoot me before you lets them take me. Hear?"

"Me neither. Regular or otherwise," Zenobia said. "Shoot everybody if that happen."

"Everybody, Zenobia?"

She looked beyond Drayton over at the little pond where, sometimes in the evenings, she used to sit beside Cally and watch her kick her tiny feet in the cool water, or try to catch the little tadpoles darting back and forth. She turned back to Drayton.

"Everybody."

"I will think on it," Drayton said.

"You do that. Now, what else we need?"

"I'm packing some tools with me, because what with the swamps being flooded the way they are, I plan to build us a raft once we get to the rivers."

"That's a good idea." Lisa Mae was looking at Drayton like he'd invented sunshine, but Zenobia had to admit he was smarter than she'd thought.

"You two pack enough food for a week for us all," he said. "Corn bread and cooked corn—things we can eat without cooking, for we scarcely going to be able to make a fire. And warm clothes, 'specially for the children."

"All right. And where we heading for?"

"Right back to Clifton. I know where lots of food is hidden. Uncle Dan is still there and he'll find some place for us to hide. We can rest, then figure how out we're going to get down to Vicksburg way."

Seemed like he'd thought of just about everything. Now it was her turn to get busy so they'd be ready to leave the next day.

* * *

"Bye, Zenobia, bye, Lisa Mae." Miss Sue's children started waving even before the wagon moved forward.

"You behave yourselves!" Zenobia shouted after them as they disappeared down the road. "You hear me?"

As soon as they were out of sight, she took Lisa Mae by the arm.

"You go down to the cabin, get the clothes. Me, I'm going back to the cook shed, pick up the children and the food. Meet me down at Drayton's cabin. Hurry now!"

* * *

Drayton, dressed like a proper coachman, was waiting for Zenobia and the children, but not Lisa Mae.

"I sent her down here to get the clothes. You didn't see her?"

Drayton shook his head and threw his hands up in the air. "We got no time to lose."

Confound it! Where was she?

"Here, get the children and the food packed away, I'm going to look for her."

She walked over to their cabin, looked in, saw the sack with all their clothes was still there. Damn. She threw it over her shoulder and went back to the wagon.

Drayton had already stowed the little packages of food in the wagon, and made the children comfortable on a bed of hay. The two brown horses hitched to the wagon were lazily flicking their tails at the horseflies buzzing around them.

"Come on, get up here with me," he said. "We got to go. Just have to leave Lisa Mae."

"Give me a few minutes. I'll find her."

Taking off his hat, Drayton slapped it across his knee, and got down from his seat. "I'm thinking this a mighty poor way to be starting."

"Drayton . . ." She took him by the arm, and her touch seemed to calm him.

"All right. But hurry. It don't bode no good for us to—"

Lisa Mae ran up to them, breathless and crying.

"What's the matter?" Zenobia said.

"Old Mary catch ahold of me and say she know I'm going and she want to go, too. Stood there asking to go, talking about she want to die free, and all the time I'm trying to get away and saying we ain't going nowhere."

Drayton said, "Where's she now?"

Lisa Mae pointed back up the hill. "She were on her knees begging when I pulled away and come running here."

Oh, Lord. She felt bad about Mary. Worried, too. Would she give the alarm?

"Zenobia, you get up here with me," Drayton said. "Lisa Mae, get in back. We leaving now. Devil take the hindmost."

Drayton snapped the whip, and they were out of the yard

and onto the muddy road. After they'd been traveling for maybe half an hour, Zenobia turned to Drayton. "No matter what happens, I am mighty grateful to you."

"You know why I'm doing this, don't you?"

"Why?"

He covered her hand with his. "Because I want to show you I'm a better man than Joe."

"There ain't no better man than Joe."

"Then why'd he run away and leave you and Cally all alone?"

She pushed his hand away. "Don't let's go into that, now. We got bigger fish to fry and—oh, Lord, look like they straight ahead of us."

The very first patrollers were galloping down the road toward them. Two riders, all covered with dust, one wearing a red hat, and one a brown hat, both carrying shotguns. One of them pointed his gun at Drayton.

"Where you niggers think you going?"

"To Clifton, Massa, take care of Miss's plantation, 'cause the Yankees done left."

"Never heard of it. How far is it?"

Drayton took out a big red handkerchief and mopped his brow. "Three days, Massa."

"How come your Miss ain't going with you?"

"Miss's children get schooling here, sir, been here for most a year now after the Yankees chased us out of Clifton."

"Guy, let's take 'em back where they come from," said the short, stocky one with the shotgun aimed at Drayton.

"Well, now, Massa, that's up to you, but Miss Kenworthy, she going to be powerful mad if you do that. Major Kenworthy, he come by here the other day and told her to send somebody back, tell everybody General Forrest say the Yankees won't be back up Clifton way for a while. He say we rules up there now."

"This major, he rides with General Forrest?"

"Yes, sir."

Guy slowly circled his horse around the wagon, stopped in front of Cally and made a face.

"Hi, little 'un."

She waved with her tiny hand and he waved back. Then she broke out in that special grin of hers and pointed at the gleaming silver medallion in the center of the harness of Guy's stallion as if she wanted to touch it. He nudged the horse up to her so she could. "Pretty horsie." Lord, was there anybody on earth who didn't love that child?

Zenobia hoped this man was also thinking he didn't want to be messing with any niggers in any way connected with General Forrest's cavalry. But he had to be thinking, too, about not losing the money due him if they were running away.

"You know, now I think on it, Guy, it don't seem likely to me these niggers would be running away dressed like they are and in broad daylight. Why, Uncle here, he dressed to kill. Let's take a look at their passes."

Drayton handed them over. The one called Guy pulled out a pair of spectacles and read each one carefully, some of them more than once.

"Well, everyone's accounted for, and the passes say they are going to Clifton over in Edmunds County." He looked at Drayton. "Now I know where you mean. You're right, we control over that way now. Reckon I'd best let you go."

The men reined in their horses and turned to ride away.

Zenobia realized she'd been holding her breath and was about to let it out when Drayton spoke.

"Massa?"

What in the world was the matter with that man? Didn't he see they were going away?

Guy turned back. "What'd you want, boy?"

"Seeing as you a big captain, and we don't want us no more trouble today, you reckon you could help us poor niggers and give us a pass that say you done seed us and looked us over? Them other folks up the road got to know a big man like you."

"Matter of fact, they do. Everybody between here and Jackson knows Guy Burr."

"Thank you kindly, Cap'n Guy, sir."

When the man had written out the pass, Drayton handed him a bottle of bourbon. "Don't reckon old colonel would mind if I give you this when you done protected his niggers so good."

"Mighty white of you, Cephus." Guy's wit sent them off riding hard and laughing big. Or maybe it was the thought of that bottle of Major Kenworthy's mellowed bourbon.

* * *

Over the next few hours, patrollers or troops stopped them just about every hour. Zenobia worried each time that they might steal the horses and wagon for some kind of soldier use, but the pass worked like magic, and by noontime they'd covered a good ten miles. They stopped in a willow grove to have something to eat and let the children pee. When they were ready to go, Zenobia put Lisa Mae up front and sat in back with the children.

Cally said, "Mommy, it hurts riding back here."

"I know, baby, come here and sit on my lap."

"What about me?" Ned asked.

Zenobia reached out and drew him close. "I ain't got but one lap. Will a hug and kiss do for now?"

Ned smiled and snuggled up close to her. "Where we going?"

"Don't ask so many questions. Less you know the better."

"But I was having fun back there at Miss Kenworthy's place, they got the best pine trees for bending and springing."

"I saw you, baby, and you was something." Zenobia believed little boys needed to feel strong, so she hadn't said a thing when he went out there in the woods and climbed a slender pine tree that stood maybe eighteen feet tall. When he got high enough, his weight bent the tree backward and he'd come falling down to the ground, holding on tight.

And don't you know, when the tree hit the ground, all that strength in its young trunk made it spring back up and send Ned flying back up into the air with it. Zenobia's heart had most dropped down into her stomach. And just as she thought, he didn't have enough strength to hold on to the tree trunk, flew through the air and landed on the ground right on his little black butt. She let him cry, and in a little while he was right back on that flying tree. Strong, determined little boy. He'd better be, considering what lay ahead of them.

By late afternoon, the children were tired and cranky. Cally would fall asleep, then the jolting of the wagon would wake her up. Ned kept wanting to get out of the wagon to run and play. The fourth time he said, "I want to pee," Zenobia saw she'd have to do some explaining.

"This ain't no game, Ned. You only eight years old, you ought to be running and playing, but you got to be a man now. If these white folks catch us today and take us back to Miss Sue, you ain't never going to see me or Lisa Mae again in life and they'll beat Mr. Drayton to death. So you hush up now. And if you got to, you pee in your pants. Because we ain't stopping no more."

About six o'clock, Drayton pulled over to the side of the road close by a plantation. A smaller road led down toward a big log cabin that stood about a quarter of a mile away.

He started tying the horses up. "Come on up here, we got to talk and make up our minds about some things."

Zenobia covered the children with a blanket. "You all just rest and be quiet."

"We in a mighty rough situation right now," Drayton said.

"Why?" Lisa Mae asked.

"These animals are tired and need rest, water, and food. You all and these chilluns need the same. Night is coming on and we can't afford to be on these roads at night, pass or no pass. And we about to get out of that man's territory."

"So what you thinking?" Zenobia said.

"That we come this far, and got two choices. We can try to find us some colored shacks around here and stay the night, or—"

"You couldn't hide all of us and the horses and wagon from Massa. Niggers would be scared enough to go tell him."

"Or we could keep on going, off into the woods, ditch the wagon and bed down for tonight. Take off tomorrow through the forest—on foot."

"That's one more night for Cally to be in the woods," Zenobia said. "And I don't want that. When exactly will Miss Sue be back?"

"Most likely day after tomorrow, in the morning—but she might be back tomorrow night. And we can't be sure about what old Mary going to do. A man galloping on a horse can easy travel three times as fast as us."

Zenobia put her hand on Drayton's. "Supposing we puts our head in the lion's mouth tonight?"

"What you mean?"

"Supposing we shows our passes and ask the overseer at this plantation to let us stay tonight in their slave quarters since we traveling back to Miss's plantation to take care of it?"

"Zenobia, you sure enough something else." He shook his head. "I ain't never disobeyed Miss before and now you got me telling all these lies, just 'cause you-all thinks she might sell you down the river. He looked at Lisa Mae. "I thinks we should go off into the woods and—"

"Well, we ain't!" Zenobia pointed down the road to the plantation. Two white men and a colored man were galloping toward them. "You better do the way I told you."

And that's just what he did. Asked them white folks couldn't these poor colored travelers have a place to stay down at the slave quarters. The overseer looked over their papers and told the colored man to see to it that they were bedded down for the night.

After sunup the next morning, and a breakfast of mush, they were ready to move on. The air was still and heavy, working up to be mighty hot as the day wore on. Just as they were about to leave, the colored man who had brought them down to the shacks the night before came riding along the path.

"Massa want you to stop up by the big house before you leave."

The overseer was waiting at the front door for them. "Good morning. How did you sleep last night?'

Zenobia didn't like the sound of the man's voice. Something was wrong.

He came down the steps and patted Ned on the head. "That's a right strong-looking boy you've got there. What's your name, son?"

"Ned, Massa."

"Mighty fine manners, too." He bent down so that his head was level with Ned's. "Where all these folks going this morning, Ned boy?"

Zenobia took Ned's hand. "We told you last night, Massa. He don't know nothing more."

"Let him speak for himself. Where you going?"

"Over to Clifton to take care of Miss Sue and Major's house, sir."

"Well, that's good." He stood up straight again and nodded a few times. Took his time looking at the rest of them, one by one.

Then his glance fell on Cally. "My goodness gracious, child, your eyes are pretty enough to drive away a cloudburst in August." Delighted, Cally stood up, clapped her hands, jumped up into the air, and fell all a-tumbling back down in the hay. "See me!"

"Why I surely do, darling. Now I got to get back to business." He turned to Zenobia.

"I have a guest going your way. His horse went lame, so you all can take Mr. Coursey over to Doylestown—that's about fifteen miles from here." He looked at Drayton. "You wait right here."

Zenobia wanted to scream, but praying seemed to make more sense under the circumstances.

Massa Coursey was a sight to see with an old grayboys' forage cap on his head and the sleeve on his right side pinned up onto his blouse. His white vest with yellow trim looked like it had been made for a stouter man, and the only thing that seemed lively about him was his red face and long black whiskers.

"Morning, folks. My good luck you came along when you did." He settled down on the seat beside Drayton. "Beautiful day for a ride. Yessiree, you-all come along just in time—old Red let me down. And that horse been dependable as the devil up to now."

Drayton said, "Always give me pleasure to help one of our brave soldiers, suh."

"Used-to-be soldier, you mean." Coursey pulled out a chaw of tobacco from his pocket and offered it to Drayton. "Here, have some."

"I surely do thank you, Massa. Them Yankees should be ashamed of themselves."

Before long they were both chewing and spitting away.

"I reckon I'm lucky to be here at all," Coursey said. "Many of my neighbors will never again see the light of day, but the Good Lord has watched over me."

Drayton nodded at the man's sleeve. "If'n you don't mind, sir, how did that happen?"

"A Yankee cannonball down at Vicksburg done it. It was almost spent but had enough left on it to mangle my arm."

Zenobia leaned forward over Drayton's shoulder. "Way I hears it, we going to get Vicksburg back. Just the way the Yankees was run out of Clifton, that's the way we going to make them leave Vicksburg. Got no right coming down here, tearing up everything like they do."

Massa Coursey smiled. "You-all are just like Lionel. He's my head nigger, real faithful. When that Yankee scoundrel Colonel Grierson came through, burning houses and all, Lionel hid my wife and some of our belongings back in the swamp. Took care of her for three days. I was mighty grateful."

Drayton grinned. "We lives to make you happy, Massa."

"Well, ain't that a nice way of putting it, now? Let's drink to that!" He pulled out a flask and offered it to Drayton.

"Lawsy, Massa!" A wide grin spread across Drayton's face soon as he'd swallowed the whiskey. "That's some mighty powerful stuff!"

Coursey cackled, enjoying the effect. "That's another thing Lionel does good—makes some of the finest corn liquor in the river country." He waved the flask at two passing patrollers on horseback going the other way. "Howdy, boys, top of the morning to you." They grinned and rode on.

Lord, that man could talk. Soon he was pointing out every little thing along the road to Drayton.

"See that house over there? Had many a dance there when I was a youngster."

Zenobia didn't see a house, only a chimney.

"Look over yonder. See them fields?" All she saw was wild-growing weeds. "Used to have cotton all over there before the Yankees come through."

That flask had to be near empty—who knew what Drayton might say with all that liquor in him?

Massa Coursey slapped him on the back. "One thing been on my mind since we started this little ride. How come you taking them youngsters back over to Clifton with you, if your old Miss want you to be taking care of her place? Ain't they going to be in the way?"

That sly white man wasn't as drunk as he pretended.

"Only Miss and a couple of old niggers left with her over at Meridian," Drayton said. She can't be worried what no children might get into."

"Been better for us if'n we could have left them there," Lisa Mae said.

Bless Lisa Mae's sweet lying heart!

Coursey drained the very last drops of corn liquor from the flask. "What you got in here?" He pointed to the carpet bag, which lay on the floor between him and Drayton.

Lord have mercy. They could do without the bourbon, but how would they ever explain the pistols and tools?

"That bag right down there between us," Coursey said. "I knowed that stuff were powerful, but I never knowed it to make a man go blind."

Drayton grinned. "Massa, I can't open that bag. That's the major's! Miss made it up special for when he come riding back through Clifton, said I was to give to him and him only. He in General Forrest's cavalry."

Coursey put his arm around Drayton's shoulder. "Well, now, how's the major going to know I opened that bag if you don't tell him?" He looked back at Zenobia and whispered, "Tell me, how is he to know? You ain't going to tell him, are you?"

She shook her head. "No, suh."

With a quick motion, Coursey reached down toward the bag.

"No, Massa. Major whip me something awful."

"Then let it be so." Coursey struggled with the buckle.

"Well, sir, if you insist." Drayton drew up the horses, then reached down and pulled out a bottle of bourbon. Coursey grabbed it.

"No wonder your Miss wouldn't let you open that. Hell, man, we got us enough whiskey to drink our way into Doylestown and way beyond. When the major asks what happened, you tell him them thieving Yankees got it!"

With all the whiskey he and Drayton had drunk, Zenobia was relieved when he said Doylestown was just a little way off now.

The sun was almost directly overhead—they'd for sure better get off into the woods soon. They couldn't count on Miss coming home tomorrow morning; they had to plan on her being there tonight and the patrollers and bloodhounds being after them, too. If only they'd taken Drayton's advice and gotten into the swamps last night. Now they had to get rid of this talking fool on the wagon.

When they drew up to Massa Coursey's house, Drayton helped him down.

"Thank you all kindly." He stumbled and almost knocked Drayton over. "Now you can go to the stables and water and feed the horses. Afterward, come on up to the cookhouse—Malindy'll give you a good meal and start you on your way."

"And we thanks you, Massa, but we'uns will just get the horses fixed up and be on our way. Miss expect us to be there by tomorrow night."

Drayton was none too steady himself, but he wasn't too drunk to know they had to get away from here.

"I'm hungry," Cally said. "I want something hot to eat."

Ned nudged her. "You ain't got to have anything hot, Cally. We need to keep on going."

"Don't poke me. I'm hungry."

Massa Coursey settled it. "Looks like we got ourselves a mutiny in the ranks. You all stay and eat. That's an order."

"Yessuh."

Drayton started the horses down the slope toward the stables. Zenobia got down from the back of the wagon and took Cally in her arms.

"Baby, don't ever talk around white peoples when us grown folks is with them. You can get us in a heap of trouble, hear?"

* * *

The sun was already beginning to set when they got back on the road. You could tell Drayton was mad by the way he took it out on the horses, whipping them along. Zenobia didn't blame him, and not just because they'd been delayed. Lisa Mae had talked long with the colored folks back on that plantation, and who knew what she might have let slip? You couldn't tell what even coloreds might do, who they might tell. Only good thing was that Mr. Coursey had given them a note vouching for them.

They were riding now on a road with open fields of corn on either side. As soon as they got a decent way up the road, Drayton reined in the horses.

"The very next time I sees a little road we turning off, and finding us a place to hide in one of these cornfields or in the woods."

"I think we should get as close as we can to Clifton before we go off in the woods," Zenobia said.

"You are one stubborn woman. Look, I know the way better than you, and just over near those hills there's a little river runs down toward Clifton, particularly when the water is as high as it is now. We can spend the night over there, and in the morning I'll get to work on a raft."

"But—"

"But nothing, Zenobia. If Miss Kenworthy gets home tonight she'll have the dogs after us before daybreak. Our best chance is on a raft when them hell hounds come."

Zenobia sighed and turned around in her seat.

"Start getting yourselves ready. Soon as Drayton find a spot, we going to go off the road and get out of this wagon."

But how would they hide the wagon so it couldn't be seen from the road? Far as you could see there was nothing but cornfields. Zenobia solved the problem about a heartbeat after Drayton did—he was going to head straight into the fields.

He waited till they came to a spot where he could see nobody was coming in either direction, then steered the horses and wagon off the road and straight up between the rows of corn. The ground was soft, and the horses strained, but on either side the corn rose so high it gave mighty good cover. There was barely room for the wagon to move, and when they got a good ways into the field, he stopped.

"Get everybody and everything out of the wagon. Quick, now."

This was it—the real beginning of the journey toward freedom. Zenobia's heart was pounding while she helped unhitch the horses and gave the reins to Lisa Mae to hold. It seemed as if everything else—all that tricking on the road and the rest of it—was a game. But now, as she helped Drayton pile corn stalks all around the wagon so you'd have to be up real close to see it, she knew they were truly runaways. On their way to freedom and no turning back.

Soon the wagon was all covered up. She picked up one haversack, handed the other to Lisa Mae, and took Cally in her arms while Lisa Mae led Ned by the hand. Drayton was loaded down with what he needed for building his raft—a hatchet, awl, chisel, hammer, and some nails. He'd also brought rope, though he said he'd just as soon use heavy vines, already soaked. They could tolerate the water better.

She watched him lead the two horses by their reins. "I thought you was going to leave them here."

"Changed my mind. Look how low the sun is. Soon as it goes down and we can't be seen, we're going to get on horseback. We'll have a heap easier time reaching those woods that way than on foot—now, don't you start arguing with me, just keep on going. We got to put distance between that road and us."

Zenobia looked up at the sky. It was beginning to look right pretty, with the white puffy clouds and that old sun a fiery red ball behind them. They reached the end of the cornfield at about the time it went down. Drayton got everybody mounted—Lisa Mae, Cally, and Zenobia on one horse, himself and Ned on the other—and off they rode into the dark of the forest. The sounds of the night were all around them, hoot owls and crickets and, far off in the distance, some kind of swamp critter roaring. Zenobia reached down into her dress, glad Drayton had trusted her with one of the pistols.

She whispered ahead to him, "How far you think it be to the river?"

"Never you mind. You just watch that horse, so he don't throw you. Should be there in about an hour."

Zenobia tried to keep her mind on the horse. But all around her was nothing but dark, and trees looking for all the world like haints—sounding like them, too, when the evening breeze rustled the branches. If there were haints out there, she prayed they were the kind that watch over you like Joe said his ancestors watched over him.

CHAPTER NINE

IN EARLY June of 1864, not far from Tupelo, Mississippi, Major Richard Kenworthy sat under a tree reading a letter from his wife. Things were really going to hell at home. Sue had sold off all the slaves she could, trusting that the ones she'd taken over to Meridian would be enough to see to her and the children's needs. And now that damned Zenobia was giving her trouble, talking back and such. Well, he'd never trusted Zenobia—any more than he trusted her son. First chance he got, he'd try and run off. That kind of thing ran in the blood.

He kept going back to one paragraph in the letter.

> Your sister wrote to say she's thinking of moving to Texas with the children and leaving Pauline in charge of the plantation. As it is, Dorothy has entrusted Pauline with the direction of the entire place, and she's doing a fine job . . .

The sight of Pauline's name was enough to excite him. He put the letter down for a minute. Had there ever been a more striking woman? Dark eyes that flashed, a beautiful face, a body that moved with incredible grace and lightness. Long hair that swirled over coffee-brown shoulders . . .

He closed his eyes and saw her as she'd been that day he caught her in her room, bathing in the wooden tub, her breasts and thighs glistening in the water. Heard her cries, felt the intensity of her struggle, then . . . What right had his father had to give her to Dorothy as a wedding present, take away from him the one woman he'd ever loved that way? Of course he loved Sue, would have laid down his life for her. But for Pauline he would have leapt over high mountains, swum through turbulent seas, walked through fire and brimstone. That's just the way she'd made him feel.

All that talk about how a Southern gentleman didn't sleep with the house slaves—what a bunch of horse manure! Especially from that hypocritical father of his who'd bedded every good-looking colored woman on the plantation at one time or another, from the high yellows to the ones so black it seemed like the color might rub off on you if you touched them. Richard liked the honey-colored ones himself, but the old man didn't care so long as they . . . Oh God, had he ever been with Pauline? The thought made Richard sick. No, she'd fought too hard, seemed to think things should be different for her. But after that first time, she'd given in to him. And left him with a memory that no woman could ever match.

He'd have her, too. He didn't care how this damn war ended—he would get up to Dorothy's plantation and have Pauline again, find some way of making her live with them. Besides, he had something she wanted very badly. What wouldn't she give to have Luke free?

"What the hell you smiling about, old buddy?" It was Clint Adams. "Considering that we're likely to get our asses blown off tomorrow."

Richard folded the letter up, put it back into his knapsack. "I'm not worried about it. The general's plan sounds foolproof."

"How foolproof can it be when Sturgis outnumbers us two to one?"

"Sturgis isn't Nathan Bedford Forrest, and that's the difference," Richard said. "Wouldn't matter if they had us ten to one—Old Bedford would still carry the field."

"I hear it's going to be Grierson's cavalry in front for them, and some nigger infantry behind him."

"I think we've shown what we can do to them. Stop worrying. Sit down and have a smoke with me. Remember that time . . ."

* * *

After Clint retired to his tent for the night Richard went down to where the colored mule-skinners sat talking around their fire.

The letter from home had started some other thoughts stirring. He called Luke out. The boy was getting tall and strong, looking more like his father every day. Could it have been that long ago that a white boy and a black boy played and tussled, growing up together at Clifton?

"How're you making out these days, Luke? I hear you do an outstanding job of blacksmithing."

"Yes, sir, Major."

The boy had Joe's ways about him. Sounded respectful enough, but there was something in the way he said it . . .

"You getting enough to eat? You a growing boy."

"Yes, sir."

"They feed you pretty good, then?"

"Tolerably well, Major."

"I should say so! I hear you get molasses and corn bread and milk every morning."

"We do, sir."

Richard put his arm around Luke's shoulder. "You miss your sister and auntie?" He felt the tense muscles. Maybe he'd finally get a rise out of the sly little bastard.

"Yes, sir, I do, Major . . . Massa Kenworthy, can I ask you something?"

"Surely."

"Do you know where my mama and daddy are?"

"Way things are now, it's hard to know where anybody is from day to day." If the boy knew where his folks were, he might take a notion to run off and find them. "Go on back and get some rest. It's late, and we got a big fight tomorrow."

* * *

Early the next morning, the smell of frying pork and hot bread wafted through the humid Mississippi air. After breakfast, when the horse holders had been assigned, Captain Clint Adams made his report.

"Battalion all present or accounted for, sir."

Richard was aware of the fine showing he himself made on such occasions, tall and proud in the saddle, and he always enjoyed addressing the men before battle.

"Men, today you're going to have the privilege and honor of whipping Yankee cavalry and infantry with your revolvers. Every man's to carry two of them, and you're going to fight on foot. Wait till they get real close and shoot low—General Forrest especially wants you to remember that. Shoot low and you'll always hit something. They got something hanging down low that's mighty precious to them, ain't it, boys?"

Laughter erupted in the ranks. "You said it, Major!"

"Now, there's something else that's pretty important for you to know. There's a lot of nigger infantry going to be fighting with them."

"We'll skin the black devils alive!"

"Oh, we going to have us a good time roasting them coons!"

The major raised his hand to silence them. "Three days ago, before they left Memphis, these niggers who are going to fight with General Sturgis got down on their knees and swore to avenge Fort Pillow, swore they would die before they surrendered. And a Yankee officer especially got up in front of them and told them they would be coming against General Nathan Bedford Forrest and his men, that they were to expect no quarter and give none!"

An angry murmur ran through the ranks.

"To show you how serious these niggers are taking this thing, they're wearing badges saying Remember Fort Pillow. Our pickets captured one of the bastards last night."

The major took his hat off and waved it around in the air.

"Make them die down on their knees, just like they were when they took that oath. Now, go with God!"

The men raised a cheer. Then he watched them, thin and raggedy but full of determination, marching off to take up their positions. He felt a surge of pride to be serving with them. A renewed sense of the rightness of what they were doing.

* * *

His faith in his men was well justified. By noon, supported by General Forrest's brilliant use of artillery, they had just about destroyed the Yankee cavalry. Richard led charge after charge, and each time they'd hurt the enemy badly.

But now, from behind a fence where he'd called a temporary halt to the pursuit, with his binoculars he spotted a new threat.

A brigade of infantry was coming fast down the road. What a sight—darkies in uniform! Shit, they had to be tired, trotting that way with this mean sun blazing down on them.

He turned to Adams. "Pass the word. Drink plenty of water, check out those six-shooters, and prepare for bayonet attacks. Because that's what's coming."

He walked up and down the line, encouraging the men. Most of them were stripped down to their waists in the heat of the day. It was hot enough to make you feel as if you were wearing the heat.

General Forrest came along on his sorrel. He was a big man, six feet tall at least, with piercing brown eyes, heavy brows, and a high forehead made higher by his receding hairline. A well-trimmed mustache blended smoothly into a perfectly manicured beard. On the shoulders of his immaculately tailored uniform he wore the two stars of a major general.

He was the picture of the gentleman soldier, and at the sight of him the men lifted a cheer.

"In three hours," he said, "we're going to have that crossroads and those cannon that have been making it uncomfortable for you up here. Just obey your orders, and we shall have the victory." He smiled at Richard. "Counting on you, my boy, same as I did at Shiloh."

"I'll do my best, sir."

Just after two o'clock, the Yankee artillery started firing and all hell broke loose. All along the line the colored regiments got up, gave loud huzzas that gave way to shouts: "Remember Fort Pillow!" A drum and fife corps came right behind them, in perfect formation, playing "John Brown's Body." Bayonets fixed, they marched across the field, straight to where Richard's boys lay waiting for them on an embankment behind a fence. To the left, an artillery battery, its guns loaded with grape, was ready to give those nigras a real warm reception.

"Wait till I give the order, men. Aim carefully. And remember—shoot low."

The band played so well it seemed a shame to spoil the sound. Had to give it to them—they looked like they were on parade. In front of the trumpets, a little darky with sergeant's stripes carried the Union colors. A tall one carried the regimental flag.

Well, parading was one thing, fighting another. In another minute, he'd see what they were made of.

"At a quick march, forward."

Not yet. Damn, they were well drilled. The steady advance picked up speed.

"Fire!"

The heavy volley swept over the Union lines like a firestorm. They staggered as if they were trying to walk into a strong north wind. All along the way, men began to go down. The flag bearer was one of the first, and another man picked up the standard.

Richard paced back and forth along the line.

"Aim carefully, Reilly."

"Thataboy, Moten."

"Steady, everybody."

Then the Negroes were among them, swinging their rifles and thrusting with their bayonets. Richard, a saber in his right hand, found himself up against a big darky with red eyes.

"I's going to kill you dead, sir."

How dare he talk to a white man like that? Richard almost dropped his guard, but he sidestepped the Negro's thrust just in time, then stuck him in the head with his saber.

A number of times it seemed as if it was over and the Negroes were retreating. The six-shooters had to be getting on their nerves.

But here they came again, still yelling about Fort Pillow.

And again.

And again.

* * *

Four o'clock. Quiet fell on the battlefield. Men drank rainwater that had gathered in rivulets. The Yankee bands had stopped playing.

When General Forrest came up, Richard wondered if he'd order the retreat. They couldn't take another assault, not in the condition his men were in.

"Men, we've got them licked. You may not know it, but the Yankee cavalry is in full retreat. And we've got some guns and men coming up over that hill there. When your officers give the command, we're going to attack and make 'em wish they hadn't."

Richard had been sure they couldn't take another assault, but the general's appearance wrought a miracle in the men's spirits. Exhausted only a minute before, they now stood up, waved their caps, and gave the Rebel yell.

Twenty minutes later, just as the general had said in the morning, they stood at Brice's Crossroads turning the captured artillery on the fleeing Yankees, white and black. The coloreds had made a brave fight to save the artillery, you had to give them that, but the field now belonged to the Confederacy.

All along the line, General Forrest galloped back and forth, yelling, "We got the scare on them, don't let it off! We'll run them back to Memphis."

The Yankees were running, all right, but every now and then someone would rally some darky troops and they'd turn and make a stand, fighting with their bayonets against the six-shooters. No contest. Soon as the artillery came up, they'd be blasted right out of position.

About four hundred yards ahead, Richard saw a bridge over a river. It was the Yankees' only means of escape, and there were dozens of supply wagons and hundreds of men still on this side of the river.

He yelled back to an artillery lieutenant, "See if you can't blow up that bridge!"

The gunners went to work, and soon shells were falling on both sides of the bridge into the masses of Yankees waiting to cross. A wagon trying to get away from the fire came barreling over the bridge too fast and turned over, dead in the center of the bridge.

"We got them," Richard said. "Right in a box." He raised his saber and led his men forward so that they weren't more than a hundred yards from the bridge. They lay down in a prone position and fired at will.

Richard watched the slaughter with mixed feelings. Those niggers and whites ran every which way trying to get out of that crossfire and away from the cannonballs falling in their midst. Horses were rearing and snorting, wagons were burning, and so many men jumped into the water that the river was soon littered with bodies floating downstream. Never saw anything like it in his life.

Then, on the other side of the river, Confederate cavalry rode up—they must have crossed the river higher up. They charged the poor devils who had managed to make it over the bridge. In what seemed liked seconds, the bridge was captured. When it had been cleared, Richard led his men over on the other side. They kept the pressure on, capturing wagons, horses, weapons, men.

As they made their advance, heavy fire came from a clump of bushes. They directed their fire there, and in about five minutes six colored soldiers emerged, led by a corporal and still wearing their Fort Pillow badges.

"We surrender, sir."

They had dropped their weapons and had their hands in the air as Richard's men hurled taunts.

"Wasn't going to take no prisoners, huh?"

"You going to have your own special Fort Pillow this day, boy."

"Take up arms against a white man, would you?"

Richard looked at the Negroes, their faces smudged with dirt and shiny with sweat. What right on earth did they have to bear arms? What a terrible and degrading thing it was for the Yankees to have given them the means to kill good men. Why, fifteen of his troopers lay dead back on the hill, most of them killed by nigger bayonets.

Before he could shout an order, shots rang out. Six Negro men lay dead on the ground.

"Come on, Major, we'll find us some more."

He turned away from the scene. "Let's get moving."

Captain Adams caught up with him, "Richard, the conventions of war."

"Shut the hell up. Just keep fighting. We'll talk philosophy some other time."

Wherever his men got the chance, they did the same thing. When he looked back down the road, all he could see was dead black bodies, dressed in blue, sprawled in all kinds of positions on the sides of the road under the blistering hot late afternoon sun.

A little later, they rode into the courtyard of a plantation and found an old white woman, still sitting and knitting a green scarf despite the war all around her.

"I'm glad you gave them such a whipping," she said. "For when they came this way, they shook their fists at us and told us they were going to show General Forrest that they were his masters. When they came back through here, they were crying and were asking me would General Forrest kill them. I told them that since they had been such naughty boys that he would surely kill them, that they deserved to die."

They rode on, around a bend in the road toward where another colored outfit had decided to make a stand. Richard ordered his men to deploy as skirmishers. As he raised his saber to lead them forward once more, a bullet smashed into his left arm and knocked him to the ground.

He looked at the blood pouring all over the ground. The last thing he remembered was Clint by his side, applying a tourniquet.

* * *

Joe could barely turn his head, so thick was the fire pouring into the embankment where the Third was surrounded. This raid up near Yazoo City looked like it might be their last time out. Nothing but Rebs all around them.

And their commander was none other than Colonel Montgomery. He had quietly led them on up into the Delta, throwing out a few patrols here and there as bait, and the Third had fallen right into his trap.

"Why in the hell couldn't you have stolen somebody else's horse?" Captain Stiles said.

All day long they'd been fighting hand to hand, pistols, sabers, bayonets, knives. Fought until they were plum tuckered out on both sides. All in front of him Joe couldn't see nothing but bodies—black men and Texas Rangers, lying at funny angles, arms and legs every which way.

It was a strange kind of fighting, real personal-like. The Rebs had been calling over all day about what they were going to do when they captured them. Talking about how they were going to kill the officers, too.

Why did these white men hate the colored so much? Because they really thought they was better? Or maybe because they knew they weren't? Hell, neither reason made any kind of sense.

Toward sundown the firing died down, and a stillness and calm settled over the field of battle. Most likely the Rebs were done for the day, figuring they'd come at them and finish them off in the morning. There wasn't too much chance that the Third could hold out. Just one more charge, and they'd have to fight with their sabers—the men had maybe ten cartridges apiece. And Joe himself—well, he knew he'd never see the light of another day if they captured this little fort. He'd heard one of those boys holler about hanging "that son of a bitch'n lying double-crossing horse-stealing black bastard."

He laughed. If he was going to hang, it might as well be for something he'd enjoyed as much as riding Princess. Just as soon not, though. He turned to Captain Stiles.

"What do you think we can do? Looks like we going down this time."

"I learned long ago, fighting in the Fourth Cavalry, not to give up hope long as you can still stand up. Many's the time a battle seemed to be lost, but then something happened, and we pulled through."

"Think that's what's going to happen here?"

"I'm counting on it."

"Well, then, I am too, Captain. Counting on it something awful."

* * *

The night came, and with it a storm. Lightning was striking all over, sometimes so hard and bright you could see the battlefield and the bodies— Third Cavalry and Rebs—lying all around. Joe had killed three men himself today, right there on the ramparts.

The Rebs would know they'd been in a fight if they took this fort. Just like the last time, the men had sworn not to surrender. They'd have to kill them to the last man—each and every one of them.

And Captain Stiles right alongside them. Joe watched him go off to officers' call and thought about his good fortune in serving under this man. Good, fair, courageous, and truth to tell, even though he was an officer, a friend. A man you wouldn't mind dying next to.

And here he came back again, not looking happy at all.

"Well, I guess you know what I'm going to tell you, Joe."

"Bet you're going to send him out again," Zack said.

"Only if he volunteers."

Joe was already reaching for the Choctaw knife scabbard under his night pack. "Right with you, Captain. And don't look so grim. I promise not to steal anything that'll get the Rebs' dander up any worse."

"I'm relieved to hear it."

"Unless, of course . . ."

"Get out of here, you crazy son of a gun! The colonel's waiting."

* * *

When he reported to Colonel Osband, he was surprised to see two other scouts. "Yes, Duckett, I'm sending three of you out. That's how bad it is."

"You hoping one of us makes it—right, sir?"

Osband nodded. "Now, listen. The main body should be somewhere down the Vicksburg road, about two hours from here. Only problem is, you got about two regiments of Reb cavalry between here and there. And there'll be lots of patrols out. I don't have to tell you how . . . well, you know the situation. We've only got half the regiment left. If you're not back by daybreak, we're goners."

"Don't worry none, Colonel," Joe said. "Why, come morning you'll not only have reinforcements, we're going to bring along some fresh eggs and bacon so you can have a breakfast what befits the commander of the Third United States Colored Cavalry."

The colonel laughed. "Just bring the troopers, Joe." He shook each man's hand, then saluted them. "Godspeed, boys!"

* * *

Joe crept up to the parapet and quietly poked his head up. Looked like about a hundred yards between him and the Rebs. The colonel had sent them out on foot, but Joe didn't relish traveling that way with fine horseflesh just standing around in the Reb's camp. Now all he had to do was find a way to get at it without getting the Rebs at *him*. Lord, the captain be some kind of mad if he knew . . .

He slid up over the parapet, nose to the ground, and began to creep along. Every time there was a bolt of lightning, he stopped. He crawled till he came up to a whole pile of bodies—dead Texas Rangers, they were— and moved around among them till he found one just about his size.

Over toward the Rebel lines it was quiet, probably they were thinking about all the niggers they were going to kill the next day. He stripped the Texas Ranger's body, and put on all his clothes. Nice gun belt, all studded with jewels, so he took that, too, and the Navy Colts with it. Shit, armed like he was, how'd that Ranger get so dead?

He laid his own clothes over the body. Wasn't right to leave him there all naked.

Bent low, he walked on tiptoe toward the Rebel lines, so quietly he couldn't hear his own step if he listened hard for it. It was awful muddy and the rain was running down into his neck, all down his back. He could even feel it in the crack of his ass. He slid down into a ditch right smack onto the body of another dead Reb, this one all covered with mud, open-eyed and staring right at Joe.

* * *

"Keep a sharp eye out, George. Sergeant says they may be trying to sneak somebody by us to go for help."

"Don't you worry. Ain't I done told you I was the champion possum shooter in my county?"

"Hell, you always bragging 'bout how you the champion this and that. You the champion at sleeping, that's what you are. Just don't let no niggers get by you tonight. I'm going on down the line."

The Reb was sitting there, comfortable-like on a saddle, a six-shooter in his hand, and he seemed to be looking directly at him. Joe calculated the distance, figured the chances of getting close enough to get him with the knife before he sounded an alarm.

He wondered how the other scouts was doing. The colonel had sent them out separate ways. Both of them was experienced, he knew that, but this here was a situation.

The rain was coming down much heavier now, the thunder booming like the cannon in the battle down at Yazoo City, the lightning making jagged rips in the sky every few seconds. The sentry stood up to tighten his shirt collar, then bent over, like he was reaching for a blanket or something to throw over his shoulders.

No sooner had he leaned down than Joe was up, quick as a cat, running right past him, then tumbling into another ditch about fifteen yards beyond and to the other side of him. He clung to the ground for about five minutes, knife in hand. Come over this way, and you'll never tree another possum . . .

He gave the sentry another few minutes, then began to crawl toward the Reb camp about a hundred feet behind their sentry lines. Not many guards around the camp itself—that's what all those pickets up close to the Third were for. Didn't expect nobody to get this close.

Joe crawled over the ground among all the sleeping soldiers. He'd crawl a little bit, rest, then crawl some more. Slow-like, doing nothing to stir anybody up. He wondered where Colonel Montgomery was—probably in that big tent over there dreaming about Princess, and how he was going to have her back tomorrow and string up the nigger who'd stolen her. Dream on, Colonel!

Creeping along at the outskirts of the camp, Joe spotted the horses in a clump of trees. "And not a soul watching over you," he said softly . . .

Now what horse was he going to take him this time? Had to be fast, though it surely wouldn't be as fast as Princess. She'd just about replaced Hawk in his favor. His eyes finally settled on a fine-looking white mustang, then he looked around to see where the saddles were piled. When he had everything all arranged in his mind, he just walked up to the picket line, took the horse he wanted, and commenced to saddle it, talking quietly.

"Now, darlin', you the prettiest thing. Me and you going to be good friends. Going to get along just fine."

"What you doing out here this hour of the night, friend?"

Joe kept his face turned away from the Ranger. "Had hard luck tonight, partner. Got to take dispatches up to General Forrest. Shit, I was asleep myself. See you."

Before the sentry could say another word or get a proper look at him, Joe was up in the saddle and riding away. He was in his home territory now, knew the way. Figured it was about another hour and a half to where the main body of the troops was. To be safe and sure, he skirted all around the Reb patrols.

He'd just about come to the place where he was going to take the cutoff that led onto the Vicksburg road when he saw two riders coming the other way.

"Halt, soldier! What you doing out here this time of night?"

"Oh, he's just one of the Rangers," the other man said when he was close enough to see Joe's uniform. "Come on in and have something to eat."

What the hell to do? Five to ten miles from the reinforcements and he had to run into these damn—what were they? Hard to tell with the rain coming down so hard and them in ponchos, most likely with shotguns under them.

"I thank you, but I don't have no time for that. Got dispatches to deliver to General Forrest."

The men drew a little closer.

"Hope you don't mind if we get a little closer look at you, do you? Everybody's suspect these days, even the Rangers."

Joe checked out the little space between the two men's horses, his hand on the trigger of the Navy Colt. No time to play with these fools. His boys were in trouble.

He brought the gun up and fired. The short man, whose hat was pulled down funny on the side of his head, gave a cry and fell right down to the ground with one foot still in the stirrup. The horse bolted away, dragging his body along.

At the crack of the pistol, the other horse whinnied and reared up—almost but not quite throwing its rider. He was trying to rein in the horse and aim his shotgun at the same time when Joe shot him in the belly.

* * *

Now Joe rode like the wind the rest of the way to the Vicksburg road. He stopped just long enough to make sure no Rebs were about, then rode on searching for the brigade. The night was still dark, the rain beating down, so he didn't see the four riders coming fast toward him until they were dangerously close. Damn.

He reined in his horse and waited. Didn't have much choice. They were sure to have seen the mustang. What had he been thinking to take a white horse?

As they drew closer he saw they were Union and raised his hand. "Hey there!"

"Hands up, or we'll shoot!"

"What the hell—" Joe said.

The first soldier, a sergeant, rode up close to Joe. "Just shut up, and keep them hands raised."

Four carbines were trained on him, but like Zenobia always said, he never knew when to keep quiet.

"Listen—"

"Listen nothing." The sergeant removed the Colts from Joe's holsters. "You're a prisoner, so just shut the hell up like I done told you, and fall in!"

"But I'm Third Cavalry!"

The sergeant laughed. "Now ain't that one for the books, caught red-handed in that ducky Texas Ranger's outfit and wants to go for the Third Cavalry, by golly!"

"You don't believe me, you take this hat off and see! I'm colored!"

The sergeant reined up his horse. "If you're lying, we'll skin you alive. Right here."

The detail stopped with Joe in the middle of them. The sergeant rode over and lifted his hat.

"Well, I'll be a son of a bitch, it is a darky! Who are you?"

"Serg—no, Corporal Duckett, Third Cavalry, carrying dispatches for General McArthur from Colonel Osband. We're surrounded and need help."

"How come you to be dressed up in that outfit?"

"I took it off a dead Ranger."

The sergeant turned to his men. "Well?"

"I don't really know, Sarge," said one.

"Sounds all right to me," said another. "Last I heard, the Rebs didn't have no colored in uniform."

"All right," the sergeant said. "Let's get on down the road, I think he's for real."

"No, he ain't," said the third soldier, a tall, skinny boy, with thin lips and a know-it-all look in his eyes. "You forgetting that the Rangers have a nigger riding and fighting with them, just like he was a white man. Don't you remember the boys in the Second talking about him when we was in bivouac? That nigger's a spy, that's what he is."

The sergeant nodded, then jabbed a finger in Joe's face. "You almost had us tricked, but it ain't going to work. Now, I don't want to hear another word out of you. When we get you back to camp, we'll get to the bottom of this. Get moving."

Joe said, "You're going to—"

The sergeant slapped him. "Shut up and get moving, I said!"

* * *

It was almost two-thirty in the morning before they arrived at the bivouac area, and another twenty minutes before Joe managed to talk his way in to see General McArthur. Thank God, the general recognized him.

"Sir, we're taken a terrible beating. Colonel Osband say he must have reinforcements by morning or they're done for."

"Captain, have the bugler blow Boots and Saddles. Joe, get a fresh mount and some Union clothes—you're leading the way back up."

In a little less than a half hour, two regiments of cavalry moved out. They rode at a steady pace, slowed down a little by the mud and the rain. Joe was anxious, kept turning this way and that in the saddle. Those Rebs was mighty bloodthirsty. And where were Singletary and Childs? Neither of them had gotten there before him, so they should have run into them on the way back.

As dawn broke, the column was about two miles from where the Third was surrounded. In the distance Joe could hear the sound of shooting. The Reb attack had started.

"At a fast trot forward . . ."

Hold out, boys, we on our way. Don't let them run you over.

When the battle scene came into view, all that could be seen were gray uniforms running up the slope toward the little fort. The Rebs were attacking on all sides, and there couldn't have been but a few men left to hold the fort. But Colonel Osband had his trumpeters blowing up a storm. And the Stars and Stripes were still flapping in the wind.

On and on the Rebs came, Colonel Montgomery at their head as usual. He was one brave old boy and he sure must want that horse something awful. Not today, sir.

General McArthur raised his saber and called back to the column of blue-clad troopers.

"Sound the charge."

Joe never saw as pretty a sight in his life. The cavalrymen went sweeping down that mountain onto the Rebs like a mighty river roaring and ranting into a levee after a thunderstorm.

A shout went up from the men in the fort, and the buglers blew even harder. The Rebs set up a skirmish line to protect the camp and allow their men to mount up and get away. They fought hard, but they couldn't stand against that cavalry charge, especially after the Third got up out of the fort and charged too.

* * *

Having lost half of the regiment, Colonel Osband didn't have much of an appetite for the eggs and bacon Joe had brought back with him. And neither did Joe, for that matter. Those other two scouts hadn't ever showed up. This war was getting mighty heavy.

CHAPTER TEN

SEATED in chairs on the after deck of the transport *Mist of the Dawn,* Captain Will Stiles and a few other officers were sipping whiskey and branch water and watching the river go by. Also on board were some civilians, including a few cotton speculators who expected to make a fine profit out of the cargo.

The boat was headed south to Vicksburg with a detachment of Third Cavalry men who'd stood guard as a load of cotton was put on board. Though Will tried to explain how important cotton was to the Union's war effort, some of the men said they'd signed up to fight, not stand around and watch over that damned white stuff.

To Will the assignment was a welcome respite. They had taken a terrible battering at the hands of Montgomery's troops outside of Yazoo City, and he definitely didn't feel like going through anything like it soon again. Ever again, for that matter. But one battle had followed another with no break to speak of, the men returning each time with cotton, Negroes they'd liberated, food supplies and, always, the wounded.

He got up from his chair, thought about going below to cheer them up a bit, but instead walked back to the stern of the boat and leaned over the rail. What an ugly river the Mississippi was, muddy as hell, nothing like the waters back home in New

York. The town he'd grown up in wasn't far from Lake George—where, of a summer day, you could swim out a ways and look down in the water and see clear to the bottom. It wasn't just plain clear either, it was blue clear.

Even on the hottest days, that lake water was always cool and bracing. He got goose bumps just thinking about how it felt to dive into it. And if you got a little thirsty, why you could drink all of it you wanted to.

The memory of days when he'd taken his canoe down from its rack, put it over his head, and carried it down to the lake, seemed to belong to another life. He'd paddle out to the center of the lake with nothing more serious to worry about than how long he'd have to wait before one of those trout struck the line and leapt out of the water, silvery brown body glistening and wriggling in the bright sunshine Silver spray, clear day, God's way!

Of course, the Mississippi had its own virtues—the sheer size of it, for one thing, and the twists and the turns, the surprises around every bend. And there was something else about the river. It was the spinal cord of this whole huge country. Knitting it together—linking cities with their factories, plains with their farms, and carrying its boats and people in a flow of commerce from one place to another. Muddy though it was, this had its own—

"Don't mind, do you, Will?" Major Cook joined him by the rail. "Couldn't leave you alone to enjoy yourself too much, just looking down there at the water."

"I'd enjoy it a lot more if we didn't have to worry about those bushwhackers shooting at us every time we get in range."

"The sharpshooters we've got posted should keep them occupied if they start up with us again." He slowly twirled the whiskey around in his hand. "Will, I've been meaning to ask you . . . You're close to these men, particularly Joe. What do they think about us—the white officers, I mean?"

"About how any group of men feel about their officers—hell, you and me were noncoms before we came over here, you know how it is. They like some of us and some of us they don't." He took a sip of bourbon. "But whatever's the case, so long as no one calls them nigger, they'll fight for him. We may be catching hell every time we go up the river, but the boys give as good as they get."

"That they do," said Major Cook, who was tugging at his uniform collar, trying without much success to loosen it. "I'd put them up against any I ever fought with. When I first came over to serve with them, I had my doubts as to whether they would fight—or even whether they could. Slavery's a hurtful thing, no question."

"None at all. And there's no denying they're ignorant—damn planters wouldn't let them learn anything. Makes me mad whenever I think about it. I mean, the slaveholders have a lot to answer for, but for some reason keeping them uneducated is what gets my blood up. It's not like they can't learn—just look at the change from what they were eight months ago. Lord, here comes our cotton speculator. Damn."

"Mind if I join you gentlemen?"

Will did mind. Lamar Chew had been up and down the river with them on these cotton-gathering expeditions before, and while his sympathies were clearly with the Rebs, all he really cared about was taking advantage of the war to make a fortune. He reeked of whiskey and had a full glass of it in his hand.

"Mighty nice view up here, isn't it?"

"That it is."

Will moved away, but Chew sidled right up to him again.

"You'd be Captain Stiles, right? Been watching you the last couple of days. It's estra . . . extraordinary, how you get along so well with those nigger troops of yours. I must tell you, I never saw anything like it."

"Mr. Chew." Major Cook stepped between them. "Perhaps you could be of some assistance to us. How navigable are the upper reaches of the Yazoo this time of the year?"

"Can't help you, Major. I'm just a cotton broker, I don't skipper the boats."

Will had moved even farther down the railing. Chew downed more whiskey and went after him. "Like I was saying, you got a real way with the nigger boys, almost like you were one of us Southern folk."

Will straightened his uniform and turned to face Chew squarely. "Mr. Chew, I have to tell you, I don't appreciate your calling my troopers niggers."

"Now, Will," Major Cook said. "I'm sure Mr. Chew meant nothing by it, that's just their way down here."

Chew patted the captain on the back. "Didn't mean to get you all riled up. Tell you what, my man—let me get you another drink. As a matter of fact, drinks for both you and the major."

They protested, but Chew lurched off in search of a waiter.

"He's drunk," Cook said. "Don't pay him any mind."

"Drunk or sober, I want no part of him."

"Will, you know our orders. We're to be courteous to all civilians, particularly these cotton brokers. We need the cotton. So—"

Chew returned, trailed by a waiter with a drink-laden tray.

"Gentlemens . . ."

"That's right, Uncle. You stay nearby in case we want some more."

They'd had only a sip or two from the fresh glasses before Chew started in again.

"Captain, seeing as you're so friendly with these nigras, how do you find their soldiering?" He leaned in closer and lowered his voice. "Do you ever think they might run out on you? I'm asking this as a close observer of human behavior, if you can call nigra behavior human."

Major Cook stepped between them again and took hold of Will's arm. "That's not a question you should be asking, Mr. Chew. If you want to stay here and drink with us in peace, that's one thing, but if you continue in this line of conversation, we'll have to leave you here."

Will shook off the major's restraining hand and glared at Chew. "My men have never quit on me yet—and never will!"

"Now, Captain, I didn't mean anything, no need to get so worked up." He took another sip of whiskey. "But tell me now, didn't I hear that up at Brice Crossroads old Bedford Forrest had the nigras running like rabbits, turned them every which way but loose?"

"Mr. Chew . . ." Will saw the glance Major Cook threw his way and gave a little nod of his head to show that he was in control. "Mr. Chew, sir, I'll have you know they gave as good an account of themselves up there as anybody else."

Chew slapped the rail with the open palm of his hand. "And I'll have you know I've supported Abe Lincoln all the way, but he went too far when he armed these . . . these nigras. Maybe Fort Pillow and Brice's Crossroads will give him and General Grant and. . . and . . . the rest of you some second thoughts about all this."

"Mr. Chew, I bid you good day. This conversation is over."

Chew stumbled, trying to grab him by the arm, but Will just sidestepped him.

"It's over because you know it's wrong—these armed nigras are a menace to white civilization, yours as well as ours."

With every drink, his voice had gotten a little louder. Now a small crowd of officers and civilian passengers was looking on.

"They'll want revenge for slavery," Chew said, "and they'll take it—on our women and children. You've already had to court-martial some of them for rape down in Vicksburg. White men should fight white men. When a white man arms a nigra, he's put himself on the level of that nigra."

"Captain Stiles, just walk away. That's an order." Major Cook turned to Chew. "Sir, my hands are tied since I'm a military officer, but if I were a civilian I'd boot you right up your civilian ass."

Chew raised his fist and shouted after the departing officers. "Say what you like, and fight with the niggers if you will, but I wish the Rebs had ten Bedford Forrests. They'd soon put an end to this race treachery!"

* * *

"That man is through," Major Cook said at the officers' table. "He'll never go up the river with us again. It's hard enough to keep the morale of the men up without this kind of thing."

"I'm glad to hear you say that, sir." Will put his fork down. He was still too annoyed to eat. "But one good thing—it's got me thinking it's about time we stopped equivocating. These soldiers aren't paid as much as the whites, and they have no Negro commissioned officers. I for one know of four men in the regiment who are officer material, proved it in combat, by any measure."

"I hear that one has already been given a field commission in the Fifty-fourth Massachusetts," Cook said. "I want you to look into this matter, Will—first identify the men who are officer material, then find out what we have to do to have them commissioned."

"Major Cook, sir!"

"What is it, Joe?"

"Better get up on deck quick, sir. The men are about to riot."

The officers, led by Major Cook, got up from the table and headed up the ladder.

On the foredeck, where just an hour earlier the men had been quietly repairing their equipment, dozens of them were now milling around. And a small group of them, urged on by Tucker, were pounding with sledgehammers on one of the doors leading below to the passenger quarters.

"I say kill the bastard."

"Throw him in the river."

"Get me a bayonet, somebody!"

"Captain Stiles, call them to order," Major Cook said.

"Attention!"

Joe looked for a bugler but couldn't see one in the confusion.

"Attention!"

"Go to hell!"

Will pulled out his Colt and fired it into the air.

The noise stopped.

"Now fall in, right there on the deck."

They obeyed, slowly forming into six ranks. A sea of sullen, angry faces looked up at Major Cook standing on the bridge.

"What the hell is the meaning of this? I just finished saying you're as fine a fighting unit as any in the whole Delta, and you start acting like a liquored-up bunch of field hand . . . I'll get to the bottom of this, then I'll deal with whoever's responsible. Captain Stiles, get them to their quarters."

* * *

Half an hour later Will reported to Major Cook, Joe and Zack at his side.

Will nodded to Zack. "Tell the major what happened."

"Well, sir, you knows I'm a sharpshooter—one of the best in the regiment, sir, many's the time I won the contest—"

"Get to the point, soldier!"

"And, and—"

With his forearms on the desk in front of him, the major leaned forward as if trying to get the words sooner.

"I was on sharpshooter duty, because Sergeant Duckett here, he want the best man to be in the bow of the boat, be the first man to get a shot at them bushwackers up there in them rocks." He turned to Joe. "Ain't that right, Joe?"

Joe nodded.

"So I was on duty, just watching them rocks, each and every one of them, 'cause you never can tell which one is going to be hiding them bushwackers—can you, Joe? And they especially likes them little cracks where there be a pine tree covering the rocks, and it take a very special kind of man with a very special kind of eye to see—"

"Corporal Bascome, get to the woman!"

Zack took a deep breath and plunged on. "Well, there I was on duty, and this high-yellow gal that been hankering after me, Rachel her name, she come and sit down on a cotton bale near me and commenced to talking."

"Your orders were not to talk to anyone while on duty," the major said.

"But, sir, I didn't. She took a seat and started talking and I just kept my eyes on those cliffs, looking out for the Rebs. But she kept on teasing me about playing soldier."

The major looked at Will. "For this we had a near riot?"

"There's more, sir. Zack, get to the point."

"Well, everybody was all sitting around just watching me, not saying nothing, just watching. And this drunk white man come up to me, had a glass of whiskey in his hand, and he say— right in front of them all—that a nigger soldier, he ain't got no rights in this world, and the least right he got is to talk to a white woman."

"What did you do?"

"I knows my duty. I just kept looking over at those hills, but next thing I know, this white man is waving around a dirk—in broad daylight, sir—and he say he going to kill me dead it I says another word to that woman."

"You'd said nothing to her up till then?"

"Well . . . she mighty pretty, like I said." Zack looked at Joe again. "Maybe just a couple of itty-bitty words."

"This man thought you were talking to a white woman and he openly threatened to kill you. Is that it?"

"That's pretty much it, sir."

"Well, is it or not?"

"Yes, sir," Joe said. "That was it, sir."

"And then what happened, Sergeant Duckett?"

"You know that troublemaker Tucker, he starts shouting at the white man and next thing you know the men are all worked up, say we'd see who did any killing, and I had to hustle the man below deck, and all the way he's yelling, 'Nigger, get your filthy hands off her.'"

"I take it this man's name was Chew?"

"Why, it is, sir. That's him all right. I was just barely able to get him away. If they'd got their hands on him, they'd of thrown him to the fishes. But how'd you know—"

"Where is he now?"

"Locked in his cabin, sir."

"Good work. Leave him there for the present." Major Cook got up from the table and looked at Zack. "You work in the mess all next week. No leave when we get back to Vicksburg. You think it's a game with those sharpshooters up there?" He sighed. "You and Sergeant Duckett are dismissed."'

"What a mess," Will said when they were gone.

"There are a hundred brave United States soldiers lying in their graves up beyond Yazoo City where they fell three days ago, and I will not permit their deaths to be in vain. Get the salon emptied out, Will. I want an officers' call there. As for Chew . . ."

Will almost smiled. He knew a pause for dramatic effect when he saw one. He also thought he knew what the major wanted with regard to Chew.

"Go up to his quarters, the sooner the better. You're to place him under arrest for making a death threat to a Union soldier while on official duty."

* * *

The officers sitting around a long table in the salon listened intently as Major Cook explained what had happened.

"Under the Articles of War and in the absence of the commanding officer, Colonel Osband, I am convening a court-martial to deal with the seditious behavior of Mr. Lamar Chew."

He stood up and rested his hands on the table. The men looked at one another, then back at him.

"Had Mr. Chew drawn a dirk on a white soldier," Cook said, "he would have been immediately shot. In this case we're going to give him the benefit of the doubt and provide him with a trial. The jury will be made up of each and every officer on board." He paused for a second. Except for one. "Captain Stiles, you'll serve as counsel for the defense."

"But, sir—"

"You started to read for the bar, didn't you? Go see your client and prepare the defense. Court convenes at two o'clock."

On the way to Chew's cabin, Will called Joe aside and filled him in.

"And I'm to defend him," he concluded.

"You, sir? But the men trust you, believe you're on their side. How will they ever—"

Will glanced skyward, then back at Joe. He'd known this would happen the second the major gave him the assignment.

"Look, Joe, there's a lot you and the men have never been taught about the way the law operates, and I don't have time to educate you on it right now. It's just that in our kind of country every man deserves a fair hearing, and the only way to do that is to give him the best defense we can. That goes for rich and poor, white, red, and black. It's got to be fair—even in the army. And I'm the only officer on board who ever cracked a law book, so I've been ordered to do the job. Now, what's the temper of the men below?"

"They just waiting to see what's going to happen, sir. Don't you worry about this none. I'll go down and explain to them about how you got to defend that man. You just following orders, doing your duty. They'll understand that."

* * *

Will found Chew on his bunk, smelling of whiskey, his eyes bloodshot but defiant. A neat pile of business papers—invoices, Will figured—lay on the desk alongside a black top hat. Chew could probably cut a pretty dashing figure in that hat and his white felt shirt and black trousers. His brown boots with their intricate Indian designs were highly polished.

He got up quickly. "Now you listen to me, Stiles. Governor Johnson, he's a personal friend of the family and he's going to see to it that you and all the other officers in this nigger outfit are court-martialed. That's a mob you've got, not a regiment."

"Sit back down, Mr. Chew, we have a few important matters to discuss."

"Discuss?" Chew advanced on Stiles, wagging his finger. "Discuss, you say? There's only one thing to discuss. Why have I, a free white man, been locked unlawfully in my cabin and denied the run of the vessel? Oh, I'll have your head for this, just you wait and see."

"I'm sorry—"

"Sorry, are you?" Chew was right up in his face. "Oh no, come with apologies to me now, and expect me not to take this up with the governor? Even if you came on your damn nigger-loving Yankee knees, I wouldn't accept an apology. Now, I'm asking you to leave—time for me to start writing my account of this matter for the governor." He pointed to the door.

"Sit down, Mr. Chew. That's an order!" Will grabbed him by the arm and forced him back onto the bunk. "Now listen to me. Damn it, man, you're in no position to make threats. I'm sorry about this whole incident, but I didn't come here to apologize to you, I came to let you know that you must stand before a court-martial in an hour—and that I'm your defense counsel."

"Court-martial? Me?"

"You."

"For calling that boy a nigger? For calling a nigger a nigger?"

"I'm afraid the charges are more serious than that. You threatened him with a deadly weapon while he was performing his official duty."

"What deadly weapon?"

"The dirk, sir. And for that, unless I can find an acceptable excuse, you'll hang."

"You're having me on, aren't you? Just trying to get back at me for all those things I said up on deck?" Chew said, standing up.

Will shook his head.

Chew eased back down onto the bunk, then dropped his head in his hands. "I got three little children at home, and a wife," he said when he looked up. "They're all depending on me."

Will sat down next to him. "I'll mention your family before the court. For now, I want to know whether you did it or not. They have the dirk, you know. And witnesses."

"You mean to say they'd take the word of a . . . Hell, man, I was defending the honor of white womanhood."

"Then it will no doubt pain you to learn that the woman in question is not white but a mulatto."

Chew's eyes widened. "A nigra?"

Will nodded.

"And I could die because of that?"

"I'll do my best to see that you don't, but it's going to be a rough haul. We took a terrible pounding up the Yazoo while we were getting this cotton for you . . ." He glanced over at the papers. ". . .and that's going to make it hard." He got up to go. "Wash your face and clean yourself up. You don't want to appear before the court in this condition."

"When the governor hears about this he'll have every nigger regiment in Mississippi busted up, you just wait and see."

"I'll be back for you in twenty-five minutes."

* * *

Half an hour later, the court convened. Twenty officers, now in dress blues and presided over by Major Jeremiah B. Cook, sat in judgment on Lamar Chew, Esquire, cotton broker, of Memphis, Tennessee.

Captain Will Stiles, resolved to defend his client as best he could, stood up as soon as the charges had been read and addressed Major Cook.

"I move for dismissal of the charges. I—"

"Dismissal? On what grounds?"

"Lack of jurisdiction, sir." With that, Will picked up a book containing the rules and regulations governing courts-martial. "Nowhere in here will you find one sentence, not even one word authorizing a military court to try a civilian so long as any possibility exists that he may be brought, in . . . uh . . . a timely fashion before a civilian tribunal. Therefore this court lacks the . . . lacks jurisdiction in this matter, and I hereby request that the court. . . I hereby request that the presiding officer dismiss the case."

"Request denied." Major Cook banged the gavel. "Proceed."

Witness after witness—Joe, Tucker, even one of the other cotton brokers on board—told the same story. Mr. Chew had threatened Corporal Bascombe with the dirk. And there was no denying that Corporal Bascombe had been performing an official duty at the time, although there did seem to be some question about just how well he had been doing it. Then Chew took the stand.

"Tell them, Mr. Chew, why you approached that sentry."

"Because I was firmly convinced that he was insulting the virtue of a Southern white woman."

Will drew closer to Chew. "Why else, sir? Why the threat and the drawing of the dirk?"

"Because I believed that he intended to touch her, embrace her, and I'd die before I'd see a nigger touch a white woman." He glared at the assembled officers. "And you all ought to, too."

Will raised his hand, but his client wasn't about to be silenced.

"Is it not absurd that this civilized nation, the creation of some of the greatest minds the world has ever known—Jefferson, Washington, Madison—is being defended by the most degraded race of all—the Africans? You come into our territory and unleash cannibals and headhunters against us, then expect—"

Major Cook banged his gavel.

"Your own officers say they cannot stop these savages from slaughter and defilement, I've heard it with my own two ears. And you accuse me—"

Major Cook pounded the desk with the gavel and stood up. "Mr. Chew, get control of yourself or I'll have you restrained. We've heard the witnesses. Now we need your account, and in an orderly—"

"My witness should be a hero like General Forrest—"

"Bind and gag him. Captain Stiles, do you have anything further to offer in this man's defense?"

"No, sir, but if I could just make another point about the question of jurisdiction—"

"You may not. This ship and all on it are governed by martial law. If you have no other witnesses to call, make your summation."

Will rose and faced his fellow officers. "Gentlemen, my client, Mr. Chew, is upset. Which of us would not be, facing the penalty he faces. I beg you not to allow his remarks, offensive though they may have been, to influence your decision." He put the manual back on the table. "In view of the refusal of the court to deny jurisdiction I ask that if you find my client guilty you punish him by means other than death. If you cannot find it in your hearts to have mercy on him, do it for his wife and children. Banish him to Rebel territory, take his cotton broker's license from him, confiscate all of the cotton he has on board, but don't condemn him to die for a failure to understand the situation he was in."

He pointed at Chew. "We don't deny that he cursed at Corporal Bascombe and threatened him with a dirk, but this was a reaction to a situation he'd never been in before—a colored soldier talking on an equal level with a woman mistakenly perceived to be white. Nothing in his experience had prepared him for such a moment. In his mind, raised as he has been raised, he had no choice but to defend her honor. Don't send him to his death because he couldn't tell the difference between a quadroon and a white woman. Hell, the poor man may have a touch of color-blindness—"

The officers erupted in laughter. Major Cook pounded the gavel for order.

Will continued. "Haven't we seen enough of death for a few days?" The room was quiet. "God knows I have."

It all seemed to have gone too fast. Will wished he had more to say, but he didn't. He sat down.

After the prosecution's summation, the major declared the court in recess and retired with the other officers to the mess to reach a decision. While they deliberated, Will sat with Chew, still bound and gagged, the four colored sentries looking on.

"When the court comes back," Will said, "I'm going to request that these restraints be removed. I'd like to at least have you treated as a man. Can you promise me there'll be no more outbursts?"

Chew nodded.

"Attention!"

When the major and the other officers were seated, Will made his request, and the gag and restraints were removed.

"Have the prisoner brought before the court," Cook said.

Will moved forward with Chew. Had to give the man credit, he was standing tall.

"The court finds the prisoner guilty of assaulting and threatening with bodily harm a soldier of the United States of America while in pursuit of his official duty."

Will felt Chew tense and took him by the elbow. And just in time, it seemed, because with the phrase "hung by the neck until dead," Chew seemed to wilt and would have fallen without support.

"To be carried out in one hour on the taffrail of the ship."

* * *

When they were back in Chew's cabin, accompanied this time by guards, Will asked Chew what he could do for him.

Chew was sitting on the bunk. "How much time?"

"About forty-five minutes, I reckon."

"Not much time to get my affairs in order."

"The major told me to give you every consideration in that matter," Will said.

Chew picked up a pen and began to scribble away. His hand trembled as it moved across the pad of paper.

"This is for my wife. It informs her where she can find my will and lists the other provisions I've made for her and the children." He looked at Will. "Reckon a condemned man could have a few shots of bourbon at a time like this?"

Minutes later, a sentry delivered a bottle of the best, courtesy of the ship's captain.

"Would you join me?" Chew said.

"I will, sir."

After his second drink, Chew put on his jacket. He looked every inch the proper gentleman.

"You know," he said, "something's changed in this country of ours. I can't exactly put my finger on it now." He laughed and pointed to the bottle. "Because it's a mite unsteady, but it's like we white people, you and me, we're being made to fight each other— by the niggers. Like they've turned the tables on us."

Will listened in silence. Death has its privileges.

"You know I always knew my big mouth would be the death of me, but I still can't believe I'm going to be hung over what I did to a nigger."

"It's a brutal war and you, my friend, just got caught in the middle of it. I truly pity you. Because there's some truth in what you say. The times changed, fast, and you didn't change with them. That's what happened." He poured them another drink. "Better get yourself ready, now. Do you want to pray? "

"I reckon I should. Will you pray with me?"

Will nodded.

"Our Father . . ."

* * *

Will accompanied Chew to the deck to the sound of drums rolling. Dusk on the river was a sight to see, the red of the sky reflecting off the water with a deep coppery glow. On the deck, row after row of Negro cavalrymen stood like their officers, ramrod-straight, eyes ahead. Up on the bridge of the ship, colored and white passengers watched a sergeant form a noose to put around the neck of Lamar Chew.

Will gripped the poor devil's elbow to steady him, for with his hands bound in front and his arms and legs lashed with rope, he was having trouble keeping his balance.

Stiles snapped to attention beside Chew as the first lieutenant in command of the execution said, "Does the prisoner have a last word?"

"I do. It's a sin to hang a man because he had one drink too many and wanted to protect the white womanhood of the South!"

At a glance from the lieutenant, the roll of the drums diminished.

The sergeant put a black hood over Chew's head, then—almost gently, it seemed—fitted the noose in place around his neck. Chew was moved into position. The drum roll got louder, but everybody heard the last of his last words:

"Damn your eyes and damn you all to hell!"

"Execute!"

The sergeant pushed him off the ship.

The line uncoiled, stiffened, and seemed to come to rest for a split second before commencing a pendulum-like swing. The ring to which it was attached made a creaking sound every now and then as the body below reached one end or the other of its arc.

The lieutenant peered over the stern. He snapped to attention, marched over to Major Cook, and saluted. It was done. The troops were dismissed and ordered below.

And the Mist of the Dawn made her way on down the river with a load of cotton, the Third Cavalry, and the body of Lamar Chew as supercargo.

CHAPTER ELEVEN

ZENOBIA woke to the long whistle of a red-winged blackbird perched on a bush nearby. The sun was just rising. She left Lisa Mae and the children sleeping and headed down to the river to see how Drayton was doing.

He was doing good. Spread out on the ground were eight good-size logs, each near long as he was tall. He was chipping away at one of them, shaving off the rough edges so it would fit in with the others. On the ground lay vines for binding them together.

"Ain't that heavy thing going to be hard to get in the water?" said Zenobia.

"And good morning to you, too, sister, you-all have a good rest?"

She laughed. "Sorry. My temper's none too sweet after sleeping on that hard ground. Probably more better than working all night, though. You doing good. Got a way with them tools."

"Maybe. But you right, it's bound to be heavy. I need something to push us off with. Look over there in the woods where I've got the horses tied, see if you can't find me a long pole."

Zenobia found a good strong limb and dragged it back. He put his awl down for a second and wiped his brow with the sleeve of his shirt.

"You got some kind of figure on you, woman. And your eyes are something to behold."

"We got no time for that foolishness. Just get that raft finished so we can leave."

"Don't you worry none. I be finished long before it's dark enough to set out."

"Dark? I think we should get out on the river as soon as you finish."

"There's going to be traffic on the river, Zenobia—small boats or something, folks is always out fishing." He looked up from his work. "Try explaining what we'd be doing with children on a raft. Don't make no kind of sense."

"And it makes sense to wait for the bloodhounds?"

"We going to have to chance they won't find us here during the day. You a big praying woman—now the time to do it."

"I reckon that's all we can do."

* * *

By the time the sun was high, the raft was finished. Drayton stood up and kicked it in a few places, testing its soundness.

"It look mighty good, don't mind if I say so myself. Come on, Zee, let's get it covered up with some weeds so won't nobody see it from the water."

When that was done and the horses fed, everybody sat down under the shelter of a big pine tree deep back in the woods to wait for nightfall. Drayton dozed off, Lisa Mae stayed with the children and Drayton, and Zenobia leaned on a tree from which she could keep an eye on both the raft and the cornfield where they'd left the wagon.

She looked up into the green leaves over her head. What was she doing out here in the middle of nowhere? Didn't even know where "here" was. And where was Luke and Milly—and Joe? Where was that lovable man of hers? Did he miss her as much as she missed him?

"What you doing here, Auntie?"

Zenobia jumped. A tall, pretty girl with her hair in cornrows stared down at her.

"Where'd you come from? I must have fallen asleep." Zenobia looked up at the sun. It was mid-afternoon. She shook her head and got to her feet, keeping a hand on the tree to steady herself. "You by yourself?"

The girl nodded. "You running away?"

"What's your name?"

"Helen."

Zenobia put her arm around the girl's shoulder. "What you doing down here all by yourself? Where the rest of the colored folks?"

"Ain't none left but me and some old aunties. And old Miz Jeffers. I just come down to see if I could catch us some fish."

"Ain't no white mens that live on the place?"

"They all gone to war. Was some mens come today while we was eating out in the cook shed, patrollers looking for some runaways. They—"

"Where are they?"

"You ain't the one. They was looking for a man and some women and children."

Putting her hands on Helen's shoulders, Zenobia turned her until they were face to face. "Where they at now?"

"They left. Miss told them to check at the Rankin plantation just down the way."

"How long ago?"

"A little while."

"Did they have dogs with them?"

"Yes, Auntie, up in the wagon."

Should she take this child back to the others? Or send her off with a warning not to tell on them? Either way, they had to get out of here now. She took Helen by the hand.

"Come with me, honey."

Drayton was already awake, making sure their food was wrapped tight in cloth bundles.

"What do we have here?" he said.

"Little sister says the patrollers is close, we got to leave now."

Drayton looked up at the sun. "Done told you, Zenobia, we can't go out on that river while the sun's still up. They'd catch us for sure." He looked at the girl. "You know any place in the river we could hide a raft?"

She pointed downriver. "Right around that bend, there's a little place where I fish sometimes, set back from the river, trees all over it. But . . ." She looked at Cally, then back at Drayton. "Where you going?"

He was already moving off. "Get the children and the food down to the raft, Zee. I'm going to run the horses away. Might throw the dogs off."

Zenobia and the others went down to the raft and pulled away the weeds. She looked out at the open water, tried to figure how long they'd be visible to anyone coming down the river before they were safe in Helen's hiding place.

Drayton came back with a rope in his hand. He tied it around one of the logs, then grabbed the other end. "Give me a hand." He turned to the two women. "Grab ahold of this rope and pull."

Zenobia and Lisa Mae each put the rope over their shoulders and pulled hard with Drayton behind them. The raft didn't budge.

"You-all got your feet planted solid?" Drayton said. "When I say pull, pull hard. One, two, three—pull!"

The raft moved just a little ways on the dirt.

"Pull again!"

Two feet forward.

"Let me help." Helen put the rope over her shoulder. "Please?"

"Me too, Uncle," said Ned.

"Me, Me!" Cally tottered forward and got under the rope.

"Pull!"

At first the raft moved an inch at a time, then it began to pick up speed. Soon they had it down by the riverside.

"All right." Drayton patted each of the children on the head. "Don't know as we'd of got it down here without you." He lowered himself into the water and held the raft tight against the slowly moving river while the women and children got on, then called back to Helen. "You go on with your fishing, child, and act like you ain't seen nobody if they ask you."

"Don't tell her that," Zenobia said. "They going to see we been here and they'll whip her if she lies. Just tell the truth, honey, only not where we going to be hiding."

Helen stood looking at them. "I want to go with you."

"No, you stay with your own."

"I ain't got no own no more."

Drayton shook his head. "Too many already."

"If we leave her here," Zenobia said, "they'll whip her anyway, just because she saw us and didn't come running to them."

Drayton sighed and reached his hand out to Helen. "At least

you can show us where that hiding place is." He shoved the raft out into the river.

"Lord have mercy!"

"Help, Mommy!"

Water was coming up through the cracks between the logs. The river was running a lot faster than it looked like from land.

"Zenobia, move over this way quick, before it turns over."

Drayton dragged the pole in the water in an effort to slow the raft down. But the river had gotten ahold of the raft and was spinning it around so fast Zenobia got dizzy. Their clothes were soaked through in no time. Thank the Lord Drayton had built four little posts on the raft—they were the only things they could hold on to.

Helen had said the water was shallow enough here for Drayton to pole them over into the hiding place, but it seemed like no matter how far he stuck the pole down into the water, he still couldn't reach bottom.

The bend in the river was coming up so fast, it looked like they were going to end up flying right past the place where they were supposed to hide. Then they'd have nothing but open river in front of them—and three hours of daylight. She must have of been crazy to get them in this fix. A bunch of field niggers, not a one of whom could swim, out in broad daylight on a raft they couldn't handle.

Helen nudged her and pointed ahead. "There, just behind where that big old rock and that long tree branch down near the water is."

They were bound to miss it by the length of a man's body. Unless . . .

She tied a big loop in one of the ropes Drayton had brought and motioned to show him what she was going to try to do. He must have understood, because he tied a knot in the other end of the rope and secured it to one of the posts.

"You're going to have to lean out to reach it," he said. "For God's sakes be careful."

"What you talking about—falling overboard?" Lisa Mae said. "You never seen the way she walk with them cotton baskets on her head?"

The limb Zenobia had spotted was coming up fast.

"Hold on tight," Drayton said. "When Zenobia loop the rope over that tree branch, this little thing going to come to a stop mighty quick."

Zenobia eyed the branch and waited. Closer . . .

Now! At first the rope slid back along the branch toward her, like it wasn't going to hold, then all of a sudden it tightened up and caught. And just like Drayton said, the raft came up tight against the rope and there was water everywhere—like the whole river was mad at them for stopping the raft and was going to sweep them all right off.

Lisa Mae lost her grip on Cally. Zenobia reached out and caught her hand, but not fast enough. Cally's wet palm slid right out of her grasp, and she tumbled off the raft into the river.

"Mama!"

Zenobia's heart had been ripped right out of her breast.

She watched as Cally's head disappeared below the surface of the muddy water, felt Drayton's strong arms around her own shoulders. "Don't, Zenobia."

She shook him off, determined to leap into the river after her daughter. But where? The river had swallowed her up whole. Zenobia brushed Drayton's arm away again and rose to jump into the river. Then she heard another splash. Helen was in the water and swimming fast to a spot about ten yards downstream. She too disappeared below the surface of the dark river.

Oh, Sweet Jesus, part them waters!

Just twigs and branches floating along on the surface like nothing had happened, like her soul wasn't suffocating down there along with Cally's. Behind her she could hear Lisa Mae praying softly. And Drayton, too.

"There's Helen, Auntie," yelled Ned.

And Cally?

The child's head slowly broke the surface of the water. She was safe in Helen's arms, but crying "Mama" between coughs and gasping for breath.

Helen pulled Cally ashore, which made them safer than the folks on the raft. With the river running so fast, that rope wouldn't hold long.

Putting Cally down on the shore, Helen ran up on the bank and called across the water to Zenobia. "Throw me that other rope—I'll pull you in."

And bless her heart, she did. When the raft was tied to land, Zenobia hugged her tight. "God sure enough sent you down to the river today. He never forget His own."

* * *

It seemed quiet under the trees, after the rush of all that water. Zenobia looked around her. Lisa Mae was holding tighter than ever now to little Cally and Ned, trying to warm their shivering little bodies with her own, which was soaking wet. Drayton was checking his revolver. Helen lay flat on the raft, looking up through the tree leaves over her head.

"What you see up there, child?" Zenobia asked.

"Nothing particular, Auntie, just waiting to see some signs of sunset so we be on our way."

Zenobia shuddered. "Lord, I don't even want to think about getting back out in the middle of that old river . . ."

She opened one of the packets of food, only to find that the water had soaked right through the wrappings. The corn bread was nothing but mush, so she passed out mussel spoons and began to feed Cally. After a few spoonfuls, Cally left Lisa Mae's arms and attached herself to Helen.

"She know how to swim and you don't," Zenobia said. She searched through the packets of supplies. "Anybody seen the cough medicine?"

"Reckon it's gone," Drayton said. "Probably went over with some other things when that rope caught and we stopped so sudden-like. Mercy, but that was something to see—you throwing that rope."

Didn't he ever stop? Silly to be making up to her when she had so much to worry about. She looked around and trembled. Cally was coughing, and there on the bank, not even twenty feet away, a pair of water moccasins slithered in and out of the water, like they were playing. At least there were no alligators. She hated their ugly leering faces. That little bitty raft wouldn't do much more than slow them down if they attacked.

"Sun getting low in the west," Helen said.

Good. The patrollers might not risk losing their hounds in strange country at this time of day, might wait until morning to let them loose. By then, according to Drayton's reckoning, they'd be at Clifton.

He held his finger up to his mouth in a signal for silence, and in a second they all knew why.

"What you figure we can catch this time of day?"

The voice came from somewhere on the opposite shore.

"Oh, I don't know, maybe some brims or mud cats. Who the hell cares? It's a good chance to get away from the house, ain't it?"

"You right about that."

"Then don't complain. Here, have a swig."

Zenobia couldn't see them, so they must be upriver a little. She took Cally from Helen's arms and pressed the shivering, soaked little body tight against her chest. Soon they were both shivering.

Time passed, what with the men fishing and talking, and every now and then breaking out into some song or another. She didn't recognize the tunes and couldn't make out the words.

The sun was almost gone.

"Reckon we'll see the niggers them patrollers is after?"

"I'd say we're as likely to see them as them patrollers. They didn't seem none too eager to me." A cackle. "The dogs were, though. Raring to go. Course, dogs ain't no good on the water. Bet those boys are going to stay down at the Pennypacker place tonight, rent them a boat there, and start down the river after those niggers in the morning."

"So what do we do if them runaways was to come floating by? Right now, I mean?"

"Me, I'd keep on fishing. Ain't going to let nothing spoil my day."

The sun had been down for a while, and Zenobia's teeth were chattering. They were lying on the raft now, warming each other with their bodies. Drayton was the only one sitting up, looking over everybody, pistol in hand. More and more, it seemed like he might sure enough be able to protect them and see them through to Yankee land.

"Well, Jeb, you ready to call it a day?"

"Day? Hell, we done run out of day."

"Womenfolk will be fussing if we still out here much longer."

Once they were gone, Zenobia could hear the whippoorwills and the crickets. And somewhere upriver, a dog barking.

Time to be on their way.

Drayton had tied ropes to the posts, four of them, and put loops in them, so everybody now had something better to hold on to. He looked over at Zenobia.

"How's Cally?"

"I'm dry now, Uncle," Cally said. "But I can't get warm."

"We'll find us a warm place by morning," Drayton said.

Zenobia hugged Cally close to her as Drayton slowly poled the raft out into the river. The current caught hold just like before, but this time it wasn't as strong. So the raft floated calm-like right on down the river. And thanks to those little ropes, there was no tossing and turning of folks all over the place.

If only the moon wasn't full, she might almost feel safe.

"Everybody lay flat down," Drayton said. "We just have to hold on now and trust God."

The raft was moving fast, the logs wet and slippery, the water bubbling up and slapping around the sides of the raft. Zenobia couldn't even remember what it felt like to be dry.

Drayton was right beside her, his leg against hers. She couldn't move away more than an inch or two—wasn't any place to go, and his leg was making hers warm. When she moved closer, he put his hand on her ass. Oh well, it felt good through the wet skirt.

They were going along just fine when the first hound dogs bayed. Zenobia squeezed Drayton's hand.

"This must be where them mens supposed to be staying for the night."

"Quiet."

The dogs soon were howling fit to wake the dead. And now a light come on in the house on the hill.

Oh, Lord . . . She looked toward the shore and saw a big rowboat tied up to a tree. The door to the house opened, and light flooded out.

"Quiet, you waking these good folks up here."

Zenobia knew it would take more than yelling to make them stop. Those nigger dogs knew they were out there. "All right, that's enough!"

As they floated at last past the house, she heard a whip crack again and again. The yelping that followed was loud enough to cover Cally's first cough of the night.

* * *

Way before sunrise, Drayton poled the raft into the little landing at Clifton. Although the air had already warmed up some, Cally was still shivering badly.

Zenobia left everything to Drayton and Lisa Mae and took Cally up to their old slave shack. She laid Cally down on the bare ground and commenced to rubbing her legs and arms. They were cold, terrible cold, even though her forehead was burning hot.

> *Ring-a-ring-a-rosies,*
> *a pocket full of posies . . .*

Cally didn't even know she was singing the song.

The others came in from the raft and Drayton looked down at Cally.

"I'm going up to the big house to see if I can find some old blankets or something. We hid some things before we left. Ned and Helen are cold too, even if they ain't complaining."

In less than a half hour, they had blankets and dry clothes. He made another trip with Lisa Mae and this time came back with cornmeal, bacon, and dried apples. A hot meal.

"Use hard wood," she said as he set off to start a fire in the old cookhouse. "It won't smoke so much."

"This ain't the first fire I ever built," he said over his shoulder.

But what if grayboys showed up? Or bandits?

She sighed. Whatever the risk, Cally had to have something hot. And if the rest of them didn't get something to eat soon, they'd end up as sick as she was.

* * *

The good, hot food soon had the children and Lisa Mae off to sleep. Zenobia and Drayton sat on the ground outside the shack and talked. The way he saw it, they had to get down the Yazoo. And the best way to do that was just to keep floating at night and hiding by day.

"Only thing is," he said, "Cally don't seem fit to travel with that fever."

"You think the patrollers will keep after us still?"

"They might, but I'm beginning to think that man up there fishing was right about them not being too eager. I'm more worried about outlaws, what with there being deserters from both armies."

"And Cally?"

"I don't propose to leave her or you," he said. "By noon-time today, we can go into the woods back of the north cotton field—remember the old slave arbor?—and stay up there till she get better."

"What about the raft?"

"Don't you worry about it, ain't nobody going to see it. I want to fix it up a little bit, meantime I'll keep it hid during the day."

"Well, since you fixing it up, I did notice one or two things that could use some improving. . . Now don't go getting your feelings hurt—it's a fine raft."

She reached up to kiss him on the cheek, but he pulled her close and covered her mouth with his. Hard to say which of them was most surprised when she pressed her body into his and kissed him back. But it was Drayton who finally broke the embrace.

"Who's that way up on the hill?"

Zenobia looked where he was pointing.

"Don't you recognize him? I wonder how long he's known we're here."

She stood up and waved. "Uncle Dan! It's me—Zenobia!"

CHAPTER TWELVE

SUE Kenworthy was standing on the porch, her arms around Laura and Gregory, when she heard the coach coming up the path. Richard was *home!* Too bad that Debbie and little Martha had been sent away to live with relatives in Alabama.

She ran down the steps to meet her husband, but the children got there first. A young colored driver helped him down. Richard put his good arm around her and drew her close for a kiss.

"We've missed you terribly," she said when he finally let her go.

"Good grief, Laura, you're almost up to my shoulders!" He held their ten-year-old daughter at arm's length, then got all tangled up trying to embrace both mother and daughter with one arm. Once disentangled he turned to Gregory, who gave a proper Confederate salute followed by a wild Rebel yell.

Richard laughed and so did the bearded sergeant who was just getting down from his horse.

"I don't know about the Yankees, son, but you sure scare the life out of me."

The only one not laughing was the Negro. Sue looked at him, then took a step closer.

"Aren't you Luke? Zenobia and Joe's boy."

"Yes, ma'am."

Sue looked at Richard. "How did—?"

"Tell you about it after dinner. Where the devil's Drayton?"

"That'll have to wait for later, too," she said, taking his arm. "Come on inside." He was bound to be angry, but she couldn't help it if they'd run off to the Yankees. That spiteful, deceiving Zenobia! It was all her doing, Sue was sure of it.

* * *

Sue and Richard sat together in the living room after the children were in bed. It was so good to have him here even for just a few days, right next to her, close enough to touch.

"Hold me?"

"Come here, sweet Sue."

She sat in his lap. "All those nights alone, I can hardly believe you're here."

He nuzzled the bare skin just above the line of her dress and shifted his body so that she rested—oh, so perfectly—in the crook of his arm. They stayed that way for a few moments without talking.

"Richard?"

"Yes?"

"Remember when I first met you?"

"With the greatest of pleasure."

"You were so handsome, all dressed up for the ball, the rising star in the state legislature. All the girls were praying you'd pick them for dancing, and then you asked me . . ."

"I didn't have a choice, you know. The way you looked at me."

He'd been so light on his feet, she'd danced more gracefully than ever in her life. It was the way they fit. Perfectly. She'd known it that first five minutes, dancing in that ballroom . . .

There would never, ever again be balls with women in beautiful dresses and champagne flowing like water and smiling nigras passing trays of delicacies. She looked into Richard's face. He looked bigger, seemed older than before he went off to war. And there was something in his eyes. . . .

She began to cry, softly at first, but before long her cheeks were wet and she couldn't seem to stop the tears.

Richard held her tight. "Oh, my poor Sue, you shouldn't have had to deal with all of this on your own. And you've held up things wonderfully with the children and all, with so little help and me so far away. I'm very proud of you."

"But, Richard, I've . . . we've lost everything."

"That's just not true." He took out his handkerchief and dabbed at her eyes—dried her cheeks.

"We have too! You're being so understanding about Zenobia and the rest. But her and Drayton, and Lisa Mae and the two children—I know that's five thousand dollars' worth of property, not to mention the ones we lost in that march over to Alabama. We're practically destitute, only ten slaves, and one of them that worthless Uncle Dan over at Clifton."

"We'll get them all back when we drive the Yankees out. The nigras will have nowhere to go."

Sue sat up and looked at him. "You surely don't believe that, do you? Why the Yankees are thicker than flies around here, raiding up and down the Mississippi and Yazoo like they owned them."

"We whipped the hell out of them at Brice's Crossroads."

"And I'm proud of you, glad you were part of it, but that devil Sherman has got people chasing our poor boys all over Tennessee and—" She stopped, resolved to get back to happier subjects. But somehow the anxious words kept pouring out of her.

"I'm sorry, but between having no money, and Clifton gone, and begging from your relatives, and now having to go to Mobile to live—it's just too much for a body."

"I know, honey," he said. "It's not easy to see everything we've worked for destroyed, or take charity from kin, or—"

She put her hand up to his mouth as if to quiet him, but he took it away and kissed it.

"Let me finish. You need to know, we've not given up. We've had setbacks, defeats, even desertions, but don't you worry. There are still men like General Forrest and me, plenty of them, who'll die before we see colored—"

She put her hand over his mouth. "Stop! I won't hear the least reference to you dying. Now, tell me how come you've got Joe's boy with you? Wasn't he over at Dorothy's place along with his sister—what's her name? Merry or Milly or something?"

"He was, but I had duty over that way, found a chance to stop over and see Dorothy. Luke's a blacksmith and the cavalry needs them, so I took him."

"Seems to me you treat him like a body servant."

"He's that, but mostly he's a blacksmith. Since Joe ran away and joined the Yankees, I find it kind of fitting to have his son serve in his stead."

"Why didn't you write and let me know you'd seen Dorothy? You know how much I love her. I should have written to let her know how things were with us, maybe even invited her to come over here and stay with us instead of up on that barren plantation all by herself."

Richard took his arm from around her waist. "I can't think of everything, you know. I did have a battalion of troops to think about, and—"

"Pauline. You had time to think about Pauline, didn't you?"

She felt his body stiffen and knew she'd caught him. Pauline was what he'd gone up there for.

"Well, how is she? Still the kind of woman that makes grown men call out her name in their sleep?"

He got up so abruptly that she almost fell to the floor, but he hardly seemed to notice! She stared at him for a moment, then turned away.

"I'm going to see about the children," Sue said.

When she got back downstairs, Richard was slumped in the chair, staring at the floor. He looked forlorn, like a little child whose favorite puppy had died—oh, why did she have to taunt him his first night home, and with his poor arm in that condition? The hero of Brice's Crossroads looked exhausted. She knelt in front of him and took his hand in hers.

"I'm sorry, Richard. Really sorry. Come on now, let's go to bed." She led him into the bedroom, stood on tiptoe, and kissed him. "You'll not hear one other unkind word from me."

Richard laid down on the bed and fell asleep, fully clothed. She gently covered him with a blanket, then laid down quietly beside him.

* * *

There were no more cross words between them. He took the children on hikes in the countryside, taught Gregory how to aim and shoot a Navy Colt, cut fresh flowers for Laura, and showered Sue with gifts—something new every day for seven days. Porcelain cups with her name on them, a silver medallion, a daguerreotype of a rose, and, best of all, a photograph of him in his new colonel's uniform. They had so much fun that she hardly thought of Pauline.

The only thing that bothered her was Joe's son. Richard treated him as if he were a trophy, a prisoner of war, and you could see from the way the boy's eyes moved that he hated his master.

"I wish you'd get rid of Luke, place him with another unit," she said one evening. "He always says 'yes' and does what you say, but he scares me. Why do you want him around you, when it would be so easy for him to get hold of a gun?"

"I told you about that day Joe stood across the river from me and taunted me. Well, I can't hurt him, he hasn't fallen into my hands—yet. But fate has given me his boy. He'll do for the time being."

"What about Milly? Why didn't you take her too?"

"She wasn't there. But if I can get my hands on her, I'll—"

"Bring her to me, Richard . . . I could use her to replace Zenobia."

"Just what I had in my mind."

"But you will keep an eye on Luke, promise me? He means you harm, I'm certain of it."

"Don't bother yourself about him. Sergeant Barclay watches him like a hawk."

"Even in the heat of battle?"

"Especially then."

* * *

The following morning a courier rode up to the house with orders for Richard.

"Well, you're going to have me around the neighborhood for a while now. I've been ordered to take command of a reinforced cavalry troop to back up the infantry regiments guarding the Big Black River Bridge. Guess the wound means I can't be galloping around the countryside with General Forrest anymore. For a while, anyway."

"Richard, that's wonder—oh, I'm sorry, darling. I know how you love your cavalry, but I'm just so happy you'll be nearby. Are you very disappointed?"

"Well, no. It's actually one of the most important assignments I've ever been given. The Mississippi Central railroad bridge on the Big Black is crucial to the running of supplies from Mississippi to General Hood's army over in Tennessee. If Hood can retake Nashville and drive the Yankees out, they'll be forced to withdraw from Tennessee and Mississippi. And that could end the war."

"Good heavens, Richard. Do you really think that will happen?"

"I do, because that tottering Abe Lincoln regime can't stand one more big defeat."

* * *

Richard, accompanied by Luke and Sergeant Barclay, was on his way to his new command early the next morning. Sue was relieved that he'd agreed to delay moving her and the children down to Mobile. And his optimism was infectious. With the bridge intact and under control of the Confederacy, Hood would crush Thomas.

"I have no intention of losing that bridge," Richard said as he got into the coach. "We've already wrecked two Yankee regiments who tried to take it. And by God we'll destroy as many as necessary to hold it."

Gregory gave a Rebel yell, and Richard put his head out the window of the coach and returned the yell.

Sue laughed and hugged Laura. "Aren't they something!" Yankees, beware!

* * *

"I don't think that there's much use even trying to make a crop next year, Miss Dorothy." Pauline held out a list of seed supplies to her. "Everything's gone. No seed, all the tools on the place stolen." Either by deserters or by Confederate regulars or by hands who'd run away. "Come on down to the stables, I'll show you what I mean."

A premature frost had left a white crust covering the earth.

Pauline showed Dorothy the one mule left on the place. "It's so thin they didn't take it." She walked over to the cow, the only source of milk and butter. Downright scrawny. And the loft that used to be filled with hay was empty—all taken by the army for fodder.

The two women, hand in hand, walked back to the big house. "I didn't know it was this bad."

"But I been telling you every day. You need to look around you—in a few days, when that stock of wood Luke cut in the spring runs out, we'll have nothing left to warm the house. And soon it won't just be chilly at night."

The two women sat down in rocking chairs in front of the fire in the living room. Finally Miss Dorothy seemed to be paying attention. She did look around.

"Oh, Pauline, when I think of what all we've lost . . ."

"I know it's sad, Miss, and I hate to worry you, but if you don't count me and Milly, there are just two able hands left here."

"It's true—something must be done. The children keep catching colds, and they're not used to eating mush every day."

Pauline poked the fire she had built that morning. "How much longer you think the teacher will be able to keep the school open?"

"It's a wonder he's still here. That old man hasn't been paid in two months, and I don't know how we can find the money to pay him. So many people have fled to Texas."

"We could shut off parts of the house. If you move the children into your room, we'd only have to heat it and the kitchen. We could save a lot of wood that way. Me and Milly can move our things into the kitchen and live there, for the time being."

Dorothy sighed. "Everything you're saying is kind and helpful, but I can see now that we're going to have to leave this place before long. The colonel is too far away to help us, and what with Atlanta gone, I doubt he'll be able to spare us any of his attention any time soon."

"I think if you are going to leave, you better do it right soon. I hate to say this, but there are some slaves up in the hills who've been raiding other plantations, stealing things out of them. They're bound to come this way sooner or later. And I wouldn't want nothing to happen to you or the children."

Pauline didn't say that the only reason they hadn't stolen everything already was because Woodson—out of love for her—had held them back. And she didn't tell her Miss that some of them were colored Yankee deserters, who were saying it was all right to burn down the mansions. Hadn't General Sherman told them to do that? There was even a white soldier among them who'd been captured by the Rebs and escaped.

"Do they hate us so? Neither the colonel nor I have ever done any harm to them. We have treated our nigras well—haven't we, Pauline? And I thought most of the danger was from our own Confederate deserters, not our own faithful nigras."

"But, Miss Dorothy, they're not your faithful nigras anymore. That's changing. The Yankees are putting different notions into their heads. Believe me, many of them would delight in being able to destroy this place. And it's sad to say, but indeed they would laugh as it burned."

"Oh, Pauline, you can't . . . I just don't believe it."

"Let me tell you a story an old lady told me once, maybe it'll help you understand how my people feel."

"Your people, Pauline? How can you talk like that? We love each other, you're more like a sister than—"

"But I'm not, Miss. I love you dearly and I do know you love me, but the colored are my people."

"How can you say that? What makes you say that?"

Pauline had been looking into the fire, but now she turned around.

"No matter the reason, sisters don't own each other." When she saw the tears well up in Dorothy's eyes, she reached for her hand. "I didn't say it to hurt you, I just—"

"That's not why I'm crying. I should have freed you long ago. And if it hadn't been for the war, I would have by now. But to give you free papers would only have placed you in more danger from my people. Now it's too late for all that, the Yankees will do it for us. I would rather I had done it myself, but I'll never have that chance." She blew her nose, sat up straighter. "Now tell me the story."

Pauline drew her shawl more tightly around her shoulders.

"Once upon a time, there was a mean old slave driver named Duncan, who carried the biggest, meanest whip for miles around and took great delight in making the slaves do anything. Well, one day his hound dog—its name was Glover—died. Many's the nigra it had caught in its lifetime, but Duncan called all the colored folks on the plantation to come to the funeral and mourn Glover's death."

"Oh, Pauline. Surely not!"

"It's true, Miss. Not everybody is as good and kind as you and the colonel. Or has as much sense. So anyway, that dog was the dearest thing in life to Duncan, and he wanted the colored people to pray and cry over this dog who'd treed so many of them when they tried to run away. You see, Duncan was convinced they had a special way of praying that would reach God—you know, pray on Glover's behalf, ask God's forgiveness for all the colored folk he torn to pieces. Duncan didn't think he could get in touch with God all on his own."

"So he had some sense, then."

"The colored people came to the funeral, just like he asked, and they had little pots of water they hid from him, and they used the water to wet their eyes, and they prayed and shouted up a storm. Old Duncan caught the Holy Spirit, and broke down in front of them and started hugging and kissing them and calling them brother and sister. He was so happy, he gave them a special ration of whiskey that night."

"Then what happened?"

Pauline's face lit up. "Well, that night, after Duncan was gone, they drank his whiskey and all night long they kept on bringing Glover's name before the Lord. 'Poor old Glover—that dog done gone and died and can't catch us no more. Give me another drink! Poor old Glover! May the gates of hell open wide! Amen, Amen!'"

The story had a different, more violent end, but Pauline

knew she'd been right to change it when her mistress laughed out loud for the first time in ages.

They were quiet again for a while, though every now and then one of them would say "Amen! Amen!" Or "Poor old Glover!" and they would both start laughing all over again.

* * *

A week later Miss Dorothy gave Pauline legal papers so she and the few others left behind would not be harassed by the authorities. When the day came for her to leave, she lingered on the porch with Pauline even when the children were in the coach. "I can't imagine waking up tomorrow without you nearby," she said. "We've spent practically every day of our lives together."

"I know, Miss. But I don't know what else we can do. You've done all you can for me and my nephew and niece, now you have to see about yourself." They walked to the coach arm in arm. "Seems like everything's changing, but the love for you and the colonel in my heart . . . well, that won't ever change."

* * *

Pauline watched until the coach was out of sight, until she could no longer see Dorothy's face framed in the tiny back window.

"Who's going to take care of us now, Auntie?" Milly asked when the coach rounded the first bend.

Pauline put her arms around Milly's shoulders and pointed to the grounds around the big house.

"See all that out there? You see how empty it looks—remember how all our folks would be working and running to and fro for Massa and Miss? That's all over now."

"They're leaving it to us?"

"Well, in a way. Come on, let's go inside."

The mansion's furniture was all covered with linen, the central fireplace dark and silent. Pauline led Milly out into the kitchen and put on a kettle of water for some tea.

"You're free now, honey. No matter what happens, slavery is finished."

Milly smiled. Lord, she was a pretty thing. Had Joe's eyes and his way of smiling.

"Oh, Auntie, everything seems so . . . It's funny, but I feel more danger now than I felt when Miss was still here."

"That's because you ain't used to standing on your own feet. It'll take a little while, but you'll get used to it. You're going to do just fine."

"Who's going to protect us now?"

The teakettle began to boil. "We're going to take care of each other. Brother Woodson and some of his people, they're going to come in tonight, going to live in the big house. The men have got guns, and they've decided that it's better to be here than out in the woods."

"What if the graycoats come by?"

"The men going to keep a sharp lookout for them. The main thing is to get all those folks in out of the cold and the rain."

Woodson and thirty other people, mostly runaways, filed into the building toward evening, looking up in wonder at the crystal chandeliers that hung from the ceilings. Most of them were young and strong, men and women who'd taken to the woods over the past two years or so and banded together. Their clothes were ragged and some had only cloth wrapped around their feet to protect them from the cold.

Soon they had a fire roaring in the main fireplace. And the kitchen was bustling with folk happy to find a real stove to cook on. Somebody began singing, "Glory, Glory, Hallelujah, When I Lay My Burden Down," and the song spread through the house:

> *"Gonna put on my shoes*
> *Walk in glory*
> *When I lay my burden down . . ."*

Pauline admired the way Woodson set things up so quick. He gave everybody an assignment. Some in the kitchen, others cleaning, the young men chopping wood, the older men—including the wounded Union veteran they had rescued—setting up defenses, sentinels around the place for a good two miles. He even laid out his plans for evacuation in case any grayboys came their way.

"And one more thing," he said. "Other folks are going to find out about us and want to come join us. Well, we're going to let them. The more of us they is, the better able we be to protect ourselves. These grayboys are on their knees now. Yankees whipping them every way they can. Our job is to save ourselves, protect these children till the Yankees get up here. Won't be long now, we just got to hold on."

"Speak on, brother," a man said. "When we get strong enough, we ought to go out and bring folks in."

"That's just what I have in mind. We going to be a beacon of light in the darkness, my brothers and sisters."

Somebody began to sing, "I'm Going to Sit at the Welcome Table, One of These Old Days."

Pauline got the fiddle out. "Anybody know how to play one of these?"

Before long most everybody was dancing, and nobody seemed to mind when the children got out of their beds and came down and joined in. Who could sleep on such a night as this?

* * *

When the house was quiet at last, Pauline left the pallet next to Milly's in a room where the women slept. As she walked through the house, she wondered where Miss Dorothy was tonight, hoped she and the children would be all right.

Most of the men lay asleep, their weapons nearby. Woodson was still sitting up, staring at what remained of the fire.

"Want to talk?" Pauline pointed to a little room off from the big hall, and they went in and closed the door. She put her hand on his knee.

"Do you really have confidence in the sentinels? We'll all be slaves again if they don't sound the alarm in time."

"We've been out in the woods for almost a year now, and they ain't caught us yet. We be all right." He put his arm around her shoulder and drew her close to him. "Long as I'm able to hold you like this, I can deal with whatever come."

She snuggled up to him. "You think the others would mind if we stayed in here together? Think they would take it unkindly, like we had privileges?"

He kissed her. "I think nobody here going to hold any happiness we make for ourselves against us."

"Then wait, I'll go get some blankets and we can make us a pallet on the floor."

"Don't be long. I got something important to ask you."

When she came back, undressed, and lay down beside him, he pulled her close to him.

"I want to care of you. Marry you. Will you have me?"

His body was very warm against hers. He was a strong man, and they were good together.

"That's a hard question to ask me on a night like this. Things changing so much—this is my first night free, remember?"

"There's no one else, is there?"

"No. Please, can't we just love each other tonight?"

CHAPTER THIRTEEN

FOR three days and nights, except when Lisa Mae or sometimes Helen would take over for a little while, Zenobia sat by a pallet where Cally lay twisting and turning and sweating.

The lean-to in the bush arbor wasn't much of a shelter. The wood planks on the muddy ground and the canvas outer covering did little more than keep out the rain that had been coming down for four days. They had a little fire in there, and a way for the smoke to get out. What they didn't have was a way to make Cally well.

"Dear God, oh God, sweet Jesus, take my life if it has to be, but let Cally live.. ." Not gone like Luke and Millie, both of them maybe dead by now. Jesus knew all about the pain and the emptiness and the fear deep down there in her soul. And Zenobia had kept on praying, hadn't she, when Joe went away and left her and Cally behind. Had stayed on her knees day and night and sang every morning:

> *"When I saw that bright sunshine*
> *I didn't have no doubt!"*

She took a damp cloth and wiped Cally's brow. Why, oh why, had she taken her on this hard, long journey to freedom? If she'd been sold down into Alabama, away from Cally, maybe she'd be someplace warm and dry now instead of in this damp, smoke-filled hiding place.

"Here, get up for a moment." Drayton put his arm around her shoulder. "I made some more of the medicine. Let's see what it will do."

He bent down and gave Cally two spoonfuls. She stared up at him and didn't even move her eyes.

Zenobia looked around her. Ned, his eyes all mournful, was poking a stick in the little fire. Lisa Mae was patching some clothes. Old man Dan, leaning on his cane and wearing those patched blue pants of his, was by the door. He came up to the arbor twice a day to see how Cally was.

Handing the damp cloth to Lisa Mae, Zenobia beckoned Drayton to follow her outside.

"I want you to take the others and go on," she said. "It's dangerous here, and even if Cally gets well she won't be able to travel for days. Go."

"Think I could make any of them in there leave you? Would Ned leave you? You been his mother since they sold DoraLee away. And Lisa Mae? She stick closer to you than a sister. Helen? She done decided to be your daughter." He took her hands. "And me?"

She stood tiptoe and kissed him full on the lips.

"What you smiling about?" she said when they broke apart.

"I love you, Zee."

She let herself be held for a minute. "You making me feel things I ain't felt for a long time. Let's go back inside. It's cold out here."

She lifted Cally out of the bed and held her while Drayton put a blanket around them both. She and Lisa Mae took turns rocking Cally's slight little body.

*"When I got down on my knees
I didn't have no doubt!"*

Such a long night. Around midnight, Uncle Dan came back. He knelt in front of Cally and Zenobia and commenced to pray.

After a while, Cally opened her eyes and smiled.

"See, Zenobia, she always do that with me, she love her uncle Dan." He waved his hand. "Hi, sweetie pie."

Cally closed her eyes again and seemed to sleep. But she breathed heavy, and Zenobia kept wiping away the sweat beading on her little forehead and soaking through her clothes.

Drayton took off his cotton shirt and wrapped it around her.

*"I knew the Lord would take care of me
I didn't have no doubt!"*

* * *

Uncle Dan bent down next to Zenobia and kissed Cally on her brow. "I be back first thing in the morning, going to pray all night, the old African way, good and loud down in my hut! Going to turn them hellhounds back!"

Drayton sat down on the floor in front of Zenobia. "Always a good sign when somebody sweat, mean the fever coming out."

"I seen it happen many a time," Lisa Mae said. "So, Zee, why don't you just lay down and sleep and let me hold Cally the rest of the night?"

Zenobia shook her head and kept on rocking. Soon Lisa Mae was sleeping on her pallet, and Drayton dozing off with his head against Zenobia's legs. And as the night wore on, Cally seemed to be resting easier. Breathing mighty fast, but she'd stopped sweating.

It was getting lighter in the hut. Far away Zenobia could hear a rooster crowing. Soon another joined in, then another. Must be Uncle Dan's birds. She bent low over Cally, couldn't hear her breathing, it was so soft. Her face looked peaceful.

> *The little baby gone home*
> *The little baby gone home*
> *The little baby gone along*
> *For to climb up Jacob's ladder.*

Through a crack in the door, she could see the sun rising all red—orange between the earth and sky.

She kissed Cally on her brow, her eyes, her little mouth, took her up, held her tight, rocked her gently.

> *For to climb up Jacob's ladder . . .*

Cally's eyes opened. She smiled pretty, just like she had for Uncle Dan, then closed her eyes. Zenobia held her breath, waiting for Cally's next one. It didn't come. And when Zenobia did breathe again it came out with a sob that woke Drayton. He held them both, mother and daughter, rocked Zenobia, who kept on rocking Cally. Rocking and crooning. Rocking and crooning.

* * *

There was a tall, spreading pine tree at the top of the hill at Clifton. Birds of all kinds liked the spot; in the springtime a red cardinal perched on the pine tree's highest branch and sang the song he used to sing when Joe and Zenobia walked up the hill and looked out over the bend in the river. "Someday we'll be free." Joe had said it so many times they'd ended up calling the place Someday.

That was where Zenobia told Drayton to dig the hole.

There was no wind. They stood around the grave, heads bowed, while Uncle Dan said a prayer.

"Oh Heavenly Father, we come before thy presence humble as we know how to come, calling upon you to have mercy on us poor sinners. And especially on the soul of your departed servant child, Cally. She ain't never done nobody wrong, were just a little bitty thing who loved to take her uncle Dan by his hand. Now we down here asking you to let her into your kingdom so she can play up there around King Jesus' golden throne.

"And, Father, we begging your mercy on us who still down here on this hard and tedious journey, asking you to look down on this grieving mother, beseeching you to console your daughter Zenobia. Put your love all around her, be unto her a fence all around, clarify her mind, give her strength for the journey. You an all-seeing God, an all-knowing God, a Burden-Bearer, Heavy Load Sharer, Mighty Waymaker. You Our Bright and Morning Star, our Wheel in the Middle of the Wheel, Our Shelter in the Time of Storm, Our Rock in a Weary Land, I say you Our Rock in a Weary Land . . ."

Lisa Mae began singing soon as Drayton tossed the dirt over the little body wrapped in cloth:

> *"Oh—Graveyard! Oh—Graveyard!*
> *You must give over to the body,*
> *Dig my grave with a silver spade*
> *You must give over to the body!*
> *Let me down with the golden chain*
> *You must give over to the body!"*

Drayton pounded a cross down into the earth.

Cally

Born 1861

Died 1864

"Let the Little Childrens Come Unto Me."

It was over. Drayton took Zenobia by the arm and led her down the hill, Lisa Mae, Ned, and Helen trailing behind. Uncle Dan stayed up on the hill, like he wanted to pray some more, maybe hold Cally's hand on her journey home.

* * *

Two days after they buried Cally, Zenobia knew it was time to go on their way. Drayton spent the morning checking out the raft again. It seemed like every day he thought of a way to make it stronger. The way Zenobia saw it, the longer they waited, the more chance that somebody would come and capture them.

She gathered up the bundle of food she would be carrying.

"You all go down to the raft," she told Lisa Mae and the others. "Drayton's down there already. I want to go up the hill one last time, then I got to stop by and tell Uncle Dan good-bye. Go on, now. I'll be along soon."

* * *

When she got to his shack Uncle Dan was sitting there, staring down at the floor. "I reckoned you'd be to see me before you left."

Zenobia hugged him. "You was the first person I met when I come here from South Carolina, remember?"

"I got something I ought to tell you, and I been meaning to do it but couldn't seem to find the right time, what with Cally passing and all."

"What is it?"

"It's about Joe. He come back here about six moons ago."

"He's alive?" Not dead, not drowned in the river when he tried to run away?

"Was the last time I saw him. Them grayboys come and captured him."

"How did he look?"

"He were a soldier with them Yankees. He against us."

Poor old man. "Did he ask about me? About us?"

Uncle Dan looked away. "I told him you and Cally gone with Miss Kenworthy over Jackson way. And he say he was going to fetch you all."

She'd known it all the time. Joe would never give them up for lost!

"What happened then?"

"Like I say, them grayboys on horses come by and caught him."

The story sounded mighty strange.

Uncle Dan reached over and took her by the hand. "If I was you, I wouldn't be going with them on that little old raft."

"It's too late for that now. It won't be long before we reach the Yankees."

"Them grayboys all around."

"We won't be leaving until dark."

"God bless you, child."

Zenobia got up to leave the hut.

"Zee?"

She turned back to him. Seemed like he was trying to say something, but the words were stuck in his mouth.

"Yes, Uncle Dan?"

"Them grayboys . . ."

"You already done told me about them, we be careful."

"But—" He was holding her by both hands, like he didn't want to let her go.

"Uncle Dan, if they knew we was here, they'd have come by now, but all the same I appreciates your worrying about us. Unless you knows—"

He released her hands. "Oh no. . . ain't nothing. You'd better run along now. It getting late."

* * *

When night came, they were all ready to go. Drayton pulled the raft from under its cover of leaves and showed Zenobia all the things he'd done to make it stronger. Proud of himself, and why not? He'd even put some planks crosswise on top so the water wouldn't come through so much. Doing his best to make it better for her, Lisa Mae, and the children.

The raft was heavier now, but with everybody pulling together, they were able to get it in the water. It looked sturdy.

"You done good." Zenobia kissed Drayton, but knew that she'd never lie with him now that she had some hope that Joe was still alive.

He tied the raft tight to the dock. "All right, everybody, get on—carefullike." He handed Zenobia the long pole. "Here, put that right there in the holder. Everything here?"

Zenobia looked around. "No, wait, I left the extra food bundles up at Uncle Dan's. I'll go get them."

"No, you won't. I don't want any more getting in and out of that raft than is necessary. I'll go up and get them, just wait here."

"Hurry."

Zenobia busied herself with arranging things on the raft. She put the foodstuffs in a little box Drayton had built to keep them dry, then checked to see that Ned and Helen were bundled up good for the night trip. Drayton had said they would need to be on the river at least two nights, then they might start running into Yankee boats.

Strange he wasn't back yet—it was only a little ways up to Uncle Dan's house.

"Lisa Mae, if he doesn't get back in a few more minutes, I'm going after him."

"Oh, Zee, you worry too much. If ever a man could take care of himself, it's Drayton."

The minutes dragged on. Full night had fallen, and Zenobia checked to see that the revolver Drayton had given her was in its special wrapping. When she drew out the gun and started to get up, Lisa Mae grabbed her arm.

"Don't leave us here all alone. If he in trouble, you the only one can get us out on the river."

"She's right, Auntie," Ned said. "If Drayton and you both gone, who going to take care of us?"

She sat back down on the raft and made herself wait, her eyes straining to see something through the dark. They all jumped when the sound of gunfire and flashes of light came from up toward Uncle Dan's house.

"Uncle Drayton in trouble?" Ned said.

"I don't know, we have to wait and see." Her grip on the gun in her lap tightened.

The firing and the noise were closer now.

"I think we got the nigger!"

"Oh!" It was Drayton's deep voice.

"Drayton, Drayton!" Zenobia screamed his name into the night.

More gunfire, then he shouted through the darkness. "Go, Zenobia, I'm shot—can't make it. I'll hold them off."

"No, we'll wait for you."

Three more shots.

"Zee, I did love—"

The sound of the shot went right through Zenobia.

She put the revolver back in its wrappings, cast off the rope, took the pole, and pushed as hard as she could.

The heavy raft barely moved.

The sounds of galloping horses and shouting men drew closer to the dock. Zenobia pushed again, harder, praying they would make it out into the current before the men reached them. By now she could make out the shapes of the men's horses.

She gave one more shove, then lay down on the raft.

Lisa Mae had her arms around the children. "Stop your crying. You got to be quiet. There ain't no moon, they might not see us. If we catch the current, we be gone before they know it."

The raft seemed to stand still, like it was stuck in a pool of molasses. Someone on shore shouted:

"All right, you niggers, the game's up. Come on back before we have to shoot!"

The raft wasn't even a hundred yards from the docks, just bobbing up and down in place. Zenobia took the revolver out and sighted it in the direction of the land.

"I know it can hardly reach them," she said, "but it might put some kind of a scare in them, anything better than just laying here."

She fired and was immediately answered with a ragged volley of shots.

"Now you niggers are dead for sure!"

Zenobia pointed the gun to fire again, but Ned tugged at her arm.

"Auntie, don't you feel it? We moving."

She looked at the water and could just see the white bubbles behind and to the side of the raft. First slowly, then faster and faster, the current drew them into the dark void of the river.

The men on shore kept firing and filling the night with their curses. They could curse and shout all they wanted to, God did have some mercy on His people.

When they were well out into the river and the noise had died out behind them, Zenobia turned her attention to her flock. They were sitting up, blankets wrapped tightly around them, all crying, holding on to each other for dear life.

Ned said, "We ain't never going to see Uncle Drayton again, Auntie?"

"Not in this life, you ain't," Zenobia said. "Only thing you can do, and me too, is pray for him. He were a good man." How good she'd never find out now.

"I used to hate him when we lived at Clifton," said Lisa Mae, who was crying. "Zee, you remember how every time you turn around, he'd be beating on somebody or another, saying Massa made him do it? And he'd always whip full measure."

Zenobia drew a hand across Lisa Mae's wet eyelids, then her own. "The Good Book say judge not lest ye be judged," she said.

"We got to say a prayer right now for Brother Drayton, forget the bad things he did and remember how he brought us over this long way and give his life out there in the field to protect us. Lisa Mae, pray a little for his soul, then I wants you all to get to sleep." When all was quiet, her mind drifted back to the words of Uncle Dan's—he must have known about the graycoats, maybe even told them.

Through the rest of the night, Zenobia watched the shore. Now and then, there'd be a light, then it would vanish. The raft was mostly dry, thanks to Drayton's good work. She wiped away the last of her tears. She could almost hear his voice: time to figure out how to reach the Yankee ships, Zee.

* * *

Early in the morning, just after daybreak, she picked up an oar when the raft rounded a bend at a narrow point in the river. She used it the way Drayton had taught her, fixing it so it bit down deep. At first, it didn't seem to make no difference, then it caught and the raft started to go in toward shore, into a clump of trees like the ones they'd stayed in when they first started out.

Soon as the raft got close enough, she poled it into the bank.

"Where are we, Auntie?" Ned asked.

"Not far enough away from them, and not close enough to the Yankees. Give me a hand, we going to try to pull the raft up here on the bank so we can hide it real good."

Ned stepped down into the water and helped her. When the raft was well covered, Zenobia climbed up the bank to see if she could find them a good hiding place for the day.

They were in luck. There must have been a big plantation here—and a little way back from the river, she could see a shack probably used for cooking meals for the hands when they were out in the fields. When she was sure there wasn't anybody about, she got the others, and they settled in for the day. By the time the sun came up, they were snug as could be.

Zenobia fixed it so one person was outside looking, especially when the others were asleep. They passed three days and three nights like that, hiding in bushes or a shack by day and floating down the Yazoo at night.

On the fourth day, while they was hiding up on a little hill in a clump of trees where they could see down to the river, some grayboys come riding down the road on horses. They were noisy, shouting to each other and singing songs and riding along like they didn't care who knew it. Like Drayton had said, the grayboys still controlled the land around here, Sherman close to taking Atlanta or not.

Behind the line of them came two pairs of horses, and they was hauling two big guns. They stopped right near where Zenobia had hid the raft and for a minute there, she thought they might find it. But looking for a raft seemed to be the farthest thing from their minds. These men were after bigger game. They drew those cannon right up to the riverbank, aimed them out at the water, then covered them over with branches and leaves.

All morning they stayed down there, not doing much, just lying around. Now and then one would go down to the river with a spyglass and look up and down. Around noontime, the one with the glasses started jumping up and down and shouting. The others come running fast as they could and started aiming the big guns.

"Look, Auntie!" Helen pointed to a long, gray boat floating down the river, with no decks for anybody to stand on and look out. "It's a Yankee ship, you can tell by the flag."

"And it's got big guns too," said Ned, who'd stood up.

Zenobia pulled him down. Thank God the soldiers were looking toward the river.

Pretty soon the air was full of smoke and noise, with some of the grayboys shooting off their big guns and some others who'd gotten up into the trees firing their rifles down at the boat.

The whole side of the Yankee boat seemed to turn into fire and smoke. There was a shrill, high whistling sound, and one of the guns and the grayboys around it was swept right off into a gully like they was little toys or something. But the other gun kept shooting—until suddenly, it was over. The Yankee boat steamed on down the river away from the Rebels.

The grayboys who were up in the trees came down and joined the others. Together they helped the wounded, buried their dead, ate, then packed up their guns and rode off in the same direction as the boat.

"Lord, that was something to see," Lisa Mae said when they were all gone.

"Do you know what I know?" Zenobia said.

"I know we going to have one hard time getting out to a Yankee boat."

"Even if we gets to see another one," Zenobia said. She called the children over. "You're going to have to do exactly what I say from now on, especially when we're on that raft. It's the only way we're going to escape to the Yankees."

They promised.

After two more nights of floating on the river and seeing three big Yankee boats go by, Zenobia made up her mind to stay in one place. They had a good place to wait, right behind a little island.

"We going to have to take our chances getting out to one of them boats," she told them. "And we ain't got no guarantee the grayboys ain't going to be around."

"What you getting at, Auntie?" Helen said.

"We going to stay right here in this place, ain't going to move no more, and when the next Yankee boat come, we going to shove off on that raft, shout to high heaven, and pray they stop and pick us up. That's the only way. If we quick enough, we might make it."

* * *

Two more days passed. Then, just after daybreak one morning, Zenobia heard the distant rumble of big boat engines coming down the river. She got up off her pine needle bed and shook everybody awake.

"Quick, now. Down to the raft."

Lisa Mae was up in a minute, but the children were tired. Helen yawned and stretched her arms. Ned started to wipe the sleep out of his eyes. The drone of the engines was getting louder. Zenobia dipped water into a bucket and splashed some of it into the children's faces.

"What you do that for?" Ned cried.

"Boats coming. Hurry!" Helen, who was already on her feet, grabbed her little bag. "I'm ready, Auntie."

Zenobia snatched up her own bag. "Run! And when we get there, don't bother with the leaves, just get on."

The boat engines were very loud now.

She ran to the edge of the little island and looked up the river. Sure enough, it was one of them Yankee boats with the guns and the big old wheels on the side.

She raced back to the raft. Her stomach felt funny. And they were leaving all the food and most of the clothing behind.

Zenobia poled the raft out into the muddy river. Lord, it was a big boat. And didn't that red, white, and blue flag snapping in the morning breeze look pretty?

"You got that white flag ready?"

Lisa Mae nodded.

"Then start waving it!"

Ned and Helen were on their knees, waving their hands.

"You two lay down before you tip the raft," she said. "You be safe soon."

They got down, but kept on shouting and waving their hands.

"Hey, boat, stop for us!"

"Auntie, can't they see us?"

Zenobia had never seen anything as big as that boat. Nor as fast. Why, it was already abreast of them and no more than a field's length away. And it was making waves big enough to send the raft sliding up one side of them and down the other. Zenobia, now on her knees, had to hold on tight to one of the ropes. She could see soldiers in blue uniforms standing on the decks. And lots of them were colored. Lord, she never thought she'd live to see the day.

The river was taking the raft fast downstream and toward the boat.

Were those men blind? How could all them eyes miss a raft with four people on it?

Another bow wave from the boat hit the raft so hard it almost tossed Zenobia overboard.

"Watch yourself, Auntie!" Helen yelled. "You can't swim!"

Zenobia clung to the rope, her feet dangling in the water.

Helen tossed a rope to her and she pulled herself up toward the center of the raft, just in time to be thrown back by the blow from another wave.

One more like that, and the whole raft would go over.

Suddenly the men on the boat started waving and yelling. Up at the top of the big boat, a man with a white hat on waved too, then turned around and yelled something to some other men in blue.

Bells clanged, whistles blew, and a big cloud of steam belched out of the smokestack.

The ship slowed, then the big wheel on its side started to turn backward. And praise the Lord if it didn't come to a stop right in the middle of the river. Somebody could sure steer that boat.

The waves still rocked the raft, but now it had floated up to the back of the boat. A colored man in a blue uniform yelled down.

"Catch this rope when I throw it and tie it to the raft! We can't stop long and can't put a boat down—they's Rebs all around."

The soldier tossed the rope down. Zenobia reached for it, and missed. The man recoiled the rope.

"Better catch it this time, sister, we can't wait for you."

He tossed the rope again. This time Zenobia kept her eye right on it, caught it, and tied it between a couple of logs.

The deck of the boat was thick with soldiers.

"Make sure it's tight!"

"You all lay down!"

"We'll bring you on board a few miles down the river!"

Ned and Helen waved at the men. Lisa Mae was crying.

"Look sharp, the captain's going to start the engines." The sailor who'd thrown down the rope never took his eye off them. "You all hang on, now, no matter what happens. It's likely to get a mite rough."

They all lay down on the raft and took a good hold on Drayton's ropes.

"Well, we done made it to the boat," Zenobia breathed. But any relief she felt vanished when bullets started whizzing over their heads and striking the wooden hull of the boat. One bullet crashed into the side of the raft itself. The rope connecting the raft to the boat got real tight, then came a hard tug on the raft as the engine sped up. Zenobia felt the sudden surge of power as the paddle wheels took hold. The boat began to move.

Too fast! So much water was coming up over the edge of the raft, it was being pulled under. The whole front part of the raft was already submerged, and so were Zenobia's legs.

"We going down!" hollered Lisa Mae, trying to scramble to the other side of the raft.

"Auntie, save me!" Ned was in water up to his chest.

Helen had been swept off the raft and was holding on to one of the ropes Drayton had made.

Zenobia grabbed Ned and held him close, but she could feel herself slipping off the raft. Couldn't hold on, not fast as that ship was going.

"Don't let go of that rope, Helen!"

Lisa Mae screamed, "I can't hold on no more." The water was up to her neck.

Zenobia said a quick prayer and prepared to die. The whole raft was under water, covered over by a mass of big white bubbles thrown up by backwash from the rudder of the ship.

But now she felt the raft lift itself back out of the water, rock a few times, then steady itself and begin to drift.

Helen crawled back on.

Lisa Mae just cried and cried. "We almost made it," she said between sobs.

Zenobia looked up and saw a sailor waving a knife in the air. Must have used it to cut them free of the transport ship.

"Thanks, mister."

Most of the soldiers who'd been waving to them were now busy returning the fire of the grayboys. But two or three of them kept on waving and one yelled, "We'll be back for you someday!"

When she looked back down, she saw that the raft was floating toward shore. It wasn't long before they were close enough to make out the guns of the white men standing on shore, waiting for them.

CHAPTER FOURTEEN

Second Report
Headquarters Cavalry Forces
Vicksburg, Miss.,
December 4, 1864

Capt. F. W. Fox,
Assistant Adjutant-General

Captain—I have the honor to report that, pursuant to orders of the major general commanding, I moved with my command to Big Black railroad bridge on the morning of the twenty-third of November. On the morning of the twenty-seventh of November we marched at daylight, and the advance of a column under Major Cook, Third U.S. Colored Cavalry, cut the telegraph on the railroad below Deasonville, and in sight of Vaughn Station, at 12:30 P.M.

The railroad bridge across Big Black lies four miles below, without any approach save the railroad track, and artillery cannot be taken to it.

I am, Captain, very respectfully, your obedient servant,

E. D. Osband
Colonel Third U.S. Colored Cavalry
Commanding Cavalry Forces,
District of Vicksburg

"I tell you," Joe said, "them infantry boys has seen some things, but the way they talked about them poor colored women and children on that raft that was cut adrift . . . well, it must have been one sad sight."

He stopped pacing long enough to take the cup of coffee Betty handed him, then sat down on the bed.

"Said it made them feel mighty bad, like they was slaves again. There wasn't nothing they could do but stand there and watch the family float over to the Rebs."

"I'm sure they did everything they could, Joe."

"One of them said he kept wishing he had wings so's he could fly down there and pluck them off the raft, bring them safe back onto the boat."

Betty sat down on the bed beside him and rested her hand on his thigh. "Bet it got you to thinking about Zenobia, didn't it?"

He nodded.

"If it's God's intention, he'll bring her back to you."

"You think?"

"What I think is you don't have no control over what's happening, any more than me."

He leaned against her, rested his head between her breasts while she stroked his neck and back.

"All I know is I love you more than I've ever loved anybody, Joe Duckett. I hate to see you looking so down."

"Don't you ever get to feeling low, Betty?" He raised his head and studied her smooth brown face. "You don't never complain, you just go to work every day, and set here and wait for me every night, even when you know I ain't getting no leave. I'm getting mighty sweet on you."

She snuggled up close to him. "Don't you be mocking me, honey."

"I ain't, trust me, I ain't. Sometimes I feel like I'm almost going crazy— like you and Zenobia is all mixed up in my mind, like you is one woman."

Betty kissed him, then took a step back and began unbuttoning his shirt. "Don't really matter to me, honey . . ." And his trousers. ". . . long as I'm the one in your arms right now."

He pulled her to him and kissed her belly, ran his tongue up, between, and around her breasts. Beneath his tongue he felt her skin contract, felt the long shudder that seemed to run the length of her.

He laid her down gently so that she was beneath him. She locked her legs around him and drew him down deep into her, moving back and forth and up and down in a way that made him think of the first time he saw her dancing.

What old war?

* * *

Joe sat at attention on Princess while Captain Stiles rode back and forth inspecting Company A. Damned if they weren't back up on the Yazoo again—by now Princess pretty much knew the way by herself once they got off the boats. Hadn't had a single easy time of it, and by the look on the captain's face this one wouldn't be no different. They'd see in a minute.

"Top of the morning to you, men!"

"A good morning to you, Captain, sir!"

"Well, now, it is my great pleasure to tell you that your Uncle Sam thinks very highly of your conduct on the field of battle. You've been good and faithful fighters, and the story of your exploits on the Yazoo has echoed through our great nation, near and far. So great is your fame, in fact, that the army has given us the distinct honor and privilege of going to destroy that very same bridge that General McArthur's boys tried to take back in June."

A groan came from the men.

"Sounds like you know the one I mean," Stiles said with a grin. "That one up there in the swamps. We're going to take that railroad bridge on the Big Black River and take it Third Cavalry style. I don't need to tell you how heavily defended it is, or how important it is to our men in Nashville that it go down. The Rebs up in Tennessee are getting all their cotton and corn and hardtack over that bridge."

His horse skittered for a second and the captain paused long enough to settle him.

"We'll just follow Major Cook's orders like we always have and carry this one off in our usual style. He's never let us down once, and we won't let him down this time."

The captain had told Joe there were close to six thousand Reb troops up here in the Delta to protect the bridge and the town of Jackson. Command must have done some heavy planning on this thing.

That very same morning, their horses had gone clattering across the pontoon bridge on the Big Black River, but they headed east toward Jackson instead of upriver and north toward the Big Black River Bridge. Just like the army to tell you they wanted you to do one thing, then change around and do another.

But the captain said Jackson, and that's the direction they took, Joe leading the column. There was less resistance from the Rebs than they expected, so they moved a good ways that day. Come nightfall, the orders were to set up good strong bonfires, and soon the whole night was lit up. Bonfires every which way you looked.

Then, around midnight, the captain had come down the line and told everybody to be quiet, and make sure the horses didn't neigh. In the dead of night they skedaddled out of there heading back west, leaving the bonfires burning behind them.

Looked like the plan was to fool the Rebs into weakening their forces at the bridge, make them think the Third was headed toward Jackson so they'd concentrate their forces there. Joe was sure of this by morning when the Third led the column up the east bank of the Big Black River, north toward Benton—back once again in the country near Clifton.

After two days of marching, the regiment was ready to make the assault. At the first sight of the bridge, Joe had taken a quick sharp breath. Holy shit! An awful lot of colored men must have died building that thing. From the hill he was standing on, he could look down and see the railroad tracks stretching far off into the distance. And there, far away—he could barely see it—was some kind of building, perched on a hill that overlooked the bridge.

The railroad track bed was broken at several points by high trestlework, maybe sixty to seventy feet in the air. The trestles were real narrow, and the ties weren't much wider than the tracks.

There was a whole lot of space between each tie, and a long way to fall if a man, running hard, tripped on one of them. And to top it all off the whole damn shebang was built on a swamp. Into which he'd bet anything the Third Cavalry would soon be descending.

For there wasn't but two ways to get to that bridge—either march directly over the railroad tracks, or go down through the swamps. Couldn't get artillery close enough to blow it up, either. The wheels of the guns and caissons would sink in the marsh.

The way Captain Stiles explained it they were going to go both ways— over the tracks and through the swamps. The captain got all the officers and sergeants down from their mounts, then here Major Cook came to draw the details in the dirt. A company—that was Joe's—was going to go through the swamps on the north side of the railroad—B company was going to do the same thing on the south side of the railroad, and Major Cook himself would lead a company straight down the railroad track.

"But, boys," he said, "we've got one little problem when we reach that bridge. The Rebs have built a blockhouse that commands its approaches. Now, we've got us a pretty good plan, but this is not going to be like your morning promenade."

He scratched a few more lines in the dirt, two straight ones about an inch apart, and a big square where the lines ended. Except the major couldn't draw too well, so the square was a little lopsided.

"See, here's the bridge, and me and an assault company are going to go straight over it, right direct at that blockhouse."

Stiles pointed the stick to the sides of the bridge he'd drawn. "And here, while we're keeping them busy on the tracks, is where you other boys are going to come up from the swamps and fire at them when they come out of the blockhouse to get us."

He stood up and grinned. "Once you give them a good dose of the carbines' medicine, all the companies will re-form on the tracks, charge them, and take the blockhouse. Simple as that. Any questions?"

Joe had one big question, but he didn't figure there was any point in asking it. If that was all there was to it, how come the Rebs done throwed back two attacks already?

* * *

It was noon before everything was ready. Joe assigned two men to stay behind with the horses and had the rest check the Sharps carbines, and their Colts. "You got to act like infantry now," he told them. "Like Sherman's boys at Chickasaw Bluffs."

Finally, Major Cook waved Joe's company off, with Captain Stiles leading. Joe looked behind him. The men, some with their hats slouched over to one side, others with brims turned up in the front, slipped one by one down into the marsh until they were knee-deep in mud. Soon they were clawing their way through a god-awful tangle of vines and slimy moss-covered limbs long ago broken off from the trees towering above them. Here and there you could see where a bolt of lightning had struck and left its jagged mark on the shattered trunk of the tree. Thorny brambles tore at their uniforms.

For a November day, it was mighty hot. Mosquitoes hummed all around them, and even though you couldn't see them, the chiggers was probably having a feast. Seemed like every time Joe looked, Zack was scratching somewhere or slapping away at his face.

"Better watch it, you might slap the little sense you got right out of yourself."

"Still leave me with more sense than you—I ain't been captured by the Rebs no three times."

"They likes my company and my home cooking. Done come to expect it."

"And they expecting you to fall into their hands one more time, Sarge," Logan said. "And when you do—"

"Whee-ho!" said another. "Whee-ho! Them Rebs going to fight to see which one gets to stretch Sarge's neck first!"

"And don't let that Colonel Montgomery win," Zack said. "Oh no. He going to have all of his boys lined up to see what he going to do to Joe. Might even call a truce so's everybody can see he done caught him the Wizard. And then—"

"Silence back there." They still had a mile to go, but Captain Stiles didn't like any horseplay come fighting time.

The mud pulled so hard at Joe's foot his boot almost came off. The water was all the way up to his waist now.

"How'd they ever build that damn bridge?" Zack whispered.

"What I want to know," Joe whispered back, "is why." God didn't intend for no bridges to be built on such land, 'specially no railroad bridges. Just weeds and muck and buzzing insects everywhere. Be glad when this war was over. Now, at home—

He almost laughed out loud.

Home? Hadn't had no home since . . . He closed his eyes and saw Zee's face, those deep-set twinkling black eyes that knew all . . .

"Pass the word back. We're stopping here."

They were right under the bridge on the side opposite the stockade. If they moved a little higher on the riverbank, up into the thick clumps of bushes that dotted the hillside on their side of the bridge, they'd have the stockade—a hundred yards away from them on the other side of the river—right in their gun sights. Same for Company B on the south side.

The captain pointed to where he wanted the troops placed, just like he'd gone over it with them before. Joe nodded, gestured with his fingers, his head, sometimes his whole body, until he had the men moved quietly into position, right where the major wanted them. They had every sally port of the stockade under their guns. Only thing they could do now was wait for Major Cook to come along the railroad track.

A few rifle shots rang out from the blockhouse.

The major and his men must be coming into sight, the Rebs probably wondering if he was a fool or just plain crazy, coming down that track on foot, high up in the air, where they had a clear shot at them. Where would they be able to hide?

Wasn't no place. Joe was glad he wasn't the one coming up those tracks.

A heavy fire came out of the stockade, then the Rebs did just what the major wanted. Thinking they had old Major Cook on the run like they done the other Yankee regiments, they stormed out, all hot to chase the major and his men back down the railroad track.

"Steady, men!" Captain Stiles held up his hand. One mess-up and the Rebs would run right back instead of whooping it on down the tracks, shooting off their guns and their mouths.

"Come on back, niggers, we'll let you have the stockade for nothing, or near about—just a little lead."

Joe and his men were looking slightly down on the Rebs, spread out all along the track, when Captain Stiles gave the order.

"Fire!"

Caught in a crossfire that had them cursing and shouting and running, the Rebs managed to get back in the stockade, leaving a lot of dead and wounded men on the tracks. But it was all they could do to get a shot off, because the Third was pouring lead into that fort. Which meant it was only a matter of time before it fell.

Back on the hill on what was now the Third's side of the bridge, Major Cook had the bugler blow assembly. Led by Captain Stiles, half the boys who'd come through the swamps scrambled onto the railroad tracks and joined Major Cook's men to form three assault companies. The rest of the men kept peppering the blockhouse with a steady crossfire.

The major yelled over to Joe. "Come on with me! Your squad will lead the way. We've got to storm that blockhouse." He turned to the bugler. "Sound the charge!"

Lord, but he was a sight to see, running over those railroad ties with his saber pointing the way. And Joe—carbine strapped across his back, and a pistol in each hand—wasn't no more than a couple of steps behind, so he could see him good. Who'd of thought the major could move that fast?

Barely a shot came out of the Reb firing ports. Thank God for the troopers up on the hill.

The feel of the ground when he reached the other side of the bridge was solid and reassuring. Another minute and they'd be at the sally ports, then into that fort.

The bugler was blowing to beat all hell. That boy sure could blow that thing.

The Rebs had abandoned the firing ports and were now up behind wooden picket fences on the parapets of the fort firing down at Joe and his troops. But Third Cavalry was pouring off the railroad track and onto the ground. Soon as a hundred or so of them were there, Major Cook raised his saber again.

"Follow me!"

He ran right through a sally port the Rebs hadn't been able to close. Joe was now no more than a half-step behind him with nothing but Rebs in front—just as fighting mad as he was, and shouting to beat all hell.

A big-assed man in a red shirt, his bayonet fixed, came right at him. His eyes were smoking and he was yelling, "Nigger! Nigger! Nigger! Triflin' son of a—"

Joe sidestepped and shot him twice in the back.

Didn't have no time to think before two more were in his face, one of them swinging his rifle. Shit, that little-assed boy belonged home with his mama. Joe leveled the Colt in his left hand and shot him, then shot the other man dead between the eyes. The Rebs were fighting hard—some swinging rifles, others thrusting with bayonets—but everywhere he looked, they was giving ground.

* * *

Captain Stiles was putting his saber to good use over there. But it looked like he needed shooting support, so Joe moved up behind him. Zack must have had the same idea.

"See behind them sandbags over there?" he said. "That's where most of the fire coming from now. What say we knock 'em out?"

"Captain?"

"I heard. Do it!"

Joe turned and called back. "Tucker, Logan, Johnson, Mendenhall, front and center!" He pointed over to the sandbag cover: "Let's take 'em."

They ran across the courtyard, bullets whizzing all around them. One burned Joe's head, he felt it go right past his ear.

Hitting the sandbags at a dead run, they were up and over in no time.

Seeing Joe and his boys come over the sandbags—yelling like crazy, running through bullets like they didn't mean nothing to them—must of put a scare into the Rebs. They threw down their rifles every which way and took off like the devil himself was after them.

And when they ran, damned if the rest of the Rebs didn't, too. Right on up the hill behind their stockade, scattering like a bunch of flushed ducks.

"Bugler, sound Recall!" Major Cook said. "Captain Stiles, Sergeant Duckett—they'll be back soon and with plenty of reinforcements. Take fifty men, advance as far up that hill as you can, and set up a skirmish line. We need enough time to soak the bridge with coal oil. We'll sound Recall when we're ready to burn it, and then you'd do well to get your asses back down here real quick."

They formed into squads and marched up the hill behind the stockade till they met fire coming from the woods less than a hundred yards away. From a position in the grass about halfway up, the Third poured a steady fire into the woods.

Then things got quiet for about half an hour. Joe hoped the hell they was hurrying with that oil stuff. Some fifty men were filling their canteens with it. That should be enough to do the job.

The fire from the woods started up again thick and heavy—reinforcements must have arrived. A trumpet sounded, drums started beating, and a line of Rebs came marching out of the woods.

And who was that leading them, saber in the air?

"It's my old master, Captain."

"We have to protect that bridge. If you kill him in a fight, well and good."

The Rebs were moving steadily forward. By now, Joe could see that their drummer boy was colored.

"Get behind our line and direct the firing," the captain said. "Keep them steady now."

Joe dropped to one knee behind the center of the Yankee line. He was surprised at how steady he was, what with Massa Richard Kenworthy marching on him, proud as a peacock, looking like the cock of the walk. And mean.

"At the order only, Joe."

The Rebs were maybe forty yards away. What was the captain waiting for?

Massa Richard whooped and raised his saber. "Charge!"

The Rebs broke into a run.

The captain yelled, "Fire!"

The Reb line staggered and wavered, but kept on coming with Massa Richard close enough now for Joe to see how old he looked.

The men waited, disciplined and ready for the captain's next order, and when it came, the Rebel line wavered again. Massa Richard's shoulder was bloody, but he was still running toward them, hell-bent on breaking their line. He'd dropped his saber now and was waving a pistol.

Joe lost sight of him when the Rebs crossed into the Yankee lines and the hand-to-hand began. No time now to worry about anything but keeping himself alive and the Rebs away from the bridge. He pulled out his Choctaw war knife and just went to work.

Saw one man out of the corner of his eye aiming a pistol at him. Ducked down low and sprang at him like a mountain cat, stabbed him quick three times, felt him drop to the ground. Turned around in time to throw the knife into the chest of a gray-haired man who was trying to bayonet Zack. He helped Zack up, retrieved the knife, and ran on.

And there was Massa Richard. He had three Rebs around him, but Joe could get to him. Yes, he could.

"Joe, I'm hurt!" Captain Stiles called out. "Take command!"

What about Massa, there? Ready to take him back into slavery, and close enough to kill. But Joe knew his duty.

"Fall back, men," he said, calm as could be. "Right down there behind those rocks. Form a new line. Zack, get the captain."

A bullet tore through his sleeve. He ducked behind a boulder and looked around to see Massa with a Colt aimed in his direction.

"I got your boy, Joe. Come get him."

Did he mean Luke? No time to think about it now.

"Steady, boys, them Rebs are hurt bad, ain't going to be asking for much more."

He detailed two men to get the captain back to the bridge and got his men into a rhythm of firing again. And sure enough, the Rebs retreated back up the hill. For the time being, they'd had enough of the Third's carbines.

Joe kept his eyes up there on the woods where the Rebs had gone, thinking, hoping it was all over now—surely it was, with Massa Richard wounded. No, there was the sound of that drum beating again. That little colored boy had been so small and they'd tried not to shoot him but here the little feller came drumming again, a line of Rebs right behind him and Colonel Kenworthy behind them.

This time he didn't have a saber, couldn't have carried it nohow. But what the hell did he have?

Joe knew the answer when he heard first one bark, then two, then . . . shit! Sounded like a whole pack of dogs. The colonel, this time on a horse, was leading a bunch of men forward, and each of them had five or six hounds on a leash.

Hellfire and damnation!

Listing to one side on his horse, Colonel Kenworthy raised his hand, and advanced on Joe's lines at a trot, followed by his pack of hellhounds— must have been thirty or forty of them.

The colonel wasn't able to keep up with his men. A sergeant took the lead, breaking into a run. Just behind the dogs was a line of infantry. They was going to use those dogs like they was cavalry.

Joe had seen his men face a lot and stand strong. But dogs? Probably nigger dogs, trained to attack colored.

"Man, do you see what's coming?"

"Sarge, them's some mean-looking bastards."

"Shut the hell up! Them ain't nothing but dogs." Joe moved along the line. "You men that's got sabers, stand up right behind the men lying down with the carbines. Dogs get in here, hack them up. We ain't letting that bridge fall!" That damn Tucker was getting up like he was going to run. "Zack, put your pistol aside Tucker's head. If he move any way but forward, shoot him."

The barking was louder, and the Rebs was about twenty-five yards away. Colonel Kenworthy had to be way back now, but he wasn't so far that his voice didn't carry.

"Joe? Can you hear me, Joe? The nigger dogs are going to chew your black asses up."

"I hears you, all right. They going to try, just the way you tried to whup me under that pine tree that day. Come on, Colonel, I ain't scared of you and I ain't scared of your damned dogs!" He dropped to his knees. "Steady, men, fire when I give the command."

They were twenty, fifteen . . .

"Joe?"

He gave the command to fire at the same time the Rebs released the dogs.

"Sic 'em, boys, make the niggers run!"

The dogs leapt forth, yelping and barking like they'd been thrown a whole pailful of bloody red beef. When the volley from the carbines hit the dogs, there was a wild confusion of yelling and barking, men and dogs all tangled and wrestling in pools of blood on the slippery grass. A hellish mingling of screams and howls, punctuated by the sound of pistols and carbines exploding with quick flashes all over the field.

Joe tried to shut it out, worked with his Choctaw knife and his revolver, tried to ignore the coppery odor of blood mixed with smoke. Everywhere he looked, was nothing but hand-to-hand fighting or hand to throat. And the worst thing was, there wasn't no line no more.

A brown and white hound leapt for his throat. He stuck his knife right in the bitch's belly, but she had no more than fallen to the ground than another one was tearing at his arm. Joe swirled around so hard the dog went flying. He shot him in mid-air with the pistol.

"Fight, you poker-loving bastards—we the Third Cavalry!" he yelled. "Take more than hellhounds to finish us."

And now he saw that a group of his men had formed around him again, that there was a line. And little by little the barking got fainter and the firing seemed thinner, till he turned and saw only one bloodhound left, standing over a fallen Third man, tearing away at his throat. Joe threw the Choctaw knife right into its side and heard his own savage yell as the dog collapsed.

The Rebs were retreating at a trot, nary a dog in sight, and Colonel Kenworthy barely keeping up with them. Must be hurt pretty bad. That bastard wouldn't be back today.

But oh, what damage he had done. All around men lay dead and dying, torn and mangled and side by side with the dogs' bloody red carcasses strewn across the green field. The baying of wounded and dying dogs filled the air.

It was another long fifteen minutes before he heard them blow Recall down there at the bridge. Gradually, what was left of his men made their way down the hill, firing back at the Rebels as they went.

Major Cook was waiting. "Was that dogs I heard?"

All Joe could do was nod, but his grim look and the men's torn and bloody uniforms said the rest.

"God will have to forgive them, for I cannot. You and the men did yourselves proud, Sergeant."

"Sir? Captain Stiles?"

"He'll live. He's on the way back to the main unit. You'll take command of the company in his absence. Dismissed."

"Yes, sir."

* * *

Fifteen minutes later he watched the bridge burst into flames. The men were cheering.

Not Joe. Too many lay there on the field amid the dogs. And glad as he was they had succeeded, he finally had time to think about what Massa Richard had said. If it was true, that bridge burning over the Black River was cutting Joe off from his son.

He turned away at Major Cook's command to march. "Zack, did you hear what Massa said about my boy?"

"Don't worry, we get him someday—me and you alone if we have to."

"We got a war to fight, Zack. Get the men lined up. Major wants to tear up the railroad line to make sure that bridge is finished good and proper, and that's what we going to do next. Right?"

"Right. But I ain't forgetting."

The dust kicked up by the lifting of the railroad ties must have been visible for miles around. But thick as it was, the smell of the dirt couldn't take away the metallic stench of battlefield blood that stayed in Joe's nostrils.

CHAPTER FIFTEEN

"HEY there, you all, won't be long before we can have us some fun!"

Zenobia and the others on the raft faced six men, every one of them waving and shouting.

"That pretty little one with them big titties, she going to be mine." The man cupped his hand over his mouth and shouted out over the water. "Ain't you, honey?"

Helen squeezed Zenobia's arm. "I'm scairt, Auntie."

Zenobia hugged her tight. No sense in telling her that in another few minutes, when the raft drifted in a little closer to land, they would be delivered into the hands of deserters and irregulars. She could tell that's what they were from the way they was all dressed different from one another and from their wild shouting and yelling. They didn't obey no man's rules.

"Here, throw me that rope, I'll pull you ashore." One of the men came splashing through the water with his boots on, his hand outstretched for the rope.

Did she have any choice? The raft had been bobbing up and down on the river for the longest time, maybe an hour or two, before drifting in close to the little inlet bordered by tall pine trees. She'd kept praying the current would pick up, carry them on down the river and away from these men. But without the oars they had no control, no way of steering.

She tossed the rope, and the man put it over his shoulder and pulled. When the raft was about ten feet from shore, he stopped and turned around.

"You all get off now and wade the rest of the way. It won't come in any closer with all that weight on board. And watch yourself, don't want none of you pretty ladies getting hurt."

Zenobia had no more than set her foot on shore when a short man in a red woolen shirt lifted the hem of her skirt with the long barrel of his rifle and nodded.

"I'm mighty pleased the good Lord sent you and your fine-looking legs floating my way." He put his hand under her chin. "Now, you didn't have no intention of going nowhere else today, did you? Who you belong to?"

"Massa Richard Kenworthy," Zenobia said. The truth could get them sent back, but by the look of these men that might be less dangerous.

"Oh, everybody in these parts has heard about him," one of the men said. "But he don't have no plantation left, way I heard it."

"Don't make no difference nohow," the short man said. "We ain't got no practical way of returning these niggers to him even if we planned to, which we don't." He turned to a long skinny man with a patch over one eye. "Take them back to camp—we'll decide later on what we're going to do with them."

Helen was trying hard not to cry. She had grabbed Ned's hand, and now Zenobia grabbed hers.

"Don't worry, honey. They take care of us, now they know we belongs to Massa Kenworthy."

"She got that right, children." The man was smiling, but all the smile did was twist his ugly features. "We sure enough going to take care of you. Now get a move on, you niggers."

* * *

Seemed like they walked all afternoon long, but it was still light when they came to a big opening in the woods with tents all over, and lots of white men. There was a little stockade for their horses. The man led them across the camp to a big fire where some colored men and women were cooking.

"Nichols, these some niggers we picked up off the river this afternoon. Take care of them till Captain Odom decides what we going to do with them."

"Yessuh, with pleasure, suh."

The white man snatched up a piece of barbecued chicken and walked off.

Zenobia glanced around her. Looked like about ten colored folk here, mostly men, except for two old ladies. It was probably their job to cook and do the laundry, take care of the horses for the white men.

"My name is Nichols Brown—what's yours, now?" His skin was yellow, and his head bald and shiny.

"Zenobia. This here's Ned. And Lisa Mae and Helen. You got any dry clothes we could put on?"

He said something to one of the colored women, who walked away and returned in a few minutes with a pile of clothes.

"Come on." She led them into a tent with eight pallets on the floor. "When you all get dressed, come outside, we give you something to eat."

"Zee, what we going to do?" Lisa Mae was trying to find a way to hold up a pair of baggy trousers.

Zenobia rummaged on the floor in the pile of rags and handed her what looked like an old sash. "Must be something in here for Ned. All of you got to put on as many extra clothes as you can. Be cold here at night, and it might be even colder where I'm thinking about going."

"You're not—"

"I surely am. We among some evil people, best to get away from them."

The woman poked her head back into the tent. "Come on out and eat."

The corn bread and bacon Nichols Brown fed them was as good as anything Zenobia had ever eaten. But even telling him what a good cook he was didn't seem to make him happy. Zenobia wondered if he ever smiled.

"Tell me about these white men," she said. "Not a one of them in uniform Who are they?"

"Thieves and robbers, that's who they are. They ain't in nobody's army. Fight everybody that come near them. On the run from everybody and stealing from everybody."

"How long you been with them?"

Nichols put his hand under his chin. "Seems like forever. I were the head man's driver for many a year, then followed him off to the wars. I been everywhere, my sister, anyplace you can think of. Up in the Tennessee mountains, over in them Arkansas swamps, and last year up in Virginny. That were the prettiest place I ever did see."

"You talk about it mighty nice," she said.

"Well, when you travels a lot, it do something to your thinking. Make you want to live other ways, do other things." He looked at her for a moment, then shrugged. "Anyways, while we was in Virginny—you know it ain't as hot up there as it is down here—the Yankees was shooting cannons at us every day."

"They does a lot of that down here too," Zenobia said.

"And finally, old Massa just got tired. Said, 'Nichols, my African friend, we going home, find us another way to pass our time. I come up here to fight Yankees, not sit here in a fort and let them fire away at us with them big guns.' Had some ideas, he said, 'bout how we going to make a living now that the plantation's gone. So we got on the railroad train and come home."

Zenobia looked around the campsite at the stacks of rifles and boxes of ammunition.

"Yep," said Nichols, following her glance. "He got the notion to stop fighting and start robbing. Done made me into a thief. And I fears my God!" He mopped his brow with a white towel he had tucked under his belt. "Feel sorry for you and the young 'uns. I'se going to do my best to help you, now he done put you in my charge. But you got to help me, too. Pull your share of the work and do what I say and it might not be so bad for you here."

He studied her face for a long moment. "Sister, you ain't even listening to me—you trying to figure a way out of here. And there ain't none!"

"I respects what you said, Nichols Brown, and I don't want to cause you no trouble, but I got to consider the children."

"Then you'll stay right here and let me figure out a way to help them," he said. "You done fell into the hands of Captain John Odom. Onliest chance you got is if he decide to sell you to some slave speculator."

He pointed with his thumb back over his shoulder to where five hound dogs were tied up.

"That man just love chasing niggers," he said. "Wait. I want you to see something." He hollered out to one of the colored men. "William, come on over here and show them your back."

From neck to waist it was nothing but big, thick scars. Looking at them, Zenobia shuddered.

"He tried to run away," Nichols said. "See now, Captain Odom, he just love the runaways. Back on the plantation, he might let folk go for two or three days just to make it harder for him to catch them. Say he don't like no easy game. But he ain't never failed to catch one yet, and when he do— once he gets his hands on you, that man sure know how to play a whip."

Some men galloped into the camp. Nichols Brown pointed to the short one in the red shirt leading them. "There he be. The one and only Captain John Odom."

"That little one in front?"

"Don't be fooled by his size. I reckon he about the meanest man alive. If they's any meaner, I hope I never meet him."

Captain Odom and his men left their horses with William and another colored man and sat down at long tables in an oak grove a fair distance from the cooking area.

"Nichols, where's the damned food?"

"Coming, Massa." He looked around at Zenobia, Lisa Mae, and Helen. "You girls stay back here and dish the food out. Better that way. Me and this boy here—your name Ned, right—we'll take these plates over to them."

"Corn whiskey!"

Nichols stumbled over himself in his haste to pour the whiskey and get the cups to them.

"Hurry up, Ned, Massa don't like to be kept waiting."

Once all the food and the whiskey were on the table, the men quieted down. Thieving and robbing all day must be hungry work. Zenobia and Lisa Mae washed bowl after bowl, stealing glances at men eating with their fingers just like they was field niggers.

They sure could drink. Seemed like no sooner had Nichols taken one jug over to them than they were hollering for another.

Zenobia counted twenty men, more ugly white people than she'd ever seen together at one time. Some had scars, others had hair like nothing on earth, and one man's beard was might near down to his belt. A few of them wore old grayboy pants. And there was one who looked like a full-blooded Indian. He wore a big round hat with a feather in its band and a big Yankee belt buckle on the front.

Captain Odom fired his pistol in the air. "Nichols, where's the music?"

"Coming, Massa. William, bring the guitar, I got the banjo. Mitchell, you get the bones."

By now other men were shooting off their pistols into the air. Must be mighty happy they'd caught some colored folks today.

"You all get in the tent and stay there," Nichols said. "He loves his women something awful."

Zenobia thanked him, then led the others into the tent where they huddled together on a cot. The men started their singing with "Dixie," and must have sung it ten or fifteen times, a little louder each time. The banjos and guitars were twinging and twanging and the coloreds was singing as loud as the whites. After a while it seemed like they were quieting down, then the captain called out: "Sing 'John Peel,' Nichols."

> *"Do ye ken John Peel*
> *With his coat so gay?*
> *Do ye ken John Peel*
> *At the break of day?*
> *Do ye ken John Peel*
> *When he's far far away?*
> *With his hounds and his horn*
> *In the morning."*

Sounded like all the white men joined him for the second verse.

> *"'Twas the sound of his horn*
> *Called me from my bed*
> *And the cry of his hounds*
> *Hath me oftimes led*
> *For Peel's view halloo*
> *Would awaken the dead*
> *Or a fox from his lair*
> *In the morning!"*

Nichols's voice floated above all the rest. Poor old Nichols, she hoped they didn't shoot him—though that might be better than . . . she remembered the fear in his voice when he talked about that whip.

"Lisa Mae, we got to get out of here right now. All of us."

"But, Zee, you heard what Nichols said. If we—"

"I heard, but I heard, too, about mens like these—know what they going to be hollering for in a few minutes."

"But, Zee—"

"And after they gets it, they's going to beat us and likely kill us. We better off with the dogs tearing us up." She was quiet for just a few seconds, busy cutting a hole in the tent with her knife. "Grab that extra blanket, and give me your feet, you-all. Quick!"

Ned giggled. "That tickles, Auntie. What you doing?"

"Hush! It's cayenne pepper. Dogs hate it. I stole it while Nichols was cooking up those barbecued ribs."

She stepped out into the darkness and looked up. Thank goodness, no moon, but there was the North Star. Which way to go? Should they try to go back to the raft? They could make it to the river in about an hour and a half. But that's the way the white men would figure they'd go. Besides, what use was it without some way to steer it? No, they'd go the other way, off into those woods there. And trust in God.

"Come on, quick now, they's starting another song."

With Ned at her side, Zenobia started walking as fast as she could, pushing bushes aside as she headed into the dark woods.

If there was a path, they never found it. The branches of the trees kept tearing at their faces, and when Zenobia touched her cheek, she found it was bleeding.

"Auntie, don't go so fast," Ned said. "I can't go so fast."

"Don't get tired, honey, don't you hear how that singing is lower now? We getting away."

They were deep into the woods before she finally looked back. No campfires in sight. No singing within earshot. But they had to keep going, put as much space between them and those men as possible.

She was sweating something awful, even though it was cold. Like the children, her feet were bare, but she was used to that. She wasn't used to being in charge of others, even herself, but God had given her Lisa Mae and Ned and Helen, and she had to lead them to freedom.

Of course, right now she was leading them all back into the land of the grayboys. But hadn't she just walked right out of that camp? And wouldn't they be some mad white boys when they came looking for their colored women?

* * *

They arrived at a little clear spot in the woods as day was breaking and sat under a big magnolia tree, its trunk spread out thick and wide, like a little seat for them. She put her arms around Helen and Ned.

"First thing we got to do this morning is thank God that He done watched over us—brought us this far. Ned, you can pray."

"But I don't know what to say."

"Just close your eyes and God will give you the words."

He scrunched up his eyes, but it took the words a while to come.

"Jesus, it was real scary out here in the woods last night. I didn't tell Zenobia, but I seen devils leaping out the trees at us with pitchforks and all. But the angels, they was dressed in white, kept telling them devils not to touch us, we God's childrens— don't touch them. And they sure enough didn't, so I thanks you. Amen, Jesus."

"I know for sure God going to hear such a sweet prayer," Zenobia said. "I don't know where we are now, and I don't know where we going to go from here. But you was all strong during the night, and I got a little surprise for you."

She pulled out some corn bread she'd wrapped in an apron and hidden under her skirt last night before they left.

"See, you learned something last night, Ned. You was tired, but you didn't give up. Now that man Nichols, he ain't no bad man, matter of fact he a good man. But them dogs and that old captain done scared him to death, so's they don't even have to worry about him running away. But we looked at them same old dogs and wasn't scared. And we ain't nothing but some womens and a little boy." She stood Ned up. "I want you to take a good look all around you, now. You see any dogs here?"

"No."

"You see anything after us?"

"Yes."

"What?"

"A lot of soldiers."

Pulling him down quick, Zenobia crept up to where he'd been and sure enough, right down there next to a road was a big camp of grayboys just waking up. As she watched, a man came out and blew a bugle to make sure they all got up.

Zenobia sat back down. They'd just wait till . . .

"Look, Zee." Lisa Mae pointed down where they'd just come from. That Injun with the Yankee buckle on his hat was headed straight for them, a rifle in one hand and the lead for one of them bloodhounds in the other.

He shaded his eyes, looked up right where they were.

"Only one thing to do," Zenobia said.

They started running down the hill, straight for the gray-boys' camp.

CHAPTER SIXTEEN

WILL Stiles raised his hand to ask a question, but Colonel Osband waved him off and continued his briefing of the officers assembled in front of him. They were on the transport *Morning Star* and would be landing in Memphis shortly.

"Gentlemen, we've got these Rebs right where we want them, and now we're going to rip the state wide open, from the Tennessee border straight down to Vicksburg. Tear up every foot of railroad track we find, destroy anything that can be used to feed or clothe the Rebs, and free every Negro we can. Every able-bodied colored man will be enlisted into the army." He nodded at Stiles. "Now, Will."

"You think that will stop all those pesky cavalry raids on our supply lines, Colonel?"

"You bet your boots it will. General Grierson's going to throw three brigades of cavalry against them. I'll be in command of the Third Brigade, and together we are going to bring these Rebs to their knees."

* * *

Three days later, Will Stiles led his company out of Memphis as part of the column. Sickness and wounds and death had depleted their numbers badly, and Will was still wearing a bandage around his head where a bullet had creased him—knocked him unconscious at Big Black Bridge.

December 21, 1864. So close to Christmas, and yet he'd almost forgotten there was anything like Christmas still left in this world. Eunice had sent a special package—Lord, he missed that sweet woman—and he had shared the cookies with Joe. And she wrote him most every day. Joe was always teasing him about her writing him so much. Probably because he never got any letters himself... of course he didn't. How could he? He and most of the men were just beginning to learn to read and write.

And even if he had been able to read well, who would he hear from? His Zenobia? His daughter? Joe had no idea where either of them was, no way of letting them—or his son Luke—know where he was.

A voice sang out:

> "*If you see my mother*
>   *Oh, yes!*
> *Won't you tell her for me*
>   *Oh, yes!*
> *I'm a ridin' my horse on the battlefield*
>   *Oh, yes!*
> *I want to see my Jesus in the morning!*"

Will looked back over the long line of colored troopers behind him. They were freshly mounted on horses recently procured from anywhere the army could find them. Fine soldiers, strong and good-natured men— but practically every one of them had a story like Joe's. Mothers, fathers, sisters, brothers, children, scattered to the wind. All they really had was the army—the United

States Cavalry. And maybe that was the way the army should function. Be their family till the real one came along.

All along the column they took up the melody.

> *"Ride on King Jesus*
> *Ride on, you conquering King!"*

They sure loved to sing. Seemed to give them a sense of peace and strength. Well, they were sure going to need it on this trip. From what the colonel had said, they'd be stirring up a hornets' nest. Easy enough to say the Rebs were almost beaten, what with Sherman about to take Savannah, but that didn't seem to make them any easier to fight. And they were particularly fierce when they were fighting colored troops.

But his men would be ready for them. This was going to be a swift-moving column—each man had two days' worth of rations and forty rounds of ammunition, with the other supplies on pack mules. They were going to live off Mississippi land. What they didn't eat, they'd destroy.

"Damn."

He felt the raindrops on his hat. Rain would make it hard on the new horses, not used to the wear and tear a trooper put on them. Will tightened the green scarf he wore around his neck and prepared for the long uncomfortable ride ahead.

* * *

That first night they camped out in a bare field. It was already a wet and soggy mess, and then the sleet started up. Since they'd packed light the men didn't have any protection from the weather except to sit around the few fires they somehow managed to get going, shivering even with blankets over their shoulders. Will was accustomed to the cold, didn't mind it so much, but what must it be like for these men so much more used to dealing with unbearable heat?

He saw Joe and Zack huddled with a group of troopers around a fire.

"Mind if I join you, men?"

"Not at all, sir," Joe said.

Will knelt down beside them. "I want you to hear this news from me. This is my last time out. I'm being reassigned to Washington for some staff work with the Bureau of Colored Troops. They seem to think my experience will come in handy."

"What?" Joe said. "When did the orders come, sir?"

"Just before we left Memphis. I told Colonel Osband I didn't want the assignment, but the army's not much interested in what I want."

He rubbed his hands together to warm them, put them to his mouth and blew on them.

"Something else. They've commissioned a colored soldier, name of Swails, in the Fifty-fourth Massachusetts. Something I've been thinking ought to be done for some time. I'm recommending that Joe take over the company as a second lieutenant. You can pass the word around. Naturally, there's a lot of channels to be gone through before he can be mustered, and Joe will remain a top sergeant in the meantime, but I thought you'd like to know."

Joe and the others sat quietly. Had to be quite a surprise to them.

"I think Joe can handle things pretty well—don't you, Zack?"

"Lieutenant Joe . . ."

They all laughed then and began patting Joe on the back.

"Yes, sir, I believe he do just fine, but we're going to miss you something terrible."

Joe looked embarrassed. "I feel the same way, but . . . well, see you fellows in the morning. Sorry I couldn't arrange better weather on this first night out." He got up. "I'll walk with you a ways, sir. I don't hardly know what to say, sir, how to thank you . . ."

"No need to, Joe. You earned it."

"All the same, I . . . I thanks you." They walked on in silence for a bit.

"Going to be rough without you, sir. You know, I don't mean the fighting, because we can do that, but you been a good friend, too."

"I'm not leaving forever. Remember? I'll be back when the war ends. You haven't forgotten what I talked about, have you?"

"No, sir, I ain't forgot. I reckon what with the other things on my mind, I just don't think too much of what it's going to be like when the war is over. There's a heap too many Rebs between me and that day, Captain."

"Well, I'm not forgetting. I'll be back."

* * *

By Christmas Day, not having met any serious resistance, the column was in Tupelo, Mississippi, dead in the center of Forrest's country. But much of the venom had been drawn out of that particular rattlesnake's mouth. While the Third Cavalry stayed in Tupelo, one of the other regiments hit the town of Verona, about seven miles away. Hit it around nightfall, and Forrest's men just disappeared. Left the town and all their supplies right there.

So while the men didn't have a real Christmas, they did have a spectacle of sorts. The whole town burned, and it was something to see, close to three hundred tons of ammunition going off, and bullets and shells exploding all over. Old Bedford Forrest must be crying somewhere. You could see the explosions easy from Tupelo. In the midst of the miserable weather it gave the men something to cheer about.

The next few days were spent tearing up the railroad tracks in every direction around Tupelo. Still no enemy resistance. Will thought it all seemed too easy, especially when they reached Okolona. Intelligence had intercepted a dispatch saying the Rebs would make a stand there, and with the railroad running into the town, General Grierson expected a hard fight.

But then the close to three thousand colored and white cavalrymen came winding out of the woods and fell smartly into formation. Line after line of blue-clad men, horses pawing the ground, the Stars and Stripes flapping in the cold December wind, and regimental standards held proudly aloft by color sergeants. Second New Jersey Cavalry, Fourth Missouri Cavalry, Seventh Indiana Cavalry, First Mississippi Mounted Rifles, Third and Fourth Iowa Cavalry; Tenth Missouri Cavalry, Fourth and Eleventh Illinois Cavalry, Second Wisconsin Cavalry, and the Third United States Colored Cavalry. When the men in the garrison saw all that, they had to have become weak of heart. Still they didn't show the white flag.

Then the trumpets—all twenty of them in the Third Cavalry—blew the charge. Will, sitting high in the saddle on his brown bay, raised his saber. At the command the bay began to trot, then canter, and with the shout "At a gallop!" the long column swept right at the town, yelling and whooping, expecting the Rebs to open fire any minute now.

Will was riding so hard his hat blew off. He took a quick glance back and saw his men galloping as fast as he was, their sabers raised high in the air. At the edge of the town the Union column split, the Third Cavalry with those going to the left. Had to sound to the Rebs like all of Hades was riding down on them, and the next thing he saw was a white flag fluttering from the ramparts of the Rebel stockade. They hadn't fired. Not a single shot.

That night another bonfire lit up the sky for miles around as the Reb supplies and ammunition, including wagons captured from the Union Army at Brice's Crossroads, were destroyed and rendered useless to the enemy. In the days that followed, they tore up more railroad tracks. And took prisoners, scores of them. By now, just a few days before the New Year, they had almost five hundred of them, including many former slaves who had been impressed into service by the Confederates.

But despite such heavy losses, the Rebs weren't finished. It was like you can be wrestling a man, and think you've almost got him, then he pulls some kind of move or you feel some strength there you didn't at first, and you know you're in for a battle. Will heard it in the hostility and smart comments of the white prisoners, sensed it in the way bushwackers hung on the flanks of the regiment. You could just feel these Rebs, whose domain had been invaded, getting together to destroy the Yankees running loose in their backyard.

You had to give them credit. They definitely made a stand at Egypt Station. Will and Joe watched from a spot where the Third Cavalry was being held in reserve. These Rebs had no intention of allowing the 1st Brigade of the Union Cavalry to advance. It took some serious fighting to drive them out of the woods and into the open plain that surrounded Egypt Station.

"I'd say those boys in the First Brigade are lining up just like they did back at Okolona, Captain."

"I just hope we get the same results. That's a lot of open space to charge across. Get the men ready. We're going right behind them as soon as the colonel gives the signal." Will raised his binoculars: "There they go."

The Union line swept forward at the trot, then the gallop. The captain swept the glasses along the fence of the Rebel stockade. It seemed unnaturally still.

The 1st Brigade was very close to the stockade when what sounded like thunder exploded from the front of that fort. It was awful. Close to a thousand men in the charge and at least that many Rebel muskets all going off at the same time. Not since Shiloh had Will seen anything like it. Union horses and men down all over the field. The charge was broken.

No time to think about that. He looked down the front of his own line. Colonel Osband had raised his saber. Will followed suit and the Fourth Illinois and the Third Cavalry moved at a fast trot to a position on the south side of the fort—away from the crushing gunfire coming from the front, where the 1st Brigade was trying to re-form itself.

The Fourth Illinois swept around the side of the fort, and Will ordered his men to dismount. Their orders were to assault the fort from the south on foot.

"Sergeant Duckett, get the horse holders up here."

The men, shouting now, moved into a long line, ready for the assault. Somebody in the fort must have decided to pay attention to them, because scattered fire began to fall among them and two or three men went down.

"On your knees, men! Make a smaller target."

Why didn't the colonel give the order for the assault? They were sitting ducks.

"Bugler, sound the charge!"

The men gave a loud hurrah and began advancing on the fort just as a white flag was raised over the stockade. A few minutes later, the men of the Fourth Illinois who'd ridden into the rear of the stockade were running up the Stars and Stripes. They'd saved the Third Cavalry what would have been a costly charge.

One minute he was saying to Joe, "Our luck seems to be holding up," and the next wishing he hadn't. A shell burst right in the middle of the company.

Joe swept his glasses over toward a train on the railroad track. Damn, a whole trainload of Reb infantry was jumping off it. They began to form up in a skirmish line about three-quarters of a mile away, lining up smartly as their band played "Dixie." Definitely regulars.

He wasn't surprised when Colonel Osband said the Third Cavalry was to be the rear guard, hold the Rebs off while the rest of the column moved off with the prisoners. So many times, out of all the companies in the regiment, his was asked to be the first one out there.

"Joe, get the men off the horses and deploy them as skirmishers. We've got to keep those Rebs off the main column. The rest of the regiment will back us when they form up."

Smooth as clockwork, the men fell in and began advancing. When they were about a hundred yards from the Reb line, Will ordered them to their knees and they commenced rapid fire.

The train must have been carrying close to four companies of men and they kept on coming. With the music going, they seemed to pick up their steps. And their fire.

Joe, behind the line, was steadying the men as usual. "We men of war— we the fighting Third."

Zack was loading, aiming, and firing like he'd been a soldier all of his life. To a man, the company was making those Sharps sing. But it wasn't stopping the Rebs. Joe saw his men falling right and left. There wasn't any cover.

Finally, at the last minute, when it looked for sure like the Rebs would overrun them, the regimental bugler sounded Recall. Will looked back and saw the whole regiment, all eight hundred of them, lined up behind him, sabers drawn. A beautiful sight to the remaining men in his company, a signal to retreat for the Rebs!

"Let's get the hell out of here, Joe."

* * *

That night, long after the rest of the column was in bed, the Third Cavalry, still acting as rear guard, came into camp.

At officers' call the next morning, Colonel Osband assigned Will to ride along the entire length of the column and report its general condition. The colonel was interested, in particular, in the prisoners and the colored refugees.

Will rode off early in the morning. First thing he saw was how few horses had survived yesterday's action. Many cavalrymen were doubled up and some were even on foot. The Third Cavalry alone had lost nearly a third of its mounts. But the friendly waves he got from the men—both black and white—as he made his way down the column was reassuring. The Third Cavalry and its officers had definitely earned their spurs, and they knew it.

Nothing he'd ever seen had prepared him for the condition of the prisoners. Even the ones who weren't obviously sick or wounded were a pitiful sight, and up close, he could only marvel that these men had offered such fierce resistance. They looked half starved, walking along in rags, most of them without shoes, some lucky enough to have Union blankets around their shoulders. They didn't look like they'd washed in months. Well, neither had the Union boys, but at least their clothes were intact.

They were marched along, guarded sometimes by colored troops who treated them with a forbearance, even kindness, that surprised him. More than once he saw them sharing food or gear, extending a hand to help a prisoner who had fallen. Will wasn't sure he would have been able to do the same if—

What the devil was that commotion up ahead? As he got closer he saw it was hogs, must have been a thousand of them, snorting and rolling in the mud while a bunch of cavalrymen tried to drive them along.

He rode up to a sergeant: "What the hell is this?"

"Orders, sir. To deny food to the Rebs. Colonel said to drive them down to Vicksburg to feed our army."

"To Vicksburg? Good God—that's at least a hundred and fifty miles from here."

"Don't I know it, sir. And these some ornery critters—got their own sense of direction."

"From what I can see, their only sense of direction is down in the mud."

The sergeant said, "Well, sir, if all else fails, we could have us one hell of a barbecue."

A little farther along Will heard a long-drawn-out moaning sound that seemed as if it was coming out of the earth. A deep sound—not a moan, a song. He reined in slightly, listened intently, and recognized the tune.

"Oh, freedom, oh freedom
Oh, freedom over me
And before I'd be a slave
I'd be buried in my grave
Go home to my lord
And be free!"

His boys sang it all the time—but there weren't hundreds of them, there weren't women and children singing. It sounded like a heavenly chorus, and when Will rode over the crest of the road and saw the mass of black men, women, and children coming behind the army, he came to a complete halt, as stunned by the sight as the sound.

Stretched out before him was what seemed to be an endless stream of Negroes, as if the Mississippi earth had opened up and borne this fruit. As far as the eye could see there was nothing but the peoples of Africa.

He edged his horse forward. Many of the men carried picks and shovels. The army was already making pioneers, construction men, out of them. Women, in white night shirts, their hair twisted in long braids, carried infants and led toddlers by the hand. Young boys and girls wore the same long shirts of coarse cotton or burlap. He looked at their feet and saw how few of them had shoes in this forty-degree weather, looked at their faces and saw the eyes of old men and women. But they pointed and smiled as he rode past, called out, "Yessuh, Yankee soldier!" And at the sight of a passing colored trooper they shouted and clapped their hands.

Riding slowly along the long column, Will stopped occasionally to smile at a child. And at a woman, one he was sure he would never forget. She was tall and beautifully made, figure and face. But what drew him to her wasn't her beauty so much as her bearing. Even here in the midst of what had to be a wilderness to her, in plain cotton and shoeless as the rest, she carried herself as if she was at home with everything. With her were a young boy, a pretty girl of about fourteen, and a young woman about twenty.

The woman looked up when Will spoke to her, but only for a second.

"Where do you come from?" he asked.

"We was washing clothes for the grayboys in Okolona."

The thought of a woman this lovely among the Rebs made him flinch.

"Is there anything we can do for you right now?"

She glanced at Will before answering. "Nothing that don't need to be done for everybody here." She waved her hand to embrace the whole column. "We all needs warm clothing and more food, but you boys are doing your best. At least we free—and that will do us just fine for now."

Will tipped his hat and rode on. He just hoped they'd be able to get them to Vicksburg safely.

* * *

When he returned that afternoon and gave his report, his voice shook a little when he described the long line of refugees and their singing. As for the hogs, he had strong recommendations. They had to be killed—they were holding up the progress of the column and could not be left behind for the Rebs. The colonel agreed to arrange it. But Will and his men wouldn't be around for the barbecue.

"Your regiment is breaking off. I want to free up the Third Cavalry for offensive action. The other two brigades will escort the refugees and the prisoners. We'll meet down in Yazoo City."

CHAPTER SEVENTEEN

JUST before going off to inspect the refugee column, Captain Stiles detached Joe to serve as a scout for a white company ordered to make a side raid on the town of Bankston, Mississippi. Said Captain Gomillion had requested him by name, because he'd heard Joe knew the country thereabouts.

Wasn't there any other man in the regiment who could scout? And in such cold weather!

He could think of lots of things he'd rather be doing than riding down the town's main street alongside Gomillion on this quiet, powerful cold night. At least the Rebs weren't shooting or otherwise raising hell.

He led a detachment on through the town, past a big cotton mill, a flour mill, and a shoe factory, scouting the area just beyond the town and posting sentries all around to give the alarm should any Rebs be coming down the road.

When he returned, Captain Gomillion was standing in front of the cotton mill. Nearby, pacing back and forth, was a tall skinny white man in nothing but his nightclothes.

"Oh, God . . ." The man stopped pacing. "Why are your men lighting those torches, Captain?"

Gomillion took no notice of him, turned instead to one of his men.

"Sergeant, take a squad through these buildings, make sure nobody is in there."

"I repeat, sir, what is the purpose of those torches?" The skinny man moved in front of Gomillion so he was between him and the building. "I demand an answer. Is it your intention to burn these buildings?"

The sergeant returned with another man in tow. "Found this fellow in there, sir, but it's all clear now."

"Thomas, you're the mayor, can't you make them stop? They're pouring tar oil all over the floors in there."

Joe almost felt sorry for the mayor. Hard to exercise authority without your clothes on. But the guy kept on trying.

"By what authority do you intend to commit this act of arson? I can have you arrested for this, you know."

The captain didn't look the least bit worried. "It's cold out here," he said. "My men have been riding all day, they need a fire to keep them warm."

"You're mad, sir, a pyromaniac. Would you burn down two buildings to keep your men warm? Take a people's livelihood away from them?"

Gomillion turned to the sergeant. "Burn them."

"I'll report this, sir, to the proper authorities. You'll be held legally responsible,"

"Well, that's as may be, sir. But next time old Bedford Forrest comes this way looking for supplies, you give him General Grierson's compliments and tell him he and his men are welcome to anything we leave behind."

* * *

By morning there was nothing left of the factories but a pile of smoldering ashes. When Joe rode by with the cavalry on their way south to tear up more railroad track, the mayor was still standing there.

"Damn you, damn you all to hell!"

Joe trotted right on past him without a trace of the pity he had felt last night. Everybody loses something in a war.

* * *

Richard Kenworthy was back where he wanted to be, protecting the lines of communication against the Yankee raids. He had been transferred, along with a regiment of men from the bridge, to General Adams's cavalry. It wasn't the same as riding with Bedford Forrest, but it was cavalry all the same.

Looking around the pretty little church in the small town of Franklin, Mississippi, he wondered if it would still be standing at the end of the day. He'd just received word that they'd practically burned Bankston to the ground and were on their way here. The loss of those factories was sure to make a bad situation even worse. Without a way to keep the troops supplied, there was no hope of slowing the tide of desertions that were hurting them worse than anything. The boys who remained still had a lot of spunk, thank God. They'd need every ounce of it, with Grierson's boys tearing down the railroad system mile by mile and destroying everything in their path. Damn Yankee locusts. They'd get a warm reception when they came down this way.

Turning his mind to the task at hand, Richard put his hand on Captain Johnston's shoulder.

"You take over here, I'm going outside to make a final check, see that all is in order. Those Yanks are going to wish they never laid eyes on this town."

After leaving the church, he rode around the other positions. The troops placed just as General Adams wanted, several companies hidden in the woods, and the junction of the road where the church stood well covered. When the Yankees came up, they'd be driven off the road and into an open field. The two companies of cavalry he'd concealed across the bridge stood ready to break the point of the Union column when they came into view. Panic them and send them scurrying back to Memphis like the rats they were.

He looked over his column. He'd fought with these men so many places now, the names had become a blur. One battle after another—didn't matter which way you turned the Yankees were always there—losing men, losing horses, but always coming back at you strong as ever. They wouldn't be satisfied until Mississippi was a barren land, smoking from one end to the other. He would never, ever understand how Christian men, white men, could harbor such malice in their hearts.

Richard glanced at his watch: twelve-fifteen. Wouldn't be long now.

He turned to Sergeant Barclay. "Send somebody back there to check on our body servants—especially Luke. Some of them boys are looking mighty restless. Make sure he keeps a sharp eye on them when the battle starts, and when they catch sight of those colored troops—"

A scout galloped up. "They're coming! A column of nigra cavalry about two miles down the road."

Good! Probably Joe's bunch.

He rode forward to where the two roads came together and took a quick look up the road with his binoculars. They were coming, all right. And they were coloreds. This time he'd be the one doing the surprising.

Richard rode back to his column. "Ready, men. Just like General Forrest taught us. No sabers, just the Colts. Going to put so much scare in those boys, they'll wish they were back on a peaceful plantation shucking corn and eating watermelon."

Not much of a joke but he wasn't surprised to hear laughter all along the line—more from tension than his wit, most likely. When the coloreds came swinging around over the bridge and down that road . . .

"Any of you see a nigra top sergeant with what looks like Injun hair, leave him to me." He raised his revolver over his head. "Column forward." He heard the sound of the pounding hooves behind him and settled into that old rhythm. He loved the smell of hot horseflesh, loved the feel of the moist skin under his hand. God, it felt good to be cantering again. Right on over the bridge.

As he passed the church, Captain Johnston waved him on. "Tan their hides good, Colonel."

The colored cavalry came into view about three hundred yards away, the Third Cavalry banner waving over them.

"Bugler, sound the charge!"

Richard spurred his horse and the entire column picked up the pace. Now the men began to yell, Richard right along with them.

The officer at the head of the coloreds held up his hand and shouted a command. The Yankee troopers broke from column formation into a solid front of at least a hundred men, carbines aimed facing his charge. Another command and they fired in unison.

At the cries of shock and pain behind him, he pulled up fast and looked back. About fifteen of his men and even more horses were lying in the road. The rest of the men were milling around, as though they were uncertain what to do.

"Forward, men, let's put them to the run." He raised his pistol again.

Another volley echoed from the colored cavalry. Beside him, a lieutenant fell and his horse bolted off to the side, away from all the smoke and fire. It was no good—more men and horses down.

"Blow Retreat." Not a moment too soon, because now the Yankee buglers were blowing their charge, and here came the Third, shouting and yelling like all get-out. Hell, one man was handling his saber as if it was nothing at all.

Richard turned his horse and galloped back down the road, barely able to keep up with his men flying right back where they'd come from, the colored troopers close behind them, shooting and yelling. On the far side of the bridge, he dismounted.

"Come on now. Damn it, you're white men."

Gradually the men settled down and began a rapid fire. They had to get that bridge back. Better wait until reinforcements arrived before making any more charges. In the meantime, his men in the church and the woods at the convergence of the roads would give the Yankees something to think about.

He rode up a little hill from where he could get a view of the whole battlefield. Damn, that little column he'd charged was nothing. There must be a whole regiment behind them—all coloreds, and they were dismounting. Instead of being driven into the open field for the crossfire he'd prepared for them, those colored devils were going to head right into the woods and try to flush his men out of there. Which meant the trap wouldn't work—couldn't work if they outflanked him. And that's exactly what it looked like they were planning to do.

Where the hell were his reinforcements?

Slowly but surely the coloreds cleaned out the woods, forcing his men into retreat, then they went to work on the detachment in the church and rooted them out. And they were still on the Confederate side of the bridge.

He scanned the position with his binoculars one more time. No question about it. When the reinforcements showed, they'd definitely outnumber the Yankees, probably about two to one. But right now his troops were taking a licking.

When a bugle sounded in the distance, he looked and saw the main body of his regiment. Thank God. Those coloreds holding the bridge had just plain overextended themselves.

He swung into his saddle one more time. "All right, men, we're not stopping till we run them back down that road."

The counterattack swept them off the bridge and out of the church. Had them on the run now, all right.

About fifty yards ahead of him, he saw that a Union flag-bearer had been unhorsed, left alone by his retreating comrades. He was sitting on the ground still trying to hold the Stars and Stripes upright.

"There, men!" Richard shouted. "Grab those colors!" He spurred his horse and pointed his saber toward the fallen man, heard the sound of his troopers galloping after him. He saw the man clearly—jet black, head upright, and blood all over his blue blouse, one arm fumbling to reach the Colt revolver that had fallen to the ground beside him.

Richard fixed his eye on him and with a maneuver of his horse that astounded even him, cleaved the man's chest open with a stroke of his saber and grabbed the flag.

"Here, Barclay, take this back to our lines!"

The sergeant went to take the flag. Richard saw the warning in his eyes before he heard him shout, "Watch out, Colonel!"

About ten troopers, sabers drawn and led by Joe, had broken away from the mass of retreating Yankees and were bearing down on him. Joe had to have recognized him. The look on his face was hard, determined, and confident, nothing like what he'd looked like back at Clifton. Hell, that was a strong-assed man galloping down on him now, and he'd damn sure better deal with him that way. That wasn't a toy saber in his hand.

"Get that flag out of here!"

Barclay grabbed the flagstaff, but by now the coloreds were on them, and Richard was face to face, saber to saber with Joe.

"It's your last day, Joe!"

"Don't let it be yours, Colonel!"

They went around and around, the horses twisting and turning, skittering off to one side and the other as the two men slashed away at each other without either one drawing blood.

The sergeant aimed his pistol at Joe.

"No! Barclay, leave him to me."

He'd noticed something on the last two passes they'd made at each other. Joe had a habit of raising that saber, lifting it high as if he wanted to get the leverage to lop off his head. Let him try it just one more time!

The next time Joe lifted the saber in that peculiar way of his, Richard spurred his horse and met the downward blow with a hard upward movement of his own. The force of his thrust combined with the horse's extra burst of speed sent Joe's weapon flying and left him open-mouthed, his eyes following its flight until it was lost in the swirling mass of men and horses fighting around the flag.

"It's all over with you, Joe!"

"I'll see you in hell, Colonel!"

Had to get to him before he got his revolver out . . .

But he wasn't going for the gun!

He was coming at him again, low down on his horse now. Damn savage had a knife out. Richard raised his saber to cut him down when he rode by, but he'd forgotten about Joe's riding tricks. Joe slipped down beneath the belly of his horse and ran his knife blade right along the side of Richard's horse, ripping the animal wide open. The noise the horse made as it stumbled and collapsed on the ground was pitiful to hear, and it was a moment before Richard realized that his legs were pinned beneath it.

The colonel looked up to see Joe grabbing the Stars and Stripes from a stunned Barclay, then galloping back toward the Yankee lines, the flag flying high.

Barclay recovered and helped get Richard free. "Here's another mount, Colonel. Better hurry up. Lots of Yanks coming back at us."

Richard shook his head to clear it, just in time to see another regiment of white enemy cavalry come into view. Led, this time, by a wild-riding redheaded captain. Back over the bridge they came. There was no stopping them. No end of them.

Driven back once more on this side of the bridge, Richard's men settled into a strong defensive position. As always he walked back and forth, trying to rally his forces to drive the Negroes from the bridge once again.

"Hell, men, this ain't no day to give up fighting. I know what you can do."

They were avoiding his eyes. "Crenshaw, remember Brice's Crossroads? Simpson, remember Tupelo? And you, Creighton, you were king of the hill at Shiloh." They'd had enough, and when the coloreds withdrew of their own free will, and departed with the rest of the Yankee column in another direction, Kenworthy let them go.

The casualty report was bad enough—a major, a lieutenant, and fifty men dead—but there must have been something else for Barclay to be looking so nervous.

"You have anything else to report?"

"Yes, sir . . . You know when that white cavalry broke us down on the flank? Well, sir, they overrun the staging area."

"Did they get any horses?"

"About ten."

"Anything else?"

"Some of the nigger teamsters, sir."

Richard drew a deep breath. "Luke?"

The sergeant was silent for a moment. "Expect we'll be getting us another blacksmith," he said finally.

"Hell's bells! I specifically gave the order that Luke in particular was to be watched."

"One of the men winged him as he was running away. I don't know how bad he was hurt."

Wounded or not, he was Joe's son and he was running. Long gone by now. Richard rubbed his eyes. God, he was tired. Tired of all of it.

"Colonel? Is there anything I can do for you?"

"What? No, Bark, no thank you. Tell the men they fought bravely today. We'll have another go at the Yankees in a few days. Dismissed."

* * *

The day after the fight at Franklin, Major Cook called Joe in. Captain Stiles had been wounded again, this time in the leg, and was in a hospital convoy on the way down to Vicksburg along with the others wounded in the battle, including some Rebs and their black teamsters.

"First I want to congratulate you, Duckett," the major said, stepping forward and taking his hand. "What with Captain Stiles being wounded, we'll have to advance the timetable a bit, so I'm officially placing you in command of Company A. Colonel Osband and myself have the utmost confidence in you."

"I won't let you down, sir."

"And now I have your first assignment."

Assignment? The regiment was supposed to be on its way back to Vicksburg.

"There's a lot of bandits and irregulars out there, riding around and raising hell with everybody and anybody. In particular, there are a couple of bands that make a practice of shooting up the Union convoys on the Yazoo. I want you to take a detachment of fifty men out in the countryside and see if you can't put a stop to some of that. You'll rejoin the regiment at Yazoo City in five days."

"Yes, sir."

"And, of course, you're under standing orders to confiscate any property of the secesh and destroy anything that can in any way be of use to them militarily. Any questions?"

"No, sir."

"Then you're dismissed."

Joe saluted and made for the door of the tent, but before he reached it the major called him back.

"Joe? I just wanted you to know that every officer in this regiment wants you to be commissioned. Let's hope the war's not over before those folks in Washington approve it."

CHAPTER EIGHTEEN

SUE Kenworthy leaned on the porch rail and looked down the long empty road. Oh, how she missed having Richard's unit nearby. Every now and then he'd send an officer by with a few men to check on her and the children, but the little messages and things they brought . . . it just wasn't enough.

Ever since her cousin had left for Mobile, all she seemed to have enough time for was worrying. What was she doing here on this little plantation with nothing but two darkies—and one of them that worthless Mary—to look after everything? The grounds and the house, chopping the wood and . . . just everything.

She dreaded the long scary nights. Gregory might be just a little boy, but he knew. He'd taken to wrapping himself in a blanket and curling up at the foot of her bed. She wanted to cry every time she saw him lying there, curled up with that toy sword in his little hand. Laura had slept beside her off and on whenever Richard was away, and now she was there every night.

About the only contact they had with people was when the sheriff, an old gray-haired man who'd lost an arm at Sharpsburg, came to pass the time of day with her. Most everybody else had left. It was him she was expecting today—probably wouldn't be here till this afternoon, though. Good thing, too—Mary was supposed to be cleaning up in anticipation of his visit.

She found the old woman right where she'd left her, sitting on a stool rinsing glasses in a round, wooden tub.

"Honestly, Mary. It's been a half hour already, and you've only washed six of the glasses. If you keep on at that pace, it'll be afternoon before they're ready."

"Yes, Miss."

"And you still have to get lunch for the children and bake some biscuits for the sheriff. You know how much he likes them."

"Yes, Miss."

"Now, tell me just how do you expect to get it all done?"

Mary kept her eyes on the water in the tub, carefully wiping down and drying each glass, and putting it on the cupboard.

"Mary, I'm speaking to you and I expect—"

"Ain't got enough help around here."

"What did you say?"

"Too much work for one soul."

This was intolerable. Mary had been a slave for fifty years, and she ought to know better.

"What has gotten into you?"

"I does my best, but you asking too much from me. Want me to make up the beds, wash all the clothes, cook all the meals, help Linus in the garden. Used to have thirty niggers to work this place, now it's only me and Linus. Ain't fair."

"Fair? Who taught you such a word?"

"And Linus, he old and crippled, can barely take care of himself."

Sue stood over Mary with her hands on her hips. "Who feeds you? Who clothes you? Who gives you a place to sleep? Who has to put up with your insolent lazy ways? Me!"

"Everybody else done left you, gone to the Yankees."

"Well, you might just as well have gone with them for all the good you are to me. I just wish you had to live one day as a mistress, then you'd see what it's like trying to . . ." She reached into the cupboard for some flour. "Never you mind about the biscuits, I'll do them myself."

* * *

"Mighty good biscuits, Mrs. Kenworthy."

The sheriff had slathered on so much hot butter and honey Sue wondered he could taste the biscuits.

"Really worth the trip over here." He wiped his sticky hands and took a long sip of lemonade.

Well, he was better than no company at all. "I'm just tickled to hear you liked them as much as usual—I baked them myself this time. Mary's been . . . out of sorts." She glanced back toward the kitchen. "I suppose that's the case with them all these days."

"As a matter of fact, it is. Them that remains, that is." He took out his pipe. "Mind?"

"Go ahead and smoke if you wish."

"I don't like to presume. Wouldn't want to offend a lady such as yourself. And while I'm on the subject, I think a lady such as yourself, like I said, and your children . . . that is, as a matter of fact, as the sheriff . . ."

"Whatever are you trying to say?"

"Well, ma'am, I'm thinking of ordering you to leave this place."

"Ordering me? My goodness!" She folded her hands in her lap. "I see no reason to do so now. It seems that one way or another, the war is about over."

"That may be, but right now things are mighty dangerous around here with these bands of irregulars robbing and plundering and . . . I don't know what all. I got no means of stopping them, just don't have enough men."

"But what about our regular forces?"

"The Yankees are a handful, and with so many slaves running loose, well, I hate to think of a lady such as yourself so unprotected."

Sue walked to the window and looked out at the children. "If Richard." She took a deep breath. "I'm grateful for your concern, Sheriff. I'll begin making arrangements."

"I'm relieved to hear it, Mrs. Kenworthy, ma'am, and I'm sure it'll make the colonel rest easier."

* * *

Sue was very busy the next few days, burying jewelry and coins—it wouldn't do to travel with them. For once Mary seemed eager to help her, as a matter of fact seemed to enjoy it, almost like it was a game. And Gregory showed her some of his favorite hiding places—behind rocks, and under little hillocks up by the creek. He kept playing with his toy popgun, dropping down every now and then behind a rock, giving the Rebel yell, and shooting at an imaginary advancing Yankee skirmish line. A few times Sue even let him shoot the revolver Richard had left behind for her protection.

On the evening before they were to leave, Sue was reading to the children, a chapter from the Tale of Two Cities. Mary was out in the kitchen eating with Linus after having served the evening meal. A good-sized fire was burning in the fireplace and Jonas, the only hound dog left now, lay in front of it. The children were sitting on the rug, Laura with her head on her mother's lap, and Gregory leaning against her legs.

> So does a whole world, with all its greatnesses and
> littlenesses, lie in a twinkling star . . .

Jonas's ears stiffened, and he began a low growl.

"Hush, Jonas!" said Laura. "What Mother's reading is so
pretty."

Sue remembered the sheriff's warning. She began again,
only slightly uneasy. A raccoon or a possum was enough to set the
hound off . . .

> Château and hut, stone face and dangling figure, the
> red stain on the stone floor, and the pure water in
> the village well—thousands of acres of land—a whole
> province of France—all France itself—lay under
> the night sky, concentrated into a faint hairbreadth
> line . . .

Jonas leapt to his feet with a growl and ran barking to the
front door.

Oh, why hadn't she left right away? Who could that be at
this hour of the night? But then maybe it was the sheriff.

She called Linus from the kitchen and told him to answer
the door. He obeyed quickly, he wasn't like that no-account Mary.

A short man in a fur jacket with a pistol strapped around his
waist pushed Linus aside and stepped right into the foyer.

"Captain Odom, to see the Miss of the house."

"But, Massa—"

Odom froze Linus with a look and walked into the large
open space in front of the fireplace, then bowed to Sue and the
children.

"I'm sorry to have to inconvenience you this way, but me and my men have been battling the Yankees for the past two days and are sore in need of food and shelter."

She looked at him. He wasn't wearing any kind of a uniform, except the gray pants. But then, times were hard and many of their men were ill-dressed.

"Get up, children. Mary will see you to bed." She kissed them. "I'll be up to tuck you in before long." She turned to Captain Odom. "How can I be of help to you?"

"Well, ma'am, I got about eighteen men left in my outfit now, and I'd be much obliged if you could put them up."

"We have plenty of room for them down in the stables—I'll have Linus show your men the way. You, of course, will do me the courtesy of staying with us in the house. Mary will prepare the guest bedroom for you." She beckoned to Linus. "Help the captain get his men settled down there."

The captain nodded to Sue and followed Linus out.

In fifteen minutes he was back again, this time accompanied by three men, one of them an Indian. With a wave of his hand, he presented them to Sue.

"My bodyguards and yours this evening."

"What—"

"Oh, you needn't worry about finding accommodations for them, they'll sleep right there by the fireplace. Won't you, boys?"

Sue was not reassured by their grunts. "But we have never . . ."

"Had an Injun to sleep in your house."

Sue nodded.

"Well, you needn't worry about this one. He's a fine soldier and a real gentleman to them he holds dear. And faithful as they come. Why, he wouldn't let me sleep in a strange house by myself!

No, we'll all be safe as houses what with him here." He smiled at Sue. "No thieving Yanks tonight."

Nevertheless, she locked the door behind her when all was settled and she was finally in her bedroom.

"Mama? I don't like those men. They don't look like the men that ride with my father," Gregory said.

"They are fighting for our freedom, Gregory. This is the least we can do for them."

"That Indian looked at me real funny. And did you see those scars on his face? Maybe he wants to scalp me."

"Hush. Some of our finest sharpshooters are Indians. I won't have you speak of them like that."

Laura was awake, too, sitting up on the bed. "Do you have the gun in here?"

"Yes, silly. But there's no need for it."

She got into bed, and drew Laura close to her. The child was trembling. Even their little warrior left his post at the foot of the bed, and the three of them fell asleep in a tangle of arms and bedclothes.

* * *

Awakened by a scraping sound, she carefully moved her arms so as not to wake the children.

The sound was coming from outside. Somebody was shoveling.

What were Captain Odom's men doing? Did he know? She slipped out of bed and put a night robe on.

When she opened her door, she saw that Captain Odom's was open too. He must have heard the same sound and gone downstairs to investigate.

She was near the bottom of the stairs before she saw how mistaken she'd been.

Linus and Mary both sat bound and gagged on the rug. The Indian was taking the fireplace apart, stone by stone, and other men were searching every corner of the room. And Captain Odom seemed to be directing the entire operation!

She had to get back to her room. And the revolver.

"Ah, Mrs. Kenworthy. Come on down—no need to alarm the children."

That odious man was aiming his pistol at her.

The Indian turned away from his project in the fireplace and smiled. Captain Odom moved to the bottom of the staircase.

"I'm sorry my men woke you. It was my intention to have been out of here before dawn without disturbing you." Still aiming the pistol, he offered his other hand and laughed when she hurried past him, head high.

"You traitor!"

"Oh no, ma'am, don't call me that, please. I've never lifted an arm against my sovereign government."

"Sir, you have taken advantage of my hospitality—and a woman's vulnerability."

He lowered the pistol. "Please sit down, ma'am. You may be able to speed us on our way. A person of your station surely has more assets than have so far surfaced here."

"We have nothing here. No gold, no jewelry, so there's no use in trying to get them from us."

"It grieves me to have to contradict such a lovely woman as you, but we both know there are things of considerable value concealed here—or somewhere nearby."

She gripped the top of her night robe and pulled it tight around her neck. All of the real money they had left was buried out there. She would not tell!

"Come now, Mrs. Kenworthy, I'm sure you don't want me to wake those children up or have my men beat the secret out of your old niggers over there." He waved the pistol in the direction of Mary and Linus. "It's only money, and what's money beside a human life? Of course, this Indian here, he don't have the same feelings about human life as us. And the worst part's that once I tell him to do something, there's no stopping him. Why, once he took a pot of scalding hot frying grease and—"

"All right."

What a mangy-looking bunch of hoodlums they were! "Just wait until daylight, and I'll show you where everything is buried. But you'll pay for this. The colonel rides with General Wirt Adams."

"I had the pleasure of riding with that gentleman myself at one time. There is naught to fear from him." He glanced at his men. "We'll wait until morning. Mrs. Kenworthy, I'll accompany you back to your room to see that you get there safely."

As she walked up the stairs, she could feel his eyes going right through her robe, so she wasn't surprised to feel his hand on her buttocks when they reached the landing.

"Would you like to sit up for a while and talk? Perhaps in that very nice guest room of yours."

She turned and with both hands shoved his shoulders so hard he would have fallen down the stairs if he hadn't grabbed the railing.

"You'll regret that." He touched her cheek with the pistol and walked into his room.

* * *

Sue awoke to a smell so delicious that she almost forgot her situation. Mmmmmm, bacon. Neither of the children was in the room. She dressed hurriedly and rushed downstairs.

That man Odom—she had no intention of honoring him with the title of captain any longer—was seated in Richard's favorite chair, drinking a cup of coffee.

"Looking for your children? They're in the kitchen eating. My men have already eaten and they're waiting down at the barn for us. Why don't you have something to eat and then we'll get to the matter of the jewelry."

Sue went into the kitchen. Mary and Linus were cleaning up after Odom's men, while the children finished their eggs and bacon.

"Mary told us these are bad men," Laura said. "Are they going to hurt you?"

Sue sat down at the table with them. "There's nothing to worry about. We're going to give them what they want and then they'll leave. I want the two of you to stay up here with Linus and Mary." She got up from the table. "I'm going now."

It was chilly outside. A touch of frost had left a light coat of white on the lawn, now overgrown with weeds. The sight of the men assembled at the stables made Sue tremble. They had already taken the shovels out of the barn.

A hound dog leapt up and down with joy when it saw Odom, who went over and patted it. "Morning, Cornpone."

These men had no right to be doing this. They were nothing but highwaymen who would run away to Texas with every last thing she and Richard had accumulated and never be heard from again.

"Sir, I implore you in the name of Southern chivalry—"

"Let's go, men. Mrs. Kenworthy will lead the way."

The odious Odom made a deep bow. Odious Odum. Sue remembered what her friend had said about her writing poetry. Merciful heavens! Was she coming unhinged, thinking about such things at a time like this?

* * *

She watched dry-eyed while they dug up the boxes of gold coins and jewelry she had buried so carefully just a few days ago. But she couldn't hold back the tears when the men passed around the diamond wedding ring made especially for her in London. She had cried when Richard gave it to her at the ceremony . . .

"All right, men," Odom said. "Don't play with that stuff. Take it back up to the house, make a regular inventory of it, and we'll divide up fair and square before we leave."

Sue glared at him. "You said you'd go if I gave you the valuables."

"Did I? Well, we'll see. Have to count what we have, then we'll decide when we're going to leave."

When they got back to the house, he ordered Mary and Linus to go upstairs with Sue and the children. He locked the door to her bedroom from the outside and posted the Indian as a sentry.

"If you-all need anything, Mrs. Kenworthy, just call."

Sue thought about the revolver. But there were too many of them. Even if she killed some of them, the rest would brutalize her and her family. She was truly at the end of her wits.

Linus and Mary lay down on the floor and slept, exhausted from the night before. Sue began again to read to the children, and soon they were engrossed enough in the story that they seemed to forget about the danger downstairs. She tried to forget, too, but the memory of her wedding ring in the hands of those men wouldn't let her.

Several hours passed with barely a sound from downstairs. When the children finally went to sleep on her bed, Sue peeked through the keyhole. The Indian was asleep on a chair.

* * *

What could be taking them so long? They had what they wanted. Why didn't they leave?

Another hour passed before Odom finally unlocked the door and marched right in without so much as a knock.

"We've finished distributing the shares and have decided to accept a little more of your hospitality. We've been doing a little scouting—there's a bit of military activity going on in the vicinity that might make it unwise for us to be on the highways right now."

"I hope they catch you."

"Now, Mrs. Kenworthy, you don't mean that. They're Yankees."

"Doesn't matter."

"Nigger Yankees."

"What?"

"Yes."

"I want you out of here, sir."

"Send the two niggers down to make lunch. And tell them to get the liquor out. We're just going to settle in here and have us a little party till the darky soldiers go away. Might even invite you to come down and join us."

Gregory walked over and stood between her and Odom. "You're a coward, sir, and my father will punish you for all of this."

"He'll have to catch me first, son, and that ain't real likely. Mrs. Kenworthy, get those servants moving, please."

* * *

By two o'clock, they were loud and raucous. Never had such profanity reached Sue's ears. They had no respect for either God or man.

By three o'clock, their singing was punctuated with the sound of breaking glass.

When would this end? Reading Dickens no longer calmed the children. Sue sat on the bed with her arms around them.

"When are they going to stop?" Laura asked.

"Never you mind. I think it's time we prayed together."

They were on their knees saying the Lord's Prayer when Odom appeared at the door with the Indian behind him, peering over his shoulder. At the sight of them, the children screamed.

And no wonder! Odom's eyes were red and his cheeks were glowing like polished apples. He had removed his bow tie and had grabbed hold of the doorknob, which he seemed to need in order to remain upright.

"Mrs. Kenworthy, my men and I beg the pleasure of your company below."

Sue had anticipated this moment and knew she had to go if the children were to remain unharmed. If she could just keep herself calm, maybe Gregory wouldn't do anything foolish.

"Sir, I'll sit with you and you alone in the guest bedroom, if you'll bring Linus and Mary up here so that they can give the children something to eat."

"Why, I'll be pleased to do that . . . I'll be right back with them."

"Don't go!" Gregory said. "Don't leave us."

Laura clung to her mother's dress, and began to sob. "You can't go with that awful man, he'll kill you."

Sue bent down and put her arms around both of them. "Now, don't worry. I don't like him either, but . . . we're just going to talk for a little while. I'll come in to check on you every now and then, and Mary and Linus will take care of you."

When she walked into the guest room, he was at least enough of a gentleman to get up from his chair. A tiny hope stirred. She watched him open a bottle of the wine Richard had had shipped from Bordeaux itself.

"These red French wines seem to be a favorite of our Southern ladies." He poured some and offered it to Sue. It wasn't even a wineglass—just a tall glass like the one he still had filled with bourbon whiskey.

She held the glass tightly, barely restraining herself from tossing its contents right into his red face. The whiskey smell on his breath hit her full blast as he took her by the elbow, trying to maneuver her over toward the bed.

"My men must have scared you with all of that racket, but there's no harm in them, just kind of playful at times."

She edged away from him. "How do you expect to live again in this territory when this war is over? Either the Yankees or our own will put an end to you."

He moved close enough to take her elbow again, the arm holding his bourbon stretched outward so that when she retreated she was forced to move back toward the bed.

"You've got beautiful skin, Mrs. Kenworthy."

She felt the gnarled wood of the bedpost pressing into her back. When he bent to kiss her on the cheek, she recoiled.

"Now, you don't want to go making it hard on yourself. Your children are in there, and we don't want my men to forget themselves, do we? I wasn't exaggerating about how wild that Injun is when he's riled up, especially with all that liquor he's got in him now. Just be sensible, and we'll be gone in a while."

Sue fell to her knees before him, folded her hands together, and began to cry. He put his hand on her shoulder.

"Now there, I'm not such an ugly man, am I? Just take a good look at me." He grabbed her chin and twisted her head so that she had to look up at him.

She stopped crying. Who was she to be spared? How many times had Richard suffered grievous wounds? Did not over half of the young men who'd formed his wedding party now lie in their graves, dead for the Cause? Yes, everyone must bear a cross. With the little dignity she was able to muster, Sue stood up.

"Turn your head around so that I may undress."

"That's a sensible girl. We'll have us a jolly good time, and then I'll be on my way." He unbuckled his belt.

"Captain Odom!" She heard footsteps on the stairs, then a sharp knock at the door. "Yankees! They're right down the road."

He was buckling his pants and his pistol belt on the way to the door.

* * *

Sue thanked God every step of the way to her bedroom.

"Look at them run, children!"

She joined them, along with Mary and Linus, at the window—just in time to see the gang mounting up. Odom was the last, but once he had mounted they all took off down the road. The hound dog was yelping and running in circles by the stable.

They were barely out of sight when a whole bunch of Yankee cavalry came just as fast down the road right behind them.

"Look, Mama—nigger soldiers."

Sue didn't know whether to cry or cheer, but considering what Odom had been about ready to do to her—

"My God! The jewelry and the gold!"

If anything had been left behind, it mustn't fall into Yankee hands. That's who she'd hidden it from in the first place. They all rushed downstairs and looked around.

"Glory, Miss Kenworthy, your wedding ring still there."

Glory, indeed. In their haste to depart, the scoundrels had left a good half of the loot on the table.

* * *

An hour later, Sue watched through the windows as the Union men wended their way up the roadway to the house. What a sight! Darky soldiers in blue uniforms with yellow piping that made their faces look even blacker, sitting astride those horses as if they had been accustomed to riding all of their lives. And not a white man with them.

Was there no end to the evil acts resorted to by the Yankees? Sending black men out on their own to devastate the land.

She stepped away from the window and went to change out of her night robe and into a dress.

"Mama, look at that nigger sergeant leading them." Gregory prided himself on knowing all the insignia in both armies.

* * *

She was ready when the knock came at the door. In her chair, with her children at her side.

"Linus, answer it."

"Joe!" she heard him say. Then, "Mary! It Joe, Zenobia's Joe, we safe!"

With a big smile on his face, he led the sergeant into the living room. At least this was a familiar Yankee. Sue smiled, too. Then she remembered.

"How do you do, Miz Kenworthy?"

Joe's uniform was dusty, but there was no mistaking the stripes on his arm or the authority in his walk. The ex-slave carpenter on their estate was now a Yankee noncommissioned officer.

Mary had slipped up next to him. "Joe, you done come to free us, ain't you?"

Joe hugged her! "Sure have, honey. Me and President Abraham Lincoln."

He released her and bowed to Sue. "You don't have to worry about nothing from us, just going to see to it that those secesh are run out of this territory, then we'll be moving on. Some of my men are still chasing them."

Sue remained silent. Her children clung to her.

"Don't worry, little chilluns," Linus said. "Joe my friend."

"That'll do, Linus." It was time for Sue to show her authority. "How long do you propose to be here?"

"We going to be confiscating those two horses down in the stable, and my men will kill the cow for dinner tonight. Any livestock we can't take will be destroyed." His speech had changed some—it was more like that of a white man.

"We were counting on those horses to get us to Alabama."

"Sorry, Miss, the needs of my command comes first."

The nerve of him! Another one appeared at the door, grinning. "Excuse me, sir, we got him, we got the leader."

"What's the joke?" Joe said.

"See, he almost got away. Left his horse and tried to run away down in the swamps. Onliest thing were, he didn't take that nigger dog of his with him. So we lets it loose and he tracks down the old master! We come up on him, standing there trying to shush that old dog of his'n away. Then he tried to shoot his way out."

"Where is he now?"

"He ain't going to be doing any more shooting. Ever."

"Good. We're bivouacking here tonight. Post the pickets and get the men fed."

"You surely don't intend to spend the night in this house!" Sue stood up. "Under my roof?"

"I'll post a sentry at the bottom of your staircase. Now I must see to some things."

* * *

She was sure she wouldn't sleep a wink, but they all went to sleep without even a page of their book. When she came downstairs the next morning, the revolver was concealed in the pocket of her gown. The children were eating breakfast with the Negro soldiers, Gregory examining the Yankee weapons. After breakfast, Joe asked Sue to come into the living room and sit down.

"Miz Kenworthy, I understands you sent the patrollers and the hound dogs after Zenobia and my child Cally. What did they report?"

That Mary had told everything. "I don't have to answer you," she said.

The muscles in his face were twitching.

"They were my legal property."

"And Milly and Luke—they was your legal property too, right?"

"I will not answer any more questions."

She started to get up, but Joe nodded to a sergeant by the door. "Be prepared to restrain her if we has to."

She sat back down. "Don't you dare put your black hands on me."

"The colonel done made my son a body servant."

Sue's upper lip began to tremble. "I bear no responsibility for his actions."

"Mary done told me about your treasure, and now I needs you to bring it downstairs. It's Federal property. Zack, you go with her."

*　*　*

They spread all the gold coins and the ring on the table in the dining room. Joe carefully itemized everything "confiscated from the secesh," then signed his name and title at the bottom.

He turned to the one he'd called Zack. "Bring those children in here."

Sue's heart sank. And when they saw the look on their mother's face, Gregory and Laura burst into tears and ran to her side.

Slipping a hand into her right pocket, Sue hooked her forefinger around the trigger of the revolver. This time she was prepared.

"Get me that wedding ring out of the bag," Joe said.

What was in that evil African mind of his? What revenge was he seeking for his children and wife?

"Give it to her."

The other sergeant slowly rotated the ring in his hand.

"That's an order."

"Yes, sir."

"Miz Kenworthy, I need you to sign this receipt for the wedding ring's return," Joe said. "If you be so kind."

She signed and he folded the receipt and bowed.

"We leaving now. Mary's going with us, but Linus wants to stay with you. Good day, ma'am, and my compliments to the colonel. His money going into the treasury of the United States Government."

From a window Sue watched him speak to another sergeant, then walk back to the house.

Joe never looked at her face this time. She could have sworn he was looking right through her shawl at the pistol as he handed her a bag of coins and another piece of paper.

"I've decided to leave the horses with you. And a hundred dollars. Your children has done us no harm and won't be made to suffer. Now I got to trouble you to sign one more time."

CHAPTER NINETEEN

ZENOBIA woke up with pain shooting from the calf of her leg straight through the rest of her body. Oh, Lord, she could barely turn over. Wouldn't be seeing Freedom Land any time soon.

They'd been walking for eight days, and the swelling had just crept up on her over the last twenty-four hours—slow at first, like always. There was no way to get heat for it, no way she could rest proper at night with nothing but that little bit of a blanket between her and the cold damp earth. And no sweet Joe to snuggle up against her real tight or rub her leg with that special oil he made up.

Lisa Mae and Ned and Helen were bundled up together, sleeping their weary young souls away. How could she ever make them go on without her? The only thing she knew to do was pray.

* * *

Lisa Mae woke up first. "You already wake, Zee? Why you not up finding us some breakfast like always?"

"Afraid this the end for me. I can't walk."

Lisa Mae laughed. "Ain't no time to be fooling with me like that, big sister."

"Get Helen and Ned up. You all got to get ready for the walking. They be leaving soon, and—"

"Wait a minute. We ain't going nowhere without you." She shook the youngsters. "You stay here and watch Auntie Zenobia. I'm going to find a soldier to help."

"Give me that bag, Ned." Zenobia reached in and took out some pieces of hardtack the soldiers had given out the day before. "Here, eat—you all need lots of strength today."

"What's wrong, Auntie? Why's Lisa Mae fussing?"

"Well, you know I been having some pain in my leg. Now it's swollen up like a big ham. No way in the world I can leave."

"You can't walk?" Ned asked.

"I think God got other plans for me today."

Helen looked like she was about to cry—in fact, they both did—but bless her heart, she took Ned by the hand. "Come on, honey."

Around them folks in the camp were up, singing and packing their little bundles for the day:

> *"I'm sometimes up, I'm sometimes down*
> *Trouble going to bury me down!*
> *Oh brethren! Poor me! Poor me!*
> *Trouble will bury me down!"*

Everybody was pretty much ready to go by the time Lisa Mae returned, riding on a horse with her arms wrapped around a white cavalry soldier. She slid down from the horse, talking a mile a minute.

"Looky here, Zee, I done fixed it. John here, he going to let you ride behind him. Lots of folks doing it up the line."

"You think you can get up here, sister?"

"Soldier man, I try anything once." The line began to move.

"If you're coming, you got to hurry," the horse soldier said. "The Rebs ain't far behind now."

Helen and Lisa Mae took her by the arms. Zenobia tried to stand up.

"It burn like fire when I move." Beads of sweat broke out all over her face. "Too much. You all go on."

The soldier leaned down from his horse. "Sister, this is your last chance, I have to get back up the line."

"Then go. And please take these young folks with you."

She could see now that the end of the line was not far away. God, give me the words to make them go. She looked up into the circle of worried faces.

"If you love me, you'll go," she said. "Break my heart if we come all this way for nothing. You got to follow the soldier man."

Helen knelt down beside her. "You my mother."

"I know it, my baby. I love you, I loves you all. But you got to obey your mother and go on like I tell you. I be all right."

"Come on, you-all, start walking," the soldier said.

"Lisa Mae, you the leader now," Zenobia said. "Be one."

Lisa Mae took their hands. "Come on, you two."

"Don't you dare look back," Zenobia said. "You hear? Don't look back!"

"May God keep you in his care, sister." With that, the cavalryman spurred his horse and rode off down the road.

* * *

"Come on in," Betty said. "The captain's right over here."

"Hello, sir."

Captain Stiles sat up. "I'm mighty glad to see you, Joe, the colonel told me you did one hell of a job after I got it."

Joe put his cap on the night table. "Was all right I guess, but we missed you like the devil. And I got a lot to learn about military tactics."

"If a general store clerk like me can learn, so will you," Captain Stiles said.

"How's my woman been treating you?"

"Couldn't have had a better nurse. Don't see how somebody pretty as her hooked up with you."

Betty said, "Now, Captain, he got a few good points."

Joe laughed and put his arm around her. "One thing for sure, I'm a lucky man."

"How're things going with the company?"

"Going good, sir. We brought down a lot of new men from those plantations up in the Delta. Zack's keeping busy whipping them into shape, but he don't have much time. We're going up to Arkansas and Louisiana soon to wipe out some of the Reb bands operating up there."

"I probably won't be here when you men get back, they're sending me home as soon as I can walk again. They think I'm too banged up to go to Washington."

"Do you think . . . You still going to be able to farm, sir?"

"Well, with that bullet where it is, I'm going to have to take it easy. But you don't think I've forgotten, do you?"

Joe grinned. "Just checking, sir. How long you think before all this be over?"

"With Savannah and Fort Fisher gone, the Rebs won't be able to hold on much longer. I'd give it another five or six months. But don't you get careless, now—a bullet can't read a calendar."

Joe squared his shoulders and shook the captain's hand. "Sir, I just want to tell you how proud I am to have served with you.

If you don't never come back this way again, me and the men, we won't never forget you."

"You made me proud too, Joe. Plenty of times."

* * *

Betty walked out with Joe. "Come along with me while I make my rounds. Might make some of them a little jealous, but still I'd like to show you off a bit."

A long shed housed all the sick and wounded who had come down the Yazoo with the brigade.

Almost as far as Joe could see, there was nothing but soldiers, colored and white, lying in those beds. For the first time he realized all the work this woman of his had to do. He thought back on the men who had started out with the Third and were now lying in their graves somewhere up there in the Delta. What a wonder he'd been spared so far, hadn't had more than a few scratches. Now he looked down the long row of beds, saw the faces, some empty, some eager, waiting for Betty's touch, her voice.

"Harrison, this my friend, Sergeant Duckett . . ."

"Corey, how you today? Let me see that bandage . . ."

"William, I brung you some candy today, made it special myself . . ."

She paused by one bed. "Brother Roland, let us have prayer together."

It wasn't long before Joe was longing to breathe some fresh air. But when Betty had finished with the short prayer, she nodded toward a far corner of the shed.

"Some real sad cases over there. Colored boys who've been with the Rebs, and they ain't had too much to eat when they come in. You boys been doing too good a job cleaning out those plantations."

One man was lying in his bed, a blanket over him, facing the wall. He had a big bandage on his shoulder.

"He like that all the time. Won't even tell me his name. So young, but he seen a lot and he pretend to be sleep all the time. He don't believe he free." She leaned over him, her voice even gentler than before. "Turn over, honey, let me feel your brow."

The man didn't wake up, didn't turn over, but Joe knew.

"Luke!"

"Oh, my God! And he been here almost a week." She reached out to wake him.

"No," Joe said. "Let me."

He touched his son's temple.

"Daddy!"

Joe was on his knees beside the bed now, stroking Luke's forehead, then kissing it. Hugging him tight when he sat up.

* * *

Betty sat on the bed and wiped away their tears—and her own—with a corner of her apron.

"Be careful, you-all, don't want that wound to open up."

Before the day was over, she had arranged to have Luke moved into her room. And now Joe had a special reason to go up into Louisiana on the raid—Milly and Pauline were there.

* * *

A few days later, just before the regiment was due to leave for Memphis on the boats, Joe asked Zack to go with him to the refugee camp just outside of Vicksburg. He'd heard there were thousands of colored folks the government was trying to put back together with their families.

He walked into the camp real slow. Being on the battlefield was a whole lot easier than to having to deal with his life and everything so scattered. What would he find in the camp this time? It was mighty scary, considering that all these folks came from right up there in the Delta where he'd spent so many years.

There were tents all over the place, set up in rows. In front of some of them, toddlers in night shifts followed after their mothers, who were gathering wood, cooking in big iron pots over fires, or mending clothing. Stray dogs darted back and forth, their barking almost drowned out by the loud and often shouted conversations of people gathered in dozens of small groups around the camp. A banjo player sat on a stump chair, surrounded by women and children who were stomping their feet and clapping their hands as his fingers plucked out the melody of "Camptown Races."

"Look at them soldier boys."

A woman with a red turban around her head was pointing at them.

Some young boys ran up. "We know you, you got that three on your collar. You from the Third Colored Cavalry."

Joe reached down and lifted one of them up. "That's right, sonny boy."

An old man, his trousers held up by a string, reached out to touch the buttons on Joe's jacket.

"Them buttons mighty pretty. Never thought I'd live to see it. Praise God!"

At the far end of the camp, where you could see down over the river, there was a big tent. As Joe and Zack approached they saw children sitting on benches trying to draw the way the teacher was drawing on the board. When she started asking them questions, they jumped and shouted to show her they knew the answers. A mighty fine thing to see them. Colored folks was on their way up, all right.

The teacher wore a tight gray dress with a high white collar. Every time one of the children gave the right answer, she clapped her hands as much as they did. Joe felt like clapping himself—he knew most of the answers. Not like two years ago. Now he could read up a storm and so could a lot of men in his company.

He and Zack had been standing watching the children for a few minutes when the teacher motioned for them to come in.

"Us?" Joe said.

"Yes, you and the sergeant there."

They took off their hats and walked over to her desk.

"Children, we're going to do something very special today." She took hold of Joe's and Zack's hands. "These men have been out fighting so that no one will ever again beat you, or call you little niggers, or sell your mothers or fathers or sisters or brothers away from you. Many lost their arms or legs or been killed by the Rebels so you can grow up as free children. Now, who wants to come up and thank them on behalf of this class?"

Every hand went up. "Me! Miss Francis!"

She looked out over them, beckoned to a girl in the back with a thin, serious face, and turned to Joe.

"It's the first time Helen has ever wanted to speak in front of the class," she said.

The girl looked up at Joe and Zack, then back down at the floor. Some of the other children tittered. Miss Francis put her fingers to her lips. "Shush!"

Joe bent down so that his face was level with the girl's and took her hands in his. "Say whatever's on your heart, darlin'."

She glanced over at Miss Francis, then back at Joe. "We is so proud of you. Most of us, we ain't knowed nothing but hurt . . ."

Joe squeezed her hand gently. "Go ahead, baby child."

"I ain't never known my mammy, never had a daddy, and my little brothers and sisters, they been sold long ago down into Alabama. Grandmama raised me and that old overseer, he would tie her to a tree and whip her. She dead now."

Joe put his hand gently on her head.

"Onliest other person I ever had were Zenobia, and now she gone too."

Joe looked at her. Could she mean his Zenobia? He didn't remember this child's face from Clifton.

"We going to study and work real hard to make you proud of us like we proud of you soldier boys. We thanks you from the bottom of our hearts."

She kissed each of them on their cheeks.

"Now our song, children," the teacher said. "Sing it good for them."

> "Walk together, children
> Don't you get weary!
> Walk together, children
> Don't you get weary!
> Pray together, children
> Don't you get weary!
> Pray together, children
> Don't you get weary!"

"Now it's our turn," Joe said. "Me and Sergeant Bascombe here, we just wants to tell you how proud we is of you." He turned to Miss Francis. "Can I have a word with Helen outside for a minute? It's mighty important."

"Is that all right with you, Helen? Class is almost over."

She nodded and followed them outside.

"Now, Helen, this Zenobia, what she look like?"

"She a mighty pretty lady. She take care of everybody."

"Was there anybody else with her?"

"Lisa Mae and Ned, and Cally and Mr. Drayton at first, only they . . ."

Joe looked at Zack. "It's her."

"You know Zenobia?" Helen said.

Joe took her hands. "Yes, darlin', I surely do. Now tell me what happened to you all."

"She can tell you better." Joe looked in the direction Helen was pointing and saw Lisa Mae walking toward them.

And she saw him and hollered at the top of her voice.

"Joe!"

They ran across the field and Joe lifted her off her feet for a hug. How many times had Aunt Garry's granddaughter stayed over in their cabin, chattering away the night with Zenobia, so tired the next morning that she could barely go back to the fields? He held on to her like if he let go they'd never see each other again in this life.

By now class was over and Miss Francis came out to join them. "Your wife?"

"No, ma'am, but she my wife's best friend." He let go and took a step back. "Now, Lisa Mae, tell me what happened . . ."

* * *

That night, the last one before they shipped out, Joe stopped by Betty's house. Luke was asleep, so they sat at the table and talked quietly.

"Want some coffee, Joe? You look like you could use it."

"No, just come on over and sit in my lap. I think this about the confusingest week of my life, don't really know which way to turn."

"Anybody wouldn't know, what with all that's happened."

"But somehow I got to make sense of all these things. See, I love you, and I love my Zenobia, too. Now, ain't that sinful when she's lying out there on some road up there in the Delta, maybe froze to death? And my little Cally gone on home to glory . . ."

"Joe—"

"How the hell am I going to tell Luke about all this? Life done dealt us a rotten hand."

She ran her fingers over his clenched fist. "I never heard you talk that way before."

"It's true, ain't it?"

"No, it's dealt a rotten hand to all those men in the sick ward. You got your health and strength and lots of people to live for, starting with me. I'm going to boil you a fine cup of coffee, then we can lie down on that pallet for a little while and maybe I can take some of that hurt out of you."

She started setting up to make coffee.

"Your men depending on you. All kinds of folks loving you and depending on you. You got to get yourself together, Joe."

"Betty?

"What is it, honey?"

"Look." He stretched out his hands.

"You shouldn't have started up drinking again, baby. You promised me—"

"Ain't had no whiskey. I'm scared. First time."

CHAPTER TWENTY

ZENOBIA watched the last soldier spur his horse and move off.

Well, that was the last of the Yankees.

She looked up the road. The Rebs, now, that was something else. She'd heard many a time how grayboys killed colored folks who tried to run off with the Yankees and failed. Once the Yankees had left so quickly they burned a bridge and left a hundred freed colored on the other side, some on their knees praying, others running into the water. The cavalry boys had a field day, cutting and slashing away at those poor souls with freedom in their heads. Killed so many it was said water from the river could have dyed a dozen bolts of white cloth crimson red.

Now here she was, watching for them. Sitting by the roadside waiting for the death angel.

Well, let them come. She didn't have any real hope of living to see another day. Didn't know if she even wanted to. Joe gone, Cally gone, Milly and Luke God knew where. At least Lisa Mae and the children were freedom bound . . .

In her head, she heard a voice. Brother Caleb's voice, at prayer meetings down in the bush. "When your burdens get heavy, my sisters and brothers, lean not to your own understanding, for He will always give you a song. May not be a song that come out of your mouth, 'cause all of us can't sing good, just may be a night sky when He make the stars to shine all at once, light up His whole big kingdom for all His chillun to see and praise His name. He will always give us a song!"

Wasn't nobody in sight, and she wouldn't care if there was. She opened her throat wide and sang the song He gave.

> *"I couldn't hear nobody pray*
> *Oh, I couldn't hear nobody pray!*
> *I was way down yonder by myself*
> *And I couldn't hear nobody pray!"*

She was still singing it when she saw the first clouds of dust down the road, heard the sound of the galloping hooves like the low rumble of far-off thunder. Not so far off, after all. Through the thickening cloud of dust she saw the flag and the horses and men, all coming right at her.

When the column was abreast of her, an officer raised his hand.

"Halt!"

His uniform was in tatters and his thin face was all splotchy and scraggy-bearded.

"Auntie, your Yankees left you here, didn't they? How long ago?"

"A long time, Massa."

He shook his head. "What's that mean, Auntie? An hour? Two hours?"

"Don't know. Long time, Massa."

The officer looked back toward his men. "Sergeant Riggins, come over here. A bite of the lash may loosen this darky's tongue, help her to remember better."

The sergeant uncoiled his whip. Zenobia winced as its hateful snap bit into the tree right above her head.

What had she to hide? Nothing she said could either help or hurt the Yankees.

"About an hour, Massa."

"That's better. Now, how come they left you here?"

"I got a sickness in my leg. Can't walk."

The sergeant unsnapped his holster and waited for the order. The captain nodded his head, the sergeant drew his Navy Colt out of its holster and pulled back the hammer.

Zenobia looked into their eyes—first one, then the other. "You mighty young boys to be killing womenfolk. How do it feel afterward?"

The sergeant placed the muzzle of the gun on Zenobia's temple and pressed. "Why, you ornery bitch!" She tried to move away from the pain, but he just pressed harder.

"Just a second there, Sergeant!" The captain put his hand on the gun. "What plantation you from, Auntie?"

"What do it matter now?" She twisted her head to look at the sergeant. "Go ahead and shoot, you look like you done had lots of practice. Too bad there ain't no more women around. And nary a child. If there was, you could let my blood flow in the same stream as theirs."

The sergeant raised the revolver again. "Sir, just let me get rid of this—"

"Not so fast." The captain smiled. "Hell, I ain't never seen nobody stand up to a gun like that. Now, dammit, woman, we ain't got time to fool with you. Tell me where you're from."

"Clifton. I'm from Clifton."

"Put away that gun, Sergeant, and let's get moving."

"But, sir—"

"Hell, man, that's Colonel Kenworthy's place. He's riding somewhere back behind us and wouldn't take too kindly to killing of his property." He looked at Zenobia. "You know Clifton's only about ten miles away from here, don't you?"

"Don't know nothing about that, neither."

"You're a real smart one, ain't you?" He turned to the sergeant. "Let's get after them Yanks."

He retook his place at the head of the column and raised his hand.

"Forward!"

Zenobia wrapped herself in her tattered blanket and watched the long column of cavalry pass by. The ribs of the horses looked about ready to push through their skin, and many of the soldiers were riding barefoot. Every one of them was ragged and dirty, and they wore all kinds of things on their heads—Reb caps, farmers' hats, bandannas, and some of them even had on Yankee caps.

A few looked at Zenobia when they passed, but most never even glanced her way. Toward evening, the number of calvary thinned out, and when nightfall came, a small detachment stopped and made camp.

A short, clean-shaven soldier came over to where Zenobia lay beneath the tree. His right eye kept blinking, like it had a mind of its own.

"Well, Suzy Mae, what you doing here?"

"Waiting till my leg get better."

"To do what?"

She pulled the blanket over her so it was almost up to her chin. "To go back to my plantation. Yankees stole me from it."

The man laughed. "One of them runaways, huh?"

They built a good-size fire and soon had a pot boiling. The smell of corn mush made her mouth water, but when they brought some over to her, it didn't have no taste. Even so, the warmth of the thin mush seemed to spread down into her leg and ease the pain some.

She awoke to a hand shoving her shoulder.

"Wake up, Suzy Mae! The night's young and we ain't even had a chance to get to know you. Tomorrow we got to be pushing on."

The man who had spoken to her earlier was holding out a cup of whiskey. "Here, take this, it'll be good for you, make the pain go away."

She took a swallow.

The rest of the men were sitting around the fire drinking and singing. "She ain't in no pain!" one of them hollered. "You know niggers is always playing sick."

He sat down next to her, that eye of his blinking up a storm. "You right good-looking, you know. What's your name?"

"Zenobia."

"Comes from the Good Book, don't it?"

She nodded. The warmth from the whiskey was spreading through her body.

"Here, have some more. You been out here all day."

He watched her take another sip.

"Zenobia, me and the boys been fighting the Yanks for the last three weeks, and we're feeling mighty poorly, just about the way you're feeling with that leg. We going to pick you up and move you over closer to the fire for the night, so's you can be good and warm."

She pulled the blanket back up to her neck. "I'm just fine here."

"Now, don't be arguing with me. Some more of that whiskey and some heat from that there fire, and you'll be right as rain." He yelled over to his comrades. "A couple of you boys come on over here and give me a hand getting Zenobia over where she can be near us and the fire."

They lifted her up, and she felt their hands all over her thighs and breasts.

"Easy with her, boys, don't want to damage the goods."

They laid her down on a bed of pine branches not far from the fire, and she pulled the blanket back around her.

"Going to need a little time to get used to our company, ain't you?" The man with the blinking eye was mighty eager to share his whiskey with her. "We ain't no bad fellows, just looking to have us a little fun tonight. Cheer you up and us too."

Some of the men were lying on their backs, others with their legs hunched up close to their chests. One was strumming softly on a guitar while another sang in a high clear voice that seemed to float into every part of the night:

> "Where the Rio Grande is flowing
> And the starry skies are bright,

"We'uns don't want to hurt you . . ."

> "She walks along the river
> In the quiet summer night."

One of the men by the fire kicked dust into it, making sparks fly up. "What the hell you doing, treating her like she's a white woman or something? Go ahead and do what you got to do. We can't be up all night if we're chasing Yankees at daybreak."

Another man said, "You ain't man enough to take her, get the hell out the way and let us have her."

"She thinks, if I remember,
When we parted long ago . . ."

"Aw, hell." He jerked the blanket off. When his hands hit her swollen calf, she cried out as pain shot through her body. "Don't fight me, girl, you'll just get the others riled up and then you don't know what they might do."

He unbuckled his belt and bent over to take his pants off.

"Touch her, and I'll shoot!" The man with the beautiful voice had stopped singing and was standing about five feet away with a revolver in his hand. "Put her skirt down and cover her up with that blanket."

"Andy, have you gone plumb out of your mind? This ain't nothing but a nigger."

"Be that as it may, you heard what I said." He had drawn another revolver, had one in each hand. "I'm sick and tired of all this killing and raping and pillaging—and I ain't having none of it tonight from you, Ben, or"—he pointed in the direction of the campfire—"any of you others."

They all stared at him. The only sound was the popping of the fire.

With a grunt, Ben pulled his pants back up and stomped off.

Andy rolled a log over to where Zenobia lay, propped his back up against it, and sat with his guns in his lap.

"I'll be watching over you tonight, Auntie. There won't no harm come to you."

Zenobia said, "I thank you kindly, Massa Andy. God bless and keep you."

* * *

In the morning, he fed her hot mush and a cup of something made out of leaves and grass.

"We're going to be on our way. Maybe somebody will come by and help you today." He gave her a gold coin. "This could come in handy."

Zenobia smiled. "That's mighty kind of you. And what with the sun coming out, this pain might go away soon."

He didn't need to know she was getting the shivers, had sweated all the night long. Let him think he had saved her.

She waved as he walked off.

* * *

Zenobia lay there for another two days, as troops, deserters, and stragglers rode by. Occasionally, somebody would leave her some hardtack, a piece of fatback, a cup of water. But nobody else tried to harm her.

Every morning she awoke shivering, her blanket soaked and dreams of Aunt Garry and Cally still in her head. And Drayton shouting, "run, Zenobia, run!" Seems like that was all she'd been doing. And Clifton no more than ten miles away! Yet so far away, so long ago. Head so hot, body so cold . . .

Propping herself up, she leaned against the log where Andy had sat guard over her. The sun was high, driving the mist off the bare fields that stretched out in the distance on the other side of the road.

She couldn't remember ever being so thirsty before. She drained the last drops of water from the canteen Andy had left her. She wiped her brow, then looked at her hand: soaking wet.

* * *

"Zenobia? Zenobia, is that you?"

Slowly she opened her eyes, then closed them again as the sun almost blinded her. And felt again a gentle nudge on her shoulder. "Wake up, Zenobia."

A thin white man with a heavy beard and bloodshot eyes dropped to his knees beside her. "That's it, Sergeant, put the compress right on her forehead."

The coolness from the damp cloth seemed to spread through her body. And the man's voice . . . she knew that voice.

"Thank you, Sergeant. Here, Zenobia, take some water, do you good." He put his hand under her neck and lifted her head so she could drink.

"That you, Massa Kenworthy? How you doing?"

"It's me all right. I'm tolerable well, but you don't seem to be."

"How you find me?"

"I didn't. The sergeant drew my attention to a woman lying here under the tree, and I came over to take a look."

Zenobia tilted her head so she could see him better. "What you going to do with me now? Send me back to Jackson?"

"I'm going to get you a wagon and have a couple of my men take you back up to Clifton. At least you'll have Uncle Dan up there to take care of you. I'll write out a pass so nobody will bother you. Once you're up there, you'll be on your own."

Andy turned to the sergeant. "We'll take a noon break here and move on in an hour. Get her some hot grub, then leave us alone for a bit. And make sure the wagon has lots of pine branches. She's a mighty sick gal."

He sat down in the dirt beside her while she ate. "Zenobia, you got swamp fever. Don't reckon I have to tell you how much rest you're going to need once you get back to Clifton."

"I know." She felt like she was burning up.

He shifted his position and picked up a twig, broke off a small piece, and then broke it into two smaller pieces.

"I got some things to tell you, Zenobia, and not much time to do it. I've been thinking a lot about things of late. Not much liking the way I feel about them."

It was hard to hear him over the ringing in her ears.

". . . anyway, I want you to know that your boy, Luke, is with the Yankees now. I think he's all right. He's hurt, but not bad enough to keep the little hellcat from running. Yankees'll know how to help him. And last I heard, Milly was safe with Pauline over in Louisiana."

"And Joe? You heard anything of him?"

"Heard of him, Zenobia?" The colonel took a deep breath and looked off into the distance. "Why, Joe's been as close to me as I am to you right now. Not more than a week ago, we liked to have killed each other. As a matter of fact, he did kill my horse."

Blood rushed to Zenobia's head, now pounding so badly she couldn't tell if the ringing had stopped or not. Joe had been so near?

"He's a soldier now, a sergeant in the Yankee cavalry—and I don't mind telling you that he's a handful when he's in battle. Don't reckon I've seen many his equal in this war."

A sergeant! "From what Joe told me, you and him been fighting from the time you was little."

The colonel laughed. "True enough, Zenobia, true enough. And you'd think we'd have learned to live peaceable once we grew up, but it's not like that. Hell, I guess we both got a kick out of having at each other out on that battlefield last week, and neither one of us would have hesitated to kill the other if we'd gotten the chance. That's the way it is out there . . ."

"You mens been through a lot, Massa."

"I have, for sure. What I want more than anything now is a good night's sleep. And maybe a chance to go to a church all by myself. Remember the stone chapel up at Clifton? I tell you, some of the things we've had to do to survive, I need to . . . There's nothing like a long and serious conversation with the Lord."

He was talking just like she should understand him, know how much hurt he felt. Maybe that happened when sudden-like you run into somebody you ain't seen for a long time and they from your same home place. Even if it was a darky you'd never had much use for.

Glancing at his watch, he hollered over to the sergeant. "Fifteen minutes!" Then he turned back to Zenobia. "And Cally, the pretty little girl with those black eyes, where is she?"

Zenobia tried to tell him. Couldn't.

"I'm so, so sorry." He reached down and took her hands, not bothering to wipe away a tear on his own cheek.

* * *

A half hour later, Zenobia was on her way back to Clifton. As night fell, they drove her up to a shack. An old colored man came out, lantern in hand.

"You Uncle Dan?"

"Yes, sir!"

"Colonel Kenworthy sent this woman for you to take care of. She's sick. Here, put the lantern down and come give us a hand."

"Wait a minute," Uncle Dan said. "I got to clean off a pallet and lay some fresh straw down for to make her an easy lying place."

The three men gently transferred her to the newly made pallet. Just before they left, one of the soldiers handed Uncle Dan some Yankee greenbacks.

"Use this to buy food and medicine for her. Courtesy of the colonel."

* * *

Once they were gone, Uncle Dan hung the lantern up by the door and sat down by her side.

"Baby child, I'm so glad they brought you back here so's I can watch over you. What you need is to have some of my bark tea and some mush. Make you feel better, you just wait and see. Mmm-hmmm."

He got up and started collecting things for cooking outside over the fire.

He returned with a steaming bowl of porridge and a cup filled to the brim with his special medicine.

"Here, take this, baby child."

Zenobia ate and drank, and whether it was that or being off the hard ground after so long, she did feel a little better.

"Uncle Dan? What happened to Brother Drayton? I got to know."

He stared down at the floor for a long moment before he looked back at her.

"Oh, he didn't suffer too long. Six grayboys shot him, still he managed to kill one of them before he died. A right brave man, according to my way of thinking. Some of the niggers come out of the bush the next day, and we buried him."

Zenobia propped herself up on one elbow. "Is there something on your mind, something else you want to tell me about what happened to Brother Drayton?"

"Ain't I always treated everybody right? Ain't I always tried to do the right thing?" He was rubbing his hands together.

"You have. None could fault you."

A tear rolled down his cheek. "Zee, I is an old man. Gets confused sometimes . . ." He was bent over, head almost to the ground, not looking at her anymore.

He'd turned Joe over to the Rebs and betrayed Drayton, sent two women and two children down the river without a man to protect them. Could she forgive him? She looked at his white head bent over like so many times in the past, remembered all the guns and whips and dogs. And his wife, Aunt Sarah, sold off by Massa many years ago. All those long hurtful years without her . . .

She laid her hand gently on his shoulder. "Well, don't worry yourself, Uncle. The good Lord knows what's in your heart, reckon I do, too. Where did you bury Brother Drayton?"

"Up aside Cally."

"Oh, if I could only get up from here and go up there on that hill and pray a minute. If I had the strength . . ."

"I goes up there every week and prays for her and him and when we got flowers, I puts them up there. You know I loved that child something awful." He smiled. "I'd be standing there with a lot of other people and she'd walk right up to me and take my hand, yes she would! Out of all them standing there, she'd come right up to me." He saw the look on her face and laughed. "Guess I done told you that a time or two before. Yessuh, I's a old man . . . a foolish old man."

He took her hand. "Now, you got to sleep, get your health and strength back. Swamp fever be a powerful foe."

Zenobia began to shake. "Could I trouble you for another blanket, Uncle?"

"I ain't got no more, Zee, but I'll cover you with my coat. Now you go on to sleep, child." He began to sing softly.

> *"There is a balm*
> *In Gilead*
> *To make the wounded whole*
> *There is a balm*
> *In Gilead*
> *To heal the sin-sick soul!"*

* * *

A warm Sunday afternoon in early spring. Massa and Miss Sue had let all the folk worship with the whites that morning, sitting right outside on the colored folks' porch while the minister preached the gospel. They walked back to the quarters, singing and shouting and having a fine time in the Lord's name. Then, after a good Sunday dinner, she and Joe left the children with Aunt Garry and walked hand in hand up to Someday.

"Zee, do you know how glad I get when I wakes up in the morning and see your face next to mine? It makes up for a whole lot of pain."

Far in the distance, she could see where the river curved down toward Yazoo City. The birds were singing in the trees that spring day with the air still light and fresh, not heavy and damp the way it got in the high summer.

"I know," she said. "And how you think I could live this life of ours if it wasn't for knowing that you're always there to take me in your arms."

She shivered as he put his arm around her and brushed his fingers against her breast, loved it a little with his fingers, right through her yellow blouse.

"Let's lay down here, baby, right in the soft grass."

It felt so good when he touched her, rubbed his fingers back and forth so slowly against her skin. She liked that about him, that he took his time loving her.

"Joe, I—"

He said "Shush" and put a finger against her mouth, kissed it, and talked to her body with his gentle, slow-moving fingers . . .

* * *

Wasn't till later in the afternoon, lying warm in his arms, that she turned her head toward the river.

"See that path down there?" she said. "I want to go down it a little ways. Can we?"

They meandered hand in hand along the bank.

"Joe, you been way down there riding horses for Massa in them races. Where do this river go?"

"To the Mississippi."

She squeezed his arm. "And then where?"

He grinned. "Straight on down to New Orleans."

"And then?"

He stopped and thought for a minute.

"Into the Atlantic Ocean, I guess."

"Joe, you ever seen the ocean?"

"A couple of times."

"Do the ocean go to Africa?"

He just looked at her.

"I want to know. Do it go to Africa?"

"I suppose. What's got into you, Zee?"

"Did you ever want to be a fish?"

"Now, that's enough!" He swatted her on the bottom and laughed.

"No, wait. Listen." She ran out a few paces ahead of him and was walking backward now with her black skirt swirling around in that way she knew made men stop and watch her as she went around the quarters of a Sunday morning. "If you was a fish, you could swim right down this river, into the Mississippi, past New Orleans, all the way to the ocean, then go into the deep blue sea, and swim anywhere you wanted to, anywhere . . ." She clapped her hands and shouted. "Anywhere! I know it!"

* * *

"Here, Zenobia, drink you some of this." Uncle Dan lifted her head with one hand, brought the cup to her lips with the other. "You must of been dreaming, baby child, now you . . . Zenobia?"

Very gently, he eased her head back down.

CHAPTER TWENTY-ONE

PAULINE awoke early that morning, sat up, and slowly rubbed the sleep out of her eyes. When she realized how high the sun was, she all but leapt out of the bed. The hogs! They should have been fed by now. Then she spied the long white dress laid out on a chair, smiled, and lay back down for a few moments. There'd be no feeding of the animals for her today—

What would Miss Dorothy think if she knew?

Hard to believe she'd been gone almost two months already. The patrollers in the area made a habit of stopping in now and then, but each time Woodson had been able to get everybody into hiding. And since Pauline had the proper papers to run the place, nothing had happened so far.

A soft knock came at the door of her room.

"Auntie?"

Must be Milly. The door creaked, then her dear face appeared, eyes sparkly with excitement. Well, a seventeen-year-old girl on the morning of a festive occasion ought to be excited.

"Can I come in?"

"Of course, baby."

"Oh, how pretty it looks!" Milly clapped her hands. "How did you make something so beautiful out of those old dresses?"

"There's enough fancy stuff up there in the attic to make wedding dresses for plenty more women—none of it good for anything else. Now let's have a look at you. Turn around."

Milly pirouetted and made a little bow.

"Good gracious, honey, you're so pretty you're going to have to beat the boys off with a stick."

She giggled. She had a sweet and lovely face, but it was the way she carried herself that drew your attention. She was Zenobia's daughter all right.

Milly had left the door open and the odors of baked sweet potatoes, ham, black-eyed peas, and apple pies all mingled and drifted upstairs. They were going to dine in style to mark this special Christmas and her wedding day. Even going to have biscuits!

Milly sat down on the bed and helped Pauline finish arranging her headdress.

"Auntie, I've been thinking . . ."

"Yes, honey?"

"When all this war is over, and the Yankees come . . . do you think you and Mr. Woodson can come back and live with us all over at Clifton, or someplace? You know, so everybody could be together?"

It would be good to live once again where she could see her darling brother Joe, every day.

"We'll just have to see about that when the time comes. Right now, why don't you run and get Ann and Jill. It's almost time for us to march in."

* * *

Pauline stood at the top of the stairs with Milly and the two little girls and looked down. A small table covered with a white cloth had been dragged to the middle of the living room. On it were two red candles; in front of the table was the big bearskin rug. A fire burned in the fireplace, and stockings stuffed with apples and homemade toys and gifts hung from the mantel. The tree Woodson had brought in was decorated with strings of berries and pine cones and any little pretty shiny thing the children could find. Pine boughs crisscrossed the mantelpiece.

The living room was so big it didn't seem as if forty people were really standing down there waiting for her, all looking up as she started down the stairs, then clapping and stomping as they parted to make an aisle for her. Everybody had dressed up their best for this day. For most of them it had been years since they'd had anything new to wear, but they'd washed and scrubbed and smoothed what they had till everything was neat and clean.

Tears came to her eyes as she took in the beauty of the many tones of color in the faces smiling at her: coffee brown, honey yellow, mahogany red, plum black, earth brown—colors made more vibrant by the glow of the fire.

And there next to old Preacher Williamson was Woodson, the only one not smiling. He looked serious and proud. Well, she felt proud to be loved by this dear good man.

When the words had been spoken and the vows exchanged, two people held the broomstick so Woodson and Pauline could jump over it together.

"I now pronounces you man and wife."

They kissed. And at last Woodson smiled and kept on smiling while they ate and drank—there was good corn liquor aplenty. When the fiddler began to play, Woodson grabbed Pauline's hands and they joined the men and the women lining up in rows facing each other. After the women curtsied, the men bowed and began to clap their hands and shuffle their feet in time to the music.

> *"Come along little children, come along*
> *While the moon is shining bright*
> *Get on board, down the river shore*
> *Gonna' raise ruckus tonight*
> *Now my old mistress promise me*
> *Raise ruckus tonight!*
> *That when she died, she'd set me free*
> *Raise ruckus tonight!*
> *She lived so long that her head got bald*
> *Raise ruckus tonight!*
> *I thought she wasn't gonna die at all*
> *Raise ruckus tonight!*
> *Oh, come along little children, come along . . ."*

Woodson bowed in front of Pauline, offered his arm, and began the promenade down the aisle between the lines of the men and women. He could really do that walk! He took a step and then jerked his face to the side, as if he were saying, "See that?" Then he stuck one leg out, bent it in mid-air, and twirled it around. Every time he did that, the folks would break out shouting and clapping and Pauline would look at him in mock amazement.

Then it was her turn. She'd shake her hips a little, throw her shoulders back, move her arms to and fro and wave her hands in the air at the same time. It took them a long while to get from one end of the row to the other, but when they finished, everybody clapped and started strutting their stuff right behind them, little children at the rear.

"Make your circle!" cried the fiddler. He sat in a rocking chair, a jug of whiskey at his feet.

Woodson led the way, going around and around that great big room. The fiddler was feeling so good, he walked right into the middle of the circle, found the prettiest girl he could—Milly, of course—and played along right beside her, making a sweet and special sound with the bow every time she twisted that young body of hers.

It was the wildest dance that Pauline, raised as a house slave, had ever seen. They'd dance all in step together, then freeze their bodies, shake their shoulders, take another step, shake their hips, take another step, clap their hands together—then everybody would twirl around in place, and start all over again.

For a while it looked as if they'd never get tired, but once a few started finding somewhere to rest, it wasn't long before all of them were sitting in various places around the room. A big man who was sweating and out of breath from the dancing held up his hands. "You all be quiet a minute, I wants you to hear this little thing I made up:

"*Run, boy, run, de pat'roller' ketch yo'*
Run, boy, run, it's almos' day.
Dat boy run, dat boy flew,
Dat boy tore his shirt in two.
Dat boy cried, dat boy lied,
Dat boy shook his old fat side,
Run, boy, run, it's almos' day."

They clapped and hollered, "More! More!" but Preacher Williamson broke in.

"Well, it's getting on to midnight now and we done had us a real good time. Tomorrow we be up and back to work, fixing up this place. It's the only home we got now and we going to keep it nice. Besides, Woodson and Pauline, they got to go to bed. Come forward here so you can face the folks and tell them good night."

Pauline walked up with Woodson, then turned around and looked right down the length of the room. "At the window!" she shouted.

A white man's face was pressed right against the glass at the far end. His eyes were big and protruding, and his beard long and bushy.

Woodson was already on his way out the door, followed by most of the men. By the time Pauline got outside, the only trace of the man was the sound of hooves fading into the distance.

"We'd never catch him in the dark with that head start," Woodson said. "Best thing for us to do is get ready for an attack. Either that or go back out into the woods. And with all these women and children—no, we'd freeze to death."

They worked the night through. Boarded over the windows, leaving openings so the men could fire through them with what muskets and carbines they had. Put great big tubs of water in the middle of the floor in case the assailants—whoever they turned out to be—decided to burn them out. Got all the livestock into a stockade at the rear of the house. Stored powder and cartridges near the windows. And brought hay in to make pallets. From now on everybody would sleep in the big house.

They set up firing posts to cover most approaches to the house and brought the pickets in closer. That would shorten their warning time, but out in the woods they'd be easy pickings for Rebs or deserters.

Toward dawn Woodson sat down with Pauline and took her hands in his.

"I'm going to mount up and do a little scouting around the neighborhood, me and Josh." He smiled and kissed her. "Not exactly what I had in mind for our wedding night."

* * *

When they returned that afternoon, he called everyone together. "We didn't see no sign of large forces out there, and the tracks of last night's visitor go off into the woods. Right now it don't look like we're in danger. Not tonight or maybe even tomorrow night. But that one white man knows we all here and they will surely come to capture us sooner or later. Josh, here, he's volunteered to take a horse and try to get through to the Yankees and tell them where we are."

He reached down and picked up a little boy who'd been pulling on his pant leg. "That's about the best we can do for now, so I want you all to pray Josh gets through. You know how to pray, little man?" He looked down at the boy, who answered by folding his tiny fingers together and leaning his head against Woodson's chest.

Woodson handed him over to Pauline and put his arms around her and Milly.

"We family here, and we going to live together or die together."

Pauline said, "Amen," and heard a chorus of Amens behind her.

* * *

Richard Kenworthy didn't like these bad feelings down inside him, but since the fall of Savannah and the report of the death in action of Clint Adams, he didn't seem to have any other kind. Now the Yankees were headed into the Carolinas. But the thing he couldn't stop thinking about was that he had failed to protect his own home. He went over and over it in his mind. That a nigger cavalry sergeant could go into his house and sleep under the same roof with his wife and children—it was just too much for a man to bear.

That and so much else didn't make sense. He'd marched off to war so proud and happy to protect the Southern way of life, and the very act of protecting that great and wonderful culture— the highest social form Western civilization had yet devised—had resulted in its destruction. And darky soldiers in his living room, giving his sweet Sue orders, putting their hands on her to restrain her! Somebody would have to pay for all this.

So it was with mixed feelings that he received orders—now that he could ride again—to report over in Louisiana to suppress the activities of the Negroes on some of the plantations. General Forrest assigning him to General Harrison's command over there was an admission that the Confederate cause in Mississippi was finished, and it was worrisome to have to leave Sue and the children so vulnerable. But one of the plantations in question was his sister's place.

Which meant he'd be able to kill two birds with one stone. Destroy some nigger enemy and renew his relationship with Pauline. Milly would be there, too. Joe's kid. The bastard had carried off most of his hard-earned money. It was stealing, never mind his damned Yankee receipt. And after he'd left Uncle Dan ten dollars for Zenobia!

* * *

He specifically requested the assignment to the Cannon plantation when he arrived in Louisiana.

The general handed him the report from the scout about the Christmas party. "It's been a while, but the darkies are probably still up there. Get to it as soon as you can and get on back here. There's a Union cavalry detachment on its way down from the Arkansas border."

"It'll take me a few days to get together some horses and equipment and food. And the men are in pitiful shape. Rags for shoes."

"Yes, Grierson's boys did a job on the shoe factory over there. One of those regiments—the Third Colored—is on its way down here."

Richard slapped his gauntlet on the edge of the general's desk. "As soon as I destroy that band up at my sister's place, I'll be back to give you a hand with the Third. I've got a few scores to settle with them."

"So do a lot of people, Colonel. Montgomery still hasn't stopped complaining about that nigger who stole his horse."

* * *

"Whoa, Princess," Joe said. "We got to wait a bit, see if Howerton can get over first."

The Third was in northern Louisiana, down near Oak Ridge, and wet as they could be. Joe looked at his hands, saw they were still trembling. God, he hoped nobody noticed. Not only that, but they were wrinkled like prunes. His and everybody else's in the regiment.

This time out, the main enemy had been water. Some days he'd glance behind him and it would almost look like the men were wading instead of on horseback. All around was nothing but water, and wasn't nothing coming down out of the sky but more of it. The Rebs seemed to have melted away in the rain.

But he was expecting that to change soon.

In the meantime, a courier had come in before they left Memphis and brought word about the folks at the Cannon plantation needing help. Since Milly was there, Colonel Osband had given Joe permission to take a detachment of fifty men and bring everybody back into the Union lines.

Pauline was there too. What a story Luke had told him, about how at the last minute when it seemed like they were going to be sold into Texas, she'd persuaded Miss Cannon to step in and buy them. Luke showed how Pauline had taught him to write his name. Hard to say who was prouder— him or Luke.

What was he going to do when he saw her? He could still close his eyes and remember how happy he'd been when Momma had called him into the hut where she lay under a blanket. "See your baby sister." Before she went off to live in the big house, she'd followed him everywhere, crawling, toddling, walking, and sometimes running after him. Then one day when she was a full-grown woman with a golden brown body, Massa Richard—

"Look at Howerton!" A shout snapped Joe out of his daydream. Howerton had volunteered to try and get across that stream, and it wasn't going to be an easy thing.

He was edging his way down the bank of the river. The water was running fast, and ripples of white were breaking all around the legs of his horse. Logs and branches—all kinds of things—were coming down the stream.

"That's it. Just ease her down," Joe said. "And let her have her head."

Howerton looked back and grinned. "How the hell I'm going to do that the way this water's running?"

"You know how."

All along the bank of the river, the horse soldiers sat cheering him on.

"You bad enough to do it, man!"

"Sarge say there some fine young womens just a-waiting to sing you to sleep on the other side!"

"Look out!" Joe cried.

Howerton was dead in the middle of the stream, and a big-assed log was running straight at him. The horse must have seen the log the same time Joe did, because it almost looked like it tried to raise its legs out of the water to miss the thing. Horse and rider fell sideways and were swept away. Wasn't nothing anybody could do to help them. One minute they were there and the next nothing but rushing water.

Everybody was quiet for a few seconds, and then all the men were looking at Joe.

* * *

Should he risk their lives and keep trying to cross the river? Every one of the men in his command knew that the assignment had been given to them because Milly and Pauline were up there.

Logan, one of the best horsemen in the Third, rode up. "I'm next."

This time, almost as if the men thought their talking had jinxed Howerton, they kept silent. Except for Tucker, who said, "My turn next." Joe looked over his shoulder and saw eight men ready to try if Logan failed. Just when he had decided that if Logan didn't make it, he'd have to find another ford.

Logan was about halfway across when he stopped. He looked back at Joe, then bent down over the horse's mane and whispered something to her. She threw her head back like maybe she'd heard something flattering. One step, two steps, three steps, then she was out of the stream and on the bank, shaking the water off her mane.

"Form into a column, men!"

They lost a few weapons and some supplies, but in a little more than an hour everybody was safely across.

By the reckoning of the Union soldier who'd come down from the plantation, they were still about twelve miles away. With all this mud and water, it was going to seem more like twenty-five—and the crossing had taken a lot out of the men.

About a mile away was an abandoned plantation where they'd be able to warm themselves and bed down for the night. Just what they all needed.

CHAPTER TWENTY-TWO

RICHARD Kenworthy looked behind him at the ragged column that called itself the Fifth Louisiana Cavalry. This was a regiment? Why, it was barely more than a few squads. Half the men on mules, some walking, not a one of them in a real uniform. Nothing about them brought to mind the fiery-eyed legions that had set out just a few years ago on high-stepping mounts to whip the Yankees to a pulp. They were subsisting on wet Yankee hardtack, rotten and full of weevils. Enough to turn a healthy man's stomach, and given the condition of these men, it was worse than no food at all.

But, by God, when he'd asked for volunteers, seventy-five men had stepped forward. If there was one thing that could still stir them, make the poor devils forget their aching bellies, it was niggers with arms. Couldn't abide the thought any more than he could.

About four miles away from Dorothy's plantation he began to recognize the countryside, though this barren land was another sorry imitation of what had been. Close his eyes and he could see the rows and rows of white cotton stretching as far as the eye could see, line after line of darkies, backs bent, putting boll after boll into the sacks over their shoulders. Dorothy and the colonel and Sue on the veranda in the evening, children playing games. A good cigar, a fine wine, and the darkies' music . . .

A blast of wind blew stinging rain into his face. He looked around for Captain Brunson.

"With night coming on, and all this mud and wet, we'd best bivouac out here. Tell Sergeant Barclay to have the men up early and ready to hit them just about daybreak. And have the scouts report back to me as soon as they get in."

"Begging the colonel's pardon," Brunson said, "but it's going to be rough sleeping out here. Half of the men are already hacking and coughing, and some of them are coming down with swamp fever. I'd just as soon we pushed on and took the place tonight. They're nothing but some nigger slaves that have never had any military training. We could just walk in and take them, get us a good night's sleep."

Richard thought about the Big Black River Bridge and Franklin. "No, we'll do it my way."

* * *

The captain was right about the conditions. Wretched. But the men were veterans, and Kenworthy knew they'd make the best of it. Somehow or other, they got a few fires going and set up some lean-tos. They'd make it, all right.

Just when he was about to fall off to sleep, the two scouts who'd been watching the plantation all day returned.

"Colonel, them niggers got pickets out all around that old place. Must be about forty or fifty of 'em living there."

"How many men in all, you reckon?"

"I'd say about twenty, the rest is women and children. No way to tell what's stashed in the house, but it don't look like they got many weapons— mostly old muskets and pikes. Won't be a problem at all."

"Well done. Get what sleep you can and we'll go in at first light. Better quarters tomorrow night, men!"

* * *

Just before the sky lightened the next morning, the detachment was on the move. It was still raining hard, but the wind had diminished, and it had gotten a little warmer. As a matter of fact, here on the third day of February 1865, you could almost feel a touch of spring in the air.

As day broke, they approached the outskirts of the plantation. Richard watched the men form into four squads—one for each side of the place— and disappear into the near dark. He had kept the command of one squad himself. They would face the front of the big house.

"Sergeant Barclay!"

"Sir!"

"We've got about fifteen minutes left. Have the men dismount and follow me."

Five men were left behind as horse holders. How strange to be approaching his sister's plantation with a group of soldiers to take it back from a bunch of nigras.

A row of hedges about thirty yards away grew around the perimeter of the place. Perfect concealment for the attack. But to reach them, they were going to have to walk down an approach road with woods on both sides.

He motioned the men forward. They crouched down and just as they began to move a volley of shots rang out.

"Son of a bitch! They bushwhacked us."

Two men fell. The rest quickly flushed out the woods on the sides, but whoever had done the shooting had made their retreat through the hedges. Probably running for the refuge of the house.

Shouts coming from the other squads confirmed that they had encountered similar resistance.

"Come on, men!"

Richard waved them into position behind the hedges, sent a runner with orders for the others to hold their fire, then had a man approach the house with a white flag.

* * *

"Don't you go out there, Woodson," Pauline said. "They just want to kill you."

"He says Colonel Kenworthy himself wants to parley with me."

Pauline's heart sank. "Him! Oh no, you mustn't go, he's ruthless."

"You see up there?" Woodson pointed to where two men stood on boxes, their muskets aimed through the firing holes in the window frames. "Anything happen to me, they'll shoot him dead. If nothing else, it'll gain us some time. What with all this flooding and stuff, it may be taking an extra-long time for the Yankees to get here."

"If they even coming. You don't know that Josh got through."

"Pauline." He touched her mouth, smoothing her bottom lip with his fingertips until she stopped biting it. "I'll be back in a little while."

* * *

Milly stood with her at a peephole and watched Woodson and another man bearing a white flag march out to meet Richard. They talked for about five minutes, then Woodson came back inside.

"See, nothing happened. The colonel says if we surrender, he'll give us safe conduct to the Yankee lines, even give us an escort to see we get there safe. He carried on about how this the property of Colonel and Mrs. Cannon—'not a refuge for slaves.' Says the only thing they want is for us to leave."

"What did you tell him?" Pauline asked.

The others had all crowded close.

"That we'd think about it."

"How much time?"

"Fifteen minutes, we all come out with our hands in the air, or they're coming in here after us."

Everybody was quiet for a moment, then milling around, trying to talk it out, see what was best to do.

Woodson called Pauline aside. "I have to tell you this— he offered safe conduct to you and Milly even if nobody else surrenders."

She took Woodson's hand and called for silence.

"My husband just told me something I think you all ought to know— Colonel Kenworthy has offered to let me and Milly go free no matter what happens to the rest of you."

Milly's head was shaking back and forth.

"But I know that man out there. You have to do what you think is right, but I have to tell you he can't be trusted and I, for one, will die before I put myself in his hands again. Those white folks like to talk about how they died at the Alamo—well, I pray it doesn't come to that, but we free now and the only way to stay that way is to fight."

"Thank you, sister!"

"Tell the truth!"

"Amen!"

"Then let's get to work!" Woodson picked up a musket and walked over to where the ammunition tables had been set up. "We have to prepare the welcome table for Colonel Kenworthy and his men. Praise the Lord!"

* * *

Joe looked out on the morning of February 3. Wasn't it ever going to stop raining? Josh had found them a good place to stay, and they'd dried off some during the night. The men wouldn't be too eager to get back out there in the wet, but it was time to get moving. Be lucky to make the plantation by nightfall with the roads the way they were.

"Send Josh out with the scouts, Zack. Give them the best mounts we've got—only way they going to deal with all this mud. If the way is clear, tell Josh to ride on in and let the people know we on our way."

The mud was so deep it hurt to see the men try to stay in column. The horses just sank in the imprints made by the mounts in front of them. Soon they were spread out over the fields on either side of the road.

By noontime, they'd made about six miles. Joe called a halt to feed the men and rest the horses. It was still pelting rain, and they were as wet and miserable as before. But when Logan, one of the scouts, came into view way down the road waving his hand, Joe was up immediately.

"A mile or so down the road, there's a crossroads," Logan said. "About fifty cavalry men come out of it. They got to be somewhere between us and the plantation. Jones and Jenkins have gone ahead with Josh."

"Boots and Saddles!" Joe didn't need to hear any more. "Good work, Logan. Zack will give you three more men and you'll make us an advance guard. Get going." He turned to Zack.

"Flankers out. Get the men dismounted. I think we'll make better time that way."

It was definitely better for the horses, though the men soon had mud all over them. The column was moving faster, but no matter how they did it, he didn't see how they could get there before evening time. He tried not to think of Milly or Pauline—they had to be left in God's hands for now.

* * *

Logan returned at four. "Sir, we got firing in our front. Jenkins got down to the plantation and met back up with us about two miles down the road. Rebs all around it, and not much shooting coming from the plantation."

"How much further for us?"

Logan looked back over Joe's shoulder at the slow-moving column of men.

"I'd say—a two-hour march, sir."

* * *

"Water, please." A mulatto man, bleeding badly from his stomach, lay on the floor looking up at Pauline.

"It will only hurt you. Here." She put a cloth into a bucket of water, wrung it out, then wiped his forehead.

She looked around the great room. Every last one of the chandeliers was shattered, and shards of glass lay all over the floor. Where boards had been nailed over the windows there was mostly nothing but splinters. Knots of little children lay flat on their bellies in a far corner of the room. One toddler, about three years old, held both hands over his ears. The women were busy with what few wounded there were.

About fifteen men had already been killed and their bodies piled in the corner of the room farthest from the children. Some women had picked up weapons—they had trained and drilled right alongside the men since Christmas. A total of eight folks were left to defend the whole house. Milly had been loading muskets, but with the ammunition almost gone now, there was little for her to do except help minister to the wounded and shepherd the children up the stairs. The firing had ceased for the moment, so she accomplished the latter task with haste. When she'd seen to it that all of the young ones were temporarily safe above, she returned to Woodson's side. He was putting the last loads into his revolver.

"I guess they'll be storming the place pretty soon. They soldiers, they know we down low now."

"Let them come," Pauline said.

"I just don't know what happened to Josh. I was sure he'd get through."

"We's just little people," said a man seated on the floor. "And we colored, don't count for nothing with nobody."

Woodson shrugged his shoulders. "Still, I thought—"

"Hello there in the house!"

That was Richard shouting out there. She'd recognize that deep, mellow voice of his anywhere.

"Hello, I say! Pauline, it's me, Richard!"

Woodson put his arm around her shoulder.

"Come on out, you and Milly. You and the rest of the women and children don't have to die in there."

Pauline took Woodson's revolver, cocked it, and walked up to the door.

"I didn't hear you good, Richard."

When he stepped out from behind the bush and cupped his hands to call to her, she fired.

"Damn you, you black bitch! We're coming in after you."

She slammed the door and leapt aside just in time. Bullets ripped through the door and into the staircase. And then they were tearing into the house from all directions.

Pauline had never heard such a racket in her life. It sounded as though somebody had lit a bunch of rockets and thrown them into a room. She wanted to cover her ears like that little child had, but her place was next to Woodson.

Through a crack in the last intact board, she saw about twenty-five of them, running across the lawn, spread out a few feet apart. What a sight they were—hair below their shoulders, bearded, ragged, ugly, and wet, screaming their lungs out. Richard was leading them, his face still handsome but otherwise looking hardly better than the rest.

She took aim with the pistol, sighted along the barrel. Easy, now . . . there he was, right in the sights—

Missed him again!

Seemed as if she could hear her heart thumping wildly over the thud of feet on the porch, the splintering sound of wood as they pounded the butts of their guns against the front door.

"Upstairs, everybody," Woodson said. "They got to come up one by one, we can hold out a little bit longer. Use those muskets like clubs, when the ammunition is all gone."

Only six able-bodied persons remained. The floor was slippery with blood; the moans and cries of the wounded mingled with the sounds of exploding weapons, of breaking glass and cracking wood.

Pauline lay down beside Woodson at the top of the stairs, behind some desks and night tables taken from Dorothy's bedroom. She grasped his hand.

"Kiss me," she said. "Just one more time."

His kiss was sweet and long—enough for her to wish for what might have been, what—

A crash louder than anything yet shook the house. Must be the huge front door.

"Here they come!" Woodson said. "But thank God Almighty, we going to die free."

* * *

Richard was the first one through the doorway. They came in low, firing as they moved.

"Cease fire!" he called when he saw that the great room was empty.

In the stillness that followed they could hear babies crying. Sergeant Barclay pointed up toward the landing. With his revolver, Richard motioned the men up the stairs.

They were about halfway when Pauline and a big nigger sprang up, shotguns firing in unison. Two of the men on the stairway tumbled backward down the stairs.

Richard fired, but he would never know if it was a bullet from his gun that killed her. The other men were firing, too, and Pauline and the man staggered under the fire and collapsed together on the spot. Richard stood looking at her until fire from somewhere above brought him to his senses and they stormed the stairs, killing two more niggers at the top.

Once upstairs, they heard the sound of children crying again. It was coming from a room at the far end of the hall—Dorothy's old bedroom. At a signal from Richard, Sergeant Barclay cautiously made his way down the hall and kicked the door open. He looked, then turned around and beckoned.

"Secure the house," Richard said, then walked down the hall to his sister's room.

About a dozen colored children ranging in age from about three to fourteen were huddled together with fifteen or so women. Most of them were staring at him, the whites of their eyes wide. He studied each face and picked out Joe's girl, who was crying without making a sound.

"Milly? Come here, child." He took her by the hand and pulled her away from the others. Why, she was almost a woman! Her hand was soft and her shoulders, too, even though he felt them tighten when he put his arm around her.

"Now, then, there's nothing to worry about. All the shooting's over. We'll get everything cleaned up and then get you to a safe place. In the meantime you all just stay up here, nobody's going to hurt you."

By the time he got back downstairs Sergeant Barclay was waiting for further orders.

"First thing to do is get all those bodies out of my sister's living room. And send someone up to choose a few women to fix us something hot to eat. The rest of them—take them down to the slave cabins and lock them in. All except the one named Milly. Leave her upstairs under guard."

Some soldiers were already at the top of the stairs disposing of the bodies. He waited at the bottom and stopped the one who was carrying Pauline.

"No, wait a second."

She was beautiful, even in death. Could it be that he had really and truly loved her? Loved a nigger woman? He reached down and closed her eyes, then took her in his arms and carried her out the front door. When he had walked a ways, he called two of his men over and handed her body over to them.

"Bury her way over there, near where those rosebushes are."

He sat down on the front porch, unmindful of the falling rain, and watched. Half an hour later, he walked to the door and called for Barclay.

"Come outside for a minute." They stepped back onto the porch.

"We've neither the time nor the supplies to deal with these captives. We'll eat, enjoy ourselves a little bit afterward, then lock them back up in the cabins and set the shacks on fire."

Teach niggers to take over other people's property!

Somebody had to pay.

* * *

The firing had ceased before Joe's detachment got within earshot of the plantation. Minutes later, the scouts he sent out were back. The Rebs had taken the big house, and it looked as though they had killed all the men. Right now they were eating and drinking and playing around with a few of the women. They had locked the rest in the slave cabins with some children. There was a guard down at the slave cabins, but they hadn't posted any sentries.

Joe listened carefully, forcing himself to remain calm. The fate of his outfit depended on him. He called Zack and the other sergeants over and sketched out the plan of assault—kill the guard down at the cabins, then storm the house Third Cavalry style.

"Careful now, we don't want to hit any of our folks. Use the sabers as much as possible."

* * *

He and Zack crept up on their bellies through the mud. From the sound of their singing he figured there must be about thirty of them in there. Having themselves a fine old time.

Joe nodded at Zack. The men took up positions at the doors and windows to await the assault signal, the firing of Joe's carbine. Joe slipped up to a window.

The first thing he saw when he peeked in the window was Kenworthy, with a woman in his lap. His pistol was laid out right on the table in front of him. The fucking bastard had a bottle of wine in one hand and the other—Oh, my God, that's Milly in his lap!

Stepping back from the window, Joe took a position in front of the door. Kicking hard, he shattered the door open and fired away with his carbine. Out of the corner of his eye, he saw Milly fall to the floor and bolt away behind a big overstuffed chair. Good girl.

In the second Joe stood watching her, Kenworthy had grabbed a carbine and was running up the stairs, firing as he went.

Rest of the poor drunken fools never had a chance. Not that they deserved one. One man on the sofa with his hand up a black woman's dress reached for his shotgun. Zack shot his hand off before it ever touched that gun. Rebs were running back and forth like the trapped rats they were. Any way they turned there was another big black man with a saber cutting into their arms, legs, bellies, necks.

Five of them who managed to get to their weapons dropped them, backed into a corner and begged for mercy. What did they know about mercy?

* * *

"Prisoners!" Joe shouted. "Take cover, men, and cease fire."

The only one still armed was Colonel Richard Kenworthy, crouched at the top of the stairs with his carbine held crosswise against his chest. His eyes were red but still strong and mean, like he weren't licked yet. When he looked down and saw who was standing there, he shook his head slowly and the damnedest grin spread over his face.

"Well, now, it's come to this, hasn't it?"

"Sure has, Colonel."

"You don't intend to take me alive, do you?"

"Now, that depends on you. I done imagined killing you many a time, but I'm a soldier now and I obeys the rules. And lately seems like I'm losing my taste for fighting and killing. You the only one left, and if you put the gun down—"

"I'm tired of all of it, too. And I never meant for Pauline to die, that's a fact."

"You done that, Colonel? You sure enough done killed Pauline?"

"Colonel!" A Reb sergeant pushed his way to the bottom of the stairs and stood next to Joe. He was unarmed, but Zack kept a close eye on him anyway.

"Colonel, sir, please surrender, don't make them kill you!"

Kenworthy made a little bow.

"Sergeant Barclay, it's my deep honor and privilege to have served our Cause with you and the other brave soldiers there behind you. Please give Mrs. Kenworthy and my children my dearest love. And see to it that my personal effects are conveyed to them. The Yankee sergeant here won't hinder you, I'm sure."

Joe nodded and for a moment nobody said anything.

"Joe, remember the time we treed that mountain jack?"

"I do, sir."

"Weren't those some high good times?"

"They was that."

The colonel looked down at the floor, like he had something heavy on his mind and wanted to think about it for a moment. Then he raised his head and looked Joe directly in the eye again.

"You're one hell of a soldier, you know."

Joe sprang to attention. "Thank you, sir."

"Now come get me!"

It was the strangest thing. Seemed like he took his time standing up in full view, brushing himself off. Only then did he raise his carbine and aim.

And only then did Joe throw the Choctaw knife.

It caught him square in the middle of the chest, and stuck there. He looked down and put both his hands on it like he might try to pull it out. And fell dead still holding it.

Joe walked across the room and wrapped Milly in his arms.

"You safe now, baby. Safe and free."

* * *

In the morning, they dug a ditch for the dead and buried them all together, white and black.

"Going to put this Reb colonel in the same grave with the rest of the folk?" Zack asked.

"He an officer, ain't he? Bury him like one."

* * *

A few hours later, after breakfast, when the column was all ready to move out, Joe walked over to Zack.

"Get going, I'll catch up with you. Me and Milly got something to do."

He took her hand and together they walked over to where

the Reb sergeant told him Pauline was buried. The rain hadn't let up, and for once he was glad. He didn't want his daughter to see him crying as much as she was.

At the grave he got down on his knees in the mud with Milly right beside him. How was he going to say good-bye to Pauline, his sweet loving sister and the savior of his children in the dark night of slavery.

"Pauline, you hear me? Me and Milly, we kneeling here beside you, we praying hard for you, and I'm praying special hard you'll forgive me that I didn't get here in time to save you. I surely do wish I could have. But we going to see you over on the other shore. Every day will be Sunday, and Sabbath shall have no end."

He stood up, took his daughter's arm, and sang:

> "*Shine on me!*
> *Shine on me!*"

Milly reached over and wiped the tears from his cheeks, then her dark husky voice joined in.

> "*Let the light*
> *From the lighthouse*
> *Shine on me!*"

* * *

Joe and Betty sat on their favorite hill outside of Vicksburg. Joe kept fingering the paper in his hand. He'd read it again and again, then had Betty read it, too, just to make sure it said that he was honorably discharged at Vicksburg on June 16, 1865. They'd also both read the letter from Captain Stiles about how he was starting a place over in Louisiana and wanted Joe as his top man.

Finally he folded the discharge paper carefully and put it in his shirt pocket. This wasn't going to get any easier, no matter how long he put it off.

"Betty . . ." He got up and stood for a moment with his back to her. "Damn!"

She looked at him but didn't say anything. Just raised her eyebrows and waited.

"I guess there ain't any way to say it good, but I got to do as my conscience tells me, got to do what's best for my children. Search for Zenobia until God tells me it's enough."

He sat back down, knees cradled between his arms. Betty laid her head against his shoulder.

"Think I don't know that? No matter what, Joe, you can go as far as life will take you, but you know I will always love you."

"You some fine woman. Luke and Milly, they done come to love you, too."

She smiled, her dimples pretty as could be. "Those children have been a blessing to have around. They so much like you, I can't help but love them to pieces." She kissed him gently on the cheek. "I'm staying on as a volunteer nurse in the army for a while, then who knows where I'll go. You can always find me through them."

"And you can find me through Captain Stiles."

"Everybody going over there with you?"

"Well, not Zack and Lisa Mae. Now they married, they want to try and make it on their own. And Helen's going with them. But Ned, he'll be coming with me and the kids. That boy, he loves Zenobia something fierce."

"When you leaving?"

"Early in the morning. Figure it's a three-day ride from here, what with the kids and all."

"Put your arms around me, darlin'." Betty's eyes were wet. "I ain't going nowhere till I hear from you one way or another. You write me, hear, and let me know."

"I will, soon as I know anything."

* * *

In the morning, Joe and Milly and Luke mounted their horses, then Ned got up behind Luke. The trip seemed long, even in the bright sunshine with the fields green again and the birds singing. And the guns all quiet. But Joe was grateful for the chance to get to know his children once again, to see how each one thought and looked at the world, to see Zenobia's strength in Luke's eyes, and her happy smile in Milly's face. And he laughed out loud when Ned said something that sounded just like Zenobia.

As he passed the places where the Third had fought so hard and where so many of his comrades had fallen, Zenobia seemed closer and closer to his heart. And it seemed like she took his hand when he passed by the spot where Lisa Mae said they'd left her, like she was riding with him. And singing, like she used to early in the morning, when the mist was still out on the field.

> "Oh, who'll go with me to that land?
> Who'll go with me to that land?
> Who'll go with me to that land
>   where I'm bound?"

Throwing her head back, ebony face shiny, eyes crinkling like she knew all about everything . . .

"Oh, won't you go with me to that land?"

Strong shoulders rising and falling all the way down the cotton row in time with the song.

"There's no kneeling in that land!"

Could be a quarter mile away from you on the way to the fields, but her voice would rise above all others.

"Peace and happiness in that land!"

And when the sun got so high and burned down so hard, and the water boy didn't come . . .

"There is joy in that land!"

Oh, Zenobia sure enough guided Joe and the children all the way up that long road to Clifton and—Glory to God Almighty!—was standing at its great iron gates, arms opened wide, tears in her eyes, when they reached their journey's end.

"Where I'm Bound!"

AUTHOR'S NOTE

THIS BOOK, first and foremost, is a work of fiction. Having said that, I'd like to note that most of the military events described in the book did take place, more or less as the author has described them. A key source for this book is Ed. M. Main's *The Story of the Marches, Battles and Incidents of the Third United States Colored Cavalry,* originally published in 1908 by the Globe Publishing Company, and reprinted in 1970 by Negro Universities Press.

I also read each and every one of the Mississippi slave narratives (WPA) as background for the book, in addition to many dozens of other works on the Civil War, the war in the Western Theater, and on black troops in general. I was already well acquainted with the history of slavery, having done research on that subject for one of my previous books, One More Day's Journey, and having taught graduate history courses on the subject for many years now.

Ed. M. Main, the author of the book on the Third United States Colored Cavalry, was a major in that unit and drew both from personal knowledge and the Official Records for his well-researched regimental history. While devoting much space to his fellow white officers, many of whom had previously served with him in the 4th Illinois Regiment, Major Main had more difficulty in recalling the names of the black soldiers and noncoms who had fought with him. This is understandable, since he had served with the white officers before, and served with the blacks for only a period of two years. Major Main stated that "There were many men in this regiment who performed deeds of heroism entitling them to special mention in the pages, but unfortunately their names cannot now be recalled." Major Main was born January 1, 1837, and was seventy-one years old at the time of publication of his work.

However, Major Main did recall the name of one black soldier, Alfred Wood, better known in the regiment as "Old Alf," primarily because he was considered an "oracle, at least in the opinion of his own people." The major wrote a sixteen-page sketch of the adventures of Old Alf, whom he called the "Wizard of the Black Regiment" and the "Secret Service of the Third United States Colored Cavalry."

This sketch, containing almost unbelievable deeds of daring by Old Alf, is the source for most of the personal escapades of Joe Duckett, duly elaborated upon and embellished by this writer. In addition, Major Main, at another place in his book, detailed the feat of two black sergeants, Washington Vincent and Isaac Trendall, in carrying dispatches through to General McArthur. This too became grist for this fiction writer's mill and part of Joe Duckett's adventures.

The big battles in which the regiment was involved, the most important of which was the assault on the Big Black River Bridge, all took place, although I have used fictional license in many places to make for a more dramatic story line.

Zenobia, on the other hand, and all of those who accompany her on her journey toward freedom are entirely creatures of the author's imagination. Old Alf did in fact have a wife, Aunt Margaret, and she, with him, escaped from slavery "undergoing many hardships and narrow escapes from capture, abandoning the horse and seeking safety in the swamps. They finally reached the Mississippi River, where, after laying in hiding for a time, they attracted the attention of a passing steamer, and were taken on board, and safely landed within the Union lines at Vicksburg." Aunt Margaret, a trained cook, became the head of the officers' mess, and in addition was a nurse for all. Major Main says, "If any of us were sick or wounded, it was the motherly hand of Aunt Margaret that ministered to us."

Colonel Kenworthy also is a creature of this writer's imagination but his relationship to Joe Duckett is patterned after the relationship of Old Alf to his former master, "one Doctor Wood, who lived on his plantation in Mississippi. The Doctor prized Old Alf largely on account of his many good qualities, trusting him largely with the affairs of the plantation. While Old Alf did his duty faithfully and well, his restless disposition led him into many difficulties, which frequently involved him in heated discussions with the Doctor."

With regard to the siege of the fort at Yazoo City, the actual historical record should show that the commanding officer at the time of the first demand for its surrender was the redoubtable Major J. B. Cook, and that at no time did he contemplate surrender. His actual reply to the Rebs was, "My compliments to General Ross and say to him that if he wants this fort to come and take it."

Later, command of the fort was taken by Major George C. McKee of the 11th Illinois Infantry, who likewise refused all efforts by the Confederates to get them to surrender the fort in this engagement of March 5, 1864. Both officers were commended for their gallantry and bravery in this encounter by Major General James B. McPherson, and this commendation was duly endorsed by Major General William T. Sherman and forwarded to the War Department on April 16, 1864.

It should also be noted that the Third United States Colored Cavalry did not always bear that appellation. It was originally mustered into service as the First Mississippi Cavalry, African Descent, in October 1863. It was redesignated as the Third United States Colored Cavalry on March 11, 1864. In order not to confuse the reader, I refer to the outfit throughout the book by the designation Third United States Colored Cavalry.

At the battle of the Big Black River Bridge, the Confederate defenders did not use bloodhounds. But they did use them against the 1st South Carolina Regiment at Pocatalago Bridge, October 23, 1862 (Joseph T. Wilson, The Black Phalanx [New York: Arno Press, and the New York Times, 1968, illustration, p. 321; original publication: Hartford, Conn.: American Publishing Company, 1890]). See also Colonel Thomas Wentworth Higginson (Army Life in a Black Regiment [New York: Penguin Books, 1997, p. 179; original publication: Boston: Fields, Osgood, 1870]), which specifically refers to "dog companies" among the Confederates, on this occasion, "mounted riflemen with half a dozen trained bloodhounds." I couldn't resist using them.

The trial and hanging of a cotton speculator by the officers of the Third Cavalry is factual. The offense that precipitated the action happened on board ship, but the actual hanging itself was done on land rather than aboard ship as I depict it.

The man's name was W. B. Wooster, and he was "hanged by the neck to a telegraph pole until dead, by Major Jeremiah B. Cook and twenty-seven line officers" on April 24, 1864, less than two weeks after the April 12, 1864, massacre of black and white troops at Ft. Pillow, Tennessee, by General Nathan B. Forrest's men.

Captain William Stiles is fictional. He is named after a college football and lacrosse coach of mine, William C. (Bill) Stiles
(1920–79), a much decorated and wounded Captain, USMC,
during World War II. He was a wonderful and brave man and
a great inspiration to me and others of my classmates at Kenyon
College in the late forties, although still suffering daily from the
effects of his wartime wounds.

In the year of my graduation from college, upon the appearance of a Marine Corps recruiter on campus and my then interest
in becoming a Marine officer, Bill Stiles said that he would be my
reference for Platoon Leaders School. That was not an insignifi-
cant action on his part, for it was 1952 and I believe I would have
been the first African-American to go through that school had I
followed through on my initial interest. Instead, I opted to accept
a Fulbright Scholarship to France, which came through at about
the same time.

I entered the U.S. Army a year later, fulfilling my military
service from 1953–55 as an NCO at SHAPE Headquarters in
Paris, but I've never forgotten Bill Stiles's action in support of
me. He was the kind of person that I imagined Major Main and
Major Cook must have been.

* * *

I did consciously consider it to be my task to give a voice to those
black soldiers who fought in the Third United States Colored
Cavalry, so as to render Major Main's wonderful work of docu-
menting the battle record of that regiment complete and whole.
I have done my level best, both as historian and fiction writer, to
tell their truths. The reader may judge how well I have succeeded.

ABOUT THE AUTHOR

DR. ALLEN B. BALLARD, taught history and African-American studies at the State University of New York at Albany. Born and raised in Philadelphia, he is a Phi Beta Kappa graduate of Kenyon College in Ohio and holds a Ph.D. in Government from Harvard University. He has served as the Dean of Faculty for the City University of New York, and was a Professor Emeritus of Political Science from that institution.

Ballard's previous works on African-American history include *The Education of Black Folk* and *One More Day's Journey, a history of Black Philadelphia*, have been praised by such literary greats as Ralph Ellison, John A. Williams, and Alex Haley.

Where I'm Bound, Ballard's first novel, won the "First Novelist" prize of the Black Caucus of the American Library Association, and was named a "Notable Book of the Year" by the Washington Post.

He is also the author of *Breaching Jericho's Walls*, an autobiography and *Carried by Six, A Novel of Urban Bravery in America*, which was the recipient of the 2010 Black Caucus American Literary Award (BCALA) Honorable Mention in Fiction.

CPSIA information can be obtained
at www.ICGtesting.com
Printed in the USA
BVHW070531170721
612147BV00005B/93

Books by Tilda Shalof

A Nurse's Story

The Making of a Nurse

Camp Nurse

CAMP
My Adventures at Summer Camp
NURSE

TILDA SHALOF

PUBLISHING

New York

© 2010 by Tilda Shalof.

Published in Canada by McClelland & Steward Ltd in 2009.

Published by Kaplan Publishing, a division of Kaplan, Inc.
1 Liberty Plaza, 24th Floor
New York, NY 10006

Library of Congress Cataloging-in-Publication Data

Shalof, Tilda.
  Camp nurse : my adventures at summer camp / by Tilda Shalof.
    p. ; cm.
Includes bibliographical references and index.
ISBN 978-1-60714-617-9 (alk. paper)
1. Shalof, Tilda. 2. Camp nursing--Canada--Biography. I. Title.
[DNLM: 1. Camping--Anecdotes. 2. Camping--Personal Narratives.
3. Nurses--Anecdotes. 4. Nurses--Personal Narratives. 5. Pediatric Nursing--Anecdotes.
6. Pediatric Nursing--Personal Narratives. WZ 305 S528c 2010]
RT120.C3S53 2010
610.73'43092--dc22
[B]
                          2009052347

Printed in the United States of America

10 9 8 7 6 5 4 3 2 1

Kaplan Publishing books are available at special quantity discounts to use for sales promotions, employee premiums, or educational purposes. For more information or to order books, please call the Simon & Schuster special sales department at 866-506-1949.

CONTENTS

AUTHOR'S NOTE

For years, I dreamed about summer camp. Since I didn't go to camp as a child, I always had a secondhand nostalgia for my friends' camp memories: sitting round a roaring bonfire, arm in arm with friends, singing songs and enjoying gooey s'mores; the tough wilderness canoe trips, after which everyone came back bonded for life. I loved hearing about the late-night mayhem and antics of hormone-crazed counsellors. As an adult, I was a camper wannabe. So, when it came time for my own kids to go to camp, I saw a way into this happy world as a camp nurse.

This is the story of my summer odyssey, told from my dual perspectives as both a nurse and a parent. These stories are all true but in order to protect patient confidentiality and preserve the privacy and anonymity of the camps and their staff, I changed names and identifying details. In some cases, I made minor changes to the order of events for the sake of conciseness.

For the past six years, for a few weeks each summer, I've taken a break from the big-city medical centre where I care for critically ill adults, and travelled to beautiful, green Northern Ontario to tend to robustly healthy children dealing with ordinary, as well as a few extraordinary, ailments. Camp nursing has given me ways to combine my experience and intuition as a mother with my skills and knowledge as a nurse. And, just as my kids have grown up at camp, I too, have grown into being a camp nurse.

To parents, camp can feel like a secret world that we send our kids into with a mixture of trepidation and relief. In my unique position of fly (spy?) on the cabin wall, I've discovered that camp is about fun and play, learning new skills, and making friends. It is having adventures, being outdoors, and yes, making mischief. Camp is a place for children to take those first steps away from home, to connect deeply with one another, and ultimately, to create a community with their peers. Now, more than ever, kids need camp to help them connect to nature and one another.

The days are getting warmer. Soon it will be summer and time for...camp.

Tilda Shalof, RN

1

THE TREATMENT FOR NATURE DEFICIT DISORDER

"There's been an accident—someone's bleeding to death! Come quickly!"

Those were the first words I heard when I arrived at Camp Na-Gee-La. I had just turned in the driveway when I was greeted by this call to action from a frantic young man wearing only swimming trunks. I parked my car, grabbed my first-aid kit, and with my two sons on my heels, followed him through a thicket of trees to where his injured friend lay, also in bathing trunks, bleeding from a large, nasty gash on his knee. A pool of dark blood was spreading on the ground beside him. I was unfazed by the sight, and even my kids were calm. They were used to Mom handling emergencies. It's what I do for a living.

While I assessed the wound I asked him his name.

"It's Zack, and I'm gushing blood!"

Dripping, yes, oozing, maybe, but definitely not *gushing*. I knew exactly what to do. I took the blue-and-white beach towel still draped around Zack's neck and pressed down on the wound to staunch the bleeding.

"Ahh, not my Toronto Maple Leafs towel!" Zack looked at his knee, winced, and looked away. "Am I hemorrhaging?"

"Don't worry, you've got plenty more blood," I reassured him. In the intensive care unit (ICU) where I've worked for the past twenty-two years, I'd seen mattresses filled with blood. I'd cared for patients whose blood poured onto the floor at my feet, blood that I sloshed around in as we worked to save their lives. This was nothing.

"How did this happen?" I asked. Zack said he'd tripped while running through the forest on the way back from the lagoon. I glanced at the flip-flops he was wearing. Not the best choice of footwear. After a few minutes, the bleeding stopped. I cleaned the wound with hydrogen peroxide from my first-aid kit and bandaged it.

"You'll have to go to the hospital for stitches," I told him once I'd helped him to his feet. A deep, jagged gash like this would need stitches in order for it to heal. "When was your last tetanus shot?" I asked. Zack hadn't a clue.

"Is it really bad?" he whimpered.

"You're going to be just fine. Are you a counsellor at the camp?"

He nodded. His friend, who'd been watching anxiously from the sidelines, now stepped forward to introduce himself.

"Hi, I'm Mike, the camp director. You must be Tilda, our nurse."

Camp director? He looked more like my kids' teenaged baby-sitter. When we'd spoken on the phone, he'd seemed older than this gawky kid, still with traces of acne and a boyish grin. Mike had told me he was doing a graduate degree in political science at the University of Toronto, so I knew he had to be in his early twenties, but he looked about sixteen.

"Welcome to Camp Na-Gee-La!" Mike said. I reached out to shake his hand, but he pulled me into a hug instead. "Good thing you arrived when you did. Man, I was freaking out."

I looked around. We were deep in the wilderness of beautiful, green Northern Ontario at a "Youth-Leading-Youth Summer Camp Dedicated to Creating a Better Society with Equality and

Justice for All!" That was its motto. I was pumped, eager for my new role as camp nurse in charge of the health and safety of about a hundred children, and their teenage counsellors, too. Apparently I was already on duty.

"Breathe deeply," I had told my kids, opening up the car windows during the drive to camp. "This is *fresh* air." We were well into our three-hour trip north from our home in Toronto to Camp Na-Gee-La on the far side of Georgian Bay, long past the suburbs with their outlet malls and bedroom communities. I glanced in the rearview mirror at Harry, age eight, and Max, age six, but could see only the crowns of their heads as they hunched over their electronic games, their thumbs a-flying. "Take a look out the window. See the *countryside*."

"Are we there yet, Mom?" Harry asked, not even looking up.

They were oblivious to the glorious view, but that would soon change. Before long, they would be living outdoors in harmony with nature, singing songs around the campfire, paddling canoes, and hiking in the woods, arm in arm with their new friends. They would be campers for the first time and I, a first-time Camp Nurse. We whizzed by farmhouses, fields of crops, and cow pastures. Then, we turned off the freeway onto a single-lane highway. On both sides of the road were the massive, craggy, pink-and-grey slabs of granite rock that I'd learned about years ago in geography class: the majestic Canadian Shield.

Camp was definitely going to be an adventure—for all of us. The outdoors was a foreign world to me. I was a city girl, at home in downtown throngs, used to breathing polluted air, idling in traffic jams, and navigating the underground subway system. The natural landscape was as familiar to me as the moon's terrain, known only from pictures I'd seen in books. I had a bad case of "nature deficit disorder."

My parents considered the outdoors a wild and dangerous place, best avoided at all costs. My mother understood Nature only in an artistic way. If the subject of "trees" ever came up, she launched into rhapsodic recitation: "I think that I shall never see / A poem lovely as a tree... A tree that may in summer wear / A nest of robins in her hair." To my father, in theory the outdoors embodied great scientific principles, but in practice, it was merely a system of passageways to get from one book-filled interior to another.

Consequently, I spent my entire childhood indoors. I spent all my time with my parents, caring for my sick, depressed mother and listening, an audience of one, to lectures from my erudite, self-educated father. My air-conditioned summers were wiled away reading in libraries, waiting in hospital lobbies, and sitting in the cool basement of our house, surrounded by piles of books and bowls of apples for sustenance. My only activities were turning pages, staring out of windows, and daydreaming. I barely moved a muscle. And summer camp was not an option. I once suggested it to my parents, but they shot that idea down right away.

"You'll get dirty," my mother fretted.

"No, my dear," my father said. "Jews and canoes simply don't mix."

When I got married and became a mother myself, I vowed that my kids would have a different kind of childhood. I wanted them to have fun and friends their own age, to play outdoors, get dirty, and appreciate wildlife. Camp seemed like the place for all of that. My kids would learn how to make a fire, build a lean-to shelter in the woods, survive in the wilderness. They would know a toad from a frog, the bow from the stern, and the Milky Way as a galaxy rather than a chocolate bar.

For most of the long drive up to camp, it was quiet in the car, apart from the cheery, tinkly muzak of the kids' games. They were cramming in as much electronic playtime as they could. They knew that upon our arrival at Camp Na-Gee-La, I would stow their games away in the car's glove compartment, not to be touched again until our drive home, three weeks later.

Suddenly, something caught my eye on the road ahead. "Hey, guys, look at that!" Directly in front of our car, slowly making its way to the opposite lane, was a turtle with a wizened dinosaur face. I slowed down and pulled over to take a closer look. My kids were fascinated, their thumbs suspended over the keys of their games, the action on pause, as they watched and waited (and waited) for the reptile—or was it an amphibian?—to make it safely to the shoulder.

I thought about my kids. My older son, Harry, was quiet, serious, and painfully shy. I hoped camp might bring him out of his shell and boost his social skills. Max, on the other hand, was high-spirited, fiercely independent, and irrepressible. I hoped camp would give him the self-discipline and structure he needed. One thing I knew for sure: my kids were not going to merely read about the world as I had—they would *live* it, first-hand. If there were dangers involved, then so be it. I've always encouraged them to try new things and take risks—within reason.

As an adult, hearing my friends reminisce about camp, I'd felt envious, nostalgic for something I'd never even experienced: the gruelling canoe trips, the zany bunk-hopping and cabin raids, and the cozy scenes of sitting round the campfire making s'mores. My friends recall their camp days with loving wistfulness, falling into a reverie whenever that touchstone comes up:

"It changed my life. My camp friends are my closest, to this day."

"I had my first kiss at camp...my first slow dance. He's my husband now, and our kids go to the same camp!"

"The best was being a counsellor. Everyone knows you go to camp to get laid!"

"I lived for camp. Those summers were the best times of my life, the happiest."

I loved hearing their stories, but I had to agree with one friend who said, "If you've never been to camp, you just don't get it." Yes, I wanted my kids to be campers, and as a camp nurse, I could vicariously fulfill my wish to be one, too.

I was pulled from these thoughts by cheers coming from the back seat of the car. The turtle had made it—*a good omen, I thought*. But as I drove on, getting closer to our destination, I began to worry.

For so many years as an ICU nurse, I had taken care of patients who had serious conditions, such as multi-system organ failure, septic shock, and respiratory failure. The stakes couldn't be higher. When I had first considered the switch from the fast-paced environment of the hospital to what I imagined would be a laid-back, easy job, I had no concerns. Surely it would be a nice break from the intensity of the ICU, leaving me lots of free time for swimming in the lake, canoeing, and hiking in the forest. How hard could it be? Taking care of healthy children who had boo-boos, sniffles, and bug bites was a far cry from treating sick patients who had life-threatening illnesses. I had developed the typical, hard-bitten humour of nurses who toss off remarks like "any day my patient isn't in cardiac arrest is a good day." I wasn't concerned about camp nursing because, after all, these weren't *sick* kids. However, I did wonder if I'd have sufficient sympathy to offer those with everyday ailments. I realized I might have to recalibrate my "compassion-o-meter."

And there might be a few other challenges at camp that I hadn't considered. First of all I had no experience with pediatrics; I'd never taken care of children, other than my own. Also, at camp I'd be isolated and working by myself, without my ICU team to back me up. I began to wonder whether my skill set was suitable for camp. I knew what to do in the event of a cardiac arrest, but I had never even seen a case of poison ivy. I could start an intravenous drip, measure central venous pressure, and analyze arterial blood gases, but I'd never removed a splinter or taped a sprained ankle. Surely I could learn these things on the job, right? As I turned off the highway and onto a quiet country lane, the road got quite bumpy. I felt as if the dark forest of trees edging the roadway was closing in on me. I gripped the steering wheel tightly and drove on. *You can do this,* I told myself.

Then I saw the sign for Camp Na-Gee-La. As we approached the entrance gate, I tried to ease my nervousness by imagining the great times awaiting us. I thought back to my conversation with Mike, the camp director, and was reassured by his words. A few weeks ago, Mike and I had had a long talk on the phone. He'd told me about the camp, focusing mostly on its socialist philosophy. He said that Camp Na-Gee-La's name came from the Hebrew, meaning "let us rejoice." Mike had been a camper there himself every summer since the age of eight. He explained how Camp Na-Gee-La was part of a youth movement, which meant it was governed by young adults. The parent council oversaw the finances and administration, but the day-to-day running of camp was done by the campers and counsellors. The parent council had voted that Mike be the camp director, and this would be his first summer in charge. He seemed eager to do a good job. He explained that it was a low-budget, no-frills camp modelled after the Israeli *kibbutzim*, or communes, of the '60s, where everything was shared, including chores, decisions, and responsibilities. It was both Zionist and pro-Palestinian, left-wing politically, and completely secular, as in no religious affiliation. "Don't worry," Mike reassured me, "there's no prayer hocus-pocus or anything like that."

It seemed like an important point to him, but I didn't feel one way or another about it. We were Jewish but not observant, so it seemed like Camp Na-Gee-La would suit me and my family just fine.

Mike told me more about their belief in the value of physical labour, living off the land, minimizing their ecological footprint, and "co-existing in a way that is respectful of the Planet." It all sounded good to me. Camp Na-Gee-La attracted the children of some of the country's finest artists, academics, and intellectuals, Mike said, "because of the way it inculcates humanistic values and promulgates a vision of equality and social justice."

"So, Nurse Tilda," he'd said playfully at the end of our conversation. "How about it? Are you in?"

I had taken only a moment to think it over. It certainly was flattering to be called Nurse Tilda. In the hospital, I was always called by my first name without any title. And I did admire Mike's passion for his camp. Admittedly, my kids were still young for any *inculcation* or *promulgation*, but it didn't seem that long ago that I had been young and idealistic, too. At forty-four years of age, I still felt young. Well, at least I was still idealistic. Though it scared me to think I'd be on my own without a doctor on hand and with the closest hospital a half-hour drive away, I reminded myself that I was an experienced nurse. I had handled many emergencies over my long career. *C'mon, you can do this,* I told myself. "Okay, I'm in," I said. *Bring it on!*

As I steered the car into the parking lot, I took a deep breath (of *fresh* air!) and readied myself for the plunge into The Great Outdoors.

2

BAND-AIDS, CALAMINE, AND A CAPPUCCINO TO GO

Camp Na-Gee-La was situated on an irregularly shaped piece of land made up of hills and valleys. At its hilly centre was a flagpole, from which a path sloped down to the waterfront. The mess hall was on another hill, and the infirmary was located on the highest hill of all. By the time I finished dealing with Zack's injury, it was late evening. Mike showed me to my new home, a room at the back of the infirmary. My kids would stay there with me for the night. Tomorrow, after all the other campers had arrived and camp officially began, they would join up with their cabin groups. I unpacked my things, organizing them on the wooden shelves provided, and tried to settle down my kids. We'd missed dinner, but I had brought some fruit and crackers with me, and we munched on those. They were excited but tired too, and soon fell asleep together on one of the two narrow cots in my room.

I sat down for a moment on the other cot to review some of my reasons for getting involved in this adventure in the first place. Camp fees can be expensive and I liked the idea of bartering my skills in exchange for them, but my real motivation was to get a ticket to the world of camp. It was too late for me to be a camper but this might be the next best thing. "Camp nurse" would also be my cover to spy on my own kids. I don't think of myself as an overprotective parent, but I admit I can get involved (too involved?) in my kids' worlds. I am the kind of mother who knew the adventures of Thomas the Tank Engine, and those of his sidekicks, Percy, Henry, James, and Edward, too. During the Pokémon craze, it was not every mother who could rhyme off the secret powers of Charmeleon, Squirtle, and Blastoise, but I could. Now, at camp, I could be on the inside and get the scoop on my kids' secret lives, while keeping a respectful, unobtrusive distance, of course. I could be a fly on the cabin wall. They would hardly even notice I was there.

Something else intrigued me about camp. I longed to learn the secrets of the successful campers. It was much easier for me to understand why someone might *not* like camp, what with the non-stop, exhausting activities, the noisy silliness, the bothersome bugs—not to mention the lack of books, solitude, and quiet time. I wanted to see for myself why so many loved it.

I went to check out the infirmary, down the hall. It consisted of a waiting room with a couch, a few plastic chairs, and a rattling old refrigerator. There were two other rooms, one with four beds for overnight patients and the other with an examining table and a desk. I took stock. There wasn't much in the way of equipment and the supplies looked like they'd fallen off the back of the proverbial truck. I found a dusty stethoscope, an antique blood pressure machine that belonged in a museum, a bottle of Tylenol long past its expiration date, a box of Band-Aids, a few bottles of rubbing alcohol, antiseptic, and a mystery bottle, unlabelled. All in all, this was not enough to supply a decent first-aid kit, let alone provide for an emergency. There was no airway (a tubular device to assist with breathing), no oxygen tank, no IV equipment or intravenous drugs. I had no medications to treat a seizure, cardiac arrest, asthma attack, or anaphylactic shock. The only thing remotely amusing about this situation was an object I discovered while rummaging in the drawer of the rickety old desk. It was a faded, cardboard disc from the 1950s called a first-aid wheel. Various injuries and ailments were listed around the perimeter of the dial. You could turn the dial and a little window revealed the treatment. I took a twirl and landed upon advice for "Choking," positioned in between the medieval-sounding "Blood-Letting" and "Dyspepsia," all seemingly equal slices of significance on the pinwheel pie:

> Loosen neckband. If object in throat, remove with finger. If child, hold upside down and slap vigorously on back. If measures fail, call doctor.

There was no mention of cardiopulmonary resuscitation (CPR), but it probably hadn't been invented when this once-useful tool had been devised. I put the first-aid wheel back in the drawer. It was a charming artifact but of little use to me.

It was getting dark, but I stood for a few moments on the porch to get a sense of the lay of the land. The campgrounds seemed rundown and shabby, but surely it would look better in the morning light?

That first night, lying on the other narrow cot in my new room, I couldn't fall asleep. All I could think of was Zack's dirty, bloody knee. I imagined it morphing into full-blown septic shock. I had seen minor wounds—even hangnails and paper cuts—develop alarmingly fast into raging infections that raced through the body at lightning speed, destroying every organ, tissue, and muscle in their way. A few of these cases had even turned out to be the devastating necrotizing fasciitis, or nec fash, as we nurses called it, generally known to the public as the flesh-eating disease. I'll never forget one patient I'd taken care of who had a swollen, inflamed toe. Within hours the infection had spread up his leg into his groin. Basically, it would have been game over if he hadn't been brought to the ICU, lickety-split.

My clinical experience was mostly treating worst-case scenarios and catastrophes. However, at least in the hospital I could
anticipate them and have everything on hand I needed. Here, I had
a feeling things would be simply coming at me, and I'd have none
of the monitors or ICU gadgets I relied upon to know my patients'
conditions and anticipate problems. My tool box was empty.

Something else threw me: When I went to make notes about
Zack's injury, I couldn't find a chart or medical records. There
was no record about any pre-existing medical history, allergies,
or immunizations. In fact, the camp should have had detailed files
for every camper and counsellor, but I only found a few health
forms and most were incomplete. The nursing credo of *not docu-
mented, not done* haunted me. This place was scaring me.

I thought of all those inviting ads for camp nurses in the back
of the nursing journals I subscribed to. "Have a fun-tastic, fun-
nomenal summer with your kids!" they promised. The best was:
"Get paid to have fun!" They had lured me in but now that I was
here I felt out of my depth and way beyond my comfort zone. This
place was more like a *danger* zone. What had I gotten myself into?

I was still tossing and turning later that night when music
started blasting out from the mess hall. I got up, threw on my
clothes, and went out to see what was happening. I stood on the
mess hall porch and peered through the window. It was Party
Central in there! The counsellors were bringing down the house
with a full-blown rave. Techno music was pouring out of a portable CD player and bodies were swaying and undulating to the
pounding, hypnotic beat. On the table were bottles of beer and
wine coolers.

Two guys rushed in past me, arm in arm, shouting, "Let's par-
tay! It's our last chance before the kids get here."

Were these counsellor-kids the ones going to be responsible
for the camper-kids? When I was sixteen, seventeen, and eighteen,
I definitely didn't have the maturity to be a counsellor—and I was

beginning to wonder if they did either. As camp nurse, was it my role to put an end to their fun? Probably. But it wasn't much of a stretch to dial up my own inner teenager and remember what I was like. I, too, had loved to cut loose and be wild. A part of me wanted to join in on the fun with them, but reluctantly, I headed back to my cabin and slept for what seemed like a few minutes.

The next thing I knew it was morning. The sun was blazing and music blared from scratchy speakers that had been placed in the trees. I stood on the porch of the infirmary to get a daytime overview of the camp from my vantage point on top of the hill. I'd been wrong: in the clear morning light of day, the place looked worse, much worse. It was a dump. The cabins were ramshackle and the mess hall, with its caved-in roof and crumbling porch, looked like a condemned building. There was garbage and empty beer bottles littered all over the ground from the party the night before. The campers' wood cabins were rundown, dilapidated shacks spread out helter-skelter in a valley. The "Nature Shack" was windblown, and the arts and crafts tent appeared to be sinking into the mud. Down, down the entire camp slumped to the one jewel of the place: the waterfront. With Camp Na-Gee-La situated on beautiful Lost Loon Lake with its sandy beach and protected cove, it made me wonder why Zack and Mike had been swimming in a pond in the backwoods.

On the porch outside the mess hall, a counsellor was strumming "Stairway to Heaven" and singing soulfully. It was way too early in the day for that intense song, but preferable, I supposed, to last night's head-banging lullabies. Other counsellors were on the grass, tossing Frisbees, and unbelievably, a few counsellors were stretched out on the lawn, covered in baby oil, "catching some early morning rays," they told me. I made a note to self to talk with them later about sun safety practices. Meanwhile, Harry and Max were amusing themselves while we all waited for breakfast.

Mike came over. "Hey, Nurse Tilda. Rough night? You look wrecked. Not a good look for you—no offence! That was your last chance to rest. The kids arrive this afternoon, so you'd better pace yourself. Did you manage to get any sleep?"

I shook my head.

"Ahh, that sucks."

"Is there coffee?" I asked.

Mike led me to the kitchen for a cup of hot tap water poured over instant decaffeinated crystals. He introduced me to the cook, a man who was a bit older than the others, which put him in his midtwenties. He had a scruffy beard and spiky, geometric tattoos depicting daggers and jagged wires along his arms. "You must be the nurse dude," he said. "My name is Gord, but everyone calls me Sarge."

I looked around Sarge's kitchen. A young woman in a do-rag, wearing an inside-out T-shirt and tattered jeans, stood at the stove, breaking eggs into an industrial-size frying pan with one hand and flipping pancakes with the other. Two gas burners were blazing with nothing on them. On the counter in the direct sunlight was an open bottle of mayonnaise. On the floor in front of the stove, glistening in the rays of sun, was a puddle of melted butter. Beside the puddle were two huge vats, one filled to the brim with peanut butter and the other with strawberry jam, over which bees were noisily buzzing. This place was a death trap if anyone had any life-threatening allergies. I would have to talk with Sarge about the hazards in his kitchen. Maybe I could also tactfully drop hints about hygiene, especially hand washing, for food handlers.

"Hey, I bet you're the nurse! Wassup?" A tall, lanky guy came over and brushed the hair out of his eyes to get a look at me. He pointed at himself. "The name's Jake but everyone calls me Wheels." He told me he was the camp driver. "I run the kids into town to the hospital and pick up supplies. I know everything about camp, so whatever you need, call on me—no explanation necessary." He hiked up his baggy pants that were slipping off his hips.

I suddenly realized how they all knew I was the nurse. I was, by far, the oldest person at Camp Na-Gee-La. My only competition for this dubious title was Anderson, a middle-aged maintenance man I'd been hearing about, who would visit the camp from time to time to do repairs. After breakfast, I left the mess hall and noticed Sarge sitting on the stoop out the back of the kitchen, surrounded by overflowing garbage cans, smoking a cigarette. I waved at him. "Hey Sarge, thanks for breakfast." He grunted in response. "What's for lunch?" I asked.

"Don't talk to me when I'm in my Zen garden," he snapped, but then added, less rudely, "Don't worry, it'll be something edible."

As I made my way back to the infirmary, I happened to meet Anderson. I found him leaning against a tree, just outside the mess hall, observing something with the focused gaze of a scientist.

"I've been standing here for twenty minutes," he said. "See that?" He pointed to a bottle of ketchup lying directly in the path of counsellors filing out of the dining hall after breakfast. They were stepping around or over it. "They won't pick it up. No one gives a rat's ass about this shit hole." He shook his head in disgust. "Nothing worse than rich socialists."

Suddenly, I heard laughter and the pounding of running feet. "They're here! The kids are here!" The sun worshippers, Frisbee-tossers, and soulful guitar-player whooped, and raced to the flagpole, the central spot in camp, where the buses were arriving and unloading the campers. As they tumbled out, each child was greeted and hugged by a counsellor. Most of them looked happy to be there, but I quickly spotted two little ones, a girl about ten and her younger brother, who seemed bewildered. In no time, the little boy found his counsellor from last

year and ran to him. The counsellor picked him up, threw him
in the air, caught him and spun him around and around. His
sister looked on the verge of tears, but then she too was found
by her counsellor and gently coaxed away to her cabin. Max
eagerly went off to the youngest cabin, the "Friends," and
Harry went off with the "Fellows." The next group, the thir-
teen- and fourteen-year-olds, were the "Comrades," and the
oldest campers, the fifteen- and sixteen-year-olds, who stood
off in a group by themselves, were "Counsellors in Training,"
or CITs.

I returned to the infirmary to wait for "business" to arrive.

They came. Children lined up to hand in their meds, and in
no time I was inundated with plastic baggies filled with pills,
capsules, and tablets; meds in film canisters, old cosmetic bags,
and Tupperware containers. Someone handed me a mysterious
herbal mixture that came in an empty jewellery box. I received
a box full of tiny bottles of homeopathic remedies, some to be
given in the event of "feelings of unease" and others for "disorientation." In a bottle decorated with Strawberry Shortcake and
Winnie-the-Pooh stickers were tablets that looked like Advil but
labelled amoxicillin, an antibiotic. One child handed me a large
business envelope containing black-and-white capsules and red-
and-white tablets, all mixed together. In an empty M&M's box,
I found ten tablets of what appeared to be Tylenol with thirty
milligrams of codeine, a heavy-duty narcotic. "They're my T3s,"
the young child told me, not too pleased to have to turn them
in to me.

Mike popped by to say "hey" and inform me that the first
day of camp was known as Safe Day. "Everyone can hand over
any contraband to you," he explained. "You know, like booze,
smokes, or drugs."

The whole scene was unnerving: I, who was used to the precise
and controlled hospital environment where I had administered

drugs in micrograms or titrated medications in milligrams or millilitres, was now expected to dispense unknown tablets by the handful?

I read through the explanatory notes some parents sent:

Jay is in tune with his body. He will let you know which pills he needs and when.

Madison experiences strange sensations at times. She'll tell you when this happens.

Phillip sometimes complains of depression, but he loves camp. Just talk him through it if it happens or if he says the "bad feelings" are coming over him.

In the hospital, I couldn't give an aspirin without a doctor's order, but suddenly, here at camp, it seemed like anything went.

Kids kept coming. After lunch, they continued to line up on the infirmary steps and then spilled onto the grass outside, waiting to hand in their meds or discuss something with me.

"Hi, are you the nurse?" A pretty little girl pushed to the front of the line. She was barefoot, in a bathing suit, her long hair wet from a dip in the lake. "Hi, I'm Micaela and I'm going to be a doctor, an interventional neuroradiologist. My mother is a microbiologist and she put me on a drug holiday for camp. I normally take a cocktail of meds, but she thought I should have a break. Hey, what's that?" She sniffed the air. "It smells like our kitchen after my mom mops the floor."

"It's the trees. Your mom must use pine-scented cleaner."

Micaela handed me a note from her mom, entitled "Presenting ...Micaela Brown." It explained that Micaela had a "touch" of attention deficit disorder and hyperactivity but was a "free spirit who needs to be allowed to do her own thing."

"I've never actually been *fond* of camp," Micaela said, "but my *hypothesis* was I would like this one because it's unique." She glanced at me to see if I was keeping up with her. "I know, I know, I use lots of *polysyllabic* words. Everyone tells me that. I've been tested, and verbally, I'm right off the charts! I'm in the ninety-ninth percentile for my age, which is twelve, going on twenty, as my mom always says."

"Have you ever been to camp before?" I said to try to interrupt the torrent of words.

"Oh, I've been going to camp, like, *forever*. Well, for the past three years, but not this camp. Now, I *live* for camp. At first, I didn't want to come, but then my mother found this place. She decided I should take a break from my meds, because it's not like school where I *need* them. My mother says nature has a calming effect, but I don't like nature. Well, I don't mind nature, per se, just the bugs."

"Where's your counsellor?" I looked around for someone to take her away, eyeing the line of kids stretching on into the afternoon.

"She knows I'm here. I love to visit the nurse. Hey, do you have ibuprofen? I get bad headaches and my head explodes. I get an aura with *scintillating scotoma*, you know, that wiggly, jiggly flashiness?" She drew a wavy picture in the air with her hands.

She was wearing me out. "Micaela, I have to see the other kids."

"I'm sorry! Sometimes I give *too much information*. Am I TMI comin' at ya? I know I talk a lot, but what can I do? My mom says I'm a turbo-talker."

For someone with attention deficit, it seemed she had an amazing ability to focus—at least, on things that interested her.

That first evening there was a singalong for all the campers around a roaring bonfire. Zack, or Moon Doggie as he was called at camp (and who hadn't, by the way, come to the infirmary to get his wound cleaned, as I had instructed), played the guitar while the kids sang "We Shall Overcome," "Give Peace a Chance," "My Song Is My Weapon" and other protest songs about the evils of materialism, the triumph of the working class, and the fight for freedom.

"That's what bugs me about Beethoven and those other old-school guys," I heard one kid say to his friend. "No lyrics." Then he caught sight of me and gave me a pitying look. "Your era must have been so boring," he said. "No cell phones, videos, or computers. What did you do all day long?"

I stifled a laugh. "It was rough, but we managed."

While the kids roasted marshmallows, Mike gave a rousing speech.

"Camp Na-Gee-La is a special place," he said. "Here we learn about sharing and caring for each other, for our community, and for Mother Earth. We are striving toward a society of equality and justice for all. For example, take candy. Any candy you have must be shared equally. Don't forget, because next week we have a trip to the jellybean factory.

"We are youth leading youth!" he called out and a great cheering roar rose up.

"We have a dream of a better world!"

"Yay! Yay!" The crowd clapped and whistled.

"Justice and freedom for all oppressed people!"

When the roar died down, Mike said, "Tomorrow you will be assigned your chores, and I expect everyone to work to the best of their ability, whether it's kitchen duty or cleaning the toilets."

"Ewww...pee-yoo!" they groaned.

"Remember, 'from each according to his ability, to each according to his needs'! *Hers*, too." He grinned.

After hugs all around, the younger campers headed to bed while the teenagers got busy with high-energy games of skateboard b-ball and gladiator dodge ball. Watching them, I remembered being their age and that feeling of boundless energy. It was fun seeing kids engaged in sports that didn't involve a coach, uniforms, schedules, and a drive to and from the event, not to mention trophies handed out for just showing up. Meanwhile, the oldest group, the CITs, went off to their evening program, which involved all of them, boys and girls together, going into the forest that surrounded the camp and staying there for over an hour. Mike called it a social mixer, a way to break the ice so that everyone would get to know each other fast. "When you're in the dark and can't see your way, you have to lean on each other. It builds trust," he explained. These goings-on weren't building any trust in me. They could be having an orgy in there for all I knew. I can't say for sure what did go on out there in the woods, but when they finally emerged, rumpled and dazed, they looked pretty pleased with themselves.

While all of this activity was taking place, counsellors who had the night off snuck away and headed for a "romp in the swamp," which included, rumour had it, skinny-dipping. Later, after it seemed that almost everyone else had gone off to get some sleep and I headed to my cabin and bed, walking past the tripping shed where they kept the paddles, canoes, and kayaks, I heard soft moans coming from inside. Two pairs of flip-flops were lying haphazardly just outside the door. I had to smile.

By the second day I felt as if I'd been there a week. I took a stroll around the grounds. In no time, I was in a scene from a "What's Wrong With This Picture?" puzzle. Wherever I looked, I saw a potential hazard, something about to break down or an accident waiting to happen. There was broken glass on the ground left from the counsellors' party. At the waterfront, I found rusty nails protruding from the dock and no sign of a lifeguard anywhere. Later that day, I cornered Mike.

"I have some concerns, things that need your immediate attention."

"I hear you, but give it time. I know it's crazy-busy at first, but trust the process." He tucked his clipboard into the crook of his arm in order to take my hands in his. "You can do it, Nurse Tilda. Be positive!"

Over those first few days I realized that if I was going to last, I'd need a daily routine. But when I tried to set infirmary hours, the kids still came and knocked on my door whenever they liked, day or night. During the brief intervals of quiet, I locked up and walked around camp. I liked to watch the activities because everyone seemed so happy, even doing their chores. My own kids were having a great time, too. Harry found a snake and kept it in a jar beside his bed, along with a pile of flat skimming stones he was collecting. Max discovered the joys of peeing in the forest, climbing trees, and hanging out with his new pal, Wheels, the camp driver, who took him for rides around camp on his BMX bike.

Why couldn't I just relax, enjoy it like everyone else?

By the third day, the flow of traffic in the infirmary had not slowed and the nights were still full of interruptions. By day the campers came; at night, it was the counsellors. At the end of each day I was exhausted but I learned that there was no point going to bed before midnight because I would only get woken up. One night, for some strange reason (sisterly bonding?), there was a run of gynecological problems. Long after midnight, a counsellor woke me up about a menstrual problem.

"I'm losing all my blood," she wailed. "It's extreme."

"How long has this been going on?"

"Weeks and weeks," she moaned.

"Is it worse tonight? Why did you decide to come to me now, so late at night?"

"I was walking past and saw your light was on."

I had taken to leaving a little light on in the hallway to help me as I fumbled around for my flashlight and jeans when I got woken up. I made a note to self to remember to turn it off. I handed her pads and tampons and promised to book her an appointment with a doctor tomorrow. "It's not easy being a girl," I commiserated.

Shortly after that girl left, another one came to the door with a "quick question" about itchiness and burning, "down there." *Doesn't anyone ever sleep at this place?* I offered to obtain the treatment for a possible yeast infection the next day.

"Okay, but if I take it, how soon after can I, you know, be with my boyfriend?"

"The over-the-counter treatment takes three nights. After that, you should be okay."

"We can't wait that long!" She burst into tears.

"Goodbye!" I showed her the door.

I would never talk to a hospital patient like this, but here, it seemed the way to go.

I dozed off, but around four in the morning, I woke up and turned on the light. *Something is not right*, I thought. Just then, Wheels carried Micaela into the infirmary. She was crying and scared. Wheels's tough-guy image and usual bluster were gone. He was gentle, holding her close and stroking her hair.

"I hate camp," Micaela said. "I am sooooo homesick. I want to go home."

"Is there anything you like about camp?" I asked.

"I only like hanging out with you in the infirmary."

"You seem happy during the day. You have lots of friends."

"It's an act. I'm faking it all the time."

She sat up, now wide awake. "Do you want to play chess?" she asked Wheels, putting her arm around his shoulder.

"Listen, Micaela, it's late. Can we discuss this in the morning?"

She nodded. I put her to bed in the infirmary, just down the hall, and she seemed pleased with that.

The late nights, the broken sleep, and my daytime worries were getting to me, and there were still two and a half weeks to go. I cornered Mike after breakfast the next day. "We need to talk," I said.

"Are you having a hard time, Nurse Tilda? You look like you could use a hug."

I dodged him and continued. "There are a few problems that need your immediate attention."

"Lay it on me, sister," he said, patting my back.

I gave him my top-ten list of what needed to be done to make the camp safer.

"Whoa!" Mike said, holding up his hands. "You're stressing out for nothing. You know what, Nurse Tilda? These are awesome suggestions. Maybe you should come to a staff meeting. We don't usually allow parental involvement because we're self-governing, but we might make an exception in your case. I'll run it by the others, put it to a vote, and if they're okay with it, you can join us tomorrow, after breakfast. Sound like a plan?" He put his arm around me. "Hang in there, Nurse Tilda."

What choice did I have?

From time to time, I checked on my kids, but there really was no need. At least *they* were enjoying camp. Harry was particularly impressed with the lake. He thought its warm currents were from an underwater heating system. I didn't correct him but did dispel the camp myth that was scaring him and the others about poisonous rainbow frogs that ate little kids' toes. As for Max, he loved everything.

"Where's Max?" I asked his counsellor one day when I was down at the lake. The counsellor was stretched out, belly up, on the dock, a towel over his face.

"No idea," he mumbled from under the towel. He looked like he was taking a nap. *Was he the lifeguard?* Did I have to supervise the waterfront too? I clenched my teeth. Mothers probably made the best lifeguards, anyway, I thought as I scanned the beach for Max.

"Nurse Tilda!" someone called. "You're needed in the infirmary." Okay, but where was Max? He was a bit of a wanderer, and though he always found his way back, I was worried. I could see kids gathering outside the infirmary at the top of the hill, waiting for me, so I headed back. *Max'll show up*, I told myself.

Just then, Wheels on his BMX bike came barrelling down the hill toward me at top speed. "Yo, Nurse! Comin' through!"

He had a passenger. Perched on the handlebars, his bare feet jutting out in front, was Max! "Boo-ya! Step off!" Wheels called out. I jumped out of the way just in time. Wheels slammed on the brakes, Max tumbled off and stood up, giggling madly.

No helmet or protective pads? I scolded Wheels.

By the time I got back to the infirmary, the place was packed. The ceramics instructor who often had just "one quick question" now had "just one more." A little girl was pale and feeling "yucky." Another kid claimed to have been attacked by a swarm of killer bees. There was a boy with a scraped arm, and a CIT who was complaining about a wart he'd had for the past three months. Zack was there, too. After my daily nagging, he'd finally showed up so I could clean his wound. (He hadn't gotten sutures and now it was far too late.)

I did what any nurse would do: triage. Mentally, I prioritized them from life-threatening conditions to emergencies, to potential serious problems, to everything else. With that logic in mind, I took the bee boy first, just in case he really had been swarmed and might be having an allergic reaction. But I couldn't find any stingers and decided the small raised bump on his arm was merely a mosquito bite. (I most definitely did not follow the advice from the first-aid wheel: *For insect stings: Remove stinger and wick the poison out with wet tobacco leaves.*) I put some soothing cream on the spot and sent him on his way. Then, I let the little girl who was feeling yucky lie down on a cot while I disinfected the boy's scraped arm. A few of his friends had by now joined him, all of them trolling for Band-Aids. I tended to be stingy with Band-Aids and doled them out seldom and reluctantly. I preferred to leave small abrasions open to air. Band-Aids seemed useless and I dreaded coming upon soggy ones in the sand or clogging up the shower drain. "I'll give you one," I told the boy with the scraped arm, "but only if you promise to dispose of it in a garbage can when you take it off." I told the CIT with the wart to wait till he got home to get treatment. Finally, I turned to Zack's knee. Although it was the most serious problem, it would take the longest to treat. The moment I saw it, red and inflamed around the open edges, oozing with thick, sticky pus, I knew it was infected. He would have to see a doctor for antibiotics. I was furious. This infection was totally preventable.

"Why didn't you come to me earlier to have this wound cleaned? This happened almost a week ago! You're a counsellor. You should know better."

Zack didn't argue. He looked sheepish. Just then, a tough-looking kid wearing purple-brown fingernail polish and filthy jeans with heavy chains hanging out of the pocket burst into the waiting room.

"Hey, do you have anything for depression?" he called out, as nonchalantly as if he was asking for a cough drop. "But please don't call my parents," he begged me. "They'll have a cow."

He wasn't homesick, he said, he loved camp, but kept having these "bad thoughts." Zack used the distraction to beat a hasty retreat, promising he'd come back again to follow up about his knee. By then, the girl who had been lying down had recovered and returned to her cabin with her counsellor, and the ceramics instructor who had only a "quick question" had gotten impatient and left, so Phillip and I had some privacy.

"Phillip, I want to call your parents. This may be something serious, something you need help for."

"Ahh, do you have to? I wouldn't have told you if I knew you'd rat on me. Don't you have a pill I could take right now, to help me sleep?"

"Come with me, let's go out." I'd learned the best way to get my own sons to talk was to get them moving. In motion, the words came. As we walked, Phillip agreed to let me contact his parents and restart his antidepressant meds if that's what they decided he needed. He promised he'd come back to talk with me again.

The next morning after breakfast, I went to the staff lounge, where the senior staff members held their morning meeting. They were lying on the filthy old couches, sinking into the deep indents made by many previous weary bodies. The guys were stretched out, their heads in the girls' laps; girls lay back with their heads in other guys' laps. Slumped into each other, the whole mess of them looked like rows of wayward dominoes. I pulled up a metal folding chair and launched into my list of concerns: waterfront safety, the importance of sunscreen, fluids to avoid dehydration, general hygiene, and foot care.

Mike stifled a yawn.

Wheels got up and walked out. "Catch ya later, Nurse Tilda!"

Carly, the head of culture and education, who everyone called Gidget and was hooked up with Moon Doggie (I figured out that their nicknames were a reference to an old TV sitcom), had been paying attention at first, but soon I lost her too. I'd already had a run-in with her the day before when she asked me to check her and her campers, but I didn't find the lice that she swore her entire cabin of little girls was infested with. She sat there, sullenly, fiddling nervously with her nose ring or else poking her fingers into her Afro, checking for lice when she thought no one was looking.

One by one, as if felled by a sedative, they tuned me out or drifted off to sleep. There was only the sound of my voice droning on about sun hats and closed-toe shoes, especially on long hikes, but no one was listening. Mike was actually snoring softly.

Let me out of here! I thought, but there was no escape. Young people usually have to inhabit the adult world, accommodate to our tastes, time tables, and rules. Here, at camp I was stuck, having to put up with their preference for late-night parties, their predilection for mac and cheese, watery hot chocolate, and ramen noodles with MSG broth, and being exposed to their unfamiliar music. I was held captive, trapped in the lonely chasm of the generation gap. Before I came here I'd thought of myself as young and hip, but now I felt like an old lady, nagging, scolding, and complaining. I was wearing jeans and a top from Old Navy but to them it was as if I was wearing polyester stretch pants, bifocals on a string around my neck, and hobbling along with a walker. I crumpled up my list and angrily lobbed it into a garbage can. Mike woke up with a start. "Hey, save a tree! Use the recycling bin," he said. He was right but I wasn't in the mood.

After the meeting, Mike came over. "Nurse Tilda, you look like you need a hug."

I stepped back. "No one was paying attention, Mike," I complained. "This is important stuff."

"Camp Na-Gee-La is all about process. We're a community of shared governance. We don't come down heavy with rules. Everyone has their say."

"Not when it comes to health and safety."

"That nurse needs to chill," someone said as I walked away.

"Yeah," her friend agreed. "She should take anger management."

Meanwhile, everyone else seemed to be having a grand old time. My own kids loved camp. Phillip was feeling a lot better after his outburst in the infirmary and our walk and talk and there were no more Micaela meltdowns. In fact, as I strolled around camp, all I ever heard were the sounds of laughter, of gleeful kids at play. I was the only miserable one. Even on rainy days, when they stayed in their cabins and had a bunk day indoors, they entertained themselves by singing funny cheers, performing silly skits, and playing board games and rock, paper, scissors for hours. It was nice to see how content they could be, whatever the weather, managing quite well without parental intervention, technology, or toys. Of course, there were many days when they got into lots of mischief, plotting and carrying out pranks such as panty raids, cabin-hopping (when they invaded another cabin or sometimes even switched over all the furniture and camper belongings), and toilet seat-greasing. One afternoon, a posse of boys burst into the infirmary, begging to borrow the stretchers and bandages so they could dress up like accident victims. They took pictures of each other to send to their parents.

But I didn't give up trying to bring them in line with what was important to me: health and safety. After they returned from a five-kilometre hike into town to buy (and, of course, share) candy, they were flushed and happy, but their arms and faces were badly sunburned and their feet were sore and blistered. Again, my lecture to the counsellors fell on deaf ears.

I noticed that the organic vegetable patch, which they called "The Farm," wasn't thriving; in fact, it was completely overgrown with weeds. During my phone interview with Mike, he had said that the garden would be used to feed the camp and the surplus would be shared with the local food bank. I doubted it would yield enough vegetables for one meal. And that wasn't the only thing being neglected. Chores around camp were done sloppily or not at all.

It wasn't because they were too busy. After the long, intense lectures the kids endured each morning on Socialism or Political Activism 101, they had lots of free fun time on their hands. Though the camp didn't own much in the way of equipment— the sports department consisted of one soccer ball and one basketball—they played a lot of the "old-school" games, as they called them, like capture the flag and hide and go seek. They also had interest groups, like folk dancing (dances of oppressed nations, only), extreme Frisbee, a rock 'n' roll club, stress-busters, a yo-yo workshop, dream interpretation classes, and the very popular Hippie Club. I wondered what they did in *that* club—smoke weed, drop acid, have sit-ins, and let the sunshine in?

"What goes on in that one?" I asked Gidget, who organized the interest groups.

"Hackey-sack, cornrow braiding, and macramé-flower pot holders."

"What about the Fear Factor Cookout?" I asked.

"Well, today they cooked up a batch of fake snot."

"What's the recipe?" I asked, half kidding.

"Gelatin, green and yellow food colouring, corn starch."

There was even a handstand class. "Not enough propulsion and you can't get your legs up. Too forceful and you'll flip right over," the instructor cautioned the kids.

I asked Mike about the daily routine. "It's a creative schedule," he explained. "We try not to impose a lot of rules. We believe kids have a right to make their own decisions about how to spend their time. We don't want to stress them out. If they want to do nothing, that's okay, too. They need down time."

"We need more safety practices," I said. "There have been too many accidents and preventable injuries."

He seemed worried. "You're not going to bail on us, are you, Nurse Tilda?" At that moment he looked like he did on that first day, a scared boy at the gate, waiting for a mother to save the day. He must have sensed how frustrated I was feeling in this chaotic, lawless place because he tried to win me over. "You're the best nurse we've ever had." It wasn't his flattery that made me stay; there was simply no way out. I didn't know how I was going to last two more weeks, but I was a nurse and would never abandon my patients.

I returned to the infirmary and sat down at the desk. For amusement, I took another whirl on the first-aid dial, my own little wheel of misfortune.

Electric Shock: Call doctor. Start artificial respiration at once. If victim is burned, apply wet baking soda or strongly brewed tea leaves to affected area.

Yeah, right, someone gets hit by lightning and I'm going to put on the kettle for tea! I tossed the wheel into the garbage... then fished it out again. Its comic relief might come in handy. I took a look at my growing shopping list. I needed a thermometer, bottles of sun block, a jar of aloe vera gel for sunburns, electrolyte replacement powder for dehydration. The days were hot and no one was drinking enough water or wearing a hat. Already a kitchen worker had fainted from heat exhaustion. I'd had to hose him down and pack him in ice.

The next time I saw Wheels, I handed him my list. He took a glance and gave it back to me. "It's all up here." He pointed to his noggin. "My memory is perfect. I hear something once and remember it for life—no explanation necessary. But I won't drive to town for just a small errand. I don't sweat the small stuff."

"So, let me get this straight," I said, exasperated. "You'll make a run to the hospital if it's an emergency and only a trip to town if it..."

"I need a real reason. Like, if a kid is in a coma or having a dying spell, then, obviously, I'll go. That's a no-brainer. No explanation necessary."

"I see," I said, gritting my teeth.

We didn't have to wait long for a "real" reason. Later that afternoon, Owen, a tall, tanned counsellor, rushed in with a female counsellor cradled in his arms.

"Becky fell," he said and laid her down gently on the couch. "She banged up her arm." Becky cradled her right arm close to her chest. She bit her lip as tears streamed down her cheeks, but managed to tell me what happened while I gently examined her.

"I was showing the kids tricks on Wheels's BMX and did a 360 into the bushes and landed on my hands. My arm broke my fall." She gasped with the pain.

Wheels appeared on the scene. I had to give him credit, he was always reliable in an emergency.

"Here's your second reason to go to town," I told him. "Becky has to be taken to the hospital for an X-ray and probably a cast." I turned to her. "What's your job at camp?"

"I'm a swim instructor."

Swim instruction? As far as I could tell, swimming consisted of a counsellor standing on the beach, bellowing into a megaphone: "Everyone into the lake!" I still hadn't even seen an alert lifeguard at the swim docks.

Becky was shivering with the pain. She was going into shock. I wrapped a blanket around her. She was about to vomit and I handed her a basin and held her hair back. "I think you've broken your arm," I told her as I created a splint out of a rolled-up newspaper. I ripped up a bed sheet and fashioned a sling to support the weight of her arm.

We loaded Becky into the van. Owen, her boyfriend, hovered over her, looking worried. He hugged and kissed her. "You're going to be all right, Becks."

"They couldn't run this place without me," Wheels said cheerfully to me, revving up the motor and turning on the car radio.

"I'm quite sure," I muttered.

"Hey, look at that!" Wheels admired my handiwork on Becky's arm. "You're more of a DIYer than I thought. You rock, Nurse Tilda! Maybe you don't need all that stuff from the drugstore after all."

"Get everything I asked for!" I practically shouted at him. "And drive carefully," I added. I wondered if I should go with them, but Becky's condition was stable and I was reluctant to leave the camp on its own if I didn't have to. I hoped my makeshift arm splint would keep Becky's bones sufficiently immobilized on the bumpy drive to the hospital.

Something else was on my mind. "Wheels, is there a coffee shop in town? Could you bring me a cappuccino?" I handed him a few bills and as I watched him drive away, I hummed the first few bars of that corny song, "Hello Muddah, Hello Faddah, here I am at Camp Grenada..." I started counting down the minutes to their return. I desperately needed a jolt of real java.

3

DANGEROUS FUN

Things got worse. Every day, the waiting room filled up and the line of kids wanting to see me snaked out the door. There were noisy coughs, stuffy noses, assorted stomach aches, and a fever that went away after a day. Two CITs were made to stay overnight in the infirmary because the camp council decided this would be a suitable punishment for their streaking through camp. However, their stay in the infirmary ended up punishing me more. Their raunchy jokes and raucous laughter kept me awake all night.

When I wasn't busy treating children in the infirmary, I was running around camp, doling out pills, bandaging wounds, or taping up sprained joints "in the field." I was either offering Band-Aids, or band-aid type solutions. I was constantly putting out fires, both figurative and literal ones. Yes, a real fire broke out. It happened in the kitchen. Sarge couldn't find the fire extinguisher, though he swore he had one... somewhere. I heard the commotion from the infirmary and rushed over, grabbed a box of baking soda, and poured it on the greasy flames that had been ignited by a splattering, overfilled deep-fryer.

So far, nothing had come up that I couldn't handle, but the sheer volume and insistence of both the campers and the counsellors' round-the-clock demands kept me hopping. The infirmary had also become a social gathering place. At first I assumed it was because of the cans of Coke I kept in the refrigerator, but the kids kept hanging out in the waiting room, long after those had been guzzled. At times, I took a breather and sat in my office with the door closed, eavesdropping on the conversations going on in the next room.

"My dad makes toilets," one girl was saying. "He taught me everything. I can work my way around a toilet like that." She snapped her fingers.

I might need her skills. Anderson still hadn't unclogged my toilet that got blocked after some kids snuck in to use it. I had caught one boy who'd forgotten to flush the evidence, just as he was making his getaway.

"Use your own!" I shouted at him.

"Yours is cleaner!" he shot back.

One day the waiting room was quiet. *Too* quiet. I went out and found a bunch of kids painting their finger- and toenails with yellow and turquoise polish, the girls doing their own nails and then polishing the boys' and talking quietly among themselves.

"Isn't camp awesome this summer?" I heard one say.

"Yeah, at home we'd never get away with half the stuff we do here," another said. I was glad I didn't know what "stuff" he was talking about. I went back to my room and spun my first-aid wheel and chuckled to myself.

Gunshot Wounds: Call doctor immediately. Such wounds may cause lockjaw.

At least I didn't have to deal with that kind of injury, but there were some serious cases, and I made sure to keep detailed notes on them. Becky's arm had a serious fracture and she needed surgery. She came back from the hospital with a cast up to her elbow and left the next day to recuperate at home. Owen, her boyfriend, trailed off after her. He was the camp's tripper so that effectively put an end to all canoe trips. A roar of "hurray" rose up because no one wanted to go anyway.

One fourteen-year-old boy suffered a mild concussion.

"My teeth got shoved into a guy's shoulder," he told me. "We were playing tackle football and I was wide receiver. The other guys forgot about the ball and one went for my stomach and the other went for my head. I'm feeling dizzy and I just threw up." He did seem a bit spaced out. That night, I set my alarm clock for every two hours to perform neurological checks on him. At first, I was tempted to ask the counsellor to help me out, but he was so dopey, I wondered if I should be doing neurological checks on him, too. It wasn't easy differentiating between a coma and a teenage stupor, but the kid at least was fine in the morning.

Then a situation came up that I'd never encountered before, and it stumped me. A twelve-year-old from Michigan needed an x-ray. (Mike had mentioned we had a few American campers, attracted by our forests and clean lakes.) The problem was, the boy was unhappy about going to the doctor and the possibility of having an x-ray.

"My mother can't afford the medical bills," he explained.

The same thing happened with a camper who had a severe stomach ache. After twelve hours the pain still hadn't abated, so I sent him to the hospital to rule out appendicitis. He was seen, blood work was drawn, an x-ray and ultrasound were done, but then he threw up and felt better. His mother was angry because she had had to pay for a hospital visit that turned out to be unnecessary.

I was uneasy when health care and business mixed. Growing up and working in Canada, I hadn't worried about the cost of health care. As a nurse I'd always been guided by what was best for patients, not by their ability to pay. Call me naive—or just call me Canadian—but that situation left me flummoxed. In over twenty years of practice, I had never had a patient who couldn't receive medical attention because of lack of funds. I'd never even seen a hospital bill.

Unfortunately, I had no one to talk to about such issues, or about anything for that matter. I was getting lonely. Overhearing the constant counsellor chatter on the walkie-talkies made me feel even more alienated because I couldn't follow the fast volley of conversation filled with private jokes, secret references, abbreviations, and codes. What I missed most of all was adult conversation and companionship, my husband Ivan's, especially. I called him one night to complain that I was homesick. He listened and encouraged me to tough it out. I knew I had to stay till the end. I had only been there a little over a week and there were still two weeks to go, but already I was thoroughly exhausted and frustrated. In some ways the work here was more demanding than in the ICU. There, at least, emergencies only took you by surprise if you hadn't prepared yourself ahead of time—something we nurses were trained to do. Almost everything that could happen to our patients was predictable. For example, if I noticed early signs of congestive heart failure, I would slow my patient's IV fluids to minimize his fluid intake and thus reduce the load on his heart. At the same time, I'd have a vial of a diuretic ready to boost the urine output if he became "wet," meaning if his lungs filled with fluid. If I was worried that pneumonia was brewing in my patient's chest, I could step up the chest physiotherapy to mobilize secretions in the lungs and maximize lung expansion. But here, I was simultaneously bombarded with the serious and the significant, the preventable and the accidental. All I could do was react on the fly.

"Lots of stuff coming at ya, Nurse Tilda?" Wheels sympathized one morning.

"You got that right," I said, sipping my coffee, back to instant after the one glorious cappuccino interlude.

He had to be tired, too. The revelry went on every night, way past midnight. Just the evening before, the counsellors were involved in some wild pagan ritual in the mess hall revolving around Wheels himself. I had peeked in to see him standing at the centre of a circle, holding up a flaming torch, surrounded by female counsellors in various states of undress and wearing crowns of dandelions and rainbow scarves wrapped around their necks and waists. They were swaying and offering up bowls of fruits and vegetables (from their rotting garden?) onto an altar. One of them was holding out a chalice of what I hoped was merely red juice.

"All hail King Wheels, God of Camp Na-Gee-La, Lord of the Lagoon!" they chanted. "Bow down to Wheels, God of camp!" they chanted.*

They said later it was a celebration of the summer solstice, but from what I could tell it was all part of their insatiable need to lose themselves in group fun. By day they looked after their campers, but the nights belonged to them.

After hours, whenever they could, they snuck off to the lagoon in the forest. Once, on an evening stroll further afield, I stumbled upon the hidden path. I followed it, led by the sounds of laughter and singing. Soon, I came to a mucky-looking pond around which male and female counsellors were whooping it up, dancing topless beside a campfire, smoking, and swigging from bottles of "hard lemonade." I stood back, out of view, wondering again if I should put an end to their fun and do everything possible to have this dangerous place closed down. But I didn't want to take on the role of morality police, and besides, the campers were safe in their cabins with counsellors who were on duty. I looked up at the sky and stars for answers. A shimmering sound, clear and bright, vibrating in the night, came from the lake, then it sounded again. Was it an echo or the call and answer

---

* I don't make this stuff up

of two birds singing to each other? I turned back to the infirmary.

The late-night merriment was definitely taking its toll on the counsellors. They were run down, getting colds, sore throats, and headaches. Whoever was in charge of the morning wake-up music was getting to it later and later and choosing more mellow selections, such as "Dream Weaver." With its ethereal synthe-sized plea about closing your eyes, getting through the night, and making it to the morning light, it was not a tune to rouse anyone out of their slumber. It seemed that the frenetic energy of the first two weeks was now starting to peter out, just as we were heading into the final stretch—the third (and my final—ever!) week at Camp Na-Gee-La.

Most evenings, there was a campfire. I went but made sure to stay back and sit just outside the circle, so as not to intrude on the intimate gathering around the fire. It felt like the campers' private space and I didn't belong. However, one evening they gave a concert at the campfire. Counsellors performed folk songs on banjos, guitars, a harmonica, and a set of drums. They played old Pete Seeger songs, Arlo and Woody Guthrie numbers, and Bob Dylan. I loved it, but I heard grumbles among the kids.

"This music is so yesterday," someone complained.

Soon the musicians switched to more modern songs about peace, many alternating between Hebrew and Arabic. There was one in particular they all loved that kept repeating the words "Peace," "Shalom," and "Salaam" over and over.

They are good kids, I thought. *Their hearts are in the right place.*

I was worried about Sarge. He didn't look well, and late at night, in his cabin at the back of the kitchen, I heard him cough-ing uncontrollably. I made him come to the infirmary and the moment I placed my stethoscope on his chest, I could hear high-pitched wheezes as he breathed in and out. "Do you have asthma, Sarge?"

In between hacking fits, he glowered at my question.

"Do you use an inhaler?" I asked.

In answer he pulled one out of his pocket and huffed into it a few times.

"Sarge, has anyone ever shown you how to use it properly?"

"I know how to use it."

"You're blowing out the medicine. Try it again."

He did it again, the same old way. "The medicine is going out into the room, not your lungs," I told him. He tried again but was getting frustrated. Then I had a hunch what might work.

"Pretend it's a joint, Sarge. Toke on it. Just suck it in and hold it."

He grinned. Now he got it.

I shook his inhaler. It was almost empty. "Do you have another?" He looked away. "This one's almost finished, Sarge. You should never be without it." He still didn't respond. "I'm going to get you a new one." He walked to the door and turned back, keeping his eyes on the ground. "Okay, but send the bill to my welfare case worker," he said, "not my foster parents. They have no more money to spend on me."

I tried to not look sympathetic because I knew Sarge wouldn't want my pity. "Okay. Will do," I said, as if what he'd just mentioned was a simple matter of account-keeping.

"Thanks, I owe you one, Nurse Dude."

"Okay, then, why don't you just tell me what's for dinner."

"Food," he snapped, back to his usual irritable self. "Ood-fay," he added in pig Latin. "Eye of newt. Mystery meat! Toxic tuna with arsenic thrown in. Are you happy, now? Didja ever wonder why the infirmary is next to the mess hall? That's so when the kids get food poisoning, they can go straight to you."

"Why won't you ever tell me what you're cooking?"
"No chef likes that question."

With the third week came even more wonky headaches, irritated
rashes, queasy stomachs, scratchy throats, and assorted bumps
and bruises. It seemed like everyone at camp had one complaint
or another. I did what I could to make things better, and luckily
the problems were fairly minor. Nothing turned into pneumonia
or septic shock, and certainly not flesh-eating disease. I handed
out a panoply of over-the-counter painkillers. I sang the corny old
song about "black flies pickin' at my bones in North On-tar-i-o,"
but of course they didn't find it the least bit amusing. Sometimes,
as a private joke, I put ordinary Vaseline on their bites and they
walked out, satisfied and cured; it soothed them just as well as
the expensive ointments, which wasn't much.* Sometimes all the
kids needed was a hug, a few moments of attention, an explanation, a short rest, distraction, encouragement, or reassurance, all
of which I could easily give.

Sometimes my nurse-patient consultations took place in the
mess hall. Hardly a meal went by when I didn't feel a tap on my
shoulder. I'd be mid-bite and a camper or counsellor would bend
down to show me some sore part of their body or divulge a private
matter. "Come see me later," I begged, "during office hours!"

An unusual dish was served up at one meal. When girls at a
nearby table started jumping up and shrieking, I went over to
investigate. It turned out the hot dog lunch was the inspiration
for one boy to place his penis inside a bun and offer it to them on
a plate. "Who wants to lick off the ketchup?" I heard him say.

"Put that back where it belongs immediately!" I shouted, but

---

* One resourceful counsellor took his itchy kids ot the kitchen to find a banana.
  He rubbed the inside of the peel on their bites and that seemed to work well, too!

no one could hear me over the roar of laughter of the entire camp.

Sometimes they came to me with problems that might actually be serious. A disturbing disclosure was made over the veggie stir-fry one time.

"I've missed my period," said a counsellor, plopping down on the bench beside me. "It's been two weeks. Should I be worried?"

"Yes!"

The sluggish, overweight ceramics instructor who always had a "quick question" for me finally got my attention when she happened to mention in passing that she'd recently been diagnosed with diabetes. "My blood sugar rate is around two point one or maybe it's twenty-one? I can't remember. Which is worse?"

"You need to see a doctor," I told her. "It could be serious."

"My diet doctor ordered vitamin B twelve shots. He said you'd give them to me."

"We don't stock that in the infirmary." I dreaded making another request of Wheels. "You'll have to get it yourself."

"What about two B six ones? Do you have those?"

"It doesn't work like that..."

I was often stumped by the kids' problems. You have to know a patient's medical history and personality in order to determine the best approach and method, and I had very little to go on. I was operating on a strictly need-to-know basis.

As for my own kids, I hadn't seen them in days. One morning, I headed down to the cabins in search of Max. His cabin was quiet and I assumed the campers were out at their activities, but I knocked first. (I didn't want a repeat of the scene when I'd walked into what I thought was an empty cabin and found two counsellors in bed, making out.) No one answered, so I opened the door and stepped into the darkened room. A burly, hairy guy was lying in Max's bed, naked under a sheet that fortunately covered up his private parts. He squinted at me and shielded his eyes against the light from the open door. "Who are *you*?" I asked.

"Who are *you*?" he grunted. "You woke me up."

"I'm the nurse. Why are you sleeping in my son's bed? Where is Max?"

"Who's Max?" Without waiting for an answer, he turned over, and settled in for more shut-eye. I slammed the door behind me and set off in search of Mike. It was a shame they'd never gotten around to giving me a walkie-talkie because I was ready to scream at the whole camp. Imagine, this scary thug, sleeping in a child's bed!

I found Mike in the staff lounge, lying back on the couch, listening to music with his girlfriend, Shona, who was draped over him, her head resting in his lap. He chuckled when I told him about the intruder. "Oh, that's Spleen. He's a legend around here." He shook his head in recollection of past heroic Spleen antics. "Spleen—what a guy! Hey, don't look so worried. He's harmless. He's buddies with Quade, Max's counsellor. Spleen's out on parole—I mean, on *vacation*. He's staying with us for a few days before he moves on."

"*Out on parole?*"

Shona giggled and turned away to hide her amusement.

"He was convicted of a B and E but I swear, he didn't do it! Spleen is awesome with kids. We're lucky to have him at camp."

I guess I didn't look reassured.

"He's not a serial killer or a child molester, I promise you that."

I wiped my brow in an exaggerated gesture of relief.

Eventually, at the waterfront I found my kids. Harry was swimming with his friends, watched over by a dopey-looking lifeguard. Max was happily playing with his gang on the beach, building sandcastles and smashing them down. I returned to the infirmary. There I found a raging, pacing Carly. She had buzzed off her 'fro and her almost-bald head was covered in a bandana do-rag.

"There are more cases of lice infestation!" she snapped at me.

"There's an epidemic going on around here and you're doing nothing about it."

"I examined your campers' heads. I didn't find a single lice— I mean louse."

"I showed you those white thingies in Sasha's hair."

"That's dandruff. Nits stick to the shaft of the hair follicle. You can't flick them off. I'm not going to treat a kid who doesn't have lice."

"Well, Wheels has already gone to town to buy me lice shampoo!"

"So, you are going to put chemicals on your scalp that you don't need?"

"My head is so itchy. I've been up all night. This is so freaking me out."

Everyone runs around barefoot, sunscreen bottles haven't been opened, your own boyfriend won't take care of the dripping, festering wound on his knee, and you're worried about harmless head lice?

"This is a serious hygiene problem," she said.

"Lice are a nuisance, not a disease. Besides, no one here has lice," I told her.

I wanted to lock the door and barricade myself in there, but of course, there were no locks on any doors in this place. I put a sign on the door that I was going for a walk. First I stopped at the mess hall to fill up my water bottle at the fountain. As I was doing that, I noticed a little rivulet on the floor of what looked like...blood! I followed the stream to a large puddle that was being fed by a continuous drip from the unplugged refrigerator. *Was there a body in there?* I yelled for Sarge. He came running.

Packages of frozen meat had been placed in the fridge to slowly defrost, but instead had melted into warm, oozing messes. When Sarge saw the bloody puddles on the floor and then the soft, grey meat he threw down his dishrag and cursed. "Damn kids! They unplug the fridge for their music at night and then forget to plug it back in again afterwards."

I looked down at the meat blood. "When was the last party?"

He stopped to think. "Not last night, but the night before. I think."

"Do not use this meat, Sarge. Throw it out immediately."

I stood back trying not to retch at the smell of warm meat blood. "It's rotten. It's been out more than twenty-four hours." I watched him thinking this over. He prided himself on his frugality and recycling. (I'd seen him make soup out of potato and carrot peelings.) Sarge didn't take suggestions about his cooking at the best of times, but this was serious. However, he wouldn't promise to dispose of it, and I stomped away, frustrated again.

In sheer desperation, I called Ivan to tell him my troubles, but he was out. I left a pathetic message, one that would make him feel sorry for me having such a terrible time while he was probably living it up, eating out at restaurants, and enjoying the single life, temporarily unfettered by any responsibilities. I returned to the infirmary to spin my first aid "Wheel of Fortune," hoping for some sage advice to miraculously appear.

I landed on "Toothache: See your dentist."

Thanks a lot! I spun it again.

Foreign Body Obstruction in Airway: If patient swallows a sharp object, get him to eat mashed potatoes to surround object. For further treatment, call doctor.

I was laughing my head off at that one when Mike burst in, the screen door banging behind him. "Hey, Nurse Tilda! Someone's on the phone from the public health department for you. Something about the water supply. Sounds majorly important."

I closed my eyes for a moment, taking in this fresh disaster.

The inspector explained that there was run-off from the septic tank leeching into the reservoir—the lagoon—at the back of the camp. The underground spring that supplied drinking water to the camp was contaminated with unsafe levels of bacteria.

"What a bummer," Mike said when I got off the phone and told him what was wrong.

I got up slowly, thinking rapidly. "From this moment on there will be no drinking water from the tap or the lake. Swimming and showering are banned. The water supply has to be turned off."

"Hey, does that include swimming in the lagoon?"

"It's a cesspool!" I glared at him. "This camp should be shut down," I muttered.

"If there are problems, we will form a task force to address them," said Mike.

"No committees! No meetings!" I thundered at him. "This is a deadly situation!"

"Watch out, guys," he warned his pals who'd gathered around us. "The nurse is going ape."

I grabbed his walkie-talkie and screamed into it. "Listen up! To everyone at Camp Na-Gee-La, there is no drinking water until further notice." I held it close to my mouth and repeated the warning. I turned back to Mike, who now looked ready to comply.

"We'll put up signs all around camp," he said.

"That's not good enough! Call Anderson! The water supply has to be shut off."

"Can it wait? He's busy fixing the roof. It's been leaking."

"No!" I stormed at him.

"Don't stress out, we're dealing with it."

"People can get seriously ill and die from contaminated water," I told him. Mike looked shocked. Was I finally getting through to him? "I want you to order a truckload of bottled water and tell Sarge to boil all water before using it for cooking or washing. This is an emergency."

At that, Mike stood there, thinking. "Does this mean the carnival is cancelled?"

I lunged forward to strangle him, but he must have thought I was zeroing in for a hug. Once again we ended up in another tangle of misunderstanding. I pulled away. No one was taking me seriously, but at least I could try to save my own kids. I raced to find them and warn them not to drink the water. I barged right into Max's cabin, and plowed through a sludge of wet towels and bathing suits, piles of grubby clothes and scattered candy wrappers. The kids were all there, a couple of them up high in the rafters, climbing the beams and swinging like monkeys. A few kids were gathered on the floor in the corner of the cabin, feeding potato chips to a family of mice. I happened to notice a nine-year-old boy wearing a dress, with his hair in pigtails and ribbons, but there was no time to inquire about that. Quade and a few other counsellors were playing poker with Spleen, while Max sat on the jailbird's shoulders, doing flips backward onto the bed, giggling helplessly each time. (Fleetingly, I had to wonder if the gambling winnings would be divvied up equitably in true socialist form.) I interrupted the game to give them the warning.

"Hey, first you tell us to drink more water and now you're telling us not to drink the water at all? I don't get it," Quade said. "Make up your mind. What's your bottom line?"

"Yeah, what gives?" Spleen said without looking up from his hand.

No time to explain! I ran out and continued to spread the word. Rain started coming down, a heavy but pleasant downpour that broke the heat wave. By late afternoon, it was still coming down. The roof was leaking in the mess hall and Anderson and Wheels were up there, trying to patch the holes. The water had been shut off and bottled water had arrived. Meanwhile, all around camp, the valleys were filling up. Two enterprising counsellors hauled up canoes from the shed near the lake and were paddling on the newly forming ponds of knee-deep water. The kids piled into the boats and others started jumping into the water with their clothes on. Kids dragged the vinyl mattresses from their beds and used them as rafts or to slide off the mess hall porch into the middle of a huge pile of mud. Pretty soon, just about everyone was deep in the mud, wearing their bathing suits or else stripped down to their underwear. I caught sight of my own kids. Max was running through the mud barefoot, looking like a feral child, while Harry was drifting around contentedly in one of the canoes, his white, mosquito-bitten arms splattered with mud. Everyone was delirious with joy! It was Woodstock, but without the drugs or music. But then someone realized that music was exactly what was missing from this scene and ran to bring the boom box from the mess hall. Soon the valley resounded with garage band grunge from what sounded like a homemade tape.

Mike joined me and gazed at the scene appreciatively. "The fun never stops around here, does it, Nurse Tilda?"

Please, make it stop! Just then I noticed that the live electrical cord running from the mess hall was lying in a foot of water and I ran off to put the kibosh on the music.

Later on, after the water emergency ended and the mud bacchanal died down, and after I'd finished treating the cuts and twisted ankles from kids slipping and sliding in the mud, there was still Zack's knee and Sarge's lungs to worry about. I had nabbed Zack at lunch, but he couldn't understand why I wouldn't examine his knee right then and there (he'd placed it right beside my tunafish sandwich).

"Bring this knee of yours to the infirmary after lunch," I'd barked at him, nudging it off the table. He didn't show up until much later. Immediately I saw that his knee was even worse. The wound was now wide open, smelly, and mushy—all signs of infection. "Okay, that's it. You're going to a doctor. This could have been prevented but now you need a deep debridement to clean all that out and antibiotics, too."

"You mean pills?"

I nodded.

He backed off. "I have issues with pills."

"How so?"

"I don't take medicine."

"You can't swallow pills? I'll crush them into applesauce for you." I was losing patience.

"My mother's a Scientologist," he said. "She doesn't want me taking pills. She believes in the body's natural healing powers."

Just then Sarge arrived, right at dinner time. "I came for my breath-a-lyzer," he said, his usual cryptic self. His lungs sounded better now that he was using his medication properly. I handed him the new inhaler I'd bought and had charged to the camp. I had him in my corner so I tried again. "What's for dinner, Sarge? Hope you saved me something tasty!"

"Spaghetti," he said, and, like the true gonzo chef he was, added, grinning sadistically, "with *meat* sauce."

4

ESCAPE FROM UTOPIA

Sarge wasn't joking. He had cooked up the rotten meat and served it for dinner.

All I could do was retreat to my room and wait for the victims to start staggering in. I hunkered down in bed under the covers, hiding from them all, and braced myself for the impending food-poisoning disaster. I left the light on in my room all night, and I stayed in my clothes so I'd be able to jump up and react even faster. I studied my textbooks, reviewing the signs of salmonella and staphylococcal food-borne infections. "Botulism," I read, "starts with diarrhea and vomiting, eventually leading to paralysis of the eyes, mouth and throat, and respiratory system." Ultimately, they would all go into cardiac arrest! Let the outbreak begin: I was ready.*

The funny thing was, that night everyone slept more soundly than ever before. It was the first night I wasn't disturbed. No one even came for an antacid tablet. The only thing I ended up nursing was my own resentment and fatigue. In spite of the ominous events, things actually improved over the next few days. Mike had gotten Anderson to board up the entrance to the lagoon in the woods. Plumbers were called in to repair the

---

* I was only marginally aware that I was losing it.

leak in the septic system. The camp's water supply was shut down and the public health authorities disinfected the system. We drank bottled water for three days and then the water was re-tested, deemed safe to drink, and the advisory lifted. The weather had turned sunny and hot, so I returned to my previous harangue about drinking lots of water to avoid dehydration and heat stroke.

I knew for sure that the camp's spirit was back to normal the morning when the wake-up music was "Walkin' on Sunshine."

There were only a few days left until the end of my tour of duty. I still fantasized about fleeing, but I was determined to see it to the bitter end. Mike and I had even become buddies.

"The buzz around camp is we're thinking of inviting you back next year," he told me. "You should take it as a compliment."

"The only buzz I'm aware of is from the mosquitoes," I shot back grumpily (though I was secretly pleased).

I had to admit, there were some delightful moments at Camp Na-Gee-La. One day I watched a group of twelve-year-old girls and boys on kitchen duty. The music was blaring, and the kids, all in their bathing suits, were laughing and dancing, spraying each other with the handheld ceiling nozzles. They were having such fun—their wet, shining faces so joyful as they threw gobs of bubbly suds at one another. I tried to not notice the slippery floor, the piles of food residue in the sink, and the partially rinsed dishes.

I also enjoyed observing the CIT "activities of leadership development." One activity was a game called "Which Would You Rather?" that posed thought-provoking questions such as: Would you rather see into the future or communicate with animals? Would you rather be famous or smart? Their Truth or Dare game must have been abandoned hastily because I kept coming upon the cards strewn all over the campgrounds, blown around by the wind.

Truth:	What do you do when you really want to punish your parents?
Dare:	Remove your top or eat a bug.
Truth:	What's a more important political issue: poverty or the environment?
Dare:	Perform your best "sick" routine you do to punk the nurse.

Another leadership session started off well but soon erupted in a messy food fight. They were making a map of the Middle East, with gumdrops for Egypt, raisins for Jordan, popcorn for Israel, and licorice sticks for the West Bank, when suddenly, they started hurtling gobs of chocolate pudding (the Mediterranean Sea) and blobs of green Jell-O (Sea of Galilee) at one another. Well, one look at that scene and anyone could see why there'd never be peace in that region!

On one of my last nights at camp there was an emergency. It was the most terrifying situation I'd ever faced as a nurse—not because I didn't know what to do, but because I had to face it totally alone and completely ill-equipped to treat it properly.

Mike banged at my window in the middle of the night during a rainstorm, shouting, "Hey, Nurse Tilda! Wake up! Come quickly! Someone's having a seizure!" I jumped out of bed, fortunately still in my clothes, and charged out the door. My heart was pounding as we raced to one of the Comrades cabins. I had no idea what to expect. I ran in and found thirteen-year-old Amanda lying on the floor in the midst of violent convulsions. This was a true full-blown or grand mal seizure. The other girls and the counsellors were gathered around her, terrified, and I pushed them aside to get to her. I knelt down and turned Amanda on her side and cleared the space around her of people, furniture, and obstacles. Had we been in the hospital, I would

have given her a shot of Valium and called a "code," to summon
the resuscitation team, but here, all I could do was try to keep
her safe while we waited it out. After a few long minutes, the
seizure eased up and she lay there, unmoving and unconscious
but breathing, slowly and deeply. I took her pulse; it was steady
but rapid. Wheels was already waiting outside the cabin in the
van. I thought about calling for an ambulance, in case Amanda
deteriorated on the way to the hospital, but I let myself be persuaded by Wheels that he could get us there faster. He came in
and helped carry her to the car. We laid her on the back seat and
I crouched on the floor, next to her.

As we drove to the hospital the rainstorm turned into a raging
electrical thunderstorm of biblical proportions. Visibility was
poor, even with the high-beam headlights on. There were no
streetlights on those winding country roads and it was only
during the intermittent split seconds when the sky cracked open
in a burst of light that we could see where we were going.

I thought through all the possible scenarios. What if Amanda
went into cardiac arrest? Mentally, I prepared myself to perform
CPR. What if her airway became obstructed? If that happened,
she would need an emergency tracheostomy; I'd have to cut into
her windpipe and breathe air into her lungs. I didn't even have a
scalpel or an airway with which to perform such surgery, much
less the qualifications or the guts to actually do it. But if I didn't
make an airway, she'd have no oxygen flow to her vital organs.
I noticed a plastic straw on the floor of the back seat, probably
from someone's trip to the Dairy Queen. I picked it up. Mentally,
I landmarked her neck for the cricothyroid membrane, the place
I'd have to slice open with a scalpel (if I had one) and then insert
the dirty straw to make an airway for her. In the hospital, I
had assisted in hundreds of these procedures on my patients,
both emergency ones and planned ones, but under completely
different conditions! I held on tightly to the crumpled straw in

one hand and to Amanda's hand with my other. *Oh, why did I listen to Wheels? I should have called for an ambulance!*

Amanda continued to breathe. I shone a flashlight into her eyes to check the response of her pupils. They were equal and reactive, which was a good sign, but when I pressed down on her breastbone, there was only a minimal response to that painful stimulus, indicating that she was still deeply unconscious.

Oh, hurry, hurry, get us to the hospital. Wheels had to drive slower than usual because it was so dark and treacherous.

"Wow, it's like Jurassic Park," he said as another bolt of lightning turned night into day and then back to night again.

"It's like a horror movie, except we're in it," I said gloomily from the back seat. What was I doing here? *I wish I was back at home, in my bed, safe with Ivan.*

"Hey, Nurse Tilda, don't be stressed. Amanda seems better, now."

"She is seriously ill."

"Oh, I've seen worse, much worse."

"This has the potential to be worse."

"Oh, well, the *potential.*"

Although she didn't appear to be seizing, I was afraid Amanda might be in a state of an underlying seizure, called *status epilepticus*, which could cause permanent brain damage. "Amanda! Wake up," I shouted at her, fruitlessly.

"She's tired, let her sleep," Wheels suggested.

"She's not asleep, she's unconscious," I said. *You fool.*

"I've brought kids to the hospital who were in way worse shape than this. Last year we had this kid who fell through a window and, like, lost almost all of his blood. I sat with him for hours in the ER. They just bandaged him up and sent us packing. Most of the people waiting in the ER don't even need to be there," he said cheerfully. "You practically have to be having a dying spell before they admit ya, these days. I'm sure they'll send us right back to camp. You'll see, she'll be back at camp tonight."

"She is staying in the hospital, and then she's going home."

"Listen, Camp Na-Gee-La has a perfect record. We've never sent a camper home. Besides, do you know who her parents are?" He told me their names, a politician mother and movie producer father. By that time we had arrived at the hospital. He pulled into the parking lot, straight into the reserved spot of Dr. McNab, Chief of Surgery. "Don't worry. He knows me. No explanation necessary." He hitched up his pants, scooped Amanda into his arms, and carried her into the emergency department.

The triage nurse took her immediately. The doctor examined her and quickly administered an intravenous drug to try to break the seizure. By then, Amanda was beginning to wake up, but was groggy and confused. She had no recollection of what had happened. They admitted her for further tests, including a CT scan of her brain. It was three in the morning, and I had to call Amanda's parents. Shocked and distraught as they were, they said they would be leaving shortly from Toronto to be with her. I went back out to the waiting room, which was indeed full, as Wheels had predicted.

"Boo!" Wheels jumped out at me from behind a plastic decorative tree. "See, what'd I tell you? Half these people don't even need to be here. Where's Amanda? Did she have a good nap?"

I gritted my teeth in response.

I tried to snooze on the drive back to camp, but Wheels played the radio and chattered nonstop. Rain was still coming down, but the heavy storm had blown over.

"I've been at plenty of other camps but this one's the best. I used to go to this Johnny Appleseed–type place, run by real Native people who were trying to take back their culture. They said Thanksgiving prayers to the trees and the wind—you know, like 'I thank the Lord for the birds and the bees and the apple trees.'" He took his hands off the wheel, clasped them, and closed his eyes in fake prayer. "Me? I'm more a rub-a-dub-dub-thanks-for-the-grub Yayyy, Ggggod! kind of guy, but hey, whatever floats your boat. That place was wild! We got to go to their sweat lodge and smoke the peace pipe."

"Keep your hands on the wheel!" I sat up to shout at him. "Watch the road!"

"Yup, my parents always sent me off to camps. I guess they needed a break from me, no explanation necessary there, ha ha ... Oh, I've been told I'm a handful. They tried to put me on meds, but I don't need them any more. Obviously, I can deal."

Just get us back safely, I prayed.

"Once they sent me to one of those 4H camps in the States. You know, all that head, heart, hands, and health stuff—it made me puke. So goody-goody! Yeah, right! One summer the nurse came up with her daughter who was a counsellor and they were both sleeping with the same counsellor. Can you believe it? Hey, anyone you dig at camp?"

At that moment, I was grateful to see the entrance to camp, thus ending Wheels's monologue.

"Good night," I said as he let me out in front of the infirmary. I was ready for bed but by now the rain had stopped, the sun was up, and it was almost time to dole out the morning meds.

Later that day, I spoke with Amanda's doctor in the hospital. The brain scan had showed a small cerebral bleed, a tiny stroke, that likely caused the seizure. She would be going home to Toronto to be examined by a neurologist and undergo more tests. She would definitely not be coming back to camp. I never found out how she was after that. It was often like that in the ICU too. We got our patients through a life-threatening situation and stabilized them. Once they progressed to the floor, they went home and we never heard how they fared. Our job was to get them through the crisis.

There were only three more days left at camp and it looked like I was going to make it! I sat reviewing my notes and making sure they were in order. I had written them one quiet day when all activities had suddenly been cancelled. (I soon found out why: The latest Harry Potter tome had arrived and everyone who could lay their hands on a copy was busy reading.)

Freddie A. Eleven-year-old with sore finger, painful after two days, improved after X-ray and ice cream cone.

Daliah C. Camper claims to have been bitten by a rattle-snake. States she heard "rattles." On examination, no findings. Possible insect bite? Camper kept overnight for observation in infirmary. Vital signs taken every four hours. Condition stable. Slept well. No signs of neurotoxic venom poisoning.

Zack D. Counsellor. Knee wound still infected. Edges are macerated and red, still not approximating and very little granulation tissue. Appointments made with a doctor in town, but he refuses to go.

Allan E. CIT. Canoe dropped on big toe, left foot. Large blood bubble under the nail. Very painful. Ice applied and drainage with sterile, sharp object.

I left it at that short note for Allan E., but I'd never forget that toe! It must have throbbed, but he tried not to let on just how painful it was, though his eyes teared up and his fists were clenched. I knew what I had to do after reading about this very thing in my first-aid book. "This is going to seem scary," I warned him, "but it will relieve the pressure." With Sarge's cigarette lighter, I heated a needle to a high temperature and inserted it into the centre of the blood spot. The hot needle melted the nail, the blood spurted out, and the pain was immediately relieved. Allan smiled, which was the biggest reward. It's so much easier to inflict discomfort when you focus on the fact that it will make things better in the end.

It was my last night at camp. There was an outdoor barbeque, but Sarge's cooking had turned me into a temporary vegetarian. (At dinner one evening, not long after the rotten meat fiasco, I had decided to take a chance on beef stew à la Sarge. My fork slid down into a decidedly un-stew-like object. I dug around and pulled out a used Band-Aid.) Eating Sarge's food was *my* "Fear Factor." So, at the barbeque, I played it safe. As I munched on a condiment burger made of ketchup, relish, mustard, pickles, and lettuce piled on a bun, Mike came over to say goodbye and graciously thank me. "Will you be back next summer, Nurse Tilda?"

No chance! I shook my head no.

"It was wild at times," he admitted, "but that's camp. I hope you felt the love. Anyway, the main thing is that everyone had fun. You had *fun*, didn't you, Nurse Tilda?" Mike asked.

I couldn't answer him right then because I was choked up with emotions. It was a mixture of relief, pent-up frustration, and gratitude that it hadn't been any worse—and it could have been so much worse. Fun was not enough for me. I needed safety measures in place, a semblance of order, and . . . well, something else. Overriding all of my emotions was a nagging disappointment. I had come to camp to get outdoors but had spent most of my time indoors. I wanted to understand the appeal of camp, yet I now understood it less. Worst of all, I hadn't connected with a single person there, and despite all the hijinks and hilarity going on around me, I'd been lonely and stressed out the entire time.

My kids had had a great time, but I knew we wouldn't be coming back here again.

That night there was a farewell campfire. It was chilly and the kids were wrapped in blankets and huddled close around the fire. I stayed just outside the circle where I could still feel the heat and watch the flames work their magic.

Afterward, I walked back to the infirmary to pack my stuff. We were leaving first thing in the morning. The door to the infirmary was closed and the screen door barricaded shut with a chair on the inside. I knocked on the door and rattled the door knob. Eventually, Gidget and Moon Doggie came out, dishevelled and flushed, their arms draped about each other. I should have known. I'd seen rumpled sheets in there before. I guess I should have been turning down the blanket and leaving condoms on the pillow like chocolate mints!

"She ruined our fun," I heard them say outside my window, "but what a great little love nest while it lasted."

They left me some poetic graffiti on the cabin wall:

We made beautiful music in here.

Gidget played the meat flute and Moon Doggie hummed on her harmonica!

The next morning, my kids were sad to be leaving. I tempted them with the promise of bubble baths, unlimited television, gourmet meals—some of the things *I'd* been missing. "When we get home, I'm going to give you kids the royal treatment," I told them.

"Mom, *you're* the royal treatment," Max said, his eyes twinkling with mirth.

The three of us were quiet as we drove out of camp. The boys looked out the windows and didn't even ask for the return of their electronic games. As I glanced into the rearview mirror and bid a silent farewell to Camp Na-Gee-La, I noticed that the recent storm had blown away the sign at the gate.

I returned my gaze to the road ahead and we got started on the drive home.

5

THE BUSINESS OF FUN

By the time January rolled around (and a bitterly cold one, at that) the unavoidable bugaboo topic came up among the mothers in the school playground. "What about summer vacation?" we asked each other. "What are you doing with your kids? Have you decided about camp?"

I came up with a radical idea and told them about it. I proposed to spend the summer at home with my kids. We'd go on fabulous excursions around town and drives out to the country. We'd equip ourselves with all the supplies needed to build Popsicle-stick picture frames, lanyards, papier mâché masks, and clay pots. We'd do everything it took to stave off the dreaded "b" word.* I'd call it Camp Mom.

"You'll never pull it off," they said.

My kids were not pleased—to say the least. They loved camp. Play dates with Mom were not going to cut it. Besides, it wasn't *my* companionship they craved. They wanted to be with their own kind, other children—and that's probably the way it should be.

I thought about sending them to camp by themselves like most parents did. It wasn't as if my kids needed, or even wanted, me

---

* There are many bad "b" words, but there's only one I can't bear and have banned from our household, and that is "bored."

there. As camp nurse, I'd have to be on call at night, face the daily mess hall feeding frenzy, and deal with attitude from rude teenagers. The freebie of the barter arrangement wasn't worth it for the work and aggravation it entailed. Still, I had this fantasy of being that iconic camp nurse—hardy, youthful, and adored by all the kids. I wasn't ready to give up my dream.

Spring came quickly and I had to make plans. I perused camp brochures and advertisements. One day I found a camp that looked like it might suit my kids, and me, too.

Camp Carson seemed in every way to be the exact opposite from dangerous, fly-by-night, bare-bones, Camp Na-Gee-La. It was an established, accredited, well-organized camp that offered every conceivable activity and amenity. At first, the name caught my attention. I assumed it was in homage to Rachel Carson, author of *Silent Spring*, a book my father loved and had given me when I was twelve. Back in the 1960s, Carson had been one of the first environmentalists and had raised the alarm about pesticides, acid rain, and the depletion of the ozone layer. I imagined Camp Carson would be a back-to-nature sort of place with homespun values. However, I soon met the camp director, *Bruce* Carson, no relation. *Oh well.*

Still, Camp Carson's glossy brochure was enticing. It was filled with photographs of smiling campers kayaking, canoeing, waterskiing, windsurfing and wakeboarding, doing arts and crafts, and horseback riding. There were also a few features I couldn't have even imagined, such as a ropes course (including a "climbing wall" and a "trust bridge"), an extreme skateboard park, a video production studio, cyber-arts workshop, and state-of-the-art music studio where kids could record their own compositions, even make a demo.

"Camp Carson—a place where friendships are formed and memories are made," was the camp slogan.

How beautiful is that?

"Providing a safe and fun summer experience for your child."
What could be better?
"A place where every child can have a *wow* experience."
Yes, wow, by all means!

In the letter to parents that accompanied the brochure, the directors stated the camp's philosophy: "Each child is unique and special. We will do everything possible to accommodate your child's individual needs. Our mature and nurturing counsellors will keep your child safe and happy. We aim to please!"

I met with Coach Carson, as he liked to be called, and his wife, Wendy, who were the owners and camp directors, for a job interview in their swanky office in downtown Toronto. "Are you ready for a fantastic summer?" Coach Carson asked me. He was a toned and tanned marathon-running man in his mid-fifties who spoke so animatedly, it was as if he were about to break into a camp cheer at any moment. "So far, we have a record-breaking eight hundred campers enrolled, which means we're filled to capacity. We even have a wait list!"

Coach Carson explained that he'd worked in the corporate world for many years, but as a "people person" and a lifelong camper, it was as a camp director that he felt he'd finally found his true calling: the "business of fun."

"*Safe* fun," Wendy interjected.

My ears perked up at this.

"Camp is in my blood," he said. "I'll never grow up. Camp keeps me young." He grinned and shrugged, raising his arms in a helpless what-can-you-do gesture.

My face was beginning to ache from excessive smiling in response, but then his tone dropped down to deep concern. "Kids these days are anxious and stressed." He shook his head sadly. "More than ever, kids need camp to escape pressures at home and at school. Camp is no longer a luxury. It's an absolute necessity."

He invited me to a screening room to view a video he'd produced, "Welcome to Camp Carson—a Cutting Edge Camp."
While he was setting it up, I studied a map of the camp and surrounding area, displayed on the wall. On the map the camp was
located on Stormy Lake, but in the brochure, it was called Lake
Serenity.

"We changed the name," he explained, "so as not to cause
undue alarm. It's a gorgeous property! Hollywood celebrities
have built stunning cottages right across the lake from us. If you're
lucky you'll catch a glimpse of one or two over the summer."

A secretary placed a plate of Rivi's Guilt Free Cookies along
with bottles of mineral water on his desk. I sank into an overstuffed leather couch to watch the video. It opened with a friendly,
rockin' medley of popular tunes in a peppy soundtrack over a
kaleidoscope filmstrip collage of happy children's faces—flushed,
glowing, covered in face paint or theatrical makeup, smudged
with pottery clay, all with huge smiles grinning out at the camera.
Everyone seemed to be having the time of their lives.

"Did that *wow* you? Are these great visuals or what?" he
asked as a perfect sunset stretched across the sky and a silhouette
of kids sitting around a campfire faded out in the final frame.

Next, I sat down with Wendy, who was the coordinator of
the camp's Medical Centre, or MC. She and Bruce met at Camp
Carson many years ago, when it was run by Bruce's father.
Wendy was fit, blonde, and pretty, decked out in stretchy yoga
wear with a pearl necklace. I couldn't imagine her getting down
and dirty at camp and she readily admitted she didn't. "I'm
mostly in the office, but all the kids know me. They call me
the 'The Tiger Lady,'" she said with a chuckle. "They say I'm
tough, but they know I love 'em and the parents know their kids
are *safe* with us."

After a review of my qualifications, Wendy Carson laid down
the law.

"Drugs, cigarettes, and alcohol are strictly prohibited. Any counsellor or staff member under the influence or found using any of these substances on campgrounds will be immediately dismissed." She looked at me to check if I was okay with that, which I was. "As for sex..." She paused to let this new subject register. "Sex is forbidden."

For a second, I paused, too. Did that apply to me? I guess it didn't really matter since Ivan wasn't planning any conjugal visits. He was looking forward to yet another carefree break from his wife and kids. I nodded my agreement.

"...as for PDA—that's what the kids call it, Public Displays of Affection—we have the four-hand rule. They must keep their hands to themselves. For example, if you see them around the campfire and suspect they're getting into mischief, tell them you have to see four hands at all times. Oh, you have to keep an eye on them. After one CIT canoe trip, we found two sleeping bags zipped together!"

Next, we turned to the medical files. "I'm a nurse, too," Wendy said, "but now I head up the office administration, marketing, risk management, and disaster planning."

Such as, what, hostage-taking, bomb threats, biological warfare? Any searches for Weapons of Mass Destruction? These guys were certainly thorough!

"We have a doctor on staff and two nurses," Wendy continued. "I don't do any hands-on nursing any more but they all come to me for hugs." She opened her arms wide to show just how welcoming those hugs were. "I know them all by name. I was the camp nurse when their parents were campers."

As I scanned the camper medical files, Wendy explained their policies about medications. "First and foremost, all drugs will be kept locked up at all times, except at meals when you take what you need to the dining hall. Only asthma inhalers and EpiPens may be kept with the camper in a fanny pack.

"Another thing," she continued, "we encourage parents to disclose everything about their children's health on the forms, but
occasionally you'll find they leave out key information, perhaps
out of fear their child will be rejected, which, by the way, would
never happen. As you can appreciate, we like to know as much
as possible ahead of time. Now, with your vast nursing experience, I'm quite certain none of their medications will faze you."

Oh no, believe me, I *was* fazed, all right. Many children
were on long lists of medications, as many meds as I'd seen on
some of my very sick hospital patients. There were children on
antidepressants, and anti-anxiety drugs, some that they took
daily and others on an as-needed basis. There were kids on a
variety of drugs for attention deficit disorder (ADD), hyperactivity, or "oppositional behaviour." Some children who were on
these drugs were also on nighttime sedation to counteract the
stimulating effects of their daytime meds. (Technically, these
drugs were stimulants, but for children with ADD they had a
calming effect.) In addition, some of these children required
liquid nutritional supplements because the ADD drugs decreased
their appetite and they didn't take in sufficient calories. Other
children—and by no means only the youngest ones—had problems with bedwetting and they took a dose of a drug called des-
mopressin before bed. It was a synthetic version of a natural
hormone and I was familiar with it from the ICU. There, I'd
given it intravenously to brain-dead organ donors to curb their
urine production prior to transplantation. I hadn't known that
as an antidiuretic it could also be used to treat bedwetting.

In addition to those meds, many children were on allergy pills
and asthma puffers and inhalers. Parents also sent their kids with
bottles of nonprescription drugs, over-the-counter painkillers
and anti-inflammatories, along with vitamin and mineral supplements. Then there was a huge range of natural products I'd
only heard of but had never administered, such as anti-oxidants,

immune-system boosters, and products that contained St.
John's wort for "mood disturbances," tryptophan and melato-
nin to "regulate the sleep cycle," and ginseng and kava-kava for
"energy boosts." Given all the medications they were on, I wondered if the kids were sickly, but as I read through their health
forms, I noted that they were all robustly healthy. Many were
high achievers—athletes, musicians, child actors, and award-
winning students.

"I'm not familiar with some of these medications," I admitted, "but I'll read up on them before camp."

Then we went through the special diets, food restrictions,
and dietary requests. Some children needed wheat-free, gluten-
free, and/or dairy-free meals. Some were strictly or flexibly vegetarian, including one whose mother stated her child didn't eat
anything that "had parents"; some just didn't eat red meat, and
one camper stated she ate everything except mammals. Some
requested kosher food, but others were okay with "kosher-style,"
which meant no bacon or cheeseburgers. There were kids with
life-threatening food allergies to peanuts or tree nuts. Others
merely had nut sensitivities. There were allergies to fish or eggs
or to common fruits, such as apples or pears, or to more exotic
fruits such as kiwi and persimmon. Some children would eat no
vegetables at all. Many parents mentioned their children's food
dislikes in lists that included beets, broccoli, and sardines—no
surprises there—but one mother wrote a lengthy letter stating
that her daughter was on a sugar-free diet, with no caffeine or
carbonated drinks, and was "highly allergic to chocolate." Her
insistent tone made me wonder if she simply didn't want her
child to have those treats.

I asked how the kitchen staff coped with so many requests and
Wendy explained.

"Trish is the Five-Star General and Johnny, her husband,
is her Commander-in-Chief. Our kitchen is run like a military

operation. Trish makes the place tick like clockwork. Each task is timed. Kitchen workers know they will be fired if they work too slowly or inefficiently. It has to be this way. Don't forget, we are feeding three meals a day to 800 campers, plus 320 staff members. By the way, kitchen staff are strictly forbidden from socializing with the campers."

That sounded like a strange rule but Wendy's authoritative tone didn't invite discussion.

Coach Carson and Wendy offered me the job on the spot. I figured if I was going to work so hard, I might as well do it in exchange for a camp that offered so many activities and such luxurious facilities. However, just before I signed the contract, Wendy asked me something that did give me pause.

"It's important that our nurses get involved in the life of camp, such as the singalongs and campfires. Our nurses must be *fun-loving*. Would that describe you?"

"What a question!" I said and plastered a big smile on my face.

A fleet of air-conditioned coach buses was lined up in the parking lot of a shopping mall, ready to transport the campers on the three-hour drive to cottage country, the clean, green, Haliburton Highlands of Ontario with its abundance of beautiful lakes, forests, and rocks. The children's duffel bags had been sent ahead earlier so that the counsellors could unpack their clothes and have their beds made up for them by the time they arrived. (I hoped they wouldn't notice I hadn't sent anywhere near the ten pairs of shorts and eight pairs of pants the clothing list dictated. My kids would have to use the camp laundry.)

I was stationed at the Medical Centre van, clipboard in hand, wearing the extra-large T-shirt Coach Carson issued me, with the Carson logo in blue, green, and gold. My job was to receive the campers' meds and ensure they were properly labelled.

Afterward, I would drive the van up to camp on my own. My kids were going with the other campers because as Coach Carson explained, "camp starts on the bus." They went according to their groups: Max, age seven, was a Hawthorne in the Wildflower Unit, and Harry, at nine, was a Polaris in the Constellation Unit.

During the intake of camper meds, I collected a huge pile of epinephrine syringes—EpiPens for short—in a large plastic laundry bin. They were the emergency treatment for those children who had allergic reactions so strong that they could go into anaphylactic shock, a life-threatening situation. These campers had to bring along extra EpiPens because for every one of them two pens were kept in the Medical Centre, another in their cabin, and a few others in strategic positions all around camp; as well, each camper carried a pen at all times. I couldn't help but reflect that in this plastic bin there was more standby epinephrine* than the total amount I'd given in treating all of my hospital patients during the hundreds of cardiac arrest cases I had participated in over the years. It was one of the first drugs we reached for when a patient's heart rate dropped dangerously low and it was used in almost every cardiac arrest. Well, we'd certainly be prepared for any cases of anaphylactic shock that might arise, but I couldn't help but wonder if a few of these EpiPens were sent "just to be on the safe side." Peanut allergies were certainly on the rise, but were all of these truly lethal allergies? I had a feeling there was also a component of parental anxiety—completely understandable when the issue is a life-threatening condition.

Along with meds, I received other items from parents. One father handed me a heavy knapsack filled with textbooks. He'd requested that a counsellor tutor his twelve-year-old, "to give him a head start on next year's material. I want him to have that edge."

---

*Epinephrine is synthetic adrenalin, a powerful emergency drug to shock the heart back into a normal rhythm and create a blood pressure.

A mother gave me an insulated food jar containing a hard-boiled egg rolling around in it. "Please give this to Justin when he arrives at camp," she said. "He needs protein after the long bus ride."

While the campers and parents said their goodbyes, I stood browsing through a growing pile of letters addressed "Attention: Camp Nurse."

Connor stutters and kids pick on him a lot. Has a hard time with letter-writing (no spell-check at camp!) so counsellors, please help. Also, very sensitive to many things, especially loud noise and flashing lights. Please, no strobe lights!

Shawna is afraid of snakes. Please ensure that she has no contact with snakes. NO SNAKES.

Wayne doesn't like to be touched. Please give him a warning if you want to hug him or pat him on the back. Must carry bug spray with him at all times. He worries about West Nile Virus. He tends to be quiet, prefers to sleep in his clothes and will not change them unless forced to by counsellors. Gets a rash if he sits around in wet bathing suit for too long. Can't handle lack of privacy. Does not respond to a sarcastic tone. He doesn't like to swim in cold water (takes a long time to get in), but drinks only cold water.

Melanie is a gifted singer. Please tell the musical director she must have a decent part in the camp play. She was overlooked last year. A HUGE mistake. It's been bad for her self-esteem!

Josh can play soccer, but not as goalie. [Was that offered as a health advisory or a game strategy?]

Shane is not officially gifted but tested VERY *close.*

If Brian can't sleep, give him two Tylenols to settle him down. Has some anger issues. Is working on controlling his temper.

Mandy has a wheat and dairy intolerance and is allergic to peas, tree nuts, and all legumes. May also be allergic to poopy [sic] *seeds? Has never had a reaction but must carry EpiPen with her at all times.*

Some notes were alarming, all the more so because of their cryptic matter-of-factness.

Darren had an isolated episode of hysterical blindness but has experienced a complete cure. Stress-related.

Michael and Jenna's father died a few months ago (suicide) and I'm hoping camp will help them take their mind off of things.

Deanna's father and I have divorced recently. She needs to be with other children of divorced parents to talk things over. Has hay fever and is in a complicated love triangle with her parents. Vomits easily and likes things organized. High anxiety if there is disorder.

Please keep an eye on Samantha. She was recently hospitalized due to weight loss. She's fine now, but FYI.

Megan recently gained fifteen pounds and needs to lose it! We're praying she'll lose weight at camp. Please make sure she doesn't lie on her bed reading all summer and weigh her once a week.

I need to be informed of everything. Notify me if you intend on giving Chad anything, even a Tylenol.

Reading these notes and seeing the parents say their good-byes made me realize how hard it must be for parents to give up control and entrust their children to the care of strangers. It brought home how huge my responsibilities would be with the children in the weeks to come and how important it would be for me to be that reassuring voice on the phone to their parents.

Most kids were handling the goodbyes fairly well, even the boy who was jumping up and down just before getting on the bus. He explained, "I'm trying to get rid of everything I learned at school." He pulled at his scalp in an attempt to expel the offend-ing material. The kids were coping, but the parents, not so well. I was just about to pack up my car when a mother in tears ran over and threw herself on me. "Please look after my darling babies!" She grasped my shoulders and pulled me close.

"What are your children's names?" *So I'll know which ones to avoid.*

"My daughter is Alexa Rose and she happens to be the pretti-est girl at camp! She's a Scorpio and her brother, Thomas Carl, is an Aries." She handed me a bottle of pills called Ativan, a sedative. "Give Alexa Rose one at night for separation anxiety and T.C. can have one too. Oh, and give them a few drops of Rescue Remedy." She handed me a small brown glass bottle containing a clear liquid. It was a tincture of distilled flowers that contained a touch of grape alcohol. She clutched her chil-dren before tearing herself away.

Just before the campers boarded the buses, they all reluctantly handed over their electronic games, cell phones, and portable computers. Turning in their hardware was the signal to say goodbye. Now, all each of them carried was a hefty tool chest (like the one Anderson had toted around at Camp Na-Gee-La but rarely used), as if they were carpenters, going off to a job site. These tool boxes were filled not with nails and screwdrivers but with bulk candy: bags of Nerds, jawbreakers, Sour Warheads, Cherry Blasters, Fuzzy Peaches, SweetTarts, and Skittles. The junk food policy at Camp Carson seemed to be to bring as much as you could possibly cram into the most gargantuan tool box you could find.

Alexa Rose's mother came back to me. "I feel like I'm abandoning them," she said as she dabbed at her tears. "This is so hard on me. I wish I was going, too." She wrung her hands as she gazed at the departing buses. She gave herself a few drops of Rescue Remedy from her own bottle. "It's hard to believe they can survive in that wilderness without me there to protect them." As the buses began to pull out of the parking lot, she ran alongside, waving at her children, now beyond her reach.

Camp Carson was every bit as impressive as the video showed, but what it hadn't conveyed was the exclusive, country club atmosphere. Even with Coach Carson's warm welcome and private tour, I felt uncomfortably like an outsider. I focused on the beautiful surroundings and learning my way around the vast property.

The camp was built on an oval, sparkling lake. All of the facilities were situated on manicured lawns spread out over sprawling grounds. First, Coach Carson took me to the Lodge, where there was a staff lounge with a TV, video games, an indoor pool, and billiard and ping-pong tables. Next, we made a loop out to the camp's periphery to see the campers' cabins. They were modern wood-and-log structures that had been freshly painted in forest-green, maroon, or navy-blue to denote the various units. Inside, the walls, ceiling, and rafters were made of unvarnished, light pine wood. There were eight single cots and four bunk beds, so there was space for sixteen people, usually twelve campers and four counsellors, two of whom were swim or water-ski specialists, for example, and only slept in the cabin. Each cabin had its own showers and bathrooms.

We walked back to the centre of camp where the dining hall was located. It was a long, grand rectangular room with several entrances and a balcony that ran right around the outside, offering breathtaking views of Lake Serenity whichever direction you looked. It was decorated in expensive-looking, but rustic, cottage-type décor, with a stuffed moose over the stone fireplace and polished pine floors. All over the walls hung bright plaques and banners from Colour War battles and victories of days gone by, all signed by campers, many of whom were probably parents of children now attending Camp Carson.

Next, Coach Carson took me to meet Trish and Johnny and see the kitchen. It was as scrupulously clean as any operating room I'd ever been in, right down to its chilled ambient temperature, white tiles, and large spotless stainless-steel tables for food preparation. A counter the full length of one wall separated the kitchen from the dining hall. Kitchen staff handed out platters of food, pitchers of "bug juice"—the ubiquitous, flavoured sugar water that was the standard camp beverage—and condiments across the counter. The kitchen workers seemed to be between sixteen and eighteen, around the same age as the counsellors. They lived in trailers at the back of the campgrounds. I wondered how they felt about working and waiting on their city counterparts whose work in comparison looked more like playing and partying.

Coach Carson pointed out the office, a modern, well-equipped log cabin, where he, Wendy, and their staff worked. Just outside of camp, down the road a short distance, was a cabin where the Carsons lived, and another for the camp doctor and his wife. To end our tour, Coach Carson showed me the Playhouse, which had a surround-sound system and plush seats. With great pride he told me about his son, Eric, who was the camp's head of drama and would be directing the camp play.

"See, I knew when you saw the camp, you'd go *wow!* So, what do you say?"

What could I say but "wow"?

We had lunch, which we inhaled at a pace that I'd come to know as camp tempo. It was a breakneck gobble of submarines-tomato-soup-Rice-Krispie-squares. Afterward, Coach Carson went up to the podium and welcomed both returning and new campers to Camp Carson, now in its thirty-fourth year. At that first lunch, I was introduced to Dr. Don Kitchen, whom every-one called "Kitch," and his wife, Marg. Kitch was a general practitioner who took his summer vacation at camp. He called it a working holiday. He'd been the camp doctor for years and knew all the kids. He and Marg had three kids who had grown up at the camp and were now counsellors. Kitch told me that every morning after breakfast, he would hold a clinic. After that, Caitlin, a newly graduated nurse in her early twenties, and I were to be available to the campers and staff at all times. We could consult with him over the phone if we had any questions. He was only a few minutes away and promised to come for emergencies. After lunch, Kitch got up and gave a stern lecture to everyone about the dangers of the sun. His words carried a lot more weight than mine ever had, but probably the scary mention of premature aging and deadly skin cancers made them listen up.

The Medical Centre was a centrally located, cozy wood cabin nestled in a grove of pine trees. There was a large, com-fortable waiting room, plus a well-equipped doctor's office, two examining rooms, and one room with six beds for girls across from another room with six beds for boys. There was also a small isolation room that had one bed in the case of a patient with an infectious disease. At the back were two small bedrooms, one for me and one for Caitlin, who had worked at the camp the year before when she was still a student nurse. After dinner that first night, Caitlin and I got to work setting up and organizing the supplies and medications. I pointed out to Wendy that some of the meds left over from the previous summer were now past their expiration date.

"Pack them up," she said, "and we'll send them off to some Third World country along with any outdated equipment. They're grateful for whatever they can get."

Caitlin lowered her voice. "The Tiger Lady is tough. She runs a tight ship with supplies and stuff and freaks out if something goes missing. She's always worried a parent might sue them for something. But she's such an old-fashioned nurse when it comes to treating the children. It's basically, *suck it up*. Like, a kid's arm could be falling right off and she'll say, 'go, have a drink of water,' or something, and it makes them laugh their heads off and forget about whatever was bothering them."

I laughed, too. *Once a nurse, always a nurse.*

The days started off with pleasant wake-up music. It was usually a selection from a mainstream repertoire, like the Barenaked Ladies, the Steve Miller Band, or the Red Hot Chili Peppers. Breakfast was at 8:00 a.m., during which Caitlin and I were on pill call duty for campers on meds. When we arrived at the dining hall, they would come at us in a mad rush. Caitlin usually stayed on "crowd control" while I gave out pills from a big picnic basket. I had to laugh as I imagined myself skipping in like Little Red Riding Hood with that straw basket over my arm!

Caitlin and I did our best to get to everyone at breakfast, or else we'd have to go hiking all around camp to track down kids who had missed their pills. If a pill accidentally dropped, the kids were quick to remind me of the five-second rule, the interval in which a dropped pill was still okay to take. (Funny, that was never covered in my pharmacology course!) After receiving their meds, the kids returned to their seats and slouched back down on the benches, beside their cabin mates, comfy in their baggy flannel plaid pants, faces hidden deep inside cozy hoodies, their feet in thick, grey woolly socks shoved into Birkenstocks.

The roar in the dining hall at meals was deafening. Conversation was impossible so I worked at reading lips and deciphering the sign language of "Please pass the Cheerios" or "More bug juice?" The food was delicious and plentiful.

After each meal, there were amusing skits and announcements about things like the swim marathon or tryouts for the camp play. Since that first week of camp fell over both July 1, Canada Day, and July 4, Independence Day in the United States, there were moments of patriotism, too. While the majority of campers were Canadian, there were some Americans. (There were few differences between the kids except the Americans referred to the tuck shop as the "canteen" and they liked to imitate the Canadians use of "eh.") On July 1, the camp dutifully sang "O Canada." But a few days later we listened to the much more enthusiastic belting out of "The Star-Spangled Banner" by the handful of Yankee campers and staff, who waved their flag and held their hands over their hearts as they sang. Our much more subdued show of national pride made me wonder if a *lack* of patriotism was one thing Canada *was* known for.

There was a definite hierarchy at this camp and you saw it clearly in the dining hall seating. The camp directors, the doctor, his wife, and their friends sat at a head table, presiding over the crowd, like at a wedding. The unit heads, who were in charge of the various age groupings, had their own tables, and the various heads of specialties such as pottery, art and crafts (A and C), or sail, sat at other tables. Counsellors sat with their campers, which was necessary so they could keep an eye on their kids and also rise up as a group when called upon, to chant in unison their own cabin's cheer. Caitlin and I sat wherever we could squeeze in. I was usually at the overflow table of swim staff, and she would angle for a spot at the trippers' table.

After an embarrassing gaffe when I mistook a camper for a counsellor and another when I mistook a counsellor for a camper, I made a concerted effort to get to know the names of the counsellors and where they sat. Soon, I also knew where each specialty was located. At the table of dance and drama instructors—known as "Divas and Drama Queens"—there were entertaining scenes featuring hysterical laughter or uncontrollable weeping over various comedies or tragedies, inevitably ending with someone getting up and stomping away. They would cry at a moment's notice and burst into song at another. They were super careful about what they ate and never took seconds. It was known that anyone scrounging for extra desserts could help themselves freely at that table.

The long table near the outside wall, right beside the balcony overlooking Lake Serenity, was where the group of trippers, most of them male, seated themselves. They would be taking the children out on hikes and four- or five-day canoe trips in the wilderness of Algonquin Park. With their scruffy beards and wearing do-rags, tight muscle shirts, and hiking boots that seemed suited to scaling Mount Kilimanjaro, they got up frequently during meals to swagger about like conquering Vikings, stretch their legs, strut along the balcony and hork spitballs over the edge onto the lawn. They were buff and stunning specimens of young male beauty. Ah, the macho glory of the trippers! They had big reputations to maintain and glorious traditions to uphold. In the camp pantheon, the trippers were at the pinnacle. But their reputations, both on and off duty, were well-earned, or so they claimed.

"We work hard, but when we're off, we're off," Jordan, the head tripper, told me.

"They're pretty hard-core party animals," Caitlin said when she saw me gazing at them. "Enjoy the eye candy while it lasts," Caitlin advised. "They are only at camp in between trips. That's when they get to lounge around and take up a lot of space being beautiful—which they do so very well, don't they?"

"Not too hard on the eyes," I said, trying not to let my admiration of the trippers' good looks be too obvious.

After lunch on the first full day of camp, Caitlin and I went from cabin to cabin, checking each camper for lice. It was the standard, first-day practice, Caitlin said. We worked steadily all afternoon and managed to get to all eight hundred heads, thanks to assistance from a fastidious counsellor from the Constellation cabin who was known as a champion nit-picker. "My whole family had lice. I know what to look for. They call me Miami, as in Miami Lice." But as it turned out, I was the one who discovered the only cases—two sisters—and felt oddly triumphant at this weird accomplishment. Camp policy dictated that they would have to be sent home and allowed back only after being treated and deemed "clear." Treating them at camp would be too time-consuming and tedious (after a few minutes of that work you have a new understanding of the phrase "nit-picking") and the risk of spread to other campers was great. Kitch explained the sensitive matter to the crushed parents on the phone.

That day, the whole camp was abuzz with excitement and jitters about the swim test that everyone had to undergo before being allowed to participate in any water sports. I had been surprised when I learned that Camp Carson had an indoor pool, situated as it was on such a beautiful, calm lake, but Coach Carson explained that it was for rainy days and those kids who couldn't get used to the weeds, the rocks, and the cool water. The Carsons had, it seemed, anticipated every possible risk of a risk and prepared for it.

For safety's sake, the Carsons also had many rules that were exactingly enforced. First, all campers had to undergo swim testing. Each child had to jump into the lake fully dressed, crawl into a canoe, tip it, swim a few lengths, and then tread water while a member of the swim staff observed and made notes about his or her swimming form. It seemed like everyone at camp, even the strong and confident swimmers and those who took private swimming lessons all year round, was nervous and on edge until they received the coveted green bracelet signifying they could participate in all waterfront activities. (They even made me take the swim test. I passed—phew!) The embarrassing yellow bracelet meant the swimmer had a conditional pass, and the red bracelets "were for losers," as one kid told me. The head of the swim staff explained to me that the red bracelet was to alert them to the kids who needed closer supervision around and in the water. That made perfect sense and it was quite a change from the non-competitive "everyone's a winner" attitude at Camp Na-Gee-La. Yet, recognition only for the star performers didn't seem right, either. How to strike a balance?

The next day was still slow in the MC so I went down to the waterfront to watch the proceedings. I've always loved being near the water but, truth be told, I was also hoping to sneak a peek at my own kids to see how they were doing on the swim test. Max had already passed it and was playing with his friends on the beach. Harry was in the midst of it. The lake was warm and now, at the age of nine, he knew that its warm currents came from the sun, not an underwater heating system.

When the swim instructors saw me near my kids, they shooed me away, so I went over to watch other kids. Most were jumping in gleefully. The few who weren't used to swimming in cold lakes were slower to jump in, but soon they too were happily splashing about. My attention was quickly drawn to Wayne, a boy I recognized from Max's cabin.

"First, I have to get psyched," I heard him saying to his swim instructor, nicknamed Cargo (her name was Carla Gordon), who was coaxing him into the water. Wayne had a high-pitched, squeaky voice. He wore glasses and had hair that was stiff and straight-up, as if he was perpetually shocked. His skinny chest showed his ribs with each breath.

"Now, Wayne, we're not going to go through this again this summer, are we? Your mom said you had lots of swimming lessons," Cargo told him. "Go for it! Jump in." Her clipboard at her waist, she was poised to tick off his swimming skills as soon as he demonstrated them to her. He was just about to jump in, then hesitated.

"Are there sharks?" His voice was higher and squeakier. "What about leeches?"

"Wayne! I'm waiting..." She took his glasses from him. "You're going in!"

Again, he made moves as if he would take the plunge, then stopped himself. "I know how to swim," he said, "just not in the deep end." He squinted out at the lake. "Which is the deep end?"

"You're stalling, Wayne!" Cargo said, her clipboard at the ready.

He stared down into the water. "It's dark in there." He looked out across the lake under a flattened hand at his brow. "Is this lake polluted? Last year, something slimy swam between my legs. Are there fish in this lake?"

"Probably, but they're harmless," Cargo answered. She tapped her foot.

"Are they endangered fish?"

"Wayne, I can't wait any longer. Just jump in. Let's see what you can do."

He stood there, thinking. "What about goldfish? Are goldfish endangered?"

"Come on!" She was getting exasperated. "The water's warm today!"

An older boy yelled out, "Hey, Waynester, watch out for the snapping turtles! They'll bite off your toes!"

"Turtles?" he gulped.

"Do a cannonball! Go for it!" someone else called out.

"Wayne, we've wasted so much time! Swim period is over!" Cargo shouted. She blew the whistle, signalling the campers to get out of the water. Wayne's ordeal was over, at least for now.

"You made it past them today," I said to him sympathetically as I wrapped his sun-warmed towel around his dry, shivering body, "but how are you going to get out of it tomorrow?" He gave a weak grin and ambled off to find his cabin.

"Who's that?" I asked Cargo, pointing to a teenaged girl sitting under a tree in the shade in her clothes, jeans and a long-sleeved shirt on this hot day.

"That's Samantha. She's weird this summer. She was here last year. She's actually a decent swimmer, but she says she's got her period."

I returned to the beach the next day after morning clinic, to see how these situations were going to pan out. I must have looked concerned because the head of the swim staff came over to talk to me again.

"It's all about safety," he said. "Kids have to learn how to swim. They have to get into the water. It has to be this way."

"It seems harsh with kids who are afraid. Kids have been coming to me, begging for swim excuse notes."

"We can't mess around. Everyone has to swim and we need to know who's safe in the water and who's not."

Fair enough, I agreed, but did they have to use such commando tactics?

Again, today, Samantha was under the tree, huddled there, clutching her knees, looking out at the lake. It was another hot, sunny day and she still wore heavy clothes. Her long sleeves were pulled down over her hands, almost to her fingertips, as if she was cold. From her sad, resolute expression, swimming seemed like the last thing she was prepared to do. I wondered how this strong-arm approach was going to work on her.

By the third day, Wayne still hadn't gotten into the water.

"You're going to rock that swim test today, buddy," Cargo said with a playful punch on his shoulder.

That day he was wearing his prescription goggles, so maybe his improved eyesight would give him the confidence he needed. He wrapped his arms around himself, then made a few diving poses as if he might really go through with it.

"Okay, Wayne," Cargo said briskly. "I talked to your mom and she says you *have* to go in. She says she spent lots of money on your swim lessons and she knows you can do it. We can't fool around with this any more. You're going in, buddy."

"No, no, no!" he shouted, digging his toes in between the cracks of the wooden boards of the dock as she pulled at him and he pushed back at her. *Splash!* Wayne was in the water, within Cargo's tight grip. She tried to get him to ride on her back like a dolphin but he remained absolutely rigid and terrified.

Mission accomplished, but whose mission and what accomplishment? It made me especially grateful that Max and Harry weren't afraid of the water. I hadn't talked with them much, but from what I could tell, they were enjoying camp. Harry tended to avoid me and slunk away, the hood on his sweatshirt suddenly up, when he saw me coming. He never liked to be singled out for attention. At first, Max bounced over every morning for a hug or to share his opinion of the meal, but his counsellors quickly came to retrieve him. They told me that seeing Max with his mother made the other kids miss theirs. I saw their point, but I also think they were having a hard time with Max and his tendency to wander off, so were trying to keep him close.

Evening pill call at the MC was much more relaxed than the mad rush at breakfast and lunch, because it was the end of a long and busy day and there were fewer pills. Mostly it was the time when the kids came for their evening sedation or antidepressants. A few teenaged girls shyly and discreetly came to receive their birth control pills (for medical reasons other than birth control, they made a point of telling me). Just before bedtime, campers came for their pills to prevent bedwetting. (The pills mostly worked, but not always, so the counsellors were expected to check the beds each morning and change the sheets if necessary while the kids were at breakfast, so as to avoid embarrassment.) I had to admire the sheer aplomb of the ten-year-old boy who told me, "Sure I wet the bed. Is there something wrong with that?"

Evening also seemed to be the time that homesickness came out. Wendy made rounds to all of the younger cabins, tucking the kids in and reading them stories. Surprisingly, it wasn't the youngest kids at camp who were the most homesick, it was the eleven- and twelve-year-olds, and frequently the teenagers. Most just needed a hug or a distraction to get them through a difficult moment, but a few kids had a bad case of it.

"Whatever you do, don't let them call home," Kitch had instructed me. "It always makes things worse."

Alexa Rose, the girl I'd met in the parking lot along with her mother, had been coming to us every bedtime in her pyjamas and furry Ugg boots, each evening more miserable than the last. She was an eleven-year-old Wildflower, a Lupin (not to mention Scorpio). Every evening I gave her a few drops of Rescue Remedy that promised on the label "to comfort and reassure" and sat with her while she sobbed.

"Can I call home?" she asked.

"It's not a good idea."

"My mother said I could call if I wanted."

"It's a camp policy. We don't let campers call home."

Phone calls home were rarely allowed and only with Coach Carson's agreement.

"But that's for everyone else. My mother said I could call home if I wanted to and if I got really homesick, she said she'd come get me."

"Does your brother know how unhappy you are?"

"He doesn't know I exist. I haven't even seen him." She tugged at her furry boots. "He's having an amazing time, so he doesn't understand me."

"Aren't you hot in those boots?" I asked, trying to distract her.

She stared back at me like I was an idiot: to her, they were the exact right temperature: cool. I looked at her forlorn face and knew exactly how she felt. For a moment, I was taken back to when I was her age and felt homesick, right in my own home. My mother was sick and depressed and my father preoccupied with her care. I was always angling to be a guest in other peoples' homes. I softened my approach. "This is only the third day of camp. Maybe give it a few more days?" I wheedled.

"Can't I just call them? If I just speak to them, I'll feel better."

"No, but you could write to your parents and tell them how you feel," I suggested.

"I feel terrible!"

"Then mention the things you *do* like about camp."

"But I don't like anything!"

"I'm sure you could think of something you like," I said, knowing I was not following Kitch's advice, which was to redirect children who were homesick rather than talk with them about it. My strategy was to try to get her to focus on the positives. It wasn't working. In between sobs, she managed to tell me all the things that were troubling her. "I'm the new girl and I don't know anyone except this one girl I know from school. We used to be BFFs, but we're so not any more. Now, I don't have a best friend at camp and everyone else does, except me. Anyway, she's jealous of me because of my stuff. She touches everything. She used my shampoo and said it was by mistake, but I mean, my nanny labelled everything, so she had to have seen my name. She knew it wasn't hers."

Perusing Alexa Rose's chart, I noted that she disliked dogs and that got me thinking. I could understand being afraid of lightning storms, or even monsters under the bed, but dogs? If forcing children to swim was a way to get over fear of the water, could playing with a friendly dog give her the courage to conquer that fear? Perhaps a dog could even help Alexa Rose with her homesickness? I had seen firsthand the comfort animals could bring. I knew a wheaten terrier who took his work as a therapy pet seriously. He helped people cope with the grief of losing a loved one. I had been impressed by the therapeutic influence of Merlin, a miniature collie who paid regular visits to residents of a nursing home. And I would never forget a dying woman in our ICU and her nurse who granted her patient's last wish to see her horse. She had wheeled her patient down to the back of the hospital, IV poles on one side of the stretcher, oxygen tank on the other. The horse was led down the ramp of the unloading docks straight to where the patient lay. He looked at her, whinnied, and stamped his hoof, as if in recognition. I don't think the patient had the energy to cry, but those of us gathered there to witness the moment did.

I looked at Alexa Rose's miserable face. "What about a dog to cuddle?"

"I hate dogs," Alexa Rose said. "They have rabies."

She didn't like any animals, she said, not even ones in the zoo. I wondered how she was going to cope at the camp's Eco

Zone with its rabbits and guinea pigs, as well as the Carsons'
poodle, Skippy. "Maybe a dog could help you with your homesickness? What if I bring Skippy on a leash? You can see how
gentle she is."

"No way! That's so not happening." She folded her arms
across her chest and looked away. She seemed ready to return
with her counsellor who'd been waiting patiently. At least I'd
managed to distract her. It's hard enough to overcome a fear you
want to overcome, much less one that you don't.

Early each morning, Caitlin got up, did yoga stretches, and at
seven o'clock knocked on my door. "Wakey, wakey, girlfriend.
Let's go!" she'd say and would drag me out of bed for a brisk
morning walk on a trail through the woods. Right before setting
out, she'd apply a layer of fruity lip gloss. "I'm addicted to
this stuff," she'd say, slipping the tube into her vest pocket for
another fix along the way. Then, she clipped the walkie-talkie
we shared to the back of her jogging pants and off we went. With
her ponytail pulled through her baseball cap, swinging back and
forth with the pumping of her muscular legs, Caitlin set a brisk
pace and I did my best to keep up.

She had grown up in a small Ontario farming town and was
used to the beauty of nature, so it didn't dazzle her as it did me.
She was impatient when I'd stop to ooh and aah over various
sights. One morning, a deer stepped out of the forest on the side
of the road and paused in front of us. I paused, too, but Caitlin
bypassed it without a break in her stride. "Keep up the pace,"
she called back over her shoulder.

Feeling so alive and healthy on those walks, I experienced
walking for the sake of being outdoors, breathing the fresh
morning air, and moving vigorously. In the woods, I allowed
myself to take in the sights around me, especially the exotic (to

me) patches of brilliant yellow, purple, and white flowers. (Caitlin
pointed out that they were weeds—buttercup, loosestrife, and
Queen Anne's Lace—but I still thought they were pretty.)

Caitlin was interested in hearing about my work in the ICU
but was taken aback when I told her how long I'd been at the
same job.

"Twenty years?" She looked at me with pity. "Isn't it time to
move on? Haven't you had enough of the bedside?"

No, I explained, I loved taking care of patients, found my
work challenging and fascinating, and felt that I still had a lot
more to learn. She said she might be interested in critical care
one day, once she got more experience under her belt, but it
sounded stressful and depressing. "And what's with the twelve-
hour night shifts and working weekends?" she asked, shaking
her head. "I don't think so, I want to have a life."

But she must have been intrigued by my stories of the ICU
because she kept asking me for more. For the first time, I found
it strange to talk about that work I loved so much with all of the
pain, suffering, and sadness it entailed, out there in that beautiful, natural setting and with the new lightheartedness I was
feeling. Should I tell her about the patient I'd cared for on my
last shift, a young man who had cystic fibrosis and was awaiting
a lung transplant? He struggled with every breath and his family
stayed at his side all day and night, waiting for news that would
save his life. I had to leave at the end of my shift without ever
finding out whether he'd received a new pair of lungs or not.
Caitlin shuddered and seemed upset when I told her about such
sad things and so I veered onto lighter topics. My two nursing
worlds never felt so far apart.

That first week went smoothly. As far as I could tell—from
a distance—my kids were content. I was enjoying myself too,
finding lots of time to get out and participate in activities
around camp. I'd spoken on the phone with Ivan a few times

and although he didn't say it, I had the distinct feeling he was missing me, which wasn't such a bad thing.

Toward the end of the first week, after lunch, Coach Carson announced it was letter-writing day. "Tell your parents about the fun you're having, your new friends, and how delicious the grilled cheese sandwiches are," he prompted them.

At first they balked, then he told them that a letter home was their meal ticket for dinner. They found letter writing and the idea of snail mail amusing.

"Wow! Stamps!" many exclaimed. "Cool."

"Letters take, like, forever," one kid grumbled, "three or four days or something. My news will be old by the time they get it."

"It's weird not to be able to text my parents," one kid told me, "but I don't miss messaging my friends 'cause I'm here with them 24/7."

Understandably, they were used to instant contact whenever the whim hit. Did they even know how to write by hand? Would they pepper their letters with electronic language like LOL for "laugh out loud," or "Camp is kewl! Camp is GR8!"*

Coach Carson told me that the lack of Internet access was problematic for parents who wanted contact with their kids. He was looking into setting it up at camp for the following summer, but in the meantime, all they had was old-fashioned pen and paper. I was curious to see how the kids would manage.

That night, at dinnertime, Coach Carson looked worried.

"Whaddup?" I asked, trying out the new lingo I was learning.

"The kids' letters have gone home."

"And your point is?"

"Brace yourself."

---

* I'd like to remind younger readers that my generation had its share of codes too. There was 2ysur, 2ysub, I CUR 2Ys4ME and SWAK for "Sealed With a Kiss" and DDDD for "Deliver De-Letter De-Sooner De-Better," so don't feel sorry for us!

"For what?"

"You'll see," he said grimly.

A few days later, I understood the reason for Coach Carson's ominous tone. The campers' letters had finally made their way home. Overnight the camp telephone answering machine and email box filled up with calls and urgent messages from parents.

6

ARTS AND CRAFTS NURSE

A boy ran up to me. "Hey, Nurse! Did ya hear? All the toilets have been stolen!"

"Is that so?"

"Yeah, the police are investigating but they have nothing to *go on*. Get it?"

"Very funny."

"Hey, Nurse," he said, now looking serious. "Did you know your wenis is showing?"

"My what?"

"Your *wenis*!"

How hilarious. This joke—which I didn't get—was on me.

"You got punk'd, girlfriend!" squealed Caitlin when I told her. Kitch had heard that one before. "Wenis is the medical term for the flabby skin on the elbow," he said. In the MC waiting room I stood in front of the mirror, fingering my wenis. Flabby, was it? I felt young at heart but they didn't see my heart, only my age. Mature, maternal Nurse Mom next to young, youthful Nurse Caitlin was not a pretty picture. What I needed was not street, but camp, cred. So, I told Caitlin it was time to kick up our morning hike a few notches. I was ready to shift into high gear! I joined an afternoon hip-hop class and in no time, was poppin', lockin', and slidin' along with the rest of them. "Work it, girl!"

The dance instructor offered encouragement as I did my best to ignore the few "what's she doing here?" looks. *I'll show them who's cool!*

By the end of the first week of camp I knew most of the campers by name and the meds they were on. A few kids stumped me, such as the identical twin brothers, Michael and Martin, each on different meds. They got annoyed when I kept asking who was who until one day I noticed that one of them, Michael, had a mole. Some kids stood grinning at me, making me guess their names. Others gave me fake names or only their first names. I guess I could have always just shouted out Michael ChristopherMatthewJoshuaNicholasAndrewDanielBradley or AshleyJessicaSarahBrittanyEmilySamanthaAmandaStephanie Nicole and *someone* would have come forward for something! The other problem was they often dragged their heels, coming late for their meds, or not showing up at all. Then I had to go after them.

"Here comes da nurse, here comes da nurse!" a CIT called out when he saw me approach with my pill basket. "Run, kids! Hide from the nurse!"

I managed to nab one camper, then I trapped another fugitive at the tennis court.

"They're just vitamins," she told me scornfully. "I don't really need them."

"Yes, but your parents want you to have them."

I hunted down one boy in his cabin who had a pretty good comeback. "Sorry!" He slapped his forehead. "I was stuck in traffic all morning."

"Here comes my connection," I heard one kid tell his friend. "She's my drug dealer. The pill pusher."

"You're not making it easy for me," I scolded another kid.

"That's why they pay you the big bucks," he quipped. "Ka-ching! Ka-ching!"

Because of these delays, the after-breakfast clinic got pushed back later and later. Kitch was understanding because he knew how many meds we had to give out. He'd calculated that roughly a third of the entire camp was on meds of one kind or another. "That's fairly typical, these days," he told me on an especially busy morning.

"It's always such a mad rush," I complained. "Are all these pills necessary?"

"Many of the kids with ADD wouldn't be able to come to camp at all without them." He disagreed with parents who put their kids on a "drug holiday" because in his experience, kids were happier staying on their meds. "Camp is a busy, structured place and they cope better if they can follow directions, wait their turn, and organize their belongings, things they can't do if they're not on their meds. Their behaviour is better and they get along with their cabin mates and therefore enjoy themselves more."

It was time to get to work. While Kitch sat in his office perusing medical journals, Caitlin and I went out to the crowded waiting room to assess the kids' problems and decide in what order they would be seen. At camp, triage wasn't strictly a matter of the severity of their medical problems. There were other factors to consider. The loudness of the whining, persuasiveness of pleading, and forcefulness of pestering didn't get anywhere with *me*—nor their "pedigree" of influential or wealthy parents—but it did influence Kitch and Caitlin, who tended to treat the high-maintenance or high-profile ones first. In my own triage system, when all medical issues were equal, campers came before counsellors and politeness was the only effective grease. I complimented one boy on his exceptionally good manners.

"Don't think I behave this well at home," he cautioned me.

For some children, it was a badge of honour how many times they frequented the MC, and for others it was more of an achievement to avoid coming altogether. I often wondered what prompted one child to rush for attention and treatment for a single mosquito bite and another to tough it out, even when covered in bug bites. Usually, I had little time to ponder such questions. Sometimes, when the waiting room was full, I asked them to write down the reason they came. It kept them momentarily occupied, but their notes weren't usually all that helpful:

Can something be done about my freckles?

Feeling crappy!

Ate evil hamburger last night. Might have Mad Cow Disease.

Eye?

Bug bite. Check it out—there's a planet on my neck!

Knee falling off [accompanied by sketch of knee, labelled with "ouch" and arrow].

In and out of consciousness.

Kitch saw each child who visited the Medical Centre, even the ones with splinters and mosquito bites that I could treat myself. At first, I assumed it was his thoroughness, or to catch something I may have missed, but Wendy explained the real reason.

"Our parents feel better knowing that a doctor has seen their child. It's what they expect. Besides, the doctor can bill for his services. He doesn't get paid if the nurse treats the child." Wendy went on to explain another situation where health care and commerce converged. "As for the American campers, it's problematic since he can't bill for his services but is still exposed legally. He takes care of them out of the goodness of his heart."

It was a pleasure working with Kitch and I had a lot to learn from him. Also, it was a relief to have him be the "enforcer." When a twelve-year-old boy needed stitches for a cut on his head, Kitch forbade him to swim until they were removed. The boy sulked, argued, and went swimming anyway. When the cut got mildly infected, Kitch stepped up to be the bad guy who scolded him. But Kitch also had the advantage of knowing the kids better than I did from having been at the camp for so many years. He could see through fabricated excuses to get out of going on a tough canoe trip. He uncovered a case of self-sabotage, when a child damaged his own braces to nab a few days home to visit the orthodontist! He was exceptionally good at identifying faked (whether consciously or not) ailments. One morning, a group of girls, all from the same cabin, showed up together with identical headaches and stomach aches. He checked their schedule and discovered they were supposed to be doing the climbing wall. He knew they didn't like that activity so he prescribed pottery class for them instead. When the dance or drama instructors came in with various injuries or muscle strains—or simply a case of rattled nerves—they often requested painkillers or something to help them relax. Kitch managed to calm them down just by sitting with them and giving them attention. He spent a lot of time talking and, perhaps more importantly, listening, to them. One day he went out to the crowded waiting room and brought in one little girl right away. "This is an MID," he told me. "A muffin in distress. All she needs is a hug."

I envied his mastery of the art and the craft—not just the science—of healing children. "So much of what I do is explaining, reassuring, and consoling," he said with a shrug, as if it were nothing.

These skills were a big part of my nursing practice, too. In the hospital I always made note of when I offered my patient "comfort measures." At camp, I recorded my intervention as

"TLC." How well I've learned that Tender Loving Care can be just as effective as a medication.

I learned a lot about sore throats from Kitch after we started to see a run on them for a few days. "More than ninety percent of sore throats are viral and therefore do not require an antibiotic. It's unlikely to be strep throat if the patient has a runny nose, stuffy ears, cough, but you can't rule it out altogether. Strep throat is worrisome because of dire complications that can develop if left untreated, such as throat abscesses, kidney inflammation, or the main one, rheumatic fever. Prudent medicine would dictate that a swab be sent for each and every sore throat, but it's not always feasible to do so." He then told me about one summer when a mysterious sore throat went around camp. The mystery was that out of one hundred and seventy-five swabs that were sent to the lab, only one came back positive and that child wasn't even symptomatic. He then had to start an antibiotic on a child who felt perfectly well.

"The question to always ask is: Is it viral, bacterial, or allergic? The answer will guide your approach," he said.

As for earaches, they always need to be examined, he explained, but few patients needed antibiotics, only painkillers to ease the discomfort, then follow-up. Most resolve by themselves. Under Kitch's tutelage, I improved my examination of the tympanic membrane inside the ear canal. We examined each child and compared notes.

"Hey, you get to see a part of me that I'll never see," one kid said, as I peered into his ear. "My eyes, too. I'll never see my own eyes, except in a mirror."

"You're right," I said. "I hadn't thought of it that way before."

There were lots of skin ailments I'd never encountered. Kitch taught me how to diagnose eczema, athlete's foot (an infection not always found on the foot), heat rash, and others, such as ringworm (which is not a worm, but a fungus). And I no longer worried that every red and swollen mosquito bite would turn into infective cellulitis or the dastardly flesh-eating disease. Nonetheless, I did a careful examination, demarcated the reddened area with a marker so I could track its progress, took baseline vital signs, gave an antihistamine, and followed up the next day.

One time I discovered a galloping skin infection by accident. I happened to bend down to pick up a dropped pill (within the allowable five seconds, of course!) and noticed a big, red, wet sore on the back of the leg of a boy named Wesley.

"Oh, that," he said. "It's nothing."

But on closer inspection, I found another sore, and then, further up his leg, a few more. His other leg was also covered in these sores.

"They're mosquito bites," he said. "They don't bother me."

"They bother *me*!" I started him on antibiotic ointment, but even so, they quickly spread onto his arms and chest. Within a few days, an entire cabin of eleven-year-old boys all had unsightly, open sores all over their bodies. Kitch took a quick glance at one of them, scanned the others, said one word—impetigo—and started them all on a ten-day course of antibiotics. "Skin infections like these are unavoidable in close quarters. We have to eradicate it—preferably before Visitor's Day," he said with a wink.

Kitch taught me a lot of practical skills. One evening after dinner, a bench fell on a young camper's foot. *Ouch!* It was bleeding under the nail and swelling up fast. "It's a subungual hematoma," Kitch said. I prepared a sterile field and assisted Kitch to perform an incision in the nail to release the blood under the nail. I didn't dare tell him about the makeshift procedure I had performed at Camp Na-Gee-La using a needle heated up by a cigarette lighter, with a first-aid book at my side.

Another skill I learned from Kitch was removing ticks. These pesky little insects got entrenched on the skin and held on fast. Together we removed a bunch of them from a young boy's legs.

"You want to make the tick squirm but not squeeze it, 'cause you'll leave the pincers embedded in the skin. Gently coax the tick to let go." He explained the importance of getting it in its entirety so as to avoid the patient contracting Lyme disease or Rocky Mountain Spotted Fever, rare infections, to be sure, but possibilities all the same.

Splinters had to be extricated with even more delicacy. A Ph.D. thesis could be written on the topic of splinter extraction! What a world of difference there was in each child's reaction to those irritating, teeny tiny logs of wood embedded in their tender skin. Some kids ignored them while others picked at them quite savagely. Another group of kids, admittedly a *splinter* group, cried so much and became hysterical at even the prospect of removing them that Kitch would apply a topical anaesthetic cream, scrub in, and perform mini-surgery while I comforted the sobbing children. Personally, I found removing splinters a very satisfying experience. I was deft with the needle and I loved seeing the pride children felt after overcoming their fear. When a child asked, "Will it hurt?" I told the truth: "Yes, it will, but I know you can handle the pain," or "Yes, but I'll help you get through it."

Headaches were very common. Kitch believed they were often stress-related and usually ran in the family. "You do a little digging and it turns out the parents have headaches too and everyone in the family is stressed out. They've all been to specialists and have had specialized scans and tests, but there are no findings. The parents are disappointed in the lack of diagnosis, but not every feeling of being unwell can be diagnosed, especially in children," he said. "Sometimes children experience a collection of vague, transient symptoms for which no particular illness can be identified. Often, they resolve with time, through no intervention whatsoever."

Stomach aches were another common problem. Often it was the same child, over and over again, complaining of them.

"Most stomach aches turn out to be nothing," Kitch said, "but you always have to be vigilant for the signs of something serious like appendicitis. Ask the kid to jump. If the kid can't jump, you know for sure the pain is severe. Another thing to remember is that the farther the pain from the belly button, the more likely it's something serious like a bowel obstruction. Always keep in mind that pain that wakes a kid up during the night almost always has a cause."

He summed it all up with an insight that captured so much about medicine and nursing, too: "You have to know what you are looking for. You only see what you know to look for." That struck me as true about many things in life.

One day, Kitch called me out on my cover-up job. He noticed that I often waved off kids who stopped by for Band-Aids for minor scrapes or cuts. I usually sent them packing without their trophy.

"Studies have come out recently proving that covering a wound helps promote healing and prevents scarring," he said.

Oh, well, evidence-based practice must prevail! I had a new respect for Band-Aids after that.

Kitch also cited scientific evidence that helped me understand another medical issue I'd been wondering about. I had asked him about the excessive number of EpiPens that had accompanied so many children to camp. "There has been an alarming increase in peanut allergies among North American children over the past few years, but I agree with you that there's probably a percentage of EpiPens that are sent purely out of parental anxiety and doctors' fear of liability. Normally, it wouldn't be a problem, but overreaction is causing a lot of anxiety in children who worry unnecessarily about dying from anaphylactic shock. Problem is, if the parents don't know for sure, they err on the side of caution and send up the drug." He shrugged his shoulders. "Who can blame them?"

Kitch was always ready to share with me his vast knowledge and grasp of the most up-to-date scientific findings, tempered by his years of hands-on, real-life work with children. He was particularly skilled when it came to treating their bones, limbs, and joints.

"I'm quite certain the locals aren't running off for x-rays as frequently as our city kids," Kitch said with a chuckle. "Our kids simply aren't used to walking outdoors. They walk in shopping malls and on paved sidewalks. They're not nimble-footed around rocks and their eyes aren't attuned to twigs or roots sticking up out of the ground."

Again, it's about seeing what you know, I thought.

"Either they don't have as many injuries as we do, or they do but suck it up and allow nature, rest, and time to heal their injuries, as they usually do, anyway. Personally, I prefer to avoid unnecessary x-rays; I'd rather take a 'wait and see' approach. But at this camp, I'll send a stubbed toe for an x-ray, otherwise parents have been known to come up here and take the kid to the hospital themselves. At times, I practise defensive medicine. I may order things that aren't necessary because I know the parents will demand it."

I wondered what the local hospital staff thought about our sending campers for x-rays for every fall, twist, or turn of a joint or limb. I found out later when I'd gone to that small (only thirty beds) but busy hospital and heard one of the nurses grumbling. "You're giving us lots of work," she said, and muttered under her breath, "Bunch of clumsy oafs and hypochondriacs at that fancy camp."

Limb injuries could be complicated. Kitch brought me in on interesting cases.

"Watch this," he said when a boy came in after an injury on the soccer field. His arm hung at his side at an odd angle. Before the child even knew what was happening, Kitch deftly popped the dislocated shoulder back into place. The boy looked shocked, then pleased to have his arm back where it belonged.

"Show us your wrist," he told a ten-year-old boy who was brought in after an accident on the baseball field.

The child winced as he placed his right hand on the table. I examined his hand gently but thoroughly, poking and prodding it and putting it through its complete range of motions. The boy held himself rigidly, his face twisted in pain. I looked carefully at his hand and arm, palpated them all over, but could find nothing abnormal.

Kitch whispered a clue. "Always examine both sides."

The boy had kept his left wrist on his lap, hidden under the table. When I took it out to examine it, he yelped in pain. He had been too scared to show me the arm that was causing him pain. However, with one look anyone could see it was fractured. It was folded back on itself with the bone poking up through the skin.

Kitch asked the boy to tell us exactly what happened. He had told me how important it was to always get a detailed account of the "mechanism of injury"—meaning, what happened. That account would always provide clues to the diagnosis. The boy said he'd landed on the palm of his hand when he fell, running for a catch in the outfield.

"Just as I thought," said Kitch. "It's a FOOSH—a Fall On Out-Stretched Hand." He pointed out the bend in the wrist. "That's a 'silver fork deformity.'" He reminded me to check the radial pulse and showed me how to make a splint that effectively immobilized the limb, snug enough to provide support, but with enough give to allow the inevitable inflammation that would soon follow and not to restrict circulation. Together we tied a sling that would comfortably bear the weight of his arm.

"But did you make the catch?" Kitch asked the boy.

"Yup," he said proudly.

"Way to go," Kitch said and high-fived him on his uninjured hand.

What a wake-up call for me! I'm quite sure I would have *eventually* discovered the obvious problem, but the incident showed me how easily one's thinking can be restricted to what the patient chooses to present. It was a reminder to stay open-minded, not limit my thinking, and be a detective, especially when examining children.

Kitch taught me how to "buddy-tape" sprained fingers together, how to make finger splints out of tongue depressors, and the differences between a sprain, a partially torn ligament, from a strain, which was a stretched ligament. "In both cases, it's the same treatment: RICE—Rest, Ice, Compression, and Elevation. After that, let pain be your guide. Pain will tell you what the child can and cannot do. The only thing is, at camp, it may be difficult to distinguish between pain and homesickness. Sometimes homesickness expresses itself as pain. We've seen them limp, moan, and groan their way in here, and after a little attention, they hop, skip, and jump out of here. For homesickness, the best thing is to keep them busy. Run them ragged all day so that they'll fall right to sleep at night."

Unfortunately, that plan wasn't working for Alexa Rose, who was busy and happy by day and homesick and unhappy by night. I was beginning to think that homesickness was a catch-all term for the process of learning to comfort oneself. At camp, far from home and parents, kids are challenged to soothe themselves. So many kids seem to have little ability to withstand discomfort, to push through the pain, or to be encouraged by the old, but oh-so-wise truism: *This, too shall pass.* They thought there was a pill for everything, even transient sadness or temporary disappointment. And it would be easy to believe that was true, what with the availability of so many over-the-counter products. I was amazed how easily so many children could describe their symptoms and request specific products. They were fluent in the language of analgesics, antihistamines, decongestants, and anti-inflammatories. They scrutinized product labels and conversed knowledgeably about ingredients. Many knew the name of the drug they wanted, requested the tablet, capsule, or syrup formulation, and could even state the dosage they took. They expected a remedy that offered quick relief. And they didn't want the pain merely blunted or diminished; they wanted it gone. Nothing less would do. They looked at me reproachfully when I couldn't make their problem go away.

"I know," Kitch said with a sigh, agreeing with me. "My patients are always disappointed if they leave my office without a prescription."

I told him about a day in town when I'd dropped by the drugstore to pick up an order Wendy had put through. The pharmacist handed me a bag of antibiotics and painkillers. "There must be some gravely ill children at your camp," he had said.

"Actually, they're pretty healthy," I said. "They just don't realize it."

I kept my eye on Wayne, the reluctant swimmer who always kept his red bracelet prominently displayed. Often he sat on the dock, watching the others swim or paddle canoes or kayaks. I never once saw him get wet. The swim staff eventually gave up and ignored him. In addition to a fear of swimming, Wayne worried about germs and infection from toilet seats. He liked to use the bathroom in the MC, but only after wiping it down first. Kitch called him an FLK—a funny-looking kid—but I knew Kitch well enough by then to know he meant it as a term of endearment.

Wayne showed up one day looking worried. "I think I have beaver fever."

I tried to keep a straight face. "Lie down, young man, and I'll examine you."

"It's an infection from beaver pee in the lake." He felt his forehead. "I may die."

"Is it by any chance swimming period?" I asked, noticing his counsellor at the door, Wayne's swim trunks, goggles, and towel in hand.

"How did you know?"

On another occasion, Wayne took me aside to tell me he was itchy.

"Where?" I asked quietly.

"Back there. You know, in the *anal* area." He squirmed around as he spoke.

I nodded and asked him a few more questions, but he refused to be examined, so Kitch had to make a guess. "We could give him Vermox in case he has pinworms. It's harmless," Kitch reasoned.

This was another drug I was unfamiliar with. "Does it have any side effects?"

"Only one," he said, his eyes twinkling. "It may cause camp-wide hysteria."

Wayne came back on another day to show me a scratch on his leg. "Does this cut look infected?" He was wearing swim trunks and a towel around his neck.

"Are you supposed to be at swim class?"

"Yeah, but this cut is bad."

"Wayne, how's it going? Other than swimming, are you happy at camp?"

"Sort of. Sort of happy. Well, happy-ish."

I sat there, waiting.

"My parents sacrifice a lot for me to come to camp. Please don't call them."

"I wasn't planning to."

"Great. Can I use your bathroom?"

After learning so much from Kitch and as I got to know the children better, I grew confident in treating them. I knew who needed a hug or a chat and who simply wanted to receive a comforting dose of some common over-the-counter product they were familiar with from home.

But Caitlin had a better connection than I did with many campers, especially the teenagers, who gravitated to her. They saw her as a friend, whereas I was more like a mother. With her banana-split-flavoured lip gloss, adorable figure, stylish clothes, and natural way of conversing in their language (casually using "phat" when it didn't mean overweight and "way cool" as a complete sentence). They identified with her. I was coming to realize that I no longer spoke the language of the people around me. They understood *my* dialect, but it was an effort for me to grasp *theirs*.

For the most part, anyone could treat the minor, everyday things the kids came to see us about. By and large, the problems they arrived with on our doorstep were all the things parents treat their own kids for on a daily basis. And when they proffered their sore finger or cut knee, what they really wanted, more than anything, was attention. Once, when a girl came to me for something I considered trivial, I asked in annoyance, "If you were home, would you go to the doctor for this?"

"No, but I would go to my mother," she answered, pouting.

Touché. Okay, I got it. At camp I was everyone's mom—except for my own kids, from whom I was expected to keep my distance. When it came to Max and Harry, I could look, but not touch. I threatened to start them on a four-times-a-day regimen of pills, just so they'd have to come for pill call and I'd get a chance to connect with them!

Happy campers came and went, but one camper who proved to have a persistent case of unhappiness was Alexa Rose. I kept an eye out for her around camp, and she seemed always to be with friends and enjoying her popularity. The other girls clearly admired her outfits, such as a pink Juicy Couture sweatshirt with camouflage cargo shorts, and designer sunglasses. But she continued to come to us every evening right before bed, asking for a few drops of Rescue Remedy. When I tried one night to get to the bottom of what was bothering her, the tears welled up instantly.

"I am soooo unhappy," she said. "This is so not a fun camp. It's more like boot camp."

"But you seem to be having fun," I countered, "at least during the day."

"There are so many rules and I miss my parents. Camp is supposed to be a vacation from your parents, but I like my parents, my mom, especially."

"What would your mom do if she were here?"

"She'd let me do whatever I want. She never makes me do anything I don't want to do."

"Anything else?"

"She'd make me feel better. She'd hug me." Her counsellor was at her side, trying to do that very thing, but Alexa Rose pushed her away. "It's not the same."

"No, it's not," I admitted, "but your counsellor can help you while you're here."

She shook her head. "No, nothing will help me."

Her counsellor, who'd been giving her lots of extra attention, was getting frustrated. "I don't know what to do. I've tried everything," she told me when we went aside to talk.

"You're doing a great job," I said. "It's not easy."

"I didn't know it would be so hard to be a counsellor," she whispered to me. "I can't wait for my day off."

We returned to Alexa Rose, who articulated her complaints only too well.

"I hate how they make us do activities all day. Why can't we relax? It's supposed to be our vacation."

"Did you want to come to camp?"

"I thought so, but not any more. Every minute here feels like an hour. I want it to go by like that!" She snapped her fingers to show just how fast. "At first, I thought the tuck shop would be good, but it's a joke. It's a hut with a few candy bars and potato chips—what is that? Like, hello! There's nothing to buy. At my other camp, there was a vending machine. And there's only three sinks for twelve girls and four counsellors. Don't you agree something's wrong with that? If I don't get there first, do you know how long it takes? Oh, how am I going to get through the next twenty-two days? I want to be in my own bed, in my clean house."

I gave up. Talking to me only gave her more opportunity to dwell on her problems.

One day I received a message from her mother.

"How's my baby doing?" she gushed into the answering machine. "I'm so worried! Alexa Rose is very sensitive and it's been so hard for me, too, because, well, we're best friends. She and I, we're practically attached at the hip, and I miss her so much, but I do think it's good for her to stay at camp. Of course, both my kids are *numero uno* in my life, but Alexa Rose is... she's special. I just want her to feel good about herself, but her letters are breaking my heart."

"Did you speak to my mom?" Alexa Rose asked the next time I saw her. "Did she say I can come home?"

"She said she wants you to stay and that...you're...*special*."

"My mom always says I'm special, but at camp, I don't feel special. Here, I feel just like everyone else." She looked dejected but ran off to join her friends.

Just like at Camp Na-Gee-La, it was not only campers who needed attention. The counsellors also got colds, sore throats, and headaches, and could be just as miserable and needy. Sometimes, the counsellors needed counselling, like the girl who returned from a day off sporting a new tattoo, a black and white Chinese yin and yang symbol, on her backside. It was inflamed and swollen, and she had a low-grade fever.

"Does it hurt?" I asked, touching it gently. "It looks sore."

"No, I don't feel a thing," she said with an odd giggle.

"Is your hepatitis vaccine up to date?" Kitch asked her.

"I don't know. Can you call my mother and find out?"

"Did you get this tattoo in a reputable place? Was it clean?" Kitch inquired, ever so sharply.

"I think so . . . The guy seemed to know what he was doing. My friend got hers there." She hiccuped loudly.

"Do your parents know about it?" Kitch asked.

"I *am* seventeen," she said, "but yeah, they know and they're cool with it, anyway. Hey, your questions are majorly freaking me out."

Kitch and I went into his office to talk privately. He told me that a tattoo in that place was called a tramp stamp, and that it was a dangerous practice. "If these girls ever require an epidural anaesthetic, during childbirth, for example, the ink can track right up the spinal column and cause serious complications. But they won't listen to reason about these things and besides, legally, they don't require parental consent. I just know that if she were my daughter, I wouldn't be too pleased."

The counsellor agreed to let me take a blood sample to send off to test for HIV and a hepatitis screen. Afterward, as I applied antibiotic ointment to the reddened area, I asked her why she got a tattoo back there where she can't see it.

"I can't, but my boyfriend can." She grinned. "He thinks it's a real turn-on."

As she got off the examining table, she stumbled, and as I reached over to steady her, I caught a whiff of alcohol on her breath. She looked at me sheepishly. She was drunk and she knew I knew it. I had to tell Coach Carson and he fired her later that day. She packed up and stormed out of camp, upset only about losing the six-hundred-dollar bonus Coach Carson gave every counsellor who completed the summer.

I would rarely treat a counsellor before a camper, but I made an exception one evening for a young woman in genuine distress. It was just after pill call and suddenly the waiting room inexplicably filled up with campers, all with minor complaints. In the midst of that, the female counsellor arrived, clearly upset and fighting back tears. I went to her right away; however, it wasn't me she wanted.

"Is Caitlin here?" She looked around.

"No, it's her day off. She'll be back tomorrow."

Face it, Caitlin is younger, prettier. Who wants the wise and witty nurse when they can get the cool and phat one?

"That sucks...but I can't wait."

"What's the problem?" I was all business, pen poised over the clipboard.

"Can I talk to you? Privately?"

"Of course." I invited her into the examining room and closed the door.

She faced me down. "You *have* to keep this one-hundred-percent under your hat. Not a word! If Coach Carson finds out, I'll be fired. You know the rule, no sex at camp."

"Yes," I nodded, "it'll stay confidential unless it involves health or safety."

She didn't look too pleased with that proviso but continued. "My boyfriend..." She twisted her hands in her lap. "He pulled out...too late. We were in the middle of it, you know...and he'd told me he was an expert in withdrawal. He said he knew what he was doing...so then I stood up right away, but..."

Together, we figured out where she was in her cycle and I convinced her to talk to Kitch, which she did, but only after swearing him to secrecy, too. He promised to obtain the morning-after pill for her, but only on condition that she and her boyfriend would come in for counselling on birth control and safe sex. "This is a one-time rescue," he warned her. "You have to make a contraceptive choice."

"No worries," she said. "We've broken up. I dumped him."

Most afternoons, Kitch took a break. "Don't hesitate to call," he always said. I didn't want to interrupt his rest, but that wasn't the only reason I didn't like to call. I had worked with doctors in hospitals for many years and was all too familiar with the nurse-doctor game. For a nurse, there's always a certain pride in figuring things out by yourself and using your own judgment. However, doctors varied hugely in the way they regarded the nurse's role. Some freely collaborated with nurses and relied upon their judgment and initiative, especially at night or during their off-hours when a capable nurse could keep them from being disturbed. Others wanted complete control and expected to be woken up for every little thing. But in many cases a nurse's hands are tied: we know what the patient needs—sometimes it may be something very basic, like a laxative—but we can't give it without a doctor's order. If I were to call the doctor in such a situation, the doctor might get annoyed with what he saw as my lack of initiative or judgment. Nurses have to be able to accurately read the doctors they are dealing with and know the degree of mutual trust and respect. They have to be confident, have excellent assessment skills, and know their own abilities and limitations. All of these are factors that go into a decision to call the doctor.

One afternoon, there was a true emergency—though it didn't appear to be one at first—for which I had to take independent, immediate action *and* call the doctor. In order to give the best care to this serious situation, we had to work together. An effective response required teamwork between Kitch and me, and luckily, by then, I had won his respect enough that we could collaborate as equals, with our separate, but interdependent roles.

It all started very quietly. I'd been sitting in the MC enjoying the air-conditioning when Jared, the water ski instructor, showed up at the door. He stood there, dazed and disoriented. He told me only a few details about what had happened.

"I was doing tricks...skiing for...to show the kids," Jared had said slowly, haltingly. "A back flip...and a tantrum, I think that's what...and went down. I wiped out and hit the water hard."

I knew immediately that this was a serious situation. I called for Kitch and then got straight to work.

"What hit the water, Jared?"

"My head." He rubbed his neck. "My back, too."

As I ran to get the spinal board from the examining room, I heard him mumble that his arms were tingling. He lifted his chin slowly. "My neck is sore."

I laid the board down on the floor and strapped him in, careful to stabilize his head and neck with the collar. Then Kitch was there and I told him what had happened and what I'd done so far. We were both thinking the same thing: spinal cord injury and possibly head injury, too.

Kitch examined Jared while I called for an ambulance. Kitch said Jared would need an emergency neurosurgical consult and a CT scan of his head and spine to rule out spinal cord compression, bruising, or even a rupture. Kitch was worried, but angry, too. "Jared, you should have known better! We've gone over emergency procedures with a waterfront injury. Would you have let a kid get up and walk after an accident like this? Don't you realize how serious this could be?"

Jared closed his eyes, wearily. He had no explanation for why he hadn't taken the proper action. Maybe he'd been stunned by the blow to his head. However, even if he'd had his wits about him, when it comes to treating ourselves, most of us lack the clinical objectivity needed to make rational decisions.

I took his vital signs frequently, including neurological checks that involved assessing the reaction of his pupils to light and the strength of his hand grips. I knew that he was at risk for "spine shock," a rapid worsening of his situation that could be fatal. It would start with a sudden drop in heart rate and other vital sign disturbances. It can lead to cardiac arrest. I stayed near and observed him closely. He remained in stable condition. Soon, the ambulance arrived and Jared was taken to the local hospital and then air-lifted from there by helicopter to a Toronto trauma centre, a hospital that specialized in treating accident victims with head and spinal cord injuries.

Later, Kitch called for the report. Jared had suffered a significant spinal cord injury. He didn't return to camp that summer, but I did hear through the grapevine that he made a full recovery, both to health and to waterskiing.

As I assessed the patient and worked to stabilize him, Kitch had backed me up by taking in the bigger picture and making the decision and arrangements to transfer him out of camp to a medical centre for treatment. It all went so well—and had a positive outcome for the patient—because we worked as partners.

Most afternoons were quiet and uneventful and I went either to my hip-hop class, down to the lake for a swim, or succumbed to the lure of a blissful nap on my bed with the wind whistling through the pine trees outside my window.

Caitlin and I took turns being on call and carrying the walkie-talkie. It crackled noisily throughout the day, and occasionally at night, with general camp chatter, most of which I ignored. But one afternoon I heard, "Is there a nurse on the walkie-talkie?" I reached for it on my hip and pressed the talk button.

"It's Tilda. I'm here."

"There's a problem at the waterfront. Can you come, like, now?"

I grabbed the spinal board, though there was one there too, plus a first-aid kit. I'd need a lot more than what was in this box if it was a true emergency. The potential for danger at the water-front was immense. When I got there, a crowd had gathered around a tall girl stretched out on the dock. It was Samantha, the girl I'd seen sitting under a tree during the swim test. She was shivering in wet clothes, trying to sit up, with two counsellors on either side helping her.

Her swim instructor and I stepped aside to talk. "It's been a week and she wasn't going in," she said. "Everyday, it was a dif-ferent excuse. She had her period, a cold, a stomach ache, a head-ache. She couldn't find her bathing suit. I don't know what her problem is, because she's an excellent swimmer. So, I gave her a little nudge, to get her in, and she panicked. It looked like she was going down, so I jumped in and pulled her out. She used her puffer because she says it's an asthma attack."

I kneeled down to examine Samantha. Her breathing was rapid. I pulled out my stethoscope and listened to her chest. It was clear of wheezes but her heart rate was only forty-five beats a minute. She was too weak to walk, so we carried her to the Medical Centre. I put her in bed and covered her with blankets. On her health form, Samantha's mother had described her as a picky eater who had been recently hospitalized for "extreme weight loss." No baseline weight was recorded, but it didn't seem appropriate to weigh her now in this fragile state. In a weak voice, she told me she didn't like camp food—"too many carbs." When I rolled up her sleeve to take her blood pressure, I saw that her arms were thin sticks, covered in goose bumps. I helped her into the dry clothes her counsellor had brought for her. Samantha sat listlessly as I lifted her top. I gasped in shock at what I saw. Running across her abdomen and upper arms was a crisscross of horizontal slashes. Some were fresh, others older. It looked like she had been violently attacked. It took me a few long moments to register the fact that Samantha had deliberately done this to herself. "Why?" I had to ask.

"I have to. It makes me feel better." Her voice was barely audible and her teeth were chattering. "It expresses how I feel inside." She looked away a moment, then directed a saddened gaze back at me. "Please don't tell anyone," she begged, and when I couldn't promise her that, she looked so disappointed. "Well, then, I guess I can't trust you. It doesn't matter; I can't trust anybody."

"Do your parents know about this?"

"There's only my mom and I can't tell her because she makes me feel worse. Grandma and Grandpa don't need to know. Mom doesn't want them upset because, you know, they're not getting any younger."

Samantha didn't want Kitch to examine her. "He's nice, but it's embarrassing."

"I understand," I said, but I didn't really understand a thing except that Samantha was not well enough to be at camp. "Do you want to be at camp?"

"If I go home my mother will make me go back to the hospital. It's better if I stay here."

I spoke with Kitch. He explained that some troubled young people use this self-abusive behaviour to substitute one pain for another and to make their distress visible. He felt that camp was a haven for Samantha, a better place for her than in her unhappy home life with an abusive father, who was now out of the picture, and a self-absorbed mother, who was in total denial about her daughter's distress. "I know the mother," Kitch said. "She travels a lot and won't be agreeable to taking her home."

That was it. Samantha was staying at camp, but I didn't believe it was the right decision.

Camp Carson had an on-site professional photographer and a videographer. They strolled around camp with digital cameras and video cameras, taking still shots and video clips of campers involved in activities. At the end of each day, they uploaded the images onto the camp website for parents to view at home. I started receiving calls from parents once they'd had a peek into their kids' world.

My son looks sad. Can you find out if he is homesick? Please get back to me.

Who do you have to pay off to get your kid's photo on the website? It's been three days now and there've been no pics of my kid.

In every shot my daughter is wearing the same yellow shirt. Were these all taken on the same day or is she not changing her clothes?

In the July 10th photograph, I don't recognize the girl my daughter is with. Could you please find out who she is?

And the photos were not the only things drawing responses from the parents. I knew the letters from the campers had arrived at home when the phone started ringing off the hook and my answering machine filled up. One mother called to complain that her child wrote only one line in her letter home: "Camp sucks." "Can you find out what's going on and get back to me?"

Another mother had a worse problem. "My son hasn't sent me a letter, not even one!"

"That's a good sign," I tried to soothe her, "they *always* write when they're unhappy."

In a recorded message, an irate father informed us that his daughter must have snuck her cell phone into camp (she'd handed over one before boarding the bus but kept a spare one hidden) and racked up a bill of over three hundred dollars of text messages to her boyfriend in the city. "Take her phone away," was the terse message.

"The parents don't seem to realize how well their kids are doing," I said to Coach Carson. *Well, most of them,* I thought.

"They'll soon get a chance to see for themselves. Visitor's Day is only two weeks away," he said, but he didn't look too happy about it.

7

HEY, NURSE!

The photographers roved around, snapping shots of happy children playing on the beach, sailing on the lake, making clay pots, and—the best photo op of all—sitting around the campfire. Needless to say, no pictures of Wayne's fearful swim test, Alexa Rose's tearful misery, Wesley's oozing impetigo sores, nor Samantha's self-mutilation made an appearance on the website photo gallery. The unhappy few were not represented. The vast majority of the campers were having a fabulous time. Everywhere I looked I saw smiling faces. Everywhere I went I heard the sounds of joyful laughter, the light-hearted banter of voices, and enthusiastic singing—even a group of kids bellowing "Stairway to Heaven" as if it were a sporting cheer. (This song was going to be ruined for me if I kept coming to camp!) When they were physically active or creating something with paint, clay, or string, the kids were content.

But if you spent each day as I did, attending to the handful of children with minor complaints, who were therefore temporarily miserable, or the even fewer individuals who were desperately unhappy (possibly at home, too?), you might forget that most kids loved camp. As a nurse, my radar zoomed in on the unhappy ones, such as Alexa Rose who now cried throughout the day (no longer just at night) and begged to go home. Wayne didn't say as much, but his sad face told the same story. Max said the other kids picked on Wayne and that he cried himself to sleep at night. There was also Hailey, a fourteen-year-old whom I hadn't yet spoken to but had certainly noticed around camp in her black clothes and dark, heavy makeup, a look that was in stark contrast to the other girls' bright, candy colours. Her counsellors told me she hated camp and was threatening to run away.

But unhappy didn't always mean homesick. Samantha, for example, had problems that went way beyond homesickness. Kitch, Coach Carson, and Wendy agreed she wasn't well but weren't as concerned as I was.

"We've been through this nonsense with Samantha before," Wendy said. "It's pure attention-getting behaviour. Princess Diana was a cutter, too. She used a lemon peeler."

She was so matter-of-fact that I couldn't tell if she was joking or not. How could they be so casual about it? The only thing that put my mind at ease somewhat was that Samantha had a tight bond with her counsellor, who promised me she'd keep a close watch on her. That was reassuring, but I saw that Samantha was too weak to participate in most activities. She stayed on the sidelines and hardly spoke. When she did, it was in a whisper and with downcast eyes. I tried to connect with her but she offered barely audible responses to my attempts at conversation.

Meanwhile, the daily routine continued. Pill Patrol still delayed the morning clinic and put us behind in paperwork, charting, and answering the growing number of phone and email messages from parents. Coach Carson tried to help out by driving me around in his golf cart in hot pursuit of kids who missed their breakfast meds. He was like the merry host of a big summer party out on a "meet and greet." He loved this opportunity to ensure everyone was having fun, and loving camp. He knew most of his "guests" by name, including their nicknames. He knew who had portaged or soloed a canoe in Algonquin Park and who had gotten up on water skis for the first time. He knew all about the CIT boys' recent late-night raid on the CIT girls' cabin.

"Don't be pulling any pranks tonight," he warned them in mock sternness as we passed by. "Tonight I'm on patrol duty and I'm not going to let you off easy. I'll make you do a hundred push-ups if I catch you out of your cabins after lights-out."

As we drove along on the bumpy ride in the golf cart, he shouted out greetings to children he saw along the way, especially, it seemed to me, the ones he deemed exceptional campers, such as the athletic, popular, talented ones, or simply the happy-go-lucky, non-complaining, content ones.

"How's it going, Blake?" he called out to one boy as we drove past and waved.

"Camp's a blast, Coach Carson!" Blake grinned and waved back.

"I love that kid! He's so *easy*." Coach Carson shook his head in admiration of a successful camper like Blake who confirmed all he believed about camp's ability to bring out the best in children.

I admired the happy campers, too. By then, I had a pretty good idea of my own what made a happy camper. Happy campers felt they belonged; they didn't question their membership in the group. They never held themselves back or apart and moved with the pack. They loved to be silly and revelled in (and often contributed to) the cacophonous noise. These extroverts adored (and wholly participated in) the relentless activity from morning to night, and didn't mind one bit the lack of personal space, privacy, or downtime. The happy campers never yearned to be elsewhere or to be doing anything other than exactly what they were doing. They knew how to find their place and fit in.

As part of my ongoing field study of the happy camper, I asked a group of boys from Harry's cabin what they liked about camp.

"I don't like camp," said one boy with an uncharacteristically grave expression. He was the joker who had kidded me about my "wenis." Then his face broke into an enormous grin. "I love, love, *love* camp! I *live* for camp!"

"Camp has made me who I am," a boy, all of ten years old, solemnly told me.

"Camp's, like, the only place where I can be myself," another boy said. "Oh, sure, there are rules and stuff, but it's nothing like at my parents' *gulag.*"

Around about the middle of the second week of camp, as I was jostling alongside Coach Carson in the golf cart on Pill Patrol, I decided to ask him about *unhappy* campers, such as Alexa and Wayne. "Aren't there some kids who aren't cut out to be campers?"

"I consider it a personal triumph to win over a camper," he said with missionary zeal. He waved to someone and gave him a thumbs-up about something.

"Do you think every child can become a happy camper?"

"Every child can be turned around."

"I'm beginning to think there are a few kids here who shouldn't be here," I persisted.

"Nonsense! What's not to love about camp?" He seemed uncomprehending. Either he wasn't seeing what I saw or just didn't want to acknowledge the downside of camp.

"But what's the benefit of making a miserable kid stay? Who wins?"

"It teaches a child the value of never quitting, of never giving up." He stopped to high-five a camper—"Hey there, D-Bomb!"—then turned back to me. "Think of the words of Winston Churchill: 'Never, *never*, NEVER give up.' Every child can succeed at camp."

"There are a few *really* unhappy kids here and I still can't see the purpose—"

"Well, their parents see a purpose," he snapped, beginning to get irritated. "A child who goes home will always regret it and look upon it as a failure. If children leave, it is *very bad* for their self-esteem."

Coach Carson had a vested interest in keeping every kid at camp. As for the parents, there was no question that the vast majority wanted their kids to stay: that was the plan, and it was what they'd paid for. Summer vacation was long, and many, if not most, parents worked and needed to keep their children safely occupied. Parents also needed time to themselves in the summer, to recharge their batteries.

After a few quiet minutes' riding together, Coach Carson reprised his beliefs about the virtues of camp, where new skills are learned, lifelong friendships made, and beautiful memories created. "Camp lays down the foundation for success in life. Camp parents understand this because many were once Carson campers themselves." He paused for a breath. "Winston Churchill also said..."

Here we go again.

"...'Success is not final, failure is not fatal; it is the courage to continue that counts.'"

He told me about his plans for improvement, such as a Camp Carson radio station and the purchase of more motorboats for the water-skiing area. His son Eric, who'd now completed university and was too old to be a counsellor any more, would be leading some of these new projects. "We've supported this theatre hobby of his for years, but starting next summer, he's going to transition into Camp Director. It's always been his dream to run the camp."

When Coach Carson had other business to attend to, and Eric wasn't too busy with play rehearsals (he was directing the camp production of the Broadway musical *Wicked*), Eric would give me a ride on his ATV to do Pill Patrol. The kids all called him "Shakespeare" because of his love of theatre. As we flew around camp, me giving out pills from the basket looped over my arm, Eric would fill me in on the social scene. Because of his widespread popularity Eric connected me to counsellors and kids who weren't the MC regulars. With Eric by my side, I didn't trigger the "incoming mom, grown-up approaching" alarms that usually sounded whenever I showed up. Eric was very good-looking, with dreamy, expressive eyes. He often dropped by the MC to ask if we needed anything or sometimes just to visit. Caitlin had developed a crush on him. I agreed with her that he was very attractive, but to me, what was most appealing about Eric was his kindness.

From Eric, I got the inside scoop on camp gossip. He gave me the skinny about all the crushes, hook-ups, break-ups, and make-ups going on around camp. He pointed out the "Sex Tree" I'd heard a lot about. It was the destination spot for heavy-duty making out. He told me who'd gotten into the university of their choice and who'd been turned down by medical school. In my role as camp nurse, it wasn't at all necessary to know any of this, but hey, I'm nosy.

One day, Eric introduced me to his buddy, Wallace, whose nickname was Einstein. He was a counsellor and also the camp tutor. Einstein wore a T-shirt with "I love π" on it and the number 3.14159265358 ... that wrapped around his chest. "Hey, did you know Tilde is a scientific symbol?" he said when he heard my name. "It means a similar or approximate value."

"Wallace is a major brainiac," Eric said with admiration.

When I had to track down kids in their cabins, Eric waited patiently outside for me. The boys' cabins were messy and smelly, with dirty clothes strewn about, bottles of insect repellant and sun screen scattered on the floor, and heaps of discarded sports equipment and damp towels. One boy, whose clothes had been sent to camp organized into separate outfits, each in a clearly labelled bag, had dumped them all out onto the floor in a tangled pile. The girls' cabins were more orderly than the boys' but crammed with considerably more stuff. Beside each girl's bed was a brightly coloured canvas director's chair—turquoise, purple, lime green—with her name spelled out in glitter on the back. Since I didn't have daughters, I found it thrilling to examine their paraphernalia—personalized stationery sets, pre-addressed and stamped; piles of teen fashion mags; tubes and bottles of makeup and hair products (was bubblegum shampoo with cotton-candy conditioner for eating or working into the scalp?); fluffy cushions (some in zebra or leopard patterns) and a rainbow of quilts and coverlets; stuffed animals; folding plastic fans in pink or orange; plush slippers; and hair dryers and curling irons. In addition to their designer clothes, assorted sports equipment, and iPods and MP3 players, there was an array of decorative trinkets, motorized mini gizmos, and novelties, such as pens with feather tops and glow-in-the-dark shoelaces.

I would never go into anyone's private things, or read a diary or a letter, but I had no compunction about reading a note left out in the open, such as the following "questionnaire" fluttering around outside a Wildflower Girls cabin.

Do you like me?

Yes   ☐
No   ☐
Not sure   ☐

Love, Me

One day I visited Alexa Rose's cabin to find out why it was so hot. "There's no AC! It's boiling in there! I can't sleep," she'd been telling me. The windows were all closed, so I opened them up, and while I was there, I picked up a few pairs of Lululemon yoga pants from the floor and put Alexa Rose's designer sunglasses that she'd left on the bed back into their case on her shelf. She was always losing her flashlight or her sunglasses, and had already lost one of her flip-flops. When I'd found Wayne's plastic water bottle and raincoat left on the porch of the dining hall in the rain, it made me wonder if perhaps it was the kids who could take care of themselves and their stuff who enjoyed camp more.

A few times, I had occasion to go into my own kids' cabins and got to peek at their stuff. I don't know many mothers who could resist that glimpse into their child's private world. As I predicted, Harry's belongings were orderly. More surprising was to see Max's clothes neatly folded on the shelf, his bed nicely made. This wasn't my kid, nor the kid his teachers knew, the one who was "all over the map." How did he suddenly manage to organize himself here at camp?

Both kids were having a great time discovering new interests. Harry was getting into breakdancing and playing the guitar, adding to his hockey and snake interests. Max was enthusiastic about everything. The way they both dived in and tried everything inspired me to try new activities myself. I took a sailing lesson and learned about the mast, mainsail, and swinging boom (discovering that the hard way). At the ropes course and climbing wall, I watched how one cabin worked together as a team to get each person across. For a moment I considered trying it out, but Harry happened to be there and looked worried.* "Please don't, Mom," he begged me. "Don't even think about it." I gave it a pass. In the Eco Zone, I made bubble bath and lip gloss from baking soda, glycerine, and rose petals and learned to identify

---

* He has worried about me ever since I attended a circus-themed birthday party for his friend Rachel when they were both six. That was when I decided to give the child-sized tightrope, four feet off the ground, a try. I executed the stunt gracefully, but upon my dismount I toppled over and broke my ankle.

poison ivy, poison oak, and sumac—"leaves of three, let it be."

"Look at you!" Eric said when he saw me taking a mountain bike from the shed. He gave me a big grin and a flash of those gorgeous eyes of his. "It's great to see you livin' in the moment. My dad'll be pleased with you. He swears he'll make a camper out of you yet."

On hot afternoons, I often went for a swim in the lake, sometimes quite far out. I always felt like I could swim forever without tiring.

At "A and C" I sat alongside the kids and made friendship bracelets out of plastic, colourful string called boondoggle or gimp. They taught me the flat stitch, zipper, and spiral. One day, I noticed a girl in dark clothes sitting by herself, away from her cabin mates, dabbling with paint and brushes. I suspected it might be Hailey, the gloomy girl I'd been hearing about. I asked her counsellor about her.

"Yup, that's Hailey. She's gone Goth. She doesn't fit in, doesn't even want to."

"Is that what she says?"

"She's, like, always saying how much she hates camp. She used to be really sweet, but this year, she's got an edge. She's managed to turn all the other girls against her."

Hailey heard us talking about her and got up and flounced away. I wanted to see what she'd painted. In dripping red was one word: *DIE*. I went outside to where she was sitting on the porch steps.

"Hailey, you look upset. What's going on? Do you want to talk?"

"Talk to you? Why should I talk to *you*? What have you done for me lately?" She said she had nothing to say to me, would never talk to me, and that I should go far away and stay away. I sat with her for a few moments, then told her I was around if she ever did want to talk.

But I wasn't going to give up that easy. Later, that night, I went to find her in her cabin. Her bunk mates were out. She was in the corner upper bunk, pretending to be asleep when I walked in. I knew she was faking it because it was still early and it would have been impossible to doze off with the commotion outside from that night's "Camp Survivor."

"Hailey." I rubbed her shoulder. "Please sit up. I want to talk to you."

She turned her back to me. I let her be for now. But the next day, right after lunch, I cornered her outside the dining hall and wouldn't let her get away.

"Hailey, can we talk?"

"About what?"

I wasn't sure myself, but she walked with me along the path away from the dining hall, then she dropped back, keeping a few steps behind me. I kept on going, hoping that by staying in motion, she'd open up to me. It never seems to fail.

"Is this a good time to talk?" I prodded gently.

"What about never? Is never soon enough for you?" She turned away from me. "I told you. I have nothing to say."

"It may help to talk. You seem really unhappy."

"Well, *d'oh*! You're just like my mother. She says I have a 'bad attitude,'" she said with air quotes. "'Change your 'tude, dude,'" she said in mock imitation. Her black-rimmed eyes were angry. "It'll probably improve *her* attitude to have me away all summer." She narrowed her eyes. "Hey, maybe you can help me. Tell me, what do I have to do to get sent home?"

"Are you homesick?"

"No, but I hate camp. My mother thinks she's doing me this huge favour by sending me here, but it's just to get me out of the picture so she can screw her asshole boyfriend all summer. They're always making out. It's *sooo* gross. I even saw them drunk one night."

"What would you do for the rest of the summer if you went home?"

"The only place I feel good is in my bedroom alone, with the door closed."

"If that's the case, it must be very hard for you at camp."

"I hate every minute here." Her voice was full of bitterness and her body was tense with rage. Even her clothes were angry. She wore a plaid grey-and-black miniskirt that was held together with a large safety pin, and a black T-shirt with a skull and crossbones on it. She had a purple streak in her hair that hadn't been there yesterday. "There's no point trying to convince me. I won't stay. Nothing you say will change that."

"So, you've made up your mind not to enjoy camp."

"That's right and I'm warning you, I'm relentless. I will not give up until they let me go home. I am so not staying at camp. Staying here is not an option." She glared at me. "I'll hurt myself if I have to."

I switched tactics. "What music are you into?"

She looked surprised at the change of topic but I knew how that question could open doors.

"Metallica. Alice in Chains. Indie bands like Burn Planetarium and The Harold Wartooth. But I can't listen to any of that music here."

"No, probably not."

"The music they play here is so *yesterday*. These people are all cheerleaders or jocks. Well, let's just say, Avril Lavigne is the extent of their angst."

How well I knew what it felt like to be on the outside. I had also been a morose, sullen kid at Hailey's age. Like her, I didn't fit in, felt angry at the world, and expressed my barely contained rage by putting myself in dangerous situations, being rude, and acting out toward authority figures. I too had been just as desperate to run away from my problems and reject everything and everyone. Perhaps Hailey sensed my empathy for her because she began to open up. Without any prompting, she told me about her biker boyfriend who was in his twenties and came from a really messed-up home and how she believed she could help him get off drugs. "Sending me to camp is my parents' twisted way of keeping me away from him," she said, "but it's not going to work. I'll run away if I have to."

"Will you promise me something, Hailey?"

"No way!" She folded her arms across her chest. The door slammed shut again.

"Please, I just want you to promise to keep talking to me, okay? Please."

That was it. We'd reached Hailey's cabin and parted ways for now.

I added Hailey to my list of kids I worried about. That list remained short compared to the number of happy campers. However, the ratio of happy to unhappy was reversed with the parents: more were displeased than satisfied. Or perhaps it just seemed that way because the dissatisfied parents were the ones I heard from the most. There were days when I spent more time on the phone with parents than I spent with their children at camp. In some cases, the child was perfectly content, but the parents were not. I remember one teenage girl who happily bounced in to phone her parents who had insisted on having her call them, and when she emerged from the private office after talking to them, her eyes were red and puffy from crying. "They said how much they missed me and now I'm worried about them," she said, wiping her face with her sleeves. "I wasn't homesick before, but I am now." It took her awhile to collect herself enough to run off and be with her cabin again.

Sometimes we called parents. It was camp policy to call parents when a child was started on a medication or stayed overnight in the MC, even if the child was already feeling better.

I was always able to reach a parent quickly, even if he or she was a busy surgeon or a lawyer. No matter what operation she was in the midst of, or what cross-examination he was involved in, I was put straight through. A call from camp took top priority! Of course, there were some parents who weren't satisfied with the nurse's report; they were reassured only after speaking to the doctor. After so many years working in the ICU, informing and counselling families about the highly technical and complex medical conditions of their loved ones, it was frustrating to hand over the phone to the doctor for him to repeat what I had just told mom and dad about their child's headache or sore throat, but that was what they expected.

Some parents called with very specific questions about their child's moods, behaviours, and interactions with others. Based on my observations of their son or daughter, they tweaked the child's medication regimens accordingly.

There were times when what seemed like a straightforward call would become more complicated. For example, once I called a mother about her child's ear infection.

"What about his leg?" she asked.

"I'm calling you about his ear. Tyler has an ear infection."

"But he had a sore on his leg when he left for camp. Has it healed? And now, he has an ear infection? How did that happen? Do you think it could be MRSA?* Did you check for that?"

"It's not something we normally check for, here at camp."

"I saw a TV special about an athlete who had MRSA in a wound and he died within twenty-four hours," she said. "I need to speak to the doctor."

Parents were hungry for any information, medical or otherwise, that I could provide about their kids. They were grateful for

---

* Methicillin-resistant staphylococcus aureus, a bacterium that is a difficult infection to treat. One of the new super bugs.

even the smallest detail, such as having seen their child eat a slice of pizza at lunch. I was sympathetic to their feeling of being cut off, because even right there at camp I felt frustrated, knowing so little about my own kids! But then I might be asked to do favours like arrange for a change in their child's bed position in the cabin or a switch to another cabin altogether. "Meaghan won't speak up for herself, so we have to do it for her," one parent explained. I was reluctant to follow through with these demands, because if there was one thing I had learned by then, it was that there were benefits in allowing kids to solve some of these problems by themselves.

Then there was Wayne, who I saw bravely, dutifully, going through all the motions required of him, and still looking miserable. His counsellor pulled me aside. "That kid reeks," he told me. "He stinks, and it's way worse in the cabin." I went to the cabin and followed my nose to Wayne's bed. Stuffed under his mattress were rolled-up soiled pairs of underwear.

"It's disgusting!" the counsellor said. "He's doing it to get sent home."

Now I understood the pinched noses and the nasty jokes I'd heard from time to time around camp:

"Hey, Wayne, have you read the bestseller *The Brown Spot on the Wall*? It's written by the Chinese author Hu Flung Poo!"

"Pee yuuuu...Hey Wayne! Haven't you heard of soap and water?" someone said.

A few kids were in the cabin and I heard them snickering as I talked to the counsellor. One kid muttered something about running the dirty underwear up the flagpole. That did it! I became incensed.

"This bullying will stop immediately!" I shouted at them. "There will be no more teasing. That goes for everyone." I glared at the counsellor and the kids and made everyone feel ashamed and guilty—I hoped! I ran to another cabin where girls had stuffed their T-shirts to mimic a girl who had large breasts, and I came down hard on them, too. Next on my crusade was a cabin known for short-sheeting the bunks, and for dipping the fingers of sleeping campers in warm water to make them pee in the bed. So far, it hadn't worked, but I let them have it, too, just for trying. All around camp, I heard their astonished reaction to my rampage.

"The nurse is going ape!"

"She's losing it!"

"She's so random!"

At the time I didn't care what they said, but, in retrospect, it probably wasn't the best way to address the problem. At least I'd had my say. I've heard some people call bullying harmless teasing; they say it's one of the rites of passage, just kids being kids. However, I suspect that it's only those who did these things themselves as kids who believe that, it's never the ones who were on the receiving end. Yeah, camp is a great place, I wanted to tell Coach Carson, unless you don't fit in. Then, camp can be torture. I've always felt an affinity for the extremely uncool.

Wayne's mother didn't seem surprised when I told her about his hygiene problem. "I feel sorry for him," she said. "We thought it would be good for him to go to camp, that it would help him with his shyness. He has no friends."

"He's in my son's cabin. He and Max are friends."

"Well, that's nice. We promised him a new computer if he stays at camp the whole summer. I've already bought it and had it set up in his room."

The next day, I took Wayne for a walk and told him I had spoken to his mother.

"Did she say I could come home?"

"No," I said gently.

"I figured they'd want me to stay," he said, despondently, as if he could see their point of view and even commiserated with them. "I just have to deal," he said to himself more than to me. He told me how he hated swimming, of course, and the bathroom stalls, because they were dirty and there was no privacy. He couldn't do *that* with other people around. I said he could use the MC bathroom whenever he wanted and could come to me at any time, even during the night. Then, impulsively—despite his mother's note that Wayne needed a "warning" before being touched—I reached over and gave him a hug. Then—what a gift—he hugged me back!

Every day after lunch, I spent the afternoon calling parents. I usually made my calls in the MC where it was quiet. The MC was officially closed, but one afternoon I forgot to lock it and a group of girls gathered in the waiting room, chatting and checking themselves out in the full-length mirror. Shamelessly, I eavesdropped.

"...we'll tell the nurse they're spider bites so she'll give us Benadryl and then we can sleep in the cabins all afternoon," one said.

"I have such a crush on Eric. He's sooo hot!"

"Don't you just want to fall into his eyes?"

(Swooning sounds and muffled sounds of surrender.)

"My counsellor and her boyfriend were doing the dirty in my cabin. I came back to get my towel for swimming. I thought she was on her day off..."

"I'm so thirsty but I can't stand camp water. We only drink Fiji water at home."

"My nanny is so clueless—she put water bottles in the freezer and then expected us to drink them. Doesn't she know they get all toxic and yucky when they're frozen?"

"I hate camp water, too. They never give us ice cubes!"

"Omigod! I hate this mirror. Look at my thighs! They're huge. I'm such a cow!"

"Get out! What are you talking about? You look great."

"I figured I'd lose weight at camp, but I've been sneaking in here, weighing myself every day, and I haven't lost a pound. I'm going on a starvation diet!"

(I wanted to smash that damn mirror. It was almost as if they were obligated to express dissatisfaction with whatever they saw in it.)

"Have you seen Samantha's legs? They're soooo thin!"

"Yeah, and she's got those leg diamonds happening, you know, that space in between her legs at the top where you can see to the other side 'cause she's so skinny."

"What about her baggy clothes? They are sooo disgusting."

"You know, she should change her name to Anna."

"Why's that?"

"You know, Anna Rexic! I think I heard her throwing up once after lunch."

"I heard she was in the hospital for it. I wish I could be anorexic, too."

"She freaks me out, but it's better than being fat. I couldn't be friends with someone who was fat, could you?"

"Which nurse is on duty?"

"I hope it's the young one."

"The old one is kind of grouchy. What's her name, anyway?"

"I dunno. They call her 'Nursezilla.' I just say 'hey, nurse' if I need something."

I opened the door. There were only three fourteen-year-old girls—all slim and pretty—but it had sounded like ten of them.

I put on my sweetest smile, stuck my hands in my pockets. "Yo, girlfriends! How're ya doin'? Just chillin'?"

The party screeched to a halt. Their horrified expressions, fired at me faster than a high-speed instant text message, made me immediately shift back to behaviour more befitting my age and status. "How may I help you young ladies today?"

"We need to talk to you. Privately."

"All three of you? Together?"

"Yes. We have the same problem."

"That's quite a coincidence," I said dryly. I took up a seat facing them.

"We have constipation," they said, practically in unison, giggling madly.

After the hilarity settled down, I asked a few questions about their condition. It turned out that what they were really doing was trolling for laxatives.

"Why not try eating more fibre?" I suggested.

"I hate fibre," said one girl.

"What *is* fibre, anyway?" asked another.

The third girl slumped into the couch, examining her split ends. "Why can't we just have the pills?"

"You don't need them and they can disrupt your system." By then they had tuned me out, so I sent them packing, each with a plastic bag of dried prunes for medicinal purposes. I wanted to tell these popular, cool girls to go easy on the others who weren't like them, but I held back from lecturing. I locked up the Medical Centre. Caitlin would be taking over and I had the rest of the day to myself. Just as I was leaving, I caught sight of myself in that mirror and stood there for a moment. I looked so *parental*. I saw what they saw: a *mother*, a ranting, raving mother.

I went to my room, put on my swimsuit, and walked down to the lake and dove in. I swam far out as if to get a distance from my disquieting feelings. Usually when I swam, campers would stand on the shore and call me back for something, but that afternoon, no one disturbed me. I knew I probably shouldn't go this far alone, but I was a strong swimmer. It's the one brave (okay, reckless) thing I do.

I swam until I reached a small island in the middle of the lake and climbed up onto the rocky shoals to sit there for a while.

Looking back, Camp Carson was so very tiny. All around me was the lake and the sky. The beautiful view buoyed my spirits. I lay back on the rock and closed my eyes.

Within minutes, a motorboat roared up. It was the camp's crash boat zooming at me like the Coast Guard in hot pursuit of a high seas pirate. The boat made a wide arc and pulled up in front of me. "Hasn't anyone ever told you not to swim alone?" the swim counsellor scolded me from the boat.

I nodded guiltily.

"You should never swim without a buddy," he continued.

"You're right." I got into the boat. By the time we returned to camp, I had a plan.

I got dressed and drove to the nearby town. First, I treated myself to a nice dinner and a glass of wine at the local diner. Then I went on a shopping spree at the Giant Tiger—"Your All Canadian Family Discount Store"—and spent over one hundred dollars on skinny jeans (for my not-so-skinny body), a halter top, a fleece hoodie with "City Grrrl" on it, sparkly eye makeup, and a bottle of Britney Spears's perfume, Curious. (Like her, I'd probably be asking myself one day, *What was I thinking?*)

Back at camp, my new look made an instant impression. Counsellors and campers alike flashed me appreciative nods. Caitlin, anxiously waiting for me, also noticed. "Hey, girl, you look freakin' fabulous!" she said, hastily applying a layer of cherry lip gloss. "I have to talk to you, like, asap!" She hustled me in and launched straight into her news.

"Samantha fainted! Eric had to carry her in. She had new cuts on her arms and legs and when I went back to her cabin to get her stuff, I saw blood all over her sheets."

"Did you tell Kitch? What about Wendy and Coach Carson?"

"I promised Samantha I wouldn't tell anyone."

"You shouldn't have done that. You have a duty to tell them."

"She'll have to go home, won't she?"

"I don't see how she can stay here. She's not well."

I went to talk with Kitch and Coach Carson about the situation. Again, Kitch dismissed my concern that Samantha was not well enough to be at camp. "We've been down this road with Samantha and her mother before."

"She feels secure at camp," agreed Coach Carson. "We'll keep an eye on her."

Wendy, the ever-cautious risk manager, suggested the cabin be checked for scissors or razors. Carson agreed with that, but Wendy went further. "I'm thinking we should remove the plastic knives from the dining hall."

"Is that necessary, dear?" he asked.

"It's a liability issue. We need to take all precautions to protect her and the others, as well."

We were way out of our depth with Samantha. I didn't have the skills or knowledge to help her, nor did anyone else there. I was uneasy with their decision to allow her to stay.

Hailey was another ongoing worry. Just that morning, Dana, her counsellor, had told me of a disturbing development. "Hailey's been scaring the other girls with these freaky notes with fake blood drops all over them," she said, handing them to me.

Things I Hate About Camp.

1. Everything
2. Everyone

This camp is history!
I'm out of here!
Who do I have to hurt to escape from this prison?

"She's getting worse," Dana said. "This morning she flew into a rage and was swearing at me for absolutely no reason. I just hope she doesn't try something stupid."

I didn't think Hailey would harm herself or others. That was my gut instinct, but I couldn't take that chance. What if I was reading her wrong? How could I know for sure?

It was Caitlin's turn to give out the evening pills, so I had time to myself. I called home. Ivan asked about the kids, but I didn't have much to tell him. Hearing his voice made me miss him. I signed off quickly and went to join the nightly campfire. I took up a place outside the circle's edge, careful not to encroach on their space. The campfire was such a unifying place—the campers were equals here, whereas in the cabins lines of loyalty and power were often drawn. It was their "nursing station," the place where they shared their stories and felt a sense of togetherness. The kids roasted hot dogs and went off in search of sticks and branches to toast marshmallows for s'mores. I stayed by the fire. I was beginning to appreciate their need to just chill. Their lives at home the rest of the year were so jam-packed and stressful. Camp was a break from all of that. I watched their noisy delight in the novelty of preparing their own food with something as primitive as fire. We were all novices with fire, coming from our fossil-fuelled homes filled with electrical appliances. None of us were used to seeing fire, much less using it.

The songleader tuned his guitar and led the campers in dances like the Cha Cha Slide or the Macarena and in singing TV theme songs from shows such as "Friends" and "Family Guy." When the youngest campers went off to bed, I got up to leave, too. I was tired but enjoyed the sensation of well-earned fatigue at the end of each active day. As we strolled away from the campfire, one girl complained to her friend.

"Tonight's E.P.* was just a campfire? How lame is that? At my other camp I got to sing 'Party Like a Rock Star' in front of everyone at talent night."

"At least a campfire is way funner than an E.T.B.,†" her friend answered.

"But still, it's the same old, same old."

Yeah, right. Another borrring day.

---

* Evening Program
† Early to Bed

8

LOST AND FOUND

"Woohoo! Lookin' fly, Nurse Tilda!"

"Check it out, fellas! Smokin' nurse headin' our way!"

"Hey, guys, who knew our nurse was such a babe?"

That was how the trippers greeted me when I visited them in their cabin one evening. It was the day after my big fashion intervention at Giant Tiger and I guess my new look was still making a hit! Perhaps they now saw me differently, or maybe, for the first time, at all. I wouldn't normally venture into tripper territory, but I needed to bring them the first-aid kits and camper medications they'd forgotten to pick up before leaving early the next morning on a six-day canoe trip.

I hesitated before knocking on the door, nervous to enter their all-male domain where, rumour had it, there were wild, late-night goings-on. Jordan, the head tripper, tall and strapping, welcomed me, along with six (or seven or eight—I couldn't count due to sudden light-headedness) trippers that crowded around me. They were wearing shorts, plus or minus muscle shirts—some in the midst of hastily pulling on those very items, as I walked in. Well, what can I say, but I was getting flustered, rather *verklempt*,* and highly *hormotional!*†

---

* A Yiddish expression meaning a crazy-making mixture of excitement and emotions.

† A more recent coinage, meaning a crazy-making mixture of hormones and emotions.

Get a grip, I told myself. *What's wrong with you? They're eighteen- and nineteen-year-old boys and you're a grown woman! Act your age!*

"What can we do you for, Nurse Tilda?" Jordan turned down the volume of the pumped-up, throbbing music playing on his boom box.

I came to my senses. "You were supposed to pick up these first-aid kits. Were you planning to wake me up at five in the morning before leaving?"

"Geez, sorry." He hit his forehead and flashed me an endearing grin. I melted.

"We also have safety information and camper medications to review."

"I know all that stuff, but you run it by the newbies here who haven't taken out a trip, yet." Jordan offered me a seat atop one of their massive knapsacks, packed for the trip. The other trippers gathered around, taking up positions at my feet, or on the edge of their bunks. They gave me their respectful attention. *Okay, this is good!*

"What about him?" I pointed at someone sprawled on his cot, softly snoring.

"Oh, the Frog Man? We went out last night and he got... *sick.*"

"Is he well enough to take kids out on a trip?"

"Oh, he'll be okay," Jordan said with another grin.

I get it, I get it. He's hungover.

We started with a review of basic first aid. I tested them on splinting a fractured limb and treating sunstroke. I watched them demonstrate taping a sprained ankle. I questioned them on bee stings, deep wounds, and blackfly bites. I put them through their paces for emergency procedures, quizzing them on the signs of anaphylactic shock and making them enact a mock CPR drill while I observed closely. I told them to double-check that they'd packed enough epinephrine and syringes. They were impressively knowledgeable and confident. They were also skilled in wilderness survival techniques, making shelters, tying ropes and knots, and predicting the weather. They knew what to do in the event of earthquakes, quicksand, electrical storms, and hurricanes.

However, when we started reviewing the camper medications, I began to lose them. Their interest waned with the move to this more prosaic topic. It's always like that: everyone prefers heroic rescues, life-saving, fixing, and curing. Nursing care, with its daily tending, monitoring, and paying close attention, takes more stamina and patience—and has no status. The guys were getting restless as I spoke about medications that could be given on an "as needed basis." One guy started juggling oranges. Others stretched out and lazed around the room. Someone turned the volume back up on the music, obviously a cue to me to cut to the chase. I continued on, all the while trying not to notice their muscular arms and legs, their strong backs and rippling chests...

What hot bodies, Caitlin would have whispered to me if she had been there. *Gorging on the eye candy, are you, girlfriend?*

As I spoke about the properties of acetaminophen versus those of ibuprofen, I was envisioning them hauling canoes out of the water and hoisting them onto their backs, getting hot and sweaty as they led the way through the wilderness. I had heard about their legendary end-of-summer trip. I knew that after the campers all went home, the trippers went out on a two-week survival trip, deep in the wild bush. *Maybe I'll join them, go off and tough it out in the wilderness...me and the trippers.*

I jumped up to clear my head and fell over one of the heavy backpacks. Jordan helped me to my feet and was kind enough not to snicker.

"Okay! Any questions about the medications?" I asked.

"Which is the drug that knocks them out?" one guy asked. "Is it this one?" He picked up a bottle of Gravol, also known as dimenhydrinate, used to prevent vomiting, and then a bottle of Benadryl, diphenhydramine, which is an antihistamine that helps to relieve itchiness or nasal congestion due to allergies. He was clearly mixing them up. It was an easy thing to do because of the similarity of their generic names and also because both drugs can cause drowsiness. However, neither is to be used for that purpose.

"Are these painkillers?" another guy asked, picking up another bottle of pills. "I'm not giving any painkillers to the wimps!" he said. "They'll have to tough it out."

They were getting me worried. I hastened to correct their misunderstanding of these drugs. Jordan asked me about a boy who was well-known for his hyperactivity and hijinks. "Where's Ryan's ADD meds?" He searched though the bags.

"Ryan isn't on any meds."

"Well, last summer he was, and man, he still needs them! That kid is majorly high maintenance." He glanced at me, trying to gauge how far he could go with this. "I think I liked him better when he was a zombie."

That cracked them right up. These guys hadn't earned the right to make these kinds of jokes. Given their cavalier attitude, these jokes were wrong, possibly dangerous. These kids were scaring me.

"You guys aren't getting it," I said. "This is a serious matter."

So many things can go wrong.

"We'll look after the kids, don't worry," Jordan said. "They love us! We won't leave them out for the wolves!"

"Listen carefully. Each of these drugs has the potential to harm a child if it is used improperly. You can *kill* someone by giving the wrong drug to the wrong person or in the wrong dose, or at the wrong time, or in the wrong way."

Now, I had their attention once again.

"You guys have the most important job at camp. Being a tripper is the job with the greatest responsibility. You take the children out of camp, into the wilderness, far from any help. If something goes wrong, you will have to handle it alone. These kids' lives are completely in your hands. It is up to you to keep them healthy and return them safely."

That did it. The room fell quiet.

I wanted to end on a positive note. So I told them about what I'd observed when a cabin of kids had returned to camp after the last canoe trip. I had stood aside, watching them bound off the bus. They looked pleased and proud of what they'd accomplished out there, roughing it in the wilderness. Overcoming the challenges they'd faced together had forged strong bonds between them. Even with their bug-bitten legs, complaints about getting rained out, and the burnt food, they were triumphant. In particular, I noticed the kids who'd been scared to go on the trip but who had gone anyway. I could see on their faces the new confidence and self-esteem they'd earned by conquering their fears.

"You taught those kids how to survive in nature and it made them stronger," I told the trippers. They listened and nodded. I was pretty sure they got my message.

It was almost midnight and time for me to go. Just then, a knock came at the door. Jordan greeted a group of swim and drama counsellors who'd shown up for a late-night rendezvous, eager for some tripper-style fun and games.

"Hey, sluts," he called out to them. "Quiet down. We gotta finish going over some stuff with the nurse. Come back in a few minutes and we'll have a cuddle party."

"We can't wait that long, you sexy beasts!" someone called back.

Involuntarily, I cringed. It was offensive to me the way they talked to each other. I don't think they even realized just how crude those words were. I'd heard this language before at camp, many times. At least they refrained from using it when campers were around. Once, I'd asked a female counsellor about it. "It doesn't mean anything. They're just words. Things we say. It's no biggie," she'd told me, but I remained unconvinced.

Jordan cranked up the music.

"Well, I see my work here is done." I got up to go.

Jordan dropped down to one knee, grabbed my hand, and placed a soda pop ring on my finger. "Hey, Nurse Tilda, will you marry me?"

"You guys really should have an early night." I tried to sound stern.

"You're absolutely right, but the thing is, there's this little party happening, like, right now," Jordan flashed me that grin again as he walked me to the door. "But thanks for coming, it was a slice!"

One tripper gave me a lazy high-five. "You da bomb, Nurse Tilda!"

"Stay real, Nurse Tilda," another called out.

I was hardly down the path from their cabin when Jordan flung open the door to bring on the girls and let the cuddle-fest begin.

The trippers left bright and early the next morning, taking two cabins of thirteen-year-old boys deep into the remote wilderness of Algonquin Park. They would be paddling canoes on its pristine lakes by day and pitching tents and setting up a campsite each night. Whenever a trip went out, Coach Carson became preoccupied and tense. He kept in touch with the trippers by satellite phone on a daily basis, but still, his campers were out of his reach. He wouldn't be able to relax until they were all back, safe and sound.

A few days later I was working in the MC. I was bent over a child's foot, soaking it in warm salt water to soften up an inflamed ingrown toenail. The walkie-talkie on the countertop crackled and a female voice came over the air. "Has anyone seen Max?"

Voices from various locations around camp volleyed back and forth: "Max who?" asked someone at A and C.

"You know, the nurse's son."

"Nope, haven't seen him."

"I think I saw down him at the waterfront... that was earlier this morning."

"Where's he supposed to be?"

"His cabin is at the ski docks."

"Hey, it's Sandy here on ski. There's no Max here."

"Shit!" someone muttered. "The kid's gone AWOL!"

Something purely primal, a deep animal instinct inside me, kicked in. I dropped the camper's foot into the basin of water, nodded at Caitlin and Kitch, and took off for the water-ski area, just south of the main swim docks.

Don't wander off! I'd told Max so many times. *Stay with the group! Follow the rules! Sit still! Listen! Pay attention!* I yelled at him in my head as I'd done many times, for real. But Camp Carson was so vast and sprawling, a child could easily go missing, and Max was someone who didn't always follow the crowd...

He wasn't at the canoes or kayaks, nor in his cabin. Others joined in the search. I knew that any minute Wendy would sound the emergency alarm and there'd be an all-out missing-person alert. Suddenly, I came to a halt and stood there, forcing myself to slow down and consider the situation rationally. I knew my kid. He was an explorer, a dreamer, and an inventor. He was full of mischief and highly distractible but neither reckless nor foolish. Max knew how to look after himself. He wasn't lost. Of course, *we* didn't know where he was, but *he* did. That's how he would see it. He'd show up, I told myself, and that calmed me down.

Less than an hour later, Max was found, sitting in Harry's cabin, surrounded by a stack of Archie comics, engrossed in reading and digging into his brother's stash of candy (his own long ago devoured). He said he'd gone off by himself to test out an idea he'd come up with for "forest hockey" using branches for sticks and pine cones for pucks. Then, he thought he'd poke around in Harry's cabin. Luckily, he was found before Wendy had a chance to enact the disaster plan, which included dragging the water, fanning the forest in a human chain, and calling the RCMP.

We barely had time to relax when, only a few hours later, there was a real emergency.

Coach Carson received a frantic call from the trippers: two boys were missing. It had been a long day of paddling and portages. When they got to the campsite, Jordan had told the kids to go off to gather wood for a fire. Two boys did not come back. They'd been missing now for three hours and night was falling. They had no flashlight, food, or water. Neither was a strong swimmer and, worst of all, a canoe was missing.

A meeting in the office was held. Kitch and I came, too. Coach Carson called the provincial police and park officials. A helicopter with searchlights and heat sensors had already been deployed and would work into the night. Then, Coach Carson had to call the parents of each of the missing boys.

"Everything is being done," he told them calmly, "we will find them."

Both sets of parents got into their cars to head up to camp immediately. They couldn't sit at home, worrying and waiting for word from the camp. "Let us know the minute you hear something," one father said. The speakerphone was on and I heard the terror in his voice.

"This can't end well!" Wendy wrung her hands.

She was losing it, but Coach Carson kept his cool. Kitch looked grim. Quietly, he and I discussed the possibilities: disorientation, shock, hypothermia, exposure, bear attack, drowning, or the worst of all, no rescue at all, only the retrieval of remains.

A few hours later, long past midnight, bolstered by cups of black coffee, we were still sitting there when one set of distraught parents burst into the office.

"We were driving so fast, I was afraid the kids would be found, only to be orphans!" one father said, nervously joking.

"I want to reassure you," Coach Carson said, "our trippers are very experienced and responsible young men. They will find your children."

A short while later, the other set of parents arrived. The parents were anxious and, understandably, inconsolable. We offered them a cabin, beds, and blankets, but all four went to a hotel in the nearby town to rest.

The light in the Carsons' bedroom burned all night.

By morning, the boys were still missing.

To avoid hysteria, no one else at camp was told about the crisis. Camp continued as usual. The few of us who knew did our best to contain our worry.

At the same time this crisis was happening, the counsellors were busy with their own secret. For the past few days, they had been staying up later than usual, preparing something big, but no one would tell me what it was. In their free time, groups of them gathered in excited huddles, busy with piles of art supplies. They were painting huge signs, drawing charts and maps, choosing captains and mascots, making costumes, writing songs, and practising special cheers.

"What's going on?" I asked one counsellor.

"I can't tell you."

"As the nurse, I *need* to know." I didn't, really, but I was curious.

She shook her head and pretended to lock her lips, throw away the key.

I glared back at her and stood my ground.

"Well, okay, I'll tell you, but you can't tell any kids. It's Colour Wars."

"What's that?"

"Get out!" she gasped. "I don't believe you."

Now, I have heard it said that many young people these days are unable to name their nation's capital city or leader and I guess I find that as appalling as this counsellor found my ignorance of her world. However, after recovering from her shock, she explained to me that Colour Wars was a huge deal, the highlight of the summer. The camp would be divided into four teams to play all-day games. If you were on the winning team, well, it totally rocked, she said in summary.

"What's the prize for the winning team?"

"Candy and a sleep-in!"

"When is this event taking place?"

"I definitely can't tell you that. It's top secret."

This girl had potential as an intelligence operative, but she'd met her match: I was a counter-intelligence agent. I gave her a menacing look.

She caved and threw me a bone. "All you need to know is when the obstacle course race happens. That's when everyone gets injured."

Thanks for the heads-up.

As I walked away, her friend went over. "You didn't tell her, did you?"

"Yeah, she made me."

"We're going to have to kill her now."

Almost a full two days after the boys had gone missing, the police called with good news. They'd been found! Sunburned, covered in insect bites, scared to death, hungry, thirsty, and in shock, but alive! After a check-up at the local hospital, they'd been discharged. They had suffered no injury from exposure. They said they had gone to gather firewood and decided to take out a canoe on their own, but on their way back they couldn't find the campsite.

Coach Carson approached one pair of now-relieved parents. "I want you to know that at no time was your son in any danger whatsoever."

"Don't bullshit us, Carson!" the father snapped. "What kind of training do these trippers have? How could they lose our child?"

"I'm sorry, what I mean is that *your* son wasn't lost. The trippers mixed up the names. It was another boy also named Brandon, not *your* Brandon."

They were stunned, unsure how to react. They hung between relief and anger. I thought about the parents whose son had been lost, who were still at home, blissfully oblivious to their possible tragedy.

After ensuring their children were all right, both groups of parents left to return home, but not before Coach Carson offered to waive all camp fees for their kids for the following summer to compensate for their emotional distress.

"I've lost ten years off my life." Coach Carson dropped down onto the couch in his office, utterly exhausted.

Wendy sighed. "At least it all ended well," she said.

Camp had been in swing for three weeks. Tomorrow was Visitor's Day, and a few days after that, my kids and I would be leaving. My days were pleasant and I was enjoying myself immensely, confidently and competently treating the daily flow of blisters, splinters, sore throats, headaches, and stomach aches.

The counsellors were still busy with their surreptitious late-night activities, but meanwhile, a daytime flurry of hustle and bustle had kicked up around camp, this one in preparation for Visitor's Day. Extra gardeners were brought in to pick up litter, mow lawns, and clip hedges. Maintenance crews spruced up the outside of the buildings. Campers and counsellors did a massive clean-up inside their cabins, followed by inspection by the unit heads. The kitchen staff was getting ready for the special lunch for the parents, and as a result breakfast was even more rushed than usual. Amid all of these distractions, Caitlin and I suddenly became aware that the picnic basket of meds, always kept on the bench with one of us, was missing. That basket held amphetamines, antidepressants, sedatives, and antibiotics. Wendy was furious at us and told us what we already knew.

"If a child gets into those meds it could be disastrous! This can't end well."

She called a camp-wide roll call and gave a stern warning to whoever had pulled this dangerous prank to come forward immediately. I noticed Hailey was missing. I ran off with a good hunch where she might be.

I had been spending a lot of time with Hailey. Almost every day, she would duck and dive when she saw me, but end up agreeing to take a walk with me. We went on the path I hiked with Caitlin in the mornings. The trail led into the woods and then out onto a quiet country road that ran alongside camp. During those walks, I gave Hailey full rein to express her unhappiness. She was still angry and defiant, more determined than ever to leave on Visitor's Day when her parents arrived. She even had her bags packed. Yet her parents had signed her up for the entire summer. I wondered who would win.

"If she comes home, she wins," her mother had explained to me on the phone.

"That girl is not coming home," her father told me in a separate conversation. "We paid for this camp. She's staying. End of discussion."

"I'm at war with my parents," Hailey said, looking resolute.

I knew I couldn't fix anything, but I also knew, from so many years of being a nurse, the value in simply listening and being open to another person's pain. Hailey had to go through it alone, but if it helped knowing there was a caring and understanding adult, I would be that.

I ran through the woods to the private spot where she and I usually sat. The moment I came upon her in the clearing, I could tell she was glad to be found, even though she scowled when she saw me. The picnic basket with the meds was at her side. I joined her on a slab of granite rock for a few minutes, talked quietly, and then we headed back to camp.

"You're the reason I've made it at camp this long. I hope you're not leaving," she said.

"Yes, after Visitor's Day. I have to get back to my job in the hospital."

"I'm going home, too. I'll do what it takes to get out of here. I warned you, I'm relentless."

After dinner that night, they held the long-standing tradition of the hilarious "Lost and Found Fashion Show," where counsellors paraded around the dining hall wearing items of unclaimed clothing and sports equipment, calling out the camper's name on the label. It was amusing to see the counsellors sporting the kids' clothes and acting silly, but there was also a sense of urgency to the game—Coach Carson and Wendy presided over it from the sidelines—of uniting those clothes and expensive items to the owners before the parents arrived the next day.

"V-Day" dawned bright and sunny. Camp Carson was abuzz with excitement. By midmorning, cars were lined up outside the gate. By noon, they were bumper to bumper in four converging rows, ready for the moment when Coach Carson opened the gate, which he did, precisely at noon. The trippers, now subdued and compliant after the disastrous trip, were very industrious. They had turned the soccer field and baseball diamond into parking lots and were directing traffic, acting as parking valets, and helping parents meet up with their children.

Caitlin ran over to tell me that a plane had landed and docked at the waterfront and someone's parents climbed out. "It's the coolest thing I've ever seen!"

Everywhere you turned, heartwarming greetings were ringing out across the Land of Camp!

"Mom!"

"Dad!"

Kids ran to their parents—and to step-parents, a slew of siblings and step-siblings, grandparents and step-grandparents. The parents looked refreshed and eager to see their kids. The time apart had been good for everyone, but how strange to see the place suddenly flooded with adults. Grown-ups were invading the kids' world!

The visitors came laden with provisions: picnic hampers and voluminous hockey bags stuffed with giant-sized bags of potato chips, boxes of party sandwiches, hamburgers (still warm from the local town's drive-thru), fried chicken, barbequed spare ribs, chocolate cakes, lemon meringue and apple pies, and cartons of lemonade and iced tea, cases of Coke, Styrofoam cups of dried noodle soups, huge slabs of chocolate, and party-sized bags of candy to replenish their tool boxes. They brought teen magazines, clothes, sports equipment, toys, games, and gadgets. Some of the things they brought the kids hadn't even been missing.

Other noteworthy visitors were the many family dogs, all well-behaved and on leashes. There were even a few purse pooches, their beribboned heads sticking out the top of their owners' handbags. I saw kids run with outstretched arms right past their parents to embrace their beloved pets. In some cases it was hard to tell if the children were happier to see their parents or their dogs, but in the end all were lavished with lots of affection.

I wondered how Alexa Rose was dealing with this canine onslaught, but Caitlin told me her parents had whisked her and T.C. out of camp for an afternoon of pampering in the local town. "She told me she was going to max out her parents' credit cards," Caitlin said. "It was the first time I've actually seen her smile."

Well, I couldn't hang around ogling and petting the beautiful dogs. I was expected to meet parents and answer any questions they had about their children's health. As I worked the crowd, I found the parents were as generous to staff as they were to their children. They tipped the counsellors—which was against camp policy but not actually enforced—and spoiled Caitlin and me with boxes of chocolates, bubble bath, gift certificates, even a voucher for a day at a spa.

The kids gave their parents the clay pots, vases, necklaces, and bracelets they'd made, showed them all around camp, and recounted their many achievements.

"I learned how to swallow pills!" said one girl as she saw me walk by. I'd obviously given her some sort of tablet. "The nurse taught me." I waved at them.

"They make us wake up at the crack of dawn," one boy said, but he didn't seem too upset about it. "We walk *outside* to check out the weather, 'cause there's no weather channel!" He told his parents about his canoe trip. "We didn't even take an alarm clock. We used the sun to wake us up!"

Another child was also excited about outdoor discoveries.

"Our cabin went stargazing! I saw a shooting star. It was way cool. Then we went out again and we saw the exact same stars in the sky. I thought every night would be different stars."

"Hey, Dad, listen to this," a kid yelled as he strummed a guitar. "I wrote a song!"

I noticed one girl who had no visitors, but it didn't seem to bother her. "At first, I thought my mom was coming and I was jiggy with that, but she nixed the idea when she thought for some reason that my dad was coming. But she should know he would never come here. His idea of nature is driving his convertible with the top down." She happily spent the day with a cabin mate and her parents.

Parents gathered around Coach Carson, bombarding him with their concerns, queries about their child's activities, requests to change cabins or counsellors, or to voice indignant complaints.

"My son had no pillowcase. Why didn't the counsellor see that?"

The counsellor probably didn't have one on his own pillow, I thought. I admired Carson's tactful restraint. He listened quietly even when a parent angrily cornered him. "There was a disgusting four-letter word on the wall of my kid's cabin. Is there no cleanup crew?"

Many parents also stopped by to tell Coach Carson and Wendy what a wonderful time their kid was having and what a great operation they were running. Perhaps it all evened out, complaints versus compliments.

"I love it when they're at camp," I overheard one mother say about her teenagers. "I don't have to worry about them. I know they're safe. My boys are telling me they don't want to come back next summer, but I told them I'd pay *them*—as well as the camp fees—if they'll just keep coming."

"I wish my son would do school as well as he does camp," a father said.

"Don't worry," Coach Carson said. "Camp is more important than school."

It was time for lunch. A sumptuous buffet was laid out. There were salads, sushi, and multigrain wraps filled with grilled veggies or smoked salmon and goat cheese. For dessert there were pastries and strawberries dipped in chocolate.

But outside the dining hall, on the front lawn, missing out on this feast, were Hailey and her parents, engaged in a furious stand-off. There were two separate combat zones: Hailey versus her mother on one side, and Hailey versus her father on the other. I went over to introduce myself, but Hailey was in the midst of arguing with her father, whom, when she addressed him at all, she called by his name, Douglas. Her mother, Eileen, whispered to me, "Hailey and I used to be so close, but she completely changed in the past few months. The boyfriend turned her against me. She's become cold and distant, like her father."

Douglas turned to me. "I don't know what she"—he pointed at Eileen—"has told you, but did Hailey tell you why we sent her to camp? I'm sure she didn't mention it was punishment for a certain house party when the police were called. We're still repairing the damage. Hailey is a liar. If I were you, I wouldn't believe a word she says, or her mother, either." He looked away in disgust. "This is a girl who has raised money for the starving children of Darfur and rescues abandoned cats, but treats her own parents like dirt." He pointed his finger at Hailey. "You are not coming home. You will stay here until the end of the summer. Case closed."

"Please stay, Hailey," Eileen begged. "Be good."

"Why don't you two just get a divorce? Get it over with." Hailey spat the words at them. "You hate each other, admit it."

No one would ever win this argument. I left them to duke it out themselves.

Toward the end of the day, Alexa Rose and her brother T.C. returned to camp with their parents. I immediately recognized their mother and her shrill voice. She was talking in an agitated way to Wendy. I went over to see if I could help.

"Someone stole my daughter's sunglasses!"

"We can't take responsibility for valuables brought to camp," Wendy countered.

"But they were stolen, here at camp. Alexa Rose told me the girls in her cabin have been touching her things. I'm expecting your insurance to reimburse us."

"Have you looked in your sunglass case?" I asked Alexa Rose. "Your glasses were left out on the bed and I put them in there last week so they wouldn't get broken or lost."

Wendy flashed me a grateful look.

Alexa Rose's mother and father were ready to take her home. "Baby doll, shall we pack up your things?"

"I want to stay," she said, surprising us all. It was as if all she needed was that small dose of her parents. She must have decided that camp wasn't so bad after all.

Her mother put her arm around her daughter and hugged her close. "My girl—she's a keeper, all right!" Next, she hugged me. "Thank you for taking care of my children! It's so hard to say goodbye. I'm a Pisces and we have issues with separation." She gave herself a few drops of Rescue Remedy.

If this Visitor's Day goes on much longer, I'm going to need a swig of that Rescue Remedy myself.

Next, I went back to Hailey and her parents, who were now taking up their problem with Coach Carson.

"Hailey takes after her father," Eileen was saying. "She doesn't express her feelings, just keeps everything bottled up."

"She's been very expressive about her unhappiness at camp," I said.

"For so many years she loved this camp, and now she's completely changed. I hardly know her. What's happened, Hailey?" She turned to her daughter and looked into her pale face and dark eyes.

"Eileen, face it," Hailey spat out, "when are you going to come clean about the boyfriend? You're nothing more than a whore. Douglas is an alcoholic." She turned away from them.

"When you get back from camp, do you want to see the therapist again?" Eileen asked. "The nice one, the one you liked?"

Hailey pointed her chin at me. "Her. She's the only one I'll talk to. The nurse."

Coach Carson told Douglas and Eileen about the prank Hailey had pulled stealing the medications. He warned them that another stunt like that would get her kicked out of camp.

"Why are dangerous medications being left lying around?" Douglas demanded to know. "That's asking for trouble. Anyone could have taken them, not just Hailey. Why should we be held responsible for *your* negligence?"

Coach Carson was silent.

"Hailey, you're staying," her father said. He pointed his car key at her. "If you come home now, that would just be one more failure." He jangled the keys. "I paid for this camp for the full session. Case closed. Carson, you keep her here."

Coach Carson shrugged and offered his handshake as a pledge that he'd do just that.

"I hate you! I hate you both!" Hailey screamed and ran off, sobbing.

"She's been given everything," Eileen said to me quietly. "I stayed home, I didn't work. She's had trips, private school. I don't understand."

Later, Hailey came to find me. Her mascara and eyeliner were smudged and she looked so vulnerable, but she spoke more resolutely than ever.

"I'll hurt myself if I have to. I'll do whatever it takes. I want to see the doctor so I can ask him how I can kill myself. What if I stop eating and drinking? How long would it take to get dehydrated?"

"You will feel the symptoms within twenty-four hours. Sooner if it stays hot."

"Will that get me home?"

"No, it will get you admitted to the hospital. Hailey, I don't see any way out for you. If you think you might hurt yourself, I'm going to have to keep you on constant watch. You've got three more weeks here. Isn't there something—anything—you could do to get you through it? Isn't there anything here you enjoy that you could focus on?"

She had no intention of considering the possibility of enjoyment. Her focus was now on escape. She stared at me in disgust as if I had gone over to their side and betrayed her. "There is no way I will enjoy this place. I hate everything and everyone here. Believe me, everyone hates me, too."

"I like you," I smiled at her. By then, I really did.

"Yeah, right."

"I mean it."

"You wouldn't if you really knew me."

I had to laugh at that. "I admire you and I like your clothes. They must have a lot of meaning for you."

She nodded thanks and looked away.

"It takes a lot of courage to be true to yourself, especially here at camp, where everyone is supposed to fit in."

"You *do* understand! Then why won't you help me get out of here?"

What Hailey couldn't possibly know and wasn't appropriate to tell her, was that I knew exactly how she felt. Hailey and I had more in common than she realized: we were both on the fringes, each for our different reasons.

I met Samantha's mother, Veronica. She was absolutely stunning, model-thin in tight jeans, with manicured fingernails and wearing tasteful jewellery and makeup. She had difficulty manoeuvring around the grassy terrain of camp in her high-heeled slides, with her frail, skinny daughter hanging on to her. Of course she noticed Samantha's dramatic weight loss (it had been only ten pounds, but Samantha was already so thin that she couldn't afford to lose *any* weight), but her child's appearance seemed to embarrass her. She blamed the camp food. "She's a picky eater. Other than that, Samantha is a perfect child. She's a champion swimmer. An A-student. She's always been so easy. In fourteen years, I've hardly had to do anything for her. She says that something has been bothering her, but now she's feeling a lot better and wants to stay at camp."

I stayed quiet about my disagreement with that decision. Samantha's condition was precarious and she desperately needed psychiatric help. Camp simply wasn't the place for her right now, in this condition, but no one saw it as I did.

Wayne and his parents were easy to spot. The resemblance to their skinny, nearsighted son was uncanny, right down to the same stiff mop of hair. Despite so many difficulties he'd endured, camp had been good for him. He had withstood the bullying and survived. Did he realize how much he'd achieved, how strong he was? I wanted to go over and tell him but he was busy with his parents. They were very sweet and doting as they said their goodbyes, so I left them alone, especially when I saw Wayne holding back tears. Besides, if I'd gone over, I'd have started crying, too.

Visitor's Day was drawing to an anticlimactic, exhausting close when I came upon two brothers wandering around aimlessly. Somehow in the commotion, no one had noticed that their parents hadn't shown up all day.

"I told Jason, Mom probably won't be able to come," the older boy told me. "She's an artist—*enormously talented*, everyone says so—and probably had to go to Paris, but Dad should be here any minute." He kept scanning the path that led from the parking area at the entrance of camp.

I went to the office and called the father's cell number. He was in Los Angeles working on a film shoot. "Tell the boys I'll try to make it up this week sometime. That is, if Carson'll let me in after Visitor's Day," he added. "Their mother, the famous *artiste*—she's *enormously talented*, I'll give her that—must have forgotten to tell me. Please buy them something extra from the tuck shop and add it to our bill."

I went to tell the kids and they seemed okay with that.

The long day still wasn't over, but it had begun to wind down as kids slowly accompanied their parents to their cars. Then, even some of the happiest of campers started losing it. Some clung to their parents and said goodbye reluctantly, with tearful faces. Others ran off, sobbing.

"I love camp," one boy told me. "I do," he added, as if to remind himself as he waved goodbye to his parents and wiped away tears.

Another boy hung back, looking shell-shocked. He had expected to stay for the entire summer, but now his parents had packed his bags and were taking him home.

"His father's company went bankrupt and we can't afford it," his mother explained to me tearfully. They had sold the house and were moving into an apartment.

One boy stood in between his parents, crying. He had been perfectly happy at camp, but after seeing his parents he wanted to go home with them.

"You are working yourself up into a state," his mother said as she headed for the car. "You know you love camp." She rushed to catch up with her husband who was already starting up the car. He opened the window and the boy leaned in, sobbing. "I want to go home."

"You brought this on yourself, son," he said, shifting into drive. "You've talked yourself into it. Come on now, be brave."

The scene was breaking my heart. I watched as the boy wiped his eyes and stumbled back from the car as it pulled away. The parents waved goodbye out their windows. They weren't being cruel, and the boy wasn't acting up on purpose. They were trying to teach their son a lesson, and he, in turn, was trying to deal with the difficult situation. It was hard all around. I went over to him and put my arm around him, but he shrugged me off and walked away, preferring to collect himself on his own.

I also saw just as many other children who had gotten their fill of whatever they'd been missing from their parents and who were very pleased to return to their cabin and counsellor and to be at camp. Some were even asking to extend their stay.

"Sure, I miss my parents," one kid cheerfully told me after saying goodbye to his parents, "but I'm not homesick."

"What's the difference?"

"I've seen them. They can go. I'm good now."

By the end of the afternoon, Visitor's Day was officially over. It was just as well, as everyone was thoroughly overwrought, some laughing, some crying, some doing both. That night, dinner was quiet, and when the campers heard that there would be a dreaded E.T.B., they were too tired to raise their usual objections. Everyone was emotionally drained and down in the dumps. I wondered out loud if Visitor's Day was such a great idea, after all. "Do we really need it?"

"Didn't you see how proud the kids are of their camp, how they love to show off all they've learned?" Coach Carson said. "Besides, we have to have Visitor's Day so the parents can sign up to guarantee them a spot for next summer. We have a ninety-four-percent return rate!"

"But there's such a drop in everyone's mood. How're we going to pick them up?"

He smiled and patted my shoulder. "I wouldn't worry about it if I were you. It's been taken care of. Just wait and see."

9

COLOUR WARS REDUX

That night I was woken from a deep sleep by shouts and screams. I bolted upright in bed. There was banging and clanging and then, of all things, marching-band music! I jumped up and dressed quickly. What was going on? A parade? A carnival? *Armageddon?*

Counsellors ran past my window shouting, "Wake up! It's Midnight Madness!"

I ran to the flagpole. The children had been assembled, still in their pyjamas, dazed from sleep. The older ones were excited and seemed to know what was going on. We all looked up at a small propeller plane circling overhead. Suddenly, hundreds of leaflets were released and fluttered to the ground. Everyone raced around, grabbing at them, scrambling to collect them all. They were lists of all their names and teams! Clues and maps leading to buried treasure! Mysteries and puzzles to be solved! Prizes to be won! Coach Carson stood at the side beaming with pride. "We do Colour Wars right after Visitor's Day but the kids forget and are always taken by surprise."

The campers were led back to bed. A ferocious battle was about to be waged between all four factions—Orange, Red, Blue, and Green—and it would begin in the morning. Everyone was so pumped up I wondered how the counsellors were ever going to get them back to sleep.

Bright and early the next day, everyone was raring to go. The counsellors had transformed the dining hall into four colourful worlds: The Orange section was decorated in Looney Tunes, with Bugs Bunny, Tweety Bird, and Road Runner as the captains; Blue was covered in comic-book characters, caped crusaders like Superman, Batman, and Wonder Woman; Red was Disney, with Mickey Mouse, Donald Duck, and Winnie-the-Pooh; and Green was plastered with the Simpsons (Homer, Marge, and Bart). Breakfast was dispensed faster than usual, including the Pill Patrol scramble, to allow the full-tilt, eighteen-hour day to get underway. The counsellors had planned every detail and activity and Colour Wars would be executed, right down to the second, like a military campaign.

Not surprisingly, no one showed up for the morning clinic. All discomforts were put on hold for such a thrilling day. Caitlin and I locked up, and I went out on my own to take in the action. Campers and counsellors alike were decked out in crazy costumes, waving scarves and banners in their team colours.

They started the day with the "cheer-off."

"Let's go gree-een, let's go!"

"Blue's the real deal! Yay, Blue!"

"Yo—Orange talks the walk, walks the talk!"

"Red has the power! Red rocks!"

After each cheer, the team punched at the air, whooped, and hollered.

For the first time, I saw all the ages mixed together on each team. It was sweet to see the little kids trying to keep up with the older ones and the older ones adjusting their pace to accommodate them as they took them on scavenger hunts, ran relays and races, played touch tag, tug-of-war, and water polo in the lake. Later, the plans included the camp's traditional buffalo stampede, treasure hunt, and Capture the Flag.

"Colour Wars is insane this year!" a kid yelled out as he ran past me.

"Yeah, it's right off the hook," his friend said.

A boy staggered along, huffing and puffing and clutching at his chest, pretending he couldn't make it, though I could plainly see he could. "I'm gonna crash and burn."

I was dreading the commotion in the dining hall that I assumed would be even more over-the-top that day. When it was time for lunch I popped a few pills myself to stave off a headache and headed over. Unexpectedly, I entered an oasis of peace and quiet. The Silent Lunch was a hallowed Colour Wars custom. However, I braced myself when I read on the schedule that after lunch was the infamous obstacle race (the one where "everyone gets hurt"). I knew where I'd be stationed the rest of the day.

That afternoon, Kitch and I worked together in the Medical Centre while Caitlin roved around camp with a walkie-talkie and a fanny pack chock full of disinfectant, bandages, and gauze so she could attend to minor injuries along the way. It was a steamy, hot day, so I was happy to stay in the air-conditioned comfort of the MC while I treated the steady stream of bumps, cuts and scrapes, twisted fingers and ankles. As the day wore on, kids with headaches and heat exhaustion started rolling in. By midafternoon, the kids were lined up on the couch and the beds were full while I rested, iced, compressed (taped), and elevated arms and legs, and medicated the children attached to those sore limbs.

A boy lay on a bed, groaning after throwing up from the lemon-eating contest.

A counsellor was beside herself with disappointment because she'd lost her voice from screaming on the chant-a-thon and wouldn't be able to lead her team.

A thirteen-year-old girl was in severe pain. Her likely fractured arm had been splinted and she was waiting to be driven to the hospital for an X-ray and probably a cast. She was moaning in pain because she couldn't swallow painkiller pills and was slowly sipping a yucky liquid substitute, trying to get it down without gagging.

A CIT boy had a possible concussion from a whack over the head during a mud-wrestling contest (he couldn't remember the injury, which was worrisome). He stayed under my close watch so I could check his vital signs and neurological status every hour.

Another camper lay on a stretcher recovering from the effects of unnecessarily injecting himself with his epinephrine syringe. What he had thought was anaphylactic shock was only extreme excitement during Human Battleship on the sports field. He'd panicked and given himself a shot in his thigh. His heart was racing and his blood pressure elevated, so I kept him for observation.

In the midst of all of this, a pack of sweaty kids barged in and rushed at me, begging for tongue depressors. I didn't have a chance to ask what they wanted them for or why they all had miniature corncobs stuffed up their nostrils, making them look like charging bulls. As I handed over the booty, an ominous call came on the walkie-talkie.

"I need help! Someone, help!"

It was Trish, the kitchen supervisor. Her voice was trembling.

"Hi, Trish, it's Tilda. What's wrong?"

"Come quick...now!"

"Can you switch to medical and tell me what the problem is?" (That was the channel we used for confidential information or to avoid camp-wide hysteria.)

"Please, just get here! Now!"

Gotcha! I grabbed the "crash box"—not the everyday first-aid kit. I had a feeling I'd need it. I'd put this box together shortly after my arrival at camp so it would be ready in an emergency. It contained plastic airways to deliver breaths in the event of an obstruction or respiratory arrest, and face masks and tubing to administer oxygen. There were lots of syringes and resuscitation drugs such as epinephrine, intravenous equipment with large-bore needles to run large amounts of fluid quickly into big veins, bags of glucose and saline, and large, thick bandages.

Kitch was out somewhere examining a child so I was on my own. "I'm coming," I yelled into the walkie-talkie. Just then, Eric dashed in and grabbed me. "Let's go!" he shouted. I jumped onto his ATV waiting outside the door and we barrelled off to the dining hall.

In the kitchen, I walked into what looked like a murder scene. Blood was everywhere: splashed against the tiled white walls, splattered on the floor, sprayed on the white aprons of the kitchen staff and head chef like some abstract paint job. They were standing around, speechless, paralyzed with fear and shock, as a young man lay on the floor writhing in a pool of blood that streamed out from his hand—what was left of his hand—hanging off the end of his arm. He was a fifteen-year-old kitchen worker who had been cleaning the meat slicer when it accidentally got turned on.

For one infinitesimal second, I paused, playing a mind game. Even after all of these years of dealing with emergencies, I sometimes need to calm myself down and I have a little technique that's very effective.

This is only a pitcher of cherry bug-juice spilled onto the floor, I told myself. *It's some joke, a Colour Wars prank from the Red team. These crazy kids are playing tricks on me!*

That second was all it took for me to come to my senses and take charge of the situation. I pulled on two pairs of vinyl gloves and rushed to the boy, careful not to slip on the slicks of blood. By the bright colour I knew that arteries had been severed. Parts of each of his fingers were missing, but the thumb hung on tenuously by a piece of fibrous tissue. Chunks of fingers were strewn across the floor. I grabbed a dishtowel and made a tourniquet on his arm. I grabbed a roll of paper towel and slapped that on the wound. Crouching beside him on the floor, I held his arm up, above the level of his heart to divert blood as much as possible from pumping out. All the while I shouted out orders, one after another, to the crowd gathered there.

"Someone, bring more towels!

"Buckets of ice, too!

"Call Kitch! Call 911 for an ambulance!

"Get the oxygen tank from the MC!"

I pointed at a gawker. "You! Gather up whatever parts of fingers you can find and put them on ice." He looked horrified but did as I told him.

The boy was now cold and clammy and had begun shivering. "Bring blankets!" I called out. The roll of paper towel was drenched in blood. Quickly, I replaced it with a new one.

"Am I going to die?" the boy mumbled.

"No!" I told him firmly. "You're going to be just fine. We're taking care of you."

I kept his hand raised high and maintained pressure on the wound, not even releasing it to check it. I kept talking to him, asking if he could feel what was left of his fingers. He couldn't. He had no movement or sensation in his arm. His pulse was fast, weak and thready, getting more difficult to palpate: I got someone to take over applying pressure, while I started an IV in his other arm and then opened the clamp to let the fluid pour in to stave off hypovolemic shock caused by such massive blood loss. Kitch arrived and nodded that I was doing everything right. Soon, the ambulance came and then the paramedics took over. By this point, the boy had lost consciousness and I realized I didn't even know his name. Trish told me it was Tom Adams. I looked at him lying on the stretcher, alone and without family or friends. I felt like a critical care nurse again, and all I knew was that I had to be with my patient and see him through to safety. I was tempted to jump into the back of the ambulance with him but decided I'd better drive my car there so that I'd have a way to get back to camp later.

In the emergency department the doctors and nurses transfused him with three units of blood. They prepared to take him into surgery to get the bleeding under control, but were also making arrangements for him to be transferred to Toronto for highly specialized surgery to re-attach his fingers by a top expert. I could hear the whirring of a helicopter on the hospital landing-pad, waiting to fly him there.

"I'll call your parents," I told Tom, who was now more alert after the transfusions and the fluid resuscitation but still groggy from painkillers.

"Don't got no parents," he mumbled. "Mom's dead and Dad's in jail."

"Who should we contact to let them know what happened?"

"I've an uncle but he don't like to be disturbed."

"What's his number?" I pulled out a piece of paper and a pen.

"He don't have no phone or nothin' like that."

"Well, give me his address and I'll go and tell him."

Instead of an address Tom gave me directions that involved a country road, a turnoff that was a "fair stretch" past a motel, a left at a tall red pine tree, and a right at a row of cedars. I got all that down just before he dozed off. I called the camp to tell them that I was going to track down Tom's relatives, but no one was picking up because they were probably still busy with Colour Wars. I left a message on the answering machine and went to my car.

I drove along the single-lane highway and was soon on that rut-filled dirt road that Tom had described. It seemed to lead nowhere. After a few minutes, I was so far off the beaten path, there was no one around to ask directions, no gas stations or pay phones. My cell phone wasn't picking up signals, and I was getting nervous. Eventually, after turning past a row of some trees, I stopped at a shack with a sagging porch. A grizzled man in bib overalls over his bare chest emerged. He stared at my car with suspicion. I got out and walked toward him. A woman came out on the porch and stared at me. Two naked toddlers were playing in the dirt. The man grunted, yes, when I asked if he was Tom's uncle. I told him about the accident but he showed no reaction. I left, shocked at what I had seen. *How could I have been unaware of such a terrible situation that existed so close to home? No one should have to live like this*, I thought, as I drove back to camp. *A nurse should know about this!*

As far back as Florence Nightingale, nurses have known how poverty causes illness and higher mortality rates. They understand the health effects of inadequate housing, sanitation, nutrition, and hygiene, and championed their reform. Tom's family was way off the grid and far beyond the protection of our social safety net. They had no running water or electricity and no access to healthy food, proper housing, health care, or education. How did they cope with our severe winters? What did they do when someone got sick or injured, like Tom? I had never come up close and personal with a case of such extreme deprivation. What a huge divide existed between the two sides of the camp's kitchen counter.

"Where *were* you?" Wendy pounced on me when I returned. I was so relieved I'd found my way back to camp that I'd completely forgotten they'd be wondering about me. Coach Carson joined her and said how worried they'd been, but they both sounded way more irritated that I hadn't been there to help on the busiest day of the summer. I explained what had happened, assuming they'd understand.

"You spent all day with a kitchen staffer and left one nurse all by herself to care for eight hundred campers?" Wendy said.

"How irresponsible! You jeopardized the safety of everyone at camp. Where were your priorities? What were you thinking?"

"That a boy needed me. I couldn't leave him. He's only fifteen."

"He's a hired worker. He's not one of ours. Your responsibility is to the campers under your care, to the parents who have paid us to keep them safe, and to us, your employers. Pills were missed at lunch and at dinner—Caitlin couldn't handle it all by herself. The MC is packed with kids who need your attention. You better get in there right away."

Kitch didn't say a word and Caitlin was quiet. She seemed miffed, though we chatted briefly about Colour Wars, but then she stopped, applied a layer of lip gloss, and turned away from me. Gone was her usually friendly demeanour and she wasn't calling me "girlfriend" any more. But she was a nurse, too; why didn't she understand the choice I'd made? I guess all she could see was that she had been left alone with a lot of extra work and that I had let her down. I later found out that not only had the MC been busy all day and the work non-stop, but in the middle of it all, Samantha had fainted once again. Kitch told me that when she returned to consciousness, she wouldn't talk to anyone or let anyone touch her, not even to take her vital signs. Kitch had called her mother and told her that Samantha's medical condition was now unstable. The camp could no longer take responsibility for her and he had no choice but to send her home.

Just as we were about to close up for the day, someone ran in to announce that the Blue team won. I didn't join the victorious celebrations, nor the evening entertainment at the amusement park that had been set up on the soccer field, complete with roller coaster and go-karts. I went to bed.

The next day Samantha's mother arrived at eleven o'clock in the morning, looking as well-groomed and glamorous as ever. Kitch told her that Samantha needed medical intervention and psychiatric treatment and that she could die from anorexia nervosa, which is what he finally concluded she had. The mother seemed far more concerned about getting back to the city in time for a business meeting. She looked at her daughter and said to me, "Sam's been given everything. I simply don't understand how this could have happened."

Just before she left, Samantha looked at me and said in her soft, wispy voice, "My mom never worries about me. She always thinks everything is okay."

"Well, we're worried about you," I said, "and we know everything isn't okay."

I hoped now she would finally get the help she urgently needed.

That day Hailey was quiet, too, but it was unlike her. The night after her parents left on Visitor's Day she had stayed in her cabin and wouldn't come out. She went on a hunger strike in protest of her "incarceration" at camp, but gave up by midmorning the next day.

I offered no sympathy but did feel admiration for this feisty girl and her rebellious spirit. Secretly, I was rooting for her, but there was no way I would condone her self-destructive behaviour. That very evening at dinner, she came up with a clever solution to her problem. We were sitting in the dining hall when someone shouted out "Hailey jumped!" There was a collective gasp and then a hush.

The trippers, whose table was closest to the balcony, leapt to their feet and ran over. Others quickly followed. People gathered at the railing, looking down the sloping hill that led into the lake below. At the bottom of the six-foot drop lay Hailey, among fallen branches and twigs, and banana peels and apple cores that the kids had thrown off the balcony. I ran down the stairs but as I approached, my pace slowed. Her eyes were tightly closed and she was breathing normally. My ICU intuition informed me that she was okay. She hadn't done any harm to herself.

"Hailey?" I knelt beside her on the ground. "Open your eyes."

She kept them pressed shut. I could tell she was fully conscious. The old phrase *the lights are on and someone is home* came to mind.* Kitch soon arrived at the scene but also saw right away that Hailey was okay. Since he knew I had a connection with her, he backed right off. She had a few scratches and he would examine her later, but for now she was okay.

"Hailey," I said firmly. "Please get up."

This is your ticket home, I thought. I helped her to her feet, brushed her off, and watched her limp away, leaning on to her counsellor's shoulder. I went to tell Coach Carson what had happened and pushed for her to be sent home.

"You're going to put me out of business," he pretended to complain, but he recognized the seriousness of a suicide attempt, regardless of how half-hearted this one was. He knew she had to go. I kept her overnight in the MC but she was angry and wouldn't talk to me. In the morning her mother called.

"Is Hailey all right?" Eileen asked tentatively.

Then Douglas came on the line. "I understand you have our daughter in your custody. How could this have happened? Why wasn't she supervised?"

"I hate them," Hailey said to me when I got off the phone, "and, I won."

---

* In the ICU, privately, quietly, among ourselves, we occasionally utter variations of this coarse shorthand about patients we're worried about. Admittedly, the phrase sounds callous—though I've never heard it used that way—but it can actually be somewhat useful. When we say that *the lights are on but no one is home,* it captures something about a certain ambiguous, often-fluctuating disturbance in a patient's level of consciousness. It conveys the notion that the patient has a partial or limited awareness that is coupled with a significant underlying neurological impairment, which may be temporary or permanent. Lastly, *the lights are off and no one is home* denotes a rare and extreme situation. If the patient has suffered extensive brain damage and rescue attempts are deemed futile, then this version may even be a description, albeit a very superficial and cursory one, of the irreversible state known as "brain death."

"Hailey, would you like me to arrange for you to get help? I know you've refused therapy in the past, but would you go now?" I asked her.

"Can you say that the camp forced me? I don't want my parents to think I'm agreeing to anything."

I said goodbye and then did something I've rarely done in my long career. I wrote down my telephone number on a slip of paper and handed it to her. I told her she could keep in touch and call me at home if she ever wanted to talk to me. I usually keep my private life separate from my patients, but my experience with Hailey helped me realize that sometimes stepping across the divide is the right thing to do. What had helped me when I was Hailey's age had been the few adults who befriended me. I wanted to be that safe adult, that sympathetic listener for other young people, and I knew I had been, however briefly, for Hailey.

But she crumpled up the paper, threw it at me, and stomped off to her parents' car.

A few evenings before that first session of camp was over, the kids put on the long-anticipated production of *Wicked*, directed by Eric, with outstanding performances by talented children and staff. I went backstage to congratulate the cast members, Eric, and his ever-present assistant Wallace but they were being swarmed by fans and I couldn't get close. The next morning, on my last Pill Patrol run, I caught up with Eric.

"I want to congratulate you on a *wicked* good performance," I said, having fun with teenage lingo.

"Can I tell you something on the down-low?" He looked at me. "I know I can." He drew a deep breath. "This is my last summer at camp. I haven't told my parents yet, but I'm not coming back."

In a flash I knew why. For some time I had sensed that Eric was gay. Why else had I instinctively held back from asking him who *he* was crushing on or had hooked up with as we drove around camp, gossiping? Why had I never teased him about joining in on the trippers' late-night parties? As for Einstein, I had a feeling that he was more to Eric than merely his stagehand. But Eric was so deeply in the closet, especially to his parents. He could never come out here at this camp. This was not an accepting or emotionally safe place for a gay person. One of the things camp teaches young people is what it is to be male or female. It can be a place to experience awakening feelings of sexuality, of which, to be sure, there are many variations. But at a camp like this there were only a few acceptable choices, and being gay was not one of them.

Eric thanked me and said goodbye. Though he didn't confide in me, I believe he knew I understood and would keep his secret safe.

On my last day at Camp Carson, early that morning, Caitlin and I went on our last hike. Again, I invited her to visit me in the ICU. "Sounds awesome," she said, but I didn't think I'd hear from her. She and Kitch never did warm up to me again after that incident with Tom.

There were certainly things I would miss about Camp Carson. I had many pleasant days there. I took one last look at myself in the MC's waiting room mirror. No, I hadn't lost any weight—the food had been too delicious—but I was fitter and trimmer. I now owned a pile of clothes that I'd never wear again, but they held good memories. I vowed to keep up my new commitment to exercise back in the city. As for all those funky hip-hop moves and grinds that I'd learned? I probably should have saved them for the privacy of home, under the dark of night, but I went ahead and did a short demonstration of "Souljah Boy" for my kids.

Harry covered his eyes. "If anyone asks, say you don't know her," he deadpanned to Max.

"Who are you and what have you done with our mother?" Max wailed.

But I had gotten what I'd wanted out of camp. I had observed first-hand the pleasures to be had if you were a part of the fun and secrets, and also the perilous position you were in if you weren't. I had a lot of sympathy for the relatively few kids I'd met who simply weren't able to join in. Sometimes they were excluded from the group, but some excluded themselves. The group wasn't always at fault; there were kids who weren't able or didn't want to let themselves in. They needed more privacy, or more rest from the constant activity and demands of having fun. Fun could be exhausting. At camp, so much depended on your ability to cut loose, lose yourself, be silly. I loved the campers' utter lack of self-consciousness as they sang the "Funky Chicken" or "Little Bunny Foo Foo" or their full-on engagement in zany antics, like the counsellor who made announcements using a banana or a broom as a microphone; a table of girls all with orange-peel smiles; Eric and Wallace sauntering around with hollowed-out watermelons on their heads like green helmets. I delighted in watching their delight.

What I really understood was the connection of kids to their counsellors. As parents, we like to believe we have the greatest influence on our kids, but I saw the power of peers and, even more so, that of the counsellors whom the kids look up to. They are the ones the kids are watching. They are the ones they idolize and try to emulate.

I knew I'd never return to this camp. Camp Carson was far too big, profit-driven, and materialistic for me. That exclusive "members-only" feel I'd picked up on the first day stayed with me the entire time. Differences were, at best, tolerated, never embraced nor encouraged. All the same, I felt proud of the work I had done there. I helped a lot of kids go through the experience of a minor illness or injury and learn that they could be cared for or comforted by someone other than their own parents. I felt grateful to Kitch for all he taught me about the "care and feeding" of healthy children. I'd met many fine, talented children and young adults who would likely go far in life. They'd been given every opportunity to succeed, every advantage that money can buy. Among them there were also some terribly unhappy, depressed, and anxiety-ridden teenagers who weren't getting the attention or treatment they needed. In some ways their lives were stressful, and in other ways they were coddled and sheltered. They faced very few hardships and even fewer opportunities to take risks or solve their own problems. Most kids overcame the difficulties they encountered at camp by themselves or with the help of their bunk mates or counsellors. However, in too many cases, children were deprived of the opportunity to solve their own problems by adults stepping in to fix things for them.

I was thoroughly exhausted and ready to go home. I needed to recover from so much fun. Was there even a place for a grown-up like me at a camp like this? I was surprised when the Carsons invited me back. Despite Wendy's annoyance with me for leaving camp during Colour Wars and the minor disagreements I'd had with Coach Carson over the summer, there must have been enough about my work that they liked for them to offer me the position of coordinator of the Medical Centre.

"You'll run the show," Wendy said. "It's time we began turning things over. Eric will soon be taking over the business, as you know."

I didn't betray Eric's secret and although I declined, Coach Carson didn't think I could resist. "You'll be back," he predicted. "You're a camper now. It's in your blood."

My own kids had a blast at Camp Carson but couldn't say they preferred it over Na-Gee-La. They simply loved camp. The day before we left, Harry ran off to the forest to release the snake and the frogs he'd caught (kept in separate jars, naturally) back into their natural habitat. Max was pleased with the new word he'd learned: "Lacoste." He begged me to buy him one of those polo shirts with the tiny green alligator, but sadly for him, he had parents who balked at spending eighty dollars on a child's shirt.

The last night farewell campfire was a stirring ceremony. A chunk of charred wood—legend was it had been salvaged from last year's campfire, and from all Carson final campfires before that—was passed carefully around the circle. A display of intertwined canoe paddles spelling out CARSON was set ablaze on the dock at the waterfront. It was a sweet moment.

After a few of the usual rollicking songs, including a final round of the "Cha-Cha Slide," the songs grew quieter and the kids became pensive as they stared into the flickering flames, their arms wrapped around each other, swaying back and forth. The last song was "Taps." The wistful mood it conjured felt strange in this usually jovial place. The children sat cross-legged around the fire. I could see my own two smiling boys sitting side by side with their friends, their arms entwined, leaning into one another as they swayed and sang the simple words.

Day is done, gone the sun,
From the hills, from the lake,
From the skies.
All is well, safely rest,
God is nigh.

Still sitting outside the circle, but singing softly along with them, I was momentarily jarred at the unexpected mention of "God." *Who said anything about God?* It seemed out of place here at this camp, which, for me, had been completely devoid of any sense of spirituality.

As the bonfire died down, my summer at Camp Carson came to an end and along with it, I decided then and there, my career as a camp nurse. It was time to get back to my work in the ICU with real patients. My camp days were done, *gone the sun*.

10

CAMP GOLDILOCKS

Sticky, heavy, humid—that's August in Toronto. A sign in the window of an industrial laundry caught my eye as I drove past on my way to work at the hospital.

Who wants to wash dirty camp clothes?
We do!

Too late—I'd already done load after load of laundry in my own washing machine at home after first dumping out my kids' duffel bags onto our back lawn to air out the rumpled, mildewed clothes; shake loose the sand, clumps of dirt, and little twigs; and set free the stowaway spiders and assorted bugs.

"They smell like camp," my kids had said gleefully, thrusting their noses into the heap to inhale traces of sun, wind, earth, and campfires. "Don't wash them," they begged.

There were also a few mysteries in those musty duffel bags. In Max's bag there was a red striped towel I didn't recognize. And who was Eli Lipton? Well, we had a pair of his swimming trunks. As for their toiletries, Max's bar of soap was bone-dry, the brand's imprint clearly intact on its smooth, untouched surface. I felt reassured about Harry's hygiene when I saw his gear, but then he told me that his stuff only *looked* used because

his counsellors had gone around on the last night of camp
dumping shampoo, squeezing out toothpaste, and roughing up
the bars of soap to fool the parents.

Camp had changed my kids in noticeable ways. Both were
stronger and more confident. They held themselves with more
assurance and were definitely sassier, with traces of new attitude, probably picked up from their teenage counsellors. They
were developing their own private lives and friendships that were
separate from me. I felt like we needed to get re-acquainted.

The boys were also going through camp withdrawal. Irritable
and restless, they wandered from room to room as if they didn't
know where to put themselves. They couldn't handle the quiet
after so many days filled with noise and laughter. After three
weeks of constantly being part of the group, sleeping, eating,
playing side by side with their friends, it felt strange to them to
be on their own. After being outdoors every day, in the lake, the
fresh air, with the wind on their faces, they were now cooped
up in the city in the close, sticky heat, breathing the smog and
pollution. I knew for sure they were missing camp the day I
found them in the kitchen trying to roast marshmallows over
the electric toaster.

August dragged on. We cooled ourselves off in chlorinated
public pools, rode the subway downtown to visit museums and
art galleries, and went on outings during which they kindly
refrained from uttering the banned "b" word. But they weren't
bored so much as longing to be outdoors with their friends,
enjoying the freedom of camp.

As for next summer, it was a long way off and I knew one
thing: my camp nurse days were over, contrary to Coach
Carson's prediction.

At the end of August I got a call from Wendy Carson. She told
me Samantha had been admitted to the hospital and was still
there, that Wayne's and Alexa Rose's parents had already signed

them up for next summer, and that Hailey had run off with her biker boyfriend and that her parents (who were now separated and had filed for divorce, as Hailey predicted) had no idea where she was. Wendy finally asked me if I would come back next year. I thanked her but declined.

A week later, when the kids went back to school in early September, I felt the relief of every frazzled parent. The school supplies store TV jingle expressed it perfectly: "It's the most wonderful time of the year!" I was happy to have them back at school but I did feel a pang as Max sailed out the door to what he jokingly referred to as "jail."

I had more understanding for kids like him who have difficulty being cooped up all day indoors, expected to sit still and quietly. In some ways, camp and school were diametrically opposed. There were many things you couldn't do at school that were allowed, even encouraged, at camp. I made a list:

- Make noise—even yell at the top of your lungs
- Dance, listen to loud music
- Daydream and stargaze
- Be messy, mess up, mess around
- Be silly
- "Waste time," putter around, or even be idle
- Try something new and screw it up, like wiping out on water-skis or making a lopsided clay pot
- Dabble in different activities and interests
- Throw your arms up in the air and shout, move around, and jump for joy

At camp, these are sanctioned, even encouraged, activities. Not at school.

I've visited schools, walked down corridors, and this is what I've heard.

- Stop talking!
- Settle down. Shhh. Be quiet. Use indoor voices only!
- Do as you're told.
- Walk, don't run!
- Settle down! Stay in your seats.
- Stop that! Don't do that!
- (And, worst of all) Sit still!

I never heard those admonitions at camp. School certainly can't be camp, but couldn't school take a lesson or two from camp? Camp does a lot of things right and is a satisfying environment for sociable, exuberant, active kids.

At school, children are expected to sit for hours on end. Their brains are exercised, their bodies so much less so. At camp, when I'd watched children in motion, their faces flushed and jubilant, smiling naturally and breathing deeply, they looked so content. I never once saw anyone look worried or anxious or heard any complaints about homesickness from kids when they were engrossed in play, actively moving, or creating something. I was beginning to think that "sitting still" was overrated.

I asked Ivan what he did during school vacation, growing up in South Africa where summer was in January and February. He told me about exploring the fields, forests, and streets of Johannesburg by foot and on bicycle, and how his mother only said "be home by dark." As for me, I had also had a great deal of independence, travelling all over Toronto on my own from the age of twelve. As a teenager I went backpacking across Europe and Israel. We both had had a lot more independence and freedom than our own kids do. We chauffeur them to organized activities and schedule every hour. So little in their lives is impromptu, spontaneous, or unsupervised. What does a child lose by all of this shuttling around and constant surveillance? What do they miss out on by not having the opportunity to explore the world, especially the *natural* world? Being out in nature is completely different from playing in playgrounds, parks, and backyards. How were our kids going to protect, much less save, our environment, if they didn't know it intimately and feel a connection to it? I was coming to the conclusion that in many ways camp was an ideal place for children.

By winter, I missed camp. Coach Carson was definitely right about one thing—camp does create memories to be enjoyed long after it's over. Images of those early morning walks, the crackling campfires, gorgeous sunsets, and singalongs burned brightly in my mind. I would also miss that little window I'd had into my kids' world.

"But you complained about it when you were there," Ivan reminded me. "Remember how homesick you were?"

Of course! I'd felt lonely and out of place. I thought about how hard I'd worked and all the nighttime interruptions. Why go back and have to learn a whole slew of kids' names along with all their nicknames? Why put up with the deafening mealtime food frenzy and running after kids who didn't bother coming for their meds? Why be exposed to the late-night antics of horny counsellors? I wasn't doing that again, but I had to find a camp for our kids. I didn't want a crazy, disorganized camp, or a big, fancy one, either. I knew I'd better choose wisely this time, because all of our flitting from camp to camp, making friends and never seeing them again, couldn't be good for anyone.

It was late April and I still had not made summer plans. I looked into camps and found a huge variety out there. There were day camps and overnight ones. Some camps had twenty kids and others sounded like little villages with fifteen hundred campers on sprawling acres of land. There were camps that specialized in magic, math, photography, sports, technology, and cyber arts; camps for budding marine biologists and others for young filmmakers. There were camps for every religion: Jewish camps of every style of observance, Christian bible camps that "teach the love of Christ to kids and have a blast doing it," as well as Islamic, Hindu, and Sikh camps. There were weight-loss camps, boot camps, wilderness survival camps, and even a grief camp for children who had recently experienced the death of a loved one. Fresh-air funds and other community charities provided a wide range of non-profit camps for kids who couldn't otherwise afford to go. Some of these were camps for kids with chronic illnesses such as asthma, diabetes, or cancer, or for kids with special needs. Some were for at-risk children and provided an escape from their homes where there was substance abuse or domestic violence. There were camps that had appealing names like Spring Lake, Pleasant Valley, Lake View; happy-sounding camps like Camp Surprise, Camp Cheerful, and New Horizons; and ones with deliriously over-the-top names such as Camp Happy Days, Summer Fantasy, and Kids' World. A handful of camps had Aboriginal-inspired names like Cherokee, Algonquin, Cree, and Mohawk, but I had to wonder if there were any real native influences at those camps, other than the fact that the land they were on probably belonged to those peoples at one time.

How did one choose a camp? I wanted to find the right fit for my kids, though truth be told, so far they'd been happy wherever I put them.

I asked my nurse friends who were parents what they were doing with their kids. Many had signed them up for day camps in the city; others were sending their children to hockey camps to improve their game. Some had summer cottages, where the grandparents would be looking after the kids. I was surprised at how many were going to let their children hang out at home, with no plans or supervision whatsoever. I wasn't so brave, but I still hadn't come up with an alternative. Soon, our options would be down to road hockey, video games, and the occasional trips to the zoo. Threats of the banned "b" word!

By June, with summer vacation only a few weeks away, I pulled out a file of brochures I'd been collecting. More and more I saw new definitions of "camp," quite different from the old-fashioned notions I still clung to. Take "Hospital Camp," whose goal was to interest teenagers in a career in health care. (Their on-line brochure stated that they held back the nursing compo-nent for the end in order to save the "best for last," but had so far managed to interest only one camper in a career in nursing.) Another camp listed a wide range of activities: "pottery, arts and crafts, tennis, dance and swim instruction, forensic science, canoeing and tennis."

Whoa! Beep, beep. Back it up. Crime scene investigation? What would that be, fingerprint examination, DNA analysis, and blood stain evidence for ten-year-olds?

There were theme camps such as "Nineteenth Century," where kids got to dress up in faithfully reproduced period cos-tumes and learned to be milliners, cabinet builders, artisans, and blacksmiths. What about the "manners and etiquette" camp? (How badly behaved were the kids who needed that? If manners were the issue, their problems were way bigger than which fork to use.) And for kids whose behaviour was really obnoxious, parents could always send them to Dr. Phil's Brat Camp. Budding performers could go to camp to learn to be a DJ, a stand-up comedian, or a circus acrobat under the Big Top.* What about Cowboy Camp? "Bring your own lariat and be a real cowhand!" There was culinary arts camp, where kids could learn the rudiments of being a chef; Camp Millionaire, where campers would devise schemes to create financial freedom; and Camp Great Masters, where children would travel to Italy to

---

* No, Harry, don't worry; I won't sign us up for that one. My circus days are over.

learn the techniques of Michelangelo. At adventure camps, children could be princesses, wizards, pirates, or astronauts. It went on and on. Did summer fun have to be complicated and expensive? I needed a simple solution: a camp that was not too big, not too small, not too chaotic, and not too sophisticated. A camp that was *juuust* right. I needed Camp Goldilocks.

Just when I was getting desperate for a camp, I got a call from Rudy Schwartz, a man desperate for a nurse. He'd gotten my number from a friend. He was the camp director of Camp Solomon, the one type of camp I'd been avoiding: a faith-based camp. As far as I knew, religion and fun didn't mix.

Camp Solomon was a liberal, Jewish camp in the beautiful Kawartha Highlands of Northeast Ontario. It offered all the standard camp activities but religious education too. I wasn't sure about that. Playing as well as praying? My first response was no; not for my kids, and definitely not for me. What kid would want to sit through classroom lectures or go to prayer services?

After only a brief chat on the phone, Rudy was ready to sign me up. "It'll be a barter system: your nursing services for the camp fees."

That was a given. He was going to have to seriously sweeten the deal. I waited.

"What activities does your camp have?" I asked to break the silence, since it didn't seem like he was going to.

"The usual. Swimming, canoe trips, a ropes course, Colour Wars. The whole shebang but more than that."

"Like what, exactly?"

"Well, man, we don't have all the latest bells and whistles," he conceded. Rudy's hippie-speak and joking manner made me guess he was smiling at the other end of the phone. "But we have enough."

I fired a few more questions at him. "How many campers do you have?"

"Around 350." I heard him shuffling through papers on his desk. "Maybe 360 or so, I can't say for sure."

Compared to one hundred individuals at the cozy but crazy Camp Na-Gee-La, and the overwhelming eight hundred campers, plus a few hundred staff members at Camp Carson, this medium-sized camp sounded manageable. "How religious is it?"

That was the defining question. Oh, I knew all about the various streams in Judaism, the main ones being Orthodox, Conservative, and Reform. Or, as my father used to say, "crazy, hazy, and lazy." Rudy explained that Camp Solomon was modern, questioning, and egalitarian. There were daily prayer services and classes led by rabbis. The food was kosher and blessings were recited before and after each meal. He explained more about the lessons, which were based on the weekly Torah portion, and lastly, he described the highlight of the week, the celebration of the Sabbath.

It didn't sound like it had too many rules and prohibitions. *Judaism Lite.* Perhaps this was the Goldilocks camp I'd been looking for. A religious camp, yes, but open-minded. Neither fly-by-night and spartan nor ostentatious and fancy. It might be *juuuust right.* I agreed to meet with Rudy at his office the next day.

As I got off the elevator in the building where the camp office was located, I was greeted by a dog. He was a mangy mutt—beagle and Lab mix, I guessed—who must have had some sheepdog in him, too, because he herded me down the hall to his master's messy, cluttered office. I found Rudy sitting in a canoe on the floor beside his desk, smoothing the inside of it with some sort of a tool. He got up to greet me and introduce his dog, Ringo. Rudy was a short, middle-aged man with a long, silver ponytail. He was wearing blue jeans, a psychedelic tie-dye T-shirt, and unappealing white socks with sandals, standard camp style. Rudy's cramped, crowded office was filled with a jumble of camping gear, musical instruments, and equipment.

It looked like he was having a garage sale. There was a junked-up desk, a tangle of life jackets on the floor, a pile of unfolded tents, and guitars and guitar cases lined up against the wall, beside music stands covered in sheet music. The wall behind his desk was crowded with plaques, diplomas, and inspirational sayings, some hanging lopsided. A few caught my eye.

Be kind, for everyone you meet is fighting a great battle.
– Philo of Alexandria.

"Who's that?"
"An old Jewish sage."

God's message to humanity is brought to life through the child.
—Rabbi Leo Baeck.

"Who's that?"
"The founder of the Reform Jewish movement."

Who is wise? He who learns from every person.
Who is happy? He who is satisfied with what he has.
– Ben Zoma.

"Who's that?"
"Some medieval rabbi dude."
I tried to decipher a quote from the Talmud written in old-fashioned Hebrew, but I knew only a smattering of the modern, spoken language. "What does that one say?"

"Something to the effect that a father's job is to teach his son how to swim. I take it to mean that as parents we have a responsibility to teach our children how to survive. Yeah, that's what camp's about."

He told me about himself. He'd grown up in a strictly religious family but had rejected the Orthodox way of Judaism. He and his wife—they'd met at camp—got into drugs and yoga and gone off to India to live in an ashram. Unfortunately, she had died of cancer a few years ago, but in his year of mourning, through the daily recitation of the traditional prayer for the dead with a small community of other mourners, he'd "found his way back." He paused to turn the tables. "How 'bout you?" He looked at me skeptically. "You don't strike me as a camp person."

How could he tell? I'd managed to fool Carson. I told Rudy about my previous summers as a camp nurse and my professional qualifications. What he didn't ask and I didn't mention, because it didn't seem like a requirement, was that I didn't go to synagogue, didn't keep kosher, and I wasn't about to start. I hadn't rejected Judaism so much as I'd never really embraced it, certainly not the rules or rituals of it anyway. My father had been an involved member of a Reform synagogue, but for him Judaism was a cerebral exercise. He loved to tussle over intellectual questions and debate issues but he didn't practise many of the observances. My mother told me repeatedly that she was against all organized religions and warned me against religion like it was something harmful. "If there were no religions, the world would be a better place," she often said. Surprisingly, in her last few semilucid years, she turned to the Baha'i faith, because, as she put it, "it's about love."

"Tell me about the campers," I asked.

Rudy picked up one end of the canoe and caressed the wood. He looked like he wanted to get back to working on it. "It's a diverse group. We have kids from wealthy families, from middle-class families, along with children who are subsidized by philanthropic organizations like the United Way. Kids who live in mansions, and others who live in public housing. We have children who are in foster care. Kids from interfaith households. Kids from same-sex parents. Kids from Jamaica, India and Ethiopia, and China. Every summer we host a contingent of counsellors from Israel. Most kids are Jewish, but not all. Oh, I almost forgot." He put down the canoe. "I should explain about our inclusion program. We have campers with various needs and abilities and we help them integrate into camp life."

"Together with the so-called normal ones?" How well I knew how needy "normals" could be.

"The new term for 'normal' kids is 'typicals.' At Camp Sol we have some campers and staff who have special needs. We do everything we can to help every kid enjoy camp to the fullest of his or her ability. We have specialized staff to support our vision of inclusion."

"You mean to help the special needs kids?"

"Not just them. There are lots of situations at camp in which someone might feel they don't fit in, don't you agree?" I nodded. "Off the top of my head..." Rudy closed his eyes to better help him recall the kids who had special needs because he clearly didn't think of them as different from all the other campers. "We have a twelve-year-old coming for the first time this summer. He's been recently diagnosed with diabetes and uses an insulin pump. The head of tennis is a paraplegic. He's competed in the Paralympics and gets around that court pretty fast in an electric wheelchair. We have a few staff with Down Syndrome who assist the counsellors. We have kids with Tourette's and a few with varying degrees of autism." He scratched his head to help him come up with the others. "We've got a fair share of kids who may act a bit strange, but everyone finds a way to fit in. Oh, yeah, we have a kid who uses a wheel-chair and comes with an attendant who lives with him in the cabin with the other boys his age. I can't understand a word he says but the kids do."

"Aren't there camps for children with special needs?"

"Our parents say they don't want their kids segregated because of their medical diagnosis. The kids themselves don't see it as a problem. It's just the way they are."

"I guess it's good for them to be there."

"At first, that's what I thought, too, but I've discovered it's even better for us." He thought about it. "It has an interesting effect on the other campers. They step up and take on more leadership. I also think it makes them behave better."

"What about bullying? How do you handle it?" Since he didn't seem to have any questions for me, I interviewed *him*.

"Bullying isn't a big issue at Camp Sol. Maybe praying together with their friends makes kids a little less likely to be cruel." He went on to explain that they provided anti-bullying training for the counsellors and had a rule that a counsellor stayed in the cabin every evening, a time when bullying often occurred and homesickness peaked. "The main thing is that every child feel included. Camp Sol isn't perfect, but we work at it. On most days, it's pretty darn good."

"What about the prayers and the study sessions? Don't the kids complain?"

"They complain a lot," he said with a playful grin, "about the food and the mosquitoes, but I've never heard them complain about a day of rest. What's there to complain about? We can all use that. Camp can get pretty hectic, as you probably know."

In theory, a day of rest wasn't a bad idea. Like most nurses, I didn't have set days off work. They occurred willy-nilly. My "weekend" could easily be a Tuesday-Wednesday. My days off were spent recovering from the night shift, shopping for groceries, or attacking my "to do" list of chores and errands that I didn't get to the rest of the week. But a *mandated* day of rest? I didn't know about that. I recalled how the counsellors at Camp Na-Gee-La had ridiculed religion. "Praying?" Mike, the director, had scoffed. "What's that all about? Is that like God's your imaginary friend?" Yet, I also recalled the discomfiting feeling

I'd had when "God" was uttered at that farewell campfire at
Camp Carson. For me, something had been missing at both of
those camps, but was it God? How would my kids take to going
to a camp where they would have to study and pray? Well, I
may have opted out of religion, but I hadn't turned away from
spirituality. "I guess it'll be good for my kids," I said to Rudy.

"That's Pediatric Judaism." He looked at me askance, like he
was suddenly having second thoughts about my suitability.

Well, perhaps a dose of religion would do me good, too. I'd
call it Medicinal Judaism.

Rudy went off on a new tangent. "When you think about it,
camp is a shock for kids these days. Sometimes I'm amazed at
how they cope with it at all." He started getting restless; putter-
ing around with papers on his messy desk, making me realize our
meeting was drawing to a close. "We throw a bunch of city kids
together in the middle of the forest, cut them off from their electronic gadgets, put fifteen or so together in close quarters. Some
have never shared a bedroom before. For many, camp is the first
time they meet kids from another neighbourhood or from a different school. It's a huge adjustment."

I noticed he hadn't mentioned "safety," even once, and I asked
him about it.

"If safety is what parents are after, they'd better keep their
kids home," he said dismissively. He picked up a wooden paddle,
walked over to his canoe, stepped into it, and kneeled down like
he was ready to push off from shore. "All of our attempts to
keep kids safe are creating the most worried, anxious, stressed-
out kids I've ever met. The only way to keep kids safe is to teach
them how to look after themselves. Those are survival skills."
He pointed back at the quote from the Talmud, hanging on
the wall. "We're all so safety conscious these days, yet no one's
feeling any safer. Camp's a place to learn how to take risks and
confront difficulties, a place where kids can go wild, yet still be

under our wing." He smoothed his hands over the wood along the inside of the canoe. "Hey, man, do the math. When you add it up, the number of camp hours is greater than school hours, considering it's round the clock, weekends, too, especially if they stay for the whole summer. Think of the opportunity to impart some good values to our kids. Sure, there's fun, but we can do much more than keep them safe and entertained."

I liked Rudy and what he'd told me about the camp. The sight of that canoe was enticing to me, too. I could feel it luring me back in . . . to camp.

"Okay, I'll come, but on one condition."

"Shoot."

"I don't have to go to prayer services."

"Hey, no pressure, man," Rudy said, backing off, his hands up as he and Ringo walked me to the door. "Do your own thing."

"One last question," I said, just before leaving. "What about candy? What's your policy there?"

"Two tuck shop visits per week and lots of treats, but no candy or junk food from home. They don't need it and it attracts critters, especially bears. Camp Solomon is right in the heart of bear country." He said all that seriously but couldn't resist slipping back to his usual big, sunny grin.

11

SURVIVAL SKILLS

It was the summer of Crocs! It seemed like just about everyone had a pair of those stubby, rubber clogs that came in every colour of the rainbow. (To me, they looked more like toys than shoes.) Harry didn't want them but Max wanted a pair in every colour. He settled on two pairs—bright yellow ones that made him look like Donald Duck (at least he could be spotted all over camp) and turquoise ones that he promptly gave away to his new friend, Ryan, underneath him on the lower bunk.

No Crocs for me. This time I wasn't going to dress to fit in—and as it turned out I didn't need to. Camp Solomon fit me as easily and comfortably as a pair of Crocs. They say "third time's the charm," and maybe it's true. At this camp, it didn't take me long to find my groove. One of the reasons was that here there were people my own age to play with. They were adult staff, or "inclusion co-ordinators," who helped the special needs kids, as well as the ordinary needs ones, to cope with camp. There were also visiting rabbis, cantors, and educators, many of whom came with their young families. The babies in high chairs and toddlers running around outside the dining hall gave the place the feeling of family. I enjoyed having adult company and sitting together at our own table, and I think we lent a certain *gravitas* to the mealtime mayhem.

Like Max, I also made an instant new friend. Her name was Alice Gordon and she wore lavender Crocs. A public health nurse with two daughters at camp, she had also left her husband back in the city while she worked to cover the cost of camp for her children. Together with Louise Mandel (navy Crocs), the camp doctor, who came with her teenaged boys to camp, we were the health care team.

Not called the infirmary as at Camp Na-Gee-La, nor the Medical Centre as at Camp Carson, at Camp Solomon it was the Health Centre, or, as the kids called it, the Health Hut. The name itself gave it a positive spin. Nearby, Alice and I had our own quarters, clean, simple dorm rooms. It didn't take long to familiarize myself with the layout of Camp Solomon. Around the periphery, nestled in the woods, were the camper cabins, connected by paths that converged onto a main road that led to the central gathering spot, "the Tent," which provided shade, and with the flaps up, a breeze. The dining hall was a polygon-shaped building with windows on all sides that ran right up to the ceiling, providing a view of leafy green trees, a wide expanse of sky, and the clean, sparkling lake.

At this camp, morning pill call was handled differently than at Camp Carson. Campers were expected to come to *us* for their meds. The onus was on them and their counsellors to make sure they got their meds, rather than on us to track them down. They were good about coming and, perhaps because they wanted to get to breakfast, they usually arrived on time.

First to show up in the morning were two nine-year-old girls, Xiu-Ling Rosenberg and Frankie Colwin. Xiu-Ling was petite with long black hair, and Frankie was also small and wiry, pale with short brown hair, and glasses that magnified her eyes and always made her look startled.

Xiu-Ling noticed me reading her name. "It's *Zweeling*," she said helpfully. "I'm from China. My parents rescued me from being drowned by some village peasant, a.k.a. my biological father," she added cheerfully. "I have ADD and Tourette's but I'll let you know if I start ticcing 'cause I'll need the chewing gum my parents sent. It helps me." She took her friend's hand. "Frankie has ADD, too. Hey, what meds are you on this summer?" she asked Frankie, who told her. "I'm on the slow-release stuff now," Xiu-Ling boasted. "It has fewer side effects and stuff. Ask your parents to switch you over." They got their meds and walked out arm in arm.

Thirteen-year-old Sharon was in a bad mood. She had a headache and was annoyed to have to come to us for the medications she took at home independently. I explained that we had to keep meds locked up, but she was impatient and left as soon as she swallowed her pills.

We were just about to lock up when Bradley arrived at the last minute. He was on daily allergy pills but preferred to take matters into his own hands. "You may not see me from time to time," he cautioned as he slapped a baseball into his catcher's mitt over and over. *Thwack!* "I decide when to take my meds. Don't worry, I'm gifted, so I know what I'm doing." *Thwack! Thwack!*

"How will we know whether to expect you or not? Will you RSVP?" I asked.

"Oh, don't worry." *Thwack! Thwack!* He launched into the history of his allergies and all the signs and symptoms but we hurried him along so we could all get to breakfast. As we were leaving, we noticed that with all of his chattering, Bradley had forgotten to take his allergy pill, the one he had come for. "I'll take it to him," I said.

"No need. I have a feeling he'll be back." Alice pointed at the baseball he'd left behind on the counter.

When I entered the dining hall for breakfast, *camp* came back to me in a wave: the noise of hungry kids, their excited voices, the breakneck speed of eating, and the hilarious post-meal announcements. But at Camp Solomon, there was one difference. I learned not to dig in to my food as soon as I sat down but to wait until everyone arrived and recited a grace together before the meal.

After breakfast, the day's routine was also familiar. A morning clinic was held for anyone who had complaints of any sort. Most mornings, by the time Alice, Louise, and I strolled back to the Health Centre, coffee mugs still in hand, a small but vocal crowd had gathered. We handed out slips of paper for the kids to write down the reason they'd come and then decided in what order to treat them.

I went out to the waiting room. "Who's got the 'fly buzzing inside his skull'?"

A sleepy-looking boy closed his comic book and waved. "Yo. That'd be, uh, me."

I checked his ears and throat, took his temperature—Louise examined him, too—but since we couldn't find anything wrong, we offered him a fly swatter, which he declined, then sent him on his way.

Meanwhile, Alice had been busy with an anxious teenage girl who had a bump on her neck and who'd written "may have cancer." Alice put her arm around her and led her in for a thorough examination, then explained that the bump was a swollen lymph node. "They help your body fight infection," Alice reassured her. Next, she took the tall counsellor with "Big wart on foot. Been there for months" and taught him a slow-acting homemade treatment that involved duct tape. However, he chose to see Louise to get a prescription medication for a speedier remedy.

I took the boy who was "all stuffed up," and gave him a decongestant, nasal spray, and box of tissues, told him to wash his hands, and that he was good to go.

A boy who had "puked all night in cabin (throw-up tasted like dill-pickle potato chips)" was looking better, but I let him lie down for a rest.

Xiu-Ling and Frankie arrived. Xiu-Ling was crying and pointing at Frankie. "We were sitting in services and she hit me over the head with a prayerbook!"

Frankie looked pleased with herself. I examined Xiu-Ling's head and felt all over for swelling but found nothing. I placed an ice-pack on the sore spot. After a few minutes, I checked. "It's fine, now, Xiu-Ling."

"But there's a bump," she wailed, "and it hurts so much."

Alice and I looked at each other and tried not to smile. I placed the ice-pack back on for a few more minutes and returned to ask how she was doing.

"Bad. Very bad," she cried. She rubbed her head and glared at Frankie.

The morning crowd thinned out, but it picked up again as the kids starting coming for their lunch meds on their way to the dining hall. During a quiet moment Alice took the opportunity to search through the drawers for medication—anti-psychotics and behavioural drugs—that a fourteen-year-old boy named Eddie was supposed to be on. He hadn't shown up for his breakfast meds and now not for his lunchtime meds either. It wouldn't have mattered because she couldn't find the meds anywhere. Alice looked worried because already—it was only the first day of camp—we'd been hearing lots of buzz about Eddie and it wasn't good.

Seth, Eddie's counsellor, had been reporting to us that Eddie had been acting up, trash talking, and making racial slurs toward Sam, one of the other counsellors in that cabin, who was from Serbia. "Serbia is the skuzziest country in the world," Eddie had said to him. He'd been bullying a boy named Mitchell, calling him names, "pantsing" him (pulling down his pants) and threatening to give him a wedgie. He'd mocked a counsellor who had special needs, for his slow, careful way of talking. Alice called Eddie's parents to ask about the meds. His mother told her that Eddie's behaviour had improved so much lately that she and Eddie's father had agreed to let him go off his meds for camp. Alice looked worried when she got off the phone.

I continued handing out the lunchtime meds.

"Hi, I'm Chelsea." A tall girl with unruly blonde hair stepped forward, her hand outstretched for her pills. She talked at top speed and her loud voice was growing louder by the moment. "You'll be seeing a lot of me 'cause I'm on three-times-a-day meds—breakfast, lunch, and late afternoon, but not too late, otherwise, I won't sleep at night." She barely paused to take a breath. "You must be the new nurse. I heard there was a new one this summer. Hey, did you forget my name?" she practically shouted. "It's Chelsea and FYI I'm bi!"

"Biracial?" I asked. "Bilingual?" *Bisexual?*

"No, bipolar and I love it! I get mood swings." She leaned over the counter to read the menu posted on the bulletin board over our desk. "Oh, it's tacos for lunch!" She waved her hands up high over her head in jubilation. "Tacos are my most favourite food in the whole wide world!" She wrapped her arms around herself in a big hug. I couldn't help but wonder if and when Chelsea would dip down to the other end of the "pole." (And it didn't take long to find out. Only two days later, I saw her at the lake, sitting at the end of the dock, sobbing into her beach towel over a perceived slight—an unintended diss—from another camper. Luckily, her counsellor arrived on the scene and managed to coax her back to the group.)

Xiu-Ling and Frankie were soon back, for their lunchtime meds. They were giggling madly as they lined up with the other campers. Xiu-Ling had completely forgotten about her sore head but now complained about itchy bug bites. She scratched at her legs, showing me just how severe the situation was.

"I'm soooo itchy! I've got way more bites than Frankie."

"I hardly have any!" Frankie crowed.

"Why do I get covered and they don't come near you?"

"I guess the mosquitoes like me so they don't bite me."

"They like me better 'cause my blood is sweeter. Hey, I'm sweet, you're sour!"

On that first day of camp, right after lunch, I had gone to check on Daniel, the twelve-year-old with diabetes who was on an insulin pump. His care was complicated, so I asked to speak with his counsellor, and Tim stepped forward. He was a shy, serious-looking guy who listened carefully while I explained that every night at midnight Daniel was to be woken up for blood-sugar testing. If it was too high, the insulin rate would need to be increased; too low, and Daniel was to be given crackers and sugar cubes. If it was *very* low, he needed to bring Daniel immediately to the Health Centre. I described the early warning signs of hypoglycemia and how, in Daniel's case, it was very serious. Tim nodded but his quizzical expression worried me. We'd been counting on a counsellor to help with Daniel's condition and I wasn't sure about Tim.

"How will I know when it's midnight?" he asked slowly, thinking it through.

"You have a watch, don't you?"

"Yes, but..." He looked at it on his wrist. "I don't know how it works."

When I told Alice about this encounter, she explained that Tim was mentally challenged. He worked as an assistant counsellor, helping out in the cabin. Seth was Daniel's main counsellor and he would be responsible for helping Daniel manage his diabetes.

Oops! I was going to have to be a lot more sensitive. Someone with special needs didn't exactly walk around with a label, now, did they?

It was Alice's third year at Camp Solomon and I was envious of the friendly greetings she received from all the kids and how she knew not just their names and medical problems but their personalities and quirks, too. I'd never spent long enough at the other camps to have built up these relationships.

Alice and I spent the rest of that first afternoon going over charts. There was a handful of kids with chronic health issues: some were hidden, others were obvious and visible. Some problems were dormant with potential for flare-ups. There were kids who managed on their own and others who needed help from us. Sophie was a thirteen-year-old, born with spina bifida, a developmental birth defect that affected her ability to urinate. She had to catheterize herself and was prone to urinary tract infections. "We probably won't even see her," Alice told me. "Sophie is extremely private. She doesn't want the other girls in her cabin to know, only her counsellors. Don't even let on that *you* know." There was Beth, a CIT, who had been recently diagnosed with Crohn's disease.* Alice and I planned to check on her daily, assess her pain and symptoms, and give her medications. Drew was a teenager with a rare metabolic disorder that he'd had most of his life. He was on morning meds and needed once-a-day monitoring but otherwise was healthy and participated in all activities. Steven was a thirteen-year-old who used a wheelchair to get around. I had seen him motoring all over camp, accompanied by his attendant, Dave. Steven had an assortment of developmental delays and physical problems. Everyone seemed to know Steven as this was his third summer at camp. His mother insisted he be treated like all the others. "Please don't make him an object lesson," she'd written in a letter to us. "And when the kids act up and are disciplined, make sure he is, too."

---

* A type of inflammatory bowel disease characterized by bouts of painful abdominal cramping and bloody diarrhea.

We were still reviewing charts when Warren, a counsellor, suddenly rushed in with a frightened little boy in his arms. "Nathan can't breathe!" Nathan was gasping for air, chugging away at forty breaths a minute.* I jumped up and took out my stethoscope, but even before placing it on his chest I could hear how tight it was, full of high-pitched whistles and wheezes. There was very little air moving through his lungs and I knew his airways were likely constricted and inflamed. Alice grabbed an oxygen mask while I put a drug to open up his airways into a nebulizer, a device that aerosolized medication, and attached it to Nathan's face. We called for Dr. Louise to come immediately.

Nathan sat hunched over, working hard at breathing. Warren held his hand and Alice, Louise, and I stood by watching closely. When his treatment was finished, Nathan was breathing more easily but looked up at us with sad eyes. He seemed so alone in the world, even with all of us comforting him.

Alice showed Nathan how to use a small, handheld inhaler for his medication. But he had difficulty managing that, so she switched him over to a different instrument called a spacer that was easier to use. Still, it was hard for him. It took all of his concentration and he squirmed, jiggled his stick legs, and twisted his feet around on the floor as he tried to master it. I sat down to read through his chart and quickly got a better understanding why all of this was so difficult. Nathan had serious developmental problems. In his chart, there was a sample of his handwriting. It was the barely legible scrawl of a child learning how to write but Nathan was twelve years old. He looked about eight.

He'd had an asthmatic attack like this at camp the previous summer but there were few details of his health the rest of the year. Alice filled me in on the horrific story of his early childhood. Nathan had been rescued from parents who had abused him, kept

---

* Around twenty per minute is normal.

him on a leash, and tied him to a chair. Two years ago he'd been placed with a loving foster family. He enjoyed coming to camp even though it wasn't easy for him to interact with other children and he was emotionally dependent on Warren—his counsellor last summer, too—who was completely devoted to him.

As they were about to leave, Nathan reached up to be carried. Tough, eighteen-year-old Warren wearing a black do-rag and multiple earrings slung him across his chest like a guitar and Nathan clung on. I said we wanted to check him again later but Nathan shook his head, no. He didn't want to come back.

"We want to prevent this from happening again," I explained, but as soon as I said that I could tell he didn't know what "prevent" meant.

As the days went on I got to know many campers well and a few parents, too, over the phone. Daniel's mother called every other day for an update on Daniel and for a report on his blood-sugar levels. There was anxiety in her voice and I tried to reassure her that her son was doing well and under Seth's close supervision. She frequently made minor adjustments to his diet or insulin regimen. Later, when I would convey these messages to Daniel, he would roll his eyes or look exasperated. "I like to stay on the down-low about my diabetes," he told me, only coming to the Health Centre if he had to change the site of his insulin needle or pick up his supplies. Usually, he came by himself, slipping in quietly so he wouldn't be noticed, but once, he brought a cabin mate with him. "I don't like needles," the friend said, giving an involuntary shudder as he watched Daniel give himself an injection of insulin into his abdomen. Daniel looked at me and I had a feeling we were thinking the same thing: He couldn't afford not to like needles. His life depended on them.

Every day after lunch was camp-wide rest time and everyone was supposed to be in their cabin, but sometimes I would find thirteen-year-old Dylan pacing around outside my door. "Can I help you?" I'd ask, but "No, I'm good," he'd say, and run off. I could tell he was trying to place me. I remembered very well where we'd met—the ICU where I worked—but decided to keep quiet about what might be a traumatic memory for him. I told him simply, "I'm here if you want to talk."

Mitchell was a more eager visitor who stopped by frequently with minor complaints or just to chat. He was thirteen, over-weight, and more at ease with grown-ups than with kids his own age. The Health Centre was a refuge for him. He came so often that we kidded him we were going to make him our mascot. Mitchell often looked sad so I asked him how things were going.

"Camp's awesome," he said with forced cheerfulness. "My cabin mates are cool, well, except for Eddie. No one likes Eddie." His face clouded over as he told me that Eddie picked on him, called him names like "fat-boy," "wuss," and "Mitchy Mouse," and said degrading things about his sister. Then Mitchell abruptly changed the topic and made disparaging jokes about his looks or his weight, such as he was so fat that when he got into the lake, the water level rose. "I've tried diets, but they never work," he said helplessly. He was worried about an upcoming canoe trip and if he'd be able to keep up, and what he'd do if he got hungry. On another occasion, he told me, "I'm starting to think I should go home." Mitchell settled into one of the couches and made himself comfortable. "I'm thinking maybe I won't stay for the whole summer." He said it like going home was an option, but we both knew his parents had signed him up until the end of August. "See, I hate the position I'm in. If I go home, I feel like a failure, but if I stay, I feel horrible. Camp isn't for me. There's no privacy and it's just go, go, go, all the time and, Eddie... well, he and I don't get along."

I felt a swell of affection for him. He enjoyed mountain biking and when I mentioned that, he visibly brightened. We talked about how Lance Armstrong had used his bike to conquer cancer and maybe he could do the same with his homesickness? Mitchell seemed to cheer up a bit with that idea and went off in a better mood, for now.

Another camper I was becoming fond of was Amy. She was a bright, creative twelve-year-old who had high-functioning autism. I'd seen her around camp, sometimes with her friends, other times standing alone, immersed in her own, very different world. Sometimes she'd stand and stare into the distance or peer down at the ground for a long time. Once I found her gazing into a single green leaf, chanting softly to herself, "back to leaves, back to leaves," over and over. Occasionally she came to us describing "weird sensations" in her body that bothered her. They usually went away on their own if we helped her take her mind off them.

Once her counsellor brought Amy in. "Amy didn't eat a thing at lunch," she said, looking worried, "well, only the parmesan cheese. That's all she put on her plate, a huge pile of parmesan cheese, but she just picked at that and kept rolling her eyes right back in her head, you know like this." She did a frighteningly good imitation. "It was freaking me right out—I mean, it was weird, even for you, Amy, no offence." She put her arm around Amy, which must have cued her to realize her counsellor was kidding, so after an awkward delay, she gave a little laugh.

Amy didn't usually volunteer much information, but that day, she did want to explain what was bothering her. "I was thinking about mud and when I think about mud, I can't eat." She gazed around the room, averting her eyes from us when she spoke. "I can only eat white foods and they can't touch each other." She spoke in chopped sentences and a monotone, saying each word in a sentence like it was on a list, every item of equal value. As if suddenly overcome with exhaustion, Amy moved over to the couch in her strange, floating way, stretched out and stared up at the ceiling, quietly describing its topography to herself. It was as if she had become the object of her rapt attention, just as I'd seen with the leaf, or another time with a handful of sand. Mud disturbed Amy greatly but she loved sand. I'd seen her sitting for hours on the beach running her fingers through the sand, chortling happily to herself. We decided to let her rest for the afternoon until she was ready to join her cabin again.

I was beginning to expand my notions of what to expect in a child; there were many different ways to be normal, and clearly there was a spectrum of normalcy. I enjoyed being at a camp that managed to accommodate a wide range of kids with a variety of abilities and to find ways to live and play together.

It was turning into a pleasant summer. Alice, Louise, and I worked well together and were a great team. Other than at meals, I didn't see much of Rudy, the camp director. He was either at the canoe docks with Ringo, his constant companion, or in his camp office, which was just as cluttered with equipment and repair jobs on the go as his city office had been.

Rudy was a quiet leader but he made his presence felt. I remember an incident in the dining hall. After each meal music was played, usually a pop or rock song, which was the signal to get up and clear the tables. As soon as the music started, the kids jumped to their feet and boogied around the room, returning dishes to the counter, scraping plates, and stacking the cups and cutlery. Then, once they were back in their seats, they launched into a longer after-the-meal prayer, this one accompanied by banging the tables, stomping their feet, clapping their hands, and making motions, each corresponding to a line of the prayer. It was fun to be in the midst of it all and I even found myself joining in from time to time. But one day, things got out of control. Kids were adding nonsense words and making rude gestures. Rudy got up and strode to the front of the room. When he spoke, his voice was so strong he didn't need to use the microphone.

"Stop!" he said sternly and silence fell. "This is a prayer, not merely a song. We're going to start over from the beginning. Pounding on the table is okay. Shouting is okay. Making noise is okay. But changing the words or making fun of it is not okay." Afterward, he kept the counsellors back. "Your kids are watching you. They take their cue from you," he reminded them. "If you show respect, they will, too."

It never happened again.

Most afternoons, Alice and I locked up and went for a walk along a trail in the woods, staying in touch with a walkie-talkie that one of us always carried. Alice was a true nature lover who appreciated the outdoors in a way I was still learning to. She was always looking around, seeing everything we encountered with a sense of wonder and delight, as if we had entered a museum full of exquisite and precious things. She showed me the delicate colours and intricate striations inside a strip of birchbark that had peeled off the tree. Once, she stopped me just in time from treading upon a large frog sitting on the path in front of us. It had huge, bulging eyes, a pulsating neck, and was so perfectly camouflaged I had almost missed it. Another time, she pointed out a bird that was chasing a persistent chipmunk away from its nest. "What chipmunk eats birds?" I asked.

"She's protecting her eggs," Alice explained.

"How do you see these things? I walk right past them."

"You're a city girl," Alice said with a chuckle.

You only see what you know. Kitch's words came back to me.

As we walked, Alice and I fell easily into intimate conversation as if we'd been friends for years. She told me about her marriage to a Jewish man and her conversion to Judaism. She hadn't converted at her husband's request nor to appease her in-laws but because she was sincerely drawn to the Jewish religion. She loved going to services at camp and felt the prayers and songs in a deeply spiritual way.

The daily services were held in an outdoor chapel in a clearing in the woods. I usually took that time to phone home to Ivan or to catch up with paperwork quietly in the Health Centre. But one day, when it wasn't in use, I went to the chapel by myself to take a closer look. Nestled in the forest, it consisted of a simple wood podium facing benches made of long, heavy logs, arranged in concentric half-circles. Interspersed among the benches were tall trees that provided shade and a canopy of leaves and branches. The blue lake could be seen through the trees. For a few minutes I sat by myself, enjoying the quiet and solitude that are usually so hard to find at camp.

Perhaps taking a few moments out of each day to express gratitude and to sit in quiet reflection did have a positive effect on all of us. Maybe it was, as Rudy had also suggested, that the presence of the special-needs children and staff brought out the best in the others. I think it also had something to do with Rudy himself. To Rudy, running a camp was a moral enterprise, not just a commercial business venture. The counsellors were a major influence, too. In many ways they were exactly like counsellors I'd met elsewhere—just as wild at night, just as mature or well-mannered, or *not*. However, counsellors here made an extra, concerted effort to ensure that each child was part of the group and no one was left out. These counsellors tried to be role models and leaders, not just babysitters or pals. On my first visit to a cabin, I saw a sign on the door, announcing, "Welcome to our crib!" Posted inside the door was a list of rules the kids had come up with under the direction of their counsellors:

1. Express yourself, but don't start drama.
2. Listen to one another.
3. Respect other people's space.
4. Don't touch anybody's stuff unless you ask first.
5. Stay clean (showers, flush toilets, etc.).
6. Tell someone if you are going somewhere.
7. No swearing unless absolutely necessary.
8. No violence or rude gestures like flipping the bird.

"Yeah, like that's all going to happen," I heard one kid say scornfully as I stood reading the list. I agreed those rules probably weren't going to be followed to the letter, but putting them in writing seemed like a good place to start.

I saw other examples of counsellors leading the way.

A spider was spotted in the dining hall and after the initial screams died down, I heard a counsellor's calm voice. "Let's take it outside and put it back into nature. That's its home." They all trooped after her to help her set it free.

I liked the gentle, low-pressure swim test and the way the staff referred to the ones who "hadn't completed their swim test, *yet*," rather than saying they'd failed.

There seemed to be an unstated acceptance that not every child was sporty or good-looking or popular. At this camp, a child didn't need certain clothes, or to be "normal" or mainstream to fit in. Here, the attitude toward competition wasn't the sloppy love-fest of "everyone's a winner," nor was it awards and accolades only for the outstanding athletes. I saw kids who didn't get a lead role in the play or make a particular sports team and how their counsellors helped them roll with the punches. Here, there was simple, modest recognition for achievement and also for trying your best. The message was, you can be whatever kind of kid you are; you can find something at which to shine.

When we discovered that Jake, a fifteen-year-old, had a bad case of lice and told him he'd have to go home to be treated, he was so angry he punched a door with his fist. "Please don't make me leave. I'll shave my head," he pleaded. "I look forward to camp all year." But when he heard that his little sister Jenny had lice too, and saw her crestfallen face, he changed his tune. "Sure, I'll go home with you, Jennster," he said, then explained to me, "Our dad works a lot and he won't have time to take care of her hair." He put his arm around her. "Don't worry, Jenny-Benny, I'll pick out the nits."

As a parent, I'm lenient about bedtimes, negligent about homework, lackadaisical about unmade beds, junk food, and crumbs on the floor, but I'm a raging dictator when it comes to my kids being respectful, kind, and considerate. It's practically the only "rule" in our household. Somehow, this camp had created a culture where kindness was the expectation. It was even expressed in writing. On a wall of names of sponsors of the camp, I read the inscription under a photograph of the Solomon family patriarch, a twinkly-eyed, distinguished-looking man: "Be Good to Each Other."

And because I wasn't needed in the Health Centre all the time, I got out and met everyone. Rudy's daughter, Layla Schwartz, was the head tripper. She was studying environmental science at university and was exactly the kind of capable, take-charge person I'd want with me if I was out in the wilderness. *She'd get me home*, I thought. Layla referred to her specialty as "survival skills" and explained it to me. "It's learning how to find your way home when you're lost in foreign territory, tie the right knot to get the job done, build a secure shelter out of next to nothing, feed yourself with potatoes you roasted over the fire, and make do with what you've got." Layla knew a lot of useful information so I asked her about something I'd been wondering about. "What should I do if I'm in the forest and I see a bear?"

"Most important: don't make eye contact. Bears feel confronted when you look into their eyes," she said straightaway. "Get up on your tippy-toes to make yourself look as big as possible and spread your arms out. Also, make a lot of noise. Shout at it."

"What should I say?" I asked, giggling.

"Go away, you bad bear!" she answered, giggling along with me.

Layla had an assistant named Alon, a husky, muscular guy who had a gentle manner and was great with the kids, especially the ones who were nervous about going out on a canoe trip. For a first-year counsellor, it was considered an achievement to be a tripper, so he must have proven himself to have made the grade.

Another rising star was Matti, the head song-leader who was something of a camp celebrity. His irresistible music and charismatic personality attracted all ages.

Seth was a terrific counsellor who had his hands full that particular summer with a challenging cabin that included Daniel, the boy with diabetes, Mitchell, who was miserably homesick, and Eddie, who was causing a lot of trouble.

Even the rabbis added a lot of pizzazz to camp! Rabbi Emily came with her partner, Cynthia, and their baby daughter. The kids adored her—she was hip, into fitness, wore funky clothes, and had a sleek, chic haircut. Rabbi Danny played folk and blues guitar, knew hundreds of songs, and was an avid waterskier who helped many children get up on skis for the first time. The rabbis swam and canoed with the kids, played soccer with them, and even went out on canoe trips with them, sharing along the way lessons from the bible about respecting our environment.

As pleasant as that first summer at Camp Solomon was for me, there was a temporary blip of mild misery for a number of kids when an outbreak of upper respiratory infections started running through camp. They were getting colds and asthma flare-ups. You could see them everywhere you looked, sniffling into tissues and giving the familiar "salute," the upward rubbing of a dripping nose with open hand. Seasonal allergic rhinitis, also called hay fever, was in full bloom, too, with lots of sneezing, itchy, runny noses, and red eyes. Many kids were started on allergy meds, puffers, and antibiotics for secondary infections. We were going through lots of boxes of tissues, cough medicine, and throat lozenges and serving up plenty of hot broth, lemon tea with honey, and sympathy. "We need more portable sink stations for handwashing," we told Rudy. The bottles of alcohol hand-sanitizers were useful, but proper handwashing with soap and water was the best way to prevent infections. We discussed ways the kids could take better care of themselves. One thing we did was set up a do-it-yourself first-aid station outside the Health Hut and encouraged them to help themselves to Band-Aids, disinfectant, and ice packs so they could treat themselves.

But there was no doubt about it, the Health Centre had become a social hub. At times it was a real hangout, and not just for sick kids. Someone passing by during evening pill call would swear a party was going on in there—and sometimes, there was! First, the Flames, the youngest campers, arrived for their meds, still flushed and excited from their evening activity and looking nowhere near ready to settle down for bed. Soon after they left, the Pioneers and Builders arrived, also high-spirited and wound-up. Lastly the CITs came for their pills and stayed on to amuse us with crazy antics. A bunch of the boys who'd complained about a mysterious ailment they called "crotch rot" started a nightly ritual to treat it. They passed around a bottle of medicated powder and gave themselves a light sprinkling down their pants without even missing a beat in the conversation. Others came to show off their special talents. One CIT girl turned off the lights, aimed the examining-table light toward the wall, and made a rooster, a cobra, and an alligator appear on the wall with hand shadows. Another CIT was a Rubik's cube expert. Someone would jumble it up and after a mere glance at the cube he'd put it behind his back and solve the puzzle, without even looking.

By the time the CITs cleared out, the counsellors started dropping by. "Hey, let's go visit the nurses," I'd hear someone say outside the window. "Yeah, chill time with the nurses!" Seth always came in to see us. "What's poppin', Nurse Tilda?" He'd flash us a smile and put an arm around Alice and me. "Just checkin' up on you two troublemakers."

Alice and I would put out snacks like licorice sticks or popcorn. Matti and other song-leaders would bring their guitars and jam right there in the waiting room of the Health Centre, filling the place with music. They all sat around telling stories of the fun and funny things that happened that day.

"I love being a counsellor," one girl said, "but I had no idea it would be this hard. It's my first job and I feel so stressed. I never have any time to myself."

The others agreed and then shared the sweet moments they'd had with their kids.

"I piggybacked this kid around all day because he had a sore foot and when I put him down, he gave me this big hug and said, 'you're the best counsellor ever!' Like, wow, that rocked my world."

"We played basketball against another camp and they played dirty, but our kids didn't retaliate. I was proud of them and I want to find a way to reward them."

At times they needed to debrief or talk through sticky situations they weren't sure how to handle. They often wanted to run something by us, or get our take on a situation, such as when Bonnie, a first-year counsellor of a cabin of twelve-year-olds, said, "I don't know what to do about my girls. They talk about sex all day!" She looked more bemused than truly exasperated.

"Well, as long as they're just talking," I joked.

"Yeah, I guess, but they're sooo boy crazy. One girl had a boyfriend and told me they broke up last night. Twelve is way too young for that, but she was crying about it today like it was a major tragedy. Puuhhh-lease...I didn't know what to say to her."

"I know what you mean," another said. "The other night my girls were talking about blow jobs and if you should swallow or not! One of the girls said, 'Only if you really like the guy.' Can you believe this? It's unreal! I think they know more than me!"

"If they're not talking about sex, they're talking about their weight," Bonnie said. "One asked me if I thought she was fat. Well, she *is* a bit chubby, but I didn't tell her that, of course. What's the right thing to say?"

"My girls are still so innocent," said a counsellor of the youngest campers, the Flames. "I came into the cabin and found them trying on my bras. It was so cute."

They discussed the children as if they were their own, worried about the homesick ones, and pooled advice on how to break up a clique or deal with a bully. They shared tips on everything from how to get the kids to settle down at night to what to do if they felt a child might have an eating disorder.

Throughout the evenings, counsellors came and went, joining in the discussions, or sometimes just sitting around, listening in. I often looked over at Dave, Steven's attendant, who didn't say much but always seemed part of the conversations. I thought about the work he did with Steven, who couldn't walk and who got around in a wheelchair. Dave helped him shower, fed him, took him to the bathroom. He was doing a job not many would choose but he did it happily, even made it seem appealing. I thought of one day when Steven was upset. The hustle and bustle in the dining hall was too much for him and he felt overwhelmed. Dave had just brought him there but Steven wanted to turn right around and return to his cabin to get away from the noise. Dave felt Steven should be a part of the group and not exclude himself. Steven begged to leave but Dave sat with him, discussing it calmly. Together they came up with a plan. I knew that Dave could have easily exerted his will over Steven or given in out of pity, but instead he negotiated with him, one on one, as equals. It reminded me of times in the hospital when I'd imposed my will on my patients, insisting, for example that they walk farther after surgery than they felt they could or shooing visitors out of my patient's room if I felt that rest was more important than socializing. I believed I was in a position to know what was best for them, but it's an aspect of my role that I've never been comfortable with. I admired Dave's equanimity in handling a similar situation with Steven.

"Typical teenager," Dave said. "He's gotta rebel, but I'm not going to butt heads with him or dominate him. Anyway, he's a great kid," he said as if that was the reason Steven commanded his respect. "Steven's really into sports," he often told me, always emphasizing his strengths, not his disabilities. They did share a love of sports, even though Steven's participation involved watching games and memorizing stats, rather than actually playing.

Those late evenings, "just chillin'" with the counsellors, gave me a window into their world. They were on the front lines, day in, day out—and throughout the nights, too. They faced many of the same challenges that parents, even nurses, face.

One way they coped with the stress of their work was to let loose on their days off. They talked openly about those wild times in the local town, even tales of drinking, drugs, and sex, feeling no need to hide it from us. Rudy must have known the score because one day, early on in the summer, he took them aside to offer a friendly cautionary message, just before a group set out for a twenty-four-hour break.

"I know you work hard," Rudy had said in his relaxed, but authoritative way, "and I want you to enjoy your day off, but if you are somewhere, anywhere, at any time, and are drinking, call me and I'll come and get you—no questions asked."

They listened to him and I hoped they'd take it to heart.

And while they claimed that sex was on their campers' minds, it was definitely on theirs, too. Some nights, they let their guard down and opened up about their own love lives. One girl explained the particular challenges of a relationship with someone at camp. "I slept with him on our day off," she said about her boyfriend, "and then it was so weird seeing him afterward every day at camp and having to work with him."

"Everyone knows who everyone is sleeping with," they all told me, complaining about the lack of privacy, then eagerly telling me who was hooked up. But often, sex wasn't the most personal or revealing topic. When they dropped down deeper and spoke of their passion for music or extreme sports like wakeboarding and mountain climbing, their attachment to their tattoos and the meaning and messages embodied in those images, or their hopes and dreams for the future, I felt they were letting me in to their true selves.

Sometimes they worried about "life after camp" and how they were going to "make it big" or what they were going to do with the "rest of their lives," by which I soon realized they meant their twenties. Many had sincere aspirations to do "something to make the world a better place" but weren't sure exactly what.

I didn't try to offer any answers to their questions or solutions, but simply listened, enjoyed their company, and treasured the connection I had with them.

As we headed into the third, and my final, week of camp, things were going well. Daniel, with Seth's supervision, was keeping his blood-sugar levels stable. The respiratory bug had run its course and most children were healthy again. Mitchell continued to show up for daily visits and to complain about Eddie. "He picks on me because I'm overweight," Mitchell said, but I wondered what would happen if Mitchell stood up for himself or gave it back to him. It was always Seth, or a cabin mate, who came to Mitchell's rescue.

There was no doubt about it—camp worked kids hard. The days were long and filled with strenuous activities. *A day at camp is like a week anywhere else*, Alice and I often said to each other. *So much happens at camp.* I'd seen this phenomenon before: by week three, the kids—and their counsellors, too—were completely rundown and worn-out. Sometimes, when children complained of a headache, or of vaguely "not feeling well," and when there was no real "diagnosis," I would lead them to a bed, cover them lightly with a sheet, and by the time I walked to the door to leave, they were fast asleep. All they needed was a break from the heat and noise and a chance to regroup. Invariably, when they awoke from the "treatment," they were refreshed and "cured."

One day a week there was a break from all that intensity. It started on Friday afternoon with preparations for the Jewish Sabbath. The frenzy of activities began to wind down. It became quiet, and as evening fell, we all gathered at the Tent. Everyone was scrubbed clean and shining, wearing their best clothes, many of the girls in skirts or dresses, some wearing jewellery and makeup. Perhaps the change in atmosphere and clothes put them on their best behaviour. As the sun set over the lake, everyone walked together to the dining hall from which wafted the aroma of freshly baked, braided bread. Candles were lit, blessings sung, and then we sat down at tables spread with white cloths and individually set places, not the usual rack of cutlery and stack of plates. A sprig of flowers was on each table and there was an exceptionally tasty meal of soup, roast chicken, vegetables, and dessert.

Afterward, the song-leaders set up their electric guitars, keyboards, and drums at the front of the room and placed amplifiers around the periphery. In no time, the dining hall was transformed into a dance hall and the entire camp burst forth into song and dance. With their arms entwined, all ages mixed, they moved together in a giant, coiling conga line that went around and around the room. They danced so hard, the floorboards shook. They sang so loudly, the beat vibrated in my chest. With flushed faces and glistening bodies, they danced and sang into the night.

Saturday mornings were for sleeping in, except for the youngest kids who got up early and scampered around, generally left to their own devices. After breakfast there was a service that involved stories, skits, songs, and prayers that the kids wrote themselves. At lunch, siblings could sit together and Max invited Ryan—who still wore his turquoise Crocs—and Harry invited Becky, his friend from school, to join us, since they didn't have siblings at camp. Becky was a gorgeous girl, with a mane of dark, curly hair, and always a huge smile. She and I laughed about her camp hair, which was wild and free, versus her city hair, which she straightened and kept perfectly coiffed. After lunch, kids attended their choice of relaxing interest groups, such as yoga, music appreciation, meditation, drumming, cloud-watching, or nature walks.

As peaceful as camp was on those days, there was one time it didn't end like that. One Saturday night, as I lingered a few moments, enjoying the campfire, I saw Seth go over to add more kindling to the fire. At the same moment, Eddie got up, too. Something about his expression made me wary, but unfortunately I didn't act soon enough to stop what happened next. Eddie held a can of insect spray in his hand and aimed the spray right into the flame where Seth was kneeling. Instantly, the flames roared up, ignited by the combustible spray, and flared straight onto Seth's face, burning his arms and face and singeing off his eyebrows and eyelashes. I rushed them both to the Health Centre and kept Eddie under my supervision while Louise treated Seth.

"Hey, I didn't know that would happen," Eddie protested, putting his feet up on the desk and lacing his hands behind his head. "I had no idea."

Rudy called Eddie's parents. His behaviour was dangerous and we couldn't keep him at camp, he told them, but they begged for him to stay, promising they'd send his behavioural medications the next day by courier. Rudy said no, but he later relented at Seth's request. Despite the pain from his burns, and the anger he must have felt at Eddie's prank, Seth persuaded Rudy to give him another chance. "I'll make sure that kid straightens out and flies right," Seth promised Rudy. "There's something about him…"

"You like a challenge, don't you, man?" Rudy looked at him in disbelief.

I have to admit, I was skeptical that Seth could make Eddie improve his behaviour and surprised that Rudy had been swayed. As for Eddie, he didn't even want to be there.

"I hope they send me home," he said. "Camp sucks. I hate how they're always shoving religion down our throats. I'm an atheist."

My heart sunk. I'd just been warming up to it, myself. But what worried me more was that Eddie seemed to feel no remorse. He sat there, scowling and unrepentant. He made me angry, but

I kept my cool and went to check on Seth. When I came back, I saw that Eddie had gone into his chart and read Louise's note recommending he restart his medications. Eddie jumped out of the chair and began enacting a furious monologue, sneering and spitting in fury.

"Thanks, Mom, thanks, Dad, for putting me on meds that have ruined my life and made me the zombie I am today! It was always so important to you that I sit still and get good grades. It's easier to put me on Ritalin, isn't it? So fuck you! If you expect me to take that shit, it's not going to happen. This place is a fucking Nazi concentration camp!" He stormed out the door, unzipped his pants, and urinated on the door of the Health Centre, yelling out obscenities as he ran off. Seth started to go after him but I held him back.

I wondered if Eddie would ever agree to go back on his meds and privately, I was glad I wouldn't have to deal with this problem. My shift at camp was almost over. I was already thinking of home and the amenities awaiting me there, comforts that, come to think of it, I hadn't missed this summer nearly as much as I had in the past. But the night before I left camp that summer, something happened that put all other problems into their proper perspective. We were working late when Layla came in with Alon, her assistant tripper. "It's nothing," I heard him say out on the porch. But when he walked in and we saw the scattering of bruises on his arms and legs and noted his pale complexion, we knew right away that he was seriously ill. A few days later, at a clinic in Toronto, the diagnosis was confirmed: leukemia. Alon's life was put on hold as he faced chemotherapy, radiation, and an uncertain future.

The next morning, Alice and I reported to the nurses who were taking over from us. As I packed up my car, campers and counsellors came to say goodbye and give us hugs. One of them, Bradley, the boy who was never without his catcher's mitt, came over to ask me, "You comin' back next summer?" We were standing in the sun and he shielded his face and squinted up at me.

"I'd like to," I said, unable at that moment to be more enthusiastic. I was preoccupied with the shocking news about Alon and I couldn't think about next year. Bradley didn't know about any of that and had no such ambivalence.

"I sure hope so," he said, waving goodbye. "Well, see you then!" He stepped out of the sunlight and onto the shaded path toward his cabin.

I was all ready to leave, but my kids hung back, crouched in a huddle with their friends—Max with Ryan and Harry with Becky, her dark curls covering her face—as they worked on some problem with a pencil and paper. At last, Becky got up and shouted out the answer. "Only 341 more days until camp starts again!"

12

SEX TALK IN THE TENT

Of course I went back the next summer. I had finally experienced camp's magic and was hooked. I was a happy camper, now!

The evening before the first day—the campers would be arriving the next morning—Rudy gathered us in the staff lounge for a meeting. The counsellors sat on the floor and Alice, Louise, and I were on folding chairs at the back. First, he welcomed everyone back and shared his excitement about making this summer the best, ever. He ended his remarks with a word of advice. "Whatever your experience was with a child last year, good or bad, forget it. Give each kid the benefit of a fresh start. Everyone changes."

He didn't name names but Alice and I looked at each other and mouthed "Eddie." We'd heard he was returning and couldn't believe it. After the terrible incident with Seth, and Eddie's ongoing obnoxious behaviour and refusal to go back on his meds, he was sent home, but not before he stole money from the camp office, destroyed someone's radio, and defecated on Rudy's cabin doorstep. Despite all of that, his parents had managed to convince Rudy to take him back, albeit on a trial basis. One incident of bad behaviour, Rudy warned them, and Eddie would be sent home.

I looked around the room. It was nice to see familiar faces and to be one, myself. I saw CITs who had graduated to being counsellors, and last year's counsellors who had been promoted to unit heads or specialists in areas such as water-skiing or swimming. There were a few CITs who had been rowdy and had pulled some crazy stunts last summer who were now back as counsellors. Alice and I wondered how they'd managed to prove to Rudy that they'd turned themselves around. How had they demonstrated that they had the leadership potential he said he was looking for?

"It takes more than a pulse to land a job at Camp Sol," Rudy always said. "You have to have the right stuff."

But at that staff meeting, they did seem to have settled down. They listened quietly as Rudy spoke. One was even embarrassed when he was reminded of his past shenanigans and insisted he no longer be called his old, tough nickname, Bones, the moniker of some cartoon villain. Now, he'd be going by his real name: Eugene. "I have to set a good example for the kids," he said.

Looking around that staff lounge, I saw my favourite counsellor, Seth. Rudy's daughter Layla was back, as was Matti, the charismatic song-leader, softly strumming his guitar (it was irresistible to him) while Rudy spoke. Rudy told us about Alon who was still undergoing treatment. His family members were being tested to see if one of them was a match for a bone marrow transplant, a procedure that offered a chance of a cure. He wasn't well enough to come back to camp any time soon.

Well, the kids might have changed, but not Alice and me—not one bit. We fell right back into our summer friendship and easy partnership.

After the staff meeting, Alice, Louise, and I had a powwow with the senior counsellors to plan strategies to keep everyone healthy. We prepared first-aid kits and placed them in each cabin and reminded the counsellors about the do-it-yourself first-aid station, which campers and counsellors could use to treat anything itchy, sore, swollen, or bruised without having to wait for us. We taught them how to handle emergencies until we could get there. We discussed ways to reduce the incidence of infections and the consequent use of prescription medications, which had been so high the previous summer, the main ways being handwashing and good hygiene.

"One sneeze sends thousands of droplets into the air," Louise told them in a scary voice. "Touch a slimy nose, then touch someone without washing your hands, and—bingo!—infection."

Perhaps a small dose of fear—or at least vigilance—is a good thing when it comes to preventing infections. Well, it certainly got camp off to a healthy start.

When the kids arrived the next day, I quickly discovered that Rudy was absolutely right about how much children can change in a year. Some of them who had been on several meds were now on fewer, or lower doses. In many cases, their medical conditions had stabilized or improved. The most noticeable changes were in the teenagers.

Daniel was back. "Yo!" he called out to us as he dropped off a trunk of equipment for his insulin pump.

"How's it going?" I asked.

"I'm good," was all he said, eager to beat it out of there. "Expect lots of calls from my mom. She's still pretty hyper," he said as he joined his group.

He was more confident dealing with his condition, so much so that he didn't even want Seth checking and reminding him about his blood-sugar testing. If his mother called to make a change in his diet or the rate on his insulin pump, he'd say, "Yeah, yeah, I'll get on to it," and walk away. A year older now, he was going to be more of a challenge to keep a close watch while still allowing him his independence.

Another teenager who seemed to have made a change—more like a complete *transformation*, from hellion to angel—was Eddie. He looked pretty much the same, still small and thin, wearing glasses this year and multiple earrings. However, what *was* different was his smile, the reliable way he showed up each morning for his meds, and his good manners. Seth had asked to be his counsellor again, eager to reinforce the strides Eddie had made. I often saw Seth point at his eyes, then at Eddie's, and back to his own, to remind Eddie he was keeping tabs on him.

Sharon continued to suffer frequent severe headaches. She still felt frustrated to have to come to us for medication she took by herself at home. Since she was a year older now and very responsible, and to practise our philosophy of encouraging children to be more self-sufficient, we decided to let her keep a small amount of medication with her in the cabin to take as she needed. Sharon was pleased with the new plan.

I saw Sophie's chart, so I knew she was back, but I'd never actually met her. Now fourteen years old, she was the camper with spina bifida who catheterized herself throughout the day to remove urine from her bladder. She was managing well and still very private about her condition.

Bradley, who still had his baseball and catcher's mitt with him wherever he went, and who still took his meds at his "own discretion," came in and gave me a big welcoming hug. "I knew you'd show," he said. He was sweet, and thankfully had stopped his annoying habit of reminding us that he was "gifted."

Mitchell seemed pleased to be back. He kept up his role of cabin clown and still always made himself the butt of his own jokes.

I saw Amy around camp, either with her cabin mates or by herself, standing and staring at objects. Not as fixated on sand as she was last year, this summer she was fascinated with weather, particularly clouds, which she watched for hours and could describe in great detail. The most dramatic change about Amy was her looks. Her hair was now long and lustrous and her body had become curvaceous. Without even being aware of it, Amy had blossomed into an attractive, even sexy, young woman.

Xiu-Ling and Frankie were back.

"I don't want to be in the same cabin with her!" Xiu-Ling said loudly, for all at pill call to hear. "All she wants to do is sit around all day and read. She's no fun."

"But you wrote on the form you wanted me to be in your cabin," Frankie whined. She turned to me. "She keeps dropping stuff from the upper bunk onto me. On purpose."

"By accident!" Xiu-Ling insisted.

"On purpose!" Frankie pouted.

"You're such a baby and you're so insensitive!" Xiu-Ling yelled at her.

"Yes, but...you're so..." Frankie stammered, trying to come up with a comeback. "You're so *sensitive*!"

"Ha!" was all Xiu-Ling said. She came over to whisper to me. "Between you and me, Frankie could use a higher dose of her meds."

I smiled at her and joined Alice who was handing out pills and welcoming new and returning campers.

Nathan was back. Much healthier this summer, he no longer needed to cling to his counsellor Warren; he now came by himself or with a friend every morning to take his inhalers and a daily pill to control his asthma.

Dylan, too, was back this summer. Now fourteen, he still occasionally paced outside my room and looked me over curiously. When I approached, he dashed off. I wasn't sure if he'd placed me yet. Two years ago, his father had died in the ICU and I had been his nurse. I remembered his horrible, painful death from liver cancer and the way his mother had fought so hard to save him, right up until her husband's last breath. When we did decide to stop treatment, because it was futile and of no benefit, she was furious. In the end, Dylan's father's death had not been a peaceful one. Seeing me must have brought back a flood of painful memories for him, but I wasn't sure he was ready to face them. I had decided to wait for a signal from him.

Alice and I kept up our daily walks. Conversation was just as easy between us, though sometimes we were simply quiet, enjoying that peaceful time in the early morning before the kids were up and the mosquitoes buzzed, before it got hot and we got busy in the clinic. We usually saw no one other than the occasional early-morning jogging rabbi or eager-beaver CIT who was into fitness. Sometimes we sat on the dock, enjoying the stillness of the lake, and watched the darting water striders on its surface. Alice taught me to identify hemlock, spruce, fir, and pine trees and laughed when I told her I'd always thought they were *all* Christmas trees! She pointed out a woodpecker poised at the side of a tree, a cedar waxwing eating red berries, and once, a regal blue heron. She caught sight of a family of minks with their silky, black fur and long tails, but I wasn't quick enough to see them before they scurried away into a cave of rocks near the lake.

One afternoon, a few days after camp started, Alice and I were just returning from a walk when a crowd ran up to tell us that Mitchell had been injured. We ran to the Health Centre where Louise was examining him. The first clue to what had happened was Eddie. He was in the waiting room with a big smirk on his face, sitting beside Seth who was steaming mad, but mostly upset at himself for not preventing the incident. "He sucker-punched Mitch," Seth said, "for no reason whatsoever."

"There *was* a reason." Eddie put his feet up on a table and Seth shoved them back off. "Mitchy Mouse was being his usual dorky self and he pissed me off, like he does everyday, but this time I'd had enough and thought, *You're going down.* So I tanked that dumb-ass kid right into next week."

I gauged the situation: Eddie's build was short and scrawny and Mitchell was hefty and solid. How much damage could Eddie have caused? But before Alice and I had a chance to hear from Louise about Mitchell's injury, Rudy came in and spoke sternly to Eddie. "Pack your things, young man. You're going home. I've called your parents and they're coming to get you." This time he made no mention of second chances, zero tolerance, or the golden rule.

"Whatever," Eddie muttered, as if he didn't care, but when he got on the phone and spoke to his parents he sounded more indignant than indifferent. "I didn't do anything," he told his father. "I have no idea why these people are on my case. They're insane. They must be on crack. The other kid's a truck. He's way bigger than me."

"You just lied to your parents," I pointed out when he got off the phone.

"Yup. I lie all the time. They say they *trust* me. Hah! Big mistake." He picked up a bottle of cough syrup from the counter. "Hey, this is the stuff they use to make crystal meth. I think I'll steal it." He made as if to pocket it before putting it back.

I tried to make conversation to pass the time until his parents arrived. "Do you have brothers or sisters?" I started off on what I hoped would be a safe subject.

"Yeah, an older brother, but he's the good one. My mother says he's going to turn out okay and I'm going to land in jail!"

"Was there anything you liked doing at camp?" I was still trying to make pleasantries.

"Yeah," he grinned devilishly, "jerking off in the forest."

How's that working for you? I wanted to retort like Dr. Phil. I was infuriated at him but still felt the need to say something therapeutic and nurse-like. I could only come up with, "Eddie, you seem unhappy. Would you like to get help for your problems?"

"Oh, they sent me to a therapist but he was an idiot. I lied to him. I didn't tell him one true thing, only lies. My mother thought he was helping me deal with my issues. What a joke! There was no way I was going to tell that guy anything personal. The problem is my fucking family. They are totally out of touch with reality. Hey, they *are* a fucking reality show."

So much bravado, but anyone could see he was hurting. Yet, try as hard as I could to be non-judgmental, I couldn't hide my disapproval.

"I suppose you want me to de-fuck my language?" he asked, grinning.

I let out a sigh of exasperation. "Eddie, your language is the least of your problems."

Soon—but not soon enough—Eddie's parents arrived, apologetic and embarrassed. They were about to rush off, but Rudy took them aside.

"Eddie has serious psychological problems," Rudy said. "There is something terribly wrong with his behaviour. He needs help."

"Oh, don't worry, he's getting help," the father said, ready to leave.

"Whatever help he's getting is not enough." Rudy held fast, wanting to make sure his message got through. "He needs more. His behaviour is abnormal and totally unacceptable. He is violent and dangerous. We cannot give him the help he needs at this camp, but we wish him well."

The parents hurried off with Eddie in tow. Only Seth came to say goodbye.

"I didn't see it coming, so I wasn't ready," Mitchell chattered nervously. He sat up on the examining table grimacing with every movement. "I got the wind knocked out of me." He clutched at his side and breathed shallowly. I gave him a painkiller and took his vital signs. Despite his discomfort, he kept up the patter. "If

I'd been ready, I could've taken the hit like a man, but hey, that's the story of my life, I never see it coming." I listened to his chest with my stethoscope and heard air moving equally in both lungs. His colour was good so he was probably getting enough oxygen, but still, I felt uneasy. Mitchell wanted to return to his cabin, which was a good sign, so we let him go. He was enjoying the attention and was given a welcoming cheer by his cabin mates, to which he gleefully responded.

"Hey, guys, did you know Harry Houdini died from a punch in the stomach?" he announced. "Maybe that'll happen to me, too!"

After pill call that evening, I went to Mitchell's cabin to check on him. He was still wincing in pain. I took his vital signs and listened to his chest. This time I detected a slight decrease in air entry on his injured side, but his colour was good and vital signs stable. He might have fractured a rib, which could have punctured his lung, causing a leak. It could heal on its own but it could also get worse, drastically. Louise agreed and drove him to the hospital late that night, where they diagnosed a small pneumothorax, which meant there was an area of his lungs that had deflated and wasn't receiving oxygen. The doctor felt the "pneumo" would heal on its own without requiring a chest tube to reinflate his lung but did admit him to the hospital for close observation. Louise and Alice congratulated me for my good call and I have to admit, I felt proud of my well-honed skills.

Two days later Mitchell returned to camp. He was well enough to re-join his cabin but wanted to stay in the Health Centre and we let him. Most of the day, he lay in bed, reluctant to walk around. He asked if we could bring in a television and kidded that he'd probably get bed sores from lying around so much. We served him noodle soups and chilled fruit juices. Seth and the cabin visited every day, bringing him treats and even Muffin, a rabbit from the nature area (and at nighttime, Mabel, the nocturnal hedgehog, who was awake and eager to play).

Mitchell was enjoying our room service and being an invalid, but he was healthy now, and after a couple of days it was time to kick him out.

It's like that in the hospital, too, I thought. We nurses always say that when our patients start playing with the buttons on the electric bed to put it into different positions or complaining about the mattress, the food, or the "service," it's time to discharge them. It may seem harsh, but the whole point is to get better and go home, isn't it?

"Why don't you take a walk to the nature area and put Muffin back in his cage?" I suggested. "You have to start moving," I reminded him, but he complained that he was still in pain and too tired.

"Don't you want to get back on the bike? Remember how it made you feel better last summer?" We talked again about Lance Armstrong but Mitchell wasn't as inspired.

Try and help yourself, I wanted to tell him.

The next day Mitchell returned to his cabin but withdrew from his friends. He left swim class or sailing, even low-key arts and crafts, to visit us, each time coming up with some tiny or implausible ailment. He began to talk about going home.

"My parents say if I come home I'll spend the summer vegging out on the couch and gain more weight."

"Is that a possibility?"

He nodded and hung his head, guilty as charged. I put my arm around him as we walked back to his cabin.

"It's weird 'cause each year I think I'm going to like camp, and I'm, like, excited—well, excited-slash-nervous—but as soon as I get here, I can't handle it. I make the best of it on the outside, but on the inside I'm sad." He brightened. "The best part was the hospital. Now, *that* was cool."

A day or two later, Mitchell did go home. His parents came and thanked us for all we'd done. They were very loving toward their son but obviously disappointed. "We thought he'd at least make it through the first week," the father said to Rudy.

"I wouldn't worry," he said. "Camp isn't the right place for every child at all times. Let's try again next year."

Occasionally I put aside my resistance and went to prayer services. Alice was always there and the counsellors, too, sitting with their campers, setting a good example. I had to ask myself, what message was I sending by not attending? *It's good for you, but not for me. You need this but I don't.* Once I got there, I realized it was pleasant to be together with the rest of the camp, and the music was fabulous. Once, a visiting rabbi played the accordion. After a few guffaws at what everyone assumed would be a corny instrument, we all got into it, moving to the cool, old-world swing sound. Another day, the song-leaders sang prayers set to U2 melodies and one to Bob Marley's "Redemption Song." The children provided a lot of entertainment, too, reading aloud prayers and poems they'd written expressing gratitude for nature, friends, family, and camp itself. Some of their thoughts were touching and a few hilarious with the odd flub or blooper.

Alice always saved me a spot on the bench beside her but I preferred to stand at the side or the back of the outdoor chapel. There was a tree that had a deep cleft running down it right to the exposed roots and I liked to lean in there against the trunk. From that vantage point, I could look out at everyone and check out who had the sniffles or was coughing and who looked homesick. I watched Xiu-Ling and Frankie and tried to figure out if they were holding hands as best friends or scowling as mortal enemies. I double-checked that the brakes were locked on Steven's wheelchair because Dave often parked it on a slope. Once, I noticed a little boy squirming in a certain way that was very familiar to me. The bathroom was a far distance, so I led him into the woods nearby and found him a private spot. "Do you enjoy services?" I asked as we made our way back.

"No, but it's better than going to synagogue at home. How can I ever go back to that boring place?" he asked. "Even my dad falls asleep."

No, these services were not boring. They were relaxing, thought-provoking, and joyful. Even talking about God didn't seem as much of a stretch of the imagination, out in nature, in this beautiful setting.

"We each understand God in our separate ways," Rabbi Emily said one day.

"I don't know if I believe in God," a young boy spoke up, "but at camp, I feel God."

"Where's God?" one kid joked. "Beats me! Let's have a scavenger hunt for God."

"If ever you're looking for God," said Rabbi Emily, "you can always touch your pulse and say, Oh, there you are." She gave time for that idea to sink in. "Or, take a deep breath. That's God moving through you."

Sometimes Amy contributed to the discussion. One sunny day, she sat up and said flatly, "It's not raining today."

Rabbi Emily nodded. "Yes, Amy, go on."

"The sky is the colour of God."

One morning during services, as I stood off to the side, watching over everyone, my eye caught a movement in the trees surrounding the chapel. Then it stopped. It was big and black. A branch shifted. Leaves rustled. It was a bear, just a few steps away! I was the only one who saw it because of where I stood, facing the woods. I had to act fast to save the camp! I was panicking, but I tried to recall Layla's advice. Was it "Make a racket! Jump up and scream!" or "Keep quiet and stare him down"? My mind raced madly for a few moments until my ICU training kicked in. I became calm and rational and knew exactly what to do. I got up, walked to the front, and whispered into Matti's ear. "Cut short the silent meditation and go straight into the music." I mentioned a particularly loud number. I bent down and cranked up the amplifier a few notches and cued Matti. Sure enough, as everyone burst into song, the bear startled, turned around, and lumbered off in the opposite direction. My scheme worked! Goldilocks had fended off the big, bad bear! I ran to tell Rudy but he wasn't the least bit concerned.

"Hey, man, you scared off Yogi Bear! He visits us every year. He's never been a problem. Well, once he broke into the kitchen and made off with a few loaves of bread."

He'd been more upset when the kids messed with the meal-time blessing!

"So, you're not worried about a bear at camp?"

"No, now that you're on top of it." He chuckled. "We can all rest easy."

It was a swelteringly hot day—we had the air conditioner roaring full blast and kids were dropping by all day to "chill," and, considering the temperature, we took that *literally*—when a counsellor came by with a special request. Could we have a "sex talk" with two of her fifteen-year-old girls? A rumour was going around that they'd been in a boys' cabin and gone too far.

For this matter, I deferred to Alice and Louise. As a public health nurse and a physician, respectively, Alice and Louise were experienced in counselling patients about sexuality. (Needless to say, the topic didn't often come up with my critically ill patients in the ICU.) However, Alice insisted I join the discussion. "We're a team," she reminded me.

That afternoon, during after-lunch rest period, we met in the Tent. Jasmine and Lee, two teenage girls in halter tops, skimpy bikini bottoms, and flip-flops, showed up with sour scowls on their pretty faces. They'd been wrongly accused and misunderstood, they said. Now, they felt, everyone was against them and their reputations ruined, all because of vicious gossip.

"Why don't you start by telling us what happened?" Alice suggested.

"It was during the Carnival and we were shaving whipped cream off a balloon without popping it," Lee said.

"Don't forget the greased watermelon relay race," Jasmine added.

"Yeah, right, we got all messy and so we went into the boys' cabin—it was the closest one—to clean ourselves off, but we didn't take showers there. See, that's the rumour, that we took our clothes off. The whole thing has gotten completely out of hand and it's soooo embarrassing! We swear, nothing happened!"

Jasmine nodded her head in vehement agreement. "They're saying we took off our tops. There's no way we did that! We're just friends with those guys," said Lee, "*not* friends with benefits. We're not skanks! Everyone's talking about us and spreading lies. One girl said we were stripping for the guys and doing lap dances. How would she know? She wasn't even there. I thought we were friends! Well, forget that!" She flounced in her seat and looked away.

"Oh, you're all against us, too, I can tell," Jasmine chimed in. She was on the verge of tears. "This whole thing has been blown out of proportion. Are you going to call our parents?"

Louise spoke first. "You were asking for trouble. You put yourselves at risk by going into the boys' cabin by yourselves, and besides, it's against camp rules." She launched into the results of a study published in a medical journal that stated that 62 percent of fourteen-year-old girls said they wished they'd waited until they were older to have sex.

"But we didn't do anything!" Lee wailed.

Louise switched gears and lightened up. "Did you ever stop and think maybe you were getting into more than you bargained for by going into the boys' cabin?"

Or, maybe exactly what we bargained for, their smiles at one another seemed to say. On the one hand they'd enjoyed themselves, but now they weren't so sure about this new bad-girl rep they were developing. *How confusing it is to be a young woman today with so many mixed messages out there!*

Next, Alice spoke. "You may be causing things to happen sooner than you are ready," she cautioned in her gentle way. "You have to know if you're ready for this." She spoke about her own daughters and her wishes for them to respect themselves and to wait until they were ready for intimate relations with the right person at the right time.

It was my turn and I wanted to contribute something useful. Louise had been the authoritative professional and Alice, the protective, concerned parent. Then there was me, who remembered all too well what it was like to feel those desires. It didn't seem so long ago that I'd done some pretty wild things myself, so it felt hypocritical to come down on them. Besides, I wanted to be the kind of grown-up who didn't stand in judgment, and who could help them sort out these complicated matters, but I wasn't sure how to do that. I'd read enough of those how-to-communicate-with-your-teenager books to know that offering advice was the worse thing. It only made them shut down, lose trust, and worse of all, it cut off the lines of communication. As a nurse, I've always been taught not to offer my personal opinion. We're supposed to merely echo back, in a neutral way, our patients' points of view and not influence them with our own values. However, here at camp, where I was both a parent figure and their nurse, that approach felt counter-intuitive. No, they didn't need judgment or information—"411" as they called it—but I wasn't sure what they *did* need.

"We're here, if you need to talk," was all I offered in the end.
After they left, we congratulated ourselves.

"They really listened to us," Louise said.

"We kept the lines of communication open," Alice murmured.

"I guess we did a pretty good job," I said.

But later, as we walked to the dining hall for dinner, we happened to fall in behind Jasmine and Lee and overheard them talking to their friends.

"So, we had this major sex convo with the doctor and the nurses," Lee was saying to her friends, "and it was *soooo* ridonkulous!"

"*Soooo* lame," Jasmine squealed.

But how bad could it have been? The very next day they came back. I was working by myself when the two of them showed up. Jasmine was still pouting but Lee came at me in her assertive way. "We want to know what you really think. I mean, like, so what if we were making out with them? Is that so bad?"

If I said the wrong thing, they'd blow me off and I'd lose them altogether. *What to say? What to say?* I looked at their low-cut jeans and bare midriffs, their breasts spilling out of their skinny tank tops. *Okay, here goes.* "You both are very attractive—" I started.

"Are you saying we brought it on ourselves?" Lee snapped. "We have the right to dress however we like. It's a free country. This isn't Iraq, you know. We're not sluts."

"We didn't do anything wrong," Jasmine said, looking tearful.

"I didn't say you did," I countered.

"So, I take it you're saying, we should wait, before, ahh, doing anything more?"

"You're not ready for more," I said firmly. "Why not wait until you are?" I said the thing I'd want another parent to say to my own kids in this situation.

"I knew you'd say that," Lee folded her arms across her chest. "Talking to you is like talking to my mother. She always freaks out, too. C'mon, Jaz, we're done here."

I'd said nothing, but already I could feel those precious lines of communication shutting down.

"I sound like a seal," I heard a girl say.

I was in the midst of giving out the evening meds when I heard a strange sound. It was coming from Naomi, an always-smiling, very popular fourteen-year-old who'd never come to the Health Centre for anything before but was now sitting in the waiting room, surrounded by a group of friends while she had fits of coughing. In between bouts of a high-pitched, insistent, squeaky coughing spell, she joked around and giggled. If this had been the ICU and a patient suddenly started coughing like that, I would have placed an oximeter on her finger (an instrument we used to measure a patient's oxygen concentration). Had she been a patient in the ICU, the sudden onset of a harsh cough like this would have garnered her a stat chest X-ray and maybe even a bronchoscopy, which involved a tube placed down into her trachea and lungs, but here, that wasn't necessary—at least not yet. Even without an oximeter, just looking at Naomi's rosy complexion and relaxed manner, I was fairly certain her oxygenation was normal.

I went out into the waiting room. Her friends were joking around with her, making her laugh. "This is not a party," I said, ushering them out.

"I can't breathe!" Naomi said, waving goodbye to her friends. I brought her into the examining room and listened to her chest and heard adequate and equal air entry on both sides, but she was breathing rapidly. "I can't swallow and my chest hurts." Her hands shook. "Is this a heart attack?" Off and on she gave that strange-sounding cough.

"No," I reassured her. "Probably your chest is sore from coughing so much."

Louise examined her thoroughly and then we went aside to speak privately. "I think it's a panic attack," she said. "You were right to throw out the friends. We want to make sure there's no acting up for an audience's attention. For now, let's try giving her a small dose of sedation."

I gave Naomi a tiny pill under her tongue and let that take effect. After about twenty minutes, we checked on her. She'd fallen asleep, and while she slept there was no cough, shakiness, or fast breathing. She must have sensed we were standing at the foot of her bed because she startled awake. As soon as she did, the cough and rapid breathing started up again. "I feel like I'm going to pass out," she yelled. I stopped in my tracks. *Someone about to pass out does not have the strength to yell. Someone about to lose consciousness is too weak to speak.*

"My heart is racing," she said, trembling. "It's flip-flopping all around!" Her hands shook violently. She clutched at her chest and took big gulps of air. "I can't breathe."

Her strange cough seemed to be gone but her pulse was racing at 120 beats* per minute and her respiratory rate was also fast at forty-five breaths a minute. I gave her a paper bag to breathe into, to try to retain the carbon dioxide she was losing by hyperventilating.

"My chest hurts," she cried. "I'm going to pass out." Before we could deal with one problem, Naomi had moved on to the next. "The room is spinning. I'm going to faint!" she shouted. I took her blood pressure and it was a robust and normal 132 over 80.

Someone about to faint would have low blood pressure, I thought.

---

* A normal, resting pulse is 60 to 80 beats per minute.

"I feel like I'm losing control of myself," Naomi said. But her words sounded false like she was repeating lines she'd learned.

"I'm sure it must feel that way," I said quietly. I felt sympathy for her because I could see she genuinely felt upset.

"My feet are numb! They're tingling. I can't feel my feet. They're paralyzed." She suddenly closed her eyes and lay there motionless.

"Naomi? Look at me! Open your eyes," I told her, feeling slightly alarmed.

"I think I just blacked out there for a moment," she said weakly.

But she hadn't lost consciousness. She had been awake and, I was fairly confident, completely aware of everything she was doing. None of this was adding up. I found myself in the situation I've always hated: suspecting a patient was "faking it." It was an especially uncomfortable feeling to doubt a child. I knew Louise was also looking for something deeper by her line of questioning.

"Is something bothering you, Naomi? Are you homesick?"

Naomi looked at her fiercely. "I love camp. I've never been homesick, not even for a minute."

"Because, if you are," Louise continued, "that can bring on these kinds of feelings and they can be really scary when you're away from home and missing your family."

"I live for camp." She turned away from us.

Louise and I spoke privately. "I can't find anything wrong," Louise said. "I think it's pure anxiety and nothing physically abnormal, especially since her memory is intact and she can describe her symptoms perfectly..." Louise's voice trailed off and I caught her drift: after a true faint, a patient can't recall events immediately prior to losing consciousness. "Let's give her another dose of sedation and watch her closely. If she worsens we'll take her to the hospital," she said, and went to call Naomi's parents.

Just then, Naomi's brother Lorne, an older camper, arrived. He rushed over to her, sat at the edge of her bed, scooped her up into his arms and held her tight. As she clung to him, their two heads of dark, curly hair mixed together like a huge, luxurious wig. He soon left to let her sleep. Naomi would stay overnight in the Health Centre. Alice was on call so I said good night.

The next morning, Alice told me it had been a quiet night. Naomi had slept and was now smiling and making light of what had happened, even apologizing for worrying us. She was dressed and eager to return to her cabin. Louise examined her and cleared her to return to her cabin. We wrote it off as a weird, inexplicable one-off episode and since she was now well and happy again, we didn't give it another thought.

I always looked forward to Saturday lunch because it was family day and I could sit with my kids.

"Where's Max?" Harry asked as he joined me. He wasn't too happy about it but grudgingly agreed to this one meal a week with me and his brother. Max soon appeared, triumphantly bearing a dripping, overflowing bowl of Greek salad he'd scored for me, because he knew I didn't have the patience to stand in the long line for this popular item, even though it's one of my favourite foods.

My kids were growing up. Their maturity brought many such delightful acts of independent thoughtfulness but it also meant they were pulling away from me and each one becoming his own person. *They grow up so fast*, I thought, and camp makes it seem even faster. It was exactly what was supposed to happen, but it was bittersweet, just the same. It was a reminder that I was getting older, too, and that they needed me less, or perhaps in a different way. Harry, especially, guarded his privacy, and now shared so little with me. Impulsively one day, I'd pumped his counsellor, prying for some insider details. He was reluctant to be an informant but eventually caved and dished.

"Harry is quite an instigator," his counsellor said with obvious pride. "He led a raid on a girls' cabin last night but took his punishment like a man."

"I guess he's coming out of his shell."

"What shell? He's the noisiest kid in the cabin. Oh, and by the way, he's quite the chick magnet. A few of the girls are majorly crushing on him."

Whoa, back off, I told myself, now uncomfortable knowing information I'd asked to know. Harry would definitely not want me hearing this. I was beginning to see why it might not be such a wonderful thing to have your mom at camp.

Late one evening a few days later, I was sitting in my room reading, when a buzz and crackle came over the walkie-talkie. "Is the nurse there?" a counsellor's voice cried out. "Someone's having a seizure!"

As I ran to the cabin, I remembered Amanda and that terrifying trip to the hospital in the thunderstorm with Wheels a few summers ago. She'd had a cerebral bleed—a mild stroke—and I prayed this wasn't going to be anything serious like that. When I got there I found Naomi, lying stiffly on the floor beside her bed, her friends and counsellors around her. I knelt down beside her. "Where are you?" I asked. Her eyes were open and I could tell she saw me but she didn't answer. This wasn't a seizure, but something was definitely wrong. "What's your name?" I asked her.

"It's Naomi," someone said. I explained I needed Naomi to answer for herself, because I was testing her level of consciousness, to see how her brain was working.

"What made you think she was having a seizure?" I asked the counsellor.

"That's what Naomi told me."

But from what the counsellor described of what she herself had witnessed, Naomi hadn't had convulsions. She was not now in a typical post-seizure state. We brought her to the Health Centre where she immediately began to flail about and breathe rapidly. Again, I gave her a paper bag to breathe into and coached her to slow down. I worried that her hyperventilation could cause her to pass out and might lead to a drop in her carbon dioxide levels so severe that it would disrupt the acid-base balance, or the "Ph," of her blood chemistry. Calcium levels would then be affected, leading to tremors and spasms, a state called tetany. I had seen the condition of "metabolic alkalosis" in my critically ill patients but never in a healthy person.

Again, Lorne, her brother, rushed in. "Naomi! Are you okay?" She stared at him blankly. "Naomi, you're going to be okay," he told her. He turned to Louise. "Is my sister okay?"

"My neck hurts," Naomi mumbled. Louise and I looked at each other grimly. Sudden neck pain was a classic indicator of meningitis, a highly infectious, deadly disease.

"Naomi, touch your chin to your chest," Louise asked her. She couldn't. It was highly unlikely she had meningitis—there were no other signs and she'd probably received the vaccine—but just in case, we closed all the doors and put on masks and gloves to protect ourselves. If it did turn out to be bacterial, or meningococcal, meningitis, it would be life-threatening for her and dangerous for us, as well as everyone at camp who'd come anywhere near her. Anyone exposed to her would have to go on antibiotics.

Naomi's counsellor went with her in the ambulance and I followed in my car. In the ER Naomi had a CT scan to examine her brain and a lumbar puncture, which involved putting a needle into her spinal column, to obtain fluid to test for meningitis. When these tests were done I went in to visit her. She was now fully conscious, sitting up, giggling, and playing a finger game called Chopsticks with her counsellor. It was as if nothing had happened. Again, she apologized for causing us worry.

I knew all the dire things that still had to be ruled out: seizure, a cerebral bleed, a serious disease, or a tumour. The ER doctor decided to keep her overnight for close monitoring and more tests. Her counsellor slept beside her in a chair, her head resting on the bed, while I headed back to camp. I had to get some sleep or I'd be utterly useless to anyone, much less myself.

13

SABBATH CHAOS

By the time I got back to camp from the hospital, it was morning. I could see Xiu-Ling, Frankie, and Nathan, along with the rest of the kids, making their way down from the cabins for pill call. One girl had beat them to it and was already there, anxiously waiting. I knew her name was Sarah but she didn't take meds and wasn't one of our "regulars." When she saw me, she ran over. "I *have* to talk to you!" I unlocked the door and she followed in, close on my heels. "I just got my period. What a nightmare! I can't believe this is happening. My mother said I probably wouldn't get it until I turned thirteen but I'm twelve so I didn't bring anything with me."

"Congratulations!" I gave a big, cheery smile to offer a warm welcome to womanhood.

"I'm so not ready for this," she moaned. "Why couldn't I just have pneumonia?"

I gave her some supplies in a brown paper bag. She waited while I finished pill call then walked with me to the dining hall for breakfast. "Do you think anyone can tell?" she asked, looking around self-consciously. "I never thought I would get it before my bat mitzvah. When does menopause start?" she asked wearily before joining up with her cabin.

After breakfast, Alice let her call her parents to tell them the news. Her cabin was planning a party complete with a red cake, and Rabbi Emily offered to take her for some private time, just the two of them, together. Sarah was very pleased with all the attention, and was it my imagination or did she now carry herself a bit more confidently?

Alice and I sat for a few minutes over coffee before starting the morning clinic. "You should have woken me," she said when I told her about the emergency with Naomi and my long night with her in the hospital. "I could have helped you. I can't believe I didn't even hear the ambulance. I slept right through it."

"That's nurse sleep for you," I said and we shared a laugh about that. I've slept through a lot of things, myself. After most night shifts working in the ICU, my entire next day would be lost to sleep. There have been days when sunlight streamed through my bedroom window, the TV blared, and my kids played game after game of mini-sticks hockey right there on the floor beside me, but I slept through it all. (Once, Ivan ran the vacuum cleaner around the bed. I only knew by the carpet marks.) Yet, when I was on call at camp, even a soft tap on the door would wake me up and I'd spring into action. As for nights when I wasn't on call, I slept soundly, just as Alice had done.

Problem was, we were both getting tired. It was only the first week of camp, which was usually quiet, but already there had been Mitchell's injury, his high-maintenance convalescence, and Naomi's baffling emergency—not to mention the late-night after-hour schmooze sessions with the counsellors, which were way too much fun to turn away—and it was all taking its toll on both of us. Now, it was Friday and things would slow down and hopefully we'd get a breather. (Mostly, I didn't even notice what day of the week it was until Friday night arrived and the Sabbath celebrations began. It gave shape to the week and reminded us of time itself. Oh, for sure, pills had to be given at certain times and clinic hours were set by the clock, but at camp, I was aware not just of clock time, but of natural time, too. I'd seen the sun rise and the sun set. I noticed the phases of the moon. In the city, I rarely paid attention to such things.)

The next morning I couldn't come up with a single compelling excuse to not go to services, so I went. It was a hot day. The lake was still and only a gentle breeze rustled the leaves in the trees. There had been no further sightings of Yogi Bear but I stayed off to the side, on guard duty—and also so I could sneak away if I wanted to. By eleven o'clock, sitting in the outdoor chapel in our good clothes, we were sweating. I'm sure everyone wanted to jump in the lake to cool off. I tried to hang in there because, eventually, there'd be cake. After the closing song, they passed around slices of delicious yellow pound cake, which I'd only heard about but hadn't actually tasted because I'd never stayed to the end. I sat for a few more minutes and then slipped off, anticipating a mid-morning snooze. But as I neared my cabin, I saw a swarm of people gathered outside on the lawn of the Health Centre.

"It's closed!" I yelled out to them. "You guys are supposed to be in services!" I said as I arrived upon a scene of utter bedlam. (Luckily, no one turned the tables on me to say, *What about you?*) Three girls were stretched out, writhing on the grass, clutching at their chests, spluttering, coughing, and gagging. A friend told me what happened.

"Tammy was sitting in services, minding her own business, and she swallowed a feather that fell off a bird! Zoe thinks she might have inhaled one, too, and just the thought of it is making Paige freak out—and can you check me, too?"

A few other "emergencies" had gathered. A little girl waved a splinter-ravaged thumb at me, begging for immediate attention. A pale, skinny girl stood patiently, but with a desperate look on her face. She gave a little wave and mouthed the words, "I don't feel well." There was Dylan, pacing around as usual, but this time not running off when he saw me. "I need to talk to you," he said urgently. Sarah, the girl who'd gotten her period, pulled me aside to whisper frantically, "I can't get the tampon out! It's stuck in there!"

I unlocked the Health Centre and they followed me in.

"I'm seeing double," cried Tammy, the feather-traumatized girl, spluttering and coughing. She and her friends were also coughing and very flushed. It *was* a hot day. Could it be sun stroke? But all three of them at the same time made that iffy. I was pretty sure this gaggle of gagging girls was okay, but they were adding to the overall chaos so I sent them off to lie down and told them I'd be with them shortly.

Just then, Daniel sauntered in. His insulin needle had fallen out of his abdomen and he had to re-insert it into his arm, but his hands were dirty and he refused to wash them. He was rude to Seth who came in to help. Was this ordinary teenage cranki-ness or a sign of a dip in his blood sugar? In Daniel's case, even slight hypoglycemia could quickly lead to a medical emergency. "Please check your blood sugar," I told him.

"Yeah, yeah, I'll get to it," he snapped at me.

"I need to know the results," I said when I saw he wasn't doing as I asked.

"Daniel, just do it," Seth said, wearily.

Alice and Louise were still at services and hadn't taken their walkie-talkies so I couldn't call them, but I knew they'd come afterward. *You can handle this,* I told myself. Out of the corner of my eye, I noticed a boy standing off to the side who had a stream of bright red blood shooting out of his nose. *Now, this is an emergency!* I ran for an ice pack, slapped it in place, and applied pressure. As the flow settled to a steady drip on the floor, I took a few minutes to assess the situation. There was a lot of commotion but nothing I couldn't handle on my own—for now. As usual, the urgent and the trivial were all mixed up. But since there wasn't anything truly serious, a part of me just wanted to gather up all their achy, needy selves into my arms, then go and put on the kettle for a cup of tea for me and a round of instant noodle soup for them. I sat there, looking at their miserable faces, taking comfort in the old ICU nurse dictum: *If the patient is breathing, the rest is gravy.* I took a deep breath and thought it through: Bleeding took priority over anxiety, but anxiety trumped a splinter and also a tampon lost in outer (inner?) space. As for the skinny, distraught girl, the sad little boy, and all the others vying for my attention, I would get to them as soon as possible. "Sit down," I told the boy with the nosebleed.

"It tastes gross."

"Lean your head forward so the blood won't drip down the back of your throat," I told him. "I wish I had some cocaine," I muttered to myself.

That got his attention. "Cocaine?" he asked. "No shit! Are you a user?"

There was no time to explain that in the hospital ER they kept a small vial of cocaine that was used to constrict the tiny arteries deep inside the nasal passages. "You'll have to go to the hospital if we can't get the bleeding under control."

"Can I have the cocaine instead?"

I went to check on the three feather girls. They were stretched out on the beds, out cold. *Once again, the magic sleep treatment cures all.*

Someone tapped me on the shoulder. I twirled around. It was the pale, worried girl. "What's wrong?" I asked, immediately regretting my abruptness. She had been waiting so patiently. *It's easy to overlook a quiet one!*

"I don't feel well."

I put my hand on her forehead. She had a fever and it was a high one. I had even more reason to apologize for my irritability when I realized who she was. It was Sophie. Catheterizing herself made her prone to urinary tract infections and fever was a sure sign of one. "I'm sorry. You *are* sick." I showed her to a bed and covered her with blankets because she was now shivering with chills.

Back in the waiting room, I was given a note from the little boy who was sitting curled up on one of the easy chairs, his legs slung over the arm, his nose deep into a comic book. It had been passed hand to hand around the crowded room, until this message in teeny-tiny letters reached me:

I'm depressed. I want to go home.

This needed time and attention, but just then Xiu-Ling and Frankie arrived, which made me glance at my watch. I thought it must be lunchtime pill call, but it was too early for that. Xiu-Ling was ticcing furiously. Her eyes were blinking, she was stamping her feet, clearing her throat, spitting on the ground, and shouting swear words. Frankie stood staring at her, stunned at this shocking scene, her eyes wide behind her large glasses. "Why is she doing that?" she asked, but there was no time to explain. I handed Xiu-Ling a package of chewing gum she'd told me helped when this happened. I had talked to her parents and they'd told me just to wait it out, it would run its course.

In the midst of all this chaos, Alice and Louise arrived, saw what was happening, and got straight to work. Alice obtained a urine specimen from Sophie to send to the lab and Louise started her on antibiotics "empirically," meaning without proof of infection, but knowing the high probability in her case. Next, Alice peeked in on the three copycat girls, still sleeping off their feather trauma. Louise took the sad boy into her office to talk to him. Alice checked on Daniel, whose blood sugar was normal and who had rejigged his insulin device, while I finished up removing the splinter and then returned to the nosebleeder. "Stop checking to see if it's still bleeding," I said. "No! Not you, Sarah!" I said, seeing her shocked face. "I didn't mean you!" Alice took Sarah into the bathroom to help with the retrieval of the lost tampon. Just then Amy appeared and said in her stiff and stilted way, "I can't stop thinking about my vulva."

"Your what?"

She leaned toward me and stared at my hair. "I'm thinking about my, you know, my va-jay-jay. I'm having... *sensations*... down there."

No, not now! No sensations now! It was likely sexual feelings that were unfamiliar to her and that she didn't understand, but this was not the time for conversation about such delicate things.

"My vagina is talking to me."

I desperately wanted to know what it could possibly be saying, but I held back from asking just to satisfy my curiosity. Luckily, I recalled that her mother told me that if she got "sensations," we should offer her Vaseline. "Tell her it's medicine," the mother had advised. I've never liked the ruse of a placebo but I was under pressure. "Here's your medicine, Amy," I told her uneasily. "Put it on, say, three times a day?"

She nodded, went into the bathroom, and then outside to sit on the porch.

Meanwhile, a counsellor came for the little boy who'd written the note. He'd walked out of Louise's office feeling better. "Can I borrow this book?" he asked.

"How will you return it if you go home?"

"Oh, I'm not going home," he said, smiling up at his counsellor.

I went to check on Amy who was now lying on the grass, motionless, staring up at the clouds. She sat up. "Can you get sick from an animal if you don't touch it or come anywhere near it?" She stared at my nose as she spoke.

I reassured her that no, she couldn't. "Are you feeling better, now?"

"Yes, I am feeling sunny, but cloudy, too."

Well, at least those *sensations* had subsided.

Louise, Alice, and I stayed in the clinic, working right through lunch. Each of us had seen this phenomenon before: a sudden, inexplicable surge in accidents, injuries, and general neediness, all at once. I've worked shifts in the ICU where the whole team was going flat out, full throttle, and in the midst of it all, we'd get word that the wards were crazy-busy, too, and that the ER was busting out. At some point, someone would chalk it up to a full moon. We'd shake our heads, laugh, and get back to work.

Dylan came forward now that things had calmed down. I motioned to Alice and Louise and they waved back to indicate they'd manage without me. I walked with Dylan down to the lake and we sat on the dock. In moments it all spilled out.

"You were my dad's nurse, weren't you? It finally hit me! You were with him when he died. I was trying to figure out where I'd seen you and it all came back to me."

"What do you remember?"

"The machines! It was like we were in the cockpit of a plane—all those dials and screens and stuff. I kept thinking he was the pilot and we were going down. My mom kept saying he was getting better but anyone could see he was a goner."

He had many questions and they rushed out all at once.

"My dad didn't squeeze my hand. If he heard me why didn't he give me a sign?

"He was so cold! When you put that warmed-up blanket on him that made him feel good.

"He was breathing weird. It was like he was choking, but was he almost dead by then or just right out of it because of the drugs?

"What drug was he on? Was he like in some la-la-land or was that a coma? Was it the drug that did him in at the end?"

I had no difficulty answering these questions even though it was over two years ago. I have an ability—most nurses do—to recall each patient's death, along with many of the specific details.

"Your dad probably heard you but was too weak to squeeze your hand. As you know, he had the tube in his mouth, so he couldn't speak to you... When a person is dying, the organs shut down and the blood moves to the body's core. That's why your father's body was cool and I put the warm blanket on him, to keep him comfortable... That gasping or choking sound is the normal breathing pattern of a dying person... The drug was morphine and I gave the doses I judged to be sufficient to keep him painfree and comfortable but not more than that, which might have speeded up his death."

I had a hunch about the question he really wanted to ask. "Dylan, are you wondering if your dad knew you were there with him?"

Dylan nodded. "Yeah, kinda. What do you think?"

"No one knows for sure but I always talk to my patients, even when they are unconscious or dying, even though I don't expect an answer. I believe your dad heard your voice and felt your presence, and then he was gone."

Dylan thought this over before he spoke. "At first, his death didn't affect me much. I was okay with it, but my mom and sister took it hard. My mom had a total breakdown. She can't handle it when I go away, but I need my space and camp is the only place I can get it."

I sat listening and looking out across the lake as he spoke. I wanted him to feel at ease, that he could take all the time he needed to share what was on his mind.

"I did everything to make my dad proud of me, and then he ended up in the cancer ward with needles and tubes stuck in him, and then in the ICU attached to monster machines." Dylan shook his head in disgust. "But, hey, I'm good now. I'm dealing. I have an awesome therapist. He says I can still have a relationship with my dad even though he's dead. It sounds unreal, doesn't it?"

"It makes sense to me."

"All I have to do is play his favourite song and it's like he's right there with me."

"What was your dad's song?"

"It's called 'Stairway to Heaven.' Have you heard of it?"

You had to ask, didn't you?

"Well, I'd better get back." He stood up to go. "My cabin's going kite-flying even though there's not much of a breeze." He felt the air with his hand. "Wouldn't it be great to be a kite?"

Naomi was still in the hospital. She was not coming back to camp. Her parents drove from their home in Montreal to be with her. Her doctors still couldn't come up with a diagnosis but she was feeling better and kept apologizing for "causing such a fuss and making everyone worry."

"It's bizarre," Louise said, "but I've seen this syndrome before. It's called *la belle indifference*. It's rare and occurs mostly in adolescent girls, usually well-adjusted, high-achievers like Naomi who have everything going for them. It usually starts with anxiety but quickly spirals out of control, as we saw."

"In between attacks, she was perfectly fine," I said, "even laughing about it."

Louise nodded. "Patients with this syndrome typically make light of their symptoms. The other feature is that each event occurs in front of witnesses and if they fall, they manage to protect themselves, so there's rarely an injury."

"What are her parents like?" Alice asked Louise, who had met them when she'd gone to visit Naomi in the hospital.

"Absolutely lovely. Beside themselves with worry, of course. There was also a younger brother and an older sister and they seemed to be a very close and caring family."

"So, it's hard to understand why..." said Alice, her voice trailing off.

We backed off and let it go. We knew and accepted the fact that there weren't always answers. Some medical mysteries never get solved. Many things get better on their own, without our doing, or understanding, anything.

Sex was on my mind. I'd been thinking a lot about it ever since the infamous talk in the Tent. I asked Alice, "Camp is a very sexual place, don't you think?"

"No, not sexual," she said, "but *intimate*, I would say."

It was a true and important distinction. Counsellors engaged in lots of friendly hugging and playful touching, but "not in a sexual way," as they pointedly, jokingly reassured us, among themselves and with their kids. Campers often walked hand in hand or with their arms entwined; counsellors held or carried their children and gave lots of hugs and pats on the back. Teenagers were in the process of growing aware of themselves as sexual beings. Everywhere you looked, you could see them blossoming right before your eyes. There was no doubt about it: sexuality was in the air. And there was something else charging up the atmosphere at camp. It was particularly special because it's something you don't see often these days and it was a pleasant thing to be around: affection, even, at times, *romance*.

Many evenings when I walked past the dimly lit staff lounge, where the counsellors played ping-pong and listened to music, I would see some couples standing off to the side or lounging on the couches, their arms around each other. I'd seen them go off to the woods, hand in hand. Late at night they shared details of their relationships, and when they got beyond the posturing and braggadocio about the hot and heavy hook-ups and the devastating breakups, they opened up and shared their real feelings—their longings, their desire for intimacy, and their disappointments, too.

Recognizing camp as an ideal place to discuss these matters that were on everyone's minds, Rabbi Emily formed a girls-only group and invited Alice and me to join a session. (A male rabbi was planning a boys' group and then a co-ed one, too.) Rabbi Emily started off by explaining that the purpose of the group was for them to explore not just their *feelings* but also their beliefs and values. She called the group "Sacred Choices," a term which at first elicited derisive eye-rolling and groans. They might not have regarded these choices as sacred but I do think most considered them important. Perhaps "choices" was also part of her message. Rabbi Emily was the perfect person to lead this group because the girls liked and respected her. She was young and cool, spoke their language, and knew many of them personally from a yoga class she took with them at camp. She started off the first group by stating it would be an "open discussion about how we make the moral choices that define us."

You don't get that in sex ed class! I thought.

She assured them they could say or ask anything and it would be confidential. It would be a safe space to talk openly and honestly. They took her at her word and didn't hold back. At the first session, Lee announced she had a new boyfriend.

"Yup, and he's here at camp! Last night I had my first kiss!"

"Wow! Your first kiss ever?" someone asked.

"Well, no." *Get real*, her eyes said. "My first kiss with him."

"Is it true love?" one girl asked.

"Maybe," she said with a smile. "He may be the one."

"Was it a French kiss," someone teased her, "or maybe an Aussie kiss*?"

"No...just a regular one."

"How does he treat you?" Rabbi Emily asked. Her question seemed to stump Lee and she sat there, mulling it over.

---

* I'd learned the kiss lexicon at Camp Carson—that was a kiss "down under."

Another girl, whose name was Tara, spoke up. "My love interest doesn't even know I'm alive. I'm *so* crushing on him but I can't even say who it is."

I had met Tara a few days ago when she'd come to the Health Centre not feeling well. "I have the flu," she'd said weakly, sinking onto the couch. She was pale and clammy and said her body "ached all over." Every few moments, she doubled over with stomach cramps. I sat down beside her and placed my fingertips on her pulse. It was pounding. She looked at me. Her face was tragic. "There's a guy I like, but I don't even register on his radar." She covered her face with her hands.

"Do you spend much time with him?"

"No, and there's no way anything could ever happen between us." She revealed her crush was on Matti, the song-leader, and Tara knew that at twenty-two years of age to her fifteen-year-old self, he was an inappropriate choice, but what could she do? I truly sympathized. How well I recalled my own attractions to older men,* not to mention days spent lolling by the phone for a boy to call!

Many questions the girls asked surprised me in their sophistication. I had to wonder, whatever happened to good ol' cooties? What about the progression of first base, second base, etcetera? Were these girls really so experienced and brazen or was it all male-imitation locker-room talk? It was hard to tell.

"Do you think a PSD—a pre-sex-discussion—is a good idea?" one girl asked. "I've heard that sex is actually better if you get to know the other person first."

"How do you get it to stop at major kiss action and go no further?" another asked.

---

* Mr. Rawlings, are you out there? Remember me? Grade 10 Science? I stayed after school, hung around the lab, and memorized photosynthesis and the Krebs cycle all for you but you never once offered me a ride home in your burnt-orange Mustang! Biology? In those days I was pure *biology!*

"Maybe you have to show some restraint before it gets that far," Rabbi Emily suggested. "You do have the right to say no."

"Yes, but do we have the right to say *yes*?" Lee asked with her usual boldness.

Before Rabbi Emily had a chance to answer, another girl jumped in with her question. "What I want to know is, how well should you know the guy for just casual sex?"

Rabbi Emily smiled and answered. "At the heart of all of these questions is knowing who you are and doing what you believe is right. You can only do that after you've given it some careful consideration."

"I'm not sure if I'm into casual sex," one girl bravely confessed, putting forward a position that suddenly seemed both quaint and radical. "I want to be at least semi-serious with the guy before I go all the way." She looked around to gauge her friends' reactions. "I mean, does that sound uptight? I know it's kind of old-school."

It must have taken courage to express this view but it also emboldened others to speak up and express their belief that, for them, too, physical intimacy was special, something they wanted to save for when they were ready and with the right person.

"I agree," said another girl. "Sex without emotions does sound empty. I'm not a prude, but I don't want to be crude, either." She looked startled, then pleased when they laughed at her accidental rhyme. "I'm so not ready for it." She looked suddenly shy in front of her friends, but they nodded their encouragement.

The questions kept coming.

"Rabbi, what's a good age to start?" a girl asked, "I mean, for going all the way? And what about oral sex? It's not really sex, is it?"

"I heard you can get re-virginized, if you lose your virginity," said another girl. "Not that I need it," she hastened to add, "I was just wondering if it's possible, in case..."

"How can you tell if you're gay?" someone else asked. "Just curious," she added.

Rabbi Emily spoke in general about sexual orientation and then openly about her own experience of coming out and how she now lived as a gay woman, married to her partner, Cynthia.

As the discussion continued, I looked around at the group. The girls were beautiful—and I wasn't just thinking about their inner beauty. In their outward, superficial shapes, sizes, colours, and even with their so-called flaws—a lisp, a stutter, excess weight, pimples, braces: the things they thought were all anyone saw—they were physically beautiful. Their beauty came from their radiant good health and from their natural, unadorned looks. Being their true selves made them shine with loveliness.

Rabbi Emily began to wind down the discussion with a few final thoughts that she prefaced by saying were her own, personal opinions. "It's important to stay true to what you believe. Having boundaries defines yourself and bestows dignity and self-respect. It comes down to, what kind of woman do you want to be? Are you prepared to make choices that are right for you, even if they are difficult or unpopular? I believe that what each of us has to offer, both inside and outside, is a gift from God and that we should value it. We've each been given a body and a soul but it is up to us to be the stewards of ourselves and take care of our health."

She had given them a lot to think about—me, too.

It was a great summer. We on the health care team congratulated each other: most kids stayed healthy and the incidence of injury and infection and the use of prescription medications were way down. Our illness prevention campaign had been a huge success. It was hard to leave, but I was feeling rested and refreshed and it was time to get back to my job in the city. My kids were staying a few more weeks on their own and were looking forward to experiencing camp as it should be, without parents around.

Harry came to see me off. "Camp is so sick, Mom."

By then, of course, I knew that in some circles, *sick* can be a good thing.

"This is the funnest camp, ever," Max said, wrapping me in a hug.

"C'mon, bro," Harry said to Max, pulling him away. "Say goodbye to Mom."

As they turned and walked off, I saw that my wish was coming true. So far the brothers were friends and looked out for each other.

Alice and I stood near our cars saying goodbye to each other. Matti came over, his guitar slung across his back, pointing down, à la Bruce Springsteen. He grabbed our hands and held them over our heads. "Ding, ding, ding," he called out. "Tied for first place we have two winners—the best nurses, ever!"

14

GONE VIRAL!

It was hard saying goodbye that summer, especially for Harry. His cabin had gone on their first canoe trip and the group of guys who went out came back as a clan of brothers. You could see it in the way they slung their arms around each other, the horsing around, and the private jokes. Even with plans and promises to stay in touch during the year, it probably wouldn't happen. Camp friends and school friends don't usually mix. Camp is a place and a state of mind that just doesn't jive with life back in the city.

That fall, there was no time for missing camp because Harry turned thirteen and preparations were underway to celebrate his bar mitzvah; we knew that if we wanted it to be a meaningful rite of passage, rather than merely a party, we had to do something about it. The first thing we did was start going to synagogue.

One Sabbath morning, who should I run into there but Eddie, last year's *enfant terrible*? He sang in the youth choir and after services saw me and came over to ask a favour. Sixteen, still thin but taller, Eddie wore ripped jeans and a black T-shirt and had a military-short, buzzed haircut. In place of multiple earrings he now had an industrial-type bar in the crunchy part of his ear. "Hey, maybe you can help me," he said. "I applied to come back to camp but got turned down. Could you speak to Rudy and give me a reference?"

"I don't think so, Eddie. You caused a lot of trouble last summer."

"But I didn't want to be there, now I do. My parents off-loaded me to camp because they couldn't handle me at home. They were going through their own shit."

"How are things now?"

"Well, for starters, my parents went splitsville."

"I'm sorry to hear that."

"It's better this way."

"I hope you're getting help for your problems."

"My *parents* are my problem, but yeah, yeah, I go to a shrink now."

"The same one you told me you lied to?"

"I *used* to lie, just randomly, but I don't any more." He looked at me to see if I bought that. "Listen, I had to lie 'cause my parents never trusted me."

"Should they have?"

"It's better to keep them in the dark. The MO in our house was *don't ask, don't tell.* My dad didn't think I knew about his affair, but I went into his computer and saw the emails—and they say they can't trust *me*! Hah! So, can you help me or not?"

I didn't know how to answer. Rudy had already turned him down and I didn't want to be the one to tell Eddie he wasn't counsellor material. "I'm pleased to hear you're doing well," I said, skirting his question for now.

"Well, it's been rough, but you just have to deal, you know? I'm still on meds and I know I need them, but I'd like to come back and be a CIT."

"You seriously injured Seth, and Mitchell, too."

"You know, someone told me I was a bully, and I'm like, you've gotta be kidding. I'm always the one being bullied. Oh, I know I did some bad stuff, the bug spray and other things, too." He looked closely at me to see what I knew but I knew enough. "I guess I used to be kind of a jerk, but I've changed."

"Well, I'm sure..." I demurred, "I guess it's possible..."

"Could you speak to Rudy and tell him that? Do you have any pull with him?"

Sure, people change. Didn't Rudy always say that? I would stand up for anyone who'd been wronged or fight for a cause I believed in, but I didn't see how I could go to bat for Eddie. "I didn't think you liked camp. Why do you even want to be a counsellor?"

"Because of Seth. He saw me as a person, not just some troublemaker loser. I want to do that for some other kid, maybe a kid who has problems like I do—I mean, *did*. Oh, you probably think I'm whacko, a freakazoid, a psycho," he said quite cheerfully.

Those were compliments compared to what I had thought of him last summer. What I thought now I wasn't sure, but he still showed no remorse, nor insight into his actions. "I'll be honest with you, Eddie, there aren't many of us who saw your behaviour last summer who'd want you anywhere near their child, and as a CIT you'd be taking care of little kids."

"But, hey, I do volunteer work in a homework club. I'm getting straight A's at school and I sing in the fucking choir! What more do you want?"

You may sing in the choir, but you're no choirboy.

"Good luck," I said, knowing it wasn't much to offer.

"That's so unfair," he said as I walked away.

I called Rudy to tell him about my conversation with Eddie. He sounded heavy-hearted about his decision. He never wanted to exclude anyone, but "Eddie's too much of a risk," he said regretfully. "I can't take the chance."

Despite the fact that there was no longer any cachet to having your mom at camp (if there ever had been), and the growing realization that Harry didn't want me there any more (but was too nice to tell me), I went back for a third summer at Camp Sol. How much longer could I keep up this camp nurse gig? My time was running out to be a grown-up interloper in this child's paradise. I figured I'd better squeeze in another summer while I could.

Time was passing fast. That fall when Harry turned thirteen, he changed almost overnight, in all the ways he was supposed to, but still, it took me by surprise. His voice deepened and he got taller. When I went to lug his heavy duffel bag from the car to heave it onto the camp bus, he took it from me easily, along with Max's too, and slid them on. He now had muscles and heft to his body. When did all of this happen?

When I arrived at camp, Xiu-Ling and Frankie ran over to greet me.

"Hi, my name is Cookie," Xiu-Ling shouted and waved at me, "and this is Cupcake." Frankie curtsied. "And that's Lollipop, Brownie, and Candy." She introduced the other girls in their cabin.

"Me likey cookies," said Frankie in a baby voice.

"Me likey cupcakes," said Xiu-Ling. "Stop! You're making me laugh!"

"No, you're making *me* laugh!" Frankie squealed with delight, which made them all dissolve into sweet giggles.

Most of the old crowd were back—Alice, Louise, Matti, and Layla. Seth came by later to say "hey." He'd lost a lot of weight and had a beard that made him look much older and serious. He seemed preoccupied. His easygoing, jovial manner was gone. He was on medication now and wanted to keep that confidential. Of course, I said, and found a place in a cupboard to store his meds.

As for Alice and me, we slipped back into our daily routine: breakfast pill call, followed by the morning clinic, which usually carried on till after lunch. Somehow we always managed to get away for a walk, a swim in the lake, or a paddle in a canoe. The first few days flew by and the kids stayed well. At night, we continued to welcome the counsellors who dropped by to chill and relax—*chillax*—serenade us with music, replenish their first-aid kits, tell us what their kids had said or done that day, and occasionally, bare their souls. It went on late but they were irresistible to us. We'd never turn them away.

That summer they seemed to have a lot more on their minds: school, travel plans, and for some, the reluctant realization that their camp days were coming to an end.

"Camp is my security blanket," one wailed, only half joking. "I have to move on but I haven't a clue what to do for the rest of my life. I wish I could stay here forever."

Matti said this was his last summer at camp. "I've got to get a decent-paying job in the city. I want to make music, but realistically I don't think I can make a living at it."

"I won't be back for sure," Layla announced. That was a surprise, because I guess we assumed as Rudy's daughter she'd always be there. "I just got into law school."

Many had a desire to give back to their communities, through volunteer work or political activism, and to find ways to tackle the big issues: saving the environment and combating social injustices such as racism and poverty. I'd attended an open-mic session in the staff lounge where a group of them talked about their upcoming mission to Guatemala with Habitat for Humanity. So many of them had big dreams of doing noble work, but one night they also enjoyed a flight of fantasy about ideal jobs such as toy designers for Lego sets, greeting card copywriters, skateboard designers, and cosmetic labellers, coming up with "Campfire Crimson" lipstick and s'mores-scented perfume. They kidded each other about becoming celebrities or being filmmakers, actors, or rock stars, and a startling number wanted to do "something related to forensics."* More than anything, they all expressed a longing to be *known* for something and to make their mark. I had a feeling many would.

One morning, at the beginning of the second week, I came in for pill call and found Alice looking worried. She'd been up all night with Murray, a counsellor. "Around one o'clock he banged on my door, but when I opened it he was gone. He'd run off to throw up. He managed to stagger back in and has been vomiting non-stop ever since."

"Was it an upset stomach? Did he eat something that dis-agreed with him?" I asked with the annoying innocence of one who's had a good night's sleep.

"He'd just returned from a day off in Toronto participating in a karate tournament. He ate dinner with his cabin, felt fine afterward, but got sick during the night."

"Sick?" I asked.

"He's sick," she said, firmly, "*really* sick."

"How sick could he be?" *C'mon, impress me, I'm an* ICU *nurse!*

"*Sick.*"

Sick is an important word and the inflection and tone are crucial. Even in the ICU where all of our patients are sick, when a nurse says a patient is sick in the way that Alice did, the serious-ness goes up a few notches. I peeked in, took one look, and had to agree with her. The fit young man I'd seen doing kicks and

---

* Possibly because of the recent explosion of shows like CSI. In fact, so many men-tioned an interest in forensics that I figure the crime rate will have to soar to keep them supplied with work.

punches in the martial arts studio was now a pathetic-looking, pale, clammy specimen, sitting at the edge of the bed, shivering, and clutching at his stomach, as he leaned into a garbage can to retch.

"I can't believe I didn't hear the commotion. Why didn't you wake me up?"

"You weren't on call," she said with a chuckle. Now, it was my turn to marvel at my own imperturbable nurse sleep.

Louise arrived to examine Murray. When she was done she came out of the room and stripped off the vinyl gloves she'd had the foresight to put on when she heard Alice's report. Louise was positive he had gastroenteritis—a stomach virus—which was very contagious. He would probably be better soon, but the main thing was to prevent its spread. Alice and I started scrubbing down all the surfaces in the Health Centre.

All that day and into the next night, Murray had a raging fever, and stomach cramps so severe he could only drag himself out of bed and crawl to the toilet, where he had uncontrollable diarrhea. I watched over him, dozing off and on, stretched out on the waiting room couch. It was about two o'clock in the morning when I heard the sound of running footsteps outside my window. I unlocked the door. One of the other counsellors in Murray's cabin stood there, trembling. "Help me," he moaned. "I'm dying." He turned his head away from me as an arc of vomit spewed from his mouth and hit the wall. He collapsed at my feet and lay there, writhing and moaning. Another counsellor who'd come with him had run off to vomit into a garbage can and was making his unsteady way back in. "What is this?" he cried. "I've never been so sick in my life."

I put on gloves and a gown and stayed with them while they went through agony, violently ill all night. By morning, they were taking turns running to the bathroom with diarrhea. Then, they stripped off their clothes, covered themselves with sheets, and flopped down on the narrow cots, one on either side of Murray, who was now peacefully asleep.

I went to wash my hands. On second thought, I decided to take a shower. Just before entering my room, I peeled off my clothes and dropped them in a heap outside my door to be boiled, bleached, and laid out in the sun later when I had the time.

After lunch, a little boy from Murray's cabin came over to me.

"I think I just threw up." He rubbed his stomach.

"You think so? You don't know if you did or not?"

"Something came out that looked like the bean burritos I just ate."

"Yeah, I saw it," his friend reported. "His yark was bright orange." He peered at the sick boy. "Hey, you look pale. Maybe you should eat some meat."

"Can I have a Tums?" the boy asked me. "That's what my mom gives me when my stomach is upset." He suddenly bolted off to find a garbage can, but—*blat!*—missed it entirely.

This was no upset stomach. This was a virus and it was spreading—fast!

"Can you give me medicine to make it better?" he called out as he ran off to the bathroom, but he didn't make it there in time, either. I went to get a mop.

Later that afternoon, I heard someone just outside the Health Centre groaning.

"Owww...my stomach hurts." I looked out the window and saw a little girl doubled over, vomiting on the ground. "I feel *sooo* yucky. I want to go home," she cried as her counsellor tried to soothe her. A few minutes later, another counsellor brought in a little girl from the same cabin. She dropped down onto the floor, sobbing and begging for her teddy bear that she'd thrown up on and that her counsellor had washed and hung outside to dry. Her counsellor held her and stroked her hair while the little girl threw up again and again. The counsellor herself looked pale and I had a feeling she'd be down soon, too.

By evening, the CITs started dropping. One boy lay on a cot while his girlfriend stood at the door. They looked like Romeo and Juliet, gazing at each other with desire, but forbidden to touch, or even come close. "I love you," she whispered.

"Love you too," he mouthed weakly as I pulled the star-crossed lovers apart.

This outbreak was escalating at an alarming rate. We could barely focus on measures to control it when we were so busy taking care of patients. We didn't even get to some of them in time and would come upon kids lying limply on their beds or even on the floor, too weak to get up. After the vomiting came diarrhea and extreme fatigue. Their eyes became red and sore from the strain of retching and their mouths were parched. We had to examine each person carefully so as not to miss any of the other things that can also cause nausea, vomiting, and diar-rhea, things such as appendicitis, a bowel obstruction, or even ordinary heatstroke. I recalled Kitch's warning that stomach pain that wakes a child in the middle of the night is always serious.

Rudy called an emergency meeting of all staff.

"This is a very aggressive virus," Louise said.

"Tell me about it," someone mumbled, going outside for air.

"It's the bubonic plague," someone said glumly. "Everyone's gonna get it."

"This thing's gone viral," Matti said, putting down his guitar. He picked it up again and wiped it all over with antiviral cleanser before putting it away in its case. He was looking unwell himself. Even those who weren't sick were feeling queasy. They also were caring for sick kids and knew the chances were high they might get the bug, too. All we could do was try to contain it with fre-quent, thorough handwashing. Isolation at camp was going to be difficult and probably already too late.

"The bad news is that it is highly infectious and if you get it, you'll feel rotten," Louise said, "but the good news is that it is short-lived and you'll all recover."

"That's great," they said sarcastically.

"After two or three days of misery, you'll get better," Louise went on to say. "It's rough—I won't lie to you—but you'll all survive. What we're going to have to do is redouble our efforts to control it, or else it will turn out to be a disastrous summer."

Many were feeling like it was already. The burden of caring for sick kids and keeping the others well and preoccupied was wearing on them, but they soldiered on.

We beefed up the handwashing blitz. Rudy installed new, portable handwashing facilities and bottles of hand sanitizer were placed on each table in the dining hall. We ordered cases of rehydration fluids to replace lost electrolytes (salts and minerals) and glucose (sugar); gallon jugs of antiviral cleaner; boxes of vinyl gloves, disposable masks and gowns; and ten-pound bags of kitty litter to absorb messes and smells. Alice and I worried about vulnerable campers like Steven whose immobility put him at risk; a girl with Crohn's disease; a boy with a metabolic disorder; and most especially, Daniel, who had diabetes. And there were others, too.

Everyone was either sick or worried sick. The virus was the main topic of conversation.

"Am I going to get it?" so many children asked me.

"I hope not, but if you do, you'll get better. Keep washing your hands."

In the midst of all of this, ordinary wounds still needed bandaging, itchy bug bites needed soothing, and twisted ankles needed icing and taping. In fact, a minor injury that occurred back on the very first evening of camp was still keeping us busy with a time-consuming follow-up. It had been pouring rain and Xiu-Ling had run in ahead of Frankie, screaming that Frankie had fallen off the porch. Frankie limped in tragically, supported on one side by her dripping wet counsellor and on the other by Xiu-Ling, who'd run back to help her. Xiu-Ling was wearing a crazy hat that had a short pole on top to which was attached an open umbrella, and she kept her head cocked at an extreme angle in order to offer Frankie cover from the rain.

"How did this happen?" I tried to keep a straight face at this comical sight.

"She fell into the bushes and they were thorny," Xiu-Ling explained.

Alice and I cleaned her up and covered her scrapes. But every evening since then, she came back to us to have the bandages changed. Painstakingly, we removed them as Frankie whimpered. "Oooh, please be careful," she pleaded. "Ouch, ouch ouch!" We told her it would be easier if we did it quickly rather than prolong the agony but she wouldn't hear of such a drastic approach. It was the third night of the gastro bug, the place was packed with sick kids, and Alice and I had no patience for the drawn-out procedure. Besides, by then, her scrapes had mostly healed. Meanwhile, we were hopping busy: kids were being carried in, the examining rooms were full, the waiting room was packed, and there was a lineup out onto the porch.

I looked at Frankie's sad face. "Frankie, can you do it yourself, tonight, please?"

"No, no!" She shook her head. "I need you to do it and it's Cupcake, remember?"

"I'll do it, but only if you let me do it fast, *Cupcake*."

"Me no likey." She backed off, her eyes large behind her glasses.

"I'm sorry, but I don't have the time, right now." *For the Band-Aid ceremony.*

"I'll do it for you!" offered Xiu-Ling. "Please let me, Cuppy-Cake? You likey?"

I stepped back to watch this play out. *Let Cookie be the bad guy.* I watched Xiu-Ling distract Frankie with another silly joke and then in one smooth motion, ripped off the bandage. "Ta-da!" Xiu-Ling held it in the air, waved it like a flag.

Frankie was stunned, uncertain how to react. Should she cry out because it was supposed to hurt? Be furious at me for allowing Xiu-Ling to do this to her? Be angry at Xiu-Ling for tricking her? Or would Frankie make another decision altogether?

I busied myself, watching them out of the corner of my eye and thinking about these everyday choices: to cope or not; to be strong or to dissolve; to choose hope or despair, rise above it or sink down low. I readied myself to celebrate or console. Finally, Frankie made her decision. She burst out laughing, the surest sign of triumph! "Yay, Frankie!" a roar went up around the waiting room. She grinned at her achievement. Cookie and Cupcake went out arm in arm, laughing hysterically.

Once again, my nursing practice was teaching me how much more we can endure, and achieve, than we think we can.

Later that night, I was working, long after midnight, and Rudy showed up unexpectedly. At first, I thought he was sick, but he looked well. He sidled over to me with a sly look in his eye. "I have the key to the tuck shop," he whispered in my ear. "What's your pleasure?"

I gasped. Was he coming on to me? "Oh, no, I don't think so," I stammered.

"What'll it be? What do you crave?"

"I couldn't...possibly..."

"Your choice: Kit Kat or Twinkie? How 'bout a Crunchie?"

I burst out laughing for having misread his intention. Anyway, I desperately needed chocolate way more than sex!

The outbreak showed no signs of abating. More and more children were getting sick and counsellors, too. Somehow, Alice and I stayed well and kept going. *Nurses can't get sick,* or so the legend goes.

Camp had become a strange and uncomfortable place. Everyone kept their distance. No hugging or holding hands, no CITs sitting in each other's laps. Visitor's Day, which was coming up in two weeks, might have to be cancelled. Camp might even have to be shut down for the rest of the summer. Worst of all was the eerie quiet. The music stopped. Silence fell over camp.

15

CAMPFIRE NURSE

The crisis continued. Kids begged to go home. The mood was bleak.

Louise, Alice, and I were stunned at how fast this thing was racing through camp. Our efforts to contain it seemed to have no effect. There were new cases every day. Rudy was worried.

"They've all lost their sparkly eyes," he said in dismay. "Morale has never been so low."

When's it gonna hit me? counsellors caring for sick kids wondered. Most kept a sense of humour—especially the lipstick namer who came up with "Pretty in Puke Pink" and "Viral Violet"—but understandably, there was also grumbling and rumbles of discontent. "I didn't sign up for this," some said. A few packed up and left. "I can't take the chance of getting sick," said one. "I'm outta here." "Me too," a friend said. "This place is contaminated! It's teeming with pestilence."

"Yeah, *right*," said Seth. He was disgusted with those who jumped ship. "They'll never be able to show their faces here ever again."

Rudy got sick and retreated to his cabin with only Ringo for company.

By the morning of Day Four we reported the outbreak to the

public health authorities. They planned to come by later that day to investigate.

We studied the situation. There had to be a logical "chain of transmission," but if we couldn't discern the pattern we had no way of knowing if our control measures were effective. I came up with an idea. I ran to the arts and crafts shed and returned with a large sheet of cardboard, markers, and stickers in assorted colours. I drew a box for each cabin and put a red dot on Murray's cabin. *Murray was the first case.* For Day Two, I put two green dots for his co-counsellors and two more for the boys in his cabin. *That makes sense, they're in the same cabin.* For Day Three, ten yellow dots. *Those kids sit together in the dining hall. The sick* CITs *had been working with that cabin.* Today, Day Four, we had thirty-five purple dots and the web was getting more intricate. It was far from over. I only hoped it would end before we exhausted our entire range of colours.

Camp had come to a standstill. Activities were cancelled. The dining hall seemed particularly empty and mealtimes were subdued. Seth, Matti, Layla, and others got on the case. They picked up their guitars and played outside the cabin windows of the sick kids and entertained them with skits, pantomimes, and juggling. They started up a drumming circle, an activity that almost everyone could do, and it got kids with bad cases of cabin-fever outdoors again. In fact, the drumming group became such a hit that long after the kids went to sleep, the counsellors kept the beat going late into the night. They reinstated the dining hall music and not just the religious songs, but their own playlist, too. "Will Santana or Sly and the Family Stone pick up the mood better?" "Does Zeppelin go better with mac and cheese, or Judas Priest?" they asked one another, considering the various pairings with the same attention a doctor gives to choosing the appropriate antibiotic. Once again, the sounds of those classic bands, along with the upbeat tunes of Great Big Sea, OutKast, and

Dispatch, boomed out of the speakers. Those who were able got up and moved to the beat as they cleared the tables after meals. Like a restorative tonic, the music brought them back to life.

Two surprise leaders were Lee and Jasmine, last summer's "bad girls" who were now CITs. They even volunteered for the cleaning squad. "We're stoked," they said, "down for whatever." The squad roved around, mopping up messes, airing out cabins, and stripping beds. They probably didn't do this kind of thing at home but here they took it on with a cheerful attitude. They squealed with delight when we issued them a walkie-talkie, and with that in hand and spray bottles of disinfectant hooked onto their shorts, they patrolled the camp, doing their chores and keeping us in the loop along the way.

"Cleanup in aisle five" or "puke puddle alert," one would say over the walkie-talkie to summon the rest of the crew to bring the bags of kitty litter, brooms, buckets, and mops.

"Nurse Tilda? Are you there? Over and out."

"Yes, Lee. I'm here."

"Hey, it's Jasmine. I'm down at the canoe docks with two little Flame girls who are spewing chunks!"

"Okay. Bring them in."

A few minutes later, I heard, "FYI: two other girls from the same cabin aren't feeling well. I think they're about to hurl."

"Bring them in, Jasmine, over and out."

"This is Lee. I'm all over it! Ten-four, Nurse Tilda!"

They didn't seem worried about getting sick themselves. They even offered to supervise our isolation ward, which had been dubbed "The Colony." They played an elaborate fantasy game with the children based on the TV show *Lost,* pretending they were survivors of a plane crash, stranded on a deserted island, having to band together to protect themselves from monsters, doomsday warriors, and evil island inhabitants. The male counsellors had their own style of fun, lining up garbage cans for duelling barf-fests, cracking lots of diarrhea jokes, and devising clever poop descriptions and fart charts.

In the afternoon the health inspector arrived. He strode in, carrying a briefcase like a detective, determined to get to the bottom of the case. First, he inspected the kitchen and found it spotless, quickly ruling out food contamination as a source of the infection. He examined my diagram charting the rapid, exponential spread and interviewed Murray, the first or "index" case, who had by then completely recovered.

"Continue exactly as you're doing," he concluded. "Disinfecting all surfaces, frequent handwashing, and minimizing physical contact is the only way to beat it." But as he got up to leave, he warned us, "If there's any escalation, you'll have to close the camp. As for Visitor's Day in a week and a half, I'd advise you to cancel it." He must have noticed our shocked faces because he added: "Go ahead if you must, but no touching."

Visitor's Day, without hugging or kissing? Unheard of!

Before parting, he offered guarded encouragement. "When the number of new cases starts to level off and you've hit a plateau, it'll be the beginning of the end."

We notified parents about the outbreak and the possibility of cancelling Visitor's Day. Some wanted to come and get their kids right away but we advised against it. They'd probably be feeling better in a day or two, and at home they'd be exposing family members, including possibly elderly grandparents or others who couldn't easily withstand a debilitating illness. Distraught, some mothers and fathers called daily. Anxiety was spreading like the virus itself. From his sick bed, Rudy composed a group email.

"The children who have gotten sick are all recovering," he wrote. "If symptoms persist once your child comes home, please contact your doctor." *And your lawyer,* I heard him mutter. He must be joking! But no, Rudy was worried that some would try to lay blame.

"It's easy to criticize but it's no one's fault," I said. "These things happen."

"You're handling this quite calmly," he remarked.

"I guess my standards are different than most people's," I admitted. "Don't forget, I'm an ICU nurse." At least here my patients weren't *dying*. I never lost sight of how bad things *could* be, and there was another reason I could keep things in perspective: I had lived through something far worse—SARS.

It was 2003. A mysterious pneumonia was suddenly making people gravely ill. Some were dying. SARS was not the first time I'd worried about my safety and what dangers I was bringing home to my family, but it was definitely the scariest. Over the years, I'd taken care of patients who'd had infectious diseases such as hepatitis, tuberculosis, and HIV-AIDS, but SARS was different. The virus that caused SARS—short for sudden acute respiratory syndrome—travelled lightning fast and was transmitted person to person by incidental, casual contact. It was lurking in the air, potentially blown your way by the wind, a breeze, a breath, or a sneeze.

Overnight, SARS turned Toronto into a ghost town. Travel was banned by the World Health Organization; hotels and restaurants emptied out, streets were vacant. Many people were quarantined. It was a new disease, and at first even infectious-disease specialists didn't know what they were dealing with. People felt confused and afraid. At a party I went to during that time, guests jumped away from me and refused to shake my hand or come near me. Mothers cancelled play dates with my kids. Those of us caring for SARS patients, doing this hazardous but essential work, felt a punishing sense of isolation.

I'll never forget how dark and quiet the hospital was during that time. Only hands-on, front-line caregivers came to work. It was mostly nurses who kept the hospital open. Wearing two pairs of gloves, gowns, plastic face shields, and heavy masks, customized to fit our individual faces and impermeable to viruses, we worked in closed, negative-pressure rooms, caring for our patients. Over the top of our masks we watched our patients, and in our eyes, patients sought assurance they would not be abandoned.

In a crisis a leader is needed, and Toronto had one. Dr. Sheela Basrur was the city's Officer of Public Health at the time and she led Toronto in the same calm, courageous manner that Mayor Rudy Guiliani guided New York City during 9/11. As more people got sick and mass hysteria threatened to erupt, Dr. Basrur reassured the public. She explained the need for the drastic quarantines and how they were the only way to stop the chain reaction. She acknowledged it was a serious situation, but not an emergency. "My job is to do the worrying," she said.

Dr. Basrur understood nursing. Like a nurse, she cared about the nitty-gritty, such as the proper handwashing technique and ensuring that we were equipped with the special masks, not the ordinary, one-size-fits-all paper ones. She was concerned that caregivers would become exhausted and unable to carry on. Then, just when the situation seemed to be coming under control, a second wave of SARS broke out. A nervous city became terrified, and again Dr. Basrur took control. Working around the clock, or so it seemed, she held daily press conferences in which she distilled complex information so it could be understood by everyone. In the end, in Toronto alone, there were over four hundred cases of SARS, the majority of them health-care workers. Forty-four people died. It was a terrible time, but many were left with a sense that it could have been much worse had it not been for the dedication of health-care workers and the leadership of Dr. Basrur.[*]

I tried to be that kind of leader, too. Together with Alice and Louise, we communicated openly with the counsellors, explaining

---

[*] Dr. Basrur resigned from her position in 2006, in order to undergo treatment for a rare form of cancer. When she died in 2008, nursing lost a great ally.

everything to them. We encouraged them to ask questions, express their frustrations, and let off steam. We acknowledged their efforts. During a lull one day, I spoke with Seth, who was looking mighty haggard. "How are you holding up?" I asked. He came in each evening, dropping by discreetly for his medication, but he didn't stop to chat or joke around like he used to.

"I'm good," he said, forcing a smile.

"It's been rough, hasn't it?"

He looked at me in surprise. "No, it's been the best summer ever. We've pulled together and are closer than ever. We're like family now."

Of course. I knew Seth loved a challenge. He was an extraordinary counsellor, an outstanding student and athlete, a terrific guy. He excelled at everything he did. I knew he'd gotten a full scholarship to university and I asked him how that was going.

"I dropped out. Couldn't hack it," he said blithely, but then sat down with me and told me the real story. "Something happened," he said, shaking his head. "I still don't get it. It was my birthday and birthdays mean a lot to me. I'd broken up with a girlfriend and none of my friends were around. I was alone in my dorm. It was August, right after camp, but before classes started. Suddenly, I snapped. I went over to the dark side. Nothing made sense. For days I couldn't even get out of bed. My parents came but they didn't know what to do. My mom cried and my dad kept telling me to pull myself together."

"What helped? You must have felt well enough to come to camp this summer."

"Camp was the only place I could be. What helped was being around people like you, Tilda. People who don't judge, who just listen, and don't tell me what to think or do. My parents are great but they give me advice when I just need them to listen."

"Are you lonely, Seth? When you're not with your kids, I always see you by yourself."

"My buddies know I need space. For awhile I was into meaningless hook-ups but no more. It was messing me up. At school, I dated someone I met on the Internet, but she'd never been to camp, so she didn't get it. I'm on my own right now and I'm cool with that." We sat together in silence for a while until he spoke again. "I've discovered you can go very far away and still make it back."

"How are you doing now?"

"I'm okay to be with kids, so don't worry, but I'm terrified the dark side will come back. I've got to make up the year I missed, so this will definitely be my last year at camp." He looked out the window as if taking it all in at once, this place he loved.

By the end of two weeks we reached the plateau the health inspector spoke about. Lab tests confirmed that, as expected, it was a norovirus, the most common culprit in this type of illness. In total, twenty per cent of the camp had gotten sick and everyone recovered. It could have been so much worse.

The night before I left, we gathered around a huge bonfire. Other than the campers and counsellors who were still recovering, everyone was there. Matti led them in this song.

O Lord, my God,
I pray that these things never end:
The sand and the sea, the rush of the waters,
The crash of the heavens, the prayer of the heart.

I looked around the circle. Everyone looked happy. Even the sick ones who'd wanted to go home were smiling once again. They were all content within themselves and connected to their friends—this was camp happiness. They were glowing with it that night.

I returned to the Health Centre and gave out the evening meds. After I locked up and headed toward my room, I heard far-off rhythmic sounds. The music beckoned me and I retraced my steps to the campfire where the counsellors had gathered. I approached tentatively. (I didn't want to crash a private ritual as I'd done once before, accidentally intruding upon a band of bare-chested CIT boys performing a war dance.) They were sitting in a circle. Some of them were holding drums—tom-toms, bongos, djembes—and some had tambourines or maracas. In unison they beat a rhythm as compelling as my heartbeat, which suddenly welled up and throbbed inside my core. A girl got up and wordlessly handed me an instrument. *No,* I shook my head, *I'll sit out and just listen,* but she kept her hand outstretched. At last I took the instrument, waited for the beat, found my place to enter, and joined in.

Later, as I left the drumming circle, I felt quietly happy—and proud, too. Finally, I'd won my place at the campfire.

16

THE CURE FOR HOMESICKNESS

"You'll never guess who's back!" Alice threw out a teaser. We were busy unpacking supplies and organizing camper meds, getting ready for the start of a new summer. By her impish grin, I knew she was also gearing up for the fun to begin.

"Who?"

"Eddie! He's a counsellor, now!"

Unbelievable. Well, Rudy always said kids can change, didn't he? Later, I heard that Eddie was Max's counsellor and I felt uneasy about that but decided to keep quiet, watch, and wait. I trusted Rudy's judgment and knew that if there was an issue with Eddie, it would be dealt with. I was getting better at letting go, at allowing my kids to solve their own problems and turn to others if they needed help. But it had taken me one more camp lesson to get that message.

I'd been strolling past Harry's cabin. It was quiet, a perfect time to sneak in for a peek—if his guitar was out, I'd know he was playing it; if his laundry bag was full, I'd remind him to send his clothes to be washed. If I could just get a glance at the skew of his flip-flops beside the bed... I mounted the creaky wooden steps and checked that the coast was clear. I knocked on the door, just to be sure. Harry's counsellor came to answer it. His eyes narrowed when he saw me. *A trespasser.*

Awhhh! Busted.

"What do you want?" he asked warily.

"Just dropping by, to, ah—visit." I squirmed.

He frowned. "Don't even think about it. This is Harry's space."

I slunk away, apologizing. "What can I do?" I said, helplessly. "He's my son."

"Yeah, but at camp, he's mine," the counsellor said, closing the door.

But later when I saw the counsellor, he tossed me a few crumbs. "Harry loves snakes. It takes a big heart to love a snake. He's friends with everyone. He knows right from wrong. What more do you need to know?"

What a comfort these connections give when we relinquish the illusion of control and learn to trust. I've heard there are now camps where the whole family can come along. "Have fun with your kids," the brochures say. But doesn't that defeat the purpose? The point of camp is to take those steps away and out into the world on your own.

At lunch, I looked around. Seth wasn't there and I missed him. Alice and Louise were back, Rudy, too, of course, but without Ringo. He'd been an old dog back when I'd first met him four summers ago and this winter he'd become unable to walk or even wag his tail. Rudy had done the kind, hard thing and taken him to the vet to have a comfortable death. He planned to get a puppy soon but had other things on his mind. He had a girl-friend now, a companion who shared his love of camp.

The first night we celebrated Alon's return to camp and his full recovery to good health. He was now head tripper, excited about implementing new "green" initiatives, such as reducing the camp's water and electricity usage and running a contest to reward the cabin that conserved the most energy.

I continued my own green awakening with Alice. One morning she stopped in her tracks, knelt down, and placed her hands gently around a large bug. She scooped it up and brought it close to show me: a shiny black beetle with long antennae and pincers that made it look like an alien from Mars.

"Isn't it beautiful?" she asked and now, at last, I could see that it was.

Most afternoons, we still managed to steal away for a swim in the lake. As I eased myself in, I commented on how cold the water was.

"Don't forget," she said, "a few months ago this lake was pure snow." I breathed in the clean smell of the air and water. "Thousands of years before that, it was a glacier."

Returning to camp was a homecoming for me. Even the noise and commotion were a familiar comfort. When I entered the dining hall, the roar engulfed me as I was immediately plunged into the midst of ecstatic, dancing bodies and a cacophony of voices, all whooping and hollering, cheering, chattering, and singing at the top of their lungs. I even joined in on one song and got up and waved my arms upward. "Oooh…ahh…" I said, swinging them back down in a swoop.

"Hey, man, you're really into it," Rudy said appreciatively, sitting down beside me on the bench.

Yes, their noisy exuberance was catchy. Why should we "sit still" or "be quiet"? *It's time to move!*

Alice and I looked at each other. How well we knew them, her smile seemed to say. Inside and out, their bodies and their souls, we knew every scrape, bump, bruise, and rash, as well as their worries, fears, and secrets, and dreams. *As nurses, we are so privileged to have this opportunity to get to know people on such an intimate level.*

At camp I learned how to care for healthy children. One malady I became skilled at treating was homesickness, especially after I understood that it's not always about missing home and doesn't only occur at camp: one can have a bad bout sitting at home.* At its core, homesickness is a yearning to be at home within ourselves. In fact, the cure for homesickness is camp itself, because at camp you can learn everything you need to know about finding your way home.

One afternoon, I had a surprise: Seth came to visit. He said he was feeling better. "I had to come back and see everyone, especially you, Tilda." He still looked wistful about camp but more hopeful about his future. "You know, I loved being a camper, but being a counsellor was the best time of my life. I'm looking into becoming a camp director."

We shared a chuckle about Eddie being a counsellor now and, from what we could tell, doing a great job. "Eddie's the best!" Max had run over to tell me—though that's what he says every summer about all of his counsellors.

Seth gave me a quick hug before leaving. "It's time for me to move on."

"You seem ready."

We hear so much bad news these days about young people in trouble, involved in delinquency, drugs, and violence. As parents we worry about the dangers and so many bad influences that are out there. Sometimes, we have doubts that the upcoming generation has the proper values or the right work ethic or sufficient motivation. Camp made me think otherwise. I met so many energetic and idealistic young people who want to do good work and give back to the community. One way they start is by being counsellors, giving the kids in their care all that camp has given them.

---

* And let's not forget late-summer campsickness, too!

At the end of my last week at camp that summer, at the Friday evening service, Rudy started off by mentioning achievements, not only of individuals, but group ones, too: a cabin that had returned from their first canoe trip; another in which everyone had passed the swim test; a successful Colour War. Then, a tall, beautiful counsellor named Dani got up to speak:

> This is my ninth summer at camp. There are so many things I love about camp: cabin bonding; stargazing; being with friends I don't see all year round (you know who you are); dancing in the rain; Sabbath cake; my summer as a CIT; meeting my cabin of girls as a counsellor for the first time; techno parties in the staff lounge; long, meaningful conversations that I would not have in the city; and seeing all of you, summer after summer. I will always and forever cherish the memories of our times together.

That says it all.

Yes, I'd probably come back next summer.

To be a camp nurse you don't have to be young, but you do have to be young at heart. At nearly fifty, I didn't feel old, but camp has made me aware of the passage of time—especially, its rush. *So much happens here. A day at camp is a week anywhere else. A week at camp is like a year,* Alice and I always said to each other.

When it was time to leave, I went up to the microphone to say goodbye to everyone at once. As I stepped down from the podium, they all rushed at me and swarmed me in hugs. Then I said goodbye to my sons and began the long, leisurely drive homeward. As I drove along that quiet, country road, I had an urge to turn around and go back, stay there forever, so camp would never end, not that summer, not ever.

ACKNOWLEDGMENTS

Thank you to:

Elizabeth Kribs, Marilyn Biderman, and Terri Nimmo at McClelland & Stewart, and Lynn Schellenberg.

Vanessa Herman-Landau and Allison Landau for your help with this book; Dani Kagen for her camp memories; Omri Horwitz of The Harold Wartooth for his vast knowledge of music; Dan McCaughey for his vast knowledge of the outdoors.

Anna Gersman, nursing partner and dear friend, along with nurses Cathy Dain, Annie Levitan, Donna Robins, Gert Rossman, and Ella Shapiro; doctors Ian Kitai, Leo Levin, Gary Mann, David Saslove, Eddie Wasser, and Georgina Wilcock; URJ Camp George staff, faculty, and counsellors—Deborah Cooper, former camp nurse and Chair of the Camp Steering Committee; Ellyn Freedland, Rabbi Daniel Gottlieb, Anat Hoffman, Karen Kollins, Marilyn Lidor, Rosalyn Mosko, Ron Polster, and Jeff Rose; Paul Reichenbach with the Union for Reform Judaism and the leaders of its Canadian region, the CCRJ; Gavin and Shirley Herman and Sam Reisman and family for their vision of a caring, inclusive camp community that is URJ Camp George of Parry Sound, Ontario.

With gratitude to the late, great leader Dr. Sheela Basrur, who understood how the public's health and hands-on nursing care go hand in hand.

To my campers and their families, especially Ariel and Liora Gersman, and Rachel Kreuter.

Most of all, thank you to Ivan, Harry, and Max Lewis, who remind me when I get homesick how fortunate I am to have such a loving home.

ABOUT THE AUTHOR

TILDA SHALOF is a staff nurse in the Medical-Surgical Intensive Care Unit at Toronto General Hospital of the University Health Network and has been there since 1987. She graduated from the University of Toronto, Faculty of Nursing back in 1983 and has worked in hospitals in New York City, Tel Aviv, and for the past 23 years, Toronto. In 1990, she achieved certification as a specialist in Critical Care Nursing from the Canadian Nurses' Association.

In 2004, Tilda published *A Nurse's Story*, a memoir of her career as a critical care nurse. It received wide critical acclaim, became a national bestseller, and has been translated into Chinese, French, Japanese, and Vietnamese. In 2007, Tilda released *The Making of a Nurse*, in which she charts the educational, intellectual, emotional, and spiritual steps in her journey of becoming a nurse. In it, she shares some of the professional and personal challenges she's faced in becoming the nurse she aspired to be. Her latest book, *Camp Nurse—My Adventures at Summer Camp* is a fond remembrance of six summers working at a variety of residential summer camps for children in Ontario, Canada. Written from the perspective of both parent and professional, it describes the joys of camp, its many benefits to children, and the ways that a camp nurse helps keep campers—and their counselors—safe and healthy.

In addition to being a critical care nurse and bestselling author, and frequent media commentator, Tilda is also a dynamic public speaker. Her presentations include insider stories from her long career as a critical care nurse and observations about the realities of clinical practice in today's healthcare environment. Tilda addresses a broad range of audiences, but her messages resonate most strongly with frontline caregivers, both professional and lay, nurses and doctors and all other healthcare roles, specialties, levels of experience, and practice settings. She is passionate about helping caregivers reconnect with their ideals, to inspiring them to excellence in their practice, and to reminding us all about the privilege it is to do this work. Tilda is dedicated to explaining nursing and healthcare to the public and to raising the awareness of the central role of nurses in ensuring the public's health and safety.

Tilda lives with her husband, Ivan Lewis, and their sons, Harry and Max, in Toronto, Canada, and can be reached through her website www.NurseTilda.com.